Business to Business Marketing Management

Business to Business Marketing Management

Frank G. Bingham, Jr.
Bryant College

Barney T. Raffield III
Oklahoma Baptist University

Homewood, IL 60430
Boston, MA 02116

Cover Illustration: Catherine Kanner

Developmental editor: Andy Winston
Project editor: Lynne Basler
Production manager: Carma W. Fazio
Cover Designer: Robyn Basquin
Compositor: Weimer Typesetting Co., Inc.
Typeface: 10/12 Times Roman
Printer: R. R. Donnelley & Sons Co.

Library of Congress Cataloging-in-Publication Data

Bingham, Frank G.
    Business to business marketing management / Frank G. Bingham, Jr.,
Barney T. Raffield III.
       p.   cm.
     ISBN 0-256-07975-7
      1. Industrial marketing—United States—Management. I. Raffield.
Barney T. II. Title.
    HF5415.13.B48 1990
    658.8—dc20   89–19935
                                               CIP

Printed in the United States of America
1 2 3 4 5 6 7 8 9 0 DO 6 5 4 3 2 1 0 9

For their patience, love, and understanding,
this book is dedicated to
Caryl and Sherrie

Preface

There is a boom in the business to business marketing area. Trade magazines and scholarly journals are giving ever more space to the special issues and concerns of business marketers and students of business marketing. The recent focus on these markets reflects the recognition that the largest part of American business is not driven by consumer business methods, but has its own practices and complexities. What's more, students are also realizing the variety of career opportunities in business marketing and are eager to prepare themselves with the practical information and theoretical principles of business marketing practices.

Business to business marketing is also in a period of transformation, reflecting the changing face of American business in general: less growth in heavy industry and more in service, the evolution of information as a product, and the increasing prominence of international opportunities. A couple of years ago this text would have been called "industrial marketing management," but smokestack industries are on the decline, and course and text titles are changing to reflect the broader range of enterprises that rightfully fall under the umbrella of business marketing. Almost every available product or service is either aimed at business users or has a business marketing facet. Financial services, company car fleets, construction cranes, trade magazines, industrial lubricants, corporate jets, convention services: the list is vast.

The business to business boom has led to a parallel rise in the number of textbooks devoted to business marketing. But quantity has not always proven to be quality. When it came time to teach this course ourselves, we were dissatisfied with the available texts, new and old. All seemed to lack either a practical grounding in the real-world activities of business to business marketers, or a full integration of the newest developments and insights into the study of this evolving discipline. So it became our custom to prepare lengthy, detailed lecture outlines to fill in the gaps with which every text seemed to be riddled. These notes, in time, became *Business to*

Business Marketing Management. We think that we have produced a text worthy of our high aspirations. We hope that you think so, too.

■ The Intended Audience for This Book

The business to business marketing course, often called business marketing or industrial marketing, is taught at trade schools, two- and four-year colleges at the junior or senior level for undergraduates, or as an MBA-level course. *Business to Business Marketing Management* is aimed at those students with a foundation in basic marketing principles. It builds upon this and focuses on the special elements and requirements of business markets.

■ What to Look For in Our Book

While the business to business market has undergone rapid change, the textbooks have been slow to do the same. We have included a number of special features and pedagogical aids in *Business to Business Marketing Management* to add structure and depth to the learning process, many of which will be new to this market.

Chapter Outlines: These are simply a supplement to the table of contents, enabling the student to see at a glance the chapter structure and content, without having to turn to the front of the book. They also reflect the way in which various topics are related, serving as a sort of "road map" to the chapter.

Learning Objectives: Each chapter begins with a listing of the major topics of the chapter and some indication of what the student should be able to glean from its coverage in the text. These are perhaps the primary points of interest in the chapter "road map."

Concept Questions: Concept Questions occur two or three times within each chapter, and are designed to give students a chance to test their recall of the preceding material. They are a simple and effective way for the student to check retention of concepts before getting to the end of the chapter.

Business to Business Marketing in Action Boxes: Each box contains a brief story of real business dilemmas or tactics that elaborates the chapter's basic concepts.

Enumerated Summaries: The summary recaps the chapter contents point by point, rather than in a cluttered paragraph format, and is numbered for easy reference.

Chapter Cases: Unlike any other book on the market, *Business to Business Marketing Management* provides two cases at the end of each chapter (after Chapter 1). The cases are generally short to medium in length, and give a more focused examination of the chapters topics and issues than do the lump of long cases provided at the back of other textbooks. The shorter length of the chapter cases allows the instructor a number of options for their implementation, such as homework or in-class assignments, test questions, or group study. Each case is followed by two or more discussion questions that help the student to probe the case scenario for causes, solutions, and lessons.

Part Cases: We fully recognize the usefulness of longer cases, and therefore, we end each part division with one or two extended cases. These cases enlarge upon the material covered in the preceding part, focusing on the attendant issues while often drawing on topics covered in previous parts. The last section of the book contains two extended comprehensive cases.

■ Unique Content

Buyers and Sellers: We have arranged *Business to Business Marketing Management* to give a uniquely strong emphasis to the unique elements of the buyer-seller connection. Following Part I, the Introduction, we move to three chapters in Part II that examine the buying function and business buyer behavior, from fundamentals of purchasing management to management of the buying function and buyer-seller relationships. This approach brings forward the factor that most clearly shapes business to business marketing: the unique needs and processes of the business buyer. It is the buyer, after all, that distinguishes consumer marketing from business marketing, a point we feel should be made early and maintained throughout the course.

Personal Selling and Sales Management: Unlike most other texts, we recognize the inescapable importance of personal selling in the business marketing process by devoting separate chapters to the selling process and the management of the process and sales force. The multitude of issues surrounding both sides of the person-to-person sales contact deserve comprehensive treatment, not to be squeezed into one chapter.

Marketing of Business to Business Services: As America's economy becomes more service oriented, the emphasis on this topic is going to grow. We think that students should be made aware of the unique problems and concerns that face marketers of services, as well as the newest practices and scholarly findings.

Ethics: If there is one change that we are proud to take a lead in, it is the increasing illumination of ethical perspectives in business textbooks. All businesses and business people must face their social and legal responsibilities. Students will take their leads from the actions of business people, their professors, and their textbooks. Therefore, we find it essential to end our discussion of business to business marketing practices with a thorough overview of the various social ramifications of business practices.

Appendices: We are fortunate to have three unique appendices on (1) careers in business to business marketing; (2) negotiating practices; and, (3) future trends in business to business marketing. All three appendices provide material found in no other competitor.

International Topics: We have taken special care to introduce global concepts and examples whenever possible and logical. This approach appeals to us more than having a separate chapter on international topics. The benefit of our arrangement, we think, is that the student, exposed numerous times to the global focus of business, will learn to look for the international facets in all areas of business.

■ Instructor's Manual

The Instructor's Manual and test bank for *Business to Business Marketing Management* consists of several features:

Chapter Teaching Materials are comprised of (1) an overview/outline of the chapter contents to facilitate lecture preparation; (2) comparison notes that correlate our chapter's contents with those of the competition to ease the conversion of class notes from a competitor's text to *Business to Business Marketing Management*; (3) answers to review questions; and (4) end-of-chapter case discussions.

Part-Ending Case Materials provide an overview of the issues presented in each case, suggestions for using the case in class, and a discussion of the case outcome, where applicable.

The *Test Bank* contains 30 multiple choice questions and 5 essay questions per chapter.

Transparency Masters of 50–75 of the most important tables and charts from the text are provided.

■ Acknowledgments

Although *Business to Business Marketing Management* was the brainchild of the authors, it would not have come to pass without the abundant help and support of our colleagues, relatives, friends, and editors. First, we would like to thank the reviewers who provided their time and expertise to help us refine our various manuscript drafts into a smoother, more cohesive whole. Those patient and hardworking individuals are:

James R. Brown
Virginia Polytechnic Institute
  and State University

David R. Lambert
San Francisco State University

Charles O'Neal
University of Evansville

S. Joe Puri
Florida Atlantic University

Zahir A. Quraeshi
Western Michigan University

Marti J. Rhea
University of North Texas

Camille P. Schuster
Xavier University

Richard Spiller
California State University, Long Beach

Fred Trawick
University of Alabama-Birmingham

Paul A. Winter
University of Northern Iowa

George W. Wynn
James Madison University

We are also thankful for the very early help given by these reviewers of our proposal materials:

Jon M. Hawes
University of Akron

J. David Lichtenthal
City University of New York—Baruch College

Wesley J. Johnston
University of Southern California

We cannot overlook the contributions of our developmental editor, Andy Winston, who has been with us all the way, and our former sponsoring editor, Elizabeth Schilling, whose savvy and energy gave us inspiration and guidance. Lynne Basler guided our manuscript through production with patience and care. We must also thank Bryant College, which provided the creative environment necessary for an undertaking such as this, and, in particular, Dr. Michael B. Patterson, Associate Vice President and Dean of Faculty for his encouragement and support. There are always numerous others who should be thanked for providing small but necessary doses of assistance or criticism. We send our thanks to all of you. Despite all the above contributions, we acknowledge that some errors and infelicities will insist on creeping into the final product. For these we assume full responsibility. Any comments or suggestions for improvement would be most welcome and can be sent to us in care of Richard D. Irwin, Inc., 1820 Ridge Road, Homewood, IL 60430.

Frank G. Bingham, Jr.
Barney T. Raffield III

Brief Contents

PART I   Introduction

1   The Business to Business Marketing Environment   2

PART II   How Buyers Buy

2   Fundamentals of the Purchasing and Materials
    Management Function   30
3   Management of the Organizational Buying Function   64
4   Organizational Buyer Behavior and Buyer-Seller Relationships   112

PART III   Identifying the Customer

5   Business to Business Marketing Research and Information Systems 156
6   Market Segmentation, Positioning, and Demand Projection   194

PART IV   Making and Moving the Goods

7   Product Development, Management, and Strategy   250
8   Business to Business Price Planning and Strategy   290
9   Business to Business Marketing Channel Participants   328
10 Business to Business Physical Distribution Management and Strategy 366

PART V   Promoting and Selling the Goods

11 The Personal Selling Function in Business Marketing Strategy   428
12 Business to Business Sales Management   470
13 Advertising and Sales Promotion Strategy in Business Markets   512

PART VI   Trends in Business to Business Marketing

14 Marketing of Business Services   602
15 Ethical Considerations in Business to Business Marketing   636

PART VII   Comprehensive Cases

Index

Contents

PART I Introduction

**1   THE BUSINESS TO BUSINESS
      MARKETING ENVIRONMENT   2**

Business to Business Marketing: An
Overview   3
  The Business to Business Market
Why Study Business to Business
Marketing?   4
How the Business to Business Market
Differs from the Consumer Market   6
  Greater Total Sales Volume
  Larger Volume Purchase
  Fewer Buyers
  Larger Buyers
  Geographically Concentrated Buyers
  Close Supplier-Customer Relationship
  More Direct Channels of Distribution
  Professional Buying
  Multiple Buying Influences
  Complex Negotiation
  Reciprocity
  Leasing
  Emphasis on Personal Selling
Characteristics of Business to
Business Demand   12
  Derived Demand
  Inelastic Demand
  Fluctuating Demand
  Joint Demand
The Nature of Business to Business
Buying Behavior   14
A Classification of Business to
Business Goods and Services   15
  Major Equipment
  Accessory Equipment

  Fabricated and Component Parts
  Process Materials
  *Maintenance, Repair, and Operating
  Supplies (MRO)*
  Raw Materials
  Business Services
Business to Business Customers   17
  Commercial Enterprises
  Governmental Organizations
  Institutions
International Customers   19
Business to Business Marketing
Planning and Strategy Formulation   22
Format of the Text   23
Appendix: Careers in Business to
Business Marketing   27

PART II How Buyers Buy

**2   FUNDAMENTALS OF THE
      PURCHASING AND MATERIALS
      MANAGEMENT FUNCTION   30**

Basic Policies and Procedures of
Purchasing   31
The Business to Business Buying
Process   33
  Recognizing the Need
  Developing Product Specifications
  *Soliciting Bids from Potential
  Suppliers*
  Making the Purchase Decision
  Issuing the Contract
  Inspecting Goods for Quality
  Evaluating Vendor Performance

Purchasing Organization   37
*Organization Related to Size of a
Company*
*Centralization versus Decentralization
of the Buying Function*

The Materials Management Concept   42
*Alternative Approaches to Materials
Management*
*Reasons for Adopting the Materials
Management Concept*

Business to Business Buying
Situations   49
New-Task Buying
Straight Rebuy
Modified Rebuy

Purchasing Record Systems   54
Catalogue File
Open Order File
Vendor Experience File
Commodity Record File

Purchasing and the Law   55
Law of Agency
Laws of Contracts

Case 2–1: The Geer Company   59

Case 2–2: American Arbitration
Association   59

3   MANAGEMENT OF THE
ORGANIZATIONAL BUYING
FUNCTION   64

Objectives of Efficient Business to
Business Buying   65
Objectives of Organizational Buyers
Seven Rights of Business Buyers
Purchasing Costs

The Buyer Center   67

Quality in Business Buying and
Selling   70
*Responsibilities of the Purchasing
Department*

Service in Business Buying and
Selling   74
Differentiation through Service
Service as a Competitive Effort

Price in Business Buying and Selling   75
Perceived Value

Value Analysis   77
What Is It?
Development of Value Engineering
Appropriate Tests Used

Make-or-Buy Analysis   80
Ascertaining Profitability
Reasons to Manufacture
Participants in Make or Buy

Negotiation   82
Objectives of Negotiation
*Negotiation Maneuvers, Strategies,
and Tactics*
The Use of Questions
*Analyzing Both Buyer and Seller
Strengths*

The Small-Order Problem   88
The Centralized-Stores System
The Petty-Cash System
The Blanket-Order System
The Electronic Ordering System

Purchasing's Impact upon Company
Profit   91

Case 3–1: John Roberts
Manufacturing Company   95

Case 3–2: Berg Raingear, Inc.   97

Appendix: The Behavior of Successful
Negotiators   99

4   ORGANIZATIONAL BUYER
BEHAVIOR AND BUYER-SELLER
RELATIONSHIPS   112

The Changing Role of the Buyer   113
*Profile of a Business to Business
Buyer*

Models of Buyer Behavior   117
The Webster and Wind Model
The Sheth Model
The Choffray-Lilien Model

Business Buying Motives   122

Evaluating Potential Vendors   124
*Basic Considerations in Evaluating
Potential Vendors*
Vendor-Rating Approaches

Environmental Forces and Buying
Decisions   131
The Economic Environment
The Physical Environment
The Competitive Environment
The Technological Environment
The Legal-Political Environment
The Ethical Environment

Social, Legal, and Ethical
Considerations   137

Case 4–1: Howell Chuck Company   140

Case 4–2: Roberts Fiber Products
Company   142
CASES FOR PART TWO
Case 1: Templeton Engine Company   145
Case 2: City of Brookings: Marketing
to the Local Government Market   147

PART III   Identifying the Customer

5   BUSINESS TO BUSINESS
    MARKETING RESEARCH AND
    INFORMATION SYSTEMS   156

Differences between Business and
Consumer Marketing Research   157
    Focus of Marketing Research
Major Tasks of Marketing Research   159
    Market Potential
    Market-Share Analysis
    Market Characteristics
    Sales Analysis
    Forecasting
    Other Applications
Marketing Research versus a
Marketing Information System   162
    Five Basic Elements of Future
    Marketing Information Systems
    Primary Uses of a Marketing
    Information System
The Marketing Research Process   167
    Planning the Research Design
    Preparation
    Field Operations
    Processing
    Tabulation, Analysis, and Interpretation
    Reporting
Using Outside or Inside Research
Specialists—Make or Buy?   170
Developing Information Sources   171
    Secondary Data Sources
    Primary Data Sources
Organization of Marketing Research   183
Conducting International Marketing
Research   184
Case 5–1: Bonita Baking Company   187
Case 5–2: The Office Boss Company   189

6   MARKET SEGMENTATION,
    POSITIONING, AND DEMAND
    PROJECTION   194

Segmentation, Positioning, and
Demand Estimation Strategy: An
Overview   195
General Market Segmentation
Strategy   196
    The Nature of Market Segmentation
Strategies for Segmentation   197
    Undifferentiated Marketing Strategy
    Differentiated Marketing Strategy
    Concentrated Marketing Strategy
Approaches to Market Segmentation   199
    Macro/Micro Segmentation
    The Nested Approach to Market
    Segmentation
Segmenting Business to Business
Markets   203
    Type of Economic Activity
    Size of Organization
    Geographic Location
    Product Usage
    Structure of the Procurement
    Function
International Segmentation   205
Evaluating Potential Segments   206
    Market Profitability Analysis
    Market Competitive Analysis
Product Positioning Strategy   209
    Perceptual Mapping
    Positioning Business to Business
    Products
Demand Projection   217
    Strategic Importance of Forecasting
    in Decision Making
    Definition of Some Basic Terminology
    Common Forecasting Problems
Selecting Forecasting Methods   220
    General Approaches to Forecasting
    Qualitative Approaches to Forecasting
    Quantitative Approaches to Forecasting
Case 6–1: Purolator Takes Aim at
Federal Express   230
Case 6–2: Apple Computer   232
CASE FOR PART THREE
Case 1: Trus Joist Corporation (B)   237

PART IV   Making and Moving the Goods

7   PRODUCT DEVELOPMENT,
    MANAGEMENT, AND STRATEGY 250

Product Strategy in Business to
Business Marketing   251
  *Effective Product Management and
  Strategy*
New Product Development   253
  *New Product Approaches
  New Product Development Process*
Organization of the New Product
Effort   260
  *Product Manager
  New Product Committee
  New Product Department
  New Product Venture Team*
The Product Life-Cycle Analysis   263
  *An Application of the Product
  Life-Cycle Model
  Life Cycle and Experience Curves*
Determinants of the Product Mix   268
  *Technology
  Competition
  Changes in Levels of Business Activity
  Operating Capacity
  Market Factors*
The Product Adoption-Diffusion
Process   273
  *Stages in the Adoption Process
  Factors Influencing the Rate of
  Adoption-Diffusion*
Product Portfolio Classification,
Analysis, and Strategy   275
  *What Is the Product Portfolio?
  Diagnosing the Product Portfolio
  Product Portfolio Strategies*
Product Deletion Strategy   278
  *Harvesting
  Line Simplification
  Total Line Divestment*
International Product Strategy   281
Case 7–1: Chemicals, Inc.   284
Case 7–2: Mathewson Machine
Works, Inc.   286

8   BUSINESS TO BUSINESS PRICE
    PLANNING AND STRATEGY   290

Business to Business Pricing: An
Overview   291
Major Factors Influencing Price
Strategy   292
  *Competition
  Cost*

  *Demand
  Pricing Objectives
  Impact on Other Products
  Legal Considerations*
Pricing Methods and Strategies   296
  *Marginal Pricing
  Economic Value to the Customer (EVC)
  Break-Even Analysis
  Target Return-on-Investment Pricing*
Demand Assessment and Strategy   301
  *Price Elasticity of Demand
  Cost-Benefit Analysis*
Pricing across the Product Life Cycle
(Life-Cycle Costing)   303
  *Introduction Phase: New Product
  Pricing Strategies
  Growth Phase
  Maturity Phase
  Decline Phase*
Price Leadership Strategy   306
Competitive Bidding in the Business
to Business Market   307
  *Closed versus Open Bidding
  A Probabilistic Bidding Model*
Leasing in the Business to Business
Market   311
  *Advantages of Leasing for the Buyer
  Advantages of Leasing for the Seller
  Types of Lease Arrangements
  Types of Leases*
Pricing Policies in Business to
Business Pricing Strategy   315
  *Trade Discounts
  Quantity Discounts
  Cash Discounts
  Geographical Price Adjustments*
International Marketing Pricing
Policy   317
Case 8–1: The Loctite Corporation   320
Case 8–2: The Gallison Company   322

9   BUSINESS TO BUSINESS
    MARKETING CHANNEL
    PARTICIPANTS   328

Functions of the Channel
Intermediary   329
  *Buying
  Selling
  Storage
  Transportation*

Sorting
Financing
Risk Taking
Market Information
The Nature of Channel Decisions   333
Direct Channels   334
Sufficiency of the Sales-Volume Base   334
Indirect Channels   335
  The Business to Business Distributor
  The Manufacturers' Representative
  (Agent)
  Sales Agents and Brokers
  Facilitating Agencies
Both Direct and Indirect Channels   345
Channel Cooperation   347
  Methods of Channel Cooperation
Channel Conflict   348
  Nature of Channel Conflict
  Conflict Management and Resolution
  A Legal Perspective of Channel Conflict
  Typical Problem Areas in the
  Manufacturer-Intermediary Relationship
International Channel Decisions   354
  Types of Indirect Channel
  Intermediaries
Case 9–1: Xerox: A Distribution
Strategy Fails   358
Case 9–2: The Childers Machine
Company   359

10   BUSINESS TO BUSINESS
         PHYSICAL DISTRIBUTION
         MANAGEMENT AND STRATEGY   366
Physical Distribution in the Business
to Business Market   367
  The Nature of Physical Distribution
Traffic Management: An Overview   370
Functions of Traffic Management   371
  Mode and Carrier Selection
  Routing
  Claims Processing
  Operation of Private Transportation
Deregulation   374
Customer Service   376
  Customer Service Standards
  Examination of Cost Trade-Offs
  The Impact of Logistical Service on
  Channel Members

Warehousing   381
  Private or Public Warehouses?
Inventory Control   384
  The EOQ Model
  Just-in-Time Concept
Order Processing   387
  The Order-Processing Cycle
  Shortening the Order-Processing Cycle
  Vendor Stocking
Intensive, Selective, and Exclusive
Distribution   390
  Intensive Distribution
  Selective Distribution
  Exclusive Distribution
International Distribution   393
Conclusion   394
Case 10–1: Gorman Products, Inc.   396
Case 10–2: Shapely Sack Company,
Inc.   397
CASES FOR PART FOUR
Case 1: S. C. Johnson and Son,
Limited (R)   403
Case 2: Rosemount, Inc.: Industrial
Products Division   415

PART V   Promoting and Selling the Goods

11   THE PERSONAL SELLING
         FUNCTION IN BUSINESS
         MARKETING STRATEGY   428
How Personal Selling Differs between
Consumer and Business Goods'
Markets   429
A Profile of Personal Selling   430
  Selling
  Cooperative Relationships with Channel
  Members
  Planning
  Decision Making
  The Management of Communication
  The Cost of Personal Selling
  The Cost to Close a Business-to-
  Business Sale
Understanding Buyer Behavior   434
  Understanding Buyer Needs
  Methods to Uncover Important Needs of
  Buying Center Members
The Selling Spectrum   437

Different Approaches to the Sales Presentation
Types of Sales Positions and Selling Styles in the Business Market

Some Contemporary Trends in Business Selling   442
The Importance of Systems Selling
The Importance of Telemarketing
The Emergence of Saleswomen
The Usage of Terminals and Laptop Computers
The Rapid Growth of Audio-Visual Aids

The Personal Selling Process: A Business Salesperson's Perspective   450
Preliminary Activities
Face-to-Face Activities
Follow-Up Activities

International Business-to-Business Selling   457

Case 11–1: Douglas & Co.   461

Case 11–2: Barton Laboratories   465

12   BUSINESS TO BUSINESS SALES MANAGEMENT   470

Business to Business Sales Management: A Leadership Challenge   471

Selecting the Sales Manager   472
Perspectives
Goals
Responsibilities
Satisfaction
Job Skill Requirements
Relationships

Basic Types of Sales Organizations   474
The Line Organization
The Line and Staff Organization
The Functional Organization
The Centralized versus Decentralized Organization
Organizing By Specialization

Staffing the Sales Force   478
Determining Sales Force Size
Recruitment and Selection

Training and Development of the Sales Force   484
Purposes of Sales Training
What the Training Program Should Cover
Who Should Do the Training?

Evaluating Sales Training

Directing and Motivating the Sales Force   491
Providing Leadership
Sales Quotas
Compensation and Motivation
Sales Force Analysis and Evaluation
Why Analyze and Evaluate Salespeople?
Who Should Analyze and Evaluate Salespeople?
When Should It Be Done?

Managing U.S. Salespeople in International Markets   498
Selection
Orientation and Training
Compensation

Case 12–1: Teletronic Electronics   504

Case 12–2: Duncan Business Machines   507

13   ADVERTISING AND SALES PROMOTION STRATEGY IN BUSINESS MARKETS   512

An Overview of Business to Business Promotion   513

Creating a Promotion Plan   515

Setting Objectives for a Promotional Plan   515

Developing the Promotion Budget   516
Prioritizing the Promotion Expenditure

Determining and Implementing the Promotion Mix   519
Advertising
Publicity
Sales Promotion

Measuring the Effectiveness of the Promotion Campaign   538
Pretesting and Posttesting
Responses to Advertisements

Following Up and Modifying the Promotional Campaign if Necessary   539

Promotional Strategy for International Markets   540
International Business to Business Advertising
International Publicity and Sales Promotion

Case 13–1: How Diminishing Returns Affect Selection of Media   544

Case 13–2: Eagle Steel Supply
Company   548
CASES FOR PART FIVE
Case 1: Henderson Service Center   553
Case 2: CSX System   572

**PART VI   Trends in Business to Business
            Marketing**

14   MARKETING OF BUSINESS
     SERVICES   602
The Marketing of Services: An
Overview   603
The Environments for Business
Service Firms   604
   Economic Environment
   Societal/Cultural Environment
   Competitive Environment
   Technological Environment
   Political/Legal Environment
Important Characteristics of Business
Services   607
   Intangibility
   Perishability and Fluctuating Demand
   Simultaneity
   Heterogeneity
Business Service Marketing—
Challenges and Opportunities   610
   *Services Marketing versus Product
   Marketing*
   Positioning
   Bundling of Services
   Service Strategy and the Marketing Mix
   New Service Development
   Classification of Services
   Seller-Related Bases
   Buyer-Related Bases
   Service-Related Bases
   Classifying Services by Clusters
   *People-Based versus Equipment-Based
   Services*
International Marketing of Business
Services   625
   *The Risks of International Marketing
   for Service Organizations*
   *Problems of Adaptation to, and
   Operation in, Overseas Markets*
   Barriers to Trade in Services

The Future of Business to Business
Services   627
Case 14–1: The U.S. Postal Service 630
Case 14–2: DataCorp of Virginia, Inc. 631

15   ETHICAL CONSIDERATIONS IN
     BUSINESS TO BUSINESS
     MARKETING   636
Marketing Ethics and the Future: An
Overview   637
   *Examples of Corporate Social
   Responsibility*
   The Individuality of Ethical Standards
Strategy and Ethics in the Business to
Business Marketing Environment   641
An Ethical Issue: The Organizational
Buying Function and Buyer-Seller
Relationships   642
   *Business Ethics Is Not a One-Sided
   Proposition*
Ethical Issues in Marketing Research 644
   Societal Rights
   Clients' Rights
Ethics and the Management of the
Pricing Function   646
   *Selling a Price That Meets Company
   Objectives, While Not Taking Advantage
   of the Customer*
   *Altering Product Quality without
   Changing Price*
   *Practicing Price Discrimination with
   Smaller Accounts*
   Price-Fixing
   *Obtaining Information on a
   Competitor's Price Quotation in Order
   to Requote or Rebid*
   Reciprocity
Ethics and the Management of the
Sales Force   649
   Ethics in Dealing with Customers
   Ethics in Dealing with Employers
Ethics and Advertising Strategy   653
   Truth in Advertising
   Comparative Advertising
Ethics and International Marketing   655
   Ethics Differ from Country to Country
   *The Complexity of International Ethical
   Issues*

Case 15–1: Manville Corporation   661

Case 15–2: Cotton Belt Exporting   662

Appendix 15A: Future Trends in
Business to Business Marketing   666
CASES FOR PART SIX

Case 1: Rogers, Nagel, Langhart (RNL
PC), Architects and Planners   671

PART VII   Comprehensive Cases

Case 1: Canadair Challenger Jet   689

Case 2: The Kingston-Warren
Company   711

Index   731

PART ONE

Introduction

Chapter 1 · The Business to Business
Marketing Environment

Chapter **1**

The Business to Business Marketing Environment

LEARNING OBJECTIVES

After reading this chapter, you should be able to:

- Discuss the differences between business to business and consumer marketing.
- Describe the characteristics of business to business demand.
- Understand the nature of organizational buying behavior.
- Distinguish among the basic types of business to business goods and services.
- Differentiate among the various kinds of organizational customers.
- Appreciate the increasing importance of international customers in business to business markets.
- Explain the pivotal importance to the business marketing effort of planning and strategy formulation.

CHAPTER OUTLINE

Business to Business Marketing:
An Overview
  The Business to Business Market
Why Study Business to Business
Marketing?
How the Business to Business
Market Differs from the Consumer
Market
  Greater Total Sales Volume
  Larger Volume Purchases
  Fewer Buyers
  Larger Buyers
  Geographically Concentrated Buyers
  Close Supplier-Customer
   Relationship
  More Direct Channels of
   Distribution
  Professional Buying
  Multiple Buying Influences
  Complex Negotiation
  Reciprocity
  Leasing
  Emphasis on Personal Selling
Characteristics of Business to
Business Demand
  Derived Demand
  Inelastic Demand
  Fluctuating Demand
  Joint Demand

The Nature of Business to
Business Buying Behavior
A Classification of Business to
Business Goods and Services
  Major Equipment
  Accessory Equipment
  Fabricated and Component Parts
  Process Materials
  Maintenance, Repair, and Operating
   Supplies (MRO)
  Raw Materials
  Business Services
Business to Business Customers
  Commercial Enterprises
  Governmental Organizations
  Institutions
International Customers
Business to Business Marketing
Planning and Strategy Formulation
  Analyzing the Environment
Format of the Text

■ BUSINESS TO BUSINESS MARKETING: AN OVERVIEW

In one way or another most large firms sell to other organizations. Companies such as Xerox and DuPont sell most of their product mix to organizations. Even large consumer products companies engage in organizational or business to business marketing. For example, General Mills manufactures a number of well-known products for the consumer market, such as Gold Medal flour, Betty Crocker cake mixes and frostings, Cheerios cereal, and Parker Brother games. Yet before these products reach the final consumer, General Mills must first sell them to wholesale and retail organizations that serve consumer markets. General Mills also manufactures and distributes other products, such as specialty chemicals, which are marketed only to industrial markets.[1]

Business to business or industrial organizations, such as Xerox, DuPont, and General Mills, constitute a vast market consisting of over 13 million organizations that buy more than $3 trillion worth of goods and services each year. Companies that sell to other organizations must do their best to understand organizational buying behavior and the buyer needs, resources, motivations, and buying processes that shape such behavior. In addition, the marketer must have a firm grasp of how some of the traditional marketing tools and techniques that have been studied, used, and written about for many years present major opportunities and challenges for business to business marketing.

The Business to Business Market

A business to business marketing transaction takes place whenever a good or service is sold for any use other than personal consumption, and all the activities involved in this process make up **business to business marketing.**

Basically, this market consists of individuals and organizations acquiring goods and services for the production of products and services that are sold, rented, or supplied to others. This market includes buyers from many types of industries—manufacturing; construction; transportation; communication; banking, finance, and insurance; agriculture, forestry, and fisheries; mining; and public utilities. The growing importance of highly technical products, the significant changes in the pattern of final demand, the rapid pace of technological change, the increasing size and complexity of the business to business firm and its customers, the growing impact of the computer and management services, and the success of foreign competition, have highlighted the need for innovative marketing strategies. All formal organizations, public or private, profit or not-for-profit, participate in the buying and selling of business to business products and services. The study of this process is what this book is all about.

■ WHY STUDY BUSINESS TO BUSINESS MARKETING?

Traditionally, business to business marketing has been a distant cousin of mainstream marketing thought. However, the employment opportunities, along with the growing importance of high-technology products and the success of foreign competition, have highlighted the need for increased marketing study in this area.

The increasing size of the business market warrants the study of this sector. In 1986 there were more than 350,000 manufacturing establishments

---

[1]Philip Kotler, *Principles of Marketing,* 3rd ed. (Englewood Cliffs, N.J.: Prentice-Hall, 1986), p. 210.

in the United States, employing over 20 million people. These firms were responsible for $2.5 trillion in sales. Another 300,000 firms provided services to businesses and other organizations, while over 400,000 firms served as assemblers, resellers, wholesalers, manufacturers' agents, and brokers. Table 1–1 provides comparative sales figures for manufacturing, wholesaling, and retailing establishments in the United States, while Table 1–2 is a general breakdown of major manufacturing industries, a $2.3 trillion market. These totals point out the unlimited career opportunities available for students of business to business marketing.

Other reasons for the increased study of business to business marketing are the significance of the international interdependence of many firms, along with the importance of the service sector of the economy, which in the United States is more than twice as large as the manufacturing sector. Deregulation, changes in professional association standards, and the application of computer technology combine to produce dramatic changes in the environment of many service industries. The increasingly competitive

■ **TABLE 1–1**   U.S. Manufacturing and Trade Sales for 1985 *(In millions of dollars)*

Manufacturing	$2,341,220
Durable goods industries	1,243,793
Nondurable goods industries	1,097,427
Retail Trade	$1,373,941
Durable goods stores	514,207
Nondurable goods stores	859,734
Merchant Wholesalers	$1,373,926
Durable goods establishments	626,749
Nondurable goods establishments	747,177

SOURCE: *1986 Survey of Current Business.*

■ **TABLE 1–2**   U.S. Manufacturers' Sales for 1985 *(In millions of dollars)*

Stone, clay, and glass products	$ 57,255
Primary metals	125,777
Fabricated metal parts	168,953
Machinery, except electrical	212,620
Electrical machinery	185,514
Transportation equipment	313,427
Instruments and related products	56,743
Food and kindred products	296,142
Tobacco products	20,606
Paper and allied products	97,565
Chemicals and allied products	214,345
Petroleum and coal products	194,030
Rubber and plastic products	48,246

SOURCE: *1986 Survey of Current business.*

nature of both the international and service sectors of the business to business market requires a new emphasis on marketing for such diverse industries as airlines and accounting, hotels and hospitals, banking and real estate brokerages, and manufacturing. Both international business to business marketing and business service marketing are covered in this text.

Finally, the bulk of academic research has focused on consumer goods marketing, while business to business marketing has been relegated to the sidelines. However, the situation is changing. This rather cavalier attitude overlooks the distinct differences between the two fields, while emphasizing their similarities. The attractiveness of the opportunities in the business to business marketing field will continue to grow because the majority of students graduating with bachelor's and master's degrees begin their careers with business to business firms, rather than with consumer goods companies.[2] (Appendix 1A details career possibilities within this marketing field.) More and more of the over 1,500 schools of business in the United States today offer business to business marketing courses, because a typical business recruiter is often faced with a pool of applicants lacking even a basic comprehension of what the world of nonconsumer goods is like. The study and understanding of business to business marketing management, out of necessity, will continue to grow.

■ HOW THE BUSINESS TO BUSINESS MARKET DIFFERS FROM THE CONSUMER MARKET

Many differences can be found between the marketing of business goods and the marketing of consumer goods. Paper Mate,[3] a division of Gillette, has traditionally manufactured and distributed medium-priced ballpoint pens to consumer markets. As this particular market became increasingly segmented into lower- and premium-priced offerings, Paper Mate decided to provide products at both ends of the price continuum.

The firm entered the business to business market by catering to the office-supplies field. Paper Mate created a special commercial sales force to market its pens to buyers. It also acquired Liquid Paper, an established brand name in office supplies. Top management viewed the business to business marketing strengths of Liquid Paper as complementary to Paper Mate's specialization in consumer markets. Paper Mate was fully aware that markets differed from consumer markets, and that the characteristics of business markets necessitated the design of new marketing strategies that would not be appropriate for use in consumer segments.

---

[2]Peter La Place, *Journal of Business & Industrial Marketing* 3, no. 1 (Winter 1988), p. 3.

[3]The Paper Mate example is from David L. Kurtz and Louis E. Boone, *Marketing,* 3d ed. (New York: Dryden Press, 1987), pp. 248–49.

Business markets have specific characteristics that differ significantly from consumer markets.[4] These are discussed below and summarized in Exhibit 1–1.[5]

Greater Total Sales Volume

Total dollar sales in the business to business market are greater than they are in the consumer market, even though there are far fewer business buyers than final consumers. An automobile bought by a final consumer is viewed as one sale in the consumer market, yet numerous sales transactions occurred in the process of manufacturing that automobile. Iron ore was mined and sold to a steel producer who, in turn, sold steel to the automobile manufacturer. Many other transactions also occurred before the automobile came off the assembly line.

Larger Volume Purchases

Business to business marketers also sell to customers who buy in larger quantities than do final consumers. For instance, Ford Motor Company buys several hundred thousand tires from different major tire manufactur-

■ **EXHIBIT 1–1**   Characteristics of Business to Business Markets as Compared to Consumer Markets

The following is a summary of the characteristics of business to business markets when compared to consumer markets:

Characteristic	Business to Business Market	Consumer Market
Sales volume	Greater	Smaller
Purchase volume	Larger	Smaller
Number of buyers	Fewer	Many
Size of individual buyers	Larger	Smaller
Location of buyers	Geographically concentrated	Diffuse
Buyer-seller relationship	Closer	More impersonal
Nature of channel	More direct	More indirect
Nature of buying	More professional	More personal
Nature of buying influence	Multiple	Single
Type of negotiations	More complex	Simpler
Use of reciprocity	Yes	No
Use of Leasing	Greater	Smaller
Primary promotional method	Personal selling	Advertising

[4]However, for an argument that consumer and business to business marketing do not differ significantly, see Edward F. Fern and James R. Brown, "The Industrial/Consumer Dichotomy: A Case of Insufficient Justification," *Journal of Marketing* (Spring 1984), pp. 68–77.

[5]This section is from Philip Kotler, *Marketing Management: Analysis, Planning, Implementation, and Control,* 6th ed. (Englewood Cliffs, N.J.: Prentice-Hall, 1988), pp. 209–11; William F. Schoell, *Marketing: Contemporary Concepts and Practices,* 2nd ed. (Boston: Allyn & Bacon, 1985, pp. 642–43; and William M. Pride and O. C. Ferrell, *Marketing,* 3d ed. (Boston: Houghton Mifflin, 1983), pp. 603–7.

ers. An electric company buys thousands of barrels of oil under a long-term contract with a distributor.

Fewer Buyers

A business to business marketer generally deals with far fewer buyers than does the consumer marketer. Firms that sell to manufacturers usually have less difficulty identifying prospective customers than do firms that sell to final consumers. For example, Allegheny International sells its specialty

■ **FIGURE 1–1**   The Geographic Distribution of U.S. Manufacturing Plants Based on Selected Criteria

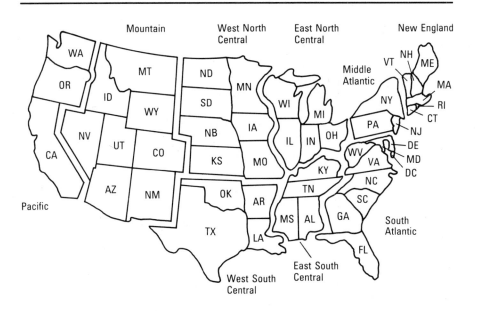

	Percent of Nation's Total in Each Region			
Region	Number of Manufacturing Plants (%)	Number of Manufacturing Employees (%)	Value Added by Manufacturers (%)	Value of Manufacturers' Shipments (%)
New England	7.2	7.6	6.8	5.5
Middle Atlantic	18.3	16.8	16.3	14.3
East North Central	18.8	22.1	23.5	23.8
West North Central	6.7	6.8	7.5	8.0
South Atlantic	13.6	15.7	14.3	13.8
East South Central	5.2	6.7	6.1	6.5
West South Central	8.9	8.0	8.8	12.3
Mountain	4.1	3.0	2.9	2.9
Pacific	17.2	13.3	13.7	12.7
Total U.S.	100.0	100.0	100.0	100.0

SOURCE: U.S. Department of Commerce, *Statistical Abstract of the United States 1987,* 107th ed. (Washington, D.C.: U. S. Government Printing Office, 1987), p. 731.

metals and electronics for jet engines to a very few airplane manufacturers, while its Oster and Sunbeam divisions sell appliances for the consumer market through thousands of distributors and retail stores.

Larger Buyers

Unlike final consumer markets, a few large buyers account for most of the purchasing in many business to business markets. In the telephone and telegraph, aircraft engines and engine parts, motor vehicles, and organic fiber industries, the top four manufacturers account for over 70 percent of total production.

Geographically Concentrated Buyers

Business to business buyers are geographically concentrated, whereas final consumers are found virtually everywhere. As Figure 1–1 shows, over two-thirds of the industrial firms in the United States are located in the Middle Atlantic, East North Central, South Atlantic, and Pacific states. Over half of U.S. business buyers are located in just seven states: New York, Pennsylvania, New Jersey, Ohio, Michigan, Illinois, and California. The aircraft and microelectronics industries are concentrated on the West Coast, and many of the firms that supply the automobile manufacturing industry are located in the Detroit area. Most agricultural output also comes from a relatively few states.

Close Supplier-Customer Relationship

There is a close relationship between sellers and customers in business to business markets because of the smaller customer base, the greater volume and cost of the average sale, and the importance and power of the larger customers over the suppliers. Sales are typically made by those suppliers who closely cooperate with the buyer on technical specifications and delivery requirements. The following "Business to Business Marketing in Action" box describes the benefits derived from the close relationship General Motors has with its suppliers.

More Direct Channels of Distribution

In consumer markets the great majority of goods are sold through a complex structure of wholesalers and retailers who serve as intermediaries between the producer and the consumer. Frozen foods, for example, are sold to several types of wholesalers or food brokers. In turn, these distributors will sell the frozen foods to supermarkets and institutional users. In most business to business marketing, however, sellers and buyers are more directly linked. When dealing with very large purchasers, marketers can make direct sales rather than go through industrial distributors or other intermediaries. However, some products sold to business buyers are commonly sold through one or two levels of wholesalers.

BUSINESS TO BUSINESS MARKETING IN ACTION

General Motors (GM), the U.S. steel industry's largest customer, buys thousands of tons of numerous types and gauges (thickness) of steel. At the beginning of each year GM traditionally awarded each of a dozen or so suppliers a certain percentage of its requirements for particular types and gauges of steel at specific plants.

More recently, GM has made some basic changes in the way it buys steel. The firm now concentrates larger purchases on a smaller number of suppliers. GM's management figured the firm would be able to work more closely with fewer suppliers, ensuring that the suppliers deliver the types and quality of steel GM needs. By placing larger orders with fewer suppliers and entering into multiyear contracts, GM may benefit in another way: it may pay lower prices because the suppliers enjoy lower production costs through economies of scale. Closer long-term relationships with its suppliers should also enable GM to lower reject rates on steel shipments received, gain manufacturing efficiencies because of the greater reliability of the steel, and operate with less inventory.

In selecting its suppliers GM ranks them in terms of traditional criteria such as product quality, ability to deliver on time, and price. But because it wants to develop closer long-term relationships with its suppliers, GM also looks at their limitations with respect to producing various widths and gauges of steel, financial strength, and commitment to remaining in the steel-making business and modernizing their facilities.

SOURCES: Steven Flax, "How Detroit Is Reforming the Steelmakers," *Fortune*, May 16, 1983, pp. 127–29; and Amal Nag, "GM Is Said to Seek Long-Term Accords with Steelmakers," *The Wall Street Journal*, May 6, 1983, p. 2. Reprinted from William F. Schoell, *Marketing*, 2d ed. (Boston: Allyn & Bacon, 1985), p. 633.

Professional Buying

Business buyers normally take a more formalized approach to buying than do final consumers. A salesperson who is selling portable typewriters in a Sears store generally deals with only one prospect at a time. Yet an IBM typewriter salesperson may have to give product demonstrations to a firm's purchasing manager, office manager, and secretaries. The professional training of purchasing personnel has resulted in a professional certification program whereby the individual earns the designation of Certified Purchasing Manager (CPM). This distinction comes after several years in the field or a degree from a recognized college or university, in addition to three years of vocational training. Such individuals must then pass a series of examinations before they can place CPM after their names. Business to business buyers are professional buyers, and selling to them requires professional salespeople.

Multiple Buying Influences

More people typically influence organizational buying decisions than consumer buying decisions. Buying committees composed of technical experts and senior management are common in the purchase of major goods. This phenomenon, coupled with the cross-functional nature of these influences, complicates the marketing communications process. Therefore, marketers must employ well-trained sales representatives, and they often use sales teams to deal with highly skilled buyers.

Complex Negotiation

Although there are a few consumer goods, such as automobiles and real estate, in which negotiation commonly takes place, considerable buyer-seller negotiation exists in the purchase and sale of more expensive business products. For example, the Ford Motor Company contracted with H. O. Smith in 1980 to manufacture the engine cradle for the 1986 Sable and Taurus models. In addition to product specifications, delivery dates, payment terms, and price were subject to negotiation. In many cases buyer representatives meet with seller representatives several times to negotiate sales contracts; and this process may continue over several months.

Reciprocity

Business buyers often choose suppliers who also purchase from them. For instance, a paper manufacturer may buy chemicals for its production process from a chemical company that buys large amounts of its paper. GM buys engines for use in its automobiles and trucks from Borg Warner, which, in turn, buys many of the automobiles and trucks it needs from GM. Reciprocity is considered to be illegal if there is a coercive use of pressure by one of the parties that results in reduced competition. Noncoercive reciprocity is legal provided it is supported by elaborate records of purchases and sales to and from other parties.[6] Governmental investigations are currently being conducted into the possibility of illegal influence in procurement in governmental organizations.

Leasing

Many business to business buyers lease their equipment rather than buy it. Computers, packaging equipment, heavy-construction equipment, machine tools, and sales-force automobiles serve as examples of this phenomenon.

---

[6]See Louis W. Stern and Thomas L. Eovaldi, *Legal Aspects of Marketing Strategy* (Englewood Cliffs, N.J.: Prentice-Hall, 1984).

The lessee is able to conserve capital, acquire the seller's latest products, receive better servicing, and gain tax advantages. The lessor often receives a larger net income and has the opportunity to sell to those customers who could not afford to purchase the equipment outright.[7] For example, General Electric leases personal computers manufactured by IBM, Apple, and Hewlett-Packard, along with related equipment and software programs, to business customers.[8]

Emphasis on Personal Selling

Because of the characteristics discussed above, business to business marketers emphasize personal selling more than advertising in designing and implementing their marketing mixes. A good salesperson can tailor presentations and highlight different product features for those individuals involved in the product purchase. The cost of a sales call can be justified because of the size, complexity, and sales volume per account of most business products, as compared to a typical consumer product. The use of personal selling, in contrast to advertising, provides immediate customer feedback, and sales representatives can adjust their promotional messages on the spot.

Concept Questions

1. What is a business to business market?
2. Why is personal selling, rather than advertising, more commonly used in business to business marketing?

■ CHARACTERISTICS OF BUSINESS TO BUSINESS DEMAND

Business to business demand can be described as derived, inelastic, and fluctuating in nature. There is even joint demand for some business goods. These characteristics are different from consumer product demand, and each will be discussed briefly.

Derived Demand

All demand for business to business goods is derived from the demand for consumer goods and services. **Derived demand** can be defined as the *demand for a business to business product that is linked to demand for a consumer good.* If the demand for consumer goods falls off, so will the demand for all the goods entering into production. For this reason, the marketer must closely monitor the buying patterns of the final consumers

---

[7]See Russell Hindin, "Lease Your Way to Corporate Growth," *Financial Executive,* May 1984, pp. 20–25.

[8]"GE Sets Business Rentals of Personal Computers," *The Wall Street Journal,* March 30, 1983, p. 23.

and the environmental factors affecting them.[9] Briggs and Stratton Corporation advertises its lawn mower engines to encourage customers to purchase lawn mowers with Briggs & Stratton engines. Additionally, the company markets its engines to original equipment manufacturers (OEM), such as the Toro Company, which uses engines as component parts in lawn mowers.[10] In the long run no business to business demand is totally unrelated to the demand for consumer goods.

Inelastic Demand

Because of the derived demand for business products, there is less opportunity for marketers to stimulate primary demand (demand for a product category) through price cuts than there is for consumer goods marketers. Therefore, the primary demand for business to business products is more price-inelastic than that for consumer products. For example, automobile manufacturers purchase headlights as component parts for automobiles. If the price of headlights goes down, the automobile manufacturers are not very likely to increase greatly their purchase of headlights. If, however, they expect the price decrease to be temporary, they may do some stockpiling. But this will result in a change in the timing of orders, and not an increase in the long-run purchase volume. Because the cost of headlights accounts for a very small part of the total cost of manufacturing an automobile, a reduction of a few cents in the selling price of cars is unlikely to stimulate new car sales. Also, the price of headlights could increase significantly before it would have much effect on the sales of headlights.[11]

Fluctuating Demand

The demand for business goods and services tends to be more volatile than the demand for consumer goods and services. This is especially true of the demand for new products and equipment. A percentage increase in consumer demand can lead to a much larger percentage increase in the demand for plant and equipment necessary to produce the additional output. This phenomenon is often referred to as the **acceleration principle.** An increase in consumer demand of only 10 percent can result in as much as a 200 percent rise in industrial demand in the next period; and a 10 percent decrease in consumer demand can cause a total collapse in the demand for business goods. This demand volatility has caused many marketers to di-

---

[9]See William S. Bishop, John L. Graham, and Michael H. Jones, "Volatility of Derived Demand in Industrial Markets and Its Management Implications," *Journal of Marketing,* (Fall 1984), pp. 95–103.

[10]William F. Schoell and Joseph P. Guiltinan, *Marketing,* 3d ed. (Boston: Allyn & Bacon, 1988), p. 176.

[11]Ibid., pp. 178–79.

versify their product lines and markets in order to achieve more balanced sales over the business cycle.

Joint Demand

The demand for a number of business products, such as raw materials and component parts, is affected by joint demand. **Joint demand** occurs when two or more items are used in combination to produce a product. For instance, a firm that manufactures hammers needs the same number of handles as it does hammer heads; these two products are demanded jointly. If the supplier of handles cannot furnish the required number, and the hammer producer cannot obtain them elsewhere, the producer will stop buying hammer heads.

■ THE NATURE OF BUSINESS TO BUSINESS BUYING BEHAVIOR

On the whole, business buyers tend to be more cautious than final consumers. Such buyers generally make a conscious and deliberate effort to act rationally and to do what is best for their companies. Table 1–3 illustrates how business customers and final consumers might view the same product differently. Business buyers, however, are not totally rational in their buying behavior. In fact, according to many marketing practitioners, selling to business buyers is very frequently a personality-oriented sales situation, as is true in final consumer transactions. Although the demand or need for business products is usually economically motivated and rational, this

■ **TABLE 1–3**   Business to Business Users and Final Consumers Evaluate the Same Products

Product	Questions Asked by Typical Business to Business Users	Questions Asked by Typical Ultimate Consumers
Typewriter	Will it increase office efficiency?	Will it help my son prepare better school reports?
	What is its capital investment value?	Will it improve my correspondence?
	Does it have special features that will help improve our company image?	Is a portable electric machine worth the extra cost?
Automobile	How efficient is the vehicle to operate?	How does it enhance my status?
	Would it be more economical to lease or purchase it?	What is its potential trade-in value?
	What is the expected working life span of the car?	Will I get reasonable gas mileage?
Telephone	Will expanded service lower the cost of communicating with our customers?	How long will it take to have one installed?
	Should our intercom system be separate from or connected to the telephone system?	Can I get three jacks and two telephones?
		What colors and styles are available?

SOURCE: John T. Mentzer and David J. Schwartz, *Marketing Today,* 4th ed. (New York: Harcourt Brace Jovanovich, 1985).

should not be confused with the actions taken to satisfy that need, or the behavioral aspects of the business to business purchaser.

Most marketers and sales managers go to great lengths to differentiate their products. Despite their efforts, buyers are unlikely to purchase from them unless the buyers are convinced of the seller's integrity and the adequacy of postsale support. Such a conviction is largely subjective in nature, and subjective judgments are seldom entirely rational in the economic sense.[12]

■ A CLASSIFICATION OF BUSINESS TO BUSINESS GOODS AND SERVICES

Business goods and services can be classified in a variety of ways. Business goods are generally classified according to tax treatment and end use. In order to appreciate the differences in demand represented by different types of products, a useful scheme for classifying business to business products might include at least the following: major equipment, accessory equipment, fabricated and component parts, process materials, maintenance, repair, and operating supplies (MRO), raw materials, and business services. Each of these is discussed below.

Major Equipment

This category, which is frequently referred to as *installations,* consists mainly of products such as machinery, computers, machine tools, stamping machines, and robots. The demand for **major equipment** is considered inelastic and is charged to a capital account because of the intent of the purchase and the nature of the product. In view of price and technical requirements, the purchase of major equipment usually requires close cooperation between the technical and sales staff of both the business buyer and seller. Installment payment schedules and leasing arrangements are common because of the large investment involved; they highlight the significant financial involvement for the buyer. The major equipment for one company may be a piece of accessory equipment for another. The seller's marketing strategy includes a strong personal selling effort, exposure to multiple buying influences in most cases, and strong engineering and service support by the salesperson or sales team.

Accessory Equipment

Accessory equipment is used to facilitate production, administrative, clerical, or marketing activities. Some examples are calculators, office equipment, and fire extinguishers. In general, accessory equipment tends to be standardized and less costly than major equipment. The demand for acces-

---

[12]This section is from W. S. Penn, Jr., and Mark Mougel, "Industrial Marketing Myths," in *Dynamics of Marketing Principles: A Reader,* ed. Thomas C. Kinnear and Kenneth L. Bernhardt (Glenview, Ill.: Scott, Foresman, 1983), p. 51.

sory equipment exhibits an elastic demand curve, and less technical service is required on the part of the seller. The purchase may be considered routine, distribution channels are usually longer, and fewer buying influences are involved in the purchase decision.

Fabricated and Component Parts

Fabricated and component parts—for example, spark plugs, timing devices, and switches—are purchased for inclusion into the final product. Although they typically become part of another product, fabricated and component parts can often be easily identified and distinguished. Business buyers purchase such items according to their own predetermined specifications or by standards common within an industry. In purchasing component parts, buyers expect the parts to consistently meet a specified quality level, and to be delivered on time so that production is not slowed or stopped.

Process Materials

Process materials differ from fabricated and component parts in that most of them cannot be identified or regrouped in the finished product. Examples of such products are chemicals, plastics, cement, asphalt, and steel bar stock. Most processed materials are marketed to customers who are original equipment manufacturers (OEM) or to distributors who, in turn, sell to the OEM market, as very few have a replacement market. Process materials are generally bought per specifications prepared by the user or bought according to standards developed by a particular trade. Certain grades of lumber and some chemicals fit into this category. Generally, price and service are important factors in the sale of process materials.

Maintenance, Repair, and Operating Supplies (MRO)

MRO supplies do not become part of the finished product, but are used up in the production process. Examples of maintenance supplies are brooms, nails, paint, cleaning compounds, and light bulbs. Repair supplies include bearings, gears, and filters. Typing paper, ink, paper clips, pens and pencils, and lubricating oils are types of operating supplies. All these supplies facilitate the production process, have a relatively short life, and are generally less expensive than most other business goods. MRO items are usually standardized, involve longer channels of distribution, expose the seller to fewer buying influences, and show a more elastic demand curve than accessory equipment.

Raw Materials

Raw materials, which are often considered the basic lifeblood of industry, are supplied primarily by the agriculture, lumber, mining, and fishing industries. Raw materials become part of a manufactured product, are generally bought in large quantities, and exhibit an inelastic demand curve. They are usually purchased on the basis of such recognized standards as grade designations or sets of specifications. Channels of distribution can be either long or short, and multiple buying influences are involved in the purchase, at least in the initial stages of the procurement cycle.

Business Services

Services provided to firms by banks, insurance companies, advertising agencies, CPA and law firms, employment agencies, and management consultants are **business services.** Let's take as an example Mead Corporation's Lexpat service, a computer-assisted patent search. Attorneys, business executives, and engineers who use this service can conduct patent searches from their own offices instead of at the U.S. Patent and Trademark Office in Washington, D.C.

Business services are expense items that do not become part of the final product. The buyer has decided that buying the service from outside specialists is less costly than having company employees perform it. Multiple buying influences may be present when the cost of a service exceeds a preestablished amount.[13]

Concept Questions

1. How is business to business demand based on consumer demand?
2. Why is business to business demand said to be inelastic?
3. When does joint demand occur in business to business markets?

■ BUSINESS TO BUSINESS CUSTOMERS

To gain a full understanding of business to business marketing, we need to examine the many different customers it serves. These customers can be broken down into three categories: (1) commercial enterprises, (2) governmental organizations, and (3) institutions. Since each of these customers buys goods and services in a different way, we need to adjust our marketing strategy to the kind of customer we have in mind.

Commercial Enterprises

Commercial enterprises consist of the following: (1) indirect channel members, (2) original equipment manufacturers (OEMs), and (3) user customers.

Indirect Channel Members. This category consists of firms engaged in reselling goods in basically the same form to commercial, governmental, or institutional markets. Some, most notably industrial distributors and dealers, take title to the goods. The functions, scope, and limitations of the channel intermediary will be discussed in detail in Chapter 9.

---

[13]Schoell and Guiltinan, p. 260.

Original Equipment Manufacturers (OEMs).   OEMs buy business goods which they, in turn, incorporate into the products they produce for eventual sale to either the business or consumer market. Thus tire producers, such as Firestone, Goodyear, or Michelin, that sell tires to Ford Motor Company consider Ford to be an OEM.

User Customers.   User customers generally buy products to support a manufacturing facility. Ford Motor Company might buy stamping equipment to form auto parts made from metal or plastic-injection molding machines to produce parts made from plastic. In addition, Ford might purchase milling machines to produce precision tooling for use with the metal stamping operation. These purchases do not become part of the finished product; they only help produce it.

Overlap of Categories.   The three categories discussed above focus on how the customers use the products. For example, one user might be a manufacturer purchasing goods to use in a manufacturing process. A second might be an OEM buying goods it intends to use in a manufactured product. A third might be a manufacturer of machinery that purchases raw materials it needs in a production process, and a fourth customer might be an OEM buying gear assemblies to incorporate into the machinery it manufactures. Here again the category of customer depends on how the product is to be used and the reason for its purchase.

Governmental Organizations

Governmental organizations include thousands of federal, state, and local buying units, and account for about 20 percent of our gross national product (GNP).[14] Much government procurement is done on a bid basis, with the government advertising for bids, stating product specifications, and accepting the lowest bid that meets the specifications. Such a procedure sometimes results in the rejection of the lowest bids. For example, the board of New York City's Metropolitan Transportation Authority must provide toilet paper in the 1,000+ restrooms included in the services of the system. When deciding whether or not to approve a $168,840 toilet paper purchase—an amount higher than three other bids—the board asked the following question of management: "Why did you reject the lower bids?" The director responded that the authority had rejected one supplier because there was insufficient tissue on the roll, while two other suppliers were ruled out because their tissue was somewhat like sandpaper and obviously not soft enough. In light of this explanation, the board approved the higher bid.

Although the governmental market could be a lucrative market for some astute marketers, many make no real effort to sell to the government be-

---

[14]Kenneth H. Bacon, "A Repeat of '29' Depression in '87 Is Not Expected," *The Wall Street Journal,* October 20, 1987, pp. 1 and 24.

cause of the red tape involved. Dealing with the government to any significant extent usually requires specialized marketing techniques and information.[15]

Institutions

Some business marketers are now paying long overdue attention to the multibillion dollar market of **nonbusiness or not-for-profit institutions.** This potentially lucrative market includes such diverse institutions as colleges and universities, museums, hospitals, labor unions, charitable organizations, and churches. These organizations, which have real marketing problems, spend billions of dollars buying products and services for their organizations.

Marketers who desire to sell to the institutional market must be aware of the diversity of this market, and tailor their marketing programs to meet the particular needs and wants of prospective customers. For instance, let's suppose that Acme Foods, a small food products marketer, wants to market its products to hospitals and nursing homes in smaller communities. Acme's primary focus would probably be on the chief dietitian, who must approve food products before the hospital or nursing home's purchasing director can contract for their purchase. However, if Acme also desires to sell its products to larger health-care institutions in metropolitan areas, it would need to target its marketing program to a diverse group of individuals (the institution's administrator, business manager, purchasing director, and chief dietitian), each of whom influences the buying decision.[16]

■ INTERNATIONAL CUSTOMERS

Most business to business organizations can no longer safely ignore international influences, as was once the case. This is because many companies have been forced to reassess their role in the world market as well as in the United States because of a threat to their domestic sales. Today major U.S. corporations export millions of dollars of goods to international markets, and such exports represent an increasingly greater percentage of such companies' total sales. Table 1–4 ranks the 50 largest U.S. business to business exporters by the dollar volume of their exports.

Many firms are finding that to be competitive nationally, they must also be competitive internationally. A number of factors are causing a growing variety and quantity of foreign goods to enter the American market, destroying the isolation from foreign competition that U.S. firms previously enjoyed. Some of these factors are increasing affluence, greater sophisti-

---

[15]See Warren H. Suss, "How to Sell to Uncle Sam," *Harvard Business Review* (November-December 1984), pp. 136–44; and David E. Gumpert and Jeffrey A. Timmons, "Penetrating the Government Procurement Maze," *Harvard Business Review* (September-October 1982), pp. 14–23.

[16]Schoell and Guiltinan, pp. 638–39.

■ **TABLE 1-4** The 50 Largest U.S. Business to Business Exporters in 1987 *(Ranked by dollar volume of exports)*

Rank 1987	Rank 1986	Company	Products	Export Sales $ Millions	Export Sales Percent change 1986–87	Total Sales $ Millions	Total Sales Fortune 500 Rank	Exports as Percent of Sales Percent	Exports as Percent of Sales Rank
1	1	General Motors, Detroit	Motor vehicles and parts	8,731.3	4.4	101,781.9	1	8.6	37
2	3	Ford Motor, Dearborn, Mich.	Motor vehicles and parts	7,614.0	5.1	71,643.4	3	10.6	30
3	2	Boeing, Seattle	Commercial and military aircraft	6,286.0	−14.2	15,355.0	20	40.9	2
4	4	General Electric, Fairfield, Conn.	Aircraft engines, medical systems	4,825.0	11.0	39,315.0	6	12.3	23
5	5	International Business Machines, Armonk, N.Y.	Computers, related products	3,994.0	30.6	54,217.0	4	7.4	41
6	6	E. I. du Pont de Nemours, Wilmington, Del.	Specialty chemicals, energy products	3,526.0	19.1	30,468.0	9	11.6	29
7	8	McDonnell Douglas, St. Louis	Aerospace and information systems	3,243.4	15.6	13,146.1	26	24.7	5
8	7	Chrysler, Highland Park, Mich.	Motor vehicles and parts	3,052.3	8.6	26,257.7	10	11.6	26
9	10	Eastman Kodak, Rochester, N.Y.	Photographic equipment and supplies	2,255.0	10.3	13,305.0	25	17.0	12
10	11	Caterpillar, Peoria, Ill.	Heavy machinery, engines, turbines	2,190.0	8.6	8,180.0	48	26.8	4
11	9	United Technologies, Hartford	Jet engines, helicopters, cooling equip.	2,017.0	−2.6	17,070.2	15	12.1	25
12	14	Digital Equipment, Maynard, Mass.	Computers, related products	1,921.0	41.8	9,389.4	38	20.5	7
13	15	Philip Morris, New York	Tobacco, beverages, food products	1,700.0	30.8	22,279.0	12	7.6	40
14	12	Hewlett-Packard, Palo Alto, Calif.	Computers, electronic equipment	1,596.0	13.6	8,090.0	49	19.7	8
15	13	Allied-Signal, Morristown, N.J.	Aircraft and vehicle parts, chemicals	1,416.0	4.3	11,597.0	28	12.2	24
16	16	Occidental Petroleum, Los Angeles	Agricultural products, coal	1,316.0	20.5	17,096.0	16	7.7	39
17	19	Motorola, Schaumburg, Ill.	Semiconductors, radio equipment	1,303.0	22.8	6,707.0	62	19.4	10
18	29	Unisys, Blue Bell, Pa.	Computers, related products	1,196.4	59.9	9,712.9	36	12.3	22
19	23	Weyerhaeuser, Tacoma, Wash.	Wood, pulp, paper, logs, lumber	1,159.0	24.4	6,989.8	58	16.6	13
20	22	General Dynamics, St. Louis	Tanks, aircraft, missiles, gun systems	1,156.9	15.3	9,344.0	39	12.4	21
21	28	Exxon, New York	Petroleum, chemicals	1,129.0	46.4	76,416.0	2	1.5	50
22	18	Westinghouse Electric, Pittsburgh	Generating equipment, defense systems	1,096.0	1.6	10,679.0	33	10.3	31

Rank	Prev.	Company, location	Products	Exports ($ millions)	% change	Sales ($ millions)		Exports as % of sales	
23	17	Union Carbide, Danbury, Conn.	Chemicals, plastics	1,064.0	−2.5	6,914.0	59	15.4	5
24	20	Raytheon, Lexington, Mass.	Electronic defense systems, aircraft	1,047.0	−9	7,659.4	53	13.7	19
25	21	Archer Daniels Midland, Decatur	Proteinates, vegetable oils, flour	981.7	−3.2	5,774.6	71	17.0	11
26	24	Dow Chemical, Midland, Mich.	Chemicals, plastics, polymer products	978.0	8.2	13,377.0	24	7.3	42
27	26	Textron, Providence	Aerospace and consumer products	391.0	13.4	5,661.4	72	15.7	14
28	25	Monsanto, St. Louis	Herbicides, chemicals, pharmaceuticals	387.0	1.6	7,639.0	55	11.6	28
29	36	International Paper, Purchase, N.Y.	Pulp, paper, wood products	777.0	45.8	7,763.0	52	10.0	32
30	31	ITT, New York	Logs, cellulose pulp	719.0	14.1	8,551.0	45	3.4	39
31	33	Minnesota Mining & Mfg., St. Paul	Industrial, electronic and health prod.	673.0	12.5	9,429.0	37	7.1	44
32	●	Hoechst Celanese, Somerville, N.J.	Chemicals, plastics, fibers	672.0	N.A.	4,596.0	91	14.6	18
33	34	FMC, Chicago	Defense equipment, chemicals	612.9	3.1	3,139.1	137	19.5	9
34	43	Honeywell, Minneapolis	Control systems, flight systems	581.0	51.3	6,679.3	63	8.7	36
35	46	Intel, Santa Clara, Calif.	Microcomputer components and prod.	537.7	46.9	1,907.1	200	28.2	3
36	37	Rockwell International, Pittsburgh	Electronic equipment, automotive parts	503.0	2.0	12,123.4	27	4.2	45
37	47	Merck, Rahway, N.J.	Drugs, specialty chemicals	492.0	35.2	5,061.3	80	9.7	33
38	39	Amoco, Chicago	Chemicals	492.0	15.8	20,174.0	14	2.4	49
39	30	Dresser Industries, Dallas	Energy related equipment	475.4	−26.8	3,119.7	138	15.2	17
40	41	Prime Computer, Natick, Mass.	Computers, related products	464.0	14.2	960.9	334	48.3	1
41	27	Lockheed, Calabasas, Calif.	Aircraft, electronic and info. systems	456.0	−41.8	11,370.0	30	4.0	46
42	42	Control Data, Minneapolis	Computers, related products	445.6	14.4	3,366.5	125	13.2	20
43	●	Cummins Engine, Columbus, Ind.	Diesel engines and parts	425.0	24.3	2,767.4	148	15.4	16
44	40	Phillips Petroleum, Bartlesville, Ok.	Liquefied natural gas, chemicals, plastics	424.0	2.2	10,721.0	32	4.0	47
45	50	NCR, Dayton	Computers, related products	410.8	18.8	5,640.7	74	7.3	43
46	45	Eli Lilly, Indianapolis	Drugs, medical equip., agricultural prod.	336.3	4.5	4,049.3	111	9.5	34
47	38	Deere, Moline, Ill.	Farm and industrial equipment	385.0	−20.4	4,134.5	108	9.3	35
48	48	Combustion Engineering, Stamford, Conn.	Steam generators and power plants	383.7	7.3	3,301.0	128	11.6	27
49	●	Ethyl, Richmond	Specialty and petroleum chemicals	367.8	16.4	1,720.3	212	21.4	6
50	●	Xerox, Stamford, Conn.	Copiers, printers, computer workstations	358.0	8.5	10,320.0	34	3.5	48
		TOTALS		$79,669.1		$767,059.4			

SOURCE: "Fifty Leading U.S. Exporters," *Fortune*, July 18, 1988, p. 71.

cation of consumers and business buying personnel, improved communication with the rest of the world, better transportation, lower tariffs on imports, and increased aggressiveness of foreign businesses.[17]

Some examples show how even small firms can be successful in exporting.

> Starting his seed company in 1974, New Yorker Mithra Newman had sales of $7 million by 1980. Over half was export, including $3 million with China.
>
> Tatus Farms of Georgia began exporting hatching eggs and baby chicks through an export broker. Subsequently, the firm sold some 70 percent of its production abroad.
>
> After a trade show in Tokyo, Gudebrod Brothers of Philadelphia began to export its dacron fishing thread to Japan, averaging $4,000 per month.
>
> EPI, Inc., a Virginia-based maker of aerators for waste water treatment plants, had one-third of its $1.1 million sales in exports with only 13 employees.
>
> Scientific Radio Systems, a Rochester manufacturer of high frequency radio transmitters and receivers, exported 60 percent of its $6.5 million in sales.[18]

■ BUSINESS TO BUSINESS MARKETING PLANNING AND STRATEGY FORMULATION

Marketing planning and strategy must begin with an analysis of the changing environment. Central to this first step is an assessment of the organization's strengths and weaknesses in relation to the competition, along with a matching of the strengths with unsatisfied customer needs in the marketplace. Effective marketing strategy must continually monitor product, price, promotion, and distribution. It must make sure that all these factors are consistent with one another, and that there is synergy, whereby the impact of the whole is greater than the sum of the parts. Again, this must be done while the marketers pay attention to other internal activities, as indicated earlier. The significance of the business goods and services classification system illustrates how planning and strategy differ by the category of goods. A marketing strategy appropriate for one category of goods or services may be entirely unsuitable for another. Entirely different promotion, pricing, and distribution strategies might be required for each, along with more or less attention being paid to other internal activities, such as manufacturing, technical service, and engineering. As an example, producers of sophisticated aerospace and defense equipment place more emphasis on the product and pricing facets of competition, and less emphasis on the sales and distribution effort than other types of business goods producers.

---

[17]Vern Terpstra, *International Marketing,* 4th ed. (Hinsdale, Ill.: Dryden Press, 1987), p. 8.

[18]Ibid., pp. 8–9.

Concept Questions

1. How can the three major categories of commercial enterprises overlap?
2. Why are an increasing amount of international goods coming into the U.S. market?
3. What is meant by achieving synergy in the business product marketing mix?

■ FORMAT OF THE TEXT

This text is organized quite differently from other books on business to business marketing. For example, we try to introduce the student to the special buyer-seller relationship early in the text by concentrating on the role of purchasing and materials management as we take up the general management of the business buying center. Purchasing procedures, organizational considerations, purchasing systems, source selection, quality determination and control, social responsibility, and ethical considerations are either covered in depth or are referred to frequently so that the student can get a feel for the language and the interaction that takes place in the buyer-seller exchange.

Next, the text focuses on the traditional tools and techniques employed in the marketing of goods and services to the business to business sector. The remainder of the text exposes the student to market segmentation strategy, product strategy, product development and product failure, pricing strategy, distribution strategy, systems selling, promotional strategy, business services marketing, international business marketing strategy, and a host of other activities to which the typical marketing student is exposed. Early in the text the thinking and attention of the student are focused on the major differences between the consumer and business to business markets—dissimilarities that, while using the same basic marketing tools and techniques, can spell the difference between success and failure in today's dynamic marketing environment.

SUMMARY

1. Business to business marketing can be defined as those activities that facilitate exchanges involving business to business products and customers. A business marketing transaction takes place whenever a good or service is sold for any use other than personal consumption.
2. Differences between business to business and consumer marketing are many and varied. Business to business marketing, as opposed to consumer marketing, is characterized by a greater total sales volume, larger volume purchases, fewer buyers, larger buyers, geographically concentrated buyers, a close supplier-customer relationship, more di-

rect channels of distribution, professional buying, multiple buying influence, complex negotiation, reciprocity, leasing, and an emphasis on personal selling.

3. The demand for business goods is derived from the demand for consumer goods and services. Business demand is relatively inelastic because demand is not likely to change significantly in the short run and tends to be more volatile than the demand for consumer goods and services. There is a joint demand for some business products when two or more items are used in combination to produce a new product.

4. Business buyers tend to be more cautious than final consumers. However, customers are not totally rational in their buying behavior. Selling to business buyers is frequently a personality-oriented sales situation, as is true in most consumer transactions.

5. Business to business goods can be classified in a number of ways. One major classification system uses the categories of major equipment, accessory equipment, fabricated and component parts, process materials, MRO supplies, raw materials, and business services.

6. There are three broad categories of business to business customers: commercial enterprises, which include indirect channel members; original equipment manufacturers (OEMs) and user customers; governmental organizations; and nonbusiness and not-for-profit institutions.

7. Most business organizations can no longer safely ignore international influences, as the potential threat to a firm's domestic market has forced many companies to reassess their role in the world market as well as nationally. Many firms are finding that to be competitive nationally, they must also be competitive internationally.

8. Marketing planning and strategy formulation begin by analyzing the firm's environment. The management should first assess the organization's strengths and weaknesses in relation to the competition. Next, the managers should try to match the firm's strengths with unsatisfied needs of customers in the marketplace.

KEY TERMS

acceleration principle

accessory equipment

business to business marketing

business to business marketing transaction

business services

commercial enterprises

derived demand

fabricated and component parts

governmental organizations

joint demand

major equipment

marketing planning and strategy

MRO supplies

nonbusiness or not-for-profit institutions

process materials

raw materials

REVIEW QUESTIONS

1. How is business to business marketing defined? What constitutes a business to business marketing transaction?
2. What are the reasons for studying business to business marketing?
3. Detail the major differences between business to business and consumer marketing. Create examples to show your understanding of derived demand, fluctuating demand, inelastic demand, and joint demand.
4. Why is business buying behavior not purely rational in nature? Give an example of a situation in which a business buyer might be more influenced by a marketer's use of emotional appeals.
5. Identify and define five major categories of business to business goods and services. Is there an alternate classification system? If so, what are the major categories of such a classification system?
6. What are the three main categories of customers? Identify three types of commercial enterprises. How can these categories overlap?
7. Why are international customers important? Why are so many international goods and services now available in American markets?
8. Why do business to business marketers need to know their firm's strengths and weaknesses as they prepare their marketing planning and strategy?

SUGGESTED READINGS

Abratt, Russell. "Industrial Buying in High Tech Markets." *Industrial Marketing Management* 15 (November 1986), pp. 293–98. A survey of 54 South African firms showed that technical personnel dominated in the decision process for medical instruments.

Berkowitz, Marvin. "New Product Adoption by the Buying Organization: Who Are the Real Influencers?" *Industrial Marketing Management* 15 (February 1986), pp. 33–43. A telephone survey concerning the decision-making process, product assessment, and the purchasing manager's role.

Hlavacek, James D. "Business Schools Need More Industrial Marketing." *Marketing News* 13 (April 4, 1980), p. 1. Reasons why schools of business should focus more attention on business to business marketing.

Kuehn, A. A., and R. L. Day. "The Acceleration Effect in Forecasting Industrial Shipments." *Journal of Marketing* 27 (January 1963). A theoretical discussion of sales and inventory implications of industrial derived demand. Applications are provided.

Matthyssens, P., and W. Faes. "OEM Buying Process for New Components: Purchasing and Marketing Implications." *Industrial Marketing Management* 14 (August 1985), pp. 145–57. Model development from eight in-depth case interviews that emphasize mapping the buying process, buying criteria, and interactions of purchasing with other departments.

Schurr, Paul H., and Bobby J. Calder. "Psychological Effects of Restaurant Meetings on Industrial Buyers." *Journal of Marketing* 50 (January 1986), pp. 87–97. A survey undertaken to determine the effects on buyers' evaluations stemming from buyer-seller meetings in ordinary and fancy settings.

Webster, Frederick E., Jr. "Top Management's Concern about Marketing: Issues for the 1980s." *Journal of Marketing* 45 (Summer 1981), pp. 9–16. A survey of business to business executives found that they see increased marketing competency as a key priority for the 1980s, and that they realize that lack of marketing expertise has been a historical weakness of business to business firms.

APPENDIX

Careers in Business to Business Marketing

More and more college graduates, particularly in the areas of business and engineering, are choosing careers in business to business marketing. This field has a large number of options available in many marketing-related areas. The following is not meant to be a comprehensive list, but rather an indication of the many and varied opportunities that are available.

Business to Business Advertising Manager. This manager supervises the firm's advertising function, which includes setting the advertising objectives and budget, developing advertisements, selecting and placing advertisements in appropriate media, and testing the effectiveness of the advertising program.

Business to Business Credit Manager. The credit manager directs the firm's credit function, which includes issuing credit, setting credit terms, handling customer complaints related to credit, and making provision for late payments.

Business to Business Designer. The designer creates the styling and production specifications for machine-made products.

International Business to Business Marketer. The international marketer works in overseas-based firms or international divisions of domestically-based firms in such areas as purchasing, materials management, sales, product management, marketing research, and promotion.

Business to Business Inventory Manager. The inventory manager establishes and controls the inventory levels of all materials used by the firm.

Business to Business Manufacturers' Representative. The manufacturers' representative works for several manufacturers that do not have their own sales forces, and markets their products and services to users.

Business to Business Marketing Research Manager. This manager directs the firm's marketing research function, which includes setting research objectives, selecting the sample, collecting data in the field, analyzing and interpreting data, and reporting results and recommendations to top management.

Business to Business Marketing Manager. The marketing manager oversees the entire marketing function of the firm in such areas as sales, promotion, distribution, pricing, and marketing services.

Business to Business Packaging Specialist. The packaging specialist designs and sets standards for durable, attractive, and cost-efficient packaging.

Business to Business Product Manager. The product manager is responsible for all activities involved with a particular product, such as research and development, market introduction, sales and promotion, distribution, pricing, financial control, and customer relations.

Business to Business Purchasing Manager. The purchasing manager directs the entire purchasing function for a firm, including the analysis and selection of vendors, setting up the order routine, inspecting the quality of incoming merchandise, and evaluating vendor and product performance.

Business to Business Sales Engineer.   The sales engineer is concerned with marketing technical products and services.

Business to Business Sales Manager.   The sales manager supervises the recruitment, selection, training, motivation, compensation, and evaluation of a sales force.

Business to Business Salesperson.   A salesperson markets products and services to intermediate customers such as manufacturers, wholesalers, not-for-profit institutions, and governmental agencies.

Business to Business Traffic Manager.   This manager oversees the purchase and use of alternative forms of transportation, and is responsible for routing and tracking shipments of merchandise.

Business to Business Warehouse Manager.   A warehouse manager directs the storage and movement of materials within a company's warehouse facilities, and coordinates both incoming and outgoing shipments.

SOURCE: Adapted from Joel R. Evans and Barry Berman, *Marketing* (New York: Macmillan, 1982), pp. A2–A6.

PART TWO

How Buyers Buy

Chapter 2 · Fundamentals of the Purchasing and
Materials Management Function

Chapter 3 · Management of the Organizational
Buying Function

Chapter 4 · Organizational Buyer Behavior and
Buyer–Seller Relationships

Chapter **2**

Fundamentals of the Purchasing and Materials Management Function

LEARNING OBJECTIVES

After reading this chapter, you should be able to:

- Discuss the steps involved in the business to business buying process.
- Explain the reasons behind using various forms of purchasing organizations.
- Understand the materials management concept.
- Differentiate between types of business to business buying situations.
- Distinguish among differing types of purchasing record systems.
- Appreciate the implications and ramifications of purchasing and the law.

CHAPTER OUTLINE

Basic Policies and Procedures of
Purchasing

The Business to Business Buying
Process
  Recognizing the Need
  Developing Product Specifications
  Soliciting Bids from Potential
   Suppliers
  Making the Purchase Decision
  Issuing the Contract
  Inspecting Goods for Quality
  Evaluating Vendor Performance

Purchasing Organization
  Organization Related to Size of
   Company
  Centralization versus
   Decentralization of the
   Buying Function

The Materials Management
Concept
  Alternative Approaches to Materials
  Management

Reasons for Adopting the Materials
  Management Concept

Business to Business Buying
Situations
  New-Task Buying
  Straight Rebuy
  Modified Rebuy

Purchasing Record Systems
  Catalogue File
  Open Order File
  Vendor Experience File
  Commodity Record file

Purchasing and the Law
  Law of Agency
  Law of Contracts

■ BASIC POLICIES AND PROCEDURES OF PURCHASING

One of the questions often asked is why business to business marketers should be concerned with **polices and procedures** established by a typical purchasing department. Many say that only experience can really teach us that there are other facets to a purchasing or buying center—that is, the persons in a buying organization directly concerned with the purchasing process—than the most obvious aspects. The policies and procedures of a buying firm determine the way in which marketing managers can usually market their products to that company. Such policies and procedures alert us to the goals the organization is striving to attain. Policies and procedures outline what is to be done by defining responsibilities and spelling out how much authority has been delegated or assigned to certain individuals. Policies and procedures indicate the intrafirm relations among subsidiaries, divisions, departments, and employees. In short, they tell the marketing manager much of what he or she needs to know to market the business product effectively. Salespeople should request statements of policy and procedures to help them in their sales efforts and to promote good supplier-customer relations. Purchasing policy and procedure manuals are often issued to appropriate parties to ensure that all participants, both internal and external, understand the "rules of the game."

Every transaction involving the transfer of a property between a buyer and seller is a contract. While some contracts are simple, others are lengthy written agreements defining in technical terms the nature of the material, the method of payment, and other conditions. The purchasing department has the authority and responsibility to buy materials and services. This assignment of duties places responsibility on those who have the interest and skill to do the work properly; their primary concern is the performance of this highly important task. Such a business practice establishes uniform policies with respect to seller relationships and assumes adequate controls over expenditures. An example of a brief, clear outline of purchasing policy is that of Hunt-Wesson Foods, Inc., which has 12 broad categories:

1. Purchasing policy and objectives.
2. Supplier contacts.
3. Negotiations with suppliers.
4. Matters of security relating to purchasing.
5. Suppliers' quotations.
6. Purchase commitments.
7. Selecting sources of supply.
8. Purchase order specifications.
9. Purchasing contracts.
10. Vendor relations.
11. Trade relations.
12. Gifts and gratuities.[1]

Hunt-Wesson's policy on supplier contacts states:

> All contacts with suppliers regarding negotiation of price, quantity, delivery, etc., are handled by purchasing. When the needs of a particular group (e.g., research development or engineering) are for information of a technical nature, and where discussions with a supplier may continue over a considerable period of time, it is not necessary for a buyer to become involved in these purchasing discussions with a vendor. However, there must be no commitment to buy on the part of these other departments, and purchasing is to be kept informed by copies of written communications between other departments and suppliers.[2]

---

[1] Paul V. Farrell and George W. Aljian, *Aljian's Purchasing Handbook*, 4th ed. (New York: McGraw-Hill, 1982), pp. 3–21.

[2] Ibid, pp. 3–22.

On the basis of this type of policy, we can easily see that it is in the best interest of the selling firm to have a firm grasp of the policies and procedures the buying organization regards as important.

We need to keep in mind that purchasing policies and procedures are not ends to themselves, but rather means to an end. They should make it easier to accomplish a task by facilitating communication and helping to coordinate the efforts of one group with another. Policies and procedures should clearly designate responsibility for each step in a process. Finally, they should permit **management by exception** by pushing down routine decision making to as low a level as possible within the organizational hierarchy.

■ THE BUSINESS TO BUSINESS BUYING PROCESS

A buying situation is created when some member of an organization perceives that a problem can be solved by purchasing a product or service. This perception can occur at any place in the organization and at almost any stage in its work. Since there are wide variations among industries, companies, products, and personnel, we cannot establish a single set of procedures applicable to all cases. Essential steps, however, must be taken in one way or another to complete a buying transaction. Each of these steps is shown in Figure 2–1 and discussed below, using General Electric company as a hypothetical example.[3] Suppose GE decides to design and build a new line of clothes dryers and needs an electric motor as a key component in the dryer. Let us track each of the stages in this purchasing process.

Recognizing the Need

After the top management of GE's appliance division decides to introduce a new line of clothes dryers, engineering and R&D personnel create a workable design that is tested and approved. They confer with the purchasing executive to reach a make-buy decision—an evaluation of whether a product or parts should be purchased from outside suppliers or manufactured by the firm itself. The group decides that the electric motor in each dryer should be bought rather than made.

Developing Product Specifications

The engineering and R&D personnel develop product specifications for the electric motor; these are detailed technical requirements the motor must meet, such as its horsepower, life in hours, and ability to operate at a stated temperature and humidity. Members of the purchasing and production departments then do a systematic appraisal of the design, quality, and performance requirements of the product to reduce purchasing costs. For

---

[3]The General Electric example is from Eric N. Berkowitz, Roger A. Kerin, and William Rudelius, *Marketing,* 2d ed. (Homewood, Ill.: Richard D. Irwin, 1989), pp. 128–29.

■ **FIGURE 2–1**   Outline of the Steps in the Business to Business Purchasing
Process

example, suppose the GE engineers conclude that at least a one-eighth
horsepower motor is needed to power the dryer. The purchasing department would recommend buying a one-quarter horsepower motor to insure
provision of adequate power.

In determining the exact product specifications needed, the purchasing
department also relies on the technical expertise of vendors in developing
appropriate design specifications. Specifications are generally stated in
terms of material, dimensions, and performance characteristics rather than
brand name. This maximizes the number of qualified vendors available and
ensures genuine competition among bidders.

The buying center must develop the necessary buying criteria for the
electric motor, which are (1) quality requirements, (2) on-time delivery, and
(3) price, in that order. The purchasing manager has the responsibility to
select the supplier and negotiate a contract for the motors.

Soliciting Bids from Potential Suppliers

The next step is soliciting bids from potential suppliers. This involves
selecting the names of vendors from a list of firms believed to be qualified
to supply a given item and sending each vendor a quotation request form

that describes the desired quantity, delivery date, and specifications of the product. A vendor analysis is typically performed so that the purchasing personnel can evaluate objectively all potential suppliers on rating sheets according to the criteria or standards they consider important. Often these criteria are given different weights to reflect their respective importance in the vendor selection process. Figure 2–2 presents a vendor rating sheet that uses a weighted scale.

Most purchasing departments maintain a separate bidders' list for each general class of items they order. These lists are updated continuously by adding potential new vendors and deleting unsatisfactory vendors. To ensure competition even further, many firms require at least three bids for purchases exceeding a specified dollar amount.

Making the Purchase Decision

While the purchase decision in a consumer buying decision, such as buying a six-pack of soft drinks, is typically short, the purchase stage in organizations could cover a period of months or perhaps years—from the vendor selection and placement of the purchase order to the delivery of the product. For example, in the GE case, the purchasing manager might perform vendor follow-up, set up an order routine, expedite the order, and renegotiate the contract terms if specification changes are made after the initial contract has been awarded.

Issuing the Contract

The contract stage of the purchasing process is the crucial part in which GE and the seller enter into an agreement that is binding on both of them. On the one hand, the seller must supply the electric motors at the agreed upon price and terms, and, on the other hand, the GE purchasing manager must accept and pay for the motors if they are received in good condition. While the purchase order forms vary tremendously as to setup and routing through the organization, the issuances of the purchase contract, no matter how involved or detailed, is more important than its format or style.

Sometimes contracts are awarded directly to vendors based on the data they provide in quotation request forms. At other times the purchasing manager may wish to negotiate with one or more bidders, particularly on high-volume, high-dollar items. Eventually, the GE purchasing manager selects a vendor and awards a contract in the form of a purchase order, which is an authorization for the vendor to provide the items under the agreed-on terms and to bill the purchasing firm.

Inspecting Goods for Quality

When the electric motors are delivered, the quality control department tests them to ensure that they meet specifications. Shortages, tampered merchandise, and goods damaged in transit must be accounted for prior to

■ FIGURE 2–2   Vendor Rating Sheet

SUPPLIER: _____ Platco Manufacturing _____

LOCATION: _____ Providence, Rhode Island _____

PLANTS SERVICED: _____ All Metal Container Division and Closure Plants _____

Rating Scale

5 - Excellent - Top 10% of all suppliers
4 - Good, but can be improved
3 - Average
2 - Below Average
1 - Poor
0 - Absolutely unacceptable

Supplier Rating: Key Supplier Rating 21.0

	Rating	Weight	Extended Rating
1. Competitive pricing	2	0.8	1.6
2. On-time delivery	1	0.9	0.9
3. Quality	4	0.9	3.6
4. Emergency assistance	5	0.9	4.5
5. Communication	1	0.4	0.4
6. Technical service	4	0.4	1.6
7. Cost-reduction suggestions	3	0.5	1.5
8. Inventory (stocking) program	2	0.3	0.6
		Total	14.7

Supplier Rating: Key Supplier Rating 21.0

Maximum Points Possible: 25
18-25   Preferred supplier - does a good job for National Can Corporation
10-17   Acceptable - room for improvement
 5- 9   Marginal - must improve to retain position. Specific programs required
 0- 5   Unacceptable - replace at once

COMMENTS: Gives excellent assistance in emergencies; however, poor
communication and missed promise dates seem to create their
own emergencies. Pricing is noncompetitive. West coast service
is particularly poor. Quality has been very good.

1/1/90	Director of Purchasing
DATE	SIGNED

SOURCE: Reprinted by permission of the publisher from D. W. Cravens and D. W. Finn "Supplier Selections by Retailers Research Progress and Needs," in William Darden and Robert Lusch (eds.) *Patronage Behavior and Retail Management* (New York: Elsevier North Holland, 1983). p. 238. Copyright 1984 by Elsevier Science Publishing Co., Inc.

the payment of an invoice. If the motors prove unsatisfactory, the purchasing manager must negotiate with the supplier to rework the items according to specifications or must arrange for an entirely new shipment.

Evaluating Vendor Performance

Experienced buyers realize that it is essential to evaluate purchase decisions. GE's purchasing manager will evaluate the vendor's performance after final delivery of the purchased items. This information is often noted on the vendor rating sheet discussed above, and is used to update the bidders list kept by the purchasing department. Performance on past contracts often determines a vendor's chances of being asked to bid on future purchases, and poor performance might result in a vendor's name being dropped from the list.

Concept Questions

1. Why are the policies and procedures of the buying firm means to an end rather than ends in themselves?
2. How is a buying situation created?
3. Why is the contract stage of the buying process so crucial?

■ PURCHASING ORGANIZATION

The **purchasing function** includes the whole process of deciding and specifying what to buy—in what quantities, at what time, from what sources, and by what procedures. It also includes the implementation of these decisions and procedures by requisitioning, authorizing, ordering, receiving, and paying for the purchases. This process is referred to as the purchasing function, but parts of it are cross-functional in the sense that other areas, such as the design, production, and user departments, not only participate in the process but may also carry the prime responsibility for elements in it. Thus organizations can be thought of in two dimensions: one dimension deals with motivating individuals and subgroups of the total organization enough to get them to contribute optimally, the other deals with the patterns of formal interrelationships that tie members of the group together. These dimensions often find expression in organization charts—an aspect of the organization of purchasing that we emphasize here.

Organization Related to Size of a Company

In a small company with a limited sales volume and variety of purchases, the purchasing department may consist of only the purchasing manager and a clerical assistant.[4] In some very large companies the department may

---

[4]Stuart F. Heinritz, Paul V. Farrell, and Clifton L. Smith, *Purchasing: Principles and Applications,* 7th ed. (Englewood Cliffs, N.J.: Prentice-Hall, 1986), pp. 71–86.

have several hundred employees. In some companies purchasing is under the jurisdiction of the production or manufacturing division, and the purchasing manager reports to the manufacturing manager. In others, the department reports to a top executive officer, such as the president, executive vice president, or general manager.

In some large companies and within some diversified industries, the purchasing operation is separated into both the operational and managerial phases of purchasing. Separate buying departments are set up at the divisional level as part of the divisional organization plan. A **general purchasing department** at company headquarters serves the entire organization as a staff facility. It counsels top management on broad purchasing and materials policies, conducts general and specific purchasing research programs that are available to all buyers, sets guidance policies for divisional purchasing departments, coordinates purchasing policies and activities throughout the company, and gives assistance on specific purchasing problems, where needed. Such a centralized purchasing department does little or no actual buying and has no responsibility for the details of procurement beyond evaluating purchasing performance at the various divisions and pointing out means for improvement. In most cases it has no jurisdiction over the hiring or firing of divisional purchasing personnel, although it usually sets up buyer-training programs and has decisive influence in the transfer of individuals with superior buying talent to other company divisions and to positions of greater responsibility and opportunity. Figures 2–3 and 2–4 show typical purchasing departmental structures in medium-sized and large companies.

■ **FIGURE 2–3**   Organization Plan of a Medium-Sized Purchasing Department

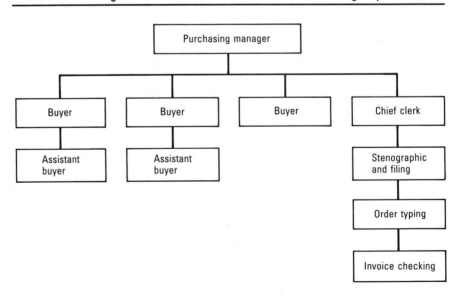

■ **FIGURE 2–4**   Organization Plan of a Large Purchasing Department

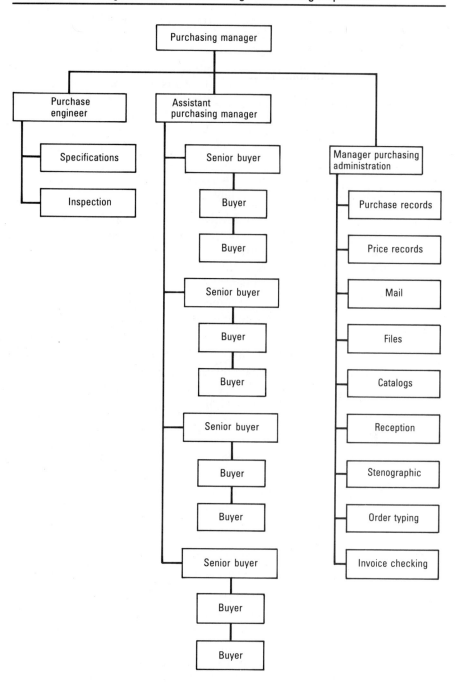

Centralization versus Decentralization of the Buying Function

We need to address the question of whether to decentralize purchasing activities in each plant of a multiple-plant firm versus centralization at the home office of the firm. In practice, virtually every company answers this question differently. Some companies centralize the activity completely, doing the buying for all plants at a central headquarters office. Others decentralize the function entirely, giving each plant full authority to conduct all its purchasing activities. Still other firms—the majority of them—develop an organizational buying structure somewhere between these two extremes. Both decentralized and centralized approaches offer significant benefits.

The reasons for having a separate plant purchasing department can be summarized as follows:

1. The plant or division manager is responsible for the profitable operation of that unit. He or she should have jurisdiction over purchasing as well as production, because a large part of costs and a major factor in the efficiency of production are represented in procurement.
2. If the division is large enough to be considered a profit center, it is usually large enough to buy in volume at favorable prices.
3. Each division may have some unique requirements and differences in operating conditions that affect material needs.
4. The public relations aspect of purchasing locally is important. Goodwill can be fostered by purchasing from nearby sources or through local distributors.[5]

However, the advantages of centralized purchasing are often so great in comparison with decentralized purchasing that almost all but the smallest of firms are centralized. Prior to centralizing its purchasing function and realizing substantial savings, General Motors spent millions of dollars each year, with more than one hundred buying locations purchasing 24 million pairs of work gloves in 225 styles from nearly 100 different vendors.

In centralized purchasing a separate individual or department is established and given authority to make all purchases (except the very unusual buy, such as a new company aircraft). The advantages to be gained from centralized purchasing are as follows:

1. Purchased parts' standardization is easier, as all decisions go through one central control point.
2. Administrative duplication is eliminated or reduced. Instead of each department head writing a separate purchase order for a product or part, the purchasing department writes only one order for the firm's total requirement.

---

[5]Ibid, p. 74.

■ **FIGURE 2–5**   A Multiple Purchasing Organization with Some Activities Centralized and Some Decentralized

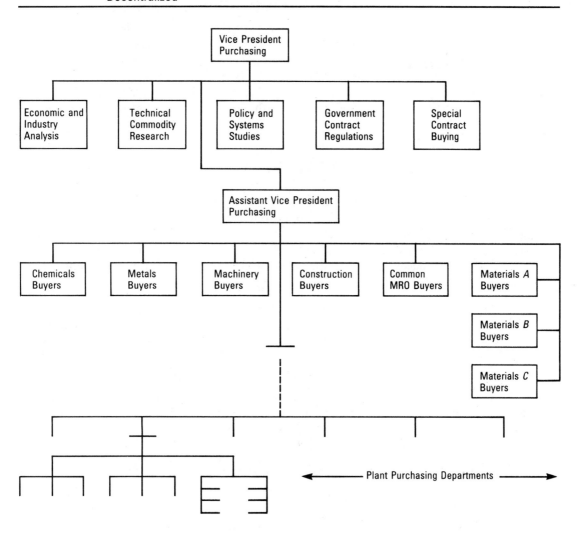

3. By combining requirements of several departments, order quantities can be increased. This may provide faster delivery, quantity discounts, and other concessions. There may also be freight savings because shipments now can be made in carload quantities.

4. This form of organization is cost-effective for vendors since they need not call on several people within a particular buying firm. This also provides better control over purchase commitments.

5. Centralized purchasing also enables the development of specializations and expertise in purchasing decisions.

As noted earlier, the purchasing organizations of some multiplant firms are found at both ends of the centralization-decentralization continuum. While most are located somewhere between these two extremes, the trend appears to be toward the general type of organization shown in Figure 2–5. This organizational arrangement includes elements of both centralization and decentralization, with the objective being to reap the major benefits offered by each approach.

■ THE MATERIALS MANAGEMENT CONCEPT

Materials management is the grouping of functions involved in obtaining and bringing materials into a production operation. (Often the concept refers to materials management as logistics, which would incorporate materials management and physical distribution.) A description of the concept offered by several leading scholars in the purchasing management field illustrates the point:

> An organization which has adopted the materials management organizational concept will have a single manager responsible for planning, organizing, motivating and controlling all those activities principally concerned with the flow of materials into an organization. Materials management views material flow as a system.
>
> The specific functions that might be included under the materials manager are material planning and control, production scheduling, material and purchasing research, purchasing, incoming traffic, inventory control, receiving, incoming quality control, stores, in-plant materials movement, and scrap and surplus disposal. Not all functions are necessarily included; the ones often excluded are production scheduling, in-plant materials movement, and incoming quality control.[6]

Because 90 percent of a typical product's cost at the Gillette Company is in the materials which compose it, the materials management team supervises inventories, warehousing, and the shipping of goods. It also assists research and development personnel in developing substitute materials.

Many observers feel that the materials management approach will be implemented by a majority of U.S. manufacturers during the 1990s. Larger firms, both those geographically dispersed domestically and those on an international level, are able to integrate centralized and operational materials management activities. This linkage, along with on-line computer systems, allows the integration of all aspects of the materials management function.

---

[6]Ibid., p. 2.

The continued adoption of the materials management concept will force many business to business marketing managers to coordinate activities affecting the materials management function of their customers. Suppliers that can manage their own production, inventory, and distribution system so as to match their customers' requirements have the best chance to establish long-range business relationships. The materials management approach to business to business buying and selling will continue to expand into the areas of raw materials, component parts, and inventory control; it will also serve as an important tool in planning and forecasting future supply needs. The organizational buying function must be directly involved in this continued trend toward integrated materials management. Business buyers initiate this movement of goods into the buying firm for use by production. As a result, the purchase timing, cost, and specific products chosen will impact the performance of this system.

Alternative Approaches to Materials Management

Critics of the materials management form of organization emphasize that it is difficult, if not impossible, for one person to coordinate and control the many variables involved in materials operations, and that effective coordination is too difficult to achieve merely by establishing a new organizational structure. Furthermore, recent literature contains much contrasting information on various approaches utilized in materials management. Some alternative approaches have been suggested.

Traditional Approach. Traditionally, inventory has been used to buffer transportation, production, distribution, and sales imbalances when availability and demand occur at differing rates. This situation is intensified with the great product variety created and, therefore, expected in our economy. Consequently, U.S. firms have emphasized materials delivery systems, and business to business marketers have reacted accordingly. The business to business sector has long been the leader in U.S. growth productivity, the wellspring of innovation, and the generator of a rising standard of living.[7] Traditionally inventory has been built into an operation to cover problems. Despite advanced control systems and the realization that inventory tied up capital, the relationship between inventory and its effects on manufacturing methods or measurement systems was seldom analyzed.

Control of inventory has historically been a problem which has been approached in different ways. Prior to the 1960s inventory was a low priority and was controlled by mathematical formulae such as economic order quantities and various reorder point techniques. However, beginning in the late 1960s and early 1970s, reduced profit margins forced management to take a more critical look at inventory. Computer-based systems of the

---

[7]"The Hollow Corporation," *Business Week* 57, March 1986.

1970s, and the advent of material requirements systems, helped take a large step toward controlling inventories. However, these steps could not hide the fact that inventory was often used to cover up problems. The best inventory control system will not compensate for the behavior of people who use inventory to cover problems.

Just-in-Time (JIT) Approach. A new form of business exchange, commonly referred to as the *just-in-time (JIT)* exchange relationship has been adopted and implemented by many original equipment manufacturers (OEMs) and suppliers of component parts and materials during the past several years.[8] The "Business to Business Marketing in Action" box discusses the major features and implications of JIT.

The objective of the JIT concept is to eliminate waste of all kinds from the production process. It requires the delivery of the specified product at the precise time and in the exact quantity needed. Variations in any of these three dimensions are considered wasteful. In theory, the product must conform to the customer's specifications every time. It must be delivered when needed—not earlier and not later; and it must be delivered in the exact quantity needed—not more and not less.[9]

Just-in-time was neither a creation of the academic community nor a development of a consulting firm. This approach was Toyota's response to managing its own internal operations and its relationship with its suppliers. The creation of JIT was driven by the vision and leadership of Taiichi Ohno, first a plant manager and later vice president of manufacturing at Toyota, along with Shigeo Shingo, head of the industrial engineering consulting branch of the Japan Management Association.

In the United States just-in-time is an approach to production and inventory management that reduces inventory. The approach is similar in terms of objective, and to a large extent in terms of practice, in the United States, Japan, and Western Europe. Thus descriptive expressions such as *stockless purchasing* or *zero inventories* are often used. Alternatively, just-in-time is defined in terms of the coincidence in time of the movement of completed work from an upstream operation to the start of work at the successive downstream operation. Two examples illustrate this approach:

> One such concept of an ideal production system is most commonly called Just-in-Time production, a name which emphasizes producing exactly what is needed and conveying it to where it is needed precisely when required.[10]
>
> The just-in-time concept appears to be the core of Japanese production management and productivity improvement. The JIT idea is simple: Produce and deliver finished goods just in time to be sold, subassemblies just

---

[8]Gary L. Frazier, Robert E. Spekman, and Charles R. O'Neal, "Just-in-Time Exchange Relationships in Industrial Markets," *Journal of Marketing 52* (October 1988), pp. 52–67.

[9]Charles R. O'Neal, "The Buyer-Seller Linkage in a Just-in-Time Environment," *Journal of Purchasing and Materials Management* (Spring 1987), pp. 7–13.

[10]Hall, Robert W. with APICS, *Zero Inventories* (Homewood, Ill.: Dow Jones-Irwin, 1983).

BUSINESS TO BUSINESS MARKETING IN ACTION

Features and Implications of JIT

Over the past two decades, American markets have been bombarded with foreign products. Japanese market-share gains have been especially pronounced in such industries as steel, office equipment, electronics, and automobiles. As American business started studying the reasons for Japanese success in manufacturing, it discovered several concepts, including just-in-time (JIT), early supplier involvement, value analysis, quality circles, total quality control, and flexible manufacturing.

JIT in particular promises to produce significant change in the relationship between suppliers and their business to business customers. The goal of JIT is zero inventory with 100 percent quality. It means that materials arrive at the customer's factory exactly at the time they are needed. It does not mean that the customer shifts inventory to the supplier, as this would not reduce total system costs; instead it calls for a synchronization between supplier and customer production schedules so that inventory buffers are unnecessary. Effective implementation of JIT should result in reduced inventory and lead times and increased quality, productivity, and adaptability to changes.

In a survey of two thousand purchasing executives in 1986, 59 percent indicated that their firm had used or planned to use JIT. General Motors, through its JIT programs, reduced inventory-related costs from $8 billion to $2 billion.

Business to business marketers need to be aware of the changes that JIT will bring about in the purchasing practices of organizations. They must position themselves to exploit the opportunities that JIT will create. The following are the major features and implications of JIT:

- *Strict quality control.* Maximum cost savings from JIT are achieved if preinspected goods are received by the buyer. The buyers thus expect that suppliers have strict quality-control procedures such as SPC (statistical process control) or TQC (total quality control). This means that suppliers need to work closely with the business to business customer and satisfy the latter that they can ship products that meet the quality standards.
- *Frequent and reliable delivery.* Daily delivery is frequently the only way to avoid inventory buildup. Increasingly, customers are specifying delivery dates rather than shipping dates, with penalties for not meeting them. Apple even penalizes for early

continued

delivery, while Kasle Steel has around-the-clock deliveries to the General Motors plant in Buick City. This means that suppliers must develop reliable transportation arrangements.

- *Closer location.* Since JIT involves frequent delivery, a location closer to the customer can be an advantage for the supplier. A close location results in more efficiency in delivering smaller lots and greater reliability in inclement weather. Kasle Steel set up its blanking mill within Buick City to serve the General Motors plant there. This means that a marketer may have to make large commitments to major customers.

- *Telecommunication.* New technologies of communication permit suppliers to establish computerized purchasing systems that are hooked up to their customers. One large customer requires that suppliers make their inventory figures and prices available on the system. It allows for just-in-time on-line ordering as the computer looks for the lowest prices where inventory is available. This reduces transaction costs but puts pressure on marketers to keep prices very competitive.

- *Stable production schedules.* Under JIT, customers provide their production schedule to the supplier so that the delivery is made on the day the materials are required. International Harvester provides one of its suppliers with a six-month forecast and a firm twenty-day order. if any last-minute changes are made, International Harvester is billed for the additional costs. This will help reduce the uncertainty and costs faced by the business to business suppliers.

- *Single sourcing.* JIT implies that the buying and selling organizations work closely together to reduce costs. This often translates into the customer's awarding a long-term contract to only one supplier who can be trusted. This makes payoffs high for the winning supplier, and very difficult for other competitors to subsequently get the contract. Contracts are almost automatically renewed provided the supplier met delivery schedules and maintained quality. Single sourcing is increasing rapidly under JIT. Thus while General Motors still uses more than 3,500 suppliers, Toyota, which has totally adopted JIT, uses less than 250. In the United States, Harley Davidson reduced its supplier base from 320 to 180 in two years.

- *Value analysis.* The major objectives of JIT are to reduce costs and improve quality, and value analysis is critical to accomplishing those objectives. To reduce costs of its product, a customer must not only reduce its own costs but also get its suppliers to reduce their costs. Thus some large manufacturers hold VA seminars for their suppliers. Suppliers with a strong VA

continued

program have a competitive edge, as they can contribute to their customers' VA program.

- *Early supplier involvement.* Business to business buyers are increasingly realizing that marketers are experts in their field and should be brought into the design process. Marketers must have qualified personnel who can participate in customers' design teams. In 1986, a survey of one thousand purchasing executives found that the major criteria for selecting suppliers to participate in design teams were quality, prior delivery performance, recommendations by the customer's engineering department, and prior value-analysis assistance.

- *Close relationship.* All the above features of JIT help to forge a close relationship between the customer and the marketer. To make JIT successful, they coordinate their efforts to maximally satisfy the customer's needs. Under JIT, the supplier is viewed as a work station that is located away from the customer's manufacturing site. To be successful, the supplier has to customize its offering for the particular customer. In return, the supplier wins the contract for a specific term. Because of the time invested by the parties, locational decisions, and telecommunication hookups, the transaction-specific investments are high. Since switching costs for the customer are high, these customers are extremely selective in choosing suppliers. A major implication is that U.S. business to business marketers must improve their skill in *relationship marketing* as compared with *transaction marketing*. Profit maximization over the entire relationship rather than over each transaction should be the objective. Otherwise the supplier may lose the customer for good.

SOURCE: Reproduced by permission from Philip Kotler, *Marketing Management Analysis, Planning, Implementation, and Control,* 6th ed. (Englewood Cliffs, N.J.: Prentice-Hall, 1988), pp. 216–17.

in time to be assembled into finished goods, fabricated parts just in time to go into subassemblies, and purchased materials just in time to be transferred into fabricated parts.[11]

The basic idea of JIT is that carrying any inventory is undesirable because it ties up capital. JIT inventory management ensures that each person involved in the manufacturing process receives what they need "just-in-time."[12] For example, a Bendix plant recently adopted a JIT system and

---

[11]Richard Schonberger, *Japanese Manufacturing Techniques—Nine Hidden Lessons in Simplicity* (New York: Free Press, 1983).

[12]Craig Waters, "Why Everybody's Talking about 'Just-in-Time,' " *Inc.* (March 1984), pp. 77–90. See also Doug Harper, "Zero Inventory Poses Questions for Distributors," *Industrial Distributor* (January 1985), p. 49; and Summar Aggarwal, "MRP, JIT, OPT, FMS?" *Harvard Business Review* (September-October 1985), pp. 8–16.

was able to convert 10,000 square feet of floor space from storage to manufacturing usage.[13] Black & Decker, IBM, Firestone, General Motors, Harley-Davidson, and other firms are experiencing decreasing costs and higher quality with the system. General Motors claims to have saved $2 billion in one year with the use of the JIT system.[14]

To be effective, just-in-time purchasing and production scheduling require very careful managerial monitoring. Undoubtedly the most important single factor to success in JIT is top management's commitment both to providing necessary resources and to an understanding of the philosophy involved. A high level of cooperation and coordination is called for between suppliers and producers, and then between production and marketing people within the manufacturing firm.[15] Also, JIT is not appropriate for all business to business buyer's operations. Therefore, it will never totally replace traditional systems relying on inventory backup.

The terms *JIT* and *Kanban* are often used interchangeably, whereas in fact Kanban is a subset of JIT. (Kanban actually means marker.) The goal of Kanban is to produce required units on time and only in the quantities necessary. The Kanban system controls production by the use of markers or cards, with the flow of materials being dependent on the Kanban cards. The "pull" card pulls work from previous work centers based on a production schedule. This "pull" system works by controlling the sequence of job activities in a manufacturing facility.

When the just-in-time philosophy takes place within a buying firm, the alert and knowledgeable business to business supplier may serve in the role of a change agent in facilitating this transition. This will require a very thorough understanding of the JIT philosophy and its translation into marketing, purchasing, and manufacturing practice.[16] Suppliers who have adopted JIT have the advantage of using their system's capabilities as a marketing tool and taking the role of adviser in working with reluctant adopters. This should put the supplier or potential supplier in an excellent position to become a preferred supplier. It should also be noted that JIT purchasing concepts can provide competitive advantages to firms in nonmanufacturing industries, as well as to those in manufacturing industries. Preliminary results obtained from research conducted by Guinipero and Keiser, using a large firm in the communications industry, indicate signifi-

[13]G. H. Manoocheri, "Improving Productivity with the Just-in-Time System," *Journal of Systems Management* (January 1985), pp. 23–26.

[14]Lewis Schneider, "New Era in Transportation Strategy," *Harvard Business Review* (March–April 1985), p. 124.

[15]For a more detailed discussion of the JIT concept, see Chan K. Hahn, Peter A. Pinto, and Daniel J. Bragg, "Just-in-Time Production and Purchasing," *Journal of Purchasing and Materials Management* (Fall 1983), pp. 2–10; and Richard J. Schonberger and Abdolhossein Ansari, "Just-in-Time Purchasing Can Improve Quality," *Journal of Purchasing and Materials Management* (Spring 1984), pp. 2–7.

[16]Larry C. Guinipero and Charles O'Neal, "Obstacles to JIT Procurement," *Industrial Marketing Management* 17, no. 1 (February 1988), pp. 35–41.

cant benefits—improved internal and external communications, improved supplier performance, and warehouse space requirement reductions.[17]

Reasons for Adopting the Materials Management Concept

There are many reasons for adopting the materials management type of organization; its greatest advantage is the improved communication and coordination between departments which such an organizational structure permits. Materials management provides a central administration in which conflicting functional or departmental interests can be balanced out in the overall interests of the company. Centralized responsibility and control also make for a smoother, faster flow of materials from the time they are requisitioned by using departments to the time they are shipped out to customers as finished products.[18]

The more specific ways in which a centrally controlled materials organization has helped a number of companies improve efficiency and reduce cost include an easier and simpler control of inventories, reduced clerical work, and fewer problems with delivery scheduling and emergency orders.

Concept Questions
1. How might the purchasing organization differ between smaller and larger organizations?
2. What are two different approaches to inventory control in materials management?
3. What is the greatest advantage in a firm's adopting the materials management concept?

■ BUSINESS TO BUSINESS BUYING SITUATIONS

Understanding buyer behavior (organizational versus consumer) becomes easier if the task is divided into phases, and these phases are then analyzed under different buying situations. This procedure enables the marketer to identify critical decision phases, the information needs of the buying organization, and various criteria buyers consider when making a buying decision.[19] Three types of buying situations have been delineated in Exhibit 2–1: (1) **New-task buying,** (2) **modified rebuy buying,** and (3) **straight rebuy buying.**[20]

---

[17]Larry C. Giunipero and Edward F. Keiser, "JIT Purchasing in a Non-Manufacturing Environment: A Case Study," *Journal of Purchasing and Materials Management* 23, no. 4 (Winter 1987), pp. 19–25.

[18]Heinritz, Farrell, and Smith, p. 90.

[19]Joseph A. Bellizzi and Phillip McVey, "How Valid Is the Buy-Grid Model?," *Industrial Marketing Management* 12 (1983), pp. 57–62.

[20]Patrick J. Robinson, Charles W. Faris, and Yoram Wind, *Industrial Buying and Creative Marketing,* Marketing Science Institute Series (Boston: Allyn & Bacon, 1977).

■ **EXHIBIT 2–1**   Characteristics of Three Buying Situations

Straight Rebuy

Continuing or recurring requirement, handled on a routine basis.

Usually the decision on each separate transaction is made in the purchasing department.

Formally or informally, a "list" of acceptable suppliers exists.

No supplier not on the "list" is considered.

Buyers have much relevant buying experience, and hence little new information is needed.

Appears to represent the bulk of the individual purchases within companies.

Item purchases, price paid, delivery time, etc., may vary from transaction to transaction, so long as these variations do not cause a new source of supply to be considered.

Modified Rebuy

May develop from either new task or straight rebuy situations.

The requirement is continuing or recurring or it may be expanded to a significant larger level of operations.

The buying alternatives are known, but they are *changed.*

Some additional information is needed before the decisions are made.

May arise because of outside events, such as an emergency or by the actions of a marketer.

May arise internally because of new buying influences, or for potential cost reductions, potential quality improvements, or potential service benefits.

Marketers who are not active suppliers try to convert the customer's straight rebuys into modified rebuys.

New Task

A requirement or problem that has not arise before.

Little or no relevant past buying experience to draw upon.

A great deal of information is needed.

Must seek out alternative ways of solving the problem and alternative suppliers.

Occurs infrequently—but very important to marketers because it sets the pattern for the more routine purchases that will follow.

May be anticipated and developed by creative marketing.

SOURCE: P. J. Robinson, C. W. Faris, and Y. Wind, *Industrial Buying and Creative Marketing* (Boston: Allyn & Bacon, 1967), p. 28. Reproduced with permission.

Figure 2–6 provides common examples of business to business goods and services purchased utilizing these three types of buying situations. Each type of buying situation must be related to the seven-stage buying process presented in Table 2–1. The exact same purchase in two different buying situations can be quite different. Therefore, marketing strategy must begin with identifying the type of buying situation facing the purchasing firm.[21]

New-Task Buying

In confronting a new-task buying situation, organizational buyers operate in an extensive problem-solving stage of decision making. They are faced here with a completely new buying situation. Let us say that the purchaser needs a new machine, part, material, or service—something he or she has had no previous exposure to. This situation presents the business to business marketer with a chance to participate in the early stages of the procurement process. (It also increases the probability of making a sale.) An astute marketer anticipates a problem even before the present or potential customer does, and is prepared to respond to the needs of new-task buyers.

[21]Earl Naumann, Douglas J. Lincoln, and Robert D. McWilliams, "The Purchase of Components: Functional Areas of Influence," *Industrial Marketing Management* 13 (1984), pp. 113–22.

■ **FIGURE 2–6**   Goods Purchased Using Three Different Types of Buying

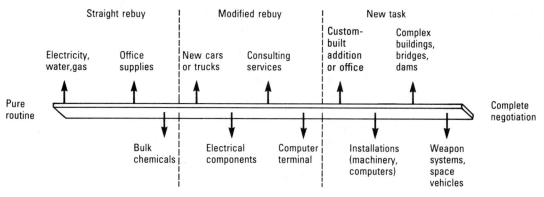

SOURCE: Ben M. Enis, *Marketing Principles,* 3rd ed. (Glenview, Ill.: Scott, Foresman, 1980).

■ **TABLE 2–1.**   Linking the Business to Business Purchasing
Process to Buying Situations

	Buy Classes		
Steps in the Industrial Purchasing Process	**New Task**	**Modified Rebuy**	**Straight Rebuy**
1. Recognizing the need	Yes	Maybe	No
2. Developing product specifications	Yes	Maybe	No
3. Soliciting bids from potential buyers	Yes	Maybe	No
4. Making the purchase decision	Yes	Maybe	No
5. Issuing the contract	Yes	Maybe	No
6. Inspecting goods for quality	Yes	Yes	Yes
7. Evaluating vendor performance	Yes	Yes	Yes

SOURCE: Adapted from Patrick J. Robinson, Charles W. Faris, and Yoram Wind, *Industrial Buying and Creative Marketing* (Boston: Allyn & Bacon, 1967).

As an example of new-task buying, consider a hospital's purchase of a computer-aided tomography (CAT) scanner—a device that x-rays tiny slices of body structures and then combines the thousands of shots into a composite picture. The scanner can pinpoint stroke-induced brain damage and also provide valuable diagnostic information about vascular structures and other soft-tissue organs. Central General, the largest of three hospitals in a medium-sized midwestern city, plans to share the CAT scanner with other local institutions.[22] The need has been recognized: the hospital can vastly improve its diagnostic work and make it available to the entire community. Moreover, the product meeting that need has been generally identified: a third- or fourth-generation scanner with high-resolution and thin-sectioning capabilities.

To characterize and write specifications for so important a purchase, the chief of staff and a hospital administrator appoint a committee under the

---

[22]The Central General example is from Peter D. Bennett, *Marketing* (New York: McGraw-Hill, 1988), pp. 138–139.

direction of the senior radiologist. One of the members, Central General's purchasing director, will record all the information the group gathers and will summarize it prior to a final decision. Each member has assigned tasks. Some will canvass hospital services, other than radiology, which will use the scanner or refer to its output: neurosurgery, cardiology, orthopedics, neurology, ophthalmology, oncology, and so on. Others will identify the CAT units available, set up interviews with potential vendors, and check out the reputation of each manufacturer with several hospitals in Chicago.

After eight weeks and as many committee meetings, several units are rejected as too difficult to service and too crude in imaging capability. Positron tomography, a technologically different option, has also been ruled out. Three units remain in contention, and marketing representatives and technical specialists are invited to make formal presentations to the committee. Marketers from General Electric will present the advantages of their model 8800; those from Varian will promote its model 360; and the group from Siements will push for its Somatom 2.

The committee, with only one dissent, votes for the GE CT/T 8800 because of its wide range of functions and convenient service provisions and because the model received high marks from current users. The chief of staff and the head radiologist, who share the burden of the final choice, concur in this decision. At a subsequent lunch hosted by GE's regional sales manager, the purchasing director talks through the details of shipping, billing, and servicing. That afternoon the purchasing director meets with GE's technical staff and the hospital's chief of building maintenance to plan the subcontracting needed to build a suitable room for the new equipment.

The cost of the CAT scanner is between $3 and $4 million; typically such expensive purchases are made through the kind of deliberative and collective process described above. The better informed marketers are about the customer's buying procedures and decision makers, the better are their chances for a successful sales effort.

Straight Rebuy

A straight rebuy situation is the most common purchasing method in business to business buying and requires little or no new information on the part of the buyer. He or she simply purchases a routine part, material, or service, with little thought or effort going into the buying process. The marketing job required of the marketer is to become a supplier for these relatively routine types of purchases. This job can be difficult because of buyer time constraints and previously established relationships. Buyers regard testing, evaluations, and approvals as costly, time-consuming, and unnecessary. Present suppliers strive to maintain product and service quality, while potential suppliers attempt to sell by offering better quality products, more reliable and efficient service, and lower prices. Table 2–2 shows the strategies of present ("in") suppliers versus potential ("out") suppliers in responding to different business buying situations.

■ **TABLE 2–2**   Reacting to Various Buying Situations: *Profiling Essential Marketing Strategies*

Buying Situation	The Supplier Who Is "In"	The Supplier Who Is "Out"
New task	Keep track of evolving purchasing needs in the organization.	
	Recognizing specific needs.	Recognizing specific needs.
	Engaging actively in early phases of buying process by supplying information and technical advice.	Engaging actively in early phases of buying process by supplying information and technical advice.
Straight rebuy	Strengthening the buyer-seller relationship by achieving organization's expectations.	Showing organizations that the potential benefits of reexamining requirements and suppliers exceed the costs.
	Adapting to evolving needs of the customer.	Trying to position yourself on an organization's preferred list of suppliers even as a second or third choice.
Modified rebuy	Correcting problems with customer.	Determining and reacting to the organization's problem with existing supplier.
	Analyzing and meeting customer needs.	Persuading organizations to try alternative offerings.

Source: Patrick J. Robinson, Charles W. Faris, and Yoram Wind, *Industrial Buying and Creative Marketing* (Boston: Allyn & Bacon, 1967), pp. 183–210.

Suppose that Central General's purchasing director buys hundreds, perhaps thousands, of items every month. Articles such as surgical gloves, rubber tubing, electronic thermometers, and paper cups are routinely reordered without approval from the hospital management.[23]

Modified Rebuy

With modified rebuy buying, the decision makers have well-defined criteria, but are uncertain about which suppliers can best fit their needs. Buyers may speculate that gains to be derived from reevaluating alternatives are significant relative to the expended effort involved. The distinctive element here is the reevaluation of alternatives—after consideration of new ones—prompted by the conviction that it is worthwhile to seek additional information and alternatives before reaching a decision. The nature of the buying requirements have changed so that the relatively routine buy or purchase is no longer routine. Because the needs have changed, the marketing effort must be changed to reply to the revised aspects of the customer's requirements.

Let us suppose that Central General is opening a new intensive-care ward in three months and needs additional help and rigorous cleaning procedures. Indeed, the chief of staff has already complained about poor hygiene in the maternity and postsurgical wards. At just this time the hospital's contract for janitorial services comes up for renewal. This situ-

---

[23]Bennett, p. 139.

ation transforms what might have been a straight rebuy into a modified rebuy. Although the purchasing director knows about janitorial services, the new requirements of the intensive-care unit and the complaints about the current vendor suggest the need to reopen the contract for bids. The chief of staff, the hospital administrator, and the head nurse in the new intensive-care unit must be consulted. The purchasing director will search for new suppliers while urging the present supplier to upgrade performance.[24]

■ PURCHASING RECORD SYSTEMS

Good record systems are a must in the daily operation and efficient planning activities of the purchasing and materials management function of a manufacturing firm, as buying decisions involve large expenditures of a firm's resources and create legal obligations. Despite the huge volume of data generated in the typical firm, much of this information can be useless in daily operations unless it is organized in a manner that makes it readily accessible. The following basic records are essential for the operation of most purchasing and materials management departments.

Catalogue File

The **catalogue file** contains product listings, catalogues, present and potential vendor promotional literature, and industrial directories of firms and products likely to be sought by the using firm. Obviously, business to business marketers must do their best to be certain that their firm's promotional data are in that file.

Open Order File

Buyers must have immediate access to all information concerning the status of open orders or purchase contracts that have not been filled. Although practice varies widely, most open order files contain all pertinent documents on outstanding orders, such as the purchase requisition, the working copy of the purchase contract, follow-up data, and all notes and correspondence about the order. This file is closed only after proper receipt of goods or services and the receipt and authorization to pay the invoice from the supplier.

Vendor Experience File

The **vendor experience file** contains background information on supplier delivery and quality performance as well as on the annual volume of materials purchased. In addition, the file lists the addresses, key personnel, telephone numbers, and other information of interest to the buying firm in its relations with suppliers.

---

[25]Bennett, p. 139.

Commodity Record File

The **commodity record file** is a reservoir of materials data maintained for each major material and service purchased repetitively. It contains a description of the purchased item, a listing of suppliers, a history of price action, and important terms such as discounts, quantities purchased, terms, etc. In deciding how much detailed information to record on a commodity card, each firm must weigh the value of the information against the cost of transcribing it.

■ PURCHASING AND THE LAW

The **purchasing-sales interchange** creates legal and binding commitments. The primary legal areas involved are those concerned with the laws of agency and of contracts. Legal considerations afford protection, and in many instances monetary recompense for nonperformance by the buyer or seller. Legal constraints exist regarding buyer-seller relationships, pricing, product liability, policies on the use of small companies and minority-owned firms, transportation, hazardous waste movement and disposal, storage, and potential personal liability of both the buyer and the seller.

Law of Agency

In buying and selling situations, the buying and selling personnel are acting as agents for their employing firms. An **agent** is any individual authorized to act on behalf of another, and yet not be subject to the other's control. Because the law of agency enters into all forms of business activity, buyers and sellers must understand the rights and duties of all parties involved, as these rights and duties create potential lawsuits.

It would be difficult to find two purchasing executives who would agree on how closely they should attend to the legal aspects of the position. One survey, for example, revealed that 40 percent of all manufacturing firms do not bother to include any terms on purchase contracts, that they do not worry about legal fine points, and that they feel that any misunderstandings which might arise with suppliers can be worked out by friendly negotiations.[25] Some buyers and sellers might blanch at such viewpoints, realizing that it is entirely possible for buyers and sellers to involve their respective companies unwittingly in legal hassles which can be catastrophically costly in terms of both money and prestige. Obviously, a working knowledge of the most important laws affecting the buyer-seller exchange is essential. Consider each of the following examples of potential legal issues.

You buy a machine from a reputable manufacturer, but the machine breaks down after an hour's work. Do you have to give the manufacturer

---

[25]*Legal Side of Purchasing*, (Waterford, Conn.: Bureau of Business Practices, 1983), p. 1.

time to remedy the situation before you can demand your money back? If so, how much time must you give? Are the answers different if every minute of the machine's downtime is costing your company thousands of dollars? Would the answers be different had the salesperson promised you that the machine would work for 20 years?

Your company needs a critical part immediately, or there is a chance that a large account will be lost. A supplier promises that the part will be on your doorstep the next morning, so you wipe your brow and sit back. The part shows up three weeks later. Can the supplier be held liable for your company's lost profits? Can the supplier be held liable at all? Are the answers different, depending on whether you talked with a sales manager or a sales representative?

You order equipment with a purchase order which says that the supplier's liability is unlimited. The equipment arrives accompanied by a sales form which says the supplier has no liability. Within minutes of installation, the equipment blows up, causing a fire that costs your company millions of dollars. Who pays for the damage—you or your supplier?

Your company refuses to pay for goods you ordered two months ago because you quit last week. So the supplier sues you personally. Can you be forced to pay for the goods out of your own pocket?[26]

Simple answers to these questions are not readily available. Although a legalistic approach to buying and selling is in most cases unnecessary, all buyers and sellers must nevertheless protect their company against potential legal problems.

Law of Contracts

The major responsibility of buyers and sellers in contractual situations is to ensure that the purchase contract is satisfactorily drawn, and that this contract is legally binding on both parties. To be valid and enforceable, a purchase contract must contain each of the following basic elements: (1) agreement ("meeting of the minds") resulting from an offer and an acceptance, (2) consideration or obligation, (3) competent parties, and (4) a lawful purpose.

The law is a vast subject. Fortunately most business to business buyers and sellers subscribe to ethical standards that make it unnecessary to conduct daily business in an atmosphere of constant legal danger. Buyers and sellers are well advised to limit application to legal principles to preventive law and recognize problems and situations that should be referred to professional legal counsel.

Concept Questions

1. How does dividing the understanding of buyer behavior into different phases aid the marketer?

---

[26]Ibid, p. 1.

2. What is the importance of good records systems to business buyers?
3. What is created by the purchase-sales interchange?

SUMMARY

1. The marketer needs to understand a buying firm's policies and procedures along with the buying process because these elements usually define responsibilities and detail both the buying authority that is delegated and to whom it is delegated. Salespeople are encouraged to examine prospects' statements of policy and procedures along with the buying process not only to help the sales effort but also to have a firm grasp on what the buying organization regards as important.

2. A buying situation is created when some member of the organization perceives a problem which can be solved through the purchase of a product or service. Seven basic steps are necessary in the buying process to complete a buying transaction.

3. The purchasing organization varies from one firm to another; some purchasing managers work out of corporate headquarters, while others operate at the divisional or plant level. In large companies the purchasing operation is often separated into both operational and managerial units. Further, the marketer needs to understand whether the buying organization decentralizes buying activities in each plant or division of a multiple-plant firm, centralizes the activity at headquarters, or uses a combination of both organizational methods.

4. The materials management concept advocates the grouping of all materials activities into a single department, and typically includes material planning and control, production scheduling, material and purchasing research, purchasing, incoming traffic, inventory control, receiving, incoming quality control, stores, in-plant materials movement, and scrap and surplus disposal. Alternative approaches to materials management include the traditional approach and the just-in-time approach.

5. The marketer who understands the organizational buying situation—that is, whether he or she has to deal with new-task buying, modified rebuy, or straight rebuy—can identify critical buying decision phases, information needs of the buying organization, and criteria considered by buyers in making their decisions.

6. Good record systems are essential in the daily operation and efficient planning of the purchasing and materials management function in a manufacturing firm. Catalogue, open order, vendor experience, and commodity record files provide important purchase-related information.

7. The purchasing-sales interchange creates legal and binding commitments; the primary legal areas involved are concerned with the laws of agency and contract.

KEY TERMS

agent

catalogue file

commodity record file

general purchasing department

management by exception

materials management

modified rebuy buying

new-task buying

open order file

policies and procedures

purchasing function

purchasing-sales interchange

straight rebuy buying

vendor experience file

REVIEW QUESTIONS

1. What is the role of basic policies and procedures in carrying out purchasing tasks? Of what value are contracts in the purchasing function?

2. Identify each of the steps in the buying process. How is a buying situation created? Create an example to show your own understanding of how a firm goes through the organizational buying process.

3. How does the organization of the purchasing department differ in regard to the size of the firm?

4. Discuss the reasons for having either a centralized or decentralized purchasing organization. Which form of organization is more commonly used by purchasing departments?

5. Define the materials management concept? Discuss why a company would adopt a materials management concept. Identify and explain two alternative approaches to materials management.

6. Identify and discuss three types of business to business buying situations. How are these buying situations related to the various stages of the procurement process? Create your own examples of business buying situations which correspond to each of the three buying situations.

7. Differentiate among four different types of purchasing record systems. What is the value of good record systems to purchasing and materials management departments?

8. Explain how contracts and the law of agency are applicable to the purchasing-sales interchange.

CHAPTER CASES

Case 2-1 The Geer Company*

The Geer company, a manufacturer of heavy-duty road-building equipment, was established in 1940 and grew slowly until 1972 when its sales volume was slightly in excess of $35 million. At that time the company "went public," and nonfamily management came into power. Aggressive management led to a tripling of volume by 1980.

During the period of slow growth, the company's purchasing department consisted of a purchasing agent, who reported to the vice president, and three buyers. One buyer bought only steel. The other two buyers bought all other items. One expediting clerk as well as the necessary clerks and typists to write purchase orders and check invoices were also assigned to the department. Inventory control was not part of purchasing, but rather reported to the production manager.

The Geer company had operated a small foundry until 1976. When this facility was closed, the responsibility for buying ferrous castings was assigned to the production manager's office and was handled by a person who had been a supervisor in the foundry.

During the period of rapid expansion the company's manufacturing facilities were inadequate, and it became necessary to subcontract a significant volume of machining operations. Two buyers responsible for subcontracts were assigned to the production manager. During the same period five new buyers and two expediters were added to the purchasing department.

The added work load in purchasing, the divided buying responsibilities, and the number of inexperienced buyers created many problems and brought complaints from the operating divisions of the company. Delays occurred in placing orders because of inexperienced employees in inventory control. Frequently the late deliveries and incorrect ordering quantities led to shortages and excesses in inventories, both of which were costly to the company. Management finally decided to engage a consulting firm to aid in reorganizing the purchasing operation and to make recommendations as to the assignment of responsibilities connected with the various buying functions.

Questions

1. As a consultant, how would you proceed to analyze this problem?
2. Prepare a recommended organization chart for the purchasing department.
3. Indicate how you would assign those functions that, while not direct buying activities, are closely related.

Case 2-2 American Arbitration Association*

The American Arbitration Association is a private, nonprofit organization established to aid businesses in finding solutions to legal disputes. Con-

---

*Gary J. Zenz, *Purchasing and Management of Materials*, 5th ed., 1981, John Wiley and Sons.

tracts between buyers and sellers sometimes contain what is called a *fu-ture dispute clause,* which establishes an agreement to settle disputes and claims in accordance with American Arbitration Association rules. Arbitration is invoked in lieu of a formal lawsuit.

The following three recent suits were submitted to arbitration:

1.   The purchasing manager (PM) contracted to buy a large supply of corrugated boxes in a size suitable for shipping a new line of merchandise her company had in production and would begin marketing in about four months. The delivery date was set at two months from the time of the agreement. Several days after she had submitted a purchase order, the PM received the order confirmation, and the deal was completely set.

Then the salesperson from the packaging company called about a week later with a special request. "Listen, we've got a warehousing problem here. We're about to rent some new space, and it would make our inventory control a lot easier if you can take delivery on that order now."

The buyer was willing, since she happened to have space to store the boxes until she needed them. However, she pointed out to the salesperson, "I can take that shipment now if I am not required to make an inspection of the merchandise until I need it." Their agreement called for any defects to be reported within 14 days, and she did not want to have to unpack all the boxes and then repack them for storage.

"That's no problem," the salesperson told her. "Your 14-day inspection time will not begin until the original delivery date."

The firm accepted the shipment of the order and stored it on its premises. Two months later, when the shipment was opened, damage apparently caused by water was discoverd. The PM immediately called the supplier and learned that the salesperson she had dealt with was no longer with the company. She then spokes to the sales manager. "These boxes we ordered from you are water damaged and can't be used."

"There's nothing I can do about it now. You've had that order for two months."

"Wait a minute," the buyer said. "We agreed to take that order early for your convenience, and your salesperson said that the inspection time did not start until the original delivery date."

"Well, he should not have made a verbal agreement like that. Look at the order confirmation. It specifically says no changes can be made except in writing."

"Well, he did make an agreement, and since he was your salesperson, you are bound to it."

"Nothing doing," was the supplier's reply. "How do we know that you didn't damage those boxes yourselves? I'm afraid it's just too late to make a claim." Both parties repeated basically the same arguments before the arbitrator.

2.   Stan Franklin, the purchasing manager for Graphics, Inc., one day felt the need for some advice on an order of paper, and went to a wholesaler for help. He discussed his needs in full, explaining that the paper he wanted was to be printed and varnished and used as box wraps. The supplier was ready with quick advice. "Got just what you need," he piped. Following the agent's recommendation, the purchasing manager ordered 27,000 sheets of a certain 34 × 57 inch paper. The cost was $1,500. Soon afterward the order was delivered, and Stan's company put the paper through the various processes to prepare it for final gluing. When the company started gluing the paper to the boxes, the results were unsatisfactory. The paper blistered and could not be made to stick.

Pressed for time, Stan went to another supplier and got paper that proved satisfactory for the purpose, and his company was able to meet its obligation to the customer. Afterward, Stan totalled up expenses of $4,000 in reprinting, finishing, and trucking the substituted paper. Then he let the first supplier know that his company had no intention of absorbing the cost. The tactic chosen by Stan's company was to deduct the expense from other invoices owed the supplier.

"You can just deduct $4,000 from what we owe you," said Graphics officials, "and next time, don't promise that a product can do a job unless you know what you're talking about."

"Who promised anything?" replied the supplier. "What I said amounted to no more than an opinion that the paper might be suitable." "In fact," he went on, "the sales contract specifically states that seller makes no warranties whatsoever, express or implied, as to suitability. That proves that you've got no gripe with me. If you couldn't make the paper perform satisfactorily, it wasn't due to any fault or defect in the paper. This is a case of bad judgment on your part, and you can't hold me responsible for that!" Stan's company decided to bring the matter to arbitration in accordance with the dispute-settlement clause in the sales contract.

3.   The sales manager of Eastville Specialty Cabinets was not in the habit of turning away business, but one day it looked as if he might have to. The prospective customer, a life insurance company, had sent in a purchase order for a large supply of metal filing cabinets for a suburban branch under construction. To prevent duplication of moving costs, the insurance company wanted the goods shipped directly to the new office during the last week of May when construction was to be completed. But Eastville officials were not happy about that kind of arrangement. They did not like the possibility of having their already limited storage space taken up by the insurance company's goods, should the new quarters not be ready on schedule. When all was taken into consideration, Eastville's sales manager felt that the order wasn't worth the trouble if his company had to risk jeopardizing the movement of other orders.

He explained the situation to the insurance company's purchasing manager, and after some discussion, they worked out a solution. It appeared in the sales agreement as Section 14: "If the buyer does not accept delivery on the date requested, then the goods will be stored at the buyer's expense."

The construction work progressed smoothly, and to the relief of both the insurance company and supplier, the building was ready on time. Eastville was notified, and the goods were shipped. But upon delivery, the purchasing manager found them less than satisfactory. Apparently, when they were crated, the cabinets had been badly marred. "Take them back," the purchasing manager told the driver. "We can't accept them in this condition."

The goods went back, and the deficiencies were corrected. When Eastville asked the purchasing manager for shipping instructions, the firm was told that the local building inspector had closed the office down pending certain repairs by the contractor. Six weeks later the manager called Eastville's sales office back. "We're in business again. Send the goods," he said. Eastville did just that, but along with the cabinets came a bill for six weeks' storage.

"We won't pay," the purchasing manager's company replied. "That storage provision in the contract applied only if for some reason we were unable to receive the goods on the date requested. We did not intend to pay storage if the goods went back because of defects."

Eastville was adamant, however, and the case eventually found its way to the American Arbitration Association.

Questions

1. How should the arbitration panel rule in each case?
2. Was there anything that could have been done to lessen the likelihood of each of these dispute's arising?

SUGGESTED READINGS

Anderson, Erin; Wujin Chu; and Barton Weitz. "Industrial Purchasing: An Empirical Exploration of the Buyclass Framework." *Journal of Marketing* 51 (July 1987), pp. 71–86. Study of the buyclass framework by querying the managers of sales forces about the behavior their salespeople encounter on the part of their business to business customers.

Bilborough, C. A. M., and B. G. Dale. "The Role and Influence of Factory-Level Purchasing within a Corporate Structure." *International Journal of Physical Distribution and Materials Management* (UK) 15, no. 1, 1985, pp. 39–48. Case studies and comparisons of corporate purchasing departments and factory purchasing departments.

Celley, Albert F.; William H. Clegg; Arthur W. Smith; and Mark A. Vonderembse. "Implementation of JIT in the United States." *Journal of Purchasing and Materials Management* 22 (Winter 1986), pp. 9–15. Comparative analysis of the just-in-time approach to materials management in Japan and the United States.

Dale, B. G., and R. H. Powley. "Purchasing Practices in the United Kingdom: A Case Study," *Journal of Purchasing and Materials Management* 21 (Spring 1985), pp. 26–33. A comparative analysis of U.S. versus British purchasing organization, performance measurement, materials management, and vendor selection.

French, Warren A.; Jan W. Henkel; John S. Kanet; and John B. Ford IV. "MRO Parts Service in the Machine Tool Industry." *Industrial Marketing Management* 14 (November 1985), pp. 283–88. MRO parts survey to include postpurchase parts and replacement policies.

Ghingold, Morry. "Testing the 'Buygrid' Buying Process Model." *Journal of Purchasing and Materials Management* 22 (Winter 1986), pp. 30–36. Study of decision making in various stages of the business to business buying process.

Jackson, Donald W., Jr.; Richard K. Burdick; and Janet E. Keith. "Purchasing Agents' Perceived Importance of Marketing Mix Components in Different Industrial Purchase Situations," *Journal of Business Research* 13 (August 1985), pp. 361–73. Systematic role-playing study of 254 business to business purchasing executives, using five product types and three types of buyclasses.

Kriger, Ruth Haas, and Jack R. Meredith. "Emergency and Routine MRO Parts Buying," *Industrial Marketing Management* 14 (November 1985), pp. 277–82. Survey of purchasing criteria and sources utilized in MRO parts buying.

LeBlanc, Ronald P. "Insights into Organizational Buying," *The Journal of Business and Industrial Marketing* 2 (Fall 1987), pp. 5–10. Research suggesting that the decision rules used to select buyers for consideration are independent of the decision rules used to make the final purchase choice.

Mast, Kenneth E., and John M. Hawes. "Perceptual Differences between Buyers and Engineers," *Journal of Purchasing and Materials Management* 22 (Spring 1986), pp. 2–6. A study of how business to business buyers and engineers differ in rating the importance of various attributes in the purchasing process.

Moller, K. E. Kristian. "Research Strategies in Analyzing the Organizational Buying Process," *Journal of Business Research* 13 (February 1985), pp. 3–15. Review and integration of strategic approaches to analyzing the organizational buying process to include decision system analysis, role analysis, information processing analysis, multiattribute choice paradigms, and social influence theory.

"MRO Buyers are Getting Better, Tougher." *Purchasing World* (30 November 1986), pp. 53–54. Analysis of trends in the purchasing of maintenance, repair, and operating supplies, with a look at systems contracting and the role of the industrial distributor.

Narasimihan, Ram, and Linda K. Stoynoff. "Optimizing Aggregate Procurement Allocation Decisions," *Journal of Purchasing and Materials Management* 22 (Spring 1986), pp. 23–30. Model development and applications using mixed-integer programming.

Shroeder, Gary D.; Gary D. Scudder; and Michael J. Pesch. "Approaches to Managing the Cost of Materials," *International Journal of Physical Distribution and Materials Management* (UK) 16, no. 3, 1986, pp. 57–69. Guidelines and case studies for purchasing and supplier relations as they relate to materials management.

Smith, David, and Rob Taylor. "Organisational Decision-Making and Industrial Marketing," *European Journal of Marketing* (UK) 19, no. 7, 1985, pp. 56–71. Guidelines for, and discussion of, strategic decision making in organizational buying behavior.

Chapter **3**

Management of the Organizational Buying Function

LEARNING OBJECTIVES

After reading this chapter, you should be able to:

- Articulate the objectives of efficient business to business buying.
- Realize the role and significance of the buying center.
- Understand the relationship among quality, service, and price.
- Appreciate the importance of value analysis in organizational buying.
- Explain the relevance of the make-or-buy decision.
- Comprehend the negotiation process from both the seller's and buyer's viewpoint.
- Distinguish among the tools and techniques used in handling the small order.
- Discuss purchasing's impact on company profits.

CHAPTER OUTLINE

Objectives of Efficient Business to Business Buying
  Objectives of Organizational Buyers
  Seven Rights of Business Buyers
  Purchasing Costs
The Buying Center
Quality in Business Buying and Selling
  Responsibilities of the Purchasing Department
Service in Business Buying and Selling
  Differentiation through Service
  Service as a Competitive Effort
Price in Business Buying and Selling
  Perceived Value
Value Analysis
  What Is It?
  Development of Value Engineering
  Appropriate Tests Used

Make-or-Buy Analysis
  Ascertaining Profitability
  Reasons to Manufacture
  Participants in Make-or-Buy
Negotiation
  Objectives of Negotiation
  Negotiation Maneuvers, Strategies, and Tactics
  The Use of Questions
  Analyzing Both Buyer and Seller Strengths
The Small-Order Problem
  The Centralized-Stores System
  The Petty-Cash System
  The Blanket-Order System
  The Electronic Ordering System
Purchasing's Impact upon Company Profits

■ OBJECTIVES OF EFFICIENT BUSINESS TO BUSINESS BUYING

Objectives of Organizational Buyers

Organizational buyers have several distinct objectives in purchasing goods and services. In general, organizational buying objectives, such as availability of items, reliability of sellers, consistency of quality, delivery, and price, are important for all types of firms. But such different organizational buyers as manufacturers, wholesalers, government customers, and not-for-profit institutions emphasize one or more of these objectives. Figure 3–1 distinguishes between general objectives commonly shared by organizational buyers and specific objectives of various types of organizational buyers. Note the dissimilarities among the objectives felt to be most important by manufacturers, wholesalers, government customers, and not-for-profit institutions.

■ **FIGURE 3–1**   Objectives of Organizational Customers

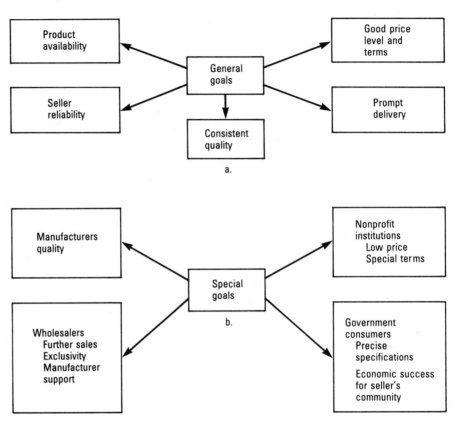

SOURCE: Joel R. Evans and Barry Berman, *Marketing,* 2d ed. (New York: Macmillan, 1985), p. 193.

Over the years people have focused much thought, attention, and research on American business organizations in order to find better ways, methods, and techniques of performing the tasks and developing the relationships essential to the realization of the full potential of a dynamic, industrial world civilization. The materials acquisition-retention cycle in the overall purchasing process is undergoing rapid change as the business to business buying process has become a time-consuming and highly involved process. Organizational buying has evolved into a complex process of decision making and communication, which takes place over time, involves several organizational members, and includes relationships with other firms and institutions. No longer is organizational buying the simple act of placing an order with a vendor or a selling organization.

Seven Rights of Business Buyers

Most purchasing and materials management textbooks provide a list of seven rights purchasing personnel use in their standard statements as to their overall objectives in meeting organizational commitments. They say that their primary objective is to purchase the right materials in the right quantity, for delivery at the right time and in the right place, from the right source with the right service and at the right price. Fulfilling this objective can be a difficult task for the business buyer and marketer as well. This is because it is not efficient to buy at the right price if the purchased parts or materials are unsatisfactory from a quality or service standpoint, or if their late arrival creates a production-line shutdown. Furthermore, the right price might be a higher than normal price for an emergency requirement when the buyer cannot adhere to a normal delivery schedule. The more rational organizational buyer must attempt to balance out sometimes conflicting objectives, and to make tradeoffs to obtain the optimum mix of these seven rights. Conflicting objectives can cause major problems for the seller, especially with regard to delivery and service. (See Figure 3–1 for a more specific statement of the overall goals and objectives of organizational buyers.)

Purchasing Costs

Purchasing costs are the largest single element in the operation of many organizations. The magnitude of the buying job becomes apparent as managers learn of the importance of the cost of purchased goods and materials versus the sales dollar. In general, the ratio ranges between 40 and 60 percent of sales revenue; reportedly it goes up to 80 percent for Xerox copiers and Chrysler automobiles.[1] Thus the purchasing decisions directly impact upon the costs and profitability of the firm. Moreover, if the trend toward automation continues in industry at its present pace, future expenditures for materials and equipment may well represent an even larger portion of a company's sales income than is now the case.

■ THE BUYING CENTER

People within an organization involved in the buying process are members of what is called a **buying center.** Only rarely is one person in any organization solely responsible for the buying decision. Usually several people are members of the buying center or decision-making unit. The astute business to business marketer must determine the appropriate buying influences for a particular situation, a task that is not always quick and easy. Several people usually play the same role (that is, there may be several influencers in a purchase decision), and one person may play two or more roles (for example, he or she may be both a decider and buyer).

The size of a buying center varies with the complexity and importance of a purchase decision; and the composition of the buying group will usually change from one purchase to another or even during various stages of

[1]Joseph L. Cavinato, *Purchasing and Materials Management* (St. Paul, Minn.: West Publishing, 1984), p. 7.

■ **EXHIBIT 3–1**   Roles of Buying Center Members in the Purchasing Process

Role	Description
Users	Those who use the product in question. Their influence on the purchasing decision can range from minimal to major. In some cases users begin the purchase process and even develop product specifications.
Gatekeepers	Those who keep a tight control on the flow of information to other members of the buying center. Can open the gate to members of the buying center for some salespeople, yet close it for others.
Influencers	Those who provide information to buying center members for evaluating alternative products or who set purchasing specifications. Normally influencers operate within the buying center, such as quality control or research and development personnel. Yet at other times influencers operate outside the buying center, such as architects who create very specific building requirements.
Deciders	Those who, in reality, make the buying decision, regardless of whether or not they hold the formal authority. A decider is often quite difficult to identify since deciders can be a company president, a purchasing director, or a research and development analyst.
Buyers	Those who are assigned the formal authority to select vendors and complete the purchasing transaction. Sometimes the prerogative of the buyer is taken by other more powerful members of the buying center. Often a purchasing manager who carries out the clerical duties of the purchase order acts in the role of the buyer.

the buying process.[2] Members of a buying center have various roles in the buying process, as shown in Exhibit 3–1.

Business to business marketers have the critical task of determining who is involved in the buying decision and the specific role played by each buying-center participant. On recognizing this, the marketers can tailor a sales presentation in terms of language, tone, and time to the appropriate role that the particular individual plays in the buying process. Marketers usually find that, while most of their contacts are with purchasing department personnel, the buying-center participants with the greatest influence are often not in that department at all. For example, Loctite Corporation, the manufacturer of Super-Glue and an industrial leader in adhesives and sealants, found that engineers were the most important buying influences in the products they were trying to market. As a result, Loctite focused its marketing efforts on production and maintenance engineers.[3] Table 3–1 illustrates some examples of typical buying influences, and shows how they may affect buying decisions and marketing strategy. Note the implied influence of the production manager, the controller, the engineer, and the plant manager. These individuals will certainly affect the buying decision and are even regarded as influencers. They may have the final say as to what is bought, especially if they are the user.

---

[2]Gary L. Lilien and Anthony Wong, "An Exploratory Investigation of the Structure of the Buying Center in the Metal Working Industry," *Journal of Marketing Research* 21 (February 1984), pp. 1–11.

[3]"Loctite: Home Is Where the Customers Are," *Business Week*, April 13, 1987, p. 63; and Bob Donath, "What Loctite Learned with Psychographic Insights," *Business Marketing*, July 1984, pp. 100–1, 134.

■ **TABLE 3–1**   Examples of Buying Influences and How They May Affect Business to Business Purchasing Decisions and Marketing Strategy

Buying Influence	Effects on Buying	Appropriate Marketing Strategy
Purchasing agent, buyer	Handles requisitions from the plant, maintains personal library of supplier's catalogs, does some discretionary purchasing, especially when delivery is critical. Usually honors sources recommended by key plant personnel.	See them regularly. Keep them informed if you see others in the plant. Keep them supplied with new product and price information. Offer them a benefit on every call. Allow them to pave the way to other buying influences in the plant.
Production manager, general foreman	Usually confined to specific production operations such as assembly, finishing. Can describe specific problems in detail.	Sell brand superiority, depth of your inventory, delivery, and your potential for contributing to productivity of production people and equipment. Leave catalog, put on general mailing list. Call only when you have a real constructive offering.
Plant controller, head bookkeeper	With purchasing department, interested in terms of sale or systems contract.	Be fully prepared with terms stated simply. Come armed with benefits offered over and above those of others.
Director or vice president of engineering	Concerned with product or process improvements. Generally involved with future changes, seldom with immediate needs. Searches continually for new, improved products. Relates heavily on library of suppliers. Also relies heavily on technical aid from vendors. Strong influence on OEM and MRO product type and brand selection.	Responds favorably to outside help in the form of new, potentially useful data and technical counsel. Offer your complete catalog. Offer technical capabilities via your own experts. Personally introduce new improved products regularly. Put on your general mailing list and keep supplied with your latest complete catalog.
Plant manager, general manager, vice president of operations, vice president of manufacturing	Key buying influence on larger plant expenditures. May direct vendors to key personnel and problem areas in the plants.	Receptive to constructive information. Often easier to reach than floor personnel. Contact periodically if possible with your management, to demonstrate your interest in serving, to sell your firm's capabilities, and to probe prospect's problems and plans. Keep informed on important product breakthroughs.

SOURCE: "Finding the Real Buying Influence," *Industrial Distribution* 67 (June 1977), pp. 36, 37, 39.

Sellers should not overlook their importance in the buying-decision process.

The buying-center membership and relative importance of different members varies from company to company. In engineering-dominated firms like Texas Instruments or General Dynamics—where constant technical innovation shortens the product life cycle—the buying center may consist almost entirely of engineers. In more marketing-oriented firms like General Foods or IBM, marketing and engineering have almost equal authority. In a small manufacturing company the buying center may consist of several individuals with very different backgrounds and demands. Members may consist of everyone from the CEO to a particular production worker, each of whom has a say about what is purchased in a particular situation. This complicates the task for business to business marketers, who may have to deal with many different personalities and interests in a selling situation. Table 3–2 lists a number of manufacturers involved in a variety of purchase situations and shows who the true decision makers are.

Concept Questions

1. How much does the typical purchasing operation spend?
2. What determines the size of a buying center?
3. What is the critical task for a marketer in dealing with buying centers?

■ QUALITY IN BUSINESS BUYING AND SELLING

In the organizational or business buying environment, value is associated with suitability and overall cost, not price. The ideal quality level purchased is the level that can be bought at the lowest total cost to fulfill the need or to satisfy the function for which the raw materials, parts, or subassemblies are acquired. Sellers should understand this distinction as the words *total cost* are used here instead of the word *price*. Price implies spending a single dollar amount as opposed to the total costs associated with a particular purchase. Transportation cost, set-up cost, training, storage, and a variety of other potential incremental costs must be taken into account when buying quality. The potential seller's input regarding quality needed is often taken as valuable input (as perhaps it should be) by members of the buying center. However, the final quality level purchased depends to a large extent on the member of the buying center who has the final responsibility for the workability of the purchased component, installation, or service. Quality really has no meaning within the spectrum of purchasing except as it is related to function and ultimate cost. If unnecessary quality is purchased, competitive pressure will force the unneeded quality out. Too much quality will lead to higher prices, which will ultimately cost the buying firm's market share. Higher quality levels than those actually needed increase cost unnecessarily. Only after the quality

■ **TABLE 3–2**   Decision Makers in Selected Buying Centers

Company	Capital Equipment	Decision Maker	Business Services	Decision Maker
Chemical manufacturer	Heat exchanger	Purchasing manager	Construction contract labor	Purchasing manager
Business to business safety products manufacturer	Automatic drilling machine	Engineer VP of manufacturing	Plant janitorial service	Purchasing manager
Steel manufacturer	Coke oven	Purchasing manager	Maintenance repair contract	Buyer
Machine tooling co.	Vertical boring mill	VP of operations	Fabricating work	Purchasing manager
Metal and wire manufacturer	Wrapping machine	Division manager	Machinery rigging for shipping	Traffic manager
Aerospace and automotive products manufacturer	Metal working machine tool	Divisional purchasing manager	Technical consultant	Director of purchasing
Paper products manufacturer	Banding system	General manager	Vending machine service	Personnel manager
Petroleum products manufacturer	Gasoline storage tank	Buyer	Printing of advertising materials	VP of marketing
Mining equipment manufacturer	Executive office desk	Purchasing agent	Training for first-line supervisors	General manager
Engineering and construction company	Cooling vessel	Job supervisor	Tar sludge removal	Buyer Purchasing manager Divisional VP
Home products manufacturer	Mixing machines	Buyer engineer	Drapery cleaning	Service manager
Building materials manufacturer	Pump	Engineer	Engineering services	Executive VP

SOURCE: Wesley Johnston and Thomas Bonoma, "The Buying Center: Structure and Interaction Patterns," *Journal of Marketing* (Summer 1981), pp. 150–51.

level needed is determined and agreed upon should price be considered. Quality, therefore, is an important ingredient in price setting.[4]

Members of the buying center need to address the issue of quality regardless of where the quality specifications originate. Purchasing personnel must challenge what they perceive as being unnecessarily high-quality levels. Buyers must work closely with external marketing personnel to help

---

[4]For more discussion of this issue, see Tom Peters and Perry Pascarella, "Searching for Excellence: The Winners Deliver on Value," *Industry Week,* April 16, 1984, pp. 61–62.

determine what constitutes acceptable quality levels. Buyers have the right to question any requests for nonstandard, higher-priced, hard-to-get items or materials. Price is only one element of the total cost, as incremental costs must also be considered.

Responsibilities of the Purchasing Department

Whether or not the purchasing department has the responsibility of originating or coordinating the quality specifications, purchasing personnel must ensure that proper quality specifications are part of the purchase contract. Within this framework, the purchasing department must accomplish the following:

1.   Know what is wanted and pass this information on to the bidders and vendors. Buyers who demand more, get more. (See the "Business to Business Marketing in Action" box.)

BUSINESS TO BUSINESS MARKETING IN ACTION

How good is incoming quality?—
How good do you demand?

Buyers who demand more get more.

That principle was driven home in the results of a recent *Purchasing* survey on how closely incoming goods meet spec. We asked buyers if they consider the rate of incoming goods meeting spec respectable. If not, we asked what they are doing about it.

Most respondents list a percentage in the 90-99% range, with the average coming in at 92.4%. But the most interesting part of the survey is the fact that buyers reporting the lowest standard of performance are not the ones doing the most complaining or taking the corrective action. No—it's the buyers with the highest conformance rates on incoming goods meeting spec who are the most determined to meet incoming goods' quality rates. In fact, many buyers with active Zero Defects programs say they are actually getting close to that elusive 100% quality acceptance goal.

In all, better than one third of all respondents say they are implementing programs to improve quality acceptance levels. Many say they are placing more of the responsibility for quality directly on the vendor, and are pushing programs with built-in penalties. Among actions most cited:

- Change or threaten to change sources.
- Restate or tighten specs and follow up with suppliers to make sure they understand what's wanted.
- Crack down on the acceptance of borderline parts.

continued

- Set up vendor certification programs with ratings that leave little question about how closely suppliers are coming to meeting requirements.
- Pare down the size of the vendor base in order to make policing of vendor performance more manageable.
- Demand specification certifications with all or most shipments.
- Request test data in advance.

Many buyers say their corrective action programs are especially geared toward promoting the concept of vendor partnership and solicitation of supplier input. High on the list of vendor partnership program approaches that feature problem-solving sessions: SPC programs; formalized vendor visitation programs; and round tables involving purchasing, QC, and buyer and vendor engineers.

Some buyers say their heaviest attention is being directed toward closer inspection of incoming parts and shipments. Focus in this area is being directed on tightening incoming inspection by upgrading the receiving department, adding more and better quality control check points, subjecting more goods to lab analysis before acceptance, and transferring more of the inspection burden to the vendor.

SOURCE: *Purchasing* 102 (February 12, 1987), p. 21.

2. See that the vendor performs according to the purchase quality specifications.
3. Take the necessary steps to protect the buyer's company against financial loss resulting from materials or parts that do not meet the purchase specifications.
4. Utilize suggestions from respected vendors in purchasing desirable product quality and reliability.[5]

To accomplish the above tasks, buyers, on occasion, will have to enlist the assistance of others, both inside and outside their respective companies, to develop and to make the purchase quality specifications workable. The final quality purchased is a measure of the degree to which the product meets the requirements of the purchaser, distributor, and ultimate user of the end product.

Let's take as an example Motorola, which is tackling a new challenge. It is taking techniques mastered to increase quality in manufacturing and insuring supplier quality, and extending them to the way it buys corporate services. Motorola purchasing executives recently completed a quality symposium for travel suppliers—car rental and travel agencies, hotels and motels—in the first step toward an overhaul of travel buying and eventually the way the corporation buys other services. It was a seminar focusing on

---

[5]Paul V. Farrell, C. P. M., and George W. Aljian, C. P. M., *Aljian's Purchasing Handbook* (New York: McGraw-Hill, 1982), pp. 9–6 and 9–7.

issues intended to create quality awareness. The idea stemmed from the trend in manufacturing to rationalize the supplier base, linking suppliers to manufacturers in cooperative partnerships for mutual benefit.[6]

■ SERVICE IN BUSINESS BUYING AND SELLING

The purchaser's desire for excellent service is a strong buying motive that can determine buying patterns. The term *service* is used here as an attribute, not a product. (Services, as a product, will be discussed in detail in Chapter 14.) Service is measured by a vendor's ability to comply with promised delivery dates, specifications, and technical assistance. Service encompasses many tangible and intangible activities, such as an assurance of supply, technical help when needed, financial assistance, and inventory holding. Businesses, government, and other institutions require such services.

Differentiation through Service

The above taxonomy, however, does not differentiate between purchased service per se, and pre- and postpurchase service, which is typically part of a product purchase. Service can and should be an important means of differentiation for the marketer. Consequently, many sellers emphasize their service as much as their products. Often a firm's only attraction to potential buyers is its service because the buyer feels that the product is so standardized that it can be purchased from any number of companies. The marketer who provides such pre- and post-service as technical assistance, reliable delivery, and a quick supply of replacement parts will have an edge over competing suppliers. Buyers who rely on the technical advice and assistance of marketers in solving their materials-use problems make it very difficult for competitors to disrupt such a relationship. The availability of replacement parts for machinery and equipment is extremely important, with speed being a vital component in the provision of this service. Sandia National Laboratories of Albuquerque, New Mexico, defines improved service level as "customers receiving frequent and timely deliveries of both stock and nonstock items, simplified ordering and receiving procedures, better product quality, immediate technical assistance, and quicker resolution of problems."[7]

Suppliers to organizational or business buyers must also place heavy emphasis on reliability of delivery. Purchasing directors, who normally receive the blame for late deliveries of materials purchased, will favor the source which always delivers as promised. Late delivery is by far a typical buyers' biggest complaint about vendor performance. Fifty-seven percent of respondents in a 1987 poll by *Purchasing* magazine stated that delivery was their biggest gripe with vendors. Respondents further reported that sup-

---

[6]"Motorola Rates Its Service Suppliers," *Purchasing* 103 (November 5, 1987), p. 13.
[7]"Sandia Bucks Low-Bid Ritual," *Purchasing* 103, (September 24, 1987), p. 20.

pliers fail to notify them when a scheduled delivery will not be on time.[8] Central Maintenance and Welding of Lithia, Florida, has found that the quality of service provided them has been deteriorating over the past three years. Reasons cited by purchasing executives include problems in timely delivery, vendor quotes, inventory availability, long lead times, reduction in vendor work force, and ignored telephone calls.[9]

Also, marketing strategy must be adapted to variations in buyer perceptions of problems in selection, introduction, and performance. For example, a marketer of computers, which present major problems to the buyer in the design of information-processing systems and in training personnel to use the equipment, should place heavy emphasis on offering technical service in system design, and on providing training in the operation and maintenance of the equipment. At the same time a manufacturer of dry copying machines, which provide essentially no procedural problems in adoption and introduction to employees, but which may provide major performance problems, would require a different strategy. For these machines emphasis would be placed upon product reliability, the provision of technical servicing, and flexibility in adjusting to buyer needs. Therefore, the supplier will relate his or her product to a prospective application and deduce the problems that the customer is likely to encounter in adopting his or her product.

Service as a Competitive Effort

At times the selling firm will even consider shifting its competitive effort to the area of service as opposed to price. This more subtle, indirect price competition is tantamount to direct competition. Prices, in effect, are reduced by the seller who agrees to perform such additional services as holding the customer's inventory, extending the time of payments, or absorbing freight charges. The amount of service that a buying firm is able to obtain, and that a selling firm is able to provide, usually correlates directly with the skills and perceptions of the buying and selling personnel. The marketer with the strongest service capabilities will certainly be in a favorable position, all other things being equal. It must be recognized, however, that service can be easily copied, but excellent service cannot!

■ PRICE IN BUSINESS BUYING AND SELLING

Professional buying personnel seldom rely on a quoted purchase price in making buying decisions. They are concerned with the **total cost of the purchasing decision,** which takes into account a variety of factors, such as the amount of scrap or waste resulting from the use of the material, the cost of processing the material, the power consumed, and a host of other variables that generate or minimize costs. For example, the price of a par-

---

[8]"Poor Delivery Performance Continues to Plague PMs," *Purchasing* 103, (November 5, 1987), p. 12.

[9]"Quality Is Up! Service Is Down!" *Purchasing,* 102 (February 12, 1987), p. 21.

ticular type of paint might be low, but it may also be costly to apply. Additionally, the coal with the low cost per ton might be high in volatile material, ash, or fusible elements, and low in BTUs. Steel is cheaper than aluminum; yet in many areas of the nation, particularly where rough terrain predominates, utility companies erect more aluminum high-voltage transmission towers than steel ones. The aluminum tower is not only cheaper to erect; since it is impervious to most types of weather, it is also cheaper to maintain.

Members of the buying center attempt to negotiate with preferred suppliers for better prices and terms before making the final selection. Innovative methods can be used to counter intense price competition. Consider the following example: Lincoln Electric has instituted the "Guaranteed Cost Reduction Program" for its distributors.[10] Under the program, whenever a customer requests a company to lower prices on Lincoln equipment to match Lincoln competitors, the company and the particular distributor guarantee that during the coming year they will find cost reductions in the customer's plant that meet or exceed the price difference between Lincoln's products and the competition's. Lincoln's sales representative and the distributor then get together, and after surveying the customer's operations, identify and help to implement possible cost reductions. If an independent audit at the end of the year does not reveal the promised cost reductions, Lincoln Electric and the distributor make good the difference, with Lincoln paying 70 percent and the distributor the rest.

Perceived Value

As noted earlier, purchasing personnel place a great deal of importance on nonprice factors, such as the quality of the product relative to their specific needs and the availability of accompanying services, such as installation, repair, and maintenance services. Product quality and service availability come before price considerations, with quality and service levels determining price.[11] Potential supplier price quotations are not the simple matching process assumed in economic theory. Quoting a price generally results from a more complicated process; it employs many factors often hidden from the marketer who does not always make a persistent investigative effort to uncover them. Marketers who investigate a variety of price-related issues before making price quotations are basing their prices on their respective product's **perceived value.** These companies see the buyer's perception of value, not the seller's cost, as the key to pricing. They use nonprice variables in the marketing mix to build up perceived value in the buyers' minds. Price is then set to capture the perceived value. Exhibit 3–2 describes how Caterpillar uses perceived value to set prices on its construction equipment. Only after the quality required to perform the function is determined does the buyer become concerned with price. The

---

[10]See James A. Narus and James C. Anderson, "Turn Your Industrial Distributors into Partners," *Harvard Business Review* (March-April 1986), pp. 66–71.

[11]See Peters and Pascarella, pp. 61–62.

■ **EXHIBIT 3–2** How Caterpillar Uses Perceived-Value Pricing

Caterpillar uses perceived value to set prices on its construction equipment. It might price a tractor at $24,000, although a similar competitor's tractor might be priced at $20,000. However, Caterpillar will get more sales than the competitor! When a prospective customer asks a Caterpillar dealer why he should pay $4,000 more for the Caterpillar tractor, the dealer answers:

$20,000 is the tractor's price if it is only equivalent to the competitor's tractor.
$ 3,000 is the price premium for superior durability.
$ 2,000 is the price premium for superior reliability.
$ 2,000 is the price premium for superior service.
$ 1,000 is the price for longer warranty on parts.

$28,000 is the price to cover the value package.
$ 4,000 discount.

$24,000 final price.

The stunned customer learns that although he is being asked to pay a $4,000 premium for the Caterpillar tractor, he is in fact getting a $4,000 discount. He ends up choosing the Caterpillar tractor because he is convinced that the lifetime operating costs of the Caterpillar tractor will be lower.

SOURCE: Philip Kotler, *Principles of Marketing,* 3d ed. (Englewood Cliffs, N.J.: Prentice-Hall, 1986), pp. 383–84.

objective here is not to minimize the importance of price in the buying decision, but rather to call attention to the many other variables vital to the determination of the ultimate cost of the good or service purchased.

■ VALUE ANALYSIS

What Is It?

Value analysis, developed by General Electric in the late 1940s, is the task of studying a product and all its components in order to determine ways of producing it at a lower cost, of improving quality, or of using a material in greater or more stable supply. It is the creative task of analyzing the purpose or function an item is supposed to fulfill. Value analysis, then, can be thought of as a scientifically organized method for reducing costs of manufactured items, and for encouraging vendor cooperation in lowering costs of purchased items. Its ultimate purpose is to secure improved performance of components at less cost. It requires a team approach. It cannot be implemented by designers without input from production, purchasing, and marketing. It also might require active supplier participation.[12]

Development of Value Engineering

Originally value analysis was intended to apply primarily to parts already in production. It soon became obvious, however, that the study of function could begin early in the design stages of a part or a product. Gradually the

[12]James Morgan, "If Cheap Products Are All You Get—You're Not Doing VA," *Purchasing* (June 16, 1988), p. 17.

scope of value analysis was expanded and refined to include preproduction functional analysis, which, in turn, became known as **value engineering.** Thus *value analysis* and *value engineering* are considered to be interchangeable terms and are so used in this text.

A value-analysis program represents an effort to integrate the commercial skills of purchasing personnel with the technical skills of engineering and production personnel. Value analysis is appropriate when new technology develops, such as a new material, adhesive coating, or chemical. The result should be significant quality improvements, a new marketing appeal, reduced costs, or just keeping the product on par with competitive products. Three years ago Wang Laboratories set out to find and implement superior protective packaging that would also be cost- and labor-efficient. At the same time, Sealed Air Corporation was in the process of developing an innovative protective packaging system and sought a company to field-test the system in a high-volume packaging environment. Working in concert with Wang, Sealed Air was able to fine-tune its new system's performance based on feedback from Wang. The result was the automated Instapak Foam 'N Fill system. According to Phil Hashway, director of distribution for field operations at Wang, previous packaging methods just did not measure up. "Our goal was to come up with a better method of packaging, and Sealed Air came in and worked with us to help meet our packaging requirements. Productivity has increased 20 percent, and we have realized a 20 percent material cost savings because the automated system dispenses the Instapak chemicals in a premeasured amount."[13] This is a good example of vendor participation in a value-analysis effort.

Quality problems during production or with the final product can also lead to value analysis. Similarly, problems with the product in the field that result in customer dissatisfaction might give rise to complete product value analysis, rather than the analysis of only one particular part or component of the product.

Value analysis is also useful when the product reaches the latter part of the market growth stage or the early part of the market maturity stage of the product life cycle. During either or both of these stages, design improvements in the basic product are often worthwhile; value analysis is often triggered by a cost squeeze experienced as a result of a flattening sales curve or of price competition.

Appropriate Tests Used

Value analysts apply a series of tests, which take the form of questions to be asked of customers, to a part, material, product, or service. Their aim is to determine whether maximum value is obtained for each dollar spent. These test questions are listed in Exhibit 3–3, which details the value analysis approach in a comparison of function to cost.

---

[13]"Protective Packaging System Proves Itself in Field Test" in Value Analysis 1988—Special Report (*Purchasing*, June 16, 1988), pp. 126B3–126B7.

■ **EXHIBIT 3–3** The Value-Analysis Approach *(Comparison of function to cost)*

I. Select a relatively high-cost or high-volume purchased item to value analyze. This can be a part, material, or service. Select an item you suspect is costing more than it should.

II. Find out completely how the item is used and what is expected of it—its function.

III. Ask the following questions:

a. Does its use contribute value?
b. Is it cost-proportionate to usefulness?
c. Does it need all its features?
d. Is there anything better, at a more favorable purchase price, for the intended use?
e. Can the item be eliminated?
f. If the item is not standard, can a standard item be used?
g. If it is a standard item, does it completely fit your application, or is it a misfit?
h. Does the item have greater capacity than required?
i. Is there a similar item in inventory which could be used instead?
j. Can the weight be reduced?
k. Are closer tolerances specified than are necessary?
l. Is unnecessary machining performed on the item?
m. Are unnecessarily fine finishes specified?
n. Is commercial quality specified?
o. Can you make the item cheaper yourself?
p. If you are making it now, can you buy it for less?
q. Is the item properly classified for shipping purposes to obtain the lowest transportation rates?
r. Can cost of packaging be reduced?
s. Are you asking your suppliers for suggestions to reduce costs?
t. Do material, reasonable labor, overhead, and profit total its cost?
u. Will another dependable supplier provide it for less?
v. Is anyone buying it for less?

III. Now:

a. Pursue those suggestions that appear practical.
b. Get samples of the proposed item(s).
c. Select the best possibilities and propose changes.

SOURCE: M. E. Leenders, H. E. Fearon, and W. B. England, *Purchasing and Materials Management*, 8th ed. (Homewood, Ill.: R. D. Irwin, 1985), pp. 57, 64.

People resist change, and often a value-analysis effort will run head-on into the natural tendency of individuals to resist changes. Value analysis should be looked upon as an aid to the buyer in that it is a technique or tool that allows the buyer to do a better job, to spend money more intelligently, and to be more creative. Marketing personnel, not only in the buyer's own organization but also those that work for present or potential suppliers, must become involved if value analysis is to be an orderly method of attacking problems that have already occurred or that could occur in the future. Value analysis is not cost- or price-oriented; it is function-oriented with involved people trying to determine the best way of doing a job at the lowest possible cost. Sellers, due in large part to their exposure to other applications of their parts, materials, or services, are in a unique position to help members of the buying center obtain maximum value for each dollar spent. Value analysis is especially appropriate in straight and modified rebuy situations, when the supplier is already familiar with what is being used and can offer suggestions for specification changes to the advantage of both buyer and seller.

The seller's knowledge includes that of materials, services, fabrication methods, and equipment. The salesperson should advise buyers on tolerances, finishes, or anything else that might affect the cost as well as the feasibility of the design. The trained marketer should be an important part of the customers' value-analysis team, understanding the objectives of their programs and earning their confidence so that no facts about predicted quantities, function, end use, and so on, will be withheld.

Concept Questions

1. What is the ideal quality level to purchase?
2. How do organizational buyers measure service?
3. What is the primary difference between value analysis and value engineering?

■ MAKE-OR-BUY ANALYSIS

The decision of whether to manufacture a product in-house or to purchase it from the outside can have a significant impact on the long-term as well as the day-to-day operation of the firm. Deciding what should be made and what should be bought constitutes what is commonly referred to as the **make-or-buy analysis.**

The make-or-buy decision can originate in a variety of ways. Salespeople may propose the alternative, and then request permission to submit quotations on components their companies are capable of producing. This decision can also result from situations of unsatisfactory vendor performance, such as an emergency created by delivery problems, poor product or component quality, or a seemingly unreasonable vendor price increase. The addition of a new product, a substantial modification of an existing one, or a value-analysis study of an existing product can suggest a make-or-buy feasibility study. Changes in sales volume and related variations in plant capacity can also prompt management to seek a make-or-buy investigation.

Ascertaining Profitability

When performing a make-or-buy analysis, buyers must be very careful not to overlook some important points. All costs, such as delivery, direct labor, plant overhead, incremental purchasing cost, and opportunity cost of capital, must be considered; otherwise, the analysis will not be correct. Also, the make-or-buy decision may not be appropriate if there is a better alternative use of available resources. Salespersons, along with buying firm personnel, such as engineering and production supervisors, should supply the buyer with pertinent data that will help in doing a thorough analysis. Aggressive sellers should be especially aware of the value of their expertise in this area.

The make-or-buy decision will determine to a large extent the profitability of the organization; and, with this factor in mind, the activity must not be taken lightly by either the buying or the selling firm. In a new product situation the analysis would be undertaken during an early stage. The postponement of this decision will, in all likelihood, require additional effort, time, and cost; so the suggestion here is that there should be a formalized approach to the decision process. The buyer's objective would be to render the make-or-buy decision that maximizes the utilization of production, managerial, and financial capabilities. Too few buyers take advantage of the vendor expertise available to them through their friends in marketing and sales. But it appears that buyers may become more creative in the future in applying this particular expertise to the make-or-buy decision area. Such creativity could mean additional market share and a long-lasting business relationship between seller and buyer.

Reasons to Manufacture

There may be good reason for a company to undertake manufacture, rather than purchase, for the following reasons: (1) the item is required in large volume; (2) it is substantially of the same nature as the regular product; (3) it is adapted to the existing production facilities; (4) it is capable of production by the company at a cost low enough to allow a savings over the price charged for the item by a supplier; and (5) it is not protected by patents so that sizeable royalties have to be paid. A company could choose to make a part even when it might cost more than buying it. This would apply to an issue such as insuring a source of supply when faced with the existence of one or more unreliable suppliers.

The decision to make, rather than to buy, is not uncommon and is frequently reported in the media.[14] Consider the following example: In 1980 the NCR Corporation announced that it would spend nearly $200 million over four years to expand its internal capacity to develop and manufacture semiconductor parts, which are used as components in its computer systems and computer terminals. Previously the company manufactured 40 percent of its needs internally. The added internal capacity enabled the company to produce 60 percent of its annual requirements. This action significantly reduced the market for outside suppliers. NCR found it desirable from a performance and cost standpoint to enlarge its in-house capabilities. The firm also believed that greater in-house component capability would enable it to control quality, respond more quickly to its target markets, and protect its supply of components in times of production shortages.[15]

[14]B. Charles Ames and James D. Hlavacek, *Managerial Marketing for Industrial Firms* (New York: Random House, 1984), p. 50.

[15]*The Wall Street Journal,* July 18, 1980, p. 5.

From this analysis of the problems involved in arriving at make-or-buy decisions, certain generalizations seem justifiable. Of course, as in all generalizations, exceptions must be made. Clearly, only in rare instances will either the make or buy argument be so conclusive as to dictate an obvious decision. Consequently, in most cases the solution will be a compromise based on judgment as to the course of action most conducive to the company's best interest. In a real sense, therefore, the correct answer to the question, "What is preferable, make or buy?" is that "it all depends upon circumstances." Nevertheless, balancing all the arguments, the burden of proof in most situations seems to rest on those urging make, rather than buy.[16]

Participants in Make or Buy

Although firms have different organizational structures, business functions usually involved in the make-or-buy decision include marketing, manufacturing, engineering, purchasing, and accounting. Figure 3–2 illustrates the decision-making process and the various functional groups involved. The marketing, management, engineering, and purchasing areas provide nonfinancial criteria, and the accounting area offers financial criteria for use in the make-or-buy decision. Because input for the make-or-buy decision comes from so many different sources within the firm, an interdisciplinary committee to implement the decision process is often advisable.

■ NEGOTIATION

Everyone at one time or another engages in some form of negotiation. The use of negotiation is almost a daily occurrence for those engaged in the organizational or business to business buying and selling process. It is no longer possible or sensible for executives to conduct negotiations totally by intuition and a few traditional guidelines. In consideration of the great importance of negotiations in contemporary buyer and seller interactions, a special appendix dealing with the behavior of successful negotiators (Appendix 3A) is at the end of this chapter.

Negotiation is a technique for communicating ideas. Both buyers and sellers attempt to convince the other party to yield to their demands, with the ultimate objective being to arrive at an agreement that will work to the benefit of both parties. Negotiation should be used in its broadest context, with quantity, delivery, payment terms, and service (among other things), being part of the purchase agreement that can and should be part of the bargaining process. The ideal negotiator, whether buyer or seller, should possess the complementary traits of understanding human nature and

---

[16]Michiel R. Leenders, Harold E. Fearon, and Wilbur B. England, *Purchasing and Materials Management,* 7th ed. (Homewood, Ill.: Richard D. Irwin, 1980), pp. 400–1.

■ **FIGURE 3–2** Participants in the Make-or-Buy Decision

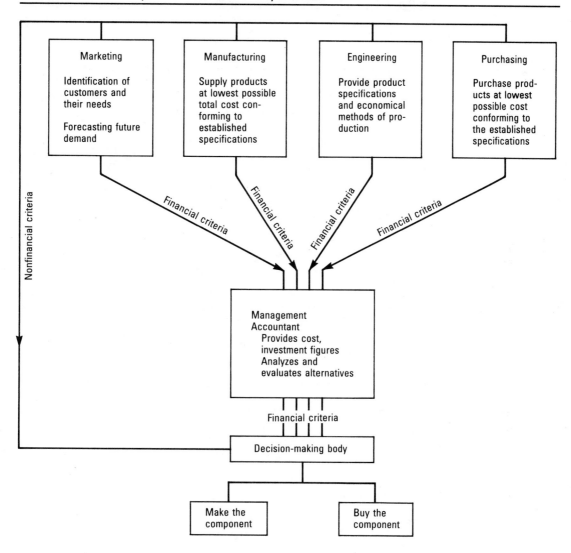

need-satisfaction, courage, confidence (high self-esteem and self-accept-ance), flexibility, great patience, humility, and charm (being likeable). In addition, he or she should have the logical traits of high tolerance for am-biguity, strong cognitive complexity (abstract thinking), high intelligence, and realistic decision-making ability. Following the negotiating process, both sides must win something, and both sides must leave the session feel-ing good; otherwise, it was not a productive session. Figure 3–3 outlines the fundamentals of successful negotiation. Note that communication is also a key element in successful negotiation.

■ **FIGURE 3–3**   Fundamentals of Successful Negotiation

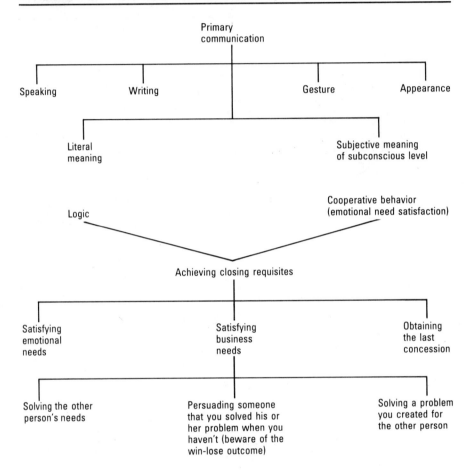

Objectives of Negotiation

Buyers use negotiations to attain desired price, quality, and/or service ends that may not be possible to acquire through other means. Some of the prime negotiation objectives are as follows:

- A price better than one available from other methods.
- Quality that is either better or of a different level or type from what is currently available on the market.
- A quantity different from normal practices.
- Vendor distribution service with special features that are inbound to the buyer's firm.
- Concessions for delivery, payment, or other buying/selling arrangements.
- Cooperation or communication reinforcement about the relationship between the two firms that is desired by the buyer, seller, or both.[17]

---

[17]Cavinato, p. 110.

Negotiations are often considered price-oriented activities. Yet almost any purchase-related feature can be sought through this process.

Negotiation Maneuvers, Strategies, and Tactics

A **negotiation maneuver** is a behavior undertaken to improve the buyer's or seller's position for the offense or the defense, while a **negotiation strategy** is a broad action plan. A negotiation tactic involves the specifics necessary to implement that plan. Table 3–3 indicates that maneuvers used in negotiations can be divided into three general classifications: (1) those that increase the negotiator's strength, (2) those that reduce the opponent's strength, and (3) those that provide leverage to the negotiator. Most of the negotiator's maneuvers attempt to increase his or her own strength.

Negotiation tactics are components of the negotiation strategy or the facets of the broad plan used to obtain the desired outcomes from the negotiation process. Figure 3–4 points out that a distinction can be made between **rational** and **irrational tactics.** Most tactics are rational; buyers and sellers engage in these behaviors to modify those of their opponents. A buyer, for instance, may challenge the seller on a recent price increase which seems to have no substantial purpose. In contrast, some tactics are not rational. For example, a negotiator abruptly changes his or her mind and walks out of a negotiation session for no readily apparent reason. **Debate tactics** are those in which the parties engage in discussions to decide jointly upon an agreement which will hopefully be agreeable to both sides. **Bargaining tactics,** in contrast, encompass behaviors that are intended to move, direct, or constrain the opponent.

The bargaining tactics can be further divided into aggressive, nonaggressive, and posturing tactics. **Aggressive tactics** portray the negotiation as tough, whereas, **nonaggressive tactics** make the process appear to be soft. Aggressive and nonaggressive tactics must be differentiated from **posturing**

■ **TABLE 3–3** Negotiation Maneuvers

Increase Negotiator's Strength	Reduce Opponent's Strength	Alter Relationships of Strength (Leverage)
Acquire status	Close opponent's outside options	Move to address opponent's weak point
Develop abilities and skills	Prevent opponent's coalitions, alliances, and support	Protect negotiator's weak point
Voice disclaimers		
Strengthen logic	Weaken opponent's stand with his or her constituency	Wait until opponent is vulnerable
Increase size of bargaining team	Disorganize opponent's constituency	Make end run
Go on record		Flank the opponent
Stockpile	Reduce opponent's status or expertise	
Strengthen stand with constituency	Prevent opponent from establishing commitments	
Make cooperative arrangements with third parties	Recruit opponent's associates	
Develop outside options	Utilize informant	

SOURCE: James A. Wall, Jr., *Negotiation Theory and Practice* (Glenview, Ill.: Scott, Foresman, 1985), p. 40.

■ **FIGURE 3-4**   Negotiation Tactics

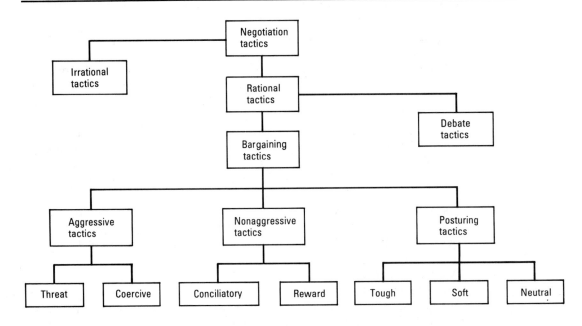

tactics, such as stares, expressed diffidence, and displayed impatience, which are primarily intended to create a mental image of the negotiation session so strong that it will alter the opponent's behavior in a manner considered positive by the other negotiating party.

Finally, in a simple negotiation a limited number of rules can be combined into a decision tree that delineates the negotiation tactics to be utilized under specific conditions. In Figure 3–5, by moving from left to right along the decision tree, by addressing each question at the top of the figure (for instance, in this negotiation, is the opponent currently engaging in inappropriate behavior?), and then by following the proper branch, the negotiation can close upon the tactical combination most suited to the current situation. Referring to Figure 3–5 again, if negotiators find that their opponents are not engaging in appropriate behavior and are uncooperative, but believe that future negotiation is important and have limited alternatives, then the negotiators should then take a tough or an aggressive stance toward their opponents in any negotiation activity.

The Use of Questions

By correctly phrasing a question, a party to a negotiation can attack an opponent's position, evade a touchy question, or control the process or trend of the negotiation session. If a buyer or a seller has the patience to ask a question, and then listen and listen well, the amount of information gained can be astonishing. To act accordingly during a negotiation process

■ **FIGURE 3-5** Appropriate Tactics for Simple Negotiation

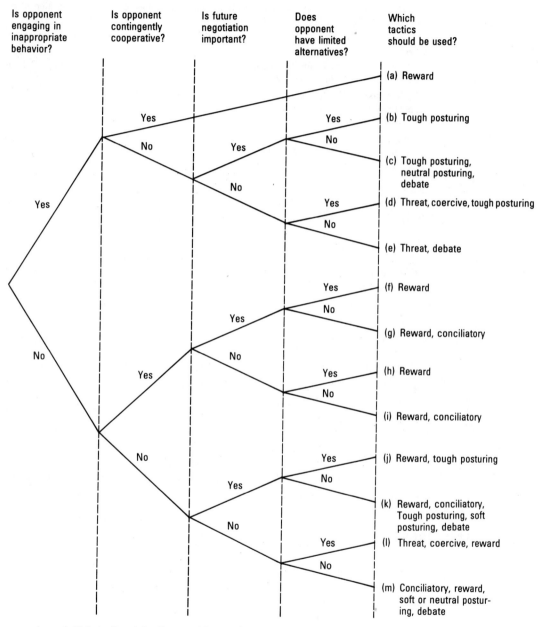

| Is opponent engaging in inappropriate behavior? | Is opponent contingently cooperative? | Is future negotiation important? | Does opponent have limited alternatives? | Which tactics should be used? |

(a) Reward

(b) Tough posturing

(c) Tough posturing, neutral posturing, debate

(d) Threat, coercive, tough posturing

(e) Threat, debate

(f) Reward

(g) Reward, conciliatory

(h) Reward

(i) Reward, conciliatory

(j) Reward, tough posturing

(k) Reward, conciliatory, Tough posturing, soft posturing, debate

(l) Threat, coercive, reward

(m) Conciliatory, reward, soft or neutral posturing, debate

SOURCE: James A. Wall, Jr., *Negotiation Theory and Practice* (Glenview, Ill.: Scott, Foresman, 1985), p. 78.

can pay large dividends, as the best questions seem to be those that probe for substantial facts and revealing information. As can be seen in Exhibit 3–4, the use of the right questions serves a number of functions, and a negotiator's ability to question intelligently and with a purpose is an art.

■ **EXHIBIT 3–4**   Five Important Functions of Questioning in Negotiation

1. Questions cause attention. Questions provide preparatory conditions for the operation of the other party's thinking (e.g., "How are you?").

2. Questions get information. Questions provide the questioner with information (e.g., "How much does it cost?").

3. Questions give information. Questions provide the other party with information (e.g.,"Did you know you could handle this situation yourself?").

4. Questions start the other party's thinking process. Questions cause the other party's thinking about the question, issue, or task at hand (e.g., "What would your suggestion be in regard to solving this problem?").

5. Questions bring the other party's thinking to a conclusion. Questions often lead a seemingly uncooperative party in a negotiation to think in terms of arriving at a conclusion acceptable to both parties involved (e.g., "Isn't it time to act now?").

Analyzing Both Buyer and Seller Strengths

We should never underestimate the strength of our adversary, for buyers or sellers who attempt to enter a negotiation session unprepared will emerge as losers. As was noted earlier in this chapter, both sides must win something, and both must leave feeling good; otherwise, the negotiation was not a productive one.

Prior to a negotiation session, the buyer must learn as much as possible about the seller's position, and the seller should do the same in regard to the buyer. Both buyer and seller must attempt to analyze the other's primary negotiating objectives, along with their minimum and maximum positions on various objectives. Figure 3–6 presents a visualization of the position of the two parties from the buyer's standpoint. Note that both the buyer and seller have maximum and minimum positions, indicating a willingness to give up certain things and an unwillingness to give up others. Note also that both have an objective, with the difference between the buyers and the sellers objectives not being that substantial. The object is to identify this area of difference, and to work to reduce it to the point where both the buyer and the seller can agree to a contract.

■ THE SMALL-ORDER PROBLEM

Small orders are a continuing matter of concern in most organizations (in both the buying and selling functions). As a general rule 70 percent of all requisitions only amount to approximately 10 percent of the total dollar volume purchased. One important consideration then becomes the cost of the system set up to handle small orders versus the cost of the items themselves. The lack of a small item may create a nuisance totally out of proportion to its dollar value; thus assured supply is the first objective to be met. Exhibit 3–5 describes a number of approaches that should be used continuously to address the small-order question. Buyers and sellers must work closely together if these approaches are to work.

■ **FIGURE 3–6**   A Buyer's Viewpoint of Both a Buyer's and a Seller's
                   Negotiating Position

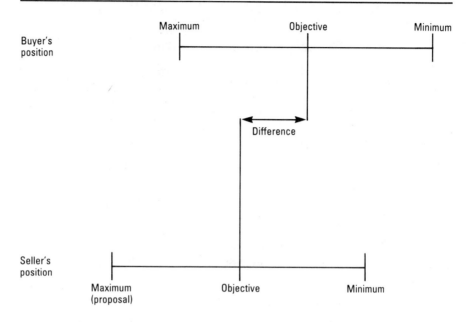

■ **EXHIBIT 3–5**   Approaches in Addressing the Small-Order Problem

1. If the fault lies with the using department, perhaps persuasion can be employed to increase the number of standardized items requested.

2. Another possibility is for the purchasing department to hold small requisitions as received until a justifiable total, in dollars, has been accumulated.

3. A third method is to establish a requisition calendar, setting aside specific days for the requisitioning of specific supplies, so that all requests for a given item are received on the same day. As an aid to the storeskeeper, the calendar also may be so arranged that practically all the supplies secured from any specific type of vendor are requisitioned on the same day.

4. Still another method or procedure is to make use of the stockless buying or systems contracting concept.* This concept has been used most widely in the purchase of MRO (maintenance, repair, and operating supply) items.

*The technique of *stockless buying* or *systems contracting* (a term registered by the Carborundum Company) is relatively new and has been used most frequently in buying stationery and office supplies, repetitive items, maintenance and repair materials, and operating supplies (MRO). This latter class of purchases is characterized by many types of items of low value and needed immediately when any kind of a plant or equipment failure occurs. The technique is built around a blanket-type contract which is developed in great detail regarding approximate quantities to be used in specified time periods, prices, provisions for adjusting prices, procedures to be used in picking up requisitions daily and making delivery within 24 hours, simplified billing procedures, and a complete catalog of all items covered by the contract.
SOURCE: Leenders, Fearon, and England, pp. 51, 64.

Because of anticipating the need for small purchases by the buyer, and the small profit or possible loss for the vendor in processing and shipping the order, specialized techniques have been designed to reduce the costs of buying and selling, while at the same time protecting the quality of the services rendered and received. The following techniques are suggested in handling small orders efficiently: a centralized-stores system, a petty-cash system, a blanket-order system, and an electronic ordering system.

The Centralized-Stores System

This technique is simply a designated, centralized area set aside and conveniently located for supply items frequently ordered in small quantities and withdrawn on an "as-needed" basis. An **ABC analysis of inventory items** indicates that the low-value C items are prime candidates for inclusion in this system (nuts, bolts, lubricants, and office supplies, etc.). A centralized store's system makes sense, especially when we consider that it costs approximately $120 to generate a typical purchase order (contract) today. One order, placed weekly, monthly, or quarterly as opposed to several orders placed weekly, would save substantial dollars, while at the same time, it would free up both the buyer's and seller's time for more important tasks. Creative buyers should consider such a system, and creative sellers who supply such items should also suggest such a system (desiring the buyer to use their products, of course).

The Petty-Cash System

Using the $120 cost per purchase order assumption, forward-thinking buyers will consider the possibility of paying cash for supplies that can be bought locally, with the allowed dollar ceiling on an expenditure being quite arbitrary. Paying cash saves time and administrative expense on the part of both buyer and seller. The major drawback to such a system would be the possible inefficiency that might arise because of a lack of buying skills. However, this problem is more than compensated for by the savings realized by both buyer and seller in not having to generate a formal purchase order, with the resulting invoice generated by the supplier firm.

The Blanket-Order System

Considerable savings in time and paperwork can be made for both buyer and seller by consolidating monthly, quarterly, or yearly requirements of a particular purchased part, subassembly, or raw material into a single agreement; and by arranging for a single weekly, semiweekly, or monthly delivery against the agreement (**blanket order**). Both creative buyers and sellers will constantly seek to make their counterpart's job easier, and this approach is a natural move in that direction.

In addition to dollar savings in paperwork and time for both buyer and seller, the lumping of requirements into a single contract will usually enable the buyer to obtain better terms. The typical contract is usually written for one year, although both longer and shorter periods are used. The immediate advantage to the vendor is an assurance of a certain work load which might allow that vendor to plan work flow better, and to make financial commitments accordingly. The immediate advantage to the buyer is the

■ **EXHIBIT 3–6**   Benefits of the Blanket-Order System of Handling Small Orders

The blanket-order system offers six important benefits to the business to business or organizational buyer:

1. It requires fewer purchase orders and reduces clerical work in purchasing, accounting, and receiving.
2. It releases buyers from routine work, giving them more time to concentrate on major problems.
3. It permits volume pricing by consolidating and grouping requirements.
4. It sometimes ensures protection against price rises during the period of coverage.
5. It centralizes purchasing control.
6. The blanket-order system helps ensure a regular and timely flow of materials in times of shortages.

SOURCE: Lamar Lee, Jr., and Donald W. Dobler, *Purchasing and Materials Management* (New York: McGraw-Hill, 1984), p. 500.

probability of a lower price for a larger, long-term contract, better delivery times, and an immediate release from routine buying tasks. As detailed in Exhibit 3–6, the blanket-order system offers a number of additional benefits to the user, ranging from lower ordering costs and less routine work to ensuring a regular and timely flow of materials in times of shortages.

The Electronic Ordering System

The pace of development in electronic systems is extremely rapid since many buyers and sellers have a desktop keyboard and a visual display unit at their disposal. Using this technology, the buyer can call up supplier records, showing each supplier's name, address, telephone number, list of salespeople, dates of recent sales visits, and transaction and performance records. These records would also usually indicate alternative supply sources, materials, and prices. Orders can be typed, changed, and eventually released for printout. Open order files can be maintained, updated, and closed as needed or as appropriate.

The uses and potential applications of electronic ordering systems will explode in the future, as the potential for dollar savings and greater profit margins through a reduction in paperwork is both challenging and exciting. The typical purchasing department in both larger and smaller firms will be using electronic ordering systems as the norm in the near future.

■ PURCHASING'S IMPACT UPON COMPANY PROFIT

Purchasing plays an important role in regard to the impacts that occur from price increases or decreases for the goods and services procured. All other things being equal, a $1 savings in the purchase price results in a $1 profit increase. A cost increase by the same amount, on the other hand, harms the firm by $1 of decreased profit.[18]

---

[18]Cavinato, p. 161.

■ **FIGURE 3–7**   Interaction of All Key Company Financial Components on Overall Profits

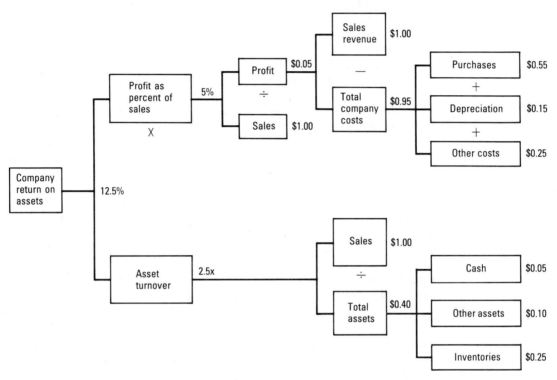

The term *profit* applies to three key measures used to describe the periodic financial performance of a firm. The first is profit as a percentage of sales. This figure is a rough measure of how much is left over from sales revenue after all costs of the firm have been paid. It is the general measure of the profit-generating potential of sales and operating activities. The second measure is asset turnover. This is a measure of how effectively the assets in the firm are being utilized. It is found by dividing total assets into the sales revenue for the year. A high asset turnover is generally considered preferable to a low asset turnover. The third key measurement is return on assets. This indicator is a measure of the profit-generating power of the firm based on the assets necessary to produce the desired profit. This figure is related to the interest people associate with savings account or money-market fund earnings. Of course, a higher return figure is far more desirable than a lower one.[19]

The interaction of all the key company financial components to the overall profit is seen in Figure 3–7. A hypothetical company is shown with a revenue of $1.00 for the year. Purchases cost $0.55; depreciation $0.15; and

---

[19]Victor H. Pooler and David J. Pooler, "Purchasing's Elusive Conceptual Home," *Journal of Purchasing and Materials Management* 17 (1981), p. 13.

other costs of operation, $0.25; for a total cost of $0.95 for the year. Profit is $1.00 less the $0.95, or $0.05. Use of assets, cash, inventories, and other assets total $0.40. Sales are $1.00, which sets asset turnover rate at 2.5 times. Profit as a percentage of sales is $0.05 (or 5 percent), and the asset turnover rate of 2.5 times causes company return on assets to be 12.5 percent. This shows how a firm could have a low return on sales but a high turnover resulting in a good overall return on assets. Another firm will have a very high return on sales, but a low asset turnover, resulting in a low return on assets. All three indicators are viewed separately as well as in a combined manner.[20]

As can be easily calculated, a reduction in the purchase price by 1 cent reduces the cost of purchases from $0.55 to $0.54, and total company costs to $0.94. Profit is now $0.06, and profit as a percentage of sales has increased from five to six percent. Return on assets is now 15 percent ($0.06 × 2.5). Therefore, a reduction in purchase price has a direct positive impact upon profit and return on assets.

Concept Questions

1. What should the buyer's objective be in the make-or-buy decision?
2. How is negotiation a technique for the communication of ideas?
3. How do cost savings and cost increases affect overall company profits?

SUMMARY

1. Organizational buying has evolved into a complex process of decision making and communication, which takes place over time, involves several organizational members, and includes relationships with other firms and institutions. The primary objective of organizational buyers is to purchase the right materials in the right quantity, for delivery at the right time and in the right place, from the right source with the right service, and at the right price.

2. People within the buying organization involved in the buying process are members of the buying center. The critical task for the marketer is to determine the specific role and relative buying influence of each buying-center participant. The buying-center membership and relative importance of different members vary from company to company.

3. Creative purchasing people must understand and appreciate the relationship among quality, service, and price. They must work with people not only within their own firms but also with sellers on the outside in challenging quality, insisting on the proper level of service, and looking at price with a very critical eye. They must determine just what is a proper price in any given situation.

4. Value analysis is a scientifically organized method for reducing the costs of manufactured items, and for encouraging vendor cooperation

---

[20]Cavinato.

in lowering costs of purchased items. Its ultimate purpose is to secure improved performance of components at less cost.

5. The make-or-buy decision will determine to a large extent the profitability of the organization. With this in mind, neither the buying nor the selling firm should undertake lightly this activity. The buyer's objective should be to render the make-or-buy decision which maximizes the utilization of production, managerial, and financial capabilities.

6. Any study of business to business marketing would not be complete without considering the negotiation process, both from the buyer's and seller's points of view. Maneuvers, strategies, and tactics along with recognized tools and techniques are used in this process. Once learned, they should make the buyer or seller a better negotiator.

7. All buyers face the so-called small-order problem. While this problem will probably never be entirely eliminated, there are tools and techniques available which will, at least, make this area somewhat more manageable. Creative buyers and sellers should recognize the opportunity involved here.

8. Purchasing plays an important role in regard to the impacts that occur from price increases or decreases for the goods and services procured. All other things being equal, a $1 savings in purchase price results in a $1 profit increase, with a cost increase by the same amount harming the firm by $1 of decreased profit.

KEY TERMS

ABC analysis of inventory items
aggressive tactics
bargaining tactics
blanket order
buying center
debate tactics
irrational tactics
make-or-buy analysis
negotiation
negotiation maneuver

negotiation strategy
nonaggressive tactics
perceived value
posturing tactics
rational tactics
total cost of the purchasing
   decision
value analysis
value engineering

REVIEW QUESTIONS

1. Why is organizational buying no longer the simple act of placing an order with a vendor or a selling organization?

2. What determines the size of a buying center? What is the critical task for marketers in their dealings with buying centers?

3. Explain the role of quality in buying and selling. In what ways can a firm's purchasing department take an active role in ensuring that proper quality specifications are part of the purchase contract?

4. Discuss the role of service in business buying and selling. Distinguish between pre- and postsale service.

5. Discuss the role of price in business buying and selling. Distinguish between price and total cost.

6. Distinguish between value analysis and value engineering. Identify the appropriate questions which should be asked in any value-analysis study.

7. What business functions are usually involved in a make-or-buy analysis? Who generally participates in a company's make-or-buy analysis? Under what conditions might a company choose to make rather than buy a particular product?

8. Why is the negotiation process so important? Identify six objectives common to all negotiation processes. Distinguish among negotiation maneuvers, strategies, and tactics.

9. How would an objective observer at a negotiation session specifically analyze the strengths and weaknesses of both buyer and seller?

10. What are the problems involved for the seller in filling small orders for the business buyer? Discuss four systems by which small orders can be handled effectively and efficiently by organizational sellers.

11. How is the purchasing function directly related to company profit? How do savings acquired by efficient and effective purchasing practices impact upon the company profit?

CHAPTER CASES

Case 3–1   John Roberts Manufacturing Company*

The John Roberts Manufacturing Company, an air-conditioning equipment manufacturer in Houston, Texas, employs 800 people. It manufactures both window-type and large industrial air conditioners.

The purchasing department is headed by Allen Harrison, director of purchases. Reporting to Mr. Harrison are four purchasing agents and one full-time expediter. The purchasing director has a secretary who handles his filing, takes dictation, and types his correspondence. There are two typists who type approximately 2,000 purchase orders and change orders each month. Approximately 65 percent of the items purchased are repetitive in nature; the balance of the items are noncompetitive and generally require considerable buyer attention. Practically all the maintenance, repair, and operating supplies (MRO) are purchased from local vendors.

---

*Gary J. Zenz, *Purchasing and Management of Materials*, 5th ed., 1981, John Wiley and Sons.

The MRO stores and the receiving and shipping functions report to the director of purchases. The company operates its own printing shop, which includes the stationery and office-supply inventories. The supervisor of the printing and stationery department also reports to the director of purchases. Responsibility for maintaining adequate inventories of stationery and office supplies as well as MRO supplies rests with the director of purchases.

An internal audit team has "spotlighted" the following problems, and management has asked the director of purchases to present a plan for correcting them:

1. A considerable number of items are delivered to the receiving department by local vendors before the receiving copy of the purchase order has reached the receiving department. This happens because deliveries are made within four to six hours on telephone orders, whereas the typed copy of the purchase order is not received until the next day. This causes confusion, wasted effort, and delays in delivery to the requisitioner, who may have an urgent need for the specific item.

2. The typists are unable to handle the peak loads of purchase-order typing. The adoption of traveling requisitions has reduced requisition writing, but not the number of purchase orders. The use of blanket orders on large-usage items provided some relief for the typists when adopted one year ago. In order to avoid serious delays in the typing and mailing of purchase orders, considerable overtime expense is incurred.

3. Although the expediter appears to be competent, many items are received late, which sometimes causes serious production delays or holds up construction of needed facilities. Deliveries of capital equipment have been as much as four to five weeks late in some instances. This has seriously delayed the start-up of some production lines. Upon investigation by the buyer, it was found that the vendor had not been expediting all items from its own suppliers and subcontractors because it had been the vendor's practice to expedite what it considered critical items, based on past experience or pressure from customers.

4. The company's value-analysis program has bogged down because the buyers say they are so busy placing orders and expediting that they do not have time for analyzing costs and devising ways to accomplish the desired functions at a lower cost while preserving or improving quality and reliability.

5. The auditors found several instances of vendor's products that did not meet specifications on physical qualities, and in some cases there were dimensional deviations. Although the suppliers replaced the material, they did not compensate the John Roberts Company for labor expended up to the point of rejection, nor for the loss of production time.

The vice president to whom the director reports has suggested that it might be possible to use the recently installed computer to overcome some of the problems. The controller supported the vice president's suggestion because of the accounting department's successful use of EDP.

Question

1. What recommendations can you make to correct the problem facing John Roberts Company's purchasing department?

Case 3–2 Berg Raingear, Inc.*

The Berg Raingear Company manufactured a complete line of men's, women's, and children's raincoats as well as umbrellas and other types of rain gear. Its annual sales were $12 million in 1980. The rain gear was of two types: (1) a rubberized fabric, and (2) chemically treated fabrics. Sales were evenly divided between the two types.

Annual purchases of Wein's rain repellent, a chemical used in treating the fabrics to induce the rain-repellency characteristics, were approximately $200,000. This product was sold by its manufacturer both to clothing manufacturing and directly to the consumer in an aerosol spray can. The latter sales were backed by heavy consumer advertising, and broad consumer acceptance of the brand name had been achieved. Berg Raingear, Inc., was authorized by Wein to attach a special label to all its garments on which the solution was used.

Shortly before a new contract was to be negotiated with Wein, Ms. Frances Adams, chemicals buyer for Berg, was approached by a salesperson of the Madison Chemical Corporation. He stated that his company had developed a new water-proofing compound for textiles that was better than anything on the market. Madison Chemical was planning to introduce it to the business to business market first, but hoped to move the compound into the consumer market through an extensive advertising campaign within 12 months. The price of this new product was competitive with the Wein product.

A sample of the new product was delivered to the company research chemist for testing purposes. He reported to Ms. Adams that this new product was equal to that currently being purchased. However, he suggested that without much trouble he could develop a similar chemical compound that would be satisfactory and could be manufactured in the Berg plant at a saving of 15 percent over the price paid to Wein. He estimated that, if this course of action were adopted, the necessary equipment could be purchased new for $11,500, or purchased used for $5,000 or less.

Ms. Adams asked the chemist to give her a list of the chemical ingredients, and their proportions, in the product. She then called on two small local chemical plants and solicited bids for a waterproofing compound made to the Berg company specifications. One bid was received at a price of 5 percent below that then paid to Wein.

Questions

1. Should Ms. Adams change suppliers?
2. Should Berg produce its own waterproofing compound?

---

*Gary J. Zenz, *Purchasing and Management of Materials*, 5th ed., 1981, John Wiley and Sons.

SUGGESTED READINGS

Clopton, Stephen W. "Microcomputer-Based Negotiation Training for Buyers." *Journal of Purchasing and Materials Management* 22 (Summer 1986), pp. 16–23. Advantages of, and guidelines for, microcomputer-based negotiation simulations.

Dillon, Thomas F., and James A. Lorincz. "Buyers Holding Good Cards in Steel Negotiations/Steel Future Is Cast in Quality, Value, and Delivery." *Purchasing World* 30 (March 1986), pp. 29–34. Industry analysis and trends related to worldwide overcapacity, competition from imports, and joint ventures.

———. "Staying Competitive Means Big Changes in Buyer/Service Center Relationships." *Purchasing World* 30 (October 1986), pp. 77/M11–80/M14. Discussion of service provided and associated costs in the steel industry.

Fodor, George M. "Orchestrating a Pricing Strategy." *Industrial Distribution* 76 (August 1987), p. 30. Product quality, delivery, and other added values generally assure success in business to business markets, but in an increasingly competitive marketplace, prices molded to buyer acceptance are a must.

Graham, John L. "The Problem-Solving Approach to Negotiations in Industrial Marketing." *Journal of Business Research* 14 (December 1986), pp. 549–66. Experiment with the problem-solving approach in negotiations, using a causal modeling approach. Outcome criteria and assessment provided.

Kapp, S. "Bearing Up against the Rising Sun." *Business Marketing* 72 (August 1987), p. 8. Industrial distributors involved in selling bearings for transmission and power products are battling low-cost Japanese imports with high-profile customer service.

Kyj, Myroslaw J., and Larissa S. Kyj. "Customer Service Competition in Business to Business and Industrial Markets: Myths and Realities." *Journal of Business and Industrial Marketing* 2 (no. 4, Fall 1987), pp. 45–53. This article reviews the premise of customer service competition. The findings are integrated into a set of guidelines for the organization contemplating the use of customer service as a competitive tool.

Perdue, Barbara C., Ralph L. Day, and Ronald E. Michaels. "Negotiation Styles of Industrial Buyers." *Industrial Marketing Management* 15 (August 1986), pp. 171–76. Survey of business to business buyer-seller relationships using a typology of five styles of negotiating behavior.

Rathbun, Craig, and Robert L. Janson. "Where Does the Time go in Purchasing?" *Purchasing World* 29 (November 1985), pp. 74–76. Survey of how purchasing people spend their time, including the negotiation process.

APPENDIX

The Behavior of Successful Negotiators*

1. Background

Almost all publications about negotiating behavior fall into one of three classes.

   a.   Anecdotal "Here's how I do it" accounts by successful negotiators. These have the advantage of being based on real life, but the disadvantage is that they frequently describe highly personal models of behavior, which are a risky guide for would-be negotiators to follow.

   b.   Theoretical models of negotiating, which are idealized, complex, and seldom translatable into practical action.

   c.   Laboratory studies, which tend to be short-term and contain a degree of artificiality.

Very few studies have investigated what actually goes on face-to-face during a negotiation. Two reasons account for this lack of published research. First, negotiators are understandably reluctant to let a researcher watch them at work. Such research requires the consent of both negotiating parties and constitutes a constraint on a potentially delicate situation. The second reason for the poverty of research in this area is the lack of methodology. Until recently there were few techniques available which allowed an observer to collect data on the behavior of negotiators without the use of cumbersome and unacceptable methods such as questionnaires.

Since 1968 a number of studies have been carried out by Neil Rackham, of Huthwaite Research Group, using behavior analysis methods. These have allowed direct observation during real negotiations, so that an objective and quantified record can be collected to show how the skilled negotiator behaves.

2. The Successful Negotiator

The basic methodology for studying negotiating behavior is simply to find some successful negotiators and watch them to discover how they do it. But what is the criterion for a successful negotiator? The Rackham studies used three success criteria.

   a.   **The negotiator should be rated as effective by both sides.**   This criterion enabled the researchers to identify likely candidates for further study. The condition that both sides should agree on a negotiator's effectiveness was a precaution to prevent picking a sample from a single frame-of-reference.

   b.   **The negotiator should have a track record of significant success.**   The central criterion for choosing effective negotiators

---

*Portions of this appendix were adapted from material developed by the Huthwaite Research Group.

was track record over a time period. In such a complex field the researchers were anxious for evidence of consistency. They also wished to avoid the common trap of laboratory studies looking only at the short-term consequences of a negotiator's behavior, and, therefore, favoring those using tricks or deceptions.

c. **The negotiator should have a low incidence of negotiation failures.**   The researchers judged that the purpose of a negotiation was not just to reach an agreement, but to reach an agreement that would be viable. Therefore, in addition to a track record of agreements, they also studied the record of implementation to ensure that any agreements reached were successfully implemented.

A total of 48 negotiators were picked who met all these three success criteria. The breakdown of the sample was:

Industrial (labor) relations negotiators	
Union representatives	17
Management representatives	12
Contract negotiators	10
Others	9

Altogether the 48 successful negotiators were studied over a total of 102 separate negotiating sessions. For the remainder of this appendix these people are called the *skilled group*. In comparison, a group of negotiators who either failed to meet the criteria or about whom no criterion data was available, were also studied. These were called the *average group*. By comparing the behavior of the two groups, it was possible to isolate the crucial behaviors which made the skilled negotiators different.

3.   The Research Method

The researchers met the negotiator before the negotiation and encouraged her or him to talk about his or her planning and objectives. For 56 sessions with the skilled negotiators and 37 sessions with the average negotiators this planning session was either tape-recorded or extensive notes were taken.

The negotiator then introduced the researcher into the actual negotiation. The delicacy of this process can be judged from the fact that although most cases had been carefully prehandled, the researchers were not accepted in upward of 20 instances and were asked to withdraw.

During the negotiation the researcher counted the frequency with which certain key behaviors were used by the negotiators, using behavior analysis methods. In all of the 102 sessions interaction data were collected, while in 66 sessions content analysis was also obtained.

4.   How the Skilled Negotiator Plans

Negotiation training emphasizes the importance of planning. How does the skilled negotiator plan?

a. **Amount of planning time.**   No significant difference was found between the total planning time which skilled and average negotiators claimed they spent prior to actual negotiation. This finding must be viewed cautiously because, unlike the other conclusions in this appendix, it is derived from the negotiators' impressions of themselves, not from their observed behavior. Nevertheless, it suggests the conclusion that it is not the amount of planning time which makes for success, but how that time is used.

b. **Exploration of options.**   The skilled negotiator considers a wider range of outcomes or options for action than does the average negotiator.

Outcomes/Options Considered during Planning (per negotiable issue)	
Skilled negotiator	5.1
Average negotiator	2.6

Skilled negotiators are concerned with the whole spectrum of possibilities, both those they could introduce themselves and those which might be introduced by the people they negotiate with. In contrast, average negotiators consider few options. An impression of the researchers, for which unfortunately no systematic data were collected, is that average negotiators are especially less likely to consider options that might be raised by the other party.

c. **Common ground.**   Do skilled negotiators concentrate during their planning on the areas which hold most potential for conflict, or do they give their attention to possible areas of common ground? The research showed that although both groups of negotiators tended to concentrate on the conflict areas, skilled negotiators gave over three times as much attention to common-ground areas as did average negotiators.

Skilled negotiators— 38% of comments about areas of anticipated agreement or common ground.

Average negotiators— 11% of comments about areas of anticipated agreement or common ground.

This is a significant finding and it can be interpreted in a variety of ways. It may be, for example, that the skilled negotiator has already built a climate of agreement so that undue concentration on conflict is unnecessary. Equally, concentration on the common-ground areas may be the key to building a satisfactory climate in the first place. A relatively high concentration on common-ground areas is known to be an effective strategy from other Huthwaite Research Group studies of persuasion, notably with "pull" styles of persuasion in selling.

In any event, potential negotiators wishing to model themselves on successful performers would do well to pay special attention to areas of anticipated common ground and not just to areas of conflict.

d. **Long-term or short-term?** It is often suggested that skilled negotiators spend much of their planning time considering the long-term implications of the issues, while unskilled negotiators showed an alarming concentration on the short-term aspects of issues.

% of Planning Comments about Long-Term Considerations of Anticipated Issues	
Skilled negotiators	8.5%
Average negotiators	4

With average negotiators, approximately one comment in 25 during their planning met our criterion of a long-term consideration, namely, a comment which involved any factor extending beyond the immediate implementation of the issue under negotiation. Skilled negotiators, while showing twice as many long-term comments, still only average 8½ percent of their total recorded planning comment. These figures must necessarily be approximate partly because of the research methods (which may have inadvertently encouraged verbalization of short-term issues) and partly because our ignorance of individual circumstances made some comments hard to classify. Even so, they demonstrate how little thought is given by most negotiators to the long-term implications of what they negotiate.

e. **Setting limits.** The researchers asked negotiators about their objectives and recorded whether their replies referred to single-point objectives (e.g., "we aim to settle at 83p") or to a defined range (e.g., "we hope to get 37p but would settle for a minimum of 34p"). Skilled negotiators were significantly more likely to set upper and lower limits—to plan in terms of a range. Average negotiators, in contrast, were more likely to plan their objectives around a fixed point. Although one possible explanation is that skilled negotiators have more freedom, which gives them the discretion of upper and lower limits, this seems unlikely from the research. Even where average negotiators had considerable capacity to vary the terms of an agreement, they usually approached the negotiation with a fixed-point objective in mind. The conclusion for would-be negotiators is that it seems to be preferable to approach a negotiation with objectives specifying a clearly defined range rather than to base planning on an inflexible single-point objective.

f. **Sequence and issue planning.** The term *planning* frequently refers to a process of sequencing—putting a number of events, points or potential occurrences into a time sequence. Critical path analysis and other forms of network planning are examples. This concept of planning, called *sequence planning,* works efficiently with

inanimate objects or in circumstances where planners have real
control, which allows them to determine the sequence in which
events will occur. The researchers found that average negotiators
place very heavy reliance on sequence planning. So, for example,
they would frequently verbalize a potential negotiation in terms
like, "First I'll bring up A, then lead to B, and after that I'll cover
C and finally go on to D." In order to succeed, sequence planning
always requires the consent and cooperation of the other
negotiating party. In many negotiations this cooperation was not
forthcoming. The negotiators would begin at point A and the other
party would only be interested in point D. This could put the
negotiators in difficulty, requiring them to either mentally change
gear and approach the negotiation in a sequence they had not
planned for, or to carry through their original sequence, risking
disinterest from the other party. In many negotiations sequences
were in themselves negotiable and it was ill-advised for the
negotiators to plan on a sequence basis.

**Typical Sequence Plan
Used by Average Negotiators**

A   then   B   then   C   then   D

in which issues are linked

**Typical Issue Plan
Used by Skilled Negotiators**

A

B

D

C

in which issues are independent
and not linked by a sequence

They would consider issue C, for example, as if issues A, B and D didn't
exist. Compared with the average negotiators they were careful not to draw
sequence links between a series of issues. This was demonstrated by observing the number of occasions during the planning process that each negotiator mentioned sequence of issues.

	Number of Mentions Implying Sequence in Planning
Skilled negotiators	2.1 per session
Average negotiators	4.9 per session

The clear advantage of issue planning over sequence planning is flexibility. In planning a negotiation it is important to remember that the sequence of issues itself (unless a preset agenda is agreed) may be subject to negotiation. Even where an agenda exists, within a particular item sequence planning may involve some loss of flexibility. So it seems useful for negotiators to plan their face-to-face strategy using issue planning and avoiding sequence planning.

5.   Face-to-Face Behavior

Skilled negotiators show marked differences in their face-to-face behavior, compared with average negotiators. They use certain types of behavior significantly more frequently while other types they tend to avoid.

> *a.*   **Irritators.**   Certain words and phrases which are commonly used during negotiation have negligible value in persuading the other party but do cause irritation. Probably the most frequent example of these is the term *generous offer* used by a negotiator to describe his or her own proposal. Similarly, words such as *fair, reasonable,* and other terms with a high positive value loading, have no persuasive power when used as self-praise, while serving to irritate the other party because of the implication that they are unfair, unreasonable, and so on. Most negotiators avoid the gratuitous use of direct insults or unfavorable value judgments. They know that there is little to gain from saying unfavorable things about the other party during face-to-face exchanges. However, the other side of the coin—saying gratuitously favorable things about themselves—seems harder for them to avoid. The researchers called such words *irritators* and found that although the average negotiator used them fairly regularly, the skilled negotiator tended to avoid them.

	Use of Irritators per Hour Face-to-Face Speaking Time
Skilled negotiators	2.3
Average negotiators	10.8

It is hardly surprising that skilled negotiators use fewer irritators. Any type of verbal behavior which antagonizes without a persuasive effect is unlikely to be productive. More surprising is the heavy use of irritators by average negotiators. The conclusion must be that most people fail to recognize the counterproductive effect of using positive value judgments about themselves and, in doing so, implying negative judgments of the other party.

b.   **Counterproposals.**   During negotiation it frequently happens that one party puts forward a proposal and the other party immediately responds with a counterproposal. The researcher found that skilled negotiators made immediate counterproposals much less frequently than average negotiators.

	Frequency of Counterproposals per Hour of Face-to-Face Speaking Time
Skilled negotiators	1.7
Average negotiators	3.1

This difference suggests that the common strategy of meeting a proposal with a counterproposal may not be particularly effective. The disadvantages of counterproposals are:

- They introduce an additional option, sometimes a whole new issue, which complicates and clouds the clarity of the negotiation.
- They are put forward at a point where the other party has least receptiveness, being concerned with his or her own proposal.
- They are perceived as blocking or disagreeing by the other party, not as proposals. (A study of 87 controlled pace negotiation exercises by the researchers showed that when one side in a negotiation put forth a proposal, there was an 87 percent chance that the other side would perceive it as a proposal. However, if the proposal immediately followed a proposal made by the other side (if in other words it was a counterproposal) the chance of being perceived as a proposal dropped to 61 percent, with a proportionate increase in the chances of being perceived as either disagreeing or blocking.

These reasons probably explain why the skilled negotiator is less likely to use counterproposing as a tactic than is the average negotiator.

c.   **Defend/attack spirals.**   Because negotiation frequently involves conflict, negotiators may become heated and use emotional or value-loaded behaviors. When such behavior was used to attack the other party or to make an emotional defense, the researchers termed it *defending/attacking*. Once initiated, this behavior tended to form a spiral of increasing intensity: one negotiator would attack, the other would defend himself, usually in a manner which the first negotiator perceived as an attack. In consequence, the first negotiator attacked more vigorously and the spiral commenced. Defending and attacking were often difficult to distinguish from each other. What one negotiator perceived as a legitimate defense, the other party might see as an unwarranted attack. This was the root cause of most defending/attacking spirals observed during the studies. Average negotiators in particular, were likely to react defensively, using comments such as "You can't blame us for that" or "It's not our fault that the present difficulty has arisen." Such comments frequently provoked a sharp defensive reaction from the other side of the table.

	% of Negotiators Comments Classified as Defending/Attacking
Skilled negotiators	1.9
Average negotiators	6.3

The researchers found that average negotiators used more than three times as much defending/attacking behavior as skilled negotiators. Although no quantitative measure exists, the researchers observed that skilled negotiators, if they did decide to attack, gave no warning and attacked hard. Average negotiators, in contrast, usually began their attacking gently, working their way up to more intense attacks slowly and, in doing so, causing the other party to build up its defensive behavior in the characteristic defending/attacking spiral.

d. **Behavior labeling.**   The researchers found that skilled negotiators tended to give an advance indication of the class of behavior they were about to use. So, for example, instead of just asking, "How many units are there?" they would say, "Can I ask you a question—how many units are there?" giving warning that a question was coming. Instead of just making a proposal they would say, "If I could make a suggestion . . ." and then follow this advance label with their proposal. With one exception average negotiators were significantly less likely to label their behavior in this way. The only behavior which the average negotiator was more likely to label in advance was disagreeing.

	% of All Negotiator's Behavior Immediately Preceded by a Behavior Label	
	Disagreeing	All Behavior except Disagreeing
Skilled negotiator	0.4	6.4
Average negotiator	1.5	1.2

This is a slightly unusual finding and it may not be immediately evident why these differences should exist. The researcher's interpretation was that, in general, labeling of behavior gives the negotiator the following advantages:

- It draws the attention of the listeners to the behavior that follows. In this way social pressure can be brought to force a response.
- It slows the negotiation down, giving time for the negotiator using labeling to gather his or her thoughts and for the other party to clear his or her mind from the previous statements.
- It introduces a formality which takes away a little of the cut-and-thrust and, therefore, keeps the negotiation on a rational level.
- It reduces ambiguity and leads to clearer communication.

Skilled negotiators, however, avoid labeling their disagreements. While average negotiators characteristically say, "I disagree with that because of . . ." thus labeling that they are about to disagree, skilled negotiators are more likely to begin with the reasons and lead up to the disagreement.

SKILLED NEGOTIATORS

| REASON/ EXPLANATION | Leading to | STATEMENT OF DISAGREEMENT |

AVERAGE NEGOTIATORS

| STATEMENT OF DISAGREEMENT | Leading to | REASON/ EXPLANATION |

If one of the functions of behavior labeling is to make negotiators' intentions clear, then it is hardly surprising that skilled negotiators avoid making it clear that they intend to disagree. They would normally prefer their reasons to be considered more neutrally so that acceptance involved minimal loss of face for the other party. But if labeling disagreement is likely to be counterproductive, why do average negotiators label disagreeing behavior more than all the other types of behavior put together? Most probably this tendency reflects the order in which we think. We decide that an argument we hear is unacceptable and only then do we assemble reasons to show why. Average negotiators speak their disagreement in the same order as they think it—disagreement first, reasons afterwards.

e. **Testing understanding and summarizing.**   The researchers found that two behaviors with a similar function, testing understanding and summarizing were used significantly more by the skilled negotiator. Testing understanding is a behavior which checks to establish whether a previous contribution or statement in the negotiation has been understood. Summarizing is a compact restatement of previous points in the discussion. Both behaviors sort out misunderstanding and reduce misconceptions.

	% of All Behavior by Negotiator		
	Testing Understanding	Summarizing	Testing Understanding and Summarizing
Skilled negotiators	9.7	7.5	17.2
Average negotiators	4.1	4.2	8.3

The higher level of these behaviors by skilled negotiators reflects their concern with clarity and the prevention of misunderstanding. It may also relate to two less obvious factors.

- **_Reflecting._**   Some skilled negotiators tended to use testing understanding as a form of reflecting behavior—turning the other party's words back in order to obtain further responses, for example, "So do I understand that you are saying you don't see any merit in this proposal at all?"

- **_Implementation Concern._**   Average negotiators, in their anxiety to obtain an agreement, would often quite deliberately fail to test understanding or to summarize. They would prefer to leave ambiguous points to be cleared later. They would fear that making things explicit might cause the other party to disagree. In short, their predominant objective was to obtain an agreement, and they would not probe too deeply into any area of potential misunderstanding which might prejudice immediate agreement, even if it was likely to give rise to difficulties at the implementation stage. Skilled negotiators, on the other hand, tended to have a greater concern with the successful implementation (as would be predicted from the success criteria earlier in this document). They would, therefore, test and summarize in order to check out any ambiguities at the negotiating stage rather than leave them as potential hazards for implementation.

f.   **Asking questions.**   The skilled negotiator asked significantly more questions during negotiation than did the average negotiator.

	Questions as a Percentage of All Negotiators Behavior
Skilled negotiator	21.3%
Average negotiator	9.6%

This is a very significant difference in behavior. Many negotiators and researchers have suggested that questioning techniques are important to negotiating success. Among the reasons frequently given are:

- Questions provide data about the other party's thinking and position.
- Questions give control over the discussion.
- Questions are more acceptable alternatives to direct disagreement.
- Questions keep the other party active and reduce his or her thinking time.
- Questions can give negotiators a breathing space to allow them to marshal their own thoughts.

g.   **Feelings commentary.**   Skilled negotiators are often thought of as persons who play their cards close to the chest, and who keep their feelings to themselves. The research studies were unable to measure this directly because feelings are, in themselves, unobservable. However, an indirect measure was possible. The researchers counted the number of times that negotiators made statements about what was going on inside their minds. The behavior category of *giving internal information* was used to record any reference by negotiators to their internal considerations such as feelings and motives.

	Giving Internal Information As a Percentage of All Negotiators Behavior
Skilled negotiator	12.1
Average negotiator	7.8

Skilled negotiators are more likely to give information about their internal events than average negotiators. This contrasts sharply with the amount of information given about external events, such as facts, clarifications, general expressions of opinion, etc. Here average negotiators give almost twice as much.

The effect of giving internal information is that the negotiators appear to reveal what is going on in their minds. This revelation may or may not be genuine, but it gives the other party a feeling of security because such things as motives appear to be explicit and above board. The most characteristic and noticeable form of giving internal information is a *feelings commentary,* where skilled negotiators talk about their feelings and the impression the other party has of them. For example, average negotiators, hearing a point from the other party which they would like to accept but doubt whether it is true, are likely to receive the point in uncomfortable silence. Skilled negotiators are more likely to comment on their own feelings, saying something like, "I'm uncertain how to react to what you've just said. If the information you've given me is true, then I would like to accept it; yet I feel some doubts inside me about its accuracy. So part of me feels happy and part feels suspicious. Can you help me resolve this?"

The work of psychologists such as Carl Rogers has shown that the expression of feelings is directly linked to establishing trust in counseling situations. It is probable that the same is true for negotiating.

h. **Argument dilution.**   Most people have a model of arguing which looks rather like a balance on a pair of scales. In fact, many of the terms we use about winning arguments reflect this balance model. We speak of "tipping the argument in our favor," of "the weight of the arguments," or how an issue "hangs in the balance." This way of thinking predisposes us to believe that there is some special merit in quantity. If we can find five reasons for doing something, that should be more persuasive than only being able to think of a single reason. We feel that the more we can put on our scalepan, the more likely we are to tip the balance of an argument in our favor. If this model has any validity, then skilled negotiators would be likely to use more reasons to back up their arguments than average negotiators.

	Average Number of Reasons Given by Negotiators to Back Each Argument/Case They Advanced
Skilled negotiator	1.8
Average negotiator	3.0

The researchers found that the opposite was true. Skilled negotiators used less reasons to back up each of their arguments. Although the balance-pan model may be very commonly believed, the studies suggest that it is a disadvantage to advance a whole series of reasons to back an argument or case. In doing so, negotiators expose a flank and give the other party a choice of which reason to dispute. It seems self-evident that if negotiators give five reasons to back their case and the third reason is weak, the other party will exploit this third reason in his or her response. The most appropriate model seems to be one of dilution. The more reasons advanced, the more a case is potentially diluted. The poorest reason is a lowest common denominator: a weak argument generally dilutes a strong.

Unfortunately, many negotiators with the disadvantage of higher education put a value on being able to ingeniously devise reasons to back their case. They frequently suffered from this dilution effect and had their point rejected, not on the strength of their principal argument, but on the weakness of the incidental supporting points they introduced. Skilled negotiators tended to advance single reasons insistently, only moving to subsidiary reasons if their main reason was clearly losing ground. It is probably no coincidence that an unexpectedly high proportion of skilled negotiators studied, both in labor relations and contract negotiation, had relatively little formal education. As a consequence, they had not been trained to value the balance-pan model and more easily avoided the trap of advancing a whole flank of reasons to back their cases.

6.   Reviewing the Negotiation

The researchers asked negotiators how likely they were to spend time reviewing the negotiation afterward. Over two-thirds of the skilled negotiators claimed that they always set aside some time after a negotiation to review it and consider what they had learned. Just under half of average negotiators, in contrast, made the same claim. Because the data are self-reported, it may be inaccurate. Even so, it seems that the old principle that more can be learned after a negotiation than during it may be true. An interesting difference between management and union representatives was observed. Management representatives, with other responsibilities and time pressures, were less likely to review a negotiation than were union representatives. This may, in part, account for the observation made by many writers on labor relations that union negotiators seem to learn negotiating skills from taking part in actual negotiations more quickly than management negotiators.

■ SUMMARY OF THE SUCCESSFUL NEGOTIATOR'S BEHAVIOR

The successful negotiator:

- Is rated as effective by both sides.
- Has a track record of significant success.
- Has a low incidence of implementation failure.

Forty-eight negotiators meeting these criteria were studied during 102 negotiations.

Planning	Negotiators	
	Skilled	**Average**
Overall amount of time spent	No significant difference	
Number of outcomes/options considered per issue	5.1%	2.6%
Percentage of comments about areas of anticipated common ground	38	11
Percentage of comments about long-term considerations of issues	8.5	4
Use of sequence during planning (per session)	2.1	4.9

Face-to-Face Skilled Negotiators	
AVOID	**USE**
■ Irritators	■ Behavior labelling (except disagreeing)
■ Counterproposals	■ Testing understanding and summarizing
■ Defend/attack spirals	■ Lots of questions

Chapter 4

Organizational Buyer Behavior and Buyer-Seller Relationships

LEARNING OBJECTIVES

After reading this chapter, you should be able to:

- Appreciate the changing role of the business to business buyer.
- Understand various models of buyer behavior.
- Discern various types of buying motives.
- Describe the process by which potential vendors are evaluated.
- Distinguish among different vendor-rating approaches.
- Realize that there are distinct types of environmental forces which influence business buying decisions.
- Evaluate the social, ethical, and legal considerations involved in buying practices.

CHAPTER OUTLINE

The Changing Role of the Buyer
    Profile of a Business to Business
    Buyer
Models of Buyer Behavior
    The Webster and Wind Model
    The Sheth Model
    The Choffray and Lilien Model
Business Buying Motives
Evaluating Potential Vendors
    Basic Considerations in Evaluating
    Potential Suppliers
    Vendor-Rating Approaches

Environmental Forces and Buying
Decisions
    The Economic Environment
    The Physical Environment
    The Competitive Environment
    The Technological Environment
    The Legal-Political Environment
    The Ethical Environment
Social, Ethical, and Legal
Considerations
    Commonly Recognized Practices

■ THE CHANGING ROLE OF THE BUYER

The role of the business buyer is constantly changing in a dynamic marketplace. The historical trend toward profit planning results in a great amount of pressure on the purchasing executive from the buying organization. The search for better methods of rating and dealing with suppliers is in the forefront of purchasing problems today, just as it has been for decades. A further problem is the trend toward decentralization and group decision making that affects the purchasing function today, and more than likely, will affect it well into the future.

Many U.S. industries spend resources for materials, direct production labor, and energy. Purchasing is directly involved in the decision to acquire materials and energy. This involvement is a key reason that sellers and buyers must work closely together, and why they must establish and maintain an enduring relationship if both are to survive. Despite the plethora of research on salesperson effectiveness, very few studies have dealt with the performance of purchasing personnel. A recent study found that buyers who were highly motivated, satisfied with their jobs, and certain of job expectations were more successful.[1] Marketing managers must keep in mind that adversarial and exploitative buyer-seller relationships are the ex-

---

[1]Peter M. Banting and Paul A. Dion, "The Purchasing Agent: Friend or Foe to the Salesperson?" *Journal of the Academy of Marketing Science* (Fall 1988), pp. 16–22.

ception rather than the rule. The erroneous adoption of the adversarial perspective can only impede the development of productive relationships with buyers.

Creative marketers are aware of the profit-making potential available to buyers, and they use this knowledge accordingly. Busy buyers who become accustomed to regular and timely assistance from creative sellers will not change sources of supply very readily. Marketing research has largely neglected the relationship aspect of the buyer-seller behavior, while tending to study transactions as discrete events. The lack of attention to antecedent conditions and processes for buyer-seller exchange relationships is a serious omission in the development of marketing knowledge.[2]

Profile of a Business to Business Buyer

In January 1986 a survey was conducted by the Organization and Planning Committee of the National Association of Purchasing Management in order to develop a profile of the typical purchasing executive. This survey, along with a study conducted and published by the Center for Advanced Purchasing Study (CAPS) in 1988, not only profiles the purchasing executive but also provides an indication of developing trends as both buyers and sellers prepare to face the challenges of the 1990s and beyond. These survey results indicated that the typical buyer is a 46-year-old Caucasian male who holds a bachelor's degree (business administration, engineering, accounting, and/or economics); who has extensive experience in buying (between 13 and 17 years); who is quite well informed about what he or she is buying; who carries the title of director of purchasing, vice president of purchasing, or manager of purchasing (as shown in Table 4–1)[3]; who is employed by a manufacturer and spends $6 to 10 million annually; and who spends more than 50 percent of the time in administrative duties. The purchasing manager receives several hundred requisitions a week; is responsible for all the company's purchases; and is in charge of an average of three other buying personnel (clerks, expediters, etc.). The average annual salary for purchasing personnel is $40,000.[4]

Purchasing magazine surveyed 2,000 purchasing executives in 1987 and found that much had changed from earlier surveys. For example, purchasing managers reported that they controlled a median average of $11.5 million of purchases, an increase over that reported in both 1982 and 1984. They are buying from fewer vendors and are traveling more to do it. Buyers made an average of 10 buying trips in 1987, up from seven in 1984. More than two-thirds of purchasing personnel have increased contract buy-

---

[2]Robert F. Dwyer, Paul H. Schurr, and Sejo Oh, "Developing Buyer-Seller Relationships," *Journal of Marketing* (April 1987), pp. 11–27.

[3]Harold E. Fearon, *Purchasing Organizational Relationships* (Tempe, Ariz.: Center for Advanced Purchasing Studies, National Association of Purchasing Management, 1988), p. 38.

[4]David Chance, C.P.M., "Profile of the N.A.P.M. Membership," Report on the January 1986 Survey, Organization and Planning Committee, National Association of Purchasing Management, Oradell, N.J.

■ **TABLE 4–1**   Title of Chief Purchasing Officer *(By organization size)*

Company Size, 1986 Sales Dollars (Percent may not add to 100, due to rounding)

Title	Under $500 million #	%	$500 mil. to $1 billion #	%	$1-1.5 billion #	%	$5.1-10 billion #	%	Over $10 billion #	%	Total #	%
Purchasing agent	2	2	—	0	—	0	—	0	—	0	2	1
Manager of purchasing	31	37	3	7	9	8	2	6	7	26	52	18
Director of purchasing	33	39	22	49	46	42	8	26	3	11	112	38
Vice president of purchasing	5	6	8	18	34	31	11	35	9	33	67	23
Materials manager	5	6	—	0	1	1	—	0	—	0	6	2
Director of material	2	2	4	9	4	4	3	10	3	11	16	5
Vice president of materials management	4	5	6	13	7	6	6	19	3	11	26	9
Other*	2	2	2	4	9	8	1	3	2	7	16	5
TOTAL	84	99	45	100	110	100	31	99	27	99	297	101

The 16 titles under "Other" were vice president, logistics (3); assistant vice president (2); director, corporate services (2); and 1 each vice president, sourcing; vice president, support services; director, operations; vice president, materials acquisition; vice president, manufacturing; vice president, supply; vice president, operations; administrative manager; and vice president, technical.

SOURCE: Harold E. Fearon, *Purchasing Organizational Relationships* (Tempe, Ariz.: Center for Advanced Purchasing Studies, National Association of Purchasing Management, 1988), p. 38.

ing, and more than three-quarters have decreased their vendor base, using fewer vendors to buy necessary parts, services, and supplies. Quality, delivery, technical service, and price have all increased in vendor rating programs, with quality showing the greatest increase. Many of these changes reflect the new and pressing demands put on those specializing in the purchase of goods and services.[5]

The marketing implications of the findings of these studies are enormous. The status of purchasing individuals within the organization seems to be rising, which is reflected not only in the title of the chief purchasing officer as previously noted but also in the functions that typically report to the purchasing executive. Table 4–2 provides job titles reporting to purchasing by organization size, and Table 4–3 provides job titles to which purchasing reports by organization size. Business to business sellers cannot avoid interaction with the purchasing person on most buying decisions, so a clear understanding and appreciation of this person's duties and responsibilities is a must. Additionally, purchasing executives are opting for more long-term buying contracts, and they will continue to buy from fewer sources. This will force many vendors (or potential vendors) to assume more responsibility for the inventory burden, which coincides with the trend toward JIT buying in many industries. Thus make and hold arrangements via long-term buying contracts, strong negotiation skills, and increased awareness of such factors as the small-order problem discussed in

---

[5]Somerby Dowst, "Profile of the Purchasing Pro: 1987," *Purchasing* 103 (October 22, 1987), pp. 63, 65.

■ TABLE 4–2   Functions That Report to Purchasing *(By organization size)*

	Total Organizations		Under $500 million		$500 million to $1 billion		$1.1-5 billion		$5.1-10 billion		Over $10 billion	
	#	%	#	%	#	%	#	%	#	%	#	%
Inbound traffic	29	10	14	17	2	4	8	7	2	6	3	11
Outbound traffic	2	1	0	—	0	—	2	2	0	—	0	—
Both inbound and outbound traffic	91	31	18	21	16	36	32	29	13	42	12	44
Warehousing or stores	102	34	31	37	14	31	40	36	8	26	9	33
Inventory control	111	37	29	35	21	47	43	39	8	26	10	37
Scrap/surplus disposal	169	57	54	64	24	53	62	56	13	42	16	59
Receiving	77	26	24	29	15	33	29	26	4	13	5	19
Incoming inspection	48	16	12	14	5	11	24	22	1	3	6	22
Other*	81	27	20	24	14	31	32	29	10	32	5	19
Number organizations responding	297		84		45		110		31		27	

*Under *Other* are included fleet management (11), personnel travel (9), production scheduling and control (6), contract administration (5), minority programs (5), office services (4), printing (4), material planning and forecasting (4), property administration (4). The following functions were indicated by three or fewer organizations: expediting, pattern shop, aircraft, security, demolition, asset recovery, agriculture, engineering standards, equipment specifications, hydrocarbon trading, packaging engineering, engineering, project management, international trading, and industrial sales.

SOURCE: Harold E. Fearon, *Purchasing Organizational Relationships* (Tempe, Ariz.: Center for Advanced Purchasing Studies, National Association for Purchasing Management, 1988), p. 38.

■ TABLE 4–3   To Whom Purchasing Reports *(By organization size)*

Number of Organizations and Percent of Organizations in Category
(Percent may not add to 100 due to rounding)

To Whom Purchasing Reports	Number of Organizations Responding		Under $500 million		$500 million to $1 billion		$1.1-5 billion		$5.1-10 billion		Over $10 billion	
	#	%	#	%	#	%	#	%	#	%	#	%
President	47	16	11	13	7	16	18	17	10	32	1	4
Executive vice president	54	18	10	12	10	22	17	16	9	29	8	31
Financial vice president	21	7	7	9	1	2	7	6	1	3	5	19
Mfg/prod/opns vice president	71	24	27	33	16	36	22	20	3	10	3	12
Materials mgt vice president	22	8	9	11	3	7	8	7	1	3	1	4
Engineering vice president	3	1	0	—	0	—	2	2	0	—	1	4
Administrative vice president	38	13	4	5	4	9	24	22	4	13	2	8
Other*	35	12	13	16	4	9	10	9	3	10	5	19
	291	99	81	99	45	101	108	99	31	100	26	101

*The 35 shown as reporting to *Other* includes division vice president (6); director of materials (3); materials manager (3); vice chairman (3); board of directors (2); vice president, logistics (2); director of support services (2); and one each to director of administration; manager of administration; director of manufacturing; director of operations; vice president, trading; vice president, systems; vice president, human resources; vice president, engineering and materials; division controller; vice president, law and public affairs; vice president, technical; vice president, marketing; assistant vice president; and manager, planning and distribution.

SOURCE: Harold E. Fearon, *Purchasing Organizational Relationships* (Tempe, Ariz.: Center for Advanced Purchasing Studies, National Association for Purchasing Management, 1988), p. 27.

Chapter 3 will put the astute seller or potential seller in a commanding position. These buying strengths, accompanied by a buyers' trend toward single sourcing, put additional pressure on vendor and sales executives.

■ MODELS OF BUYER BEHAVIOR

The business buying environment is influenced by budget, cost, and profit considerations, and involves many people in the decision process. There is much interaction among these individuals, who have many different immediate goals. For the marketer, models of buyer behavior are useful in identifying factors which influence the buying decision process. Any useful framework for analyzing organizational buying behavior will help in designing marketing strategy.

The three models of behavior presented in Figures 4–1, 4–2, and 4–3 do not describe specific buying situations, and cannot be quantified. However, they do present a view of buying that will enable the marketer to evaluate the relevance of specific variables and permit additional insights into buying behavior.

The Webster and Wind Model

Figure 4–1, which was developed by Frederick Webster and Yoram Wind, is a general model identifying the classes of variables that must be examined by students of organizational buying behavior.[6] The fundamental philosophy underlying the model is that organizational buying is a decision-making process carried out by individuals who interact with other people in the context of a formal organization.[7] The organization, in turn, is influenced by a variety of forces in the environment, including individual, social, organizational, and environmental forces. Within each class there are two broad categories of variables: those directly related to the buying problem called *task variables*[8] and those that extend beyond the buying problem

---

[6]Frederick E. Webster, Jr., and Yoram Wind, "A General Model for Understanding Organizational Buying Behavior," *Journal of Marketing* 36 (April 1973), pp. 12–19. See also Harold J. Leavitt, "Applied Organizational Change in Industry: Structural, Technical and Human Approaches," in *New Perspectives in Organization Research,* ed. William W. Cooper, Harold J. Leavitt, and Maynard W. Shelly II. (New York: John Wiley & Sons, 1964), pp. 55–71.

[7]See Thomas V. Bonoma, "Major Sales: Who Really Does the Buying?" *Harvard Business Review* 60 (May-June 1982), pp. 111–19.

[8]See Richard M. Hill, Ralph S. Alexander, and James M. Cross, *Industrial Marketing* (Homewood, Ill.: Richard D. Irwin, 1975), pp. 54–58; E. Raymond Corey, *Industrial Marketing: Cases and Concepts* (Englewood Cliffs, N.J.: Prentice-Hall, 1973), pp. 59–63; J. Patrick Kelly and James W. Coaker, "Can We Generalize about Choice Criteria for Industrial Purchasing Decisions?" in *Marketing: 1976 and Beyond,* ed. Kenneth L. Bernhardt (Chicago: American Marketing Association, 1976), pp. 33–43; William D. Perreault, Jr., and Frederick A. Russ, "Physical Distribution Services in Industrial Purchasing Decisions," *Journal of Marketing* 40 (April 1976), pp. 3–10; and Lamar Lee, Jr., and Donald W. Dobler, *Purchasing and Materials Management* (New York: McGraw-Hill, 1971), pp. 90–91.

■ **FIGURE 4–1**   The Webster and Wind Model of Buying Behavior

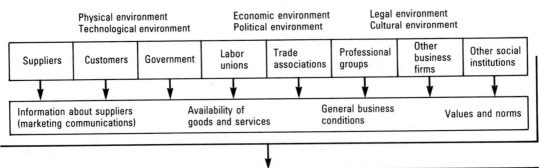

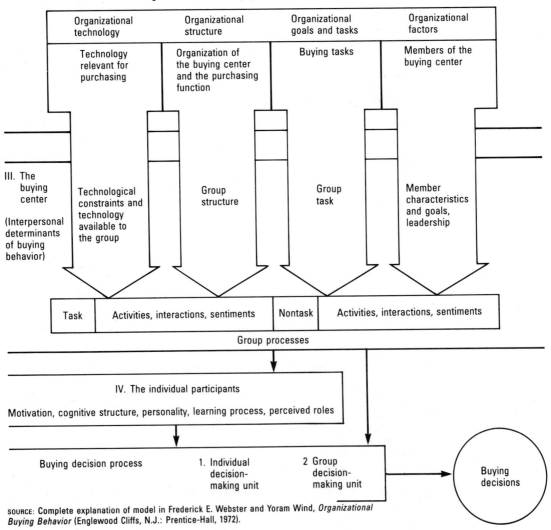

SOURCE: Complete explanation of model in Frederick E. Webster and Yoram Wind, *Organizational Buying Behavior* (Englewood Cliffs, N.J.: Prentice-Hall, 1972).

called *nontask variables*.[9] The distinction between the two variables applies to all of the classes and subclasses of variables, and it is seldom possible to identify a given set of variables as exclusively task or nontask; rather, any given set of variables will have both task and nontask dimensions. One such dimension is often predominant.

The Sheth Model

Figure 4–2, a buyer behavior model developed by Jagdish N. Sheth, is a general model that attempts to describe most types of business buying decisions.[10] This model explicitly describes a joint decision-making process. Sheth has attempted to: (1) broaden the vision of research on organizational buyer behavior so that it includes the most salient elements and their interactions, (2) to act as a catalyst for building marketing information systems from the viewpoint of the business buyer, and (3) to generate new hypotheses for future research on fundamental processes underlying organizational buyer behavior. He has attempted a reconciliation and integration of existing knowledge into a realistic and fairly comprehensive model of organizational buyer behavior.

The Choffray-Lilien Model

In the basic model developed by Jean-Marie Choffray and Gary Lilien (Figure 4–3), attention is focused on the relationship between an organizational buying center and three major stages in the individual purchase process to include the following: (1) the screening of alternatives which do not meet organizational requirements, (2) the formation of decision participants' preferences, and (3) the formation of organizational preferences.

Individual members of the buying center use different evaluative criteria and are exposed to different sources of information. These informational sources influence the suppliers included in the buyer's evoked set of alternatives. The evoked set comprises the alternative suppliers a buyer remembers when a need arises, and represents only a few of the many suppliers who might be available.[11]

---

[9]See Thomas V. Bonoma and Wesley J. Johnston, "The Social Psychology of Industrial Buying and Selling," *Industrial Marketing Management* 17 (1978), pp. 213–34; Delbert J. Duncan, "Purchasing Agents: Seekers of Status, Personal and Professional," *Journal of Purchasing* 2 (August 1966), pp. 17–26; and George Strauss, "Tactics of Lateral Relationships: The Purchasing Agent," *Administrative Science Quarterly* 7 (1978), pp. 161–86.

[10]Jagdish N. Sheth, "A Model of Industrial Buying Behavior," *Journal of Marketing* 37 (April 1973), pp. 50–56.

[11]John A. Howard and Jagdish N. Sheth, *The Theory of Buyer Behavior* (New York: John Wiley & Sons, 1969), p. 26. See also Ronald P. LeBlanc, "Environmental Impact in Purchase Decision Structure," *Journal of Purchasing and Materials Management* 17 (Spring 1981), pp. 30–36; and Lowell E. Crow, Richard W. Olshavsky, and John O. Summers, "Industrial Buyers' Choice Strategies: A Protocol Analysis, *Journal of Marketing Research* 17 (February 1980), pp. 34–44.

■ **FIGURE 4–2** The Sheth Integrative Model of Buyer Behavior

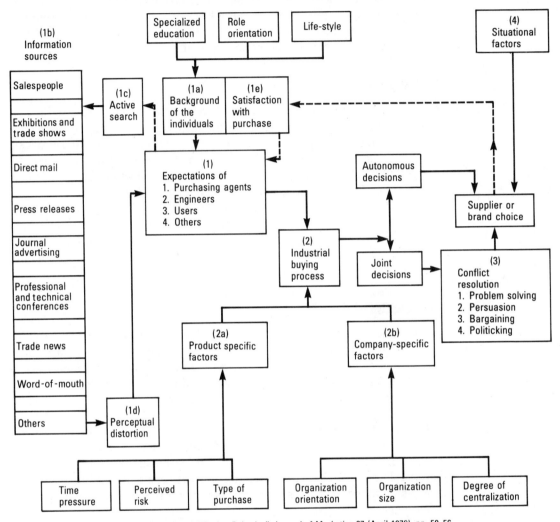

SOURCE: Jagdish H. Sheth, "A Model of Industrial Buying Behavior," *Journal of Marketing* 37 (April 1973), pp. 50–56.

Environmental constraints and organizational requirements influence the procurement process by limiting the number of product alternatives which satisfy organizational needs. For example, capital equipment alternatives which exceed a particular cost (initial or operating) might be eliminated from further consideration. The resulting choices become the feasible set of alternatives over which individual preferences are defined. The interaction structure of the members of the buying center, who have different criteria and responsibilities, leads to the formation of organizational preferences, and, ultimately, to organizational choice. An understanding of the organizational buying process allows the marketer to play an active rather

■ **FIGURE 4–3**   The Choffray-Lilien Model of Buyer Behavior

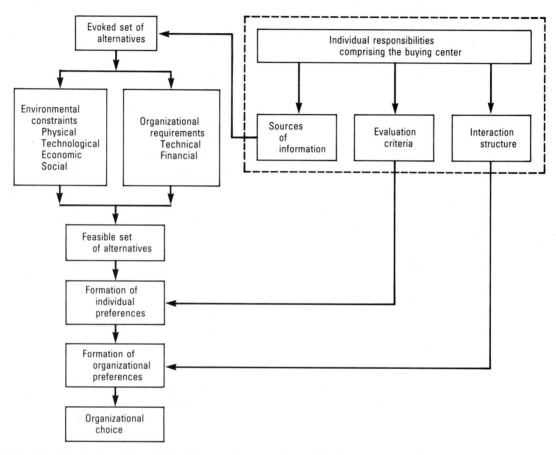

SOURCE: Jean-Marie Choffray and Gary L. Lilien, "Assessing Response to Industrial Marketing Strategy," *Journal of Marketing* 42 (April 1978), p. 22.

than a passive role in stimulating market response.[12] Exhibit 4–1 provides a more detailed application of the Choffray-Lilien model of organizational behavior.

The reader needs to realize that all buying decisions are not the result of a systematic approach to the decision-making process depicted in the models cited above. For the majority of purchases, model building is neither relevant nor useful. However, the reconciliation and integration of existing knowledge into a realistic and comprehensive model of organizational behavior is useful to describe and explain many types of

[12]W. C. Buss, "A Comparison of the Predictive Performance of Group-Preference Models," *Proceedings of the American Marketing Association* 47, Chicago: American Marketing Association, 1981, pp. 174–77; and Jean-Marie Choffray and Gary L. Lilien, "Assessing Response to Industrial Marketing Strategy," *Journal of Marketing* 42 (April 1978), pp. 20–31.

■ **EXHIBIT 4–1**   An Application of the Choffray-Lilien Model

The Choffray-Lilien model of buyer behavior can be applied to the specific case of the adoption of solar air conditioning. This study examined how members of the buying center differed in their perceptions of available product alternatives, how groups of decision participants (i.e., those occupying similar buying roles) differed in their evaluation of criteria, and how these criteria influenced actual preferences. Sophisticated research methodology was used to measure participants' perceptions of product attributes, and to assess the differences among the perceptions of various groups. The existence of substantial perceptual differences was confirmed. Analysis of these differences revealed several interesting conclusions, among them that groups with more decision responsibility used more decision criteria and different criteria than groups with less responsibility. For example, corporate engineers were found to place the most importance on reliability and initial cost, but plant managers felt that modernness, fuel savings, and low operating cost were most significant. Another interesting observation was that the assumptions appropriate in analyzing consumer preference data (e.g., that consumers use homogeneous evaluation criteria but have different preference parameters) might be inappropriate in analyzing business to business buyers' preferences.

These findings have clear implications for product design decisions and for promotional strategy. For example, they can help management decide on the trade-offs among various product parameters and to design advertising and selling strategies that would be responsive to the information needs of various decision influencers. More important, however, these findings contribute significantly to the development of a methodology for measuring and analyzing buyer preferences, and using these data for new product development and marketing communication. This methodology is clearly more appropriate to the complexity of the business to business buying process than any borrowed from consumer marketing.

SOURCE: Jean-Marie Choffray and Gary L. Lilien, "Industrial Adoption of Solar Air Conditioning: Measurement Problems, Solutions, and Marketing Implications." Working paper, 894–76, Sloan School of Management, Massachusetts Institute of Technology, June 1976.

buying decisions. The buying behavior models exhibited above are shown primarily to illustrate research in this area of study. Although these macro-models provide overall impressions of the underlying nomological network of general categories of personal, organizational, and environmental variables that might influence the organizational buying process, they do not explicitly specify key variables and their interrelationships with respect to the buying process.[13]

Concept Questions

1. Why are contemporary purchasing personnel different from their counterparts of only a few years ago?
2. What is the primary utility of buyer behavior models for the marketer?

■ BUSINESS BUYING MOTIVES

Several different approaches are found in the literature which reflect different behavioral schools of thought applied to understanding and explaining the buyer behavior and motives of purchasing personnel. It is not unusual to find purchasing, engineering, manufacturing, and marketing personnel involved both individually and jointly at various phases in the buying de-

---

[13]Ronald E. Michaels, Ralph L. Day, and Erich A. Joachinsthaler, "Role Stress among Industrial Buyers: An Integrative Model," *Journal of Marketing* (April 1987), pp. 28–45.

cision process, particularly in a new-task or a modified-rebuy buying situation.

If uncertainty is involved with a purchasing decision, research studies have found that decision makers avoid as much risk as possible by remaining loyal to existing suppliers they know and trust. For instance, a number of business observers credit IBM's success in marketing personal computers to this tendency of business to business buyers. Many purchasing directors who were considering the purchase of personal computers in the early 1980s seemed overwhelmed by having more than 150 different computer manufacturers competing for their business. Therefore, to minimize their risk level, many turned to IBM as a trusted name with consistently reliable products.[14] A large number of purchasing managers frequently utilize one or more of the following activities in an effort to reduce or remove perceived risk:

1. ***Reduce Uncertainty.***   Uncertainty can be reduced by gathering additional information, such as consulting with other influencers or visiting potential suppliers' plants.

2. ***Play the Odds.***   Sophisticated quantitative methods of vendor analysis and selection, involving expected value analysis and considering both the probability and magnitude of consequences, are available. As a result, the business buyer will often **play the odds** by selecting the supplier with the most favorable expected value.

3. ***Spread the Risk.***   The consequences of choosing the wrong supplier can also be reduced through **multiple sourcing,** which enables buyers to choose the proportion of risk to be assumed by allocating it among different suppliers.[15] For example, Loctite holds an 85 percent market share in anaerobic adhesives. A number of other companies have entered the industry by taking advantage of the hesitancy of Loctite's customers to depend solely on a single source of supply.[16]

Unlike consumer products, business products do not necessarily make anyone look or feel better, and they generally do not have significant aesthetic value. These products are bought to help the users manufacture, distribute, or sell more effectively in order to improve their respective economic and competitive positions. As such, firms tend to emphasize price and quality checks and balances in the buying process that often do not exist in the typical household purchase situation. Examples of exceptions

---

[14]"Computer Shock Hits the Office," *Business Week,* August 8, 1983, p. 46.

[15]Robert R. Reeder, Edward G. Briety, and Betty H. Reeder, *Industrial Marketing: Analysis, Planning, and Control* (Englewood Cliffs, N.J.: Prentice-Hall, 1987), p. 113. See also T. W. Sweeney, H. L. Mathews, and D. T. Wilson, "An Analysis of Industrial Buyers' Risk-Reducing Behavior," *Proceedings of the American Marketing Association* (Chicago: American Marketing Association, 1973), pp. 217–21; and D. T. Wilson, "Industrial Buyers' Decision-Making Styles," *Journal of Marketing Research* 8 (November 1971), pp. 433–36.

[16]"Loctite: Ready to Fend Off a Flock of New Competitors," *Business Week,* June 19, 1978, pp. 116, 118.

■ **EXHIBIT 4–2**   Goals Influencing Buying Decisions

Personal Goals	Organizational Goals
Want a feeling of power.	Control cost in product use situation.
Seek personal pleasure.	Few breakdowns of product.
Desire job security.	Dependable delivery for repeat purchases.
Want to be well liked.	Adequate supply of product.
Want respect.	Cost within budget limit.

---

to this practice would be the buyer with the latest EDP System (signifying a position of power within the organization), and a salesperson with a new Mercury Sable as a company car (signifying status within the organization). In developing marketing strategy, both existing and potential suppliers should be aware of buyers' decision strategies in reducing uncertainty, and of how such strategies affect the choice of a supplier.

Using another perspective, final consumers buy for their own use or for use by people close to them. As such, personal goals are important to consumers in making their purchasing decisions. Business buyers purchase for their organizations, not for themselves. However, since people are still doing the buying in organizations, both personal and organizational goals may play a role in buying.[17] The presence of both types of goals can somewhat complicate the marketing effort. A vendor's sales representatives can have difficulty in ascertaining whether personal or organizational goals hold more importance for the buyer. For example, a buyer of metal cans, a product which does not greatly differ from one vendor to another, considers organizational goals such as cost control, package safety, and delivery time when choosing a supplier. Simultaneously, that buyer also considers personal goals, such as the desire for power and job security, when making a buying decision. Exhibit 4–2 compares personal and organizational goals.[18] As can be seen from this illustration, personal goals and organizational goals are not usually the same. A vendor has little choice but to reorganize and respond to both types of goals.

■ EVALUATING POTENTIAL VENDORS

Basic Considerations in Evaluating Potential Vendors

The use of suppliers with whom there is no previous experience requires, at the least, some initial work by the buyer. In many instances, if the supplier is to provide a significant part or material, the evaluation may be a rather exhaustive process. Four basic considerations many buyers use for this process are discussed below.

---

[17]Thomas V. Bonoma, "Major Sales: Who Really Does the Buying?" *Harvard Business Review* (May-June 1982), p. 116.

[18]David W. Cravens, Gerald E. Hills, and Robert B. Woodruff, *Marketing Management* (Homewood, Ill.: Richard D. Irwin, 1987), pp. 160–61.

Performance Considerations.   A potential supplier's total ability to fulfill the requirements of a purchase contract as it relates to price, delivery, quality, and service, must be predicted. These points generally revolve around the potential vendor's financial capabilities. An independent analysis of a potential vendor's financial statements will be in order. A buying executive must be able to obtain information on a supplier's financial stability, pricing cushion, and general operating efficiency by applying the tools of ratio analysis to the vendor's balance sheets and income statements.

Plant Visits.   A business buyer will learn a great deal by a plant visit to a potential supplier. Insight into the type of facilities, personnel, housekeeping, and procedures will reveal the level of efficiency maintained as well as provide an indication of potential problems which could affect the prospective supplier's ability to provide necessary presale and postsale services. Care must be taken to insure that the plant visit did not simply provide the potential supplier with an excuse to clean up the plant. Usually, a superficial plant cleanup will be obvious since a team with cross-functional members will perform a relatively comprehensive audit of the plant and its operations.

Geographic Location.   Shipments from distant suppliers are subject to more and greater risks of interruption from accidents, strikes, and acts of God. Thus the geographic location of the supplier becomes important in many buying situations. Most geographical disadvantages can be overcome by creative marketing, including special transportation arrangements, inventory make-and-hold service, etc. The increased adoption of the JIT philosophy is making geographic location of the supplier a much more important consideration.

Capacity.   Production capacity available to the buyer becomes an important consideration, especially during times of high business activity. In evaluating reserve facilities, the buyer needs to consider technical and managerial skills as well as physical plant and facilities. Therefore, in comparing suppliers, the buyer will analyze in detail the facilities various potential suppliers have to offer as a criterion for the service they will supply.

Continued potential vendor evaluations are critical in the development of effective long-term relationships and performance. A total cost approach—one which is significant to long-term sourcing decisions and ultimately to bottom-line profitability—recognizes that the purchase price is only a fraction of the cost of materials. The buying focus must shift from primarily a unit-price-oriented evaluation to a cost-based-performance evaluation of potential suppliers, incorporating quality, delivery, and other related costs as measurable factors to be included when evaluating the total purchase costs of buying from various suppliers.[19] If a supplier fails to meet delivery, quality, and price requirements, additional costs are in-

---

[19]Robert M. Moncka and Steven J. Trecha, "Cost-Based Supplier Performance Evaluation," *Journal of Purchasing and Materials Management* (Spring 1988), pp. 2–7.

curred by the buying organization to correct these deficiencies. These excess costs, both direct and overhead, have an immediate impact on the buying firm's available resources.

Vendor-Rating Approaches

The purchasing department performs an economic function, and as noted earlier, is a vital profit-enhancing unit for the company. Its services disseminate advanced technological techniques, methods of manufacturing, and other pertinent data from vendors to proper echelons within the company. As an economic function, purchasing has a responsibility through its delegated authority from management to evaluate properly both potential and active vendors through all phases of the procurement cycle. Computer as-

■ **EXHIBIT 4–3**   Ranking of Factors Motivating Purchasing Managers in Choosing Vendors of a Standard Product

Accounting Department
1. Providing volume discounts
2. Achieving quality specifications consistently
3. Responding promptly to all communications
4. Offering competitive prices
5. Dealing with product rejections equitably
6. Providing necessary information when requested (e.g., bids)

Production Control Department
1. Rapid delivery in times of emergency
2. Shipping products when desired
3. Achieving quality specifications consistently
4. Cooperating willingly in face of unforseen problems
5. Providing assistance in emergency situations

Purchasing Department
1. Achieving quality specifications consistently
2. Counseling about potential trouble
3. Using honesty in dealings
4. Supplying goods in shortage periods
5. Cooperating willingly in face of unforseen problems
6. Shipping products when desired
7. Providing necessary information when requested
8. Providing assistance in emergency situations

Manufacturing/Engineering Department
1. Delivering goods as promised
2. Using honesty in dealings
3. Supplying goods in shortage periods
4. Achieving quality specifications consistently
5. Delivering rapidly in times of emergency

Quality Control Department
1. Achieving quality specifications consistently
2. Using honesty in dealings
3. Giving credit for scrap
4. Supplying goods in shortage periods
5. Providing low percentage of rejects

Specialty Machinery/Engineering Department
1. Supplying goods in shortage periods
2. Achieving quality specifications consistently
3. Providing low percentage of rejects
4. Delivering goods as promised
5. Using honesty in dealings

Tool Design Department
1. Using honesty in dealings
2. Offering technical ability and knowledge
3. Dealing with product rejections equitably
4. Giving credit for scrap
5. Invoicing properly
6. Supplying goods in shortage periods
7. Responding promptly to all communications

*Duplicate numbers indicate ties in rankings.

SOURCE: Stanley D. Sibley, "How Interfacing Departments Rate Vendors," *National Purchasing Review* 6 (August-October 1980), p. 11.

■ **FIGURE 4–4**   A Vendor Visitation Form Providing Data for Vendor Evaluation

Company visited: Date:

Purpose of visit:

Representatives contacted:

Survey: If vendor has not been surveyed in 12 months, acquire following information:

  a. Size of plant (square feet):
  b. Equipment (Acquire facility list, if available):
  c. Housekeeping:
  d. Labor situation:
  e. General atmosphere:
  f. Product lines:
  g. Shipping—Mode:
  h. Organization (Acquire organization chart, if available):
  i. Growth plans:
  j. Purchasing–Cost evaluation:
  k. Quality Control—Q.C. manual: Organization chart:
  l. Research & development:
  m. Exchange cost-cutting ideas:

Observation:

Suggestions:

If you go there:

                          Reported by:

SOURCE: Frederick E. Webster, Jr., *Industrial Marketing Strategy,* 2d ed. (New York: John Wiley & Sons, 1984), p. 46.

sistance allows for a thorough evaluation of vendors on a regular basis, as actual performance must be evaluated. Buyers need to rate supplier performance in assessing the quality of past decisions, in making future vendor selections, and as a negotiating tool to gain leverage in buyer-seller relationships.[20] As can be seen in Exhibit 4–3, purchasing managers will frequently prepare a rank-ordered list of the desired supplier attributes and their relative importance. The real test of vendor selection is, of course, the test of experience, or satisfactory performance by the vendor once the order has been placed. It is most often the deciding factor in whether the selected vendor will continue to receive the buyer's business or be replaced by another source.[21] Figure 4–4 offers a vendor visitation report, and provides evaluation data when it has been some time since the last rating of a particular supplier.

Vendor rating systems generally involve three basic considerations: quality, service (delivery), and price. The most common methods used to eval-

[20]David Bonneville, "Vendor Analyzers Pack a Punch in Negotiations," *Purchasing World* 27 (March 1983), pp. 32–34.

[21]Stuart F. Heinritz, Paul V. Farrell, and Clifton L. Smith, p. 103.

■ **TABLE 4–4**   Illustration of the Categorical Method of Vendor
Performance Rating

Performance Characteristics

Vendor	Cost	Product Quality	Speed	Total
A	Good (+)	Unsatisfactory (−)	Neutral (0)	0
B	Neutral (0)	Good (+)	Good (+)	+ +
C	Neutral (0)	Unsatisfactory (−)	Neutral (0)	−

Source: E. Timmerman, "An Approach to Vendor Performance Evaluation," *Journal of Purchasing and Materials Management* (Winter 1986), pp. 2–8.

uate suppliers are (1) the categorical plan, (2) the weighted-point plan, and (3) the cost-ratio plan.[22]

The Categorical Plan.   In the **categorical plan,** buyers keep notes on their dealings with suppliers as events occur. At monthly buyer meetings (or at some other convenient time interval), notes are compared, and suppliers are categorized as being in the good, neutral, or unsatisfactory category. This method is highly subjective, but it is easy to understand and is easy to use. The simplicity of the plan is its most desirable feature. The simple recording, reporting, and analytical techniques also allow evaluation at a minimum cost. As is shown in Table 4–4, in this approach a list of significant performance factors is developed for evaluation purposes, with the buyer assigning a grade in simple categorical terms, such as *good, neutral,* and *unsatisfactory,* indicating the vendor's actual performance in each area. In this example Vendor B appears to have generated the best performance record.

The big disadvantage of this approach is that it is largely an intuitive process, relying heavily on memory, personal judgment, and the experience and ability of the buyer.

The Weighted-Point Plan.   In the **weighted-point plan,** quality, price, and service (or other relevant criteria) are assigned weights. Quality might be assigned a weight of 40 points, price 35 points, and service 25 points. This point offering must be adjusted to fit a particular organization's needs. Flexibility is an important feature of this plan, as point values can be changed to suit special requirements without changing the workings of the plan.

Sellers are rated on each factor; the resulting ratings are then changed to a composite, which becomes a portion of 100 percent. One seller will have a composite closer to 100 percent than will the others.

Table 4–5 shows the relative simplicity of arriving at the quality portion of the rating. In Table 4–6 the price factor is illustrated as being more complex, since one must first determine delivered cost, as shown in Part A. Then the buyer must convert this cost into a merit value, as shown in

---

[22]The following discussion is based on Paul V. Farrell and George W. Aljian, *Aljian's Purchasing Handbook* (New York: McGraw-Hill, 1982, pp. 6–24 to 6–28. Also based on National Association of Purchasing Management, *Guide to Purchasing,* pp. 1.6.10–1.6.18.

■ TABLE 4–5   Quality Rating under the Weighted-Point Plan

Quality

(Insert drawing and part number)	Lots Received	Lots Accepted	Lots Rejected	Percentage Accepted × Factor	Quality Control Rating
Supplier A	60	54	6	90.0 × 40	36.0
Supplier B	60	56	4	93.3 × 40	37.3
Supplier C	20	16	4	80.0 × 40	32.0

Note: To rate lots closer, a system of fractional lots can be used. Thus if an unacceptable lot is only one-half or one-tenth bad, it could be said that 0.5 or 0.1 lots were unacceptable, etc. This would distinguish between suppliers with a total lot unacceptable, and those with only a small part of the lots unacceptable.

SOURCE: Douglas V. Smith, "Vendor/Supplier Evaluation," *Guide to Purchasing,* vol. 1, Article 1.6 (Tempe, Ariz: National Association of Purchasing Management, 1967), p. 1.6.15.

■ TABLE 4–6   Price Rating under the Weighted-Point Plan

Part A

	Price				
	Unit Price	− Discount	+	Transportation Charge	= Net Price
Supplier A	$1.00	10%	($ .90)	$.03	$ .93
Supplier B	1.25	15%	($1.06)	.06	1.12
Supplier C	1.50	20%	($1.20)	.03	1.23

Part B

	Lowest Price	÷ Net Price	= Percentage	× Factor	= Price Rating
Supplier A	$.93	$ .93	100%	35	35.0
Supplier B	.93	1.12	83%	35	29.1
Supplier C	.93	1.23	76%	35	26.6

Source: Douglas V. Smith, "Vendor Supplier Evaluation," *Guide to Purchasing,* vol. 1, Article 1.6 (Tempe, Ariz: National Association of Purchasing Management, 1967), p. 1.6.15.

■ TABLE 4–7   Service Rating under the Weighted-Point Plan

Service	Promises kept	× Service factor	= Service rating
Supplier A	90%	25	22.5
Supplier B	95	25	23.8
Supplier C	100	25	25.0

Note: As in the quality factor, a closer or finer evaluation of service can be used. Fractional lots delivered on time can be so reported; for example, the final percentage might be based on 11.5 lots of 14 received on time, etc.

SOURCE: Douglas V. Smith, "Vendor/Supplier Evaluation," *Guide to Purchasing,* vol. 1, Article 1.6 (Tempe, Ariz: National Association of Purchasing Management, 1967), p. 1.6.15.

Part B. Here the lowest cost is rated as 100 percent, and the others are rated relative to the lowest cost.

In Table 4–7 the service factor has been tabulated as in the quality rating. By combining these factors, as in Table 4–8, an optimum choice of suppliers can be made (Supplier A). Table 4–9 provides an example of the

■ **TABLE 4–8**   Composite Rating under the Weighted-
             Point Plan

Composite Rating

Rating	Supplier A	Supplier B	Supplier C
Quality (40 points)	36.0	37.3	32.0
Price (15 points)	35.0	29.1	26.6
Service (25 points)	22.5	23.8	25.0
Total rating	93.5	90.2	83.6

SOURCE: Douglas V. Smith, "Vendor/Supplier Evaluation, *Guide to Purchasing,* vol. 1, Article 1.6 (Tempe, Ariz: National Association of Purchasing Management, 1967), p. 1.6.15.

■ **TABLE 4–9**   Weighted-Point Method of Supplier Evaluation

Factor	Weight	Actual Performance	Performance Score
Quality	40	90% acceptable	$40 \times .9 = 36$
Delivery	30	90% on schedule	$30 \times .9 = 27$
Cost-reducing suggestions	20	% of total received = 60	$20 \times .6 = 12$
Price	10	125% of lowest price $100/125 = .8$	$10 \times .8 = 8$
		Total composite score =	83

SOURCE: Adapted from Gary J. Zenz, *Purchasing and the Management of Materials* (New York: John Wiley & Sons, 1981).

weighted-point plan. The majority of buyers are satisfied with the simple but effective weighted-point plan, which has been modified to suit specific conditions.

The Cost-Ratio Plan.   With a **cost-ratio plan** all activities in a supplier's performance are valued in terms of dollars and cents. The **total cost of buying** is determined, including the cost of such things as letters, telephone calls, visits, etc. Buyers can then select future vendors on the basis of the lowest total cost incurred. The total (real) cost of the same item from several sellers will vary with the skill and dependability of the seller. This method evaluates supplier performance by using the tools of standard cost analysis. The total cost of each purchase to be evaluated is calculated as its selling price plus the buyer's internal operating costs associated with the quality, delivery, and service elements of the purchase.[23] The calculation methodology involves a four-step approach. Table 4–10 illustrates the use of the technique in comparing the various elements of cost for four competing vendors.

In the cost-ratio plan the first step is to determine the initial costs associated with quality, delivery, and service. Next, each is converted to a cost ratio, which expresses the cost as a percentage of the total value of the

---

[23]E. Timmerman, "An Approach to Vendor Performance Evaluation," *Journal of Purchasing and Materials Management* (Winter 1986), pp. 2–8.

■ **TABLE 4–10** Cost Comparison Utilizing the Cost-Ratio Method of Vendor Rating

Company	Quality Cost Ratio	Delivery Cost Ratio	Service Cost Ratio	Total Penalty	Quoted Price/ Unit	Net Adjusted Cost
Abraham S.	1%	3%	−1%	3%	$86.25	$88.84
Winston Inc.	2	2	3	7	83.25	89.08
Plough Co.	3	1	6	10	85.10	93.61
Barron	2	1	2	5	85.00	89.25

SOURCE: E. Timmerman, "An Approach to Vendor Performance Evaluation," *Journal of Purchasing and Materials Management* (Winter 1986), pp. 2–8.

purchase. The third step is to sum the three individual cost ratios to obtain an overall cost ratio. Finally, the overall cost ratio is applied to the vendor's quoted unit price to obtain the net adjusted cost figure. As can be seen in Table 4–10, any costs of doing business with a vendor are assessed as a penalty, which has the effect of raising the overall price and making it less attractive.

Operationally this approach is complex, requiring a comprehensive cost-accounting system to generate the precise cost data needed. Further, it assumes the ready availability of such data to the purchasing department.

Concept Questions

1. Why does the presence of both personal and organizational goals complicate the marketing effort?
2. What are the four sources of input buyers can utilize in evaluating suppliers they have not used before?
3. Under what types of conditions do organizational buyers rate potential and/or current vendors?

■ ENVIRONMENTAL FORCES AND BUYING DECISIONS

Marketing success depends upon developing a sound marketing mix (the controllable variables) adapted to the trends and developments in the **marketing environment** (the uncontrollable variables). The marketing environment presents a set of largely uncontrollable forces to which the company must adapt its marketing mix.

The purpose of **environmental analysis** is to identify and assess threats and opportunities as they are evolving in the marketplace. The company itself is part of the changing environment, since it develops and refines its basic competence in interaction with its customers' evolving needs. Virtually every aspect of the firm's marketing activities, and the competitive and customer response to them, will have some effect on the structure and functioning of the marketplace, especially in regard to its pricing policies, distribution strategies, and new product marketing efforts.

Environmental analysis requires a continuous flow of information from a potentially limitless variety of sources. Any piece of information has value if it contributes to increased management awareness and understanding of the forces shaping the economy, the industry, and the market. The typical manager relies on a number of regular reports and publications for this type of information. From these information sources he or she shapes a set of assumptions about the future that provide a basis for setting objectives and for the development of plans and programs. Among the most obvious sources of information are sales representatives, customers, distributors, trade associations, universities, government publications, the general business press, management associations, trade journals, professional publications, management consultants, and other managers within the firm.[24]

Buyers and sellers must understand the environment within which they operate, and must communicate with each other so that they can monitor, adapt to, and develop strategies to meet environmental change that impacts either or both the buying and selling organizations. Many firms are beginning to employ environmental scanners because of constant changes in their external environments. An **environmental scanner** is defined as a person who collects, studies, and analyzes data on the company's external environments. This person monitors changes in the economic environment, the physical environment, the competitive environment, the technological environment, the legal-political environment, and the ethical environment.

The Economic Environment

This environment includes factors both at home and abroad, along with variables which determine the income and wealth-generating ability of the economy. Because of the derived nature of demand, few business buyers and sellers are immune to its effects. The dangers of derived demand for suppliers when final consumers' demand for a product produced by these suppliers' customers begins to decline must be understood and monitored. For example, Uniroyal, which has the smallest sales volume of the five largest U.S. tire makers, was hit hard by the energy crisis of the early 1980s. The fact that people were driving less, resulting in less wear on their tires, and the introduction of the 40,000-mile radial tire caused Uniroyal's sales to decrease markedly. Top management decided to eliminate its weakest plants and to concentrate on its more profitable specialty chemical businesses.[25]

The Physical Environment

This environment contains not only the geographic and raw material characteristics of the country or region of the country where the firm operates but also the political stability of the country within the international en-

---

[24]Frederick E. Webster, Jr., *Industrial Marketing Strategy,* 2d ed. (New York: Ronald Press, 1984), p. 294.

[25]M. Casey, "Tire Makers Survive Radial Changeover, Energy Crisis," *Houston Chronicle,* April 15, 1984, p. 16.

vironment, and its location and transportation infrastructure. As transportation costs increase, buyers will generally prefer suppliers whose mining, manufacturing, and storage facilities are nearby.[26]

The Competitive Environment

All other sellers who are competing for the patronage of the same buyer are included in this environment. Many firms find themselves in intensely competitive industries, where astute responses to competitive pressures are critical for such firms to maintain and/or improve their market positions. For example, in 1985 GTE's Sylvania Division built a computer data base which can constantly monitor activities of 51 competitors. The Management Information of Competitor Strategies (MICS) supplements information from filings of the Securities and Exchange Commission and articles found in industry publications with assessments and reports made by GTE's field staff.[27] Additionally, some smaller firms remain viable in highly competitive markets by creating a unique product offering. For example, Steiger Tractor Company has netted sales well over $100 million by manufacturing a large articulated tractor. The articulated tractor differs from most farm tractors in that it has four-wheel traction for handling larger loads, and bends in the middle for easier and smoother turning. Farmers can reduce their labor costs by as much as 33 percent per acre by using such a product.

Both domestic and global actions of competitors can greatly affect the firm's selection of target markets, product mix, distributors, and even the overall marketing strategy. For several years now, as productivity has been declining and labor costs have been rising, U.S. businesses have been losing market share to foreign rivals both at home and abroad.[28] For example, to compete in the world's largest automobile market, Mazda Motor Corporation has invested millions of dollars to modernize Ford's idled plant in Fort Rock, Michigan. Along with Toyota, Nissan, and Honda, Mazda (the fourth largest Japanese automobile maker) is now building compact cars in the United States.[29]

The Technological Environment

This particular environment consists of the application of science to develop new ways of doing various tasks. For instance, IBM, GTE, and Corning Glass are developing superconductors which will reduce the size of the quickest computers to no more than that of a shoebox, and will

---

[26]Niran Vyas and Arch G. Woodside, "An Inductive Model of Industrial Supplier Choice Processes," *Journal of Marketing* 48 (Winter 1984), pp. 30–45.

[27]"Intelligence Update," a newsletter published by Information Data Search, Inc., Cambridge, Mass.

[28]"Drastic New Strategies to Keep U.S. Multinationals Competitive," *Business Week,* October 8, 1984, pp. 168–76.

[29]"Mazda to Build Compact Cars in U.S., Following Other Japanese Auto Firms," *The Wall Street Journal,* November 30, 1984, p. 2.

BUSINESS TO BUSINESS MARKETING IN ACTION

Tech-Type Buyers Are Needed to Keep the Lid on Inflation

The only way to keep inflation under control for keeps is to assure that buyers understand the basic technologies of what they're buying. Otherwise, says Wayne C. Evans, they can't say "no" to opportunistic price hikes—and they can't help suppliers get "yes" answers on usable ideas presented to in-house technical people.

"That doesn't mean converting liberal arts or business graduates into engineers," says Evans, an industrial engineer who is director of purchasing for the Homelite division of Textron in Gastonia, N.C. "But they should be able to talk the language of those they're dealing with in design, manufacturing, quality, and vendor firms.

"They should be able to look at prints and relate them to the specifications," Evans continues. "It's especially important as far as tolerances are concerned, because new types of equipment are making it possible to achieve new tolerances—often at lower costs. As a bare minimum, buyers must be able to understand what is critical, and what is less so."

Hit the books again. Local schools and colleges often offer evening courses that will beef up buyers' technical know-how, Evans points out. He currently has three buyers taking what he calls "engineering-oriented" night courses at nearby institutions.

Moreover, this training is supplemented by in-house education. Every other Monday morning, the first hour of the work day is set aside for a group get-together of the 20-person purchasing staff. Evans himself leads some sessions, but he also schedules presentations by execs from design, manufacturing, quality control, etc.

"If nothing else, we go over systems and documentation," says Evans, "and at least every quarter we have critiques and exams."

Common language helps. According to Evans, it's the "exchange of information" that's a vital part of purchasing's mission, and the department can truly live up to it only when buyers talk the common language of specifiers and suppliers.

"Every one of my buyers," he says, "is on either a new product team, or a product improvement team. The other team members come from design engineering and manufacturing engineering. The directors of the other departments and I make the assignments from our staffs so that no team gets overloaded."

Under the team arrangement, the buyer's job is supplier communication, and vendors' technical contributions—especially early in the design process—go a long way toward cutting costs and saving time.

continued

"We know we won't design ourselves into a corner," says Evans, "if the supplier who's going to make a part gets a chance to comment on the specs. Make-or-buy studies, also, are more accurate when buyers and everyone else on a team understand the manufacturing processes."

In addition, says Evans, the early involvement of suppliers, brought in by technically competent buyers, can trim literally "months" off new product development times. This is especially important to a company such as Homelite, which has introduced 28 new products in the past year." If you don't hit the 'window,' you miss the season."

Saying 'no' to inflation. By the same token, he stresses, it takes a buyer who knows what he's talking about—in technical as well as economic terms—to deny unrealistic supplier demands for price increases.

"The inflationary pressures are already building," he says. "We're seeing it in some of the basic raw materials that are the drivers for fabricated goods: petroleum, resins, copper, and aluminum. For some producers, the very first sign of an upturn in business means it's time for a price increase."

As Evans sees it, the problem stems from too much emphasis on short-term bottom line results. Also alarming is the fact that the push for price hikes is in some cases accompanied by a fall-off in quality, as vendors seek to "ship everything they can sell."

The only way to keep all aspects of inflation down for the count, Evans concludes, is for buyers to stand fast against price increases and be equally tough about quality miscues. Perhaps, in some cases, cooperative value analysis work with suppliers can lower their costs and enhance their reliability. But a technically minded buyer still has to be the catalyst for such cures," he says.

SOURCE: Somerby Dowst, in *Purchasing,* September 10, 1988, p. 43.

---

enable trains to travel smoothly and comfortably at a speed of 300 miles per hour.[30] High technology, with the resulting **knowledge explosion,** has presented buyers and sellers with different sets of marketing problems and deserves special attention. Significant new developments in manufacturing technology have the potential for altering buyer-seller relationships. The increase in the number of high-tech marketing articles and entire issues offered by the more traditional business press, such as *Business Marketing, The Wall Street Journal,* the *New York Times,* to name but a few, serve to illustrate this point.

High technology represents a whole new arena for marketing theories, practices, and research. The requirement of a technical background for

---

[30]Anthony Ramirez, "Superconductors Get into Business," *Fortune,* June 22, 1987, pp. 114–18.

sales and buying personnel has been especially noted in such areas as bio-technology, electronics, medical instrumentation, ceramics, and robotics. As discussed in the "Business to Business Marketing in Action" box, buyers in the types of areas just cited must have the required technical training not only to understand the technologies of what they are buying but also to talk the language of those with whom they are dealing, and to keep inflation under control by being able to say no to opportunistic price increases. Researchers in one particular survey found that the typical educational background of a robotics' salesperson included an engineering degree. Some 77 percent of robotics' executives interviewed indicated that an engineering degree was required for selection to their respective sales forces.[31] This focus on a technical background rather than one in business or marketing (or a combination of the two) has potential implications for the buyer-seller relationship that are of much concern to those in the business-to-business sector.

The Legal-Political Environment

Included in this environment are the rules and regulations society has imposed on business firms and the political interest groups that affect the environment. Additionally, the environment includes international trade restrictions, government attitudes toward business and social activities, and government funding of selected programs.

Buyers and sellers are regulated by agencies responsible for protecting businesses, consumers, and other interests in society from unrestrained business behavior. The dictates of agencies, such as the Food and Drug Administration, the Federal Trade Commission, the Environmental Protection Agency, and the Federal Communications Commission must be adhered to by both buyers and sellers in the development of their products and overall marketing strategies.

Manufacturers must carefully consider product safety and ecological impact in the design of products and the location of plants, or face the same situation as Aerojet General. So far Aerojet General has spent more than $20 million in attempting to clean up its environmental pollution. TCE, a cancer-causing chemical used by Aerojet in the manufacture of rockets, was discovered in the groundwater underneath its California plant—a plant which has been called California's worst toxic-waste site.[32]

The Ethical Environment

The norms or moral behavior society imposes on business and marketers comprise the ethical environment. As key links between their organizations and their customers, business to business salespeople encounter sit-

---

[31]William L. Shanklin and John K. Ryans, Jr., *Essentials of Marketing High Technology* (Lexington, Mass.: Lexington Books, 1984), p. 100.

[32]Bruce Ingersoll, "SEC Begins Inquiry of General Dynamics' Disclosure of Cost Overruns to Submarines," *The Wall Street Journal,* October 3, 1984, p. 16.

uations which might lead to ethical conflict. Chapter 15 will take up in detail additional ethical problems within business to business marketing management.

■ SOCIAL, LEGAL, AND ETHICAL CONSIDERATIONS

Ethics can be thought of as the principles of conduct governing an individual or a professional group. Through contracts and dealings with vendors, purchasing managers are custodians of their company's reputation for courtesy and fair dealing. The ultimate act of selecting a vendor and awarding an order is essentially an act of patronage. Thus a high ethical standard is essential.

There are seven types of ethical improprieties in purchasing: commonly recognized practices, sharp practices, reciprocity, competitive bidding, negotiations, acceptance of presale technical services and samples, and vendor relationships.[33]

Commonly Recognized Practices   Gifts and kickbacks should not be offered, nor should buyers purchase from family members since, in such circumstances, a buyer's loyalty can be misdirected. Likewise, buying from, or selling to, a firm in which the buyer is an owner or part owner can create conflicts of interest.

Sharp Practices   The term **sharp practices** is typically thought of as engaging in evasion and indirect misrepresentation. In today's buying and selling environment, which is based on mutual confidence and integrity, such practices are frowned upon just as severely by the buyers themselves as by the sales organizations with which they deal. It is a sharp practice if, for example, a large number of bids are solicited in the hope that the buyer will be able to take advantage of a quotation error. It is a sharp practice to attempt to influence a seller by leaving copies of bids or other confidential correspondence, where a seller can see them.

Reciprocity   **Reciprocity** occurs when a buyer gives preference to a supplier who is also a customer, and makes good business sense when important factors such as price and service are equal. In general, reciprocity is found in industries where products are homogeneous and/or where there is not a high degree of price sensitivity. Industries such as chemicals, paints, and transportation are most affected by reciprocity practices. For example, General Motors purchases transmissions from Borg-Warner, and Borg-Warner buys automobiles and trucks from GM. It must be kept in mind, however, that the practice can be judged as illegal should the courts determine that restraint of trade is involved.

Competitive Bidding   In **competitive bidding** there is a fundamental implication that the low bidder will receive the order. However, this does not

---

[33]See Robert I. Felch, "Proprieties and Ethics in Purchasing Management," *Guide to Purchasing* 4.7 (Oradell, N.J.: National Association of Purchasing Management, 1986), pp. 3–8.

always happen. If a firm contemplates awarding a bid for reasons other than low price, it should announce that such is the case in the solicitation, and alert all suppliers that other factors will also be determinants in the selection process.

Acceptance of Presale Technical Service and Samples   A question of ethics frequently raised is the proprietary interest of a supplier who does valuable and extensive preliminary engineering services that produced a design or product adapted to the buyer's need. Is the buyer justified in sending out blueprints of such designs, product samples, or formula specifications for competitive bids, or does the supplier who originated them have a continuing claim upon the business?[34] When an offsetting order is not forthcoming, the seller might feel that the buyer has taken an unfair advantage. This seeming breach of faith on the part of the buyer can cause bad buyer/seller relationships.

Vendor Relationships   Improprieties buyers should avoid when dealing with vendors on a day-to-day basis include (1) keeping a seller waiting for a protracted period of time if the sales interview is to be denied; (2) not seeing to it that samples received are given a prompt and fair test; and (3) neglecting to give the seller a report on the test with an indication of the buyer's possible use of the product. The regular use of courtesy and consideration by purchasing personnel can influence the effectiveness of their relationships with vendors.[35]

Concept Questions

1. What is the major purpose of environmental analysis?
2. Why are some business firms now employing environmental scanners?
3. What are the seven types of ethical improprieties in purchasing?

SUMMARY

1. Marketers are increasingly confronted today by a well-educated, more sophisticated purchasing executive. In light of the strong competition present within the business to business sector, marketers need to make every effort to learn as much about their customers as possible. Buyer profiles are very useful in this endeavor and enable the marketer to tailor strategy to particular buyers and markets more easily and effectively.

2. The buying environment is influenced by budget, cost, and profit considerations, and usually involves many people in the decision process. There is much interaction among these individuals, who have many

---

[34]Heinritz et al., p. 388.

[35]Victor P. Gravereau and Leonard J. Konopa, "Activities of Salesmen Toward Industrial Buyers and Purchasing Policies," *Journal of Purchasing Management* (August 1970), pp. 28–29.

different immediate goals. Buyer behavior models provide a useful method of identifying factors that influence the buying decision process. Three organizational buying models are offered as tools for the marketer in designing and developing appropriate marketing strategies.

3. In developing marketing strategy, both existing and potential suppliers should be aware of buyers' decision strategies in reducing uncertainty, and of how such plans affect the choice of suppliers. Purchasing personnel will often develop a rank-ordered list of desired supplier attributes so as to facilitate comparisons among competing vendors.

4. Use of suppliers with whom the buyer has had no previous experience requires some initial work by the buyer. This includes analysis of potential vendors' financial position, visits to prospective suppliers' plants, analysis of possible vendors' geographic locations, and study of the production capabilities of various potential suppliers.

5. As part of its economic function, purchasing has a responsibility through its delegated authority from top management to evaluate both potential and present vendors through all phases of the procurement cycle. Three models of vendor evaluation are presented.

6. Salespeople must recognize the existence of environmental forces which can have an impact upon the buying decision. Environmental scanners are being employed to collect and study data on economic, physical, competitive, technological, legal-political, and ethical environments that affect the firm's decision-making process. Education, intuition, and the seller's assistance can indeed help the buyer surmount some different obstacles identified by the environmental scanning process.

7. Social, legal, and ethical implications of how both buyers and sellers conduct themselves on the job are essential to the initiation, fostering, and maintenance of good buyer-seller relationships. Potential ethical improprieties should be recognized and avoided in a buyer-seller relationship.

KEY TERMS

categorical plan

competitive bidding

cost-ratio plan

environmental analysis

environmental scanner

ethics

knowledge explosion

marketing environment

multiple sourcing

play the odds

reciprocity

sharp practices

total cost of buying

vendor rating systems

weighted-point plan

REVIEW QUESTIONS

1. Describe the typical purchasing professional. In what areas of the purchasing executive's job have the major changes occurred?

2. Distinguish among three different models of business buyer behavior. What are the major features of each model? Try to take the best features of each model and integrate them into one of your own. What are the major difficulties you encountered in so doing?

3. Identify three methods by which buyers attempt to minimize or avoid risk in selecting suppliers. How can personal and professional goals of organizational buyers create conflict for the marketer?

4. Discuss the four basic sources of input purchasing managers frequently utilize in evaluating vendors with whom they have had no previous experience.

5. Why is the evaluation of vendor performance referred to as an economic function? Identify the major features of the categorical, weighted-point, and cost-ratio plans of vendor evaluation.

6. What is the role of an environmental scanner in marketing? Identify and briefly explain the significance of each of the six major external environments for the marketer.

7. Discuss five areas of social, legal, and ethical concern for purchasing executives. Why is the ultimate act of selecting a vendor and awarding an order essentially an act of patronage?

CHAPTER CASES

Case 4–1   Howell Chuck Company*

The Howell Chuck Company is a manufacturer of chucks and similar accessories for original machine-tool equipment and replacement purposes. Approximately 500 employees work for the company. The purchasing department consists of the purchasing agent, who also functions as treasurer, two buyers, and two clerical employees. Inventory records for raw materials and stores items are maintained in the purchasing department.

The purchasing agent and two buyers make all financial decisions about sources of supply, although heads of operating departments are permitted to recommend suppliers, and the buyers often follow their recommendations. All salespersons are interviewed in the purchasing department. Where the situation seems to warrant it, the buyers arrange for the head of a department to interview a salesperson.

Over the years the Howell Chuck Company has developed and followed a policy of loyalty to established suppliers. The experience of the company during periods of short supply convinced the purchasing agent of the wis-

*Gary J. Zenz, *Purchasing and Management of Materials*, 5th ed., 1981, John Wiley and Sons.

dom of this policy. On many occasions the agent was able to secure deliveries of items that competing firms had difficulty in securing because they had patronized many suppliers. The purchasing agent felt so strongly on this point that the buyers were instructed not to shift from an established supplier unless a price differential of more than 10 percent existed. If products were defective or unsatisfactory, the agent would notify a supplier that the company was on probation. If no additional problem shipments were received during the next six-month period, the supplier was retained. If a second unsatisfactory shipment was received, the supplier was called in for an interview before a drop decision was made.

During May a requisition was received from the supervisor of the heat-treatment department for a new welding outfit. The requisition recommended the make and model, which was priced at $36,000. The proposed supplier was a recognized firm in the field, although the company had not previously bought from it. The company bought similar equipment from Ace Welding Company, a local firm with which it had dealt for more than 20 years. The proposed supplier did not sell the gas used by the welding equipment, but such gas was available from five local suppliers, including the Ace Welding Company.

The buyer who was processing the requisition called in the supervisor of the heat-treatment department and asked why the new supplier was recommended. According to the supervisor, an inspection of the new equipment and discussions with the salesperson convinced him that the equipment of the proposed supplier was clearly superior to that sold by Ace Welding Company. The new equipment sold for $3,000 less than the equipment available from the old supplier. During the discussion it developed that the new salesperson had gone to the heat-treatment department supervisor without the consent of the purchasing department.

The purchasing agent had never made visits to supplier plants, but had recently decided to change that policy. After discussion with his buyers, he had prepared a policy statement to govern plant visitations. Pertinent excerpts from this statement are quoted:

1. Visits shall be made only to suppliers who receive orders totaling more than $20,000 annually.
2. Usually each supplier should be visited annually.
3. Supplier visits should be made by purchasing department personnel only.
4. Potential suppliers shall only be visited if the proposed volume of purchases exceeds $20,000 annually.
5. Initial contact for a plant visit shall be made through the supplier's plant representative.
6. No undue entertainment or favors shall be accepted by purchasing personnel during a plant visit.

Questions

1. What should the buyer do about the requisition for the welding equipment?

2. Should steps be taken to prevent direct contact of salespersons and operating personnel within the company?

3. Is the Howell Chuck Company policy with respect to supplier loyalty sound?

4. Evaluate the proposed policies dealing with plant visitations.

Case 4–2   Roberts Fiber Products Company*

The Roberts Fiber Product Company operates 20 plants throughout the Midwest. The company manufactures fiberboard, and in some plant locations also manufactures corrugated paper containers. Management is decentralized, each plant being under a vice president in charge of manufacturing. Mr. Ward, purchasing agent for the plant in Capitol City, reports directly to the vice president in charge of manufacturing.

Mr. Ward's most important responsibility is the purchase of straw and wastepaper, the two principal raw materials used by the plant. In purchasing these commodities he is guided largely by market prices published in trade papers in the two fields. Mr. Ward also processes all purchase requisitions involving expenditures in excess of $250.

Reporting to Mr. Ward are Mr. Bond, inventory and control clerk, and four clerical employees. Mr. Bond is authorized to purchase items not exceeding the $250 limitation. It is also his responsibility to requisition materials and parts on which he maintains inventory-control cards. It is left to his discretion to determine the reorder point.

As insurance against plant shutdowns and slowdowns in the plant, the company maintains an inventory of replacement parts and fittings for its machinery and equipment. Each replacement part is tagged as it is received with such information as the part number and the supplier's identification. When a part is issued from stock, Mr. Bond is expected to make an entry on the tag, which is removed, noting the date and the equipment for which it is being used. He is then required to forward the tag, along with a requisition for replacement, to the purchasing agent.

Stock items may be requisitioned by any employee, and the requisition is then sent to the purchasing agent for processing. Requisitions involving purchases in excess of $10,000 are treated as capital expenditures. Requisitions for capital expenditures can be initiated only by the purchasing agent, the plant manager, or the plant superintendent and must be approved by the vice president. All such requisitions must be accompanied by a form showing the estimated costs, the reasons for the expenditures, the annual savings anticipated, and the proposed disposition of any old machinery or equipment.

A recent purchase of forklift trucks illustrates the procedure of the purchasing agent, Mr. Ward, with respect to the selection of a supplier for such items. The plant superintendent initiated the approved requisition. Mr.

---

*Gary J. Zenz, *Purchasing and Management of Materials*, 5th ed., 1981, John Wiley and Sons.

Ward then visited several fiberboard plants to determine the types of trucks they were using. He next arranged for three suppliers to send in demonstrator models so that his workers could try them. His choice of supplier was based largely on the preference expressed by the workers who used the forklift trucks.

Mr. Ward says that he likes to keep paperwork to a minimum because of the small size of the purchasing department. The two most frequently used forms are the purchase-order requisition and the purchase-order form. The requisition form has space for identifying the item, quantity desired, the department initiating the requisition, the purpose for which the item will be used, and the date by which the item is required. The individual initiating the requisition fills in all this information. There is also a space on the requisition for the purchasing agent to fill in the name of the supplier, the purchase-order number, the price, terms of sale, and shipping information.

The purchase order is typed in triplicate by one of the clerical employees from the requisition form. One copy is sent to the supplier, one to the receiving department, and one is kept for the purchasing department files.

A postcard is used when follow-up of an order is indicated. The printed card contains a simple request for information as to the expected shipment date of an order, which is identified by purchase-order number.

A special form is used when a fixed asset is being requested. This form is called the *fixed-asset expenditure recommendation*. In addition to identifying the asset and its proposed plant location, the form provides a space for the description of an item, reasons for making the acquisition, estimated costs, detailed information about any assets to be retired because of the purchase, and the recommended supplier.

Questions

1. Evaluate the purchasing procedures used by the company. Would you suggest any changes in procedures?
2. Evaluate the procedure followed by Mr. Ward in selecting the supplier of forklift trucks.
3. Can the follow-up procedure of this company be improved?
4. Should the company make use of the fixed-asset expenditure recommendation form for all purchases of fixed assets?

SUGGESTED READINGS

Bates, Bryan. "Buying-Decision Research: A Case." *Industrial Marketing Digest* (UK) 11 (Third quarter 1986), pp. 107–16. Survey of European buyers focusing on supplier characteristics, quality, service, delivery, and price.

Carusone, Peter S. "Buying Extractive Products: Criteria and Influences." *Journal of Purchasing and Materials Management* 21 (Winter 1985), pp. 28–36. Survey of purchasing behavior, decision processes, buying constraints, environmental considerations, and marketing strategy formulation of purchasers of natural resources.

Dale, B. G., and R. H. Powley. "Purchasing Practices in the United Kingdom: A Case Study." *Journal of Purchasing and Materials Management* 21 (Spring

purchasing function, materials management, and performance management between the United Kingdom and the United States.

Dillon, Thomas F. "Vendor-Rating System Boosts On-Time Delivery." *Purchasing World* 30 (July 1986), pp. 62–64. Case study of a vendor performance record related to delivery service.

Farmer, John Haywood, and Michiel R. Leenders. "Psychological Need Profile of Purchasers." *Journal of Purchasing and Materials Management* 22 (Winter 1986), pp. 23–29. Survey of purchases, high-level and low-level needs, negotiations, and purchasing behavior trends among business to business buyers.

Grassell, Milt. "What Purchasing Managers Like in a Salesperson . . . and What Drives Them up the Wall." *Business Marketing* 71 (June 1986), pp. 72–77. Survey of purchasing managers' perceptions of both positive and negative attributes exhibited by business to business sales representatives.

Gregory, Robert E. "Source Selection: A Matrix Approach." *Journal of Purchasing and Materials Management* 22 (Summer 1986), pp. 24–29. Case study of Texas Instruments' approach to supplier evaluation and selection.

Jackson, Ralph W., and William M. Pride. "The Use of Approved Vendor Lists." *Industrial Marketing Management* 15 (August 1986), pp. 165–69. Vendor analysis and background checks of various-sized firms in five industries.

Krapfel, Robert E., Jr. "An Advocacy Behavior Model of Organizational Buyers' Vendor Choice." *Journal of Marketing* 49 (October 1985), pp. 51–59. An experiment using a causal model to explain information diffusion, attributed source credibility, and source factors.

Meredith, Lindsay. "Developing and Using a Customer Profile Data Bank." *Industrial Marketing Management* 14 (November 1985), pp. 255–68. Discussion of the decision-making task, daily sales decisions, buyer mix analysis, and on-line information systems.

Shealy, Robert. "The Purchasing Job in Different Types of Businesses." *Journal of Purchasing and Materials Management* 21 (Winter 1985), pp. 17–20. Survey of job task similarities among business to business buyers in various types of manufacturing concerns and service specialties.

Cases for Part Two

CASE 1: Templeton Engine Company

The Templeton Engine company, located in eastern Wisconsin, was a major producer of aircraft jet engines. On December 15, 1984, Dave Giltner, Sales Manager for Precision Cutting Tools, called Neil Carlson, a purchasing supervisor for Templeton, to tell him that Precision planned to increase its prices 6 percent across the board on February 15. When he replaced the telephone, Neil wondered how to respond to this news in view of Templeton's plan to reemphasize its cost reduction program in January.

■ THE COMPANY

The Templeton Engine Company produced turbo-jet and turbo-prop engines for use on small- and medium-sized jet aircraft. It did not compete in the commercial jet engine market, although it did produce smaller engines used to power auxiliary equipment on commercial airliners. Templeton's sales totaled approximately $1 billion per year, divided roughly 80–20 among private and governmental purchasers. The firm employed 6,200 people, including approximately 50 professionals in the purchasing department. Because of the technical character of its products, over the years the company developed a strong engineering orientation which pervaded all aspects of its operations.

■ PURCHASING ACTIVITIES

Templeton spent approximately $600 million a year for materials, most of which were used in producing its finished products. All buying activities were based on material specifications generated in the firm's various design engineering department. As a general rule, technical factors were the controlling considerations in specification development.

When considering potential new suppliers for major purchases, the purchasing department coordinated an extremely

This case was written by Donald Dobler during the Case Writing in Purchasing Workshop. Copyright © 1984, The National Association of Purchasing Management, Inc., P.O. Box 22160, Tempe, Arizona. Reprinted by permission.

thorough investigation of the operations and capabilities of each firm reviewed. In addition to an investigation of the normal commercial and service considerations, personnel from Templeton's quality-assurance and manufacturing-engineering departments carefully analyzed each vendor's production and quality-control operations. The objective was to evaluate both effectiveness and efficiency, as well as compatibility with Templeton's requirements. After selection, when a supplier proved its ability to meet the buyer's requirements consistently, Templeton frequently utilized a vendor certification program that allowed the supplier to perform a great deal of its own part's inspection and acceptance.

Templeton's buyers used both competitive bidding and negotiation techniques in determining price, depending on the prevailing buying and market conditions. Since some of Templeton's products were sold to federal agencies, buyers must follow government regulation, which stipulated the use of competitive bidding and negotiation, and set the guidelines for its use. The Defense Contract Audit Agency periodically audits such purchases to ensure compliance. Once a vendor was selected, however, buyers frequently negotiated numerous contract details and service arrangements with the vendor.

An additional complication faced by some buyers stemmed from a Federal Aviation Agency (FAA) requirement. Each of Templeton's products and related components produced by specific suppliers had to be tested and certified initially by the FAA. Whenever a new supplier for such a part was used, Templeton was required to subject the new item to a rigorous and costly 150-hour operating test. Hence, buyers did not change suppliers without considerable analysis and effort to rectify problems with existing suppliers.

Like many major firms, over the years Templeton's purchasing philosophy evolved to view suppliers as partners that, in reality, functioned as extensions of its own production operations. Thus, while buyers evaluated a supplier's performance rigorously, they worked closely with the supplier to optimize the benefit of the relationship for both organizations. When it was advantageous, buyers liked to utilize long-term contracts—often up to three years in duration—to assure compliance with quality and pricing objectives. As a rule, Templeton's buyers had responsibility for the full range of activities involved in their respective transactions—everything from market research to expediting.

■ COST AND QUALITY

For obvious reasons, quality requirements in the jet engine industry were stringent and extremely important. No producer of shoddy work survived for long. At the same time, however, competition among major producers had become increasingly intense. Consequently, the incentives to keep costs down were substantial. For this reason, buyers at Templeton diligently sought out potential opportunities to reduce material costs without jeopardizing quality. The company, in fact, was currently in the process of reemphasizing its corporate-wide cost reduction program.

THE PURCHASE OF TOOLING

The Templeton manufacturing organization used approximately $1 million in tooling each year. Because of the tight tolerances required in the manufacturing process, tooling that performed with precision and reliability was essential.

The special tooling supplied by Precision Cutting Tools was a major dollar item for Templeton. In addition, after extensive testing, Templeton's design engineers specified the Precision organization as a sole-source supplier.

As Neil Carlson pondered the pending 6 percent price increase on Precision's special tooling, he was acutely aware that he had less than 60 days to resolve the problem.

CASE 2: City of Brookings: Marketing to the Local Government Market

BACKGROUND

Brookings, California, a suburb of a major city in northern California, has a population of over 100,000. The city has been incorporated for over 10 years and has grown substantially during the 1980s. City management has evolved in a smooth fashion during this time, and its departmentalization is typical of most cities of its size. The local government of Brookings is much like that found in other towns of the same size in the state.

It has come to the attention of Lars Bloomquist, the city's street maintenance supervisor, that to keep in contact with an ever increasing field staff, an updated communications system is needed. The present system cannot adequately serve the communication needs of his growing department. Simply stated, Bloomquist needs a system that enables him to contact all field staff as well as providing a way for field staff to contact the department office if the need arises. The present system does not have this capability.

Bloomquist's department includes 60 field maintenance operators, all of whom need their own communications devices. In addition, 23 vehicles in the city's maintenance fleet require installation of two-way radios. Some type of base station is also needed.

Case contributed by Steven Turtletaub, Graduate Assistant, San Diego State University.

The design of a two-way communications system is a highly sophisticated and complex task. The two-way communications industry is extremely competitive, and there are a large number of suppliers from which to choose.

Lars Bloomquist has requested a meeting with Milo Bates, the city communications officer. He wants to discuss with Bates the needs of the street maintenance department. After extensive discussion, Bates, who is presently bogged down in the development of the communication system for the city's department of emergency services, agrees that something must be done to enhance the inadequacy of the maintenance system.

The system presently used by the maintenance department is an older Mason Electronics system that the city had purchased years before from the neighboring suburb of Clayton. The transaction took place when Clayton purchased a new system and sold the old one to Brookings. The system was adequate at the time, but with Brookings's rapid growth, the city had simply outgrown it. Before working for the city of Brookings, Bates had worked for Mason Electronics, and he still has a number of contacts in that firm. He suggests to Bloomquist that they contact Mason and conduct some fact findings before proceeding. Bates considers telephoning Rodney Slinger, his former boss at Mason. He tells Bloomquist that Slinger, who has been promoted to Mason's senior sales engineer, is likely to be willing to meet with them.

Before meeting with Slinger, Bloomquist and Bates meet and develop a list of questions that they want to have answered. They hope that Slinger's answers to these questions will aid them in their decisions. Some of the major questions are as follows:

1. Can the city keep the equipment now in service and simply add on to the existing system?
2. If adding on is possible, what will be the cost to bring the system up to the city's requirements?
3. What are the expansion possibilities of any such add-on system?
4. How long will it take to build an add-on system once a contract is awarded?
5. If adding on is not feasible, what is the cost of a new system to meet the city's needs?
6. What are the expansion possibilities of any new system?
7. What lead time is involved with a new system?
8. What, if any, personnel requirements are required by either system?
9. If additional personnel are needed, what salary requirements may be involved?
10. Will training programs be involved with either system?

With the development of these questions, Bates telephones Slinger to arrange a meeting.

■ THE TELEPHONE CALL

Milo Bates places a call to Rodney Slinger at Mason Electronics.

"Hello Rod, this is Milo Bates."

"Hello Milo, how is life in the municipal sector treating you?"

"Well Rod, it is never boring. The reason I am calling you is that our maintenance department is considering an overhaul of their two-way system. I would like your input, if that is possible. Please understand that we are just in the initial stages—all we are doing right now is fact finding."

"That sounds good. Let's meet for lunch if you would like." As he spoke, Rod Slinger was calling up the city of Brookings's listing on his computer database. "Is Lars Bloomquist still with the department?"

"Yes he is."

"Good. I think it would be a good idea for him to be at the meeting. Would next Wednesday at 11:30 be good for the two of you?"

"It is fine with me, but I will have to check with Bloomquist and get back to you."

"OK Milo, I'll talk to you soon. Take care."

"Good-bye."

Milo hangs up the phone and calls Lars Bloomquist to set up the appointment.

■ THE LUNCHEON MEETING

At the Wednesday meeting, it becomes apparent to Lars Bloomquist that there is no feasible way for Mason Electronics to expand the current system. Slinger states that the cost of expanding is so close to the cost of buying a totally new system that there is little justification to updating the old one. By the end of the meeting, Lars Bloomquist is ready to begin preparing a proposal for a new communications system.

■ THE DELAY

Three weeks pass since the fact-finding luncheon with Slinger, and no real progress takes place on the development of a proposal despite Bloomquist's good intentions. Bates has been very involved in a battle between the emergency services department and city hall in regard to updating the communications system for fire and paramedic units. Thus, he has not had time for the maintenance department's problems. Bloomquist too has been busy. Severe winter storms have kept him occupied, even though the lack of an adequate communications system consistently hampers road repairs. When Slinger telephones Bloomquist to inquire about progress of the proposal, he is told that the project has been put on the back burner due to more pressing concerns.

With the delay, Lars Bloomquist feels continually frustrated with his inadequate communications system. Two months after the luncheon meeting, he still, however, has not begun to work on the proposal. He decides to call Rodney Slinger.

"Hello Rod. I have been unable to put much thought into development of a system proposal. As you know, this has been an unusually bad winter, and Bates has been embroiled in the emergency services confrontation. We still really do need a new system—it would make my job and everybody else's jobs much easier. We would get roads repaired quicker, and the whole city would benefit."

"I would like to help in any way I can," said Slinger as he listened intently.

Bloomquist continued,"I think you understand our needs. What I would like you to do is write up a complete proposal, specifications, personnel requirements, arguments for a new rather than an add-on system, growth potential, etc."

"Do you also want cost estimates?" Slinger asked.

"Yes, but you need to understand that this will go out to bid."

"Of course. I can begin work on the proposal right away and should have it ready for you in a couple of weeks."

"Thanks Rod, I will look for it. Take care of yourself."

"Good-bye Lars, I will be in touch."

With that, Slinger goes to work on the proposal.

Within two weeks, Bloomquist receives Slinger's finished proposal. This proposal sets specifications around a patented two-way communications system belonging to Mason Electronics. The cost of the equipment alone is $46,000, with an additional $5,000 for installation and training. Bloomquist then submits the proposal to the city's purchasing department for action. He hopes his proposal will start the wheels turning that will provide his department with its badly needed communications system.

■ ·A PROBLEM ARISES

Gail Fenster is the purchasing officer for the city of Brookings. On receiving her copy of the proposal, she is taken by surprise, since the proposal is the first she has heard of the entire situation. After reading the plan thoroughly, she calls Mason Electronics to get more information about the system. One week later, she sends Milo Bates and Lars Bloomquist copies of the interoffice memorandum shown in Exhibit 1.

Two weeks later, Fenster, Bates, and Bloomquist meet in regard to Slinger's proposal. The main problem discussed at the meeting is that although Mason Electronics has always provided the city with quality equipment, the specifications in the proposal are drawn so tightly around the Mason system that competitive bids will be difficult to obtain. There are a number of locally owned communications companies that Fenster believes should have the opportunity to submit bids on the system. She feels strongly about supporting local businesses whenever possible. In addition,

■ **EXHIBIT 1**   Memo from Fenster to Bates and Bloomquist

CITY OF BROOKINGS
Purchasing Department

TO: Milo Bates, Communications Officer
          Lars Bloomquist, Street Maintenance Supervisor

FROM: Gail Fenster, Purchasing Officer

DATE: February 1, 1989

PURCHASING PROCEDURES

The primary function of the Purchasing Department is to assist the City departments in securing supplies, services, and equipment necessary to carry out their duties at the most economical cost.

The staff of the Purchasing Department acts as a liaison between the departments and the vendors and contractors serving them. The duties and responsibilities of the Purchasing Department are carried out in accordance with the legal requirements established in the Brookings Municipal Code and by the general laws of the State of California.

It is my belief that the Maintenance Department has circumvented specific purchasing procedures, believing such avoidance of procedures would facilitate the implementation of a badly needed communications system.

Gentlemen, there are inherent problems with the proposal that has been submitted for the communications system. I suggest a meeting between the Purchasing Officer, Communications Officer, and Street Maintenance Supervisor. Specific problems regarding the ethicality and practicality, along with purchasing procedures, will be the topic of discussion at the meeting.

I suggest you review pages 1–18 of the City purchasing manual and sections 3.28.001–3.28.180 of the Brookings Municipal Code prior to the meeting.

Gail Fenster
Purchasing Officer

---

she claims that Mason bids in the past have been much higher than those of many other competitors.

City regulations require that competitive bids be obtained on any product or service involving over $500. In addition, on items costing over $10,000, formal bidding must take place.

There is general agreement among the three that something has to be done to alleviate the maintenance department's communications problem. They also agree that due to increasing workloads, neither Milo Bates nor Lars Bloomquist has the time to develop a detailed request for proposal. Although Lars knows what his department needs, he does not have the time to research alternatives to the Mason system or to write up the specifications. The following conversation takes place. "Although cost is always a factor," Fenster states, "I feel that if Lars can write up the specific needs of his department, a consultant may be very valuable in this situation."

(Gail Fenster does not like having to hire consultants, but she feels it is justified in this case.) "Do you agree, Milo?"

Bates responds, "A consultant seems to be the quickest way for us to develop an unbiased request for proposal (RFP). I have an excellent list of communications consultants."

"I have an outline," says Bloomquist. "I can have a description of the department's needs to Gail by the end of next week."

"Good," responds Fenster, "you give me your description, and I will put together an RFP for the consultant. Milo, I would appreciate a copy of your list of consultants. That will make my job a lot easier. I have another meeting to go to now. Thanks for your time this morning."

Gail Fenster leaves the room.

"Well Lars, it's in the works. Hopefully, you will have your system in four or five months."

"Great! Just in time for next winter," chuckles Lars.

■ THE RFP IS SENT TO THE CONSULTANTS

Gail Fenster's proposal is 25 pages in length and is mailed to all 30 consultants on Bates's list. The RFP describes the city's purchasing procedures and the general needs of the street maintenance department. In addition, respondents are asked to include (1) prior history of dealing with similar systems and in what capacity they served, (2) sample plans and specifications, (3) a time schedule, (4) costs, (5) a list of employees who will be involved in the project and their backgrounds, and (6) a brochure or written description of the firm giving pertinent information, especially financial. A cost summary sheet is included with the proposal. Respondents are to use this sheet to total all costs. A 30-day time period is set for responses.

Of the 30 consultants on Bates's list, 7 respond within the 30-day time period. Five of the 7 arrive on the last day via overnight mail. The proposals are opened, and proposed consulting fees are read in public from the prepared summary sheets. The purchasing department's secretary keeps track of the bids on a bid summary sheet. Three of the consultants are present at the bid reading and take notes. The bids range in price from $7,000 to $28,000. Total time elapsed in the reading of the bids is seven minutes. After reading the final bid, Gail Fenster states:

"The choice of consultant will be based on qualifications, past performance, and cost of service. The city has a standard consultant agreement that we will use when the selected consultant is hired. We will review all of these proposals and have a decision two weeks from today. Thank you all for attending."

■ A CONSULTANT IS SELECTED

Thirty-five days following the bid opening, the field of seven consultants is narrowed to just two. These finalists are requested to make presentations to the city council. Both Bates and Bloomquist attend the presentations. Two weeks following these presentations, the consulting project is awarded to the consulting division of Amos & Fitch, Inc. This firm has a large division dedicated to consulting for a number of California municipal governments. The contract is awarded for $16,000.

Reporting to Fenster and Bates, the consultant's staff assigned to this project will spend the next 60 days interviewing field and supervisory staff. Interviews at the communications centers of neighboring communities will be carried out to establish a degree of compatibility with their communications systems. In addition, consultant staff will investigate the market and find a range of products, companies, and services from which to choose. The staff will then write a request for proposal, which will be mailed to potential suppliers of the communications system. A bid list of potential suppliers will be obtained from the city's purchasing department, and it will be incorporated into the consultant's own bid list. Notices inviting bids will be placed in local newspapers and journals 15 days prior to the formal bid opening.

As stated earlier, the solicitation of competitive bids is required in the selection process by city charter. Since any system purchases will cost over $10,000, the city council has the authority to execute the bid award.

■ THE BIDDING PROCESS TAKES PLACE

The Amos & Fitch consulting team prepares an 85-page RFP that is mailed to 25 communications companies qualifying under the conditions developed by the consulting firm. Respondents are given 60 days to present their proposals. At that time, all proposals will be opened, and the bid prices will be read publicly.

Twelve of the 25 companies respond with proposals. Only 4 of them send representatives to the bid opening. Of these 4 firms, 3 are from companies based in Brookings. The other is headquartered in the neighboring city of Amherst. Bid prices range from $29,000 to $67,000. These prices include installation and training. Amos & Fitch's consulting team will then take 30 to 45 days to evaluate the proposals, at which time their selection will be presented to the city council for final approval.

By now, almost one year has passed since Bloomquist and Bates first discussed the overhaul of the street maintenance department's communications system. The Brookings City Council awards the contract to Brookings Communications, a locally owned dealer of Standard Communications equipment. The contract price is $31,000. The system will be compatible with the communications system of two nearby suburbs, so that in case of emergency, the three cities can pool their resources. In addition, system expansion is available at a fraction of the cost of any of the other systems considered. Brookings Communications will order the equipment and begin work installing the system.

■ FINAL COMMENTS

Lars Bloomquist stands outside his second-floor office looking out over the mountains to the east. An early winter storm is threatening. Brookings Communications has begun work installing two-way radios in vehicles as planned. The base station, however, will not arrive for another week. Milo Bates is discussing something with the installation supervisor down in the parking lot. Lars turns to watch them. As he puts his hand out over the railing to catch the first few rain drops, Milo Bates turns his head toward the mountains and then up to Lars.

"Maybe we should requisition some umbrellas for the work crews," Milo calls up to Lars.

"Don't you have a friend at K mart who could write up specs for us?" Lars calls back.

"Do you think it is necessary? They say next winter is going to be a dry one," Milo counters.

Questions

1. Compare the purchasing practices of Brookings with those found in private firms. Can you identify similarities and differences?

2. Analyze the buying influences involved in this case. What role does each play in this purchasing situation? Which of the buying influences do you consider to be key buying influences? Explain.

3. The city saved only a few thousand dollars by not using the Mason Electronics system that it could have purchased a year earlier. What do you think the city gained and lost by taking the time to go through such a long and complicated process?

4. If you were Rodney Slinger at Mason Electronics, what would you do if you found out that the contract was awarded to Brookings Communications?

5. In terms of specific points, what has this case taught you about marketing to local government customers?

PART THREE

Identifying the Customer

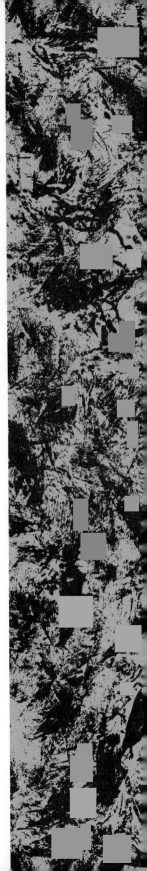

Chapter 5 · Business to Business Marketing
Research and Information Systems

Chapter 6 · Market Segmentation, Positioning, and
Demand Projection

Chapter **5**

Business to Business Marketing Research and Information Systems

LEARNING OBJECTIVES

After reading this chapter, you should be able to:

- Differentiate between business and consumer marketing research.
- Ascertain the major areas in which marketing research is used.
- Identify the similarities and differences between marketing research and a marketing information system (MIS).
- Discuss the steps involved in the marketing research process.
- Recognize when it is appropriate to use either inside or outside marketing research specialists.
- Realize the differences between primary and secondary sources of research data, and become aware of the disadvantages and drawbacks of each.
- Understand the reasons behind the often widely differing organizational designs and staffing needs of research departments.
- Appreciate the role of marketing research in international marketing.

CHAPTER OUTLINE

Differences between Business and
Consumer Marketing Research
  Focus of Marketing Research
Major Tasks of Marketing Research
  Market Potential
  Market-Share Analysis
  Market Characteristics
  Sales Analysis
  Forecasting
  Other Applications
Marketing Research versus a
Marketing Information System
  Five Basic Elements of Future
   Marketing Research Systems
  Primary Uses of the Marketing
   Information System

The Marketing Research Process
  Planning the Research Design
  Preparation
  Field Operations
  Processing
  Tabulation, Analysis, and
   Interpretation
  Reporting
Using Outside or Inside Research
Specialists—Make or Buy?
Developing Information Sources
  Secondary Data Sources
  Primary Data Sources
Organization of Marketing Research
Conducting International Marketing
Research

■ DIFFERENCES BETWEEN BUSINESS AND CONSUMER MARKETING RESEARCH

There are many differences between business and consumer marketing. However, is there a difference between business and consumer marketing research? This question can be answered by looking at the types of marketing research studies conducted, and by comparing the types of research techniques used by consumer companies with those employed by business to business marketers. Table 5–1 presents a summary of such studies and comparisons.

Table 5–1 shows that marketing research is widespread with some important commonalities as well as some significant differences in the types of marketing research activities in both consumer and business to business companies. Consumer goods companies use marketing research in testing products, improving packaging, determining brand attributes and brand personality, improving the efficiency of advertising (both as to content and selected media), measuring the flow of sales, setting sales quotas both for products and for territories, and analyzing distribution costs. Business goods' manufacturers are less remote from their markets, and both their current and their potential customers are fewer and more easily identified

■ **TABLE 5–1**   Research Activities of 798 Companies

Subject of Studies	Percentage of Reporting Companies Doing Easy Type of Research		
	All Reporting Companies	Consumer Product Companies	Business to Business Product Companies
1. Sales and market research			
Market potential measurement	93	97	97
Market characteristics	93	92	97
Market-share analysis	92	96	97
Sales analysis	89	96	97
Establishing sales quotas and territories	75	91	95
Distribution-channel studies	69	86	87
Sales-compensation studies	60	78	79
Test markets, sales audits	54	83	43
Promotional studies	52	73	32
2. Business economics and corporate research			
Business-trends analysis	86	79	97
Short-range forecasting	85	90	98
Long-range forecasting (over one year)	82	87	96
Pricing studies	81	88	93
Plant and warehouse location	71	76	84
Acquisition studies	69	81	47
3. Product research			
Competitive product studies	85	93	95
New product acceptance and potential	84	94	93
Testing existing products	75	95	84
Packaging research	60	83	65
4. Advertising research			
Ad-effectiveness studies	67	85	47
Media research	61	69	43
Copy research	49	76	37
Motivation research	48	67	26
5. Corporate responsibility research			
Legal constraints on advertising and promotion studies	51	64	60
Ecological-impact studies	33	40	52
Social values and policies	40	43	40
Consumers' right-to-know studies	26	32	21

Data reported by 798 companies to the American Marketing Association.

SOURCE: Adapted from Dick W. Twedt, ed., *1978 Survey of Marketing Research* (Chicago: American Marketing Association, 1978), pp. 41, 43.

than those for consumer products. Business to business markets are more sensitive to economic fluctuations, and the marketer has more opportunity to learn buyer preferences on a first-hand basis. When the channel of distribution is shorter, as is the case with most business products, communication becomes easier. For example, a machine tool producer or a specialty steel house has more direct customer contact than does a toothpaste manufacturer such as Procter & Gamble or Colgate-Palmolive.

Focus of Marketing Research

Marketing research focuses less on product attributes than on such questions as what is the potential in different areas and for different products; who makes buying decisions; who are members of the buying center; and which trade journals provide the biggest return per advertising dollar spent. Since this market is generally more sensitive to economic fluctuations than the consumer market, product-line forecasting is correspondingly more important. Business companies use less advertising research than consumer companies, and they rely more on the personal selling aspect of the promotional mix than do consumer firms. Business services of all kinds, such as industrial cleansing services or freight carriers, conduct research on customer wants and needs. A mortgage banker will consider establishing a research department because it might be easier to arrange financing when the borrower's activity has been formally and objectively analyzed. A truck leasing agency, such as Ryder Truck, will consider conducting operating cost research to demonstrate the value of its service to a prospective customer. Another way to compare business with consumer marketing research is to break down the various aspects of the research survey process. Table 5–2 compares the process of business versus consumer research, pointing out some of the more important differences between the two.

Surveys often encounter different problems than those found when conducting consumer research. As such, the survey process is often very different. In Table 5–2 the student will note the special difficulties associated with respondent accessibility and cooperation. These are important differences, given the prevalence of the personal interviewing technique.

■ MAJOR TASKS OF MARKETING RESEARCH

The extent to which companies use marketing research is wide and varied. Below are the major areas where marketing research is conducted.

Market Potential

Research must clarify the maximum total sales and profit potential of product-market opportunities. This clarification will help direct the resources available for new product introduction and product deletion decisions.

■ TABLE 5–2 Consumer versus Business to Business Marketing Research
(What are the differences?)

	Consumer	Business to Business
Universe population	Large. Dependent on category under investigation but usually unlimited. 72.5 million U.S. households and 215 million persons.	Small. Fairly limited in total population and even more so if within a defined industry or SIC category.
Respondent accessibility	Fairly easy. Can interview at home, on the telephone, or using mail techniques.	Difficult. Usually only during working hours at plant, office, or on the road. Respondent is usually preoccupied with other priorities.
Respondent cooperation	Over the years has become more and more difficult, yet millions of consumers have never been interviewed.	A major concern. Due to the small population, the respondent is being over-researched. The purchaser and decision makers in the business firm are the buyers of a variety of products and services from office supplies to heavy equipment.
Sample size	Can usually be drawn as large as required for statistical confidence since the population is in the hundreds of millions.	Usually much smaller than consumer sample, yet the statistical confidence is equal due to the relationship of the sample to the total population.
Respondent definitions	Usually fairly simple. Those aware of a category or brand, users of a category or brand, demographic criteria, etc. The ultimate purchaser is also a user for most consumer products and services.	Somewhat more difficult. The user and the purchasing decision maker in most cases are not the same. Factory workers who use heavy equipment, secretaries who use typewriters, etc., are the users and, no doubt, best able to evaluate these products and services. However, they tend not to be the ultimate purchasers and in many cases do not have any influence on the decision-making process.
Interviewers	Can usually be easily trained. They are also consumers and tend to be somewhat familiar with the area under investigation for most categories.	Difficult to find good executive interviewers. At least a working knowledge of the product class or subject being surveyed is essential. Preferably more than just a working knowledge.
Study costs	Key dictators of cost are sample size and incidence. Lower incidence usage categories (for example, users of soft moist dog food, powdered breakfast beverages, etc.) or demographic or behavioral screening criteria (attend a movie at least once a month, over 65 years of age, and do not have direct deposit of social security payments, etc.,) can up costs considerably.	Relative to consumer research, the critical element resulting in significantly higher per-interview costs are: the lower incidence levels, the difficulties in locating the "right" respondent (that is, the purchase decision maker) and securing cooperation, time, and concentration of effort for the interview itself.

SOURCE: Martin Katz, "Use Same Theory, Skills for Consumer, Industrial Marketing Research," *Marketing News,* January 12, 1979, p. 16.

Market-Share Analysis

Marketing research is assigned the task of determining the ratio of sales revenue of the firm to the total sales revenue of all firms in the industry, including the firm itself. The competitive environment is dynamic, making market-share analysis a regular standard against which to compare the firm's current objectives and future performance.

Market Characteristics

Marketing research helps identify opportunities and set objectives in this area as well. Much of what was studied in Chapters 2, 3, and 4 in terms of buyer behavior, buying organizational changes, and so forth, will be researched and reported on. How successful a firm has been in penetrating particular markets, and more important, why they have or have not been successful, are important pieces of data when setting objectives and direction for the future.

Sales Analysis

Marketing research is also a tool used in controlling marketing programs in which actual sales records are compared with sales goals to identify strengths and weaknesses. Sales analysis, also called **microsales analysis,** traces sales revenue to its sources such as specific products, sales territories, or customers. Common research breakdowns would include the following:

- Customer characteristics: reason for purchase, type of firm, and user versus middleman.
- Product characteristics: model, size, and accessory equipment bought.
- Geographic region: sales territory, city, state, and region.
- Order size.
- Price or discount class.

This analysis helps the marketing manager determine future efforts regarding product profitability, sales territory changes, product deletion decisions, and the like.

Forecasting

Both short-range and long-range forecasting are vital inputs to the marketing planning process. The amount a firm expects to sell during a specific time period under specific conditions and to specific segments affects both the controllable and uncontrollable factors that influence future business. Forecasts form the basis of all planning activity within the organization. The Conference Board has described the importance of sales forecasting in this manner:

The sales forecast is an essential tool of management in any business. Those in charge—the hot dog vendor no less than the members of senior management at General Motors—require some means of gauging the probable direction and level of future sales. Lacking such predictions, there is no realistic starting point for setting the enterprise's course and safeguarding its profits.[1]

Forecasting is critical for cash flow estimates, plant expansions, projected employment levels, decisions regarding product line changes, distribution channel changes, and a host of other decision areas about which the firm must act upon regularly.

Other Applications

In addition to the above, the subjects to which companies apply their marketing research efforts have been studied and reported upon regularly by the American Marketing Association for over thirty years.[2] Additional data researched include studies on sales quotas and territories, pricing, test marketing audits, business trends, new product acceptance, advertising research, and competitive differences. For instance, the "Business to Business Marketing in Action" box describes how a construction company was able to use a marketing research study to position itself as "the contractor of choice" by asking its customers, architects, and designers questions about the worst features of its competitors. Marketing research can certainly be described as a widely diverse marketing function.

■ MARKETING RESEARCH VERSUS A MARKETING INFORMATION SYSTEM

Whereas marketing research is problem- or project-oriented, a **marketing information system** (MIS) combines procedures, hardware, and software. It then accumulates, interprets, and disseminates important data through reports to key marketing decision makers. It is imperative today for every firm to manage and disseminate marketing information as effectively as possible. A marketing information system is a computerized model providing timely, accurate information to improve marketing decisions. It is a set of procedures and methods designed to generate, analyze, and distribute marketing decision-making information on a regular basis to key marketing executives involved in the decision-making process.

An important point to remember about MIS is that it gathers important information from the disciplines of finance, production control, accounting

---

[1]David L. Hurwood, Elliott S. Grossman, and Earl L. Bailey, *Sales Forecasting* (New York: Conference Board, 1988), p. 1.

[2]These studies are conducted at five-year intervals by the American Marketing Association, Chicago, Illinois.

BUSINESS TO BUSINESS MARKETING IN ACTION

Quiz Customers for Clues about Competition

John Grubb wanted to distinguish his San Francisco construction company, Clearwood Building Inc., from a host of competitors. So, in early 1983, he and his brother Robert started talking to Clearwood's customers: the architects and designers who hired their services.

What, the brothers asked their customers, were the worst features of Clearwood's competitors? The answer: Bad manners, workers who tracked dirt across carpets, and beat-up construction trucks, which high-class clients objected to having parked in their driveways.

Those seemingly small points were the signal for a repositioning. The brothers decided to make Clearwood the contractor of choice among the Bay Area's upper crust. The company bought a new truck and kept it spotless. Its estimators donned jackets and ties. And its work crews, now impeccably polite, began rolling protective runners over carpets before they set foot in clients' homes. In less than two years, Clearwood's annual revenue jumped to $1 million from $200,000.

Keeping an eye on the competition, of course, is a vital part of running any business. But the way it is done is changing, particularly for small businesses. Increasingly, business owners are strengthening their ties to customers in the hope of gaining insights about competitors that they can turn to their advantage. "It's the difference between acquaintance and commitment," Robert Grubb says of the stronger links being forged.

The strategy of drawing closer to customers is a lesson some businesses are learning from Japan. There, tight bonds between suppliers and manufacturers have produced flexibility, cost savings and quality levels that translate into export advantages. But the approach is also spreading because the notion of strategic planning, long practiced by big U.S. companies, is percolating down to smaller concerns. Owners are taking a longer-term view of their companies and a more disciplined approach to analyzing the players in their markets.

Robert Grubb, for example, was studying strategic planning at a business school when he began mapping competitive moves for Clearwood Building. He has since become president of DTM Products Inc., a Boulder, Col., plastic injection-molding concern, where he is using a similar approach. "We are looking at the competition by focusing on the customer," he says.

continued

In DTM's case, the current concern is foreign competition. One major customer, for instance, recently told the company that an Italian competitor had delivered a "beautiful" sample mold.

"We said, 'Look, we are committed to you guys as a team member," Mr. Grubb says. "Rather than being defensive, we say, 'That's great. What do you think the advantages are?' Through that kind of questioning, we can find out what they *can't* get overseas. We start realizing what we need to focus on in order to be their suppliers two, four, six, ten years from now.'"

SOURCE: Reprinted by permission of *The Wall Street Journal,* © Dow Jones Company, March 3, 1986, p. 17. All Rights Reserved.

(and others) and translates it into useful form. Some information, such as certain data on competition or data regarding a particular market may not exist within the firm. Often the sales force plays a key role in gathering market data via sales control systems, such as call reports, quotes submitted, lost order reports, and the like. Some of this data may be available in published sources (secondary data), but they may be difficult to find in accurate relevant form. Other data necessary to make a decision may not exist at all and may be obtained only after expending much time and effort along with many dollars generating primary data. In short, gathering marketing information is time-consuming and may be difficult, with the firm spending much time and money on the effort. MIS is designed to perform even more comprehensively by additionally gathering, analyzing, processing, and distributing marketing information gathered from marketing research. In most firms marketing research departments have been created so that data not currently in existence can be obtained, although marketing research represents only one source of information for a marketing information system.

Figure 5–1 illustrates the marketing-information interface with the marketing decision-making process. Notice that data which would be in the form of facts, figures, and numbers is fed to data organization, analysis, and report generation. Key marketing executives now have the necessary information to make decisions concerning market share, entry into new markets, product adaptations, and the like. This information increases the likelihood of making good decisions.

Five Basic Elements of Future Marketing Information Systems

The MIS of the 1990s will emphasize the need for the system to be user-friendly and will have five basic elements:

1. A **data bank** or a collection of libraries of information. In marketing these include sales by type of outlet and geographic area as well as customer data reported to the sales force as a result of sales calls.

■ **FIGURE 5–1**   Schematic View of a Marketing Information System

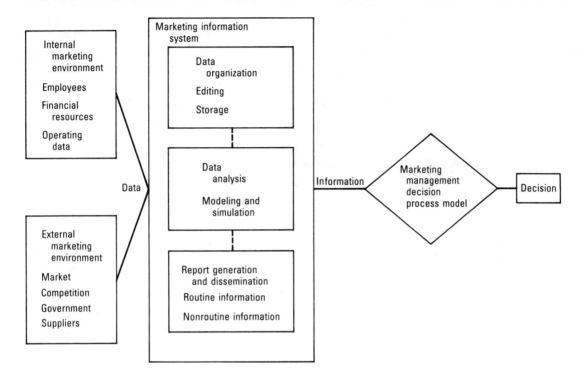

2. **Models** or ideas or hypotheses about the relationship between the factors a marketing manager controls and the results sought.
3. **Links,** which are a means of tying the data bank to other models.
4. **Optimization,** which is a goal of improving the marketing decision maker's measure of success—whether it is increasing sales and profits or reducing expenses.
5. A **systems interrogation** or a means of communicating with the entire system so that the manager can ask questions and get answers quickly—a reason for direct access to the system through a terminal or personal computer on the manager's desk.

Primary Uses of a Marketing Information System

The 1990s and beyond will introduce an MIS that will serve as a nerve center, providing instantaneous information and monitoring the marketplace continuously so that management can adjust activities as conditions change.

Some marketing executives think that their organizations are too small to use an MIS because their marketing research department can provide adequate research data for effective decision making. However, as noted earlier, marketing research itself is typically focused on a specific problem or project; its investigations have a definite beginning, middle, and end. A marketing information system is much wider in scope. Figure 5–2 shows the various information inputs which serve as components of a typical firm's MIS. Information sources are broad and varied, and although all primary and secondary data are not included in the diagram, a brief review of Figure 5–2 will give the reader an overview and a better understanding of the depth and importance of a good MIS. (Primary data are organized and collected for a specific problem, have not been collected previously, and must be generated by original research. Secondary data already exists).

■ **FIGURE 5–2**   Sources of Input to a Marketing Information System

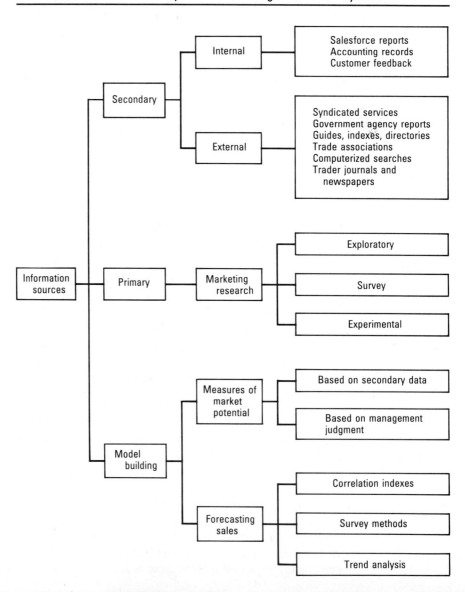

■ **FIGURE 5–3**   A Marketing Information System with an Example of Its Use

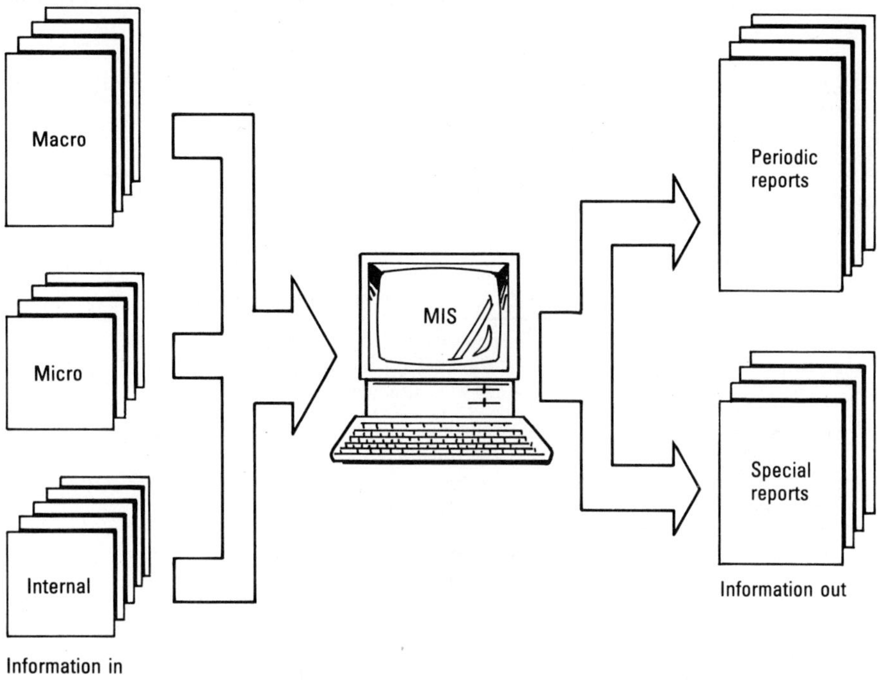

Finally, an effective MIS will enable the marketing manager to make more effective decisions in overall marketing strategy. Making marketing decisions without input from the marketplace is dangerous if we consider the degree of competition encountered by most U.S. firms. An MIS is intended to provide information about customer problems and dissatisfactions, potential problems with intermediaries, competitive actions, and other external and internal factors before crisis situations are reached. A properly formulated MIS can be preventative as well as curative for problems or potential problems commonly faced by the practicing marketing manager. Figure 5–3 illustrates the use of a marketing information system.

Concept Questions

1. What is the major focus of business to business marketing research?
2. What is the role of sales analysis in marketing research?
3. How does an MIS serve as a nerve center for the business firm?

■ THE MARKETING RESEARCH PROCESS

Marketing research is undertaken to gather reliable marketing information to facilitate planning and control. Such research must be viewed as a process of primary phases and steps. Exhibit 5–1 shows the six primary

■ **EXHIBIT 5–1**   Primary Phases in the Course of
a Research Project

Planning the Research Design
1. Recognize and define problems
2. Research design and project proposal

Preparation
3. Sampling plan
4. Data-collection and questionnaire-design considerations

Fieldwork
5. Scheduling interviews
6. Conducting interviews
7. Check-in, editing, and validation

Processing
8. Coding and keypunching data
9. Constructing the computer file

Tabulation, Analysis, and Interpretation
10. Generate tables
11. Analysis
12. Interpretation

Reporting
13. Written report oral presentation
14. Follow-up

phases and the 14 principal steps needed to take a marketing research project from initiation to completion. Each step is important, so each will be examined in detail.

Planning the Research Design

Planning the research design has often been called the most important phase of a research project as many, if not all, of the qualitative and quantitative aspects of the study are conveyed by the chosen design. The problem recognition and definition step is critical because if the research problem is not properly defined, the information produced by the research process is unlikely to have any value. **Problem definition** involves specifying the types of information needed to solve a problem, while the design process culminates with a written project proposal that conveys the essence of a study to management. The typical proposal contains a clear explanation of the study's objectives and value, and statements of the research method to be used, what is to be measured, how the data will be analyzed, and the projected cost with a schedule of when various aspects of the project will be completed.

Preparation

If information to solve a problem cannot be found in internal or external published data, the research must then rely on primary data collected from the field specifically for the study. This process may require taking a sample of the target population. Deciding on sample size requires that the sample size necessary to answer the research question with the required precision and confidence be calculated within a framework of time and cost restrictions. For example, a marketing researcher needs data concerning the salability of a new feature on an automatic packaging machine. Because secondary data are not available, the researcher must talk to potential users to determine whether or not the proposed new feature is wanted or even needed by the target market. The sample size will be small, as a check of just a few potential users will provide enough information to make a decision. Questionnaire construction is a critical step here, as the respondent will be technically oriented, and the questions to be asked must be worded accordingly.

Field Operations

This activity involves meeting with the respondents and administering the questionnaire. The interviewer must insure that all questionnaires are completed properly, and that the number of completed interviews meets the research design specifications for cost and schedule. To insure the validity of the research findings, the researcher needs to check whether the interviews were conducted according to the specifications of the research design. If this is not done, poorly worded questions will produce answers that may cause the firm to make a wrong decision as to the marketability of a new product or new product feature.

Processing

In this phase the researcher codes and prepares the data for tabulation and analysis. **Coding** is the process by which numerical values or alphanumeric symbols are assigned to represent a specific response to a question. Either closed-ended or open-ended questions are generally used. With closed-ended questions the respondent has a limited number of answer choices, while answers to open-ended questions are not limited by the researcher beforehand. Respondents can say whatever they want and in their own words.

Tabulation, Analysis, and Interpretation

After gathering the data, the researcher proceeds to draw conclusions by logical inference. **Tabulation** presents the data in tabular form, which allows the marketing researcher to communicate effectively with the marketing executive. **Analysis** attempts to turn numbers into data, and then to turn data into attainable marketing information which can be well utilized by the marketing executive. **Interpretation** involves a clear statement of implications derived from the study's findings. These implications define the alternative courses of action consistent with the objectives and nature of the study. With the example previously mentioned, data are now available to make a recommendation and decision as to the marketability of the new feature on the automatic packaging machine.

Reporting

Although the technical research work has ended by interpreting the data into findings relevant to the problem, the researcher's work has not yet ended. Much of the acceptance the research results receive depends on the way in which they are presented. The report is often all the marketing executive sees of the project, and is usually a source of great pride to the researcher.

The **reporting phase** of a research study typically involves a written report, an oral presentation, and a follow-up. All of these should focus on the marketability of the new packaging machine feature, while justifying the dollar outlay for the research study. The follow-up should try to measure the efficiency of the research project as a whole. This measurement should involve questionnaire analysis and respondent analysis, among other things. The aim is to improve the entire research process so as to improve the decision-making process as well.

■ USING OUTSIDE OR INSIDE RESEARCH SPECIALISTS— MAKE OR BUY?

Who should conduct the marketing research studies? Should the firm depend on internal specialists or should outside sources be employed? This decision is not too different from the make or buy analysis studied in Chapter 3.

It is not unusual for firms to have marketing research studies or portions of studies, such as the interviewing phase, conducted by outside organizations. Many organizations perform research activities on a contract or fee basis, including most advertising agencies, marketing research firms, management consulting firms, some universities, and trade associations. Seven factors are involved in the typical marketing research "make or buy" decision:[3]

1. *Economic Factors.* Can an outside firm provide the information more economically?

2. *Expertise.* Is the necessary expertise available internally?

3. *Special Equipment.* Does the study require special equipment not currently available in the firm?

4. *Political Considerations.* Does the study involve deeply controversial issues within the organization? Studies designed to help resolve bitter internal disputes or that might reflect

---

[3]L. Adler and C. S. Mayer, *Managing the Marketing Research Function* (Chicago: American Marketing Association, 1977), pp. 56–70.

unfavorably on some segment of the organization should generally be conducted by an outside organization.

5. ***Legal and Promotional Considerations.***   Will the results of the study be used in a legal proceeding or as part of a promotional campaign? In either case, the presumption (which is not necessarily correct) that an outside firm is more objective suggests that one be used.

6. ***Administrative Facets.***   Are current work loads and time pressures preventing the completion of needed research? If so, outside firms can be employed to handle temporary overloads.

7. ***Confidentiality Requirements.***   Is it absolutely essential to keep the research secret? As the need for confidentiality increases, the desirability of using an outside agency decreases.

■ DEVELOPING INFORMATION SOURCES

Information sources available to the marketing researcher can be classified broadly as either primary or secondary, as previously defined. **Primary data** are organized and collected for a specific problem, have not been collected previously, and must be generated by original research. **Secondary data** already exist. They are historical data previously gathered by people either inside or outside the firm to meet their needs. If those needs are similar to those of the researcher, there is no reason to collect primary data. Secondary data are usually cheaper and quicker to collect than primary data, but marketing researchers must always consider their relevance, accuracy, credibility, and timeliness.

Secondary Data Sources

Internal Secondary Data Sources.   Inside sources include marketing plans, company reports, and marketing information system (MIS) reports. Firms produce, assemble, distribute, and store enormous amounts of internal literature and statistics. Such reports can range from a simple, informational type of memorandum to a several-hundred-page report describing some future direction the firm will likely take. In reality, personnel in the accounting and sales departments are generally the most prolific producers of internal secondary data.

External Secondary Data Sources.   More general, more diverse, and simply "more" secondary data exist in sources outside the decision maker's firm. Sources of external secondary data include governmental, commercial, professional, and other sources.

Governmental Sources.[4]   Federal and state government provide so much useful literature and statistics that they collectively account for more sec-

---

[4]This section is from James E. Nelson, *The Practice of Marketing Research* (Boston: Kent Publishing Company, 1982), pp. 73–78.

ondary data than any other source. Governmental agencies publish a number of census studies and other documents used extensively by marketing researchers. Examples include the following: *Census of Agriculture, Census of Business, Census of Manufactures, Census of Service Industries, Census of Transportation, Census of Wholesale Trade,* and *Census of Population.*

The Standard Industrial Classification Code.   Business-oriented census data, such as the development of the **Standard Industrial Classification (SIC) System** has greatly enhanced the ability of the business to business marketing researcher to conduct marketing research and to gather marketing intelligence. The Standard Industrial Classification System, published by the Office of Management and Budget and distributed through the U.S. Government Printing Office, divides the nation's economic activities into broad divisions, using two-digit major groups, three-digit subgroups, and four-digit detailed industries. For example:

Division	Manufacturing	SIC Code
Major group	Good and kindred products	20
Industry subgroup	Canned and preserved fruits and vegetables	203
Detailed industry	Frozen fruits, fruit juices, and vegetables	2037

Beyond four-digit detailed industries, the researcher can find data on five-digit product classes (for example, 20371 stands for frozen fruits, juices, and ades). The researcher can also find data on seven-digit products (20371–71 stands for frozen orange juice, concentrated).

The Standard Industrial Classification system is a numerical system set up by the federal government to classify the total economy into different segments. It was developed in the mid-1930s to make it both easier and quicker for those collecting secondary data from the government to find information about their specific areas of interest. The system categorizes business activities into several broad divisions, and then subdivides them into major groups, subgroups, and detailed four-digit subgroups, as illustrated above. The SIC number assigned is based on the product produced or operation performed by each establishment. Firms with similar products, or those engaged in comparable production activities, are grouped together. The manual is periodically updated to improve on the code, although updates are infrequently made. The last three major updates occurred in 1957, 1972, and 1987. Although two firms may have different seven-digit codes for a specific industry, both would use the same four-digit code as a base, thereby providing a uniform system that can be easily used as a tool for research.

In order to make the code workable, all economic activity within the United States is first divided into eleven separate categories. One of the eleven is an open category set up for nonclassifiable establishments. These major areas of activity are considered *divisions,* and each of the eleven groups is given a unique alphabetical letter ranging from A to K to represent the division. Within each division two-digit codes are given to break the industry down into *major groups*. The number of two-digit groups depends on the size of the division that is being broken down. Within each two-digit code, the major groups are again divided into lower level subgroups by adding a third code number. This three-digit level classifies *industry groups*. Finally, the last digit is generated by dividing the three-digit codes down; the resulting four-digit code relates to *specific industries*. By having the system set up in this way, researchers are given an inverted funnel structure to use as a basis and starting point for their research.

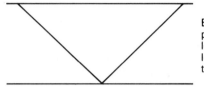

By using this inverted funnel structure in the research process, a researcher will start with the most general level of information and work down to the most specific level. This provides a quick and logical manner in which to secure data.

Expanded versions of the SIC code follow the same system; the only difference is that additional sublevels have been established to an even more specific level. This same pattern is repeated to produce six- and seven-digit codes. The major reasons for collecting data with the SIC code are: (1) to collect information on a specific target market to be reached; (2) to research the competition within a specific market; and (3) to obtain information on a specific market and compare that information over time in order to note market trends within a specific industry.

Advantages of the SIC code.   Using the SIC code has many advantages, the greatest of which is that the system itself is uniformly set up. Therefore, if researchers want to find data on companies within a regional area, they can cross-reference the location with the specific code for the industry of interest. By doing so, they can easily find similar information from all secondary data journals searched. The benefits can be found in the code's uniformity because it greatly reduces the amount of work to be done by the researcher. In the above-stated scenario, the researcher would need only to look at a limited amount of reference materials, thereby eliminating information and not having to worry about overlooking a prospect. The next major advantage can be found in its ease of use. With the inverted funnel structure shown above, a researcher can quickly channel an area of interest down to a specific industry. Without the SIC code we would have to search for the specific industry first, which can be difficult, especially when an industry has more than one product or when its products go by more than one technical name. Additionally, without the SIC code, a researcher may spend much time in trying to find information rather than in collecting and analyzing it. Because the SIC code is easy to use, information can be gathered quickly, thereby providing a major advantage to those who use it.

Limitations of the SIC code.   Although the SIC code has many advantages, it is not without limitations. One of its first limitations relates to the data itself:

> Because the total output of a multiproduct establishment must be assigned to a single 4-digit industry (an unavoidable consequence of this type of system), the shipment's total for that industry will be somewhat overstated.[5]

Another limitation relates to the Code's method of identification of an industry when a company produces many products. The SIC code lists industries under the major product they produce; the result is that many firms within that market may be omitted. A third limitation is the nondisclosure rule which:

> Bars the Census Bureau from publishing data that may disclose the operations of an individual employer. In other words, a large establishment that dominates a county's statistical listing cannot by law be listed, since the data for the county would constitute a virtual profile of this company's business operations. Because the largest establishments in a county are often affected by this rule, their shipments/receipts totals would be excluded from the Census Bureau's industry totals, leading to an understatement at the local level.[6]

This situation can be especially dangerous for researchers trying to compile industry trends.

A fourth limitation relates to the code's current revision. Although the latest SIC manual has been improved greatly, many secondary data sources will not be updated for several years. Because of this fact, researchers must put up with the faults of the old code until the new revisions are used. A fifth limitation also relates to the topic of revisions. As times change, revisions are especially needed in highly technical industries entering new fields on a regular basis. Because the system is not updated on a regular basis, great amounts of information are left out of the code until the next revision is made.

Steps involved in using the SIC code.   At this point we need to explain how to use the SIC code to target a specific market and to acquire information on it. The first step is to define the market to be reached. Once a specific industry has been selected, the researcher should obtain a copy of the 1972 version of the SIC manual. After it has been searched, the updated 1987 version should be used for the collection of data, but only from the secondary data sources that have been updated in the 1987 version. Until all sources are in the 1987 version, it is easier to start with the 1972 version of the SIC manual.

The next step is for the researcher to open the SIC manual to its table of contents, which lists each of the divisions as well as the major groups

---

[5]Richard Kern, editorial director, *Sales and Marketing Management,* April 27, 1987, p. 36.
[6]Ibid.

within each division. Each of the major groups has a corresponding two-digit SIC code, and it is here that the research actually begins. The researcher should choose the division closest to the industry being researched. This industry may not be included as a specific division, so the open category must be looked at if this situation arises. Once the division has been selected, the researcher needs to choose from the many major groups. He or she should select the major group closest to the industry that is being studied. If more than one area can be selected, the researcher ought to make a note on a piece of paper of the other choices. This may occur when researching closely related topics, especially as the researcher gets closer to a specific topic. If the search does not come close to the industry that is sought, the researcher needs to go back to the other selections and work through the system again. Once the specific industry has been selected, research using the SIC manual is over. The researcher should record on a piece of paper all the codes used to get to the specific industry and then put away the SIC manual. We need to note that the specific industry selected may not be the one that is being searched, but the closest one to it. When looking at secondary data journals, we might find the exact industry to be studied through an expanded version of the SIC code. A limitation to these expanded versions of the code, however, is that not all of them are uniform. Thus a code developed by one census may not give the same exact industry in another, but it will always be accurate to the four-digit code.

With the SIC codes at hand, the researcher needs only access the secondary data. There are many books, journals, and censuses which provide the secondary data on specific industries. Although some may include only a two- or three-digit SIC code, we should not underestimate their potential usefulness. For example, a regional census for a state that lists only two-digit codes may provide more than enough information on a specific industry. Other censuses use expanded versions of the SIC code. If this is the case, we will need to find extended code numbers. The process is the same as looking up the four-digit code in the SIC manual; we need to just work from the broadest topic to the most specific. Once a source to search has been found (for example, *Dun's Census of American Business* or *Predicasts Basebook*), all that remains to be done is to look up the SIC code, given the number of digits to be used, and record the data for analysis. Although this process is relatively easy, collecting the information can be tedious and can take a substantial amount of time.

In summary, the SIC code provides an organized way to catalog statistical data. Because it is a uniform system, its use can save great amounts of time. Although the SIC code is successful in achieving the objectives it was created to meet, it still has major limitations, which have been mentioned. One significant limitation of the 1987 modifications was that the code did not include enough industry classifications. Currently many individuals believe that the SIC code is not as effective as it should be and that additional changes must be made:

Recent surveys conducted by the Direct Marketing Association indicate that among mailers who use the SIC for list selection, only one in three find it an effective system.[7]

Currently, a new coding structure, which will be called the *SIC + 2 + 2 enhancement*, is under development. Under this new system two more digits will be added to the government's four-digit codes. As a result of the added levels it will be possible to obtain SIC codes for almost any industry by using this eight-digit system. However, researchers need to continue with the current system until the new coding system has been completed. Despite some limitations, the code remains one of the best tools in use today when conducting basic industrial marketing research.

Additional governmental sources.   Other relevant government publications are the following: *Business Conditions Digest, Construction Review, Federal Home Loan Bank Board Journal, Federal Reserve Bulletin, Monthly Labor Review, Survey of Current Business, Weekly Business Statistics,* and *U.S. Industrial Outlook.*

Commercial sources.   Several publications are distributed by the private sector. Among them are the following sources: *Funk and Scott Index of Corporations and Industries, Annual Survey of U.S. Business Plans for New Plants and Equipment, Sales and Marketing Management, Survey of Industrial and Commercial Buying Power, Survey of Buying Power,* and *Thomas' Register of American Manufacturers.*

Professional publications.   Professional associations exist in many fields of business, service, and technology, and most of them are interested in securing and disseminating information among people with common, work-related interests. **Academic publications** cut across industries and provide an exchange of ideas among marketing people; usually such publications have an intellectual orientation. Some publications like *Marketing News* resemble newspapers and report current marketing events and issues. Others, such as the *Journal of Marketing, Journal of Marketing Research, Journal of the Academy of Marketing Science, Journal of Business and Industrial Marketing,* and *Journal of Industrial Marketing* contain more details and are of greater interest. Still other forms of academic publications include the proceedings of professional meetings, research reports, monographs, and working papers. Exhibits 5–2 and 5–3 will assist the student in locating secondary data in academic publications and government documents, respectively. **Trade publications** focus on a particular industry and exchange both ideas and statistics among decision makers; they usually have a pragmatic orientation. Most trade publications contain articles describing trends in their industry, case histories of successful firms, procedures to improve a firm's performance, and industry statistics. Most are listed in *Business Publication Rates and Data,* a publication of Standard Rate and Data Service, Inc. Each of the more than 300 trade publication entries in this publication contains the publication's address, advertising costs, circulation, and other useful data.

---

[7]Jerry Reisberg, "An Expanded SIC Code: Let's Do It Ourselves!" *Direct Marketing,* October 1987, pp. 148–156.

■ **EXHIBIT 5–2**   A Search Process for Secondary Data in Academic Publications

1. Start your search by examining current marketing texts. Consult both introductory texts and advanced texts as well as texts on component parts of marketing consumer behavior; marketing management; marketing research and product price; distribution; and promotion strategy. Use tables of contents and indexes in these books to locate the topic. Depending on the level of the text and its scholarship, you will find varying levels of topic treatment. In the more rigorous texts you will find footnotes and suggested readings that lead to more detailed sources.

2. Pursue these footnoted and other referenced sources. Read them but also use them to search for work published later and earlier. If the source is a journal, check later and earlier annual indexes usually found as part of the last issue of each journal's annual volume. If the source is a proceedings, check later and earlier editions by scanning their tables of contents and indexes. While reading, be alert for other references to other related work.

3. Be especially alert for literature review articles and annotated bibliographies referenced in the preceding sources. Both of these identify and describe (and often evaluate) past research on the topic.

4. Refer to other published guides to academic publications, three of which are described here: One is the "Marketing Abstracts" section found in each issue of the *Journal of Marketing*. This section summarizes marketing literature in over 200 journals, trade magazines, university monographs, government reports, and business persons' speeches. Entries appear in numerous classes under seven main headings; they report details on the articles' original publication, summarize the article, and often comment on its significance. The second is a separate publication, *The Marketing Information Guide*. This periodical reviews over 100 marketing-related books, journals, pamphlets, and government reports every other month. Entries summarize the articles, appear in numerous classes under three main headings, and show original sources, including addresses and reprint prices. Finally, try the *Business Periodicals Index*. This monthly publication indexes nearly 300 business journals and trade magazines. It does not summarize indexed articles.

5. Obtain and review publications brochures of the American Marketing Association and Marketing Science Institute. Both of these list and describe special publications on many marketing topics.

SOURCE: Walter Gross, "Research and Other Applications of the Marketing Abstracts," *Journal of Marketing* 42 (April 1978), pp. 32–37.

Other sources.   The reader should be aware of sources of standardized market research information other than data supplied by governmental, professional, and commercial service publications. Such database sources are shown in Table 5–3. For example, public utilities can supply information on the number of new customer hookups and related data. Database sources such as the *Directory of On-Line Databases* (Santa Monica, Calif.: Cuadra Associates, Inc.), *Information Industry Marketplace* (New York: R. R. Bowker), and *Encyclopedia of Information Systems and Services* (Detroit: Gale Research) are useful because they are periodically updated. In addition, the researcher may wish to consult an information specialist who works with on-line services in a library or corporate information center. Here, a specific database is accessed through a contract with an intermediary (referred to as *on-line vendors*) rather than directly from the data-

■ **EXHIBIT 5–3**   A Search Process for Secondary Data Published by the Federal Government

1. If you have absolutely no idea about where to find data, start with the most recent edition of the *Statistical Abstract of the United States.* This annual publication summarizes social, political, and economic statistics for the nation and states in each of its more than 30 sections. You may find the data you seek in one or more of the nearly 2,000 tables contained in these sections. If not, you will find *references at the foot of each table* leading to more complete and less aggregate sources. Pursue them.

2. If you know that data belong to a particular census, by all means start instead with those publications. Look for more current data in appropriate interim report series. . . .

3. If you have found nothing so far, check appropriate *subject bibliographies* issued by the Superintendent of Documents. Over 270 are currently available, free— individually treating such subjects as marketing research, the *Census of Population* educational statistics, how to sell to government agencies, patents and trademarks, prices and the cost of living, retirement, statistical publications, and women, for example. All refer to thousands of reports, articles, and statistical sources of potential interest to marketing researchers.

4. If you still have found nothing, begin the somewhat tedious task of searching through cumulative issues of the *Monthly Catalog to U.S. Government Publications.* This monthly publication indexes by author, by title, and by subject, everything the U.S. government disseminates to the public. It functions as the card catalog as well, giving you call numbers to locate the publication in your library.

    Searching a privately published work, the *Index to U.S. Government periodicals,* completes this step. This monthly publication indexes articles in over 160 federal government periodicals. . . . Entries identify subject, author, title, periodical, and *Monthly Catalog* entry number to allow retrieval.

    Step 4 is mandatory to locate government literature as distinct from government statistics.

5. If you meet little success so far, contact the appropriate government unit directly. Most offer help quite willingly; the Bureau of the Census even employs data "ombudsmen" and publishes a list of "Telephone Contacts for Data Users" as services for information seekers.

SOURCE: Walter Gross, "Research and Other Applications of the Marketing Abstracts," *Journal of Marketing* 42 (April 1978), pp. 32–37.

base producer. The advantages of accessing a database through an on-line intermediary are as follows:[8]

1. One contract with the vendor can usually provide access to many different databases.

2. Because there is only one contract, billing for the use of various databases is simplified with one periodic invoice.

3. Search protocol is generally standardized over all of the databases on the vendor's system, thereby simplifying the research process itself.

---

[8]William R. Dillon, Thomas J. Madden, and Neil H. Firtle, *Marketing Research in a Marketing Environment,* (St. Louis: Times Mirror/Mosby College Publishing, 1987), p. 97.

■ **TABLE 5–3**   Database Sources of Secondary Data

Database	Description	Producer
Predicasts' Terminal Service	Provides national and international data regarding articles published in 2,500 sources, forecasts, and time series. Covers industries, companies, products, and services. Firms are classified by SIC code, by name, and by several other methods. Data are updated weekly.	Predicasts, Inc.
EBIS	Provides information on firms that account for over 90 percent of product and service sales in the United States.	Economic Information Systems, Inc.
Chase Databases	Provide multiple databases that cover all major sectors of the U.S. economy as well as much international data. Used by over half the *Fortune* 500 companies.	Chase Econometrics
Disclosure On Line	Provides extracts on more than 12,000 companies based on their Securities and Exchange Commission reports.	Disclosure, Inc.
Frost & Sullivan Defense Market Measures	Provides data on U.S. government purchasing. Covers new and proposed as well as existing projects. Data include negotiations, awards, companies involved, and sources sought.	Frost & Sullivan
System Trade Opportunities Weekly	Provides data regarding foreign firms and governments that want to buy or act as representatives for products and services. Specifications, quantities, and names of firms and their home countries are supplied.	U.S. Department of Commerce

SOURCE: Selections from *Encyclopedia of Information Systems and Services: 1988*, 8th ed., edited by Amy Lucas and Annette Novallo, Copyright © 1971, 1974, by Anthony T. Kruzas, © 1978, 1981, 1982, 1985, 1987, 1988, by Gale Research Company. Reprinted by permission of the publisher.

   4. The availability of an on-line database index may assist the researcher in pinpointing the individual databases most appropriate for a specific research.

While there are hundreds of on-line vendors, a few of the larger ones include the following:

- Bibliographic Retrieval Service (BRS)
- Compuserve, Inc.
- Dialog Information Service, Inc.
- Dow Jones News Retrieval
- Mead Data General
- News Net
- System Development Corporation (SDC Search Service)
- Telmar Media Systems
- Vu/Text Information Services, Inc.

These on-line vendors provide access to over 200 databases in a variety of disciplines, including science and technology along with business and economics. Some provide electronic access to the full text of hundreds of business databases, newsletters, company annual reports, and investment firm reports. New information technologies such as these will continue to revolutionize the acquisition of secondary-source market information, as access to these sources becomes a necessity in the world of business marketing research.

Disadvantages and drawbacks of secondary data.   Secondary data were developed for purposes other than the particular study under consideration. Therefore, those data must be scrutinized for applicability and accuracy. Quotations or excerpts from secondary data are often misleading, and when taken out of context, a portion of secondary data can have different relationships and different interpretations. The very nature of secondary data makes it imperative that they be evaluated carefully before making any use of them. The series of steps a marketing researcher can use in evaluating the helpfulness of secondary data are presented in Figure 5–4. The questions listed below need to be answered.

1. *How recent are the data?*   Obsolescence is often a factor to be considered in the use of secondary data. Some secondary data are collected periodically; hence, the latest available data may already be obsolete.

2. *Is the coverage of data adequate for present purposes?*   This question relates not only to geographic coverage but also to the type of products or establishments included in the data. For example, in studying the composition of an industry as reported by a trade organization, it is important to determine whether the data cover all members of an industry or are restricted to members of the association. The question of coverage becomes especially important in studying production data for individual products. In past censuses of manufactures, plants were generally classified according to their principal products. As a result, products that were produced widely but as by-products of other goods received relatively little mention. This was the case with a product like nails, which are a by-product of some iron and steel plants.

3. *In a sample survey, was an adequate sample used?*   This is especially important in the case of a mail survey where most of the sample members may not have replied, and bias in the data may have been substantial.

4. *Might the data have been biased because of the nature of the sponsor or the objectives of the original study?*   This danger may arise when trade associations conduct attitudinal or profit studies. Association members may be reluctant to provide confidential data. Alternatively, if the association in a questionnaire indicated that a study had certain objectives, such as to show how poor a dealer's profit margins were, the results are likely to bear out the objectives. Here, the marketing researcher should seek a copy not only of the original questionnaire but also of the cover letter.

■ **FIGURE 5–4** Evaluating Secondary Data

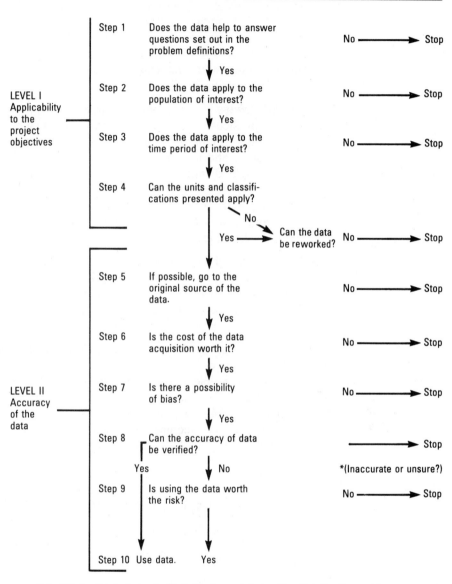

SOURCE: Robert W. Joselyn, *Designing the Marketing Research Project* (New York: Van Nostrand Rheinhold, 1977).

Primary Data Sources

Although business to business marketing researchers must rely heavily on secondary data sources, research objectives may also dictate the collection of primary data. Primary data should only be generated after secondary data research sources have been exhausted. This is because there is always the problem of the availability and accessibility of respondents because of travel requirements, the need to schedule appointments, and the like. The most common method of obtaining primary data for the business to business market is through surveys. Three survey methods commonly used with respondents are: (1) the personal interview, (2) the telephone, and (3) the mail. Table 5–4 compares these three survey methods as to cost, time, information quality, information quantity, the nonresponse problem, and the interviewer bias.

Personal Interviews.   In the personal interview the interviewer is in the presence of, or face-to-face with, the respondent. This allows maximum versatility of questioning methods (structured or unstructured, disguised or nondisguised), and a variety of question types. Interviews attempt to uncover content and intensity of feelings and motivations beyond the rationalized overt responses to structured questions. Because tape recordings are frequently used, interviews take a long time to complete, transcribe, and read, and must be analyzed by an experienced practitioner who knows both the technique and the product category under study.

Telephone.   A telephone survey is the most convenient means of reaching respondents, even though it is not so flexible and versatile as the personal interview. Drawbacks of the telephone medium relate particularly to the lack of anything visual. Distance is not a serious obstacle, nor is cost with the use of WATS lines.

Mail.   In a mail survey there is no interviewer to explain the purpose of the study, to induce cooperation, to ask questions, to record answers, and to cope with any problem that may come up. This is the main difference between mail and the other two methods; the mail method puts a great deal of importance on the construction of the questionnaire and any transmittal letters that may accompany it. Mail cannot be used to conduct an unstructured study in which an interviewer can improvise the questioning

■ **TABLE 5–4**   Comparing Business to Business Survey Methods

Criteria	Personal Interview	Telephone	Mail
Cost	Highest respondent	Second highest respondent	Least respondent
Time	Most	Least	Moderate
Information quality	In-depth, complex information	Complex information with prior contact	Somewhat complex information
Information quantity	Much	Little	Moderate according to respondent interest and the effort required
Nonresponse problem	Limited due to face-to-face contact	Hard to ensure contact with proper respondent	Hard to control
Interviewer bias	Difficult to identify and control	Difficult to identify and control	Controllable through rigorous pretesting

SOURCE: William E. Cox, Jr., *Industrial Marketing Research* (New York: John Wiley & Sons, 1979).

as the interview progresses. Once a mail survey is put in the mail, the researcher can only let it run its course. If research results must be obtained quickly, mail is not the data collection method to use. However, mail is cheaper per completed interview as cost is confined to mailing lists, forms, and postage. Also, more confidential information may be divulged.

Disadvantages and Drawbacks of Primary Data.   Collecting primary data can be, and usually is, expensive. While versatility is a plus, speed and cost along with an unwillingness (or inability) of the respondent to provide information can be a disadvantage. Mail and telephone surveys lack flexibility, and the use of unstructured questionnaires and questions is difficult. The accuracy of information obtained can be questioned, and sequence bias, in which the respondent can change an answer after seeing a later question, will occasionally present a problem. In answering open-ended questions, respondents will tend to be more brief and more general in mail surveys than in personal or telephone interviews. Complex questions with rating scales or other confusing procedures tend to draw more "no answers" in mail surveys. Finally, despite the improving returns reported on mail surveys, many such studies still have a large number of non-respondents.

Concept Questions
1. How does an MIS serve as a nerve center for the firm?
2. Why has planning the research design been referred to as the most important phase of the marketing research project?
3. Of what value is the Standard Industrial Classification (SIC) System?

■ ORGANIZATION OF MARKETING RESEARCH

The organization and staffing of marketing research departments varies greatly, depending largely on the size and organization structure of the individual company. These variations are the result of many factors, including the assignment of certain research activities to other departments, the type of products and markets involved, the relationship between the firm and its advertising agency regarding who does what research, the extent of new product development, the personalities and attitudes of top operating executives, and the maintenance of a research library. Thus we cannot state categorically how the ideal research department should be staffed.

Generally speaking, large business to business research organizations take a variety of organizational forms. The three most common types are listed below:

1. *Research organization set up by area of applications.*   Examples would be units established by product line, by customer segment, or by geographic area.
2. *Research organization set up by function performed.*   Examples would be sales analyses, advertising research, or product research.

3. *Research organization set up by research technique or research approach used.*   Examples would be mathematical and/or statistical analysis, field interviewing, or questionnaire design.

Many large firms may combine two or more of these research organization structures.

Some firms do some or all of their own research, whereas others depend heavily on outside sources. (See the make-or-buy decision studied in Chapter 3.) Some firms have only a single marketing research department responsible for all research projects. Others have decentralized research activities, with decision making spread among several people at different levels or operating units. Whether centralized or decentralized, large or small, the marketing research function depends on the relative importance of that function within the firm, and on the scale and complexity of the research activities to be undertaken. Again, there is no optimum method of organization for business to business marketing research. The best organization depends on the firm's needs and on the way it has organized its marketing function and other functions.

■ CONDUCTING INTERNATIONAL MARKETING RESEARCH

Accurate, effective decision making often depends on the quality of information provided. Marketing research plays an essential role in providing accurate and useful information, and the job becomes somewhat more difficult when the researcher must conduct marketing research overseas.

Foreign politics or the politics of the host country can range from very friendly to very hostile and even dangerous. The host country may view inputs negatively, even if the product is needed to advance or modernize a local industry. (An adverse contribution to the balance of payments would be a reason for such a viewpoint.) For example, IBM learned that lesson quickly when it planned to build a computer plant in Mexico; the Mexican government objected to IBM's policy of having 100 percent ownership of all off-shore facilities. Marketing researchers need to take also into account potential domestic politics (i.e., criticism) before an overseas venture is begun. Some labor and political organizations might accuse the firm of exporting both capital and jobs. Often foreign investment is based on moral principle. The citizens of some countries might prohibit investment in South Africa because of that country's policy of apartheid. Knowledge of this public attitude would be critical information for the domestic marketing researcher in view of the tremendous investment the firm might have to make in such an effort.

The political risks involved in a foreign expansion must be researched. The threat of confiscation, expropriation, and domestication all apply to any potential future acts by a host government. Potential social unrest and an analysis of the political climate must be considered. Problems of this type may help explain why 12 U.S. firms decided to leave El Salvador during the 1980s.

Marketing researchers need to conduct awareness and reputation (image) research studies that measure the effectiveness of a firm's overall policies and communications. Such studies would include research on advertising, promotion, and public relations. In the mid-1980s Westinghouse International authorized image studies of competitive manufacturers of electrical equipment and components in five high-priority foreign markets in an effort to strengthen the overall position of its international operations. Because the competitive image studies were conducted throughout the world (Europe, the Middle East, and South America), the services of a large international research firm (supplier) were required to ensure consistent and reliable data from country to country and to maintain the anonymity of the client.

In summation, a systematic attempt must be made to ascertain both opportunities and potential pitfalls when considering overseas expansion or export. Although the marketer might face a complex and difficult political environment, his or her task will become somewhat easier if marketing research is conducted prior to launching the new venture.

Concept Questions

1. How does a firm select the appropriate research organization structure?
2. How can the international marketing researcher's environment be made less complex and less difficult?

SUMMARY

1. A number of major differences exist between consumer research and business to business research. Business marketers, who are closer to their markets than are consumer marketers, can ascertain buyer preferences more easily. Business marketing research focuses on buying decisions and the buying center, whereas consumer research emphasizes product attributes and buyer motivation.

2. The extent to which companies use marketing research studies is wide and varied. Marketing research usually falls within one or more of the following major areas: market potential, market-share analysis, market characteristics, sales analysis, and forecasting.

3. Whereas marketing research is problem-oriented or project-oriented, a marketing information system combines procedures, hardware, and software; it then accumulates, interprets, and disseminates marketing information as effectively as possible.

4. Marketing research is undertaken to gather reliable marketing information to facilitate planning and control. Marketing research should be viewed as a process of primary phases and steps that include planning the research design; preparation; field operations; processing; tabulation, analysis, and interpretation; and reporting.

5. Firms often utilize outside firms on a fee or contract basis to do either some or all of their marketing research. The decision to use either inside or outside marketing specialists is somewhat similar to the make-or-buy decision.

6. Information sources available to the researcher are of two types: primary or secondary data. Secondary data sources include both internal and external data. Internal secondary data include marketing plans, company reports, and marketing information system (MIS) reports. External secondary data involve governmental documents, commercial sources, professional publications, and a variety of other sources. There are a number of disadvantages and drawbacks to secondary data which the researcher must consider. Primary data sources include personal interviews, telephone surveys, and mail surveys. The researcher needs to be aware of the disadvantages and drawbacks to using primary data.

7. The organization and staffing of marketing research departments varies greatly, depending largely on the size and organizational structure of the individual company. These variations are the result of many factors, including the assignment of certain research activities to other departments, the type of products and markets involved, the relationship between the firm and its advertising agency regarding who does what research, the extent of new product development, the personalities and attitudes of top operating activities, and the maintenance of a research library.

8. A systematic attempt must be made to ascertain both opportunities and potential pitfalls when considering overseas expansion or export. The international marketer's political environment is complex and difficult, but can be made easier if prior marketing research is conducted.

KEY TERMS

academic publications

analysis

coding

data bank

interpretation

marketing information system

microsales analysis

models

optimization

primary data

problem definition

reporting phase

secondary data

Standard Industrial Classification (SIC) System

systems interrogation

tabulation

trade publications

REVIEW QUESTIONS

1. Define marketing research. Point out the major differences between business to business and consumer marketing research.

2. Identify and elaborate upon the five major tasks of business to business marketing research.

3. Distinguish between marketing research and a marketing information system. What are the basic components of a marketing information system, and how is it used?

4. What is the general purpose of marketing research? Identify and briefly discuss the six phases involved in a research project.

5. Distinguish between primary and secondary data, and between internal and external secondary data. Identify three primary types of external secondary data. Identify the steps involved in using the SIC code. How can computer technology assist the researcher in locating relevant external secondary data?

6. Distinguish between personal interviews, telephone surveys, and mail surveys as methods of collecting primary data. Discuss some of the major disadvantages of both primary and secondary data sources.

7. What are the fundamental reasons for the sometimes wide variations among the organizational structures of research departments within business to business companies? Discuss the three most common organizational forms for the business marketing research function.

8. Give an example of how foreign investment can be based on moral principle. What is included under awareness and reputation (image) research?

CHAPTER CASES

Case 5–1 Bonita Baking Company*

Frank Fortunada, Jr., is the sales manager of Bonita Baking Company, a moderate-sized regional bakery in southern California that specializes in breads and bread products for markets, restaurants, and institutional accounts. Established in 1910 by Frank's grandfather, Vito Fortunada, Bonita bakes and sells a number of world-known brands of bread under licensing agreements. Among these brands are Holsum, Butter-top, and Hillbilly bread and rolls. Since his grandfather's retirement many years ago, Bonita has been run by Frank's father. To this day, everyone refers to them as Frank and Frank, Jr., (except in the latter's presence).

Frank Fortunada, Jr., has been involved in the bread business all his life. As a boy he cleaned up at the bakery and later drove a route truck while attending high school. After serving four years in the U.S. Navy (as a baker), Frank, Jr., continued to work as a routeman while attending college on a part-time basis. A year after graduating with a degree in marketing from the local state college, Frank was appointed by his father as sales

---

*William G. Zikmund, William Lundstrom, and Donald Sciglimpaglia, *Case in Marketing Research*, 1982, The Dryden Press.

manager in charge of 65 driver salespeople. Within two years Frank, Jr., was put in charge of both retail and commercial accounts. As such, Fortunada was the ranking marketing person at Bonita Baking; his father was in charge of the operations of the bakery.

■ THE MARKETING PROBLEM

About 10 years ago Bonita Bakery introduced a line of specialty bread under the name of Bonita Health Bread. Specialty bread is made from special or mixed grain flour and is heavier than regular bread. Not only have specialty breads been a rapidly growing segment of the bread market but they also are a higher gross margin product. Industry trade publications identified the specialty bread consumer as someone from upper-income households and as more highly educated than the typical bread consumer.

Fortunada knew that Bonita's specialty breads were high quality and should be selling well, but sales figures indicated otherwise. The Bonita Health line was apparently losing market share rapidly to the national brands and to another regional brand, Orowheat, which was the market leader. All, including Bonita Health, were actively promoted with advertising, coupons, and price deals. Also bothersome was the fact that many supermarket chains were also selling their own private brands of specialty bread. Fortunada's salespeople could offer no real insight as to why Bonita Health was doing poorly.

Fortunada decided to do something that had never before been attempted at Bonita—to undertake some marketing research. He knew that he would have trouble selling the idea to his father, but he also knew that he needed more information. Except for his own sales records and the trade publication reports, he decided that he knew very little.

Fortunada knew almost nothing about the growth rates of the specialty bread market in his area. He had no idea who bought his brand or those of his competitors, or how much customers bought or how often. Except for his own experience, he really didn't even know who requested specialty bread or who selected the bread. Another point that troubled him was not knowing the relative awareness of Bonita Health and its image among customers. Lastly, since he hadn't been on a bread route in some time, Fortunada thought that he had better get to know retailers' attitudes toward other brands and associated marketing practices.

Questions

1. How would you define the problem at Bonita Baking Company?
2. What are some objectives of any research to be conducted with customers?
3. Why do you think that research has not been done previously at Bonita? Why will Fortunada have difficulty convincing his father of the need for research now?

Case 5–2   The Office Boss Company*

A new customer survey. The market research department of the Office Boss Company, which makes and sells dictating equipment, set up a questionnaire and distributed it to a representative sampling of new customers. The purpose of this questionnaire was to determine why a particular article had been purchased.

A response of 62.5 percent was received, which would seem to indicate that people were quite willing to answer this type of questionnaire—in fact, were glad to do so. A tabulation of the results showed the following summaries of replies to the questions asked:

I.   What one reason do you feel was most important in first developing your interest in dictating machines?

23%—Have seen the equipment used in other companies.
20 —It was recommended by friends or associates.
19 —Have personally used the equipment previously in other organizations.
12 —Advertising literature created interest.
8 —Have been canvassed by a salesperson.
5 —In use elsewhere in the organization or subsidiaries.
13 —Miscellaneous other reasons.

II.   What do you feel was the main reason for your purchase?

35%—To help operator handle work faster and more conveniently.
22 —For after-office-hours use in office.
18 —To help secretary get the work done.
9 —For traveling or home dictation.
8 —To reduce office overhead costs.
5 —For use in recording conference and telephone calls.
3 —Miscellaneous other reasons.

III.   Did you investigate any other types of dictating machines?

64%—Yes   36%—No

IV.   Why did you buy the Office Boss in preference to other makes?

Those Answering Yes to Question III	Those Answering No to Question III
21%—Reliability and reputation	25%
19 —Superior operation and appearance	4
13 —Availablility of service	9
13 —Type of recording media	9

*Ralph S. Alexander, James S. Cross, and Ross M. Cunningham, *Industrial Marketing*, 2nd ed., © 1961, R.D. Irwin. Used by permission.

Those Answering Yes to Question III	Those Answering No to Question III
11%—Recommended by friends or associates	18%
9 —Portability	9
6 —Previous use in other organizations	13
2 —In use elsewhere in the organization	7
6 —Other	6

V.   Are you thus far satisfied with your Office Boss?

83%—Yes, extremely so.
16 —Moderately so.
1 —No.

Once the results of the new customer survey were received, the next step was for the marketing department to make use of all that information.

A study of territorial coverage.   Making use of published information, the market research department decided to compile a listing of manufacturers in 11 different sales territories. After looking over this listing, the researchers were able to quickly eliminate companies that, because of their small size, were unlikely prospects for the Office Boss. Next, all the names of companies remaining on the listing were checked against sales records compiled by salespersons and branch offices in the 11 territories. The results of this check are shown below in Exhibit I.

■ EXHIBIT I

City	Number of Salespersons	Total Number of Names of Possible Prospects	Names on Customer List	Names Already on Prospect List	Unknown
A	1	396	93	56	247
B	1	429	103	107	219
C	2	818	86	126	606
D	1	832	108	284	440
E	4	763	87	215	461
F	4	1,601	198	714	689
G	1	446	24	28	394
H	4	1,480	200	393	887
I	1	380	77	87	216
J	6	866	247	259	360
K	6	1,426	293	644	489

Question

Do you feel the results have any significance for sales management? If so, what do you think they mean, and what do you propose to be done about it?

An analysis of advertising effectiveness.   Next, the market analysis department made a study over a two-year period during which advertisements of the same size and color treatment were placed in the same list of publications. The market research department developed an index of advertising effectiveness that shows the percentage of space cost for advertisements that was recovered from sales of the Office Boss to individuals who had sent in inquiries about it. The results of this analysis are shown below in Exhibit II.

■ EXHIBIT II   Analysis of Campaigns and Individual Advertisements*

	Advertisement No.	Cost per Inquiry	Index of Effectiveness
Group A:	Product prominently displayed appeal: This is a wonderful product—Why not try it yourself?		
No. 1		$ 39	145%
No. 2		37	119
No. 3		54	116
No. 4		44	90
No. 5		47	61
No. 6		49	57
No. 7		70	67
Group B:	A single operating feature of the product was presented.		
No. 8		$ 95	97%
No. 9		62	57
No. 10		63	48
No. 11		102	31
No. 12		176	12
Group C:	Testimonial type—featuring a prominent individual who personally uses the product.		
No. 13		$ 73	43%
No. 14		98	21
No. 15		122	42
No. 16		52	15
No. 17		130	18
Group D:	Appeal: Increased efficiency and cost reduction.		
No. 18		$106	23%
No. 19		107	12
No. 20		138	12
No. 21		89	17
No. 22		97	34
No. 23		438	46

*Each advertisement is listed together with its cost per inquiry and index of effectiveness.

Question

Based on this information alone, what conclusions do you draw as to the advertising of the Office Boss Company? What recommendations do you have?

SUGGESTED READINGS ───────────────────────────

Alwin, Duane F., and John A. Krosnick. "The Measurement of Values in Surveys: A Comparison of Ratings and Rankings." *Public Opinion Quarterly* 49 (Winter 1985), pp. 535–52. A literature review, theoretical discussion, and empirical study of ratings and rankings of values in survey research.

Bartran, Peter. "The Communication of Results: The Neglected Art in Marketing Research." *Marketing Intelligence and Planning* (UK) 3 (no. 1, 1985), pp. 3–13. Guidelines for simplification and clarification in the presentation of research data.

Crispell, Diane. "Your Marketing Consultant." *American Demographics* 8 (September 1986), pp. 64–65. Marketing research-oriented software review that emphasizes a combination software/data package.

Goldstein, Frederick A. "A Practical Guide to Gathering USA Market Information and the Current Status of Marketing Research in the U.S." *Journal of the Market Research Society* (UK) 27 (October 1985), pp. 243–59. Discussion of the most effective means of gathering market information in the United States, and a look at current trends in marketing research in the United States.

Goyder, John. "Face-to-Face Interviews and Mailed Questionnaires: The Net Difference in Response Rate." *Public Opinion Quarterly* 49 (Summer 1985), pp. 234–52. A review of response rates between face-to-face interviews and mailed questionnaires in both the United States and abroad.

Grabowski, Daniel P. "Building an Effective Competitive Intelligence System." *Journal of Business and Industrial Marketing* 2 (Winter 1987), pp. 39–44. There seems to be little need to establish an active competitive intelligence function as an integral part of a corporation's existing operations structure. An intelligence system can be organized utilizing existing resources, and an example of how such information can be used to predict a competitor's actions is presented.

Gross, Irwin. "Critical Uses of Research in Business Marketing." *Industrial Marketing Management* 14 (August 1985), pp. 165–70. Discussion of the trends in marketing research for business marketing, and a look at the academic and professional activities of the Marketing Science Institute.

Hague, Paul. "Market Research 1976–1986—Swings and Roundabouts." *Industrial Marketing Digest* (UK) 11 (First quarter, 1986), pp. 85–91. Current trends in industrial research, including a shifting away from outside consultants.

Jobber, David. "Improving Response Rates in Industrial Mail Surveys." *Industrial Marketing Management* 15 (August 1986), pp. 183–95. A review of prior notification, incentives, stamps, and various other techniques.

———. "Questionnaire Factors and Mail Survey Response Rates." *European Research* (Netherlands) 13 (July 1985), pp. 124–29. Review of guidelines related to questionnaire construction for the improvement of responses to mail surveys.

Lidington, Simon. "Market Research—The Emotional Side of the Corporate Buyer." *Industrial Marketing Digest* (UK) 11 (First quarter, 1986), pp. 147–54. A discussion of psychographically segmented market segments and business to business buying decisions as they are affected by emotional considerations.

Narus, James, and Tor Guimaraes. "Computer Usage in Distributor Marketing." *Industrial Marketing Management* 16 (February 1987), pp. 43–54. A study of decision making uses of results of mail surveys and personal interviews by industrial distributors.

Piercy, Nigel. "The Corporate Environment Marketing Management: An Information-Structure-Power Theory." *Marketing Intelligence and Planning* (UK) 3 (No. 1, 1985), pp. 23–40. A theoretical discussion of a new model in marketing which deals with organizational influences in decision making and information processing theory.

Welch, Joe L. "Researching Marketing Problems and Opportunities with Focus Groups." *Industrial Marketing Management* 14 (November 1985), pp. 245–53. Guidelines for, and applications of, the use of focus groups in business to business marketing research.

Chapter **6**

Market Segmentation, Positioning, and Demand Projection

LEARNING OBJECTIVES

After reading this chapter, you should be able to:

- Appreciate the difficulty of successfully segmenting business to business markets.
- Distinguish among undifferentiated marketing, differentiated marketing, and concentrated marketing.
- Differentiate between the micro/macro and the nested approaches to market segmentation.
- Understand how to evaluate potential market segments.
- Discuss six approaches by which the firm can position its products.
- Recall the purpose, problems, and general methods of sales forecasting.

CHAPTER OUTLINE

Segmentation, Positioning, and Demand Strategy Estimation: An Overview

General Market Segmentation Strategy
The Nature of Market Segmentation

Strategies for Segmentation
Undifferentiated Marketing Strategy
Differentiated Marketing Strategy
Concentrated Marketing Strategy

Approaches to Market Segmentation
Macro/Micro Segmentation
The Nested Approach to Market Segmentation

Segmenting Business to Business Markets
Type of Economic Activity
Size of Organization
Geographic Location
Product Usage
Structure of the Procurement Function

International Segmentation

Evaluating Potential Segments
Marketing Profitability Analysis
Market Competitive Analysis

Product Positioning Strategy
Perceptual Mapping
Positioning Business to Business Products

Demand Projection
Strategic Importance of Forecasting in Decision Making
Definition of Some Basic Terminology
Common Forecasting Problems

Selecting Forecasting Methods
General Approaches to Forecasting
Qualitative Approaches to Forecasting
Quantitative Approaches to Forecasting

■ SEGMENTATION, POSITIONING, AND DEMAND ESTIMATION STRATEGY: AN OVERVIEW

Segmenting business to business markets is a difficult job, much more difficult than segmenting consumer markets. To be successful, the marketer must be able to identify, analyze, and evaluate potentially attractive segments; target the segments to be served; and then develop and communicate a positioning strategy that will differentiate the firm's offerings from those of others. This is no easy task indeed! Customers are widely dispersed, yet geographically concentrated in certain areas of the United States. These customers differ greatly in many ways, making it difficult to discern which strategies are important and which are less important in developing marketing strategy in general, and in segmentation, positioning, and demand estimation strategy in particular.

■ GENERAL MARKET SEGMENTATION STRATEGY

Few marketers or academicians have written extensively about business to business segmentation strategy. Thus, some concepts from psychology and sociology, which most consumer marketers have found useful in their segmentation strategies, have received only limited application in business segmentation strategy and planning. In fact, segmentation can assist firms in several areas:

- *Analysis of the market.*   Better understanding of the total marketplace, including how and why customers buy.
- *Selection of key markets.*   Rational choice of market segments that best fit the company's capabilities.
- *Management of marketing.*   The development of strategies, plans, and programs to meet the needs of different market segments profitably, and to give the company a distinct competitive advantage.[1]

Firms have different needs and wants, have different structures within the procurement function, are of different sizes, engage in different types of economic activities, and are in different geographic locations. **Market segmentation** is the practice of dividing up the total market into distinct groups (1) that have common needs, and (2) that will respond similarly to a specific set of marketing actions. Firms use segmentation strategy to increase sales volume, profit, and return-on-investment, among other things.

The Nature of Market Segmentation

Figure 6–1 shows how the process of segmenting a market and selecting specific segments as targets is the link between the needs of various buyers and the organization's marketing actions. Market segmentation is only a means to an end: in an economist's terms, it relates supply (the organization's actions) to demand (customer needs). A basic test of the usefulness of the segmentation process is whether it leads to tangible marketing actions.[2] In business to business marketing, segmentation is achieved generally by forming user segments (identified by SIC code), customer size segments, geographic segments (defined by boundaries between countries or by regional differences within them), product segments (based on technological differences, production economics, or product use), and the makeup of the buying center. The primary task for the marketer is to choose a variable or variables which so divide the market that prospects in a particular segment have similar responsiveness to some aspect of the marketing strategy. Once segments have been identified, the decision must be made as to which segments should be selected and pursued. Choices for selected segments should be ones in which the maximum differential in

[1]Benson P. Shapiro and Thomas V. Bonoma, "How to Segment Industrial Markets," *Harvard Business Review* 62, no. 3 (May–June 1984), pp. 104–10.

[2]Eric N. Berkowitz, Roger A. Kerin, and William Rudelius, *Marketing* (St. Louis: C. V. Mosby, 1986), pp. 191–92.

■ **FIGURE 6–1**   Market Segmentation Links Market Needs to an Organization's
Marketing Actions

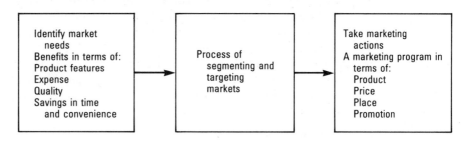

competitive strategy can be developed, and ones capable of being isolated
so that a competitive advantage can be preserved.[3]

The choice of identifying, analyzing, and pursuing wanted segments is
not a straightforward task. Marketers must weigh their strengths and
weaknesses as compared with the competition. It also requires analytical
marketing research to uncover specific market segments in which the identified strengths can be significant, and in which the identified weaknesses
can be overcome.

■ STRATEGIES FOR SEGMENTATION

Marketing managers must determine what strategy will be used for different market segments. Three alternative market-selection strategies are
available regarding segment similarities and differences: undifferentiated
strategy, differentiated strategy, and concentrated strategy.[4]

Undifferentiated Marketing Strategy

An **undifferentiated marketing strategy** uses the concept of market aggre-
gation, wherein the total market is treated as if it were but one homogeneous market segment. Marketing management creates a single marketing
mix to serve potential customers within this market. Therefore, only one
distribution framework, one promotional program, and one pricing strategy are needed. This approach focuses on what is common in the needs of
buyers rather than on what is different. An example would be a cleaning or
industrial waste removal firm. The price per hour or per pickup would be
the same for all potential users of the service, and the same promotional
package would be aimed at buyers in several different industries. Undifferentiated marketing is defended on the grounds of cost economies, with the

---

[3]Subhash C. Jain, *Marketing Planning and Strategy,* 2d ed. (Cincinnati, Ohio: South-
Western Publishing, 1985), pp. 222–33. For an advanced overview, see B. F. Shapiro and
T. V. Bonoma, "How to Segment Industrial Markets," *Harvard Business Review,* May–June
1984, pp. 104–10.

[4]See Philip Kotler, *Marketing Management: Analysis, Planning, Implication, and Control,* 6th ed. (Englewood Cliffs, N.J.: Prentice-Hall, 1988), pp. 302–4.

narrow product line keeping down production, inventory, and transportation costs. This particular strategy also lowers the cost of marketing research and product management. An undifferentiated marketing strategy might be adopted by firms which offer a nondifferentiated staple product, such as gasoline and industrial lubricants, where product usage varies little by customer type.

Undifferentiated marketing strategy will expose the firm to competitive attack by firms that do differentiate. Although this strategy is reasonable where homogeneity exists, the situation is relatively infrequent in reality.

Differentiated Marketing Strategy

A **differentiated marketing strategy** is the strategy by which one firm attempts to distinguish its product from competitive products offered to the same aggregate market. An example of a firm using a differentiated marketing strategy is IBM, which offers many hardware and software variations to different segments in the computer market. By differentiating its product or product line, the firm identifies several potential target markets. Each of these target markets may be attractive in demand, but they may differ substantially in other important aspects (such as size, product application, and technical expertise). With this strategy the firm hopes to engage in nonprice competition and thus avoid, or at least minimize, the threat of severe price competition. Differentiated marketing strategy is justified when each segment is distinct; when there is very little cross-elasticity of demand; and when the potential size of each segment is large enough to provide a satisfactory return.

Although it can usually be shown that total sales may be increased with the marketing of a more diversified product line, such activity increases the cost of doing business. The following costs are likely to be higher when the firm elects to pursue a differentiated marketing strategy:[5]

1. *Product modification costs.*   Modifying a product or product line to serve different segment requirements usually involves additional research and development, engineering, and/or special tooling costs.
2. *Production costs.*   The longer the production set-up time for each product, and the smaller the sales volume of each product, the more expensive it becomes. If each product is sold in large volume, however, the higher costs of setup time can be quite small per unit. However, innovative technology, including setup time reduction, flexible automation, and computer integrated manufacturing has offset some of these additional production costs when pursuing a differentiated marketing strategy.
3. *Administrative costs.*   When a differentiated strategy is used, the firm must develop separate marketing plans for different segments.

---

[5]Ibid., p. 303.

Such a requirement usually means additional effort in marketing research, forecasting, sales analysis, promotion planning, and channel management strategy.

4. *Inventory costs.* Managing inventories under a differentiated strategy is generally more costly than managing an inventory of only one product. Each product or product line must be carried at a level which reflects basic demand plus a safety factor to cover unexpected variations in demand. The sum of the safety stocks for several products will exceed the safety stock required for one product.

5. *Promotion costs.* Differentiated marketing strategy involves trying to reach different market segments with different variations of the promotional mix. Each segment may require separate creative advertising planning, sales strategy, and so forth.

Concentrated Marketing Strategy

Concentrated marketing strategy is practiced when the firm selects one or a relatively few segments on which to focus all its marketing effort. Through concentrated marketing the firm hopefully achieves a strong market position in the chosen segment because of its greater knowledge of the segment's needs. Furthermore, the firm enjoys many operating economies through specialization in its production, distribution, and promotion functions. Such operating economies can help the firm earn a high return on its investment.[6]

Concentrated marketing is, however, not without risk. A particular market segment's demand can turn downward or a competitor may decide to enter the same segment. A good example of this situation can be found in the defense industry. General Dynamics has one primary customer—the United States government, with its Electric Boat Division located in Connecticut and Rhode Island, which builds submarines for the U.S. Navy. If defense spending is curtailed in this area, the effect will be felt by many thousands of the firm's employees. Also, the recent addition of the Newport News, Virginia, facility as a competitor for both the fast attack and Trident submarine programs, has added a competitive element. For these reasons some firms decide to operate in more than one segment.

Figure 6–2 summarizes the key differences among undifferentiated marketing, differentiated marketing, and concentrated marketing.

■ APPROACHES TO MARKET SEGMENTATION

Two fundamental means of segmenting business markets are macro/micro segmentation and the nested approach. Each of these is discussed below.

---

[6]Ibid., p. 301.

■ **FIGURE 6–2**   Three Alternative Market
                    Selection Strategies

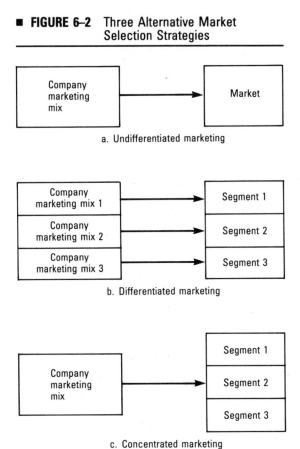

a. Undifferentiated marketing

b. Differentiated marketing

c. Concentrated marketing

Macro/Micro Segmentation

Macro segmentation involves dividing the market into subgroups based on overall characteristics of the prospect organization (usage rates, SIC categories, etc.). Micro segmentation, on the other hand, pertains to characteristics of the decision-making process, and the buying structure within the prospect organization (buying center authority, attitudes toward vendors, etc.). The marketer would identify subgroups that share common macro or micro characteristics, and then select target segments from among these subgroups.[7]

---

[7]For especially helpful discussions of market segmentation in industrial settings, see Arch G. Woodside and Elizabeth J. Wilson, "Large Scale Application of Industrial Market Segmentation" in *A Strategic Approach to Business Marketing,* ed. R. E. Spekman, and D. T. Wilson (Chicago: American Marketing Association, 1985), pp. 40–42; Thomas V. Bonoma and Benson P. Shapiro, *Segmenting the Industrial Market* (Lexington, Mass.: Lexington Books, 1983); Peter Doyle and John Saunders, "Market Segmentation and Positioning for Specialized Industrial Markets," *Journal of Marketing* 49 (Spring 1985), pp. 24–32.

The Nested Approach to Market Segmentation

Thomas Bonoma and Benson Shapiro have developed a more detailed approach to industrial market segmentation, which they refer to as a **nested approach.**[8] Their premise is that the distinction between macro segments and micro segments (as noted above) leaves out a number of potentially valuable segmentation variables. The nested approach stresses segmentation according to the amount of investigation required to identify and evaluate different criteria. Layers are arranged so as to begin with organization demographics as the area easiest to assess. Then come increasingly complex criteria, including company variables, situational factors, and personal characteristics, as diagrammed in Figure 6–3. The method integrates and builds on previous schemes for segmenting markets and offers an approach which enables not only the simple grouping of customers and prospects but also a more complex grouping of purchase situations, events, and personalities. The approach assumes a hierarchial structure which moves from broad, general bases to very specific bases. As illustrated in Figure 6–3, macro bases are in the outermost squares, with micro characteristics in the innermost squares. (More specific customer characteristics are nested inside the broader organizational basis.)

An Application of the Nested Approach.   We can give an example to help people understand this approach. Assume that a firm is selling copiers and initially wishes to segment the potential market on broad organizational characteristics, such as company size, SIC category, or general location. The firm may decide to concentrate only on companies with several hundred or more employees, or companies engaged in manufacturing, or companies located in the northeastern United States. However, rather than stop here and focus on all companies that meet the desired criteria, the firm further segments the potential market on operating variables, such as whether the firm has a centralized copy center, buys or leases present equipment, or uses copy equipment. If the firm focuses only on prospects who have a centralized copy center, it might go one step further and target only prospects that emphasize low price as a purchasing criterion, and so on. The marketer can move through all five phases of the nesting model if more specialization is needed or can stop at any point. After several attempts at working completely through the nesting process, most firms will discover which segmentation criteria are likely to yield the greatest benefits.

Another word of caution is in order. The outer-nest criteria are generally inadequate when used by themselves in all but the most simple markets because they ignore many significant buying differences among customers. Overemphasis on the inner-nest factors, however, can be too expensive and time-consuming for smaller markets. Shapiro and Bonoma suggest achieving a sense of balance between the simplicity and low costs of the outer

---

[8]Shapiro and Bonoma, "How to Segment Industrial Markets," p. 104.

■ **FIGURE 6–3**   Major Potential Bases for Segmentation (Nesting)

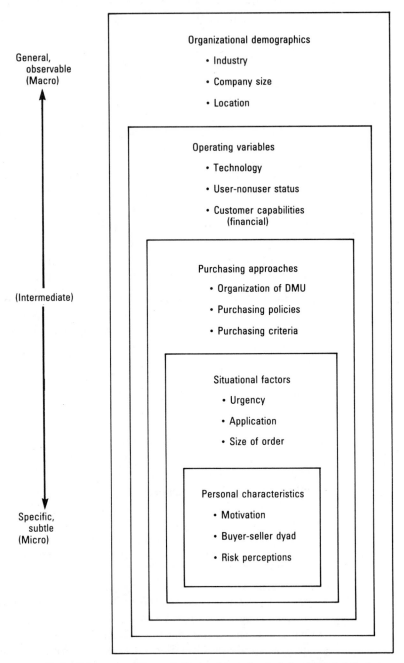

General,
observable
(Macro)

Organizational demographics
- Industry
- Company size
- Location

Operating variables
- Technology
- User-nonuser status
- Customer capabilities
  (financial)

(Intermediate)

Purchasing approaches
- Organization of DMU
- Purchasing policies
- Purchasing criteria

Situational factors
- Urgency
- Application
- Size of order

Specific,
subtle
(Micro)

Personal characteristics
- Motivation
- Buyer-seller dyad
- Risk perceptions

SOURCE: Thomas V. Bonoma and Benson P. Shapiro, *Segmenting the Industrial Market,* (Lexington, Mass.: Lexington Books, D. C. Heath, 1983). Reprinted by permission of publisher.

nests and the richness and expense of the inner ones by making the choices explicit, and the process clear and disciplined.

Concept Questions

1. What two conditions are necessary for a particular segment to be of interest to a business to business marketer?
2. What is the fundamental difference between a macro segmentation strategy and a micro segmentation strategy?
3. What is the basic premise of the nested approach to market segmentation?

■ SEGMENTING BUSINESS TO BUSINESS MARKETS

Many of the variables generally used by the marketer to segment the consumer market can also be used by the marketer to segment the organizational market (e.g., user status, degree of customer loyalty, and customer attitude toward the product). To expand upon the discussion of market segmentation discussed above, some of the categories of variables for segmenting organizational markets are identified in Figure 6–4 and are also discussed below.

Type of Economic Activity

The Standard Industrial Classification System (SIC) discussed in Chapter 5 is a useful starting place to segment firms according to primary economic activity. In addition to SIC data, several other sources of secondary data, also discussed in Chapter 5, will identify prospects for the marketer's products or services.

Size of Organization

Segmentation on the basis of size, using variables such as volume of shipments, number of employees, market share enjoyed, etc., may be a useful technique for market segmentation. However, a note of caution is in order. Segmentation based on size alone is rather risky, as the prospect may or may not be a viable target. Just because an organization is large does not necessarily mean that will be a large or heavy user of the product. However, segmentation on the basis of size is quite useful as a segmentation tool for the marketer.

Geographic Location

Segmentation on the basis of location can also be used in segmenting organizational markets, as some industries such as textile manufacturing and furniture manufacturing, are concentrated geographically.

■ **FIGURE 6–4**   Examples of Segmentation Variables for Organizational Markets

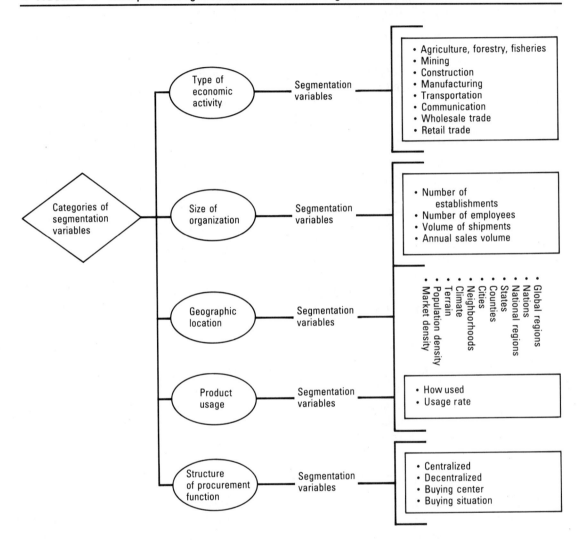

Product Usage

Many products are used in a number of different ways, making it possible to segment a market on the basis of product application. The manufacturer of a component, such as an industrial fastener, may attempt to market it to industries incorporating the product into machine tools, precision instruments, office equipment, and missile systems. Additionally, segmentation is possible by usage rate (light, moderate, and heavy user).

Structure of the Procurement Function

Market segmentation strategy can also be affected by the manner in which the buying organization is structured. The buying behavior of the firm which centralizes the buying function is quite different from that of one which uses decentralization. In a centralized situation members of the buying center are in a stronger position to buy in larger quantities and to make quicker buying decisions; and they are attractive targets to many potential competitors. When the buying decision is decentralized, the potential order size will be smaller, the number of potential competitors will be limited geographically, and a final decision on the price and quality aspects of the decision (especially in a modified rebuy or new-buy situation) may need final authorization from a centralized authority. Also, large buying organizations respond to the seller's marketing mix and marketing stimuli differently from smaller firms. The composition of the buying center can also present considerable demographic and psychographic differences among members of the center, which the marketing manager has to consider. Finally, segmentation across buyclasses (as presented in Chapter 2) will impact segmentation strategy. As noted, the effort necessary to appeal to buying center members in new task situations is very different from that needed to appeal to buyers in a straight rebuy situation.

■ INTERNATIONAL SEGMENTATION

The World Bank lists 126 countries. When a firm decides to expand into foreign markets, it must evaluate all possible markets to identify the country or group of countries presenting the greatest opportunities. Initially, the firm may opt to enter one or a few countries; eventually, it may broaden that base as it brings other countries within its fold. Research on international investment decisions has shown that the four critical factors affecting market segmentation are market size and growth, political conditions, competition, and market similarity.[9] The firm must systematically evaluate all these factors, both initially and on a regular basis, to be sure that company assets are directed toward the countries with the best opportunities. The screening process enables the firm to evaluate information about these factors regularly, thus becoming the basis for the development of an international market strategy.

Generally speaking, international market segmentation provides additional opportunities over and above domestic business. Massey-Ferguson decided long ago to concentrate on sales outside North America rather than competing with firms such as Deere & Company, International Harvester Company, and Ford Motor Company for the farm equipment market. It took Massey-Ferguson many years, but it now derives about 70 percent of its sales outside of North America. In 1975 Massey-Ferguson's return

---

[9]William H. Davidson, "Market Similarity and Market Selection: Implications for International Market Strategy," *Journal of Business Research* 11 (December 1983), pp. 439–56.

was more than the combined return for both Deere & Company and International Harvester Company.[10] The entire industry sustained losses in the 1980s, but Massey-Ferguson still fared better than its competitors.

For a product or service to be successful in any market, it must satisfy the customer's needs. American business to business marketers should understand that they must change or at least slightly adapt their marketing strategies when selling abroad. For companies that have committed seriously to international needs via market segmentation, performance can be quite encouraging. Du Pont has done well in Japan (a market misunderstood by many) by recognizing the importance of market segmentation. The company, for example, maintains 13 laboratories in Japan that work closely with specific customers to tailor particular products to meet particular customer needs.

■ EVALUATING POTENTIAL SEGMENTS

Market segmentation reveals potential market opportunity facing firms, and what would appear to be the most attractive markets the firm can serve. Before target markets can be chosen, the marketing manager has to decide which segments and how many segments will provide the best return, given limited resources. The relationship between marketing strategy and financial performance must be examined, as it would seem appropriate to select market segments which appear profitable and to disregard segments which seem less profitable. Chosen segments must be able to be served at a reasonable cost to the firm, thus providing the necessary or required return on investment. Additionally, a competitive analysis should be undertaken to assess both the strengths and weaknesses of competitors within a segment and to identify further areas of opportunity for the firm. We will now examine briefly a competitive analysis and a profitability analysis as potential tools in the overall evaluation of potential segments.

Market Profitability Analysis

A market segment might have desirable size and growth characteristics and still not be attractive from a profitability point of view. (Many marketers would cite government defense procurement as an example of this phenomenon.) Michael Porter has identified five forces which determine the intrinsic long-run attractiveness of a whole market, or any segment within it. His five-force model is shown in Figure 6–5. The model shows that the firm must assess the impact on long-run profitability of five groups: industry competitors, potential entrants, substitutes, buyers, and suppliers. The collective strength of these five competitive forces determines the ability of firms in an industry to earn, on average, rates of return on investment in excess of the cost of capital. The strength of these five forces varies from industry to industry, and can change as an industry evolves. The strength

---

[10]"Massey-Ferguson's Success Story," *Business Week,* February 1976, p. 40.

■ **FIGURE 6–5** Elements of Industry Structure

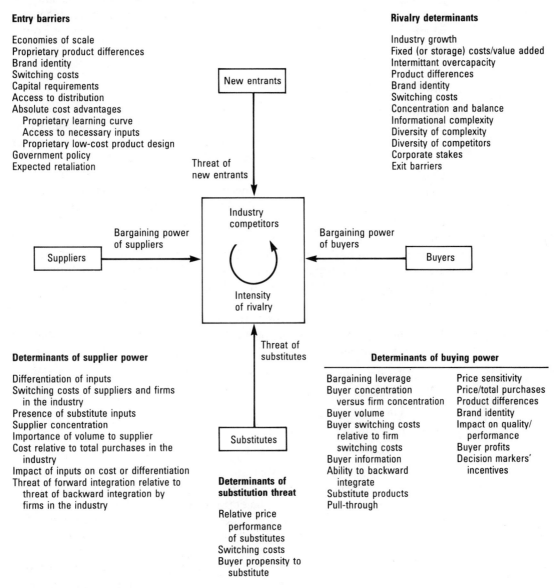

Entry barriers

Economies of scale
Proprietary product differences
Brand identity
Switching costs
Capital requirements
Access to distribution
Absolute cost advantages
    Proprietary learning curve
    Access to necessary inputs
    Proprietary low-cost product design
Government policy
Expected retaliation

Rivalry determinants

Industry growth
Fixed (or storage) costs/value added
Intermittant overcapacity
Product differences
Brand identity
Switching costs
Concentration and balance
Informational complexity
Diversity of complexity
Diversity of competitors
Corporate stakes
Exit barriers

Determinants of supplier power

Differentiation of inputs
Switching costs of suppliers and firms
    in the industry
Presence of substitute inputs
Supplier concentration
Importance of volume to supplier
Cost relative to total purchases in the
    industry
Impact of inputs on cost or differentiation
Threat of forward integration relative to
    threat of backward integration by
    firms in the industry

**Determinants of
substitution threat**

Relative price
    performance
    of substitutes
Switching costs
Buyer propensity to
    substitute

Determinants of buying power

Bargaining leverage	Price sensitivity
Buyer concentration	Price/total purchases
versus firm concentration	Product differences
Buyer volume	Brand identity
Buyer switching costs	Impact on quality/
relative to firm	performance
switching costs	Buyer profits
Buyer information	Decision markers'
Ability to backward	incentives
integrate	
Substitute products	
Pull-through	

SOURCE: Michael E. Porter, *Competitive Advantage: Creating and Sustaining Superior Performance,* (New York: Free Press, 1985), pp. 4–8, 234–36. Used with permission.

of each of the competitive forces is a function of industry structure or the underlying economic and technical characteristics of an industry. The five-forces framework does not eliminate the need for creativity in finding new segments within which to compete in an industry. Instead, it directs managers' creative energies toward those aspects of industry structure which are most important to long-run profitability; thereby, it raises the odds of discovering a desirable strategic innovation and the particular segment within which to market it. Further, even if the segment fits the firm's objectives, the firm must consider whether it possesses the skills and resources to succeed in that segment. The firm should avoid market segments where it cannot produce some form of superior value, resulting in predetermined profitability objectives.[11]

Market Competitive Analysis

Demand and profitability are not the only key variables in a marketing plan, as the number and types of competitors must also be analyzed. Competition both within and between segments is stronger today than ever before, partly because of the increasing strength of both domestic and foreign marketers. Foreign competitors are strong and important factors to consider in the markets for machinery, steel, and chemicals, to name only a few. Competition cannot be avoided, and the actions of competitors cannot be controlled. Thus profit potential depends to some degree on a careful analysis of the strengths and weaknesses of existing or potential competitors. In evaluating market segments, the marketing manager should ask, "Who are the top competitors? What are the target competitors' strategic weaknesses? What are the design vulnerabilities of the target competitors?"[12]

The traditional view of competition can be expanded by reexamining Figure 6–5 and by recognizing again the five competitive forces which determine performance within a segment:

1. Rivalry among existing firms.
2. Threat of new entrants.
3. Threat of substitute products.
4. Bargaining power of suppliers.
5. Bargaining power of buyers.

The first force recognizes that an industry's performance is greatly affected by interfirm competition, and the second force points out that an industry will be stimulated by the entrance of a new competitor, regardless of any attempts by established competitors to erect barriers to entry. The third force suggests that the availability and suitability of substitute products, which indicate an elastic product demand, can pose a threat to existing products in the industry, and the fourth shows that firms in a particular industry can be influenced by the potential bargaining power of suppliers. The fifth and final force acknowledges the potential bargaining power of buyers relative to suppliers within an industry. A major consequence of this view of competition is that the competitive arena may be altered over time because of the impact of the five forces upon the industry. For example, in the case of diamonds, all five forces are at low or negligible levels of

[11]Michael E. Porter, *Competitive Advantage: Creating and Sustaining Superior Performance* (New York: Free Press, 1985), pp. 4–8, 234–36.

[12]Ian C. MacMillan and Patricia E. Jones, "Designing Organizations to Compete," *Journal of Business Strategy* 5 (Spring 1984), pp. 11–26.

intensity because of DeBeer's global control of diamond distribution. In contrast, where low barriers of entry exist, the number of firms tends to increase, leading to greater rivalry among competitors. Strategies of individual firms can also influence the five forces.[13]

In formulating strategy, we need to study the existing and potential competitors' strengths in the areas of research and development, finance, technical service, sales force development, advertising, distribution, and organizational design before the firm makes a commitment to enter a particular segment. "Competitors are in business to defend or take market share from rival firms, and their ability to do so varies with their individual strengths and weaknesses."[14]

Concept Questions

1. How can the structure of the procurement function affect market segmentation strategy?
2. What is necessary for a product or service to be successful in any market?
3. What is the role of a competitive analysis?

■ PRODUCT POSITIONING STRATEGY

Once potential markets have been identified, analyzed, and properly segmented, if appropriate, marketers must carve a position or niche for their respective products in the minds of prospective customers. **Product position** is the way the product is defined by customers on important attributes or the place the product occupies in the customer's mind relative to competing products. When National Cash Register (NCR) dubbed itself the computer company in a major advertising campaign, the promotional effort failed because people thought of NCR only as a manufacturer and marketer of cash registers. IBM could more easily have used this advertising copy, but did not need to, since the general public already identified with IBM in this regard.

This term *positioning* refers to the placing of a product in that part of the market where it will have a favorable reception compared to competing products. Positioning means different things to different people. To some, it might mean the segmentation decision, while to others it might address the image question. To still others, it might mean selecting which product features to emphasize. As a matter of strategy, a product should be matched with the segment of the market where it is most likely to succeed. The product should be so positioned as to stand apart from competitive products, reflecting the firm's unique combination of marketing variables which differentiate the product from competitive offerings. The "Business to Business Marketing in Action" box describes how Inmac, a large Cali-

---

[13]David W. Cravens, "Strategic Forces Affecting Marketing Strategy," *Business Horizons*, September–October 1986, pp. 77–86.

[14]MacMillan and Jones. "Designing Organizations to Compete," p. 11.

BUSINESS TO BUSINESS MARKETING IN ACTION

Inmac's Creative Approach to Positioning

Inmac is a large, California-based supplier of computer accessories to the business to business market. It launched an ambitious effort in 1987 to attract and hold large-volume customers to bolster its 10 percent share of the highly fragmented computer aftermarket. Largely thanks to Inmac's popular, plain-talking catalog—it plays up product benefits in simple, nontechnical language—the mail-order company got its foot in more than a few doors during 1987. Observes catalog consultant Dick Hodgson, president of Sargeant House of Westtown, Pennsylvania, "Inmac forgets that they are in the computer field, and treats the catalog as if they are selling to someone who doesn't know anything about computers." CEO and founder Kenneth Eldred relied primarily on direct mail to deliver the firm's message of dependable quality and service. "We started the company with a pad and pencil in one hand, and a copy of David Ogilvy's *Confessions of an Advertising Man* in the other," Eldred says.

The company's corporate image seems to be a natural by-product of what they do. Boasts Eldred, "We really count on our catalog for the better part of our image." Splashed with color and irreverent humor, the catalog has won several design awards and is believed to be the key reason why solicited customers respond with enthusiasm. Experts say its ability to translate complex product data into pointed customer benefits has helped Inmac tap into a broad cross-section of potential customers. Instead of getting bogged down in detailing the advantages of an accessory for printers, for instance, catalog copy asks the provoking question, "Does your printer sound like a machine gun?"

Those with questions can call a toll-free hotline for information on how to make their new computer accessories work the right way. "They don't have blinders on when it comes to people," says Hodgson. "They're a direct marketing business, run like a marketing-oriented business."

With 60 employees working full-time at three separate research facilities to design new products—90 percent of the products sold carry the Inmac label—Inmac hopes to continue as the most comprehensive computer aftermarket source in the business. The company also shoots for newly designed products comprising 20 percent of total annual sales.

SOURCE: "Eldred's Afterlife," *Marketing & Media Decisions* 23, no. 3 (March 1988), pp. 85–88. Used with permission.

fornia-based mail-order supplier of computer accessories, uniquely uses its popular, plain-talking catalog and finely honed direct-mail techniques to deliver the company's message of dependable quality and service.

Perceptual Mapping

A technique for examining a product's position, relative to strengths and weaknesses of the product and compared to competitors, is called **perceptual mapping.** Perceptual mapping attempts to uncover how buyers evaluate a set of competing products by identifying the relative dimensions or features of each one. As is evident in Figure 6–6, this map has opposite levels of one dimension on the ends of the X- and Y-axes, such as the strong to weak customer service programmed on the end of the X-axis, and excellent to low product durability on the ends of the Y-axis. Perceptual mapping can be accomplished by using statistical tools, with the most popular being multidimensional scaling (MDS). Buyers rate sellers' products or services on specified attributes, thereby evaluating the firm's position relative to the competition.

■ **FIGURE 6–6**   Two-Dimensional Perceptual Map of Vendor Attributes of Copier Supplies

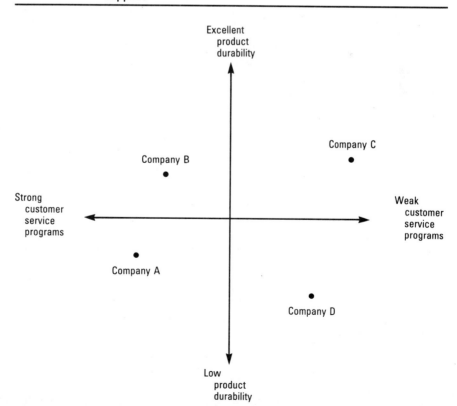

The perceptual map presented in Figure 6–6 illustrates the positions of four manufacturers of copiers. Product durability and customer service are the most important attributes in this market, with marketers within this industry trying to position their respective products favorably on those attributes in relation to the competition. Customers interviewed clearly perceive Company A as having a better service program than any of the competitors. However, Company A's product durability level is not rated highly. Company C, on the other hand, is perceived as having the best product durability, but its product service is rated poorly. Company B has the strongest combined performance on both attributes. Company D is perceived by the buyers as having low product durability and a weak customer service program. With such data, sellers are at least in a position to attempt control of their own destiny with regard to positioning strategy in relation to the competition.

Positioning Business to Business Products

Positioning business to business products is often more difficult and subtle than is the corresponding task with consumer goods. Positioning represents the place that a product occupies in a particular market and is determined by researching the organizational buyer's perceptions and preferences for a product in relation to the competition. While advertising is the primary tool used to position products and services in consumer markets, personal selling, advertising, and trade shows are used in the business market.

To evaluate the position of individual products or product lines relative to the competition requires not only extensive knowledge of the competitor's offerings but also access to the various members of the buying center. Few firms recognize what their actual position is, nor do they understand how their customers perceive their position. Lack of top management support and managerial ignorance of the concept of positioning are generally responsible for this lack of awareness. Consequently, few business to business organizations purposely employ positioning strategy.

An initial step in understanding the opportunity of positioning alternatives is to study some of the ways in which a product positioning strategy can be conceived and implemented. As shown in Figure 6–7, six possible approaches emphasized by the marketing strategist include positioning by technology, price, distribution, service, quality, and image. We will discuss each of these in turn. Several additional positioning strategies can be used in select situations, depending upon the particular industry (or segment), competitive structure, marketing expertise, etc.

Positioning by Technology. The high-tech marketer must ascertain which industries or buying groups can use the firm's products, and then array them in an ordered fashion. A high-technology firm should be able to determine which industries offer the greatest potential; which firms in these industries would benefit most from its products or processes; and which markets, in rank order, it will attempt to exploit. Often there is a multitude

■ FIGURE 6–7   Approaches to Positioning Strategy

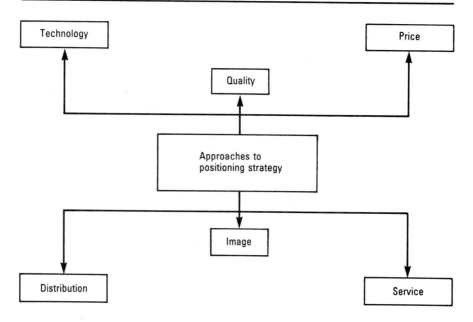

of possible applications for any technology the firm could employ. In the computer software field, with a broad range of applications and industries to pursue, Cullinane first offered data retrieval systems running on IBM computers, and then branched out to applications for banking.[15] Positioning by technology also highlights the time problems that are experienced by a high-tech business marketer. The nature of many high-technology products or processes suggests that the marketer can be described as having each of the following:[16]

- A limited product/process life cycle.
- A limited lead time before competition responds with an equal or greater breakthrough or improvement.
- A desire to control the portions of the new technology it introduces during any single time period or to any single target market.

Rapid change puts tremendous pressure on the marketer and emphasizes the selection and the establishment of priorities for target markets.

Positioning by Price.   Astute marketers know what their respective firms' total costs are (fixed, variable, and incremental), and will set prices accordingly. They will avoid unwittingly cross-subsidizing product lines or underestimating overhead. By achieving the lowest delivered-cost position relative to competition (including freight charges and installation expense),

---

[15]Andrew Pollack, "Computers: The Actions in Software," *New York Times,* November 8, 1981, p. 7–1.

[16]William L. Shanklin and John K. Ryans, Jr., *Essentials of Marketing High Technology* (Lexington, Mass.: Lexington Books, 1987), p. 148.

the firm can build a strong position in that the lowest costs generally provide the highest margins. Higher margins, in turn, present additional opportunities for future cost, price, or promotional battles with the competition. **Price positioning** requires the development of large economies of scale in purchasing, manufacturing, selling, and distribution, using cumulative experience and increases in efficiency and volume to keep costs down. A number of firms have used the lowest delivered price as a key positioning strategy, not only to gain market share but also to combat challenges to their market leadership.[17] Texas Instruments (TI) used this form of leverage as the leader in new solid-state technology in the early 1970s to bring calculator production costs progressively lower. Lower costs provided opportunities to decrease price, which, in turn, opened up successively larger volume market segments. This phenomenon increased demand, and again forced costs down. TI's success with the Experience Curve Strategy to achieve the lowest delivered cost position was such that by 1977 TI had gained market leadership in the personal calculator market—a position it held until the mid-1980s by maintaining its cost leadership strategy.[18]

Positioning by Quality.   Although organizational buyers resist paying for unnecessary high quality, they generally will not compromise quality for a lower price. In recent years the relationship between price and quality has been questioned by those who claim that improvements in product quality need not increase product costs.[19] For example, Ericsson, a major international firm in telecommunications equipment has developed a new quality culture, a major quality program triggered by the CEO of Ericsson. The rationale behind the program was a strong conviction that quality was to become the most important weapon in the firm's marketing arsenal.[20] This type of thinking has liberated product quality, making it a separate strategic variable which the firm can use in its positioning strategy. Earlier explanations describing the relationship between profitability and sales volume focused on the experience curve and the relationship between volume and cost. The works of Phillips, Chang, and Buzzell have shifted the focus to product quality.[21] This study found that product quality had a positive impact on performance measures, such as market share, profit, and ROI. It was observed that high market share means high volume, which leads to lower per unit product costs. Given this phenomenon, high quality can lead to lower costs through a favorable influence on market position. Some

[17]Barrie G. James, *Business Wargames* (New York: Abacus Press, 1985), pp. 77–78.

[18]Ibid., p. 78.

[19]David J. Curry and Peter C. Riesy, "Price and Price/Quality Relationships: A Longitudinal Analysis," *Journal of Marketing* 52 (January 1988), pp. 36–51.

[20]Evert Gummesson, "Using Internal Marketing to Develop a New Culture—The Case of Ericsson Quality," *Journal of Business and Industrial Marketing,* Summer 1987, pp. 23–28.

[21]Lynn W. Phillips, Doe R. Chang, and Robert D. Buzzell, "Product Quality, Cost Position, and Business Performance: A Test of Some Key Hypotheses," *Journal of Marketing* 47 (Spring 1983), pp. 26–43. Also see David J. Curry, "Measuring Price and Quality Competition," *Journal of Marketing* 49 (Spring 1985), pp. 106–17.

firms will have the delicate task of retaining the image of low price, while simultaneously trying to upgrade their quality image. In this situation the firm runs the risk that the quality message will obscure the basic low price, value position. **Quality positioning** is a difficult, but frequently a highly lucrative, positioning strategy to employ.

Positioning by Image.   **Image positioning** strategy stresses the importance of creating an exclusive image for a product by establishing a distinctive quality perception of the product category that will place it in a class above all other products in the category. It should also be noted that image positioning is vulnerable to more specific product-oriented concepts by the competition.

In some cases a successful company image in one market may be a handicap in another. IBM, for example, had built a blue-chip name in the world of office equipment, but in the mass market it was perceived as cold and efficient. To launch its first mass-market product, the Personal Computer (PC), to small business concerns as well as to final consumers, IBM knew it had to humanize its image. The company decided to use Charlie Chaplin's Little Tramp in its advertising campaign to make the company and the product seem less threatening. The strategy worked. By combining its traditional aggressive marketing with low-cost production and a new, friendly image, IBM, in two years time, rocketed to number one in sales in the personal computer industry.[22]

Positioning by Distribution.   Many firms think of distribution as a dilemma or possibly as an unpleasant problem. Management's difficulties with distribution can often be traced to the fact that it has not made up its mind whether distribution should be part of the sales organization, the manufacturing organization, or the executive group. Too often distribution is the neglected side of marketing. In contrast, some companies have outstripped their competition with imaginative strategies for getting products to their customers, and other marketing executives can learn from such creativity. The Federal Express system is so innovative and formidable that it might be considered a model even beyond the small-package delivery industry. Federal Express has successfully positioned itself in the package delivery business by promising the customer delivery within a specific number of hours. If they fail, the customer receives a full refund. American Hospital Supply has gained the edge over its competition by linking up to hospitals and clinics with a sophisticated system of data processing, while Steelcase has set a standard for delivering complex office furniture installations, complete and on time.[23] There are still many opportunities available in which the firm can employ **distribution positioning** and gain a competitive edge through efficient distribution.

Positioning by Service.   Positioning by service describes an attribute provided by the marketer to assist the ongoing activities of the buyer. This

---

[22]"Softening a Starchy Image," *Time*, July 11, 1983, p. 54.

[23]Louis W. Stern and Frederick D. Sturdivant, "Customer-Driven Distribution Systems," *Harvard Business Review*, July–August 1987, pp. 34–37, 40–41.

category can include technical assistance, repair services, information, delivery, parts availability, and financing as well as advisory services such as tax or legal counsel. It can also include adding services to the present offering or providing a higher level of quality of present services offered. Federal Express provides a good example of service positioning. Finding that its once unique overnight-package-delivery system had been emulated by numerous competitors, Federal Express executives rethought and redefined service as "all actions and reactions that customers perceive they have purchased." They proceeded to develop a sophisticated, centralized customer-service function to handle information provision, order taking, tracing, and problem solving. Federal Express executives believe that they can provide a higher level of service than the competition, and they also note that it would be extremely expensive for competitors to install the equipment and systems needed to duplicate Federal Express's approach.[24] **Service positioning** is an important means of differentiation for the business to business marketer, and management's ability to use service positioning effectively to place a product in the market correctly could be a major determinant of company profit.

When a firm or provider establishes and maintains a distinctive place for itself and its offerings in the market, it is said to be successfully positioned. In the increasingly competitive business sector, effective positioning is one of marketing's most critical tasks.[25] While the concept of positioning strategy is not new, its application in the business sector has multiplied with the proliferation of products, many with similar characteristics. All this activity has given credibility to the theory of positioning. The identification of an exclusive niche in the market or the creation of a unique perception of the product or service that satisfies an unfulfilled customer need can serve to distinguish the product or service from competitive offerings.

Finally, how does the firm get started on a positioning strategy? To help this thinking process, six questions (simple to ask, but difficult to answer) should be asked.[26] Specific questions the firm should attempt to answer include the following:

1. *What position does the firm now own?*   Determining what position the firm already holds in the mind of the prospect allows the marketer to tie the product service or concept to what is already there.

2. *What position does the firm want to own?*   This question involves the marketing manager's assessment of what is the best position to hold from a long-term point of view. Head-on positioning should be avoided by all but the strongest of firms.

---

[24]Christopher H. Lovelock, *Managing Services: Marketing, Operations, and Human Resources* (Englewood Cliffs, N.J.: Prentice-Hall, 1988), pp. 263–64.

[25]G. Lynn Shostack, "Service Positioning through Structural Change," *Journal of Marketing* 51 (January 1987), pp. 34–43.

[26]Al Ries and Jack Trout, *Positioning: The Battle For Your Mind* (New York: McGraw-Hill, 1981), pp. 219–26.

3. *Whom must the firm outgun?*   Generally the marketing manager will attempt to avoid the competitor's strengths, while exploiting obvious weaknesses. The marketer will try to select a position no one else has a firm grip on or owns.

4. *Does the firm have enough resources?*   A big obstacle to successful positioning is attempting to establish a position with limited resources that can be committed to the effort. It generally requires substantial resources to establish a position and even more resources to maintain it.

5. *Can the firm stick it out?*   The marketing environment changes regularly and rapidly, so it is important for the marketer to develop a long-range point of view, to determine the positioning strategy desired, and then to stick to it. Indeed, a strong argument can be made that the firm should not change its basic positioning strategy unless forced to by elements in either the internal or external environment. Only tactics or short-term maneuvers that are intended to implement long-term strategy should change. Once a firm's position is lost, it may be difficult or even impossible to get it back again.

6. *Does the firm match its marketing mix with its stated market position?*   In determining a positioning strategy, the marketing manager must be able to match the elements of the marketing mix creatively with the stated position. Does the firm's advertising campaign, for example, match the firm's overall positioning strategy?

A business to business firm must have a good idea of the basic segments of the market it can satisfy with its product or product line. Some marketing practitioners would argue that some of the above-mentioned positioning strategies should be used and that others will serve no useful purpose. Many of these arguments would depend on the firm's position within the industry. Is the firm a leader or a follower, an innovator or a laggard? The main point is that product positioning studies are useful for giving the marketing manager a clearer idea of customer perceptions of market offerings.

■ DEMAND PROJECTION

When marketers have successfully carved out a position for each product in all their product lines, they are then ready to forecast potential sales volume (i.e., estimate demand) for each product. There are both qualitative and quantitative methods of sales forecasting available for use, depending on the nature and reliability of the data desired. Before discussing each of these methods, there should be a preliminary discussion of the strategic importance of forecasting, some commonly used forecasting terminology, and some of the typical problems found in the forecasting function.

Strategic Importance of Forecasting in Decision Making

With increasing complexity, competition, and change in the business environment, organizations need more reliable performance forecasts to be able to maintain favorable market position.[27] Few would deny that forecasting is one of the most important activities undertaken by the firm, and that there are few other activities as shrouded in mystery and as misunderstood. **Forecasting** is used in the analysis, measurement, and improvement of current marketing strategy, and in the identification and/or development of new products and new markets. Forecasting promotes and facilitates the proper functioning of the many aspects of the firm's activities (i.e., production, marketing, finance, research and development, purchasing, etc.). Accurate sales forecasting helps the marketing manager plan strategies and tactics and compile a marketing plan to achieve realistic profit targets or other objectives in the short, medium, and long run. It further assists the marketer in integrating a firm's mission, operating plans, and objectives with opportunities in existing and/or potential markets or market segments. In short, accurate sales forecasting is an absolute must in the business to business sector.

Definition of Some Basic Terminology

Before we can discuss forecasting methods, we need to define several terms, as there is a tendency to use these terms rather loosely in the business market sector.

Market Factor. A market factor is something which exists in a particular market or segment that can be measured quantitatively, and that is somehow related to the eventual market demand for a particular product or service. As an example, the number of copiers three years old and older is, or may be, a market factor underlying the demand for replacement copiers. A market factor is something that affects the number of replacement copiers that can be either sold or leased in the immediate or short-term future.

Market Index. A market index is simply a market factor that is expressed as a percentage, relative to a base figure. To illustrate, one market factor might be the number of firms owning the copier model X. In 1988 the market index for this factor was 155 (relative to 1986 equals 100). A market index might also consist of several market factors, such as the number of model X copiers five years old and older, where they are located based on geographic segmentation, types of substitutes available, etc.

Market Potential. The market potential for a product is the maximum possible sales of the product or product line by all firms in a particular market or market segment, within a given environment over a period of

---

time. Market potential basically sets the upper limit for industry sales, and serves as important data in helping the marketing executive evaluate which opportunities should be pursued, based on interest, income, and segment size. Market potential in the copier industry can refer to total expected sales of copier model X within an entire market or for only a segment of that market over a period of one year.

Sales Potential.   Sales potential refers to the maximum amount that the firm expects to sell in relation to the competition. It is an ideal. For example, the marketer of copiers may speak of the number of units expected to be sold for copier model X on the West Coast over the next fiscal year.

Market Share.   Market share refers to the actual measurement of sales, by percentage, in relation to total industry sales. For example, the marketer might claim that the firm captured (or will capture) 20 percent of the market during the firm's 1991 fiscal year.

Market Demand.   Market demand refers to the absolute amount of product that might be bought or leased by a particular customer segment within a very defined geographical area during a particular time period and using a specific marketing program. For example, the marketer might refer to the sales potential of copier model X that would be bought or leased by health care facilities within three southwestern states during the first quarter of 1991, using a special, one-time only sales promotion.

Market Forecast.   A market forecast refers to the expected sales of a particular product or product line within a given environment or specific environment over a specific time period by all marketers in the particular industry. For example, the marketer would define expected shipments of all copiers competing with copier model X by all marketers of copier machinery within territory C during the first quarter of 1991. The assumption is that all will utilize a fairly uniform promotional technique.

Sales Forecast.   Sales forecasting refers to anticipating what organizational buyers are likely to purchase of a specific product or product line within a specific market or market segment over a given time period and under a given set of conditions. To generate an accurate sales forecast, marketing strategy must be decided upon in advance. For example, the marketer might estimate how many model X copiers will be sold or leased in the midwestern territory within the first quarter of 1991, using a preplanned promotional and pricing strategy.

Common Forecasting Problems

Before general sales forecasting techniques are discussed, we will present an overview of the basic problems encountered by marketers in dealing with sales forecasting techniques.[28]

---

[28]This section is from George C. Michael, *Sales Forecasting* (Chicago: American Marketing Association, Monograph Series no. 10, 1979), pp. 1–4.

Forecasting Mystique. Many marketers, uninitiated and untrained in forecasting techniques, are apprehensive about forecasting methods for three primary reasons: (1) forecasting techniques range from simple to complex; (2) from qualitative to quantitative; and (3) from traditional to very nontraditional methods. Keeping current with these techniques in light of daily pressures is difficult.

Forecasting Accuracy. Business to business marketers tend to be optimistic doers, with the result often being a forecast that is unrealistically high overall and lacking accuracy of detail.

Forecasting Inconsistency. The continual subjective modifications made by both forecasters and other decision makers tend to cloud forecasting data, which, in turn, impacts results. Modifications to a submitted forecast might range from adjusting or throwing out data because of unusual variations within the market or individual market segment, to adjusting the forecast because of a known bias by one of the participants in the forecasting process. While these modifications will usually make the ending forecast more accurate, the motive for these changes is often difficult to understand and explain.

Forecasting Accountability. In some situations the decision maker who develops a forecast does not have to live with a forecast decision that greatly impacts the line organization. Forecasting and the line organization become two different functions—one area being responsible for developing the forecast and the other area being responsible for achieving the forecast.

Forecasting Implementation. Forecasts are the best estimates of sales in a given period. However, the distinction between forecasts and sales quotas, targets, and goals is not always made. This increases the likelihood of misunderstanding and consternation between the people responsible for making the forecast and those responsible for carrying it out.

■ SELECTING FORECASTING METHODS

General Approaches to Forecasting

Preparing a sales forecast is intrinsic to the management function, with some marketers making a forecast on a short-term basis (from one to six months); others preparing them on an intermediate-term basis (from six months up to two years); and still others preparing them on a long-term basis (over two years) in combination with one or the other above. There is, however, a measure of commonality here; marketers prepare sales forecasts on a routine basis because the performance of the marketing manager is determined and measured (to a certain degree at least) by the accuracy of their forecasts.

Two very subjective, very basic categories of sales forecasting methodology, based on management judgment in estimating potential are: (1) the top-down method and (2) the bottom-up method (also called the build-up method). With the **top-down method** management begins by developing an aggregate measure of potential that is then disaggregated. Sales potential is first estimated, sales quotas are developed, and then a sales forecast is constructed. The initial estimate includes an analysis of economic and specific industry variables that might influence the sale of the firm's products, including indicators like gross national production (GNP), capital expenditures, price indices, and others. A model or mathematical equation is often created to link economic and industry variables to individual company sales, and it serves as a starting point in the forecasting process. An area of concern that inhibits the expanded use of this general approach is the assumed correlation of economic variables and quantity demanded, along with the assumption that this observable relationship will continue. However, it is a macro approach, is initiated by top management decision makers, and is appropriate in many situations.

The **bottom-up method** of forecasting originates with the sales force and is a process of estimating the number of potential buyers by adding the individual estimates by product line, geographic area, or customer group. Potentials are estimated at the field level and then tallied to obtain total sales predicted. The logic behind this approach is that salespeople have a better feel for customer product requirements, customer inventory requirements, and conditions within specific sales districts or territories. An area of concern with this approach is that since sales forecasts eventually will lead to the establishment of sales quotas in most firms, the salesperson may underestimate the sales potential of a territory or, if he or she is an optimist, the salesperson may tend to overestimate the sales potential. Perhaps the combination of both the top-down and the bottom-up approaches is best in most situations.

Qualitative Approaches to Forecasting

Qualitative approaches to forecasting employ managerial judgment to determine future expectations and are often used when data are scarce; or when perhaps there is no relevant sales history, as in the case of a new product. Such approaches are also used when good information is virtually nonexistent. These techniques rely primarily on qualitative or judgmental information, with the objective being to bring together in a logical, unbiased, and systematic way, all information and judgments relating to the factors under evaluation. Techniques for qualitative analyses include: (1) jury of executive opinion (sometimes called *executive panels*); (2) sales force composite (sometimes called *sales force estimates*); (3) survey of buyer intentions (sometimes called *market survey of user expectations*); and (4) the Delphi method.

Jury of Executive Opinion.   The jury of executive opinion consists of combining and averaging the outlooks of top executives from internal disciplines such as finance, production, marketing, and purchasing. It can be an effective method, especially when the top executives are knowledgeable about situations which might influence sales and are open-minded and realistic concerning the future. A major criticism of this approach would be comments concerning ivory-tower thinking and the very real possibility that executives are not in tune with some of the realities faced by field sales personnel.

Sales Force Composite.   Among business to business firms the most often used technique or approach to sales forecasting is the sales force composite. This approach combines each salesperson's estimate of future sales in a particular territory into a total company sales forecast. This total forecast is analyzed, adjusted, and perhaps compared with forecasts from other sources; it is then adjusted upward or downward if deemed necessary by high-level marketing management. Advantages associated with this method include the assignment of forecasting to those who will be held responsible for results, the utilization of specialized knowledge of people in the field, and the greater reliability and accuracy usually obtained. Disadvantages include using people who are not trained in forecasting and who may not view the function as an important part of their job; estimates that are either too optimistic or too pessimistic (as mentioned earlier in the discussion of the bottom-up approach); and the lack of potential salesperson perspective for future planning, which may result in forecasts based on present rather than future conditions.

Survey of Buyer Intentions.   A survey of buyer intentions anticipates what buyers are likely to do under a given set of conditions and suggests that, at the least, major buyers should be surveyed. In the business to business sector various agencies carry out intention surveys regarding plant, equipment, and materials purchases, and the two best-known surveys are conducted by the U.S. Department of Commerce and the McGraw-Hill Book Company. Most of the estimates, surprisingly enough, have been within 10 percent of the actual outcomes. Advantages include giving the marketer a continual feel for the market and its needs, keeping the marketer abreast of competition, and the possibility that, as a side benefit, the approach will indicate where additional advertising, promotion, and personal selling pressure may be needed. Disadvantages of this approach include the likelihood that many buyers may not know, or may be unwilling to reveal, their buying intentions; users may be too numerous, too hard, or too expensive to locate; and if indirect channels of distribution are used, distributors and representatives may not be willing to take on the extra work of tracing and questioning customers or potential customers on future buying intentions.

Delphi Method.   The Delphi method is a group forecasting method that is a modified version of the expert-opinion approach. It is accomplished by questioning experts individually and then providing them with anonymous feedback information from others in the group until there is a convergence of the estimates or opinions of the total group. (This approach was developed during the late 1940s by the Rand Corporation.) Any set of information available to some experts is passed on to each of the other experts, enabling them to have access to all information pertinent to the forecasting function. All questioning is handled impersonally by a coordinator, and the technique eliminates almost all committee activity. This reduces the influence of certain psychological factors, such as specious persuasion, unwillingness to abandon publicly expressed opinions, and the bandwagon effect of majority opinions.[29] A coordinator analyzes forecasts submitted, sends an averaged forecast back to participants, and asks each expert to submit another forecast. This process continues until a near-consensus is reached. Advantages of this approach include accuracy, as results will tend to be better than other methods that neither employ the same level of detail nor give the necessary attention to obtaining unbiased estimates. It is also an attractive approach when the budget for sales forecasting is limited, and when the risk or consequences of serious error in forecasting is low. Disadvantages of using this approach include the length of time needed to develop the consensus sales forecast, the tendency to use guesswork, and the possibility of infringing too much on valuable executive time. At International Business Machines Corporation this technique is used to estimate if a market is ready for certain new equipment. IBM's own experts, chosen for their diverse backgrounds and knowledge of the market, get together in some isolated spot so that they can concentrate without interruption. Their anonymous estimates are quickly totaled by computer, a process which is repeated until consensus is reached.[30] Table 6–1 summarizes the qualitative forecasting techniques considered in this chapter.

Quantitative Approaches to Forecasting

Quantitative approaches to forecasting tend to be of a statistical/mathematical nature, and can be divided into two broad categories: time-series techniques and causal techniques. **Time-series techniques** focus on historical data, while **causal methods** rely on the relationship among various factors, both past and present, within the marketing environment. Five different time-series techniques will be introduced here. They include: (1) trend fitting, (2) moving average, (3) exponential smoothing, (4) adaptive control, and (5) Box-Jenkins. Six different causal techniques will be introduced: (1) regression, (2) econometrics, (3) leading indicators, (4) diffusion index, (5) input-output analysis, and (6) life-cycle analysis.

Time-Series Techniques. *Trend fitting.* Trend fitting is a popular technique, with the forecaster fitting a trend line to a series of deseasonalized sales data. Once the line is established, the forecaster simply extends it farther to project sales for the future. To put it another way, the analyst estimates the trend from past data and adds this figure to current sales to obtain a forecast. Trend fitting is very accurate for short-term forecasting, and is usually reproduced in graph form.

Moving average. With the moving average method of forecasting, the forecaster computes the average volume achieved in several recent periods

---

[29]John C. Chambers, Satinder K. Mullick, and Donald D. Smith, *An Executive's Guide to Forecasting* (New York: John Wiley & Sons, 1974), p. 44.

[30]Harry R. White, *Sales Forecasting: Timesaving and Profit-Making Strategies That Work,* Sales Executives' Club of New York (Glenview, Ill.: Scott, Foresman, 1984), pp. 31–33.

■ **TABLE 6–1**   Summary of Qualitative Forecasting Techniques

Technique	Approach	Major Advantages	Major Disadvantages	Potential Application
Jury of Executive Opinion	Combines and averages the opinions of top executives.	Limited budget. Executives are usually experienced and have a feel for customer needs.	Possibility of ivory-tower thinking. Use of valuable executive time. Lack of the use of a standard procedure.	New product forecasts. Medium to long-range forecasts.
Sales Force Composite	Combines salesperson's estimate of future sales.	Assignment of forecasting to those who will be responsible for results. Utilization of the knowledge of people in the field. Good reliability and accuracy.	Salespeople not usually trained in forecasting techniques. Salespeople may view the function as unimportant. Possibility of estimates either too optimistic or too pessimistic. Lack of planning ability.	Short to intermediate range forecasts. Effective when intimate knowledge of customers' plans are necessary, as in the case of probable buying plans on large proposals or bids.
Survey of Buyer Intentions	Anticipates what buyers are likely to do under a given set of conditions.	Provides a continual feel for the market. Keeps abreast of the competition. Indicates where additional advertising, promotion, and selling pressure may be needed.	Buyer may not know or may be unwilling to reveal intentions. Users may be too numerous, too hard, or too expensive to locate. Channel intermediaries may be unwilling to participate.	With a well-defined or limited market. When intermediaries play an important role in the buy-sell exchange.
The Delphi method	Group forecasting method using feedback from others until a near-consensus is reached.	Accuracy. Limited budget for forecasting. Used when risk and consequence of serious error is low.	Length of time required. Tendency toward the use of guesswork. Use of valuable executive time.	Intermediate to long-term forecasting. New product forecasts. To indicate future technological events that might affect a market.

and uses it as a prediction of sales in the next period. The approach assumes that the future will be an average of past achievements, with the earliest period being dropped and the latest being added. Forecasters usually employ moving averages in conjunction with other methods, as it is good for short-term forecasting only. The data generated are in quantitative form, which is very explicit.

Exponential smoothing.   Essentially, exponential smoothing is a moving-average technique with past forecast errors being adjusted by a weighted moving average of past sales by periods. This average is modified or weighted in proportion to the error in forecasting the previous period's sales. The new forecast is basically equal to the old one, plus some proportion of the past forecasting error. The more recent the observation, the heavier the weight assigned. This method is effective when the more recent period's sales are better predictors of the next period's sales than are those of earlier periods. Data generated are quantitative, definitive, and easily applied to forecast situations. Exponential smoothing normally provides a highly accurate, short-term forecast.

Adaptive Control.   Adaptive control is similar to exponential smoothing, with the difference being that optimum weights that reduce the statistical error are derived from historical data. These weights are then used to forecast future demand. With each forecasting period, actual sales data are used to recalculate the optimal weights. Forecasts are more sensitive to historical data than the moving average and exponential smoothing techniques. This method is good for short- to intermediate-term forecasting. Output is explicit, and is shown in either quantitative or graph form.

Box-Jenkins.   Box-Jenkins, the most comprehensive time-series analysis/projection technique, enables the computer to select the statistical model of the time series that gives the best fit. The forecaster fits a times series with a mathematical model, which is optimal in the sense that it has smaller errors or variability than any other model fitted to the data. It is a very accurate, but costly and time-consuming computational procedure. However, the data are quantitative and easily applicable to forecasting problems.

Causal Techniques.   *Regression.*   Regression models, the most widely used causal models for forecasting, attempt to relate sales predictions to elements of the system that explain some of their variation, such as economic, competitive, or internal variables (e.g., level of advertising or sales visits made). Accuracy is excellent for short-term forecasting; cost of use is reasonable; and the technique is not overly complex. Output is in quantitative form and is quite explicit.

Econometrics.   Econometrics is the application of regression analysis to business and economic problems, and the applications are similar to regression analysis. The model is a system of interdependent regression equations which describe an area of economic or profit activity and provide good forecasting accuracy for short-, intermediate-, and long-term time periods. Data derived is in quantitative form and is quite explicit.

Leading indicators.   A leading indicator is a time series of an economic activity whose movement in a given direction precedes the movement of some other time series in the same direction. If the company has products with a dependent relationship on a variable whose changes precede changes in the firm's sales, profitable use can be made of this indicator. Accuracy for leading indicators is fairly good for short-term forecasting,

■ **TABLE 6–2**   Summary of Time-Series Forecasting Techniques

Technique	Approach	Major Advantages	Major Disadvantages	Potential Application
Trend fitting	Estimates trend from past data and extend them to project future sales.	Low-cost technique. Excellent short-term accuracy. Easy to use. Quick.	Many observations required for accuracy. Not effective in identifying turning points.	Good technique for products in the maturity phase of the product life cycle
Moving average	Computed with the average progressing forward in time, as the earliest period is dropped and the latest is added.	Low-cost. Short-term accuracy. Easy to use. Quick.	Will not forecast turning points. Not accurate for long-term forecasting.	Often used for inventory control for standard or low-volume items.
Exponential smoothing	A moving-average technique with recent data being given more weight.	Low-cost. Easy to use. Quick.	Will not forecast turning points. Not accurate for long-term forecasting.	Best used to forecast a highly stable sales series, similar to the application presented with the moving-average technique.
Adaptive control	Similar to smoothing with the addition of optimum weights that reduce statistical error.	More sensitive to historical data than previous methods. Short-term accuracy.	Costly. More time-consuming than methods mentioned above.	Excellent for forecasting sales demand on a monthly basis.
Box-Jenkins	A mathematical technique whereby the computer selects the statistical model of the time series that gives the best fit.	Short-term accuracy. Easy to use.	Costly. Time-consuming. Not accurate with long-term forecasting.	Best used in production and inventory control of large volume items and forecasts of cash balances.

but is questionable for intermediate- and long-term forecasting. Output is produced in quantitative form and is very explicit.

Diffusion index.   A diffusion index is the percentage of a group of economic indicators that are going up or down. A succession of low index numbers over a number of months in an expansionary period should precede an economic downturn. Short-term forecasting accuracy is only fairly accurate at best, and costs can be high with this method. Output is in quantitative form and is very explicit.

Input-output analysis.   Input-output analysis is concerned with the interindustry or interdepartmental flow of goods or services in the economy, or in a company and its markets. This method is not appropriate for short-term forecasting, is costly, and is time-consuming. The output is quantitative.

■ **TABLE 6-3**   Summary of Causal Forecasting Techniques

Technique	Approach	Major Advantages	Major Disadvantages	Potential Application
Regression	Relates sales predictions to elements of the internal and external environment.	Low-cost technique. Short-term accuracy. Easy to use.	Data generated are only as good as the data from which derived. Lacks accuracy for long-term forecasting.	Prediction of overall market demand for a generic product type.
Econometric	An application of regression analysis. A system of interdependent regression equations that describe an area of economic or profit activity.	Good for short-, intermediate-, and long-term forecasting.	Costly. Time-consuming.	Used in the prediction of overall market for a generic product type.
Leading indicator	A time series of an economic activity whose movement in a given direction precedes the movement of some other time series in the same direction.	Will identify turning points. Will forecast overall business conditions.	Accuracy is questionable. Limited application. Costly. Time-consuming.	Forecasting changes in overall business conditions.
Diffusion index	The percentage of a group of economic indicators that are going up or down.	Will identify turning points. Fair to good short-term forecasting accuracy.	Costly. Time-consuming. Poor long-term forecasting accuracy.	Used for forecasting sales of overall product classes.
Input-Output analysis	Concerned with interindustry and interdepartmental flow of goods or services.	Will identify turning points. Good for intermediate- and long-range forecasting.	Costly. Time-consuming. Poor short-term forecasting accuracy.	Forecasting sales of Business products and services over long periods of time.
Life-cycle analysis	Phases of product acceptance are analyzed.	Good for forecasting new-product sales. Good for intermediate forecasting.	Limited accuracy. Will not identify turning points. Costly. Time-consuming.	Forecasting of new-product sales.

Life-cycle analysis.   Life-cycle analysis consists of an analysis and forecast of new-product growth rates based on S-shaped curves. Central to the analysis is the phase of product acceptance by the various groups such as innovators, early adapters, early majority, late majority, and laggards. A growth curve is estimated and is reviewed as sales data are corrected. Forecasts are made by reading future points along the S-curve.

Tables 6–2 and 6–3 summarize the quantitative forecasting techniques considered in this chapter.

Concept Questions

1. What is meant by product positioning?
2. What does perceptual mapping attempt to uncover?
3. What is the general role of forecasting or demand estimation?

SUMMARY

1. Segmenting business to business markets is a difficult job. To be successful, the marketer must be able to: (1) identify, analyze, and evaluate potentially attractive segments; (2) target the segments to be served; and (3) develop and communicate a positioning strategy which will differentiate the firm's offerings from others. Market segmentation is the practice of dividing up a market into distinct groups that have common needs, and that will respond similarly to a specific set of marketing actions.

2. Marketing managers must determine what strategy to use for different market segments. By adopting a strategy of undifferentiated marketing, the organization treats its total market as a single entity. Differentiated marketing is the strategy by which a firm attempts to distinguish its product from competitive brands offered to the same aggregate market. Through concentrated marketing the firm achieves a strong market position in the segment because of its greater knowledge of the segments' needs.

3. Macro segmentation involves dividing the market into subgroups based on overall characteristics of the prospect organization, while micro segmentation pertains to characteristics of the decision-making process and the buying structure within the prospect organization. The nested approach stresses segmentation according to the amount of investigation required to identify and evaluate different criteria. This method integrates and builds on previous schemes for segmenting markets, and offers an approach that enables not only the simple grouping of customers and prospects but also more complex grouping of purchase situations, events, and personalities.

4. Many of the variables generally used to segment the consumer market can be used by the business to business marketer to segment the organizational market. Five primary ways of segmenting business markets include type of economic activity, size of organization, geographic location, product usage, and structure of the procurement function.

5. When a firm decides to expand into foreign markets, it must evaluate all possible markets to identify the country or group of countries presenting the greatest opportunities. The firm must systematically evaluate market size and growth, political conditions, competition, and market similarity of each country on a regular basis to be sure that company assets are directed toward the countries with the best opportunities.

6. Before target markets can be chosen, the marketing manager must decide how many segments and which segments will provide the best return, given limited resources. A competitive analysis should be undertaken to assess both the strengths and weaknesses of competitors within a segment so as to identify further the areas of opportunity for the firm. Porter's five-force model shows that the firm must appraise the impact upon long-run profitability of five groups: industry competitors, potential entrants, substitutes, buyers, and suppliers. In formulating strategy, the existing and potential competitors' strengths in the areas of research and development, finance, technical service, sales force development, advertising, distribution, and organizational design must be studied.

7. Positioning refers to the placing of a product in that part of the market where it will have a favorable reception compared to competing products. Six approaches in positioning strategy include positioning by technology, price, quality, image, distribution, and service.

8. Because of the increasing complexity, competition, and change in the business environment, organizations need more reliable performance forecasts to be able to maintain a favorable marketing position. Forecasting, or demand estimation, is used in the analysis, measurement, and improvement of current marketing strategy, and in the identification and/or development of new products and new markets. Common forecasting problems faced by marketing managers include forecasting mystique, forecasting accuracy, forecasting inconsistency, forecasting accountability, and forecasting implementation.

9. There are two major techniques for forecasting business to business demand. Qualitative approaches to forecasting employ managerial judgment to determine future expectations, and are often used when data are scarce, or good information is virtually nonexistent. Quantitative approaches to forecasting tend to be of a statistical/mathematical nature, and can be divided into time-series and causal techniques. Time-series techniques focus on historical data, while causal methods rely on the relationship among various factors, both past and present, within the marketing environment.

KEY TERMS

bottom-up method

causal methods

concentrated marketing strategy

differentiated marketing strategy

distribution positioning

forecasting (demand estimation)

image positioning

market segmentation

nested approach

perceptual mapping

price positioning

product position

quality positioning

service positioning

time-series techniques

top-down method

undifferentiated marketing
   strategy

REVIEW QUESTIONS

1. In what kinds of areas can segmentation assist business firms? How is segmentation achieved in business to business marketing? What are three criteria in selecting market segments?

2. Differentiate among undifferentiated marketing, differentiated marketing, and concentrated marketing as market segmentation strategies.

3. Distinguish between macro segmentation and micro segmentation. What is the nested approach to market segmentation? What is its major premise? Why are outer-nest criteria generally inadequate when used alone to segment markets?

4. Identify five ways in which markets can be segmented. Can you think of any additional ways in which a business to business market might be segmented?

5. What is the first thing a firm should do when considering expansion into foreign markets? What are the four critical factors that affect market segmentation in international markets?

6. What is the role of a competitive analysis in market segmentation? Distinguish between a market profitability analysis, and a market competitive analysis as preconditions to selecting market segments.

7. What is meant by product position? Why is perceptual mapping used? Identify six ways by which a company could position a product. What six questions should the firm ask in getting started with a positioning strategy?

8. When is forecasting used? What is the value of accurate sales forecasting?

9. Identify each of the following terms: (1) market factor; (2) market index; (3) market potential; (4) sales potential; (5) market demand; (6) market forecast; and (7) sales forecast.

10. Discuss five common problems encountered by marketing managers in sales forecasting.

11. Distinguish between the top-down and the bottom-up methods of sales forecasting. Discuss four qualitative methods of sales forecasting.

12. Differentiate between time-series techniques and causal methods of quantitative sales forecasting. Identify and explain five types of time-series techniques and six types of causal methods.

CHAPTER CASES

Case 6–1   Purolator Takes Aim at Federal Express

It's hard to top Federal Express Corp. in advertising, as the overnight-delivery company's competitors freely admit. Airborne Freight Corp. even has publicly conceded that in a recent commercial—before slyly turning the compliment into a gibe. "Federal Express does advertising," the 10-second spot says, "so Airborne has to give you better service."

The latest express service to step up against Federal is Purolator Courier Corp., whose new TV commercials began recently. They combine hard-sell price comparisons with soft-sell humor in an attempt to differentiate Purolator from Federal, and from others competing in the $2.5 billion industry. Purolator should already be better known than it is. Although only half as large as Federal in revenue from parcel shipments, Purolator handled 37 percent more packages last year. Largely because of stingy ad budgets and forgettable messages, though, Purolator is familiar to only about one third of its potential customers, while Federal "is right up there with Coke" in recognition, says a competitor.

Purolator hasn't any delusions about making people forget Federal. "Its advertising has been brilliant; there's no getting around that," says Kenneth Olshan, chairman of Wells, Rich, Greene Worldwide, Purolator's ad agency. "It's made Federal the generic."

Federal's ads have succeeded because the company was the first in the industry to recognize that its customers were secretaries and executives rather than purchasing agents or shipping departments. Federal used TV to reach them and spent heavily—$35 million in the fiscal year just ended. Ally & Gargano, Federal's advertising agency, skillfully used humor to make its point. Best known is the commercial with mile-a-minute talker John Moschitta as a harried executive. That and other spots showing hapless slobs doomed by their choice of the wrong courier helped Federal grow to a $1 billion company and turned the agency into a warehouse for advertising awards.

Federal's competitors have yet to beat its sales ability. Airborne has tried to be funnier; Emery Worldwide strives to be just the opposite; and DHL Corp. relies on testimonials from prominent executives. Visual tricks abound: United Parcel Service showed one of its brown trucks changing into a plane, and United Airlines had animated packages deliver its spiel.

The common denominator of these ads is emphasis on the same claims—reliability and speed. Numerous surveys show these factors to be most important to overnight-delivery customers. Purolator, however, has decided that express-delivery customers assume that any company will provide acceptable service and reliability. Furthermore, because Federal has emphasized those attributes the longest and loudest, Mr. Olshan says, competitors that stress reliability and speed "are helping Federal, and not distinguishing themselves."

Purolator, instead, is touting its prices in its two fairly recent commercials, which open with an obvious parody of the industry leader. Both show three identical employees of "inflexible Express." Bald and wearing black-rimmed glasses, they're reminiscent of the oddballs in Federal's commercials. A customer calls to ask the price of an overnight letter and is shocked when told it is $12.50.

SOURCE: Bill Abrams, "Purolator Courier's New Ads Take Aim at Federal Express," *The Wall Street Journal,* September 29, 1983, p. 33. Copyright © 1983, by *The Wall Street Journal.* Used by permission.

"Absolutely, positively," each of the inflexible men whine. The scene then switches to a Purolator delivery man—as normal and friendly as can be—who touts his company's $8.75 price. In the second commercial the inflexible employees chortle as they add surcharges to packages lacking ZIP codes or account numbers. The blue-suited Purolator spokesperson is there again for contrast, bragging how Purolator "delivers more packages overnight than any other courier." The campaign slogan: "You want it. You got it."

Because Purolator uses trucks to transport many of its packages between cities, the company is a low-cost competitor and can tout its prices. Purolator has tried that strategy before unsuccessfully. (Actor Ben Gazzara was the spokesperson, and "overnight, not overpriced" was the slogan.) Competitors say their research shows that the claim is irrelevant. "Secretaries, executives, and other occasional shippers have said over and over again, 'Don't tell me what it costs. If it doesn't get there on time, my boss doesn't want to know that I saved $4,' " says Jerry Della Femina, head of Airborne's agency. He adds that Purolator can't follow other couriers that promise 10:30 A.M. deliveries because its distribution system won't support that promise—a point that Purolator concedes.

Questions

1. How would you segment the market for overnight delivery services?

2. How could Purolator use the SIC system to identify market opportunities and to evaluate their effectiveness to date?

3. What criteria do you think are important in the purchase of overnight delivery services? Given these criteria, what can Purolator do to increase its marketing effectiveness?

4. What type of buying situation is represented? What are the steps in the purchase decision process for this product?

Case 6–2   Apple Computer*

Since its beginnings in 1976, Apple Computer has been the most successful start-up company in the United States. By the mid-1980s it had won more than a million households with its pioneering personal computer, the Apple II. Along with Tandy's Radio Shack, it assumed a dominant position in the personal computer field. Indeed, for the year ending September 26, 1984, Apple's overall sales had reached $1.5 billion.

Apple Computer has often straddled the delicate line between boldness and arrogance. In discussing the "Apple knows best" attitude that many customers have found offensive, one industry analyst said of Apple's cofounder, Steven P. Jobs: "Jobs judges more on what is right with a capital 'R,' than on what the market wants, and what will sell best. Like many brilliant visionaries, he is arrogant." Whether bold or simply arrogant,

---

*Peter D. Bennett, *Marketing*, 1988, McGraw Hill.

Jobs and Apple certainly had reason to be proud of their success in competing with IBM in the home computer market. In view of IBM's difficulties in selling its PC to households, and the retailing fiasco of IBM's PC Jr., Apple can claim that it was the first competitor to truly defeat IBM in a head-to-head competition.

By the mid-1980s, however, Apple had focused on an even more ambitious goal: challenging IBM's dominance of the office market for personal computers. According to one estimate, businesses buy about two-thirds of the personal computers sold in the United States. Apple achieved little success in its efforts to win over business buyers with two of its more powerful personal computers, the Apple III and the Lisa. As a result, it has attempted to turn its Macintosh computer, first offered in 1983, into a formidable office alternative to the IBM PC.

In 1984, the first year of this Macintosh campaign, Apple sold 275,000 Macs. While industry analysts viewed this as a respectable first-year figure, Apple failed to achieve critical sales to the *Fortune* 500 companies. Despite impressive graphics and computing power—despite being somewhat easier to use than the IBM PC—the Macintosh did not "take off" because it lacked business software and was not IBM-compatible.

Initially, Jobs and other Apple executives had brashly predicted that Macintosh would come to rival the IBM PC, which accounts for more than 75 percent of all desktop computers in *Fortune* 500 companies. In 1985 Apple had been forced to scale down its predictions (and its bold rhetoric); its goal was simply to win 50 orders from major corporations during the year that would serve as showcase accounts. Industry sources suggest that smaller companies account for more than 80 percent of sales of personal computers to businesses. Even while conceding that IBM would continue to dominate sales to the *Fortune* 500, Apple hoped to reach the target market of smaller business buyers by showing that it had at least some impressive big-company Macintosh users. Apple did receive major Mac orders from Federal Express, General Motors, GTE, Honeywell, and Motorola.

Perhaps the critical stumbling block was the issue of IBM compatibility. "What has made the Macintosh seductive is that it's easier to use for basic functions than IBM's PC," noted John Hammitt, vice president of information management at Pillsbury. "But like it or not, we live in an IBM world. People who don't plug into that world are not going to have a long-term place with us." Apple hoped to resolve this problem partly through its Macintosh Office (a device that will allow Macs to communicate with PCs) and other new offerings.

Software was another key problem, and here Apple faced a vicious cycle. Until it sells many more Macintoshes to business clients, it will have great difficulty convincing software writers and producers to develop programs for the Mac. Yet without an extensive array of programs, it will continue to be difficult to sell the Mac to major companies. IBM clearly enjoys a dramatic advantage over Apple in terms of software. In 1983, for example, five times as many programs were written for the IBM PC than for Apple computers.

Apple's advertising has hardly been a spectacular success with potential corporate customers; even the firm's whimsical name seems to contrast unfavorably with that of International Business Machines. A controversial Apple commercial (aired during the 1985 Super Bowl) showed a procession of apparent business executives blindly following IBM and marching single file off a cliff. Only the last executive in line, presumably a Macintosh user, pulled off his blindfold and avoided imminent death. Advertising experts were highly critical of the commercial, viewing it as one more example of Apple's arrogance. "It insulted the very people Apple was trying to reach," observed the president of a New York-based market research firm.

Another key weakness was poor relations with independent dealers. Apple's salespeople were apparently offering cut-rate Macs to potential corporate customers at prices that dealers couldn't match. "We didn't feel we were getting a fair shake," remarked the director of a California-based chain. With such complaints in mind, Apple's national salespeople were instructed to seek only "highly visible reference accounts," and to leave smaller orders for dealers.

By mid-1985 it had become clear that Apple was in severe trouble, partly because of the disappointing performance of the Macintosh campaign. The firm was forced to take its first quarterly loss as a public company and to dismiss 20 percent of its employees. Shipments of the Mac were running at only 10,000 per month—far below Apple's 80,000 per month capacity for making the computer. As matters grew worse, chairman John Sculley (formerly a protégé of Donal Kendall at Pepsico) wrestled control of Apple from ousted co-founder Steven Jobs.

While some business customers advised Sculley to stick to the education market and drop its attempt to challenge IBM with the Macintosh, he rejected such counsel. "The Mac was one of the major reasons I came to Apple in the first place. I had to fall back on what I knew best." He began a new marketing campaign for the Mac, personally lobbied for the machine with buyers for major corporations, and pleaded with software companies to write better programs for the Macintosh.

By early 1987 Sculley's efforts seemed to be paying off. One industry analyst estimated that shipments of Macintoshes doubled in 1986, while worldwide personal computer shipments increased by only 9 percent. Although the Mac still holds only about 7 percent of sales to business firms, its noted user-friendly style is apparently being noticed. Moreover, Apple has benefited from two important developments: the success of desktop publishing, a method for printing typeset-quality documents that the Macintosh pioneered; and the success of Excel, a spreadsheet program that allows the Mac to challenge the Lotus 1–2–3 program that can run on the IBM PC.

While IBM's 1986 earnings fell, Apple's jumped 151 percent to $154 million in the fiscal year ending September 30, 1986. By early 1987 Apple's shares on the stock market—which sold as low as $14 per share in mid-1985—were trading at over $40 per share, a three-year high. Analysts projected that Apple's earnings would rise by 15 percent in 1987; some Wall

Street sources claimed that the company's stock would reach $60 per share by the end of 1987.

Of course, Apple still faces a rather formidable threat from the always dangerous IBM. In early 1987 a leading IBM executive told an industry gathering that future PCs will offer "a new level of user-friendliness." IBM certainly has the potential to co-opt the key strengths and selling points of the Macintosh, just as it took business away from the successful Apple II in the early 1980s.

Another lingering question facing Sculley is whether Apple can maintain its present sales approach. "Apple is up against the direct-sales forces of IBM and DEC," noted one industry analyst. "I don't think it's possible to sell successfully in the business market without a direct-sales force." Thus far, Sculley continues to disagree. He insists that Apple can attract business customers by carefully selecting its dealers, and by restricting the company's more complex products to the more sophisticated outlets. But Sculley has made one concession: he placed 40 salespeople across the nation to link up dealers with corporate customers.

Questions

1. Why did Apple decide that it was important to shift its focus from the home computer market to the office computer market?

2. What were the major reasons for Apple's difficulties in penetrating the office computer market?

3. What do you think are two or three major changes that Apple made in its marketing program in order to become more successful in the office computer industry?

SUGGESTED READINGS

de Kluyver, Cornelius, and David B. Whitlark. "Benefit Segmentation for Industrial Products." *Industrial Marketing Management* 15 (November 1986), pp. 273–86. Detailed example and guidelines for practical segmentation.

Hlavecek, James D., and B. C. Ames. "Segmenting Industrial and High Tech Markets." *Journal of Business Strategy* 7 (Fall 1986), pp. 39–50. Discussion of, and guidelines for, identifying and selecting business to business segments.

Hlavecek, James D.; B. C. Ames; and N. Mohan Reddy. "Identifying and Qualifying Industrial Market Segments." *European Journal of Marketing* (UK) 20 (no. 2, 1986), pp. 8–21. Presentation of a three-stage model for segmenting by business to business product application.

———. "Identifying and Qualifying Industrial Market Segments." *Marketing Intelligence and Planning* (UK) 3 (no. 1, 1985), pp. 41–56. Discussion of market segmentation guidelines using a product application.

Lauer, Joachim, and Terrence O'Brien. "Sales Forecasting Using Cyclical Analysis." *Journal of Business and Industrial Marketing* 3 (Winter 1988), pp. 25–32. Presentation of a forecasting method involving construction and interpretation of the business cycle.

Michman, Ronald D. "Linking Futuristics with Market Planning, Forecasting, and Strategy." *Journal of Business and Industrial Marketing* 2 (Spring 1987), pp. 61–68. Association of the science or art of anticipating and planning for the future with marketing planning and forecasting.

Plank, Richard E. "A Critical Review of Industrial Market Segmentation." *Industrial Marketing Management* 14 (May 1985), pp. 79–91. A literature review, current status, and outlook for business to business market segmentation.

Robles, Fernando, and Ravi Sarathy. "Segmenting the Commuter Aircraft Market with Cluster Analysis." *Industrial Marketing Management* 15 (February 1986), pp. 1–12. Survey of business travel and cargo in regional airlines.

Shostack, G. Lynn. "Service Positioning through Structural Change." *Journal of Marketing* 51 (January 1987), pp. 34–43. Within service systems a structural process design can be used to engineer services on a more scientific, rational basis.

Smith, Paul. "The Who, What, Why of Industrial Segmentation (Part 2)." *Industrial Marketing Digest* (UK) 10 (Second Quarter, 1985), pp. 122–27. Guidelines for different types of market segmentation.

Stryker, Charles W. "Data, Decisions, and Development/1985 U.S. Totals/1985 State and County Totals/Guide to Using S&MM's Survey of Industrial and Commercial Buying Power." *Sales and Marketing Management* 136 (April 28, 1986), pp. 6–7, 48–108. Annual survey of the purchasing power of many industries.

Wheeler, David R., and Charles J. Shelley. "Toward More Realistic Forecasts for High-Technology Products." *Journal of Business and Industrial Marketing* 2 (Summer 1987), pp. 55–64. Examination of the problem of overoptimistic forecasting in the high-technology arena to include reasons for this bias, and suggestions as to how to make such forecasts more realistic.

Case for Part Three

CASE 1 Trus Joist Corporation (B)

Mr. Mike Kalish, salesman for the Micro = Lam® Division of Trus Joist Corporation, had just received another moderately sized order for the product Micro = Lam laminated veneer lumber; however, the order held particular interest for him. The unique feature of the order was that the Micro = Lam was to be used as a truck trailer bedding material. This represented the second-largest order ever processed for that function.

Earlier in the fall of 1978, Mr. Kalish had spent some time in contacting prospective customers for truck trailer flooring in the Northwest and Midwest; however, the response from manufacturers had been disappointing. Despite this reception, smaller local builders of truck trailers were interested and placed several small orders for Micro = Lam laminated veneer lumber. The order Mr. Kalish had just received was from one of the midwestern companies he had contacted earlier, thus renewing his belief that the trailer manufacturing industry held great potential for Micro = Lam laminated veneer lumber as a flooring material.

■ COMPANY BACKGROUND

The Trus Joist Corporation, headquartered in Boise, Idaho, is a manufacturer of structural wood products, with plants located in the Pacific Northwest, Midwest, Southeast, and Southwest. Annual sales, which totaled over $78 million in 1978, were broken down into three major product categories: the Micro = Lam Division, contributing 7 percent of sales (the majority of Micro = Lam sales were internal); the Commercial Divisions, with 82 percent of sales; and the Residential Sales Program, with 11 percent of sales.

In the late 1950s Art Troutner and Harold Thomas developed a unique concept in joist design, implemented a manufacturing process for the design, and then founded the Trus Joist Corporation. By 1978 the company employed over 1,000

This case is produced with the permission of its author, Dr. Stuart U. Rich, Professor of Marketing and Director, Forest Industries Management Center, College of Business Administration, University of Oregon, Eugene, Oregon.

people, of whom about 180 were sales personnel. The majority of sales-people were assigned to the regional Commercial Division sales offices; four outside salespeople were assigned to the Micro = Lam Division. The functions of selling and manufacturing were performed at each of the five geographically organized Commercial Divisions; therefore the salespeople concentrated on geographic selling. The Micro = Lam Division was more centralized in nature, conducting all nationwide sales and manufacturing activities from Eugene, Oregon.

In 1971 Trus Joist first introduced and patented Micro = Lam laminated veneer lumber. The product is made of thin $\frac{1}{10}$-inch- or $\frac{1}{8}$-inch-thick veneer sheets of Douglas fir glued together by a waterproof phenol formaldehyde adhesive. Under exact and specified conditions the glued sheets are heated and pressed together. The Micro = Lam lumber, or billet,[1] is "extruded" from specially made equipment in 80-foot lengths and 24-foot widths. The billets can be cut to any customer-desired length or width within those limiting dimensions. The billets come in several thicknesses ranging from $\frac{3}{4}$ inch to $2\frac{1}{2}$ inches; however, $1\frac{1}{2}$ inches and $1\frac{3}{4}$ inches are the two sizes produced regularly in volume.

■ MARKETING MICRO = LAM

When Micro = Lam was first introduced, Trus Joist executives asked an independent research group to perform a study indicating possible industrial applications for the product. The first application for Micro = Lam was to replace the high-quality solid sawn lumber 2 × 4-inch trus chords[2] in its open-web joist designs and the solid sawn lumber flanges[3] on its wooden I-beam joist (TJI). Into the fall of 1978 this still represented the majority of Micro = Lam production. The findings of the research report suggested that Micro = Lam could be used as scaffold planking, mobile home trus chords, and housing components. These products accounted for about 25 percent of the Micro = Lam production. Mr. Kalish had also begun to develop new markets for Micro = Lam, including ladder rails and framing material for office partitions.

When marketing Micro = Lam to potential customers, Trus Joist emphasized the superior structural qualities of the product over conventional lumber. Micro = Lam did not possess the undesirable characteristics of warping, checking, and twisting; yet it did show greater bending strength and more structural stability. (One ad claimed, "Testing proves Micro = Lam to be approximately 30 percent stiffer than #1 dense select structural Douglas fir.") In some applications, Micro = Lam offered distinct price advantages over its competing wood alternatives, and this factor al-

---

[1]Micro = Lam is manufactured in units called billets, and the basic unit is one billet foot. The actual dimensions of a billet foot are 1 foot × 2 feet × 1½ inches, and one billet is 80 feet × 24 feet × 1½ feet.

[2]Trus chords are the top and bottom components in an open-web trus incorporating wood chords and tubular steel webs.

[3]Flanges are the top and bottom components in an all-wood I beam. Refer to Exhibit 1.

■ **EXHIBIT 1**   End of an All-Wood I Beam (TJI)

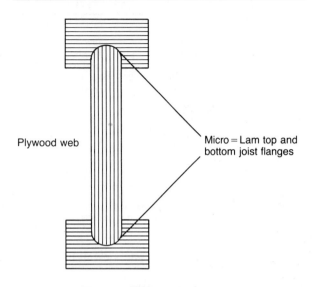

Plywood web

Micro = Lam top and
bottom joist flanges

ways proved to be a good selling point. Manufacturers were often concerned about the lead/delivery time involved in ordering Micro = Lam.
Trus Joint promised to deliver within one to three weeks of an order, which
was often a full two weeks to two months ahead of other wood
manufacturers.

The industrial application report had also suggested using Micro = Lam
as a decking material for truck trailers. This use became a reality when
Sherman Brothers Trucking, a local trucking firm that frequently transported Micro = Lam, made a request for Micro = Lam to redeck some of
its worn-out trailers. To increase the durability of the flooring surface, the
manufacturing department of Trus Joist replaced the top two veneer sheets
of Douglas fir with apitong. Apitong was a Southeast Asian wood known
for its strength, durability, and high specific gravity. This foreign hardwood
had been used in the United States for several years because of the diminishing supplies of domestic hardwoods. (See Exhibit 2.)

The pioneer advertisement for Micro = Lam as a trailer deck material
had consisted of one ad in a national trade journal and had depicted the
Micro = Lam cut so that the edges were used as the top surface. (See Exhibit 3.) The response from this ad had been dismal and had resulted in
only one or two orders. The latest advertisement depicting Micro = Lam as
it was currently being used (with apitong as the top veneer layers) had
better results. This ad, sent to every major truck or trailer manufacturing
journal as a news release on a new product, resulted in 30 to 50 inquiries
which turned into 10 to 15 orders. Approximately 15 decks were sold as a
result of the promotion.

Everyone at Trus Joist believed that the current price on Micro = Lam
was the absolute rock bottom price possible. In fact, most people believed
that Micro = Lam was underpriced. The current price of Micro = Lam in-

■ **EXHIBIT 2**   Mechanical Properties of Wood Used for Trailer Decking

Common Name of Species	Specific Gravity (percent moisture content)	Modulus of Elasticity (million psi)	Compression Parallel to Grain and Fiber Strength Maximum Crush Strength (psi)
Apitong	0.59	2.35	8,540
Douglas fir	0.48	1.95	7,240
Alaska yellow cedar	0.42	1.59	6,640
White oak	0.68	1.78	7,440
Northern red oak	0.63	1.82	6,760
Micro = Lam*	0.55	2.20	8,200

*Micro = Lam using Douglas fir as the veneer faces of the lumber.

SOURCE: *Wood Handbook: Wood as an Engineering Material,* USDA Handbook No. 72, rev. ed., 1974; U.S. Forest Products Laboratory.

■ **EXHIBIT 3**   End View of Remanufactured Micro = Lam

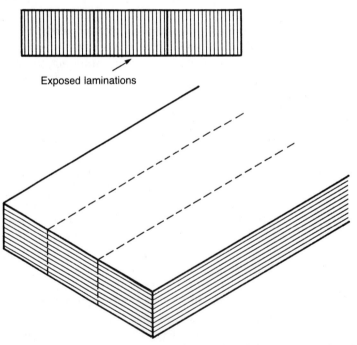

Exposed laminations

Original Micro = Lam billet depicting the cutting path (--------) during the remanufacturing process

cluded a gross margin of 20 percent. The price of 1¼-inch-thick and 1½-in-thick Micro = Lam was based on the costs of a 1½-inch billet. The total variable costs of a 1½-inch material were multiplied by five sixths to estimate the same costs of 1¼-inch material. There had recently been some discussion over the appropriateness of this ratio. Some of the marketing

■ **EXHIBIT 4** Truck Trailer Shipments and Dollar Value (by calendar year)

	1975	1974	1973	1972	1971
Complete trailers and chassis	67,888	191,262	167,201	141,143	103,784
Value	$613,702,000	$1,198,520,000	$956,708,000	$795,500,000	$585,264,000
Containers	4,183*	10,108*	18,626	18,166	8,734
Value	$18,071,000	$27,343,000	$60,159,000	$51,527,000	$26,514,000
Container chassis	2,936	12,883	12,790	15,498	9,775
Value	$14,898,000	$42,076,000	$33,143,000	$39,028,000	$24,999,000
Total units	75,007	214,253	198,617	174,807	122,293
Value	$646,671,000	$1,267,939,000	$1,050,010,000	$886,055,000	$636,777,000

Author: Truck Trailer Manufacturers Association. Data for 1975 preliminary and subject to slight possible change.
*Containers not reported June—October 1974 and January—March 1975.
SOURCE: *Ward's Automotive Yearbook, 1978*, p. 91.

personnel believed that a more appropriate estimate of the variable costs for the 1¼-inch Micro=Lam would be the ratio of the number of veneers in a 1¼-inch billet to the number of veneers in a 1½-inch billet, or ¹⁴⁄₁₆. At the present time, the costs of veneer represented 55 percent of the selling price. Glue cost was approximately 13 cents/square foot; fixed overhead represented 14 cents/square foot; and other variable costs amounted to approximately 12½ cents/square foot. The total variable costs were divided by 0.80 to cover all selling and administrative expenses and to secure a profit.[4]

In 1977, truck trailer manufacturers ordered and used 46 million square feet for installation in new truck trailer construction. This figure was understated because redecking or replacement of worn-out floors of trailers had not been incorporated, and there was little organized information to determine what this potential could be. As of 1975, 236 truck trailer manufacturers produced $646.7 million worth of trailers. (See Exhibit 4.)

The problem Mr. Kalish saw with this aggregate data was that it was not broken down into the various segments of trailer builders. For example, not all of the 236 manufacturers produced trailers which used wooden floors. Among those not using wooden floors were tankers and logging trailers. Mr. Kalish believed that the real key to selling Micro=Lam in this industry would be to determine the segment of the trailer industry on which he should concentrate his selling efforts. Mr. Kalish also knew that he somehow had to determine trailer manufacturers' requirements for trailer decking. The Eugene-Portland, Oregon, area offered what he thought to be a good cross-section of the type of trailer manufacturers that might be interested in Micro=Lam. He had already contacted some of those firms about buying Micro=Lam.

■ **GENERAL TRAILER COMPANY**

Mr. Jim Walline had been the purchasing agent for General Trailer Company of Springfield, Oregon, for the past 2½ years. He stated, "The engi-

---

[4]All cost figures have been disguised.

neering department makes the decisions on what materials to buy. I place the orders after the requisition has been placed on my desk."

General Trailer Company was a manufacturer of several different types of trailers: low-boys, chip trailers, log trailers, and flatbeds. In 1977 General manufactured five flatbeds and redecked five flatbeds. General did most of its business with the local timber industry; however, it sold three flatbeds in 1977 to local firms in the steel industry.

The flatbeds General Trailer manufactured were 40 to 45 feet long and approximately 7 feet wide. Log trailers were approximately 20 to 25 feet long.

General Trailer manufactured trailers primarily for the West Coast market, although it had sold a few trailers to users in Alaska. On the West Coast, General's major competitors were Peerless, Fruehauf, and Trailmobile, all large-scale manufacturers of truck trailers. Even though General was comparatively small in size, it did not feel threatened, because "we build a top-quality trailer which is not mass-produced," as Mr. Walline put it.

General had been using apitong as a trailer decking material until customers complained of its weight and its expansion/contraction characteristics when exposed to weather. At that time, Mr. Schmidt, the general manager and head of the engineering department, made the decision to switch from apitong to laminated fir.

Laminated fir (consisting of solid sawn lumber strips glued together) was currently being used as the material for decking flatbeds, and Pacific Laminated Company of Vancouver, Washington, supplied all of General's fir decking, so General would only order material when a customer bought a new trailer or needed to have a trailer redecked. Mr. Walline was disappointed with the two- to three-week delivery time, since it often meant that much more time before the customer's trailer was ready.

Laminated fir in 40-foot lengths, 11¾-inch widths, and 1¼-inch thicknesses was used by General. General paid approximately $2 to $3 per square foot for this decking.

Even though Pacific Laminated could provide customer-cut and -edged pieces with no additional lead time, General preferred shiplapped fir in the previously noted dimensions, with the top two layers treated with a waterproof coating.

The different types of trailers General manufactured required different decking materials. Low-boys required material 2¼-inch thick and General used 3 × 12-inch rough-cut fir lumber. Chip trailers required ⅝-inch-thick MDO (medium density overlay) plywood with a slick surface.

Mr. Walline said General had used Micro=Lam on one trailer; however, the customer had not been expecting it and was very displeased with the job.[5] Therefore, the current policy was to use only laminated fir for the

---

[5]After purchasing Micro=Lam, General Trailer modified the material by ripping the billets into 1½-inch widths and then relaminating these strips back into 12-inch- or 24-inch-wide pieces of lumber. This remanufacturing added substantial costs. Also, the laminations were now directly exposed to the weather. Moisture could more easily seep into cracks or voids, causing swells and buckling. (See Exhibit 3.)

local market unless a customer specifically ordered a different decking material. Trailers headed for Alaska were decked with laminated oak, supplied by a vendor other than Pacific Laminated.

Mr. Walline said that if he wanted to make a recommendation to change decking materials, he would need to know price advantages, lead times, moisture content, availability, and industry experience with the material.

■ SHERMAN BROTHERS TRUCKING

"We already use Micro=Lam on our trailers," was the response of Mr. Sherman, president of Mayflower Moving and Storage Company, when asked about the trailer decking material his company used. He went on to say, "In fact, we had hauled several shipments for Trus Joist when we initiated a call to them asking if they could make a decking material for us."

Mayflower Moving and Storage owned 60 trailers (flatbeds) which it used to haul heavy equipment and machinery. It had been in a dilemma for eight years about the types of materials used to replace the original decks. Nothing seemed to be satisfactory. Solid apitong was tough, but it was too heavy and it did not weather very well. Plywood did not provide adequate weight distribution and had too many joints. Often the small wheels of the forklifts would break through the decking, or heavy equipment with steel legs would punch a hole through the decks. Laminated fir was too expensive.

Mayflower Moving and Storage was currently redecking a trailer per week. It usually patched the decks until the whole bed fell apart; then the trailer would sit in the yard waiting for a major overhaul. By this time the trailers needed to have the crossbeams repaired and new bearings as well as a new deck.

Mr. Sherman went on to say, "The shop mechanic just loves Micro=Lam. This is because it used to take the mechanic and one other employee two days to redeck a trailer, and now it just takes the shop mechanic one day to do the same job." Advantages (over plywood and apitong) of the 2-foot × 40-foot Micro=Lam pieces were ease of installation, excellent weight distribution due to the reduced number of seams, and reduced total weight of the bed.

Mr. Sherman explained that Mayflower Moving and Storage usually purchased four or five decks at a time, and warehoused some of the materials until a trailer needed redecking.

Mr. Sherman thought the original decking on flatbeds was some type of hardwood, probably oak, which could last up to five years; however, a similar decking material had not been found for a reasonable price. The plywood and fir decks used in the past 8 to 10 years had lasted anywhere from 1 to 2 years, and some had worn out in as little as six months. After using Micro=Lam for six months, Mr. Sherman expected the decking to last up to three to five years.

When asked about the type of flooring used in the company's moving vans, Mr. Sherman emphasized the top care that those floors received. "We sand, buff, and wax them just like a household floor; in fact, we take

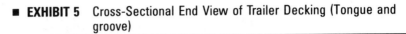

■ **EXHIBIT 5**   Cross-Sectional End View of Trailer Decking (Tongue and groove)

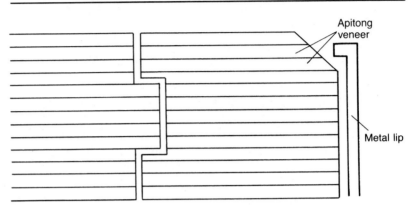

such good care of these floors they will occasionally outlast the trailer." The original floors in moving vans were made out of a laminated oak and had to be kept extremely smooth, allowing freight to slide freely. The local company purchased all of its moving vans through Mayflower Moving Vans. The only problem with floors in moving vans was that the jointed floors would occasionally buckle because of swelling.

The fact that Micro=Lam protruded ⅛ inch above the metal lip[6] which edged the flatbed trailers posed no problem for Sherman Brothers. "All we had to do was plane the edge at 40 degrees. In fact, the best fit will have the decking protrude a hair above the metal edge," Mr. Sherman said. Just prior to this, Mr. Sherman had recounted an experience which occurred with the first shipment of Micro=Lam. Because the deck was too thick, Mayflower Moving and Storage had about ⅛ inch planed from one side of the decking material. However, the company shaved off the apitong veneer, exposing the fir. Mr. Sherman said that he laughed about it now, but at the time he wasn't too pleased.

■ PEERLESS TRUCKING COMPANY

"Sure, I've heard of Micro=Lam. They [Trus Joist salespeople] have been in here . . . but we don't need that good a material." This was the response of Mel Rogers, head of Peerless' Purchasing Department, Tualatin, Oregon, when asked about the use of Micro=Lam as a truck decking material. Mr. Rogers, a 30-year veteran of the trailer manufacturing industry, seemed very skeptical of all laminated decking materials.

The primary products manufactured by Peerless (in Tualatin) required bedding materials very different from Micro=Lam. Chip trailers and rail-car dumpers required metal beds to facilitate unloading. Low-boys required a heavy decking material (usually 2 × 12-inch or 3 × 12-inch rough

---

[6]Refer to Exhibit 5.

planking) as Caterpillar tractors were frequently driven on them. Logging trailers had no beds.

Approximately 60 decks per year were required by Peerless in the manufacture of flatbeds and in redecking jobs. Micro=Lam could have been used in these applications, but fir planking was used exclusively, except for some special overseas jobs. Fir planking was available in full trailer lengths, requiring eight labor-hours to install on new equipment. Usually five or six decks were stocked at a time. The estimated life of a new deck was two to three years.

Fir planking was selected for decking applications on the basis of price and durability. Peerless purchased fir planking for $1,000 per MBF. Tradition supported fir planking in durability, as it was a well-known product.

Decking material thickness was critical, according to Mr. Rogers, as any deviation from the industry standard of 1⅜ inch required extensive retooling.

Any new decking materials for use in original equipment manufacture had to be approved by the Peerless engineering department. Alternative decking materials could have been used locally if specified by the customer.

Mr. Rogers was certainly going to be a hard person to sell on the use of Micro=Lam, Mr. Kalish felt. "Why use Micro=Lam when I can buy fir planking for less?" Rogers had said.

■ FRUEHAUF TRUCKING COMPANY

"I'd be very happy if someone would come up with a durable [trailer] deck at a reasonable price," was the response of Wayne Peterson when asked about Fruehauf's experience with decking materials. Mr. Peterson was service manager for Fruehauf's factory branch in Milwaukie, Oregon. Fruehauf Corporation, with its principal manufacturing facilities in Detroit, Michigan, was one of the nation's largest manufacturers of truck trailers.

The manufacturing facilities in Milwaukie produced 40-ton low-beds as well as assembled truck bodies manufactured in Detroit. The low-beds were subjected to heavy use, often with forklifts, which required a decking material of extreme strength and durability. Laminated decking materials then available were therefore excluded from this application.

The decking materials used in the truck bodies were specified by the sales department in Detroit, based on customer input. Generally, apitong or laminated oak was installed at the factory. Any new product to be used in original equipment manufacture had to be approved by Fruehauf's well-developed factory engineering department.

The Milwaukie operation also did about 15 redecking jobs per year. The decking material was specified by the customer on the basis of price and weathering characteristics. The materials used were laminated oak (11½ inches wide × 40 feet), apitong (7 inches × ⅛ inch—random lengths), Alaska yellow cedar (2 inches × 6 inches T&G), fir planking (2 inches × 6 inches T&G), and laminated fir (24 inches wide × 40 feet). Alaska yellow cedar was priced below all other decking materials, followed (in order) by fir planking, laminated fir, laminated oak, and apitong.

Fruehauf's suppliers of decking materials were as follows: laminated fir—Pacific Laminating, Vancouver, Washington; Alaska yellow cedar—Al Disdero Lumber Company, Portland, Oregon; and apitong—Builterials, Portland, Oregon. There were no specific suppliers for the other materials.

A minimum inventory of decking materials was kept on hand to allow for immediate repair needs only. Orders were placed for complete decks as needed.

A redecking job typically required 30 labor-hours per 7-foot × 40-foot trailer, including the removal of the old deck and installation of the new one. Decking materials that were available in full trailer lengths were preferred, as they greatly reduced installation time, improved weight distribution, and had fewer joints along which failure could occur.

The use of alternative products, such as composition flooring of wood and aluminum, was not under consideration.

Alaska yellow cedar and fir planking had the best weathering characteristics, while apitong and laminated oak weathered poorly. Oak and apitong did, however, have a hard, nonscratching surface that was desirable in enclosed use. When asked about the weathering characteristics of laminated flooring in general, Mr. Peterson responded, "It's all right for the dry states, but not around here."

■ COMPETITION

There were a large number of materials with which Micro=Lam competed in the trailer flooring market, ranging from fir plywood to aluminum floors. Trus Joist felt that the greatest obstacles to Micro=Lam's success would be from the old standard products like laminated fir and oak, which had a great deal of industry respect. For years oak had been the premier flooring material; recently, however, supplies had been short and delivery times long (two months in some cases), and prices were becoming prohibitive. (See Exhibit 6.)

■ **EXHIBIT 6** Decking Material Prices, November 1978

Product	Price	Form
Alaska yellow cedar	$650/MBF	2″ × 6″ T&G 15′ lengths
Apitong	$1.30–2/lineal foot*	1⅜″ × 7″ random lengths
Fir planking	$1/bd. ft.	2″ × 6″ T&G random lengths
Fir, laminated	$2.50/sq. ft.	1¼″ × 11¾″ × 40′
Micro=Lam	$1.30/sq. ft.	1¼″ × 24″ × 40′
	$1.50/sq. ft.	1½″ × 24″ × 40′
Oak, laminated	$2.20/sq. ft.	1⅜″ × 1½″ × 40′

*Lineal foot = price per unit length of the product.
SOURCES: Al Disdero Lumber Company, Portland, Oregon; Builterials, Portland, Oregon

Mr. Kalish had found that in the Northwest, Pacific Laminated Company was one of the major flooring suppliers to local manufacturers. Pacific Laminated produced a Douglas fir laminated product that was highly popular; however, like oak, it was relatively high priced. Despite the price, Pacific Laminated could cut the product to dimensions up to 2 feet wide and 40 feet long. Delivery time was excellent for its customers, even with special milling for shiplapped or tongue and groove edges and manufacturing to user thickness.

■ CONCLUSION

Although Mr. Kalish had had limited success marketing Micro=Lam to truck trailer manufacturers, he was concerned with the marketing program for his product. Several trailer manufacturers had raised important questions concerning the price and durability of Micro=Lam compared to alternative decking materials. He knew Micro=Lam had some strong attributes, yet he was hesitant to expand beyond the local market. Mr. Kalish was also wondering about the action he should eventually take in order to determine the additional information he would need to successfully introduce Micro=Lam nationally as a trailer decking material. One thought that crossed his mind was to define the company's marketing strategy for this product. Meanwhile, small orders continued to trickle in.

PART FOUR

Making and Moving the Goods

Chapter 7 · Product Development, Management, and Strategy

Chapter 8 · Business to Business Price Planning and Strategy

Chapter 9 · Marketing Business to Business Channel Participants

Chapter 10 · Physical Distribution Management and Strategy

Chapter **7**

Product Development, Management, and Strategy

LEARNING OBJECTIVES

After reading this chapter, you should be able to:

- Recognize the two major approaches to new product development.
- Describe four methods of organizing the new product development process.
- Relate how experience and learning curves can determine what happens to a product as it matures.
- Explain what forces impact upon a firm's decision to expand, contract, or maintain its product mix.
- Understand how quickly prospects will adopt a new product, and to what extent they will replace the old one.
- Discuss strategic alternatives for each of the strategic business units in a company's product portfolio.
- Describe three options for product elimination.

CHAPTER OUTLINE

Product Strategy in Business to
Business Marketing
Effective Product Management and
Strategy
New Product Development
   New Product Approaches
   New Product Development Process
Organization of the New Product
Effort
   Product Manager
   New Product Committee
   New Product Department
   New Product Venture Team
The Product Life-Cycle Analysis
   An Application of the Product Life-
    Cycle Model
   Life Cycles and Learning Curves
Determinants of the Product Mix
   Technology
   Competition

Changes in Levels of Business
 Activity
Operating Capacity
Market Factors
The Product Adoption-Diffusion
Process
   Stages in the Adoption Process
   Factors Influencing the Rate of
    Adoption-Diffusion
Product Portfolio Classification,
Analysis, and Strategy
   What is the Product Portfolio?
   Diagnosing the Product Portfolio
   Product Portfolio Strategies
Product Deletion Strategy
   Harvesting
   Line Simplification
   Total Line Divestment
International Product Strategy

■ PRODUCT STRATEGY IN BUSINESS TO BUSINESS MARKETING

Product development, management, strategy, and deletion are important parts of the business to business marketing process, with the major concerns being both to measure and predict success and to execute proper strategy over the life of the product. Success is more likely if the organization can develop a unique or superior product or service, has knowledge of the market, and has a well-managed marketing effort.

Effective Product Management and Strategy

Effective product management and strategy are more important today than ever as the business sector positions itself to counter offshore competitors that have impacted the domestic market for several years and show no sign of abatement. New product development, a greater marketing orientation, more sophisticated marketing research, improved new product introduction efforts, better attention to service marketing, a closer linkage with

with customers, and an increased global marketing effort, all are keys to meeting this challenge. New product development success is the principal component through which the firm can align its resources with the market environment to achieve organizational objectives. Figure 7–1 shows that new products have significantly contributed to profits in every industry

■ **FIGURE 7–1** Contribution of New Products to Profit by Industry

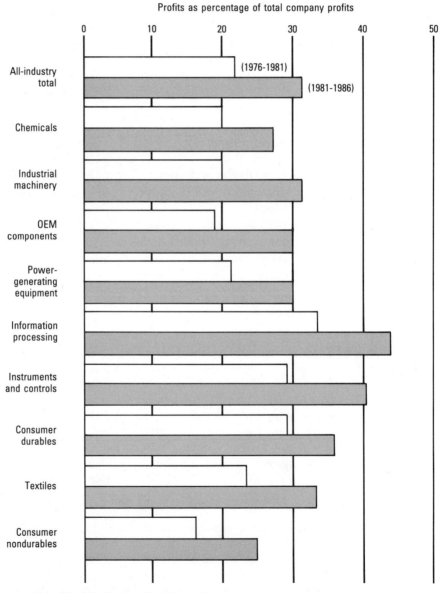

listed.[1] At the same time, it must be recognized that approximately two thirds of all commercialized new products fail in the marketplace for a variety of reasons. This situation is not likely to change.

■ NEW PRODUCT DEVELOPMENT

In many firms the design of new products and services (especially scientific and technical products) is the sole responsibility of people within the engineering discipline. However, much marketing literature argues that marketing managers should play a major role in the design (development) of new products through the guidelines marketing research can provide as to customers' wants and needs. It appears that the important role of marketers in the design and development of new products and services is finally being recognized.

Some of the past reluctance to use marketing personnel for new product development is justified, given the lack of research training and the questionable quality of many marketing research projects in the past. Many "quantitative" studies were based on approaches not necessarily appropriate for the identification and quantification of customers' wants or needs. At the other extreme "qualitative" market research studies provide some insight into customer wants and needs, but there has been some understandable and justifiable reluctance to use the resulting recommendations as guidelines for specific decisions.

Developments in mathematical psychology have introduced other tools such as the conjoint analytical approach, which among other tools makes it possible to obtain rigorous quantitative insights into customer needs and wants and their relative importance. These approaches have provided designers with valuable guidelines for the design of new products and services.

New Product Approaches

Most new product development efforts follow, and can be classified as belonging to, one of two approaches: the technology push process or the market pull process.

Technology Push.   When the perceived value of a particular technology is great, **technology push** usually results. Once the product or process has been developed, the marketing function becomes important. The marketer has some form of technology and a vague notion of possible applications, and usually not much more. Most of the truly great inventions of the period 1830–1915 fall into this category (e.g., the steam turbine, triode, and telephone). With a great invention, it is difficult to estimate the ultimate size of the market. Who, at the outset, could have estimated the market

[1]*New Products Management for the 1980s* (New York: Booz, Allen & Hamilton, 1982), p. 7.

■ **EXHIBIT 7–1**   A Comparison of Two New Product Approaches

Traditional Customer-Driven Process	Technology-Driven Process
1. Identify customer values.	1. Identify technology.
2. Creatively identify solutions and approaches.	2. Creatively identify possible customers/ applications.
3. Do homework.	3. Do homework.
4. Validate with market research.	4. Validate with market research.
5. Test.	5. Test.
6. Launch.	6. Launch.

for computers or xerography? In fact, Sperry Univac is purported to have initially estimated that the size of the total computer market by the year 2000 would be 1,000 or 2,000 machines.[2] This type of product, in effect, follows Say's Law in economics: "Supply creates demand." This kind of success inspires all technology push efforts, whether warranted or not.

Market Pull.   **Market pull** is primarily the result of marketing research methodologies of interviewing potential users about their needs, and then developing solutions to those perceived market needs. This method carries the least business risk because there is less of a chance that the developed product cannot be sold. This approach is considered more difficult to manage than technology push because it requires more input and coordination from both the internal and external environments. Exhibit 7–1 shows a comparison of these two approaches. Note that the only differences between the two approaches are in the first and second steps. The market pull approach identifies customer values, and then creatively identifies solutions and approaches; the technology push approach identifies technology, and then creatively identifies possible customers/applications.

There are more similarities between these two processes than differences, and the point should be made, whether the new product development process is technology push or market pull, is that it is a process; and the key to success lies in pursuing each step of the process thoroughly, professionally, and objectively.

New Product Development Process

New product success has long been valued as an essential factor in maintaining the economic health of a business unit, and as a critical means for improving business performance. As noted earlier in this chapter, approximately two thirds of all commercialized new products fail. This discussion will explore seven stages in the new product development process. These stages include new product strategy development, new product idea gener-

---

[2]Eugene F. Finkin, "Developing and Managing New Products," in *Marketing Management Readings, from Theory to Practice,* vol. 3, ed. Benson P. Shapiro, Robert J. Dolan, and John A. Quelch (Homewood, Ill.: Richard D. Irwin, 1985), pp. 263–75.

ation, initial screening, business analysis, product development, product testing, and product commercialization (product introduction).[3]

New Product Strategy Development.   The successful implementation of this phase requires cooperation among different groups, such as finance, research and development, corporate staff, and marketing personnel. This situation makes product strategies difficult to develop and implement.[4] The point can be illustrated with reference to what was said about the Chrysler Corporation in the 1970s—that its engineering department had such dominance that all other considerations were subordinated. As a 1975 *Fortune* article noted:

> Engineering considerations . . . dictate what kinds of cars the company makes. In the late fifties, when the auto makers were developing their first compacts, Chrysler's management wanted to build a rear-engine compact to compete with GM's Corvair. "Our engineers were not willing to go into the weight distribution that it would entail. There was no way this management could have even ordered the engineering department to do a rear-engine car." A decade later, as Ford and GM were preparing subcompacts, Chrysler's engineers concluded they could not design one that would be both competitive in styling and meet their standards for interior comfort.[5]

According to this article, too much engineering emphasis in arriving at strategic decisions was one of the major reasons for the Chrysler Corporation's poor showing in the turbulent 1970s. A fairly recent and much quoted survey of company practice with regard to new product development, found that over three quarters of all firms have a specific new product development strategy guiding their new product development process.[6]

Idea and Concept Generation.   This stage involves the search for product ideas or concepts which meet company objectives. These new ideas usually come from the customer, although the sales department's distributors, suppliers, and other employees play an important role in this effort. One very interesting way for a firm to get new product ideas is by copying its competition. Exhibit 7–2 describes how Ford Motor Company conducts "autopsies" on competitors' products in a search for new product ideas. However, this can be risky as patent infringement lawsuits can badly tarnish a firm's image.

   Many marketing analysts suggest that an open perspective is essential for generating new ideas. For example, a 3M employee came up with the idea for notepaper that could be stuck to telephones, desks, paper, and walls by a small adhesive strip on the back. The employee thought of the

---

[3]Booz, Allen & Hamilton Inc. can be credited as the authors of this particular scheme in their report entitled *Management of New Products*, 1968. Also, see the updated version, *New Products Management for the 1980s*, New York, 1982, p. 7.

[4]Subhash C. Jain, *Marketing Planning and Strategy*, 2d ed. (Cincinnati, Ohio: South-Western Publishing, 1985), p. 637.

[5]Peter Vanderwicken, "What's Really Wrong at Chrysler," *Fortune*, May 1975, p. 176.

[6]Booz, Allen & Hamilton Inc., *New Product Management for the 1980s*, 1982.

■ **EXHIBIT 7–2**   Conducting Autopsies: Sources for New Product Ideas

What does it mean to be a "destruction engineer"? To find out, take a look at Robert Cameron of Ford Motor Company.

New ideas don't mean sending lots of dollars into research and development. As a matter of fact, they might even come from copying competitors. Cameron purchases new competing models from local dealers and spends two weeks disassembling each one. Along with his pool of mechanics, he takes an automobile apart and catalogs and inspects each of its 30,000 parts.

When he discovers a product innovation, such as Nissan Stanza's wheel base, Cameron sends it through a battery of tests. In the case of the Stanza wheel base, he found that even a vise could not bend it out of shape. As a result, he sent the idea to the Ford management team, which decided to adopt it for use in their own cars.

Ford Motor Company is well known for advertising that it has better ideas. But where do these new ideas come from? A new method for rolling up windows by GM and a one-unit alternator and regulator by Toyota are good examples. Disassembling automobiles has also helped Ford's engineers to uncover competitors' mistakes, which would not then be repeated by Ford.

Although this type of activity might seem unethical and unfair, similar practices are also employed by GM and Chrysler. In a concern for patent infringement, the major automakers frequently trade rights to certain improvements. Ford, for instance, swapped its innovative two-way tailgate to GM for the right to several of GM's patents.

SOURCE: Based on Kevin Totus, "Auto Makers Look for Ideas in Rivals' Cars," *The Wall Street Journal,* July 20, 1982, p. 29. Reprinted by permission of *The Wall Street Journal,* © Dow Jones & Company, Inc. (1982). All rights reserved.

idea because his place mark kept falling out of his hymnbook during choir practice. Today, annual sales of Post-it-notes are around $40 million.[7] Top managers at Lockheed Corporation also encourage entrepreneurship among their staffs. They open their doors to new ideas for products and processes from all workers and give individuals and groups seed money to nurture those ideas. These entrepreneurs are given timetables to prove their ideas have merit. They are not penalized for failure, but are encouraged to learn from their mistakes and to try again.[8] A new product idea collection system ought to be a well-defined process for communicating new product ideas from various sources to a collection point within the firm.

Screening and Evaluation.   This step involves an analysis to determine which ideas submitted are pertinent and merit a more detailed study as to potential feasibility and market acceptance. For its internal screening and evaluation in its search for new products, Medtronic, a high-technology medical firm, has developed the weighted-point system shown in Table 7–1. This system establishes screening criteria and assigns weights to each one used to evaluate new product ideas. The 17 specific factors in the figure are grouped into six categories commonly cited as reasons for new product failures. Medtronic believes that a score of at least 120 is needed on the "hurdle" in the point system to find a winning new product.[9]

[7]Lawrence Ingrassia, "By Improving Scratch Paper, 3M Gets New-Product Winner," *The Wall Street Journal,* March 31, 1983, p. 31.

[8]Patrice Apodaca, "Flatter Organizations, Challenge Executives," *Investors Daily,* October 17, 1988, pp. 1, 34.

[9]Eric N. Berkowitz, Roger A. Kerin, and William Rudelius, *Marketing* (St. Louis: C. V. Mosby, 1986), pp. 238–39.

■ **TABLE 7–1** A Weighted-Point System Used by Medtronic to Try to Spot a Winning New Medical Product

General factor	Specific factor	Scale	Total points
Size of target market	Incidence of malady	Undefinable — 10,000s — 1,000,000s ✓ — 100,000,000s (0, 5, 10, 15, 20)	12
	Product usage	One per many patients — One per patient ✓ (0 ... 5)	5
	Cost-effective for health care system	No — Yes ✓ (0, 5, 10)	7
	Application of product	Other ✓ — Spine — Brain — Brain/heart — Heart (0, 5, 10, 15, 20)	3
Significant point of difference	Treatment evaluation	Similar to existing approaches — Better than existing approaches — Clearly superior to existing approaches ✓ (0, 5, 10)	10
	Clearness of function	Questioned or uncertain — Direct cause and effect ✓ (0, 5, 10)	8
Product quality	Restore natural physiology	Partial ✓ — Total (0, 5, 10, 15, 20)	6
	Restore viability	Partial — Full ✓ (0, 5, 10, 15, 20)	13
	Characteristic of product	External — Implantable. Capital equipment → Permanently worn → Totally implanted ✓ (0, 5, 10, 15, 20)	20
	Mode of operation	Chemical ✓ — Mechanical — Electrical-mechanical — Electrical (0, 5, 10, 15, 20)	7
	Product development team	Physician only — Engineer only — Physician and engineer ✓ — Physician with engineering training (0, 5, 10)	6
Access to market	Physician users know Medtronic name?	No — Same (50%) — Yes (all) ✓ (0, 5, 10)	10
	Inventor's ability, willingness to be champion	Not well known Not willing to promote — Well known Willing to promote ✓ (0, 5, 10, 15, 20)	8
Timing	Technologies in place	No — Partially ✓ — Yes (0, 5, 10)	6
	Entrepreneur in place	No — Partially ✓ — Totally (0, 5, 10)	4
	Social acceptance	Negative — Positive ✓ (0, 5, 10)	8
Miscellaneous	Gut feel about success	Uncertain — Good chance — Positive ✓ — Highly positive (0, 5, 10, 15, 20)	12
Total			145

SOURCE: Ed Bakken and Medtronics, Inc. Used with permission.

We can indicate the nature of this part of the analysis by the following questions that are meant to be informative, but not exhaustive:

1. Do we have or can we develop access to the necessary raw materials?
2. Is the project of a scope that is feasible within our existing financial capability?
3. Is there some synergy within our existing product line?
4. Is it likely that our present customers represent a potential market, or must we develop entirely new markets?
5. Could the product be marketed through our existing sales force and distributor organization?
6. Does the idea appear to be within the capability of our product development organization?
7. What impact would the successful development of this product have on our existing products, markets, and marketing organization?
8. Would the new product be capable of manufacture within our existing production facilities, and with our existing skills?[10]

Negative answers to several of these questions or recognition of the fact that significant new financial, managerial, marketing, production, or supplier resources would be required would reduce the attractiveness of the idea.

Business Analysis. This step, along with the remaining steps in the process, is the expansion of the idea or the concept through creative analysis into a "go" or "no-go" recommendation. Return-on-investment criteria are examined along with competition and the potential for profitable market entry. A more specific list of considerations during the business analysis stage would include demand projections, cost projections, competition, required investment, and profitability. Business marketers sometimes use the break-even analysis, discounted cash flow, Bayesian decision model, and simulation models to assess the likely profitability of promising new product ideas.

Product Development. This stage involves taking the product from an idea generated during a brainstorming session to a state of readiness for product and market testing. Activities during this particular stage are often more difficult and time-consuming than expected. Something which looks great on paper can fail miserably when scientists, engineers, and production technicians try to create the physical product. Many new product ideas are either abandoned or sent back for more study at this point in the new product development process. Exhibit 7–3 discusses the activities involved in the development of a new agricultural product; it gives an indication of the time involved and the difficulties encountered during this phase of the process.

---

[10]Ibid., p. 123.

■ **EXHIBIT 7–3**   Developing and Using a New Farm Product

Canadian wheat farmers in both Saskatchewan and Alberta have long used the practice of fallow-ing, which means leaving fields free of crops in alternating years. Fallowing allows the dry Cana-dian soil of the regions to accumulate extra moisture during the alternate years; as a result, crop yields are usually greater. Yet fallowing also permits the growth of weeds which rob the fields of much of this stored moisture. Farmers typically use mechanical cultivation to eradicate the weeds, causing yet another depletion of moisture.

To solve this problem, Elanco Products, a division of Eli Lilly Canada, Inc., created a new product called HERITAGE Wheat Production System. This system uses herbicides to assist the farmer in improving crop yields over each two-year cycle. Use of the system also tends to aid moisture conservation, reduce soil erosion, reduce cultivation, and increase wheat yields.

Elanco understands that the adoption process is an immediate outgrowth of the new product development process. When the HERITAGE system was first introduced as a product, Elanco solic-ited growers to experiment with HERITAGE on their fields. The company hoped that these "bell cow" growers would model the benefits of HERITAGE to their fellow growers.

Dick Greschuk, a "bell cow" who farms 4,000 acres, stated, "I like technology. I'll use anything that helps save money and works for me."

SOURCE: Based on Jeff Lieb, "Product Repositioning in the Face of Tradition: How Elanco Created a New Herbicide Market Niche," *Business Marketing,* November 1984, pp. 64–68. Used by permission.

Product Testing.   Commercial experiments necessary to verify earlier business judgments are conducted during this stage. Product testing takes place both in the laboratory and the field, and involves pilot production testing as well as presentation to the market for an indication of accept-ance or rejection. Following satisfactory results in market testing, many companies will commercialize the product by listing it in their catalog and turning it over to the sales force. More and more companies are now turn-ing to market testing to indicate such things as the product's performance under actual operating conditions, how different buying influences react to alternative prices and sales approaches, the market potential, and the best market segments. Some market-test methods commonly used by business to business marketers in the new product development process include product-use tests, trade shows, distributor and dealer display rooms, and test marketing. While product testing is necessary to some degree, there is a real risk of tipping the firm's hand to the competition during field testing.

Product Commercialization and Introduction.   This stage includes launch-ing the new product through full-scale production and sales, and by com-mitting the company's reputation and resources to the product's success.

The new product development process is complex, difficult, interdiscipli-nary, challenging, and expensive. However, it is also a vital process that is necessary to sustain the profitable growth of the firm. A primary purpose of this process is to eliminate new product ideas which do not seem feasible before extensive resources are expended on a potential product failure. New product ideas within the new product development process follow a characteristic decay curve with a progressive elimination of product ideas during each stage of the process. Figure 7–2 gives an indication of this product idea elimination as it moves through the stages of the new product development process.

■ **FIGURE 7–2**   Mortality Rate of New Products by Stage of Development

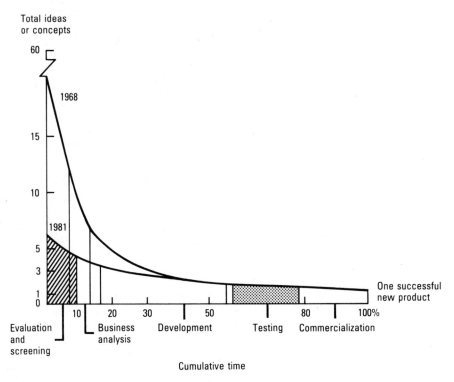

SOURCE: Booz, Allen & Hamilton Inc., 1982. Used with permission.

■ ORGANIZATION OF THE NEW PRODUCT EFFORT

New product development, evaluation, and management must follow good management practice if we expect to achieve effectiveness, efficiency, and a reasonable likelihood of success. In most firms the new product development effort involves a complex structure of line and staff relationships, and several departments are usually involved in the development of new product ideas. Fusing these groups together in a manner that will bring their efforts to maximum productivity for the new product without destroying their effectiveness in producing and marketing mature existing products is one of the most difficult problems facing management. However, if profits are to be realized from new products, this problem has to be solved. As discussed below, a number of options or alternatives are available to management.

Product Manager

Product managers are in charge of planning, organizing, implementing, and controlling new product development, along with the management of the product as it travels through its life-cycle. Product managers can greatly enhance their product line management through the form of integrated new product development they choose. The **product management concept** requires the product manager to move the new product from the idea generation stage to the product introduction stage, complete with service, technical assistance, and performance feedback. Union Carbide, Bell Helicopter, Texas Instruments, Uniroyal, and General Dynamics have all subscribed to the product management concept.

The product manager is a tactician who orchestrates the new product effort, very much the way the advertising manager, sales manager, distribution manager, sales promotion manager, and marketing research manager do. Product managers in the business to business market are often considered the equivalent of brand managers in the consumer market. Table 7–2 shows one view of the duties and responsibilities of the business product managers. Note the wide variety of tasks for which product managers are responsible and the technical nature of some of the tasks they most commonly perform.

■ **TABLE 7–2**   Duties and Responsibilities of Product Managers in the Business to Business Market

Duty/Responsibility	Percent of Respondents Having This Duty or Responsibility
Oversees product(s) progress	91
Decides the nature of or initiates changes in ongoing products	70
Initiates product reengineering	67
Determines product deletion	65
Determines product phaseout	65
Determines markets to enter or depart	64
Initiates and controls new product conceptualization	64
Responsible for product profitability	62
Develops and presents product's budget requests	61
Initiates price changes	58
Preserves promotional strategy	57
Initiates market research analysis	57
Sets pricing strategy	55
Develops sales goals and objectives	55
Attends product committee meetings	52
Develops product control criteria	45
Has chief responsibility and decides which new products are added	42
Determines product's channel of distribution	39
Chairs product committee	36
Decides the type of promotional mix	35
Controls package changes	25

Note: Responses exceed 100 percent due to multiple answers.

SOURCE: Robert W. Eckels and Timothy J. Novotney, "Industrial Product Managers' Authority and Responsibility," *Industrial Marketing Management* 13 (1984), p. 73. Used with permission.

New Product Committee

The **new product committee approach** involves a top management committee, consisting of representatives from marketing, production, accounting,
engineering, and other areas who review new product proposals. Though
not involved in the actual development process, the committee is charged
with evaluating new product proposals. This approach allows for a minimum of organizational disruption. However, a disadvantage to this organizational structure is the possibility that demands of departmental priorities
might supersede those of the committee. Committee participation is generally considered a part-time activity that is secondary to the major needs
of a particular department within the firm. Most firms must feel that the
advantages outweigh the disadvantages because the new product committee is the most common form of organizational structure for managing new
products.[11]

New Product Department

The **new product department approach** creates a specific department to
generate and evaluate new product ideas, to direct and coordinate development work, and to implement field testing and precommercialization of
the new product. This arrangement allows for a maximum effort in new
product development, but at the expense of major overhead costs incurred
at the outset. The department head typically has substantial authority and
relatively easy access to top management. One research study revealed that
of 2,000 large firms in several industries, 869 had formed new product
departments.[12]

New Product Venture Team

The **new product venture team approach** involves forming a task force representing various departments, and giving responsibility for new product
implementation to a full-time staff. This task force is brought together and
charged with the responsibility of bringing a specific product to the market
or a specific new business into being. The venture team is normally dis-
solved once a new product is established in the market. Signode Industries,
Inc., creates independent venture teams in which half the members have a
technical background, and half are drawn from marketing and sales. The
company, which was founded in 1916 and went private in recent years in a
leveraged buyout, is a $750 million producer of steel and plastic strapping
systems along with other business products. How do its teams work? After
two weeks of listening to outside experts talk about trends and possible
opportunities, a team spends about six months searching for unmet or un-
perceived market needs. Its only preconceived direction is that they need

---

[11]Robert Hisrich and Michael P. Peters, *Marketing Decisions for New and Mature Products: Planning, Development, and Control* (Columbus, Ohio: Charles E. Merrill Publishing,
1984), p. 29.

[12]Booz, Allen & Hamilton, *New Product Management for the 1980s*, p. 20.

to emphasize the company's strategic strengths. The full-time task of the team members, which they perform away from the company, is to generate new product ideas. They are challenged to be creative and to encourage one another in the solicitation of new product ideas. Searching widely for information and ideas, they are sensitive to research and development (R&D) but also use a market-driven, customer-oriented approach. After narrowing their list of ideas down from a few hundred to two or three, they eventually carry a product to market.[13]

Concept Questions

1. What is the principal component through which the firm can meet its organizational objectives?
2. What does the new product development process involve in most business to business companies?

■ THE PRODUCT LIFE-CYCLE ANALYSIS

Regardless of the type of product organization chosen by the firm, the management of new products throughout their useful lives is of paramount importance. The product life-cycle model, along with the importance of new product development, has been utilized frequently in the marketing literature to show how sales of a product vary over time, and how every product eventually ends in obsolescence. Figure 7–3 points out that sales

■ **FIGURE 7–3**   How Sales and Profits of a Business to Business Product Vary over Time

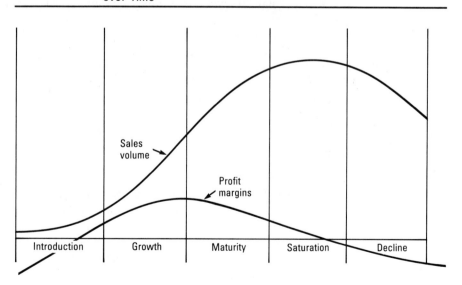

[13]Robert O. Null, "The Team Approach to Business Expansion," presentation to the Chicago chapter of the Product Development and Management Association, February 26, 1986.

grow sharply during the market growth stage, but begin to flatten out during the market maturity stage. Sales reach their peak during the saturation stage and dramatically fall off during the decline stage. This information has been used to suggest effective marketing strategies over a product's projected life span. While the shapes of the sales volume and profit margin curves vary from product to product, the basic shapes and the relationship between the two curves are as illustrated in Figure 7–3. Note that profit peaks during the growth stage, whereas sales top out during the saturation stage.

Management must recognize what part of the life cycle a product is in at any given time. The competitive environment and resultant marketing strategies ordinarily differ, depending upon the stage of the product life cycle.[14] Some strategic elements to consider in this connection would be competitive action, return on investment, distribution decisions, and advertising strategy and emphasis.

An Application of the Product Life-Cycle Model

Technological advances can move products more quickly through their life cycles, often necessitating a product deletion decision. Product life cycles for IBM's mainframe computers seem to be getting shorter; it introduced two computers in six years, and then four more in the following four years. On a price-performance basis, IBM's latest 4381 computer is about 40 times better than the 360 it introduced in 1964, and Hewlett-Packard's latest model 41 CX calculator is over 100 times better than its model 35, which was introduced in 1972.

A particular life-cycle period may be quite short, as it is in the electronics field where new product development and introduction are daily events; or it may be quite long (a decade or more), as it has been for some products such as milling machines, standard fasteners, and industrial gears. However, sooner or later, all products yield to new technology and are made obsolete by new technology that either reduces costs or improves performance characteristics.

Sandia National Laboratories in New Mexico has developed a novel supercomputer which relies on a controversial technology called *massively parallel processing*. The theory behind the system is elegantly simple. Conventional computers require only one number-crunching processor; for most jobs, such as word processing and spreadsheets, that is enough. However, the problems tackled by supercomputers require billions of computations, and scientists have tried to improve performance by hooking 10s or 100s of processors together. With all the processors working simultaneously, the parallel computer solves the problem faster than its single predecessors. As a test, the Sandia team took three sample problems and

---

[14]For a discussion of strategies for reviving declining products and also some ideas for reintroducing abandoned products, see William Layer, Mushtag Luqmani, and Zahir Quraeshi, "Product Rejuvenation Strategies," *Business Horizons*, November–December 1984, pp. 21–28; and Mark N. Vamos, "New Life for Madison Avenue's Old-Time Stars," *Business Week*, April 1, 1985, p. 94.

smashed the speed limit each time. One example was calculating the stresses inside a building beam supported only at one end. The problem would have taken a powerful minicomputer 20 years to solve; the new machine finished in a week.[15]

Life Cycles and Experience Curves[16]

Learning curve analysis, linked with the product life cycle, is another base for developing product strategy. This concept is based on the discovery that costs (measured in constant dollars) decline (usually from 10 to 30 percent) by a predictable and constant percentage each time accumulated production experience (volume) is doubled. The curve illustrated in Figure 7–4 is an 85 percent **experience curve.** With every doubling of experience, costs per unit drop to 85 percent of their original level—a 15 percent reduction in costs for every doubling of cumulative production. Different products and industries experience different learning rates. The experience curve phenomenon has been supported in studies of numerous industries, including the chemical, steel, paper, and electronics industries. The concept is especially relevant in high-technology markets such as semiconductors and computer memories.[17]

The learning curve phenomenon, which was discovered in the 1920s in the aircraft industry, was reported in 1936.[18] Simply stated, the rate of learning is such that as the quantity of units manufactured doubles, the number of direct labor hours it takes to produce an individual unit decreases at a uniform rate.

In a related concept *economies of scale* (often confused with the experience curve), refers to the production efficiency attained as increased units are produced. It is a fixed-cost phenomenon as seldom does an increase in production require an equivalent increase in capital investment, size of the sales force, or overhead costs. In a stable environment the firm can realize economies of scale by producing a uniform product, with perceivable demand, thereby guaranteeing efficiencies and higher profit levels. Learning per se helps the firm not only to increase profit levels but also to lower the break-even quantity. The result is a reduction in fixed costs as they are spread over many additional units.

---

[15]"Faster than a Speeding Chip: A Novel Supercomputer," *Newsweek,* March 28, 1988, p. 63.

[16]This section is from Louis E. Yelle, "Industrial Life Cycles and Learning Curves: Interaction of Marketing and Production," *Industrial Marketing Management* 9 (1980), pp. 311–18; taken from Manoj K. Agarival, Philip C. Burger, and David A. Reid, eds., *Readings in Industrial Marketing,* (Englewood Cliffs, N.J.: Prentice-Hall, 1986), pp. 104–11. Also, see George S. Day and David B. Montgomery, "Diagnosing the Experience Curve," *Journal of Marketing* 47 (Spring 1983), pp. 44–58; and Hans B. Thorelli and Stephen C. Burnett, "The Nature of Product Life Cycles for Industrial Goods Businesses," *Journal of Marketing* 45 (Fall 1981), pp. 97–108.

[17]George S. Day and David B. Montgomery, "Diagnosing the Experience Curve," *Journal of Marketing* 47 (Spring 1983), pp. 44–58.

[18]T. P. Wright, "Factors Affecting the Cost of Airplanes," *Journal of Aeronautical Sciences* 3 (February 1936), pp. 122–28.

■ **FIGURE 7–4**   An 85 Percent Learning Curve Requiring 1.0 Direct Labor Hour to Manufacture the First Unit (K = 1)

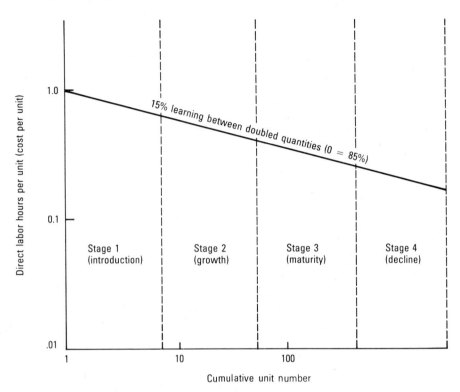

SOURCE: George S. Day and David B. Montgomery, "Diagnosing the Experience Curve," *Journal of Marketing* 47 (Spring 1983), pp. 44–58. Used with permission.

The task at hand is to explore what happens to a product as it proceeds from one stage of the product life cycle to the next. The model relationships discussed next examine how the learning curve can help clarify the product life cycle.

Introduction.   Product introduction, the initial phase of the learning curve, represents the highest cost stage. Initial costs are high, but drop rapidly with additional units produced. This phenomenon is vividly demonstrated for three different learning curves in Table 7–3. Given an 85 percent learning curve, if the cost to make the first unit is $10.00, the cost to make the 1,000th unit will be only $1.98.

This phase of the learning curve is labeled Stage 1 so that it can coincide with the introductory stage of the product life cycle shown in Figure 7–4. Sales are lowest here while the innovative firm tries to drive its costs down, as shown by the slope of the learning curve. As cost and price decrease, the product appeals to more users, and this results in increased sales.

Market Growth.   In the market growth stage of the product life cycle, rapid growth occurs, accompanied by the dramatic cost decreases shown

■ TABLE 7-3   Cost of a Specific Unit for Three Different Learning Curves All Having a First Unit Cost of $10.00

Cumulative Number of Units Made	90% Learning Curve	85% Learning Curve	80% Learning Curve
1	$10.00	$10.00	$10.00
2	9.00	8.50	8.00
3	8.46	7.73	7.02
4	8.10	7.22	6.40
8	7.29	6.14	5.12
16	6.56	5.22	4.10
32	5.90	4.44	3.28
64	5.31	3.77	2.62
1,000	3.50	1.98	1.08
10,000	2.47	1.15	.52
100,000	1.74	.67	.24
1,000,000	1.22	.39	.12
10,000,000	.86	.23	.06
20,000,000	.78	.19	.04

SOURCE: George S. Day and David B. Montgomery, "Diagnosing the Experience Curve," *Journal of Marketing* 47 (Spring 1983), pp. 44–58. Used with permission.

in Table 7–3. During this stage the innovative firm should be utilizing cost decreases, as described by the learning curve, to its advantage in keeping costs below those of the competition. If the firm manages to succeed in this effort, it can expand its market share, use price as a competitive weapon, and still generate an adequate profit margin.

Market Maturity.   During this stage cumulative volume has reached the point where costs are about as low as they are going to get. (The data in Table 7–3 demonstrate this point.) For example, if a firm is riding an 80 percent learning curve and has built up a cumulative volume of 10 million units, an increase in volume to 20 million units would only drop its cost by two cents (i.e., for a first unit cost of $10.00). Because further significant cost decreases are difficult to achieve, market penetration into new user segments is very slow. What the learning curve adds to understanding the maturity stage of the life cycle is that lower costs are associated with market penetration, which means increased sales. In Stage 3 of the learning curve (see Figure 7–4), cost reductions are progressively harder to achieve; thus maturity occurs.

Sales Decline.   The sales decline stage is associated with Stage 4 in Figure 7–4. As the market becomes saturated, sales drop off. When this happens, it becomes impossible to achieve large enough increases in cumulative production to lower costs significantly in an attempt to stimulate sales. Marginal producers then drop out of the market.

Other learning curve variations and their hypothesized effect on the product life cycle have been explored in depth.[19] One theory contends that

---

[19]Yelle, "Industrial Life Cycles and Learning Curves," pp. 311–18.

more frequent use of the learning curve leads to enlightened marketing strategies and policies by fostering closer cooperation between the production and marketing functions within business firms. The experience curve can create the tendency to formulate marketing policies in a vacuum because it deals with price and not costs. Hence, the use of the learning curve in the marketing strategy selection process should help circumvent this apparent tendency.

■ DETERMINANTS OF THE PRODUCT MIX

The act of planning implies a course of action that has been thought through in advance so as to result in a consistent pattern of decisions regarding profits, market share, sales, and cash flow. This planning identifies the fundamental determinants of the product mix of a firm, including product line depth and product mix width, which would include the total number of items and lines offered by the firm. The difficulties faced by management in formulating a sound product mix will become evident. Management's role consists of adjusting to these forces as skillfully as possible in light of the resources of the enterprise, and of guiding the firm along product paths that lead to future growth and profits. The determinants discussed here are limited to those of a basic nature, and no effort has been made to treat in detail the various specific reasons or motivations underlying product action.

Technology

In times of rapid technological and market change, successful firms are the leaders not only in adopting new technology but also in introducing new technology for competitive reasons. New technology provides the means for effective product innovation. The "Business to Business Marketing in Action" box explains that Apple Computer has recently introduced a new generation of software that for the first time allows users who have never programmed a computer to create "stacks" of "interactive information." The release of this product has prompted Apple's competitors to accelerate testing their own competitive models.

New product development can be inspired by technological change as well as by customer need. However, product development should not lead to companies' emphasizing either a technological focus or a customer focus. The emphasis should be on achieving the proper coordination between the two areas.[20] Technical excellence is not a sufficient basis for success in product innovation. Innovation requires a mix of activities as the new technology is reshaped. (Capital, facilities, and perhaps new personnel are needed.) The electronics industry is a prime example of a field in which a myriad number of inventions have led to dynamic changes in products.

---

[20]Roland W. Schmitt, "Successful Corporate R&D," *Harvard Business Review* 63 (May–June 1985), pp. 124–28.

BUSINESS TO BUSINESS MARKETING IN ACTION

Yes, But What Does It Do?

A guide to a new software generation

On his lecture tours, Bill Atkinson, father of the much-touted HyperCard program, likes to ask how many people have used his new computer software. Then he asks: "How many of you know what it *is*?" At a recent meeting in New York, more than 400 hands were raised in answer to the first question. When the second was asked, all but a few dropped—and the crowd roared with laughter. And how does Atkinson describe his baby? Is a "software Erector set" any help?

HyperCard is only the first in a new generation of software that defies the familiar categories of word processor, spreadsheet or database—and is giving the marketing folks fits. Another program, Agenda, has been termed "a spreadsheet for words"; a third, Ize, is called a "textbase." All blend qualities of traditional programs to help users master mountains of information—and strip away the rigid rules that limit the flexibility of older programs. "The next great wave of applications is going to be these information systems," says Mitch Kapor, whose Lotus 1–2–3 helped kick off the personal-computing revolution. Esther Dyson, whose Release 1.0 newsletter covers the computer industry, says, "It's stupendous stuff."

But what do the programs *do*? Atkinson's HyperCard allows users who have never programmed a computer to create "stacks" of "interactive information." With a "stack" about fishing, a reader could instantly get facts on a particular species—or even cause an image of a carp to pop up on the screen. Though Apple Computer released HyperCard only in August, Macintosh owners have already used it to create thousands of "stacks"—many of which are being sold or swapped to other HyperCard users.

Like science fiction: Test versions of two other as-yet-unreleased programs help people find needles in the information haystack. Lotus's Agenda acts like a personal secretary, making sense of the notes you scribble to yourself. The user can ask to see only items about "Bill," or "beetles." If Bill collects beetles, Agenda can link the topics. It even "intuits" some links automatically; it recognizes that "next Friday" and "December 18" are the same and will consult both in compiling a to-do list. The Royal Bank of Canada uses Agenda to sort through news-agency stories. Some trial and error is involved. Hoping to gather stories on foreign political problems, bank employee George Goodwin had Agenda gather wire copy containing the word

continued

"stability." He got stories about gold and oil prices, but none about political stability.

Ize, from the Madison, Wisc.-based Persoft, offers another way to take arms against a sea of data. It builds ingeniously detailed indexes. Attorney Leland Hutchinson in Chicago uses Ize to help associates pinpoint thousands of paragraphs from contracts giving them a guide for their own work. Personal-computer consultant Roy Freborg says the program reminds him of computers in science fiction, which figure out what you mean when you ask them a simple question. He recalls seeing it for the first time and thinking, "Yes! This is what you should be able to do with a computer!"

The history of software is littered with good ideas that never caught on, and the success of these products will be tallied at the cash register. Apple gives HyperCard away with each new Macintosh—perhaps to get around having to explain it. Lotus, however, will charge a hefty $400 for Agenda, and Persoft plans to charge $445 for Ize.

As good as the new programs may be, they may offer only a hint of what's to come. Kapor, who began the work on Agenda before leaving Lotus, is now putting together an even more extensive program for the Macintosh. Every new category of software defied description at first, from spreadsheets to desktop publishing. Analyst Dyson predicts that the more information people have to assimilate, the more easily they will adapt to these information managers. Atkinson would agree. More and more, he says excitedly, his audiences are responding to his "what is it" question. "I'm getting a bunch of people raising their hands and shouting, 'A software Erector set!' " At least *they* understand it!

SOURCE: *Newsweek;* December 14, 1987. Used with permission.

Technological shifts in product use and application require the maintenance of continuous contact with customers. Customer activities must be observed and monitored in order to determine variations and changes in customer needs and wants—those suggesting technological shifts in product use and application. These are the vital signs of impending product change. They signal opportunity for product variations or improvements, and new products altogether. The Muffco case is an interesting example of technological shift and resultant change in product requirements.

Muffco is a manufacturer of mufflers and air cleaners for heavy-duty trucks, and construction and mining equipment. Muffco's business is divided into two components by type of distribution: direct to original equipment manufacturers (DEMs) and distributor sales to the aftermarket.

Muffco's customer service department has been under considerable stress for several years. Business has been at a high level, but internal departments have not kept pace with demand. In an attempt to create order out of chaos, the customer service manager has isolated different activities and initiated reports that illustrate trends in various vital signs of the business:

- Orders-received and order-aging reports
- Time-required-for-shipment and back-order sales
- Reports of complaints or compliments received by letter or telephone
- Technical-information-request report

In analyzing these reports, the customer service manager discovered two distinctive characteristics in the complaints about products and requests for technical information: first, that a new category of complaints began to develop regarding the contribution of air filters and mufflers to energy inefficiency; and second, that the number of requests for technical information about air filters and mufflers to improve energy efficiency had increased substantially.

He reviewed these data with the engineering department manager and found that both developments preceded, by approximately six to twelve months, negotiations with DEM customers for products having performance characteristics that would improve the energy efficiency of their engines.[21]

This illustration does not conclusively prove that vital signs such as complaints and information inquiries are precursors of technological shifts and changes, but the thesis certainly seems logical. Muffco's management accepts this idea, and now periodically reviews complaint and technical-information-request reports as part of its routine search for information and ideas that suggest the need for product changes and additions.

The automotive and homebuilding industries have experienced extensive energy-related change in their products. In both industries dramatic technological shifts have resulted from product use and application requirements imposed by energy-conscious consumers, architects, homebuilders, and government agencies.

Blue-collar workers, technicians, engineers, scientists, supervisors, and managers are all constantly searching for ways to cut costs and to improve efficiency, effectiveness, productivity, and timeliness. (See the section on value analysis in Chapter 3.) This never-ending search by millions of people results in changes in product uses and applications—technological shifts that alter or abort life cycles, often causing new products to come into being.

Business to business marketing managers must continuously monitor the customer environment and search for evidence suggesting technological shifts. The marketplace yields these vital signs to the astute marketer.[22]

---

[21]Dick Berry, *Industrial Marketing for Results* (Reading, Mass.: Addison-Wesley Publishing, 1981), pp. 42–43.

[22]Ibid., pp. 42–43.

Competition

A second important determinant of a firm's product mix is the changes in product offerings of the competition. A change in a competitor's product mix could represent a major challenge to the company; and if that change is truly a significant improvement, such as a technological breakthrough, it may prove disastrous unless it can be matched or surpassed within a reasonable length of time.

In recent years American companies have experienced dramatic changes in their domestic competitive environment. Small specialized competitors have exited or been swallowed up by larger multi-industry companies, often resulting in stronger, financially solvent, but more unpredictable competition. Foreign and multinational competitors have taken aim at the critical and more profitable U.S. markets, which are easier to penetrate and pivotal to worldwide success, while building and maintaining barriers to entry by U.S. companies themselves.[23] This competitive change has not been limited merely to new configurations of traditional competitors; it has also included a considerable number of new companies and complete substitution by new types of products.

Changes in Levels of Business Activity

Most firms must deal with changes in business activity as a result of business cycles and seasonal variations. Many such firms expand their total product offering by adding product lines with different seasonal patterns to offset those of their present lines. Thereby, they are able to smooth out their production level and sales volume throughout the year. In somewhat similar fashion some firms add product lines that are less sensitive to business cycle variations than their existing lines.

Operating Capacity

A firm will often expand its product mix if it discovers underutilized capacity in any part of its business. The underutilized capacity might be in any number of functional areas, such as production, sales, or research. For example, when new equipment is bought, there may be a time when it is not totally utilized in satisfying existing demand, and there is pressure on management to find new products to keep such equipment busy. Similarly, when a marketing organization is set up to serve a particular market for a single product line, it often becomes apparent that the sales force could handle other lines as well. Then pressure is generated to find new products that can also be sold profitably to that market.

---

[23]William E. Rothschild, "Competitive Analysis: The Missing Link in Strategy," in *Marketing Management Readings,* vol. 3, eds. Benson P. Shapiro, Robert J. Dolan, and John A. Quelch (Homewood, Ill.: Richard D. Irwin, 1985), pp. 235–47.

Market Factors

Several market factors impact the selling firm's product mix. A change in the buyer's product mix as a result of competitive action or technological innovation could present an opportunity for the sale of additional quantities of various products or an opportunity to capitalize on additional business. Additionally, the migration of industry into an area economically served by the producer might offset losses from outward migration. Such activity, along with an increase or decrease in production capabilities, can lead to changes in the product mix.

Concept Questions

1. What does the new product development process involve in most companies?
2. What is the fundamental marketing value of product life-cycle analysis?
3. What is the role of competition in determining a firm's product mix?

■ THE PRODUCT ADOPTION-DIFFUSION PROCESS

Business to business marketers are assigned the responsibility of not only assessing new product success or failure time estimates but also the responsibility of evaluating the substitution factor for a proposed new product. If a company decides to expand its product mix, marketers must assess how quickly prospects will adopt a new product and to what extent they will replace the old.

The **adoption process** is the decision-making activity of the buying firm through which the new product or innovation is accepted. The diffusion of the new product, innovation, or service, is the process by which the product or service is accepted by an industry over time. There are many similarities between the consumer in the consumer adoption process and members of the business buying center, as both groups go through a basic five-step process in deciding whether or not to adopt something new.

Stages in the Adoption Process

The stages in the adoption process are discussed below.

Awareness.   The buyer first learns of the new product or service, but lacks much information about it. Awareness might come about by being exposed to sales promotion, by talking with other buyers, or by casual conversation with another member of the buying center.

Interest.   The buyer seeks out additional information about the product or service by requesting either additional data from the potential seller or perhaps by requesting a member of the potential supplier's sales team to make a sales call.

Evaluation. Here, the buyer (or another member of the buying center) considers, or makes a mental evaluation of, whether the new product or service would be useful. Consideration might be given to a value analysis project or quite possibly to a make or buy situation.

Trial. In this stage, adoption of the innovation takes place on a limited basis, as the buyer who makes a trial purchase carefully evaluates the correctness of the decision. If the new product or service is very expensive, radically new, or quite complex, the prospect might perceive the risk of a trial purchase as greater than its benefits. Less expensive and less complex products might be distributed as free samples, with the goal being to induce prospects to try the new offering by reducing perceived risk,

Adoption. If the trial purchase worked as expected, then the decision is made to make regular use of the product. If the trial did not work as expected, then the product or service is rejected, at least for the time being.

As can be seen, the adoption process is a series of stages that a member of the buying center (or an individual in the case of consumer goods) goes through in deciding whether to buy and make regular use of a new product or service. The **diffusion process** represents the spread of a new product, innovation, or service throughout an industry over time. The speed with which the diffusion process takes place varies among industries; it is very fast in the electronics industry and possibly quite slow in the domestic steel industry. As in the adoption process, there are many similarities between the consumer group proceeding through the diffusion process and buying center members as a group (representing a particular industry) proceeding through the diffusion process over time. In the diffusion process a few firms adopt at first (innovators), and then the number of adopters increases rapidly (early adopters and early majority) as the value of the product, innovation or service becomes apparent. The rate finally diminishes as fewer potential buyers (late majority and laggards) remain in the nonadopter category. By the time laggards adopt something new, it may already have been discarded by the innovator group in favor of a newer idea or technological idea.

Factors Influencing the Rate of Adoption-Diffusion

The development and acceptance of new products and the time spent in the introductory stage vary greatly among firms. Some products diffuse very slowly into a particular market, while others may almost bypass this stage. Perceived advantage and perceived risk would play a part, along with common barriers to adoption, such as marriage to an existing facility or incompatibility with existing products. Products that require major changes in manufacturing processes or those that require a large outlay of capital tend to diffuse slowly.

Another factor is technological uncertainty. Will the technology function as expected when placed into volume production? How about the perceived likelihood of technological obsolescence? What about the unpredictable quality of a new product or innovation, or other emerging technologies that can provide similar advantages? These and other factors force some potential customers to take a "wait and see" attitude before committing to a new product adoption.

■ PRODUCT PORTFOLIO CLASSIFICATION, ANALYSIS, AND STRATEGY

The business marketer must regularly review the product portfolio, developing strategic alternatives for each of the company's current products, businesses, and new business possibilities. The concept of the product portfolio stresses the importance of viewing products not individually but as parts of the total system. This perspective allows for management's regular review of strategic alternatives and for corresponding resource allocation decisions.

What Is the Product Portfolio?

A product portfolio is the firm's offering of products or divisions, each of which can be identified as a **strategic business unit** (SBU); most of which operate as a separate profit center, with its own management, its own set of identifiable markets and competitors, and its own marketing strategies. The firm's product portfolio typically consists of related businesses and/or products that are grouped into SBUs that are homogeneous enough to control most factors affecting their performance. Resources are allocated to SBUs in proportion to their contribution to the corporate objectives of growth and profitability. The challenge of the 1990s will be to identify the SBUs within the firm's product portfolio that will enhance the overall corporate mission, while withdrawing support for those that will not.

The basic concept of the product portfolio was first put forth by the founder of the Boston Consulting Group, Bruce Henderson, in a booklet published on the subject in 1970.[24] Henderson looked at a firm's products or divisions as a mix of businesses that strategically interact and influence one another, principally in terms of their uses of resources and their development of resources against threats in a competitive marketplace. He described and evaluated products and divisions in terms of three dimensions:

1. The attractiveness of the market, especially in light of the SBU's stage in the product life cycle.
2. The firm's position in the market in terms of market share.
3. The firm's acknowledged or perceived strengths and weaknesses, relative to competitors.

---

[24]Boston Consulting Group, "The Product Portfolio" in *Perspectives on Experience* (1970).

■ **FIGURE 7–5**   Matrix Quadrants of Four Categories of Strategic Business Units

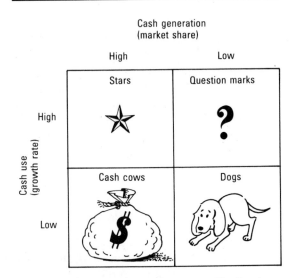

One of the earliest and most widely implemented approaches is the cash quadrant or share/growth matrix developed by the Boston Consulting Group.[25]

Diagnosing the Product Portfolio

As shown in Figure 7–5, strategic business units can be classified into four categories. Businesses in each category exhibit different financial characteristics and offer different strategic choices. The four types of SBUs specified by the growth rate matrix include *stars, cash cows, question marks,* and *dogs*. If market share and growth behave as expected, then this portfolio matrix tells a compelling cash-flow story with important investment and strategy implications. However, this is only one approach to portfolio analysis, and it is rather limited.

Product Portfolio Strategies

In a typical business to business company, products are scattered in all four quadrants of the portfolio matrix. An appropriate strategy for products in each cell is given briefly in Table 7–4. First, a primary goal of the company should be not only to secure a position with cash cows but also to guard against the frequent temptation to reinvest in them excessively.

[25]See Bruce D. Henderson, *Henderson on Corporate Strategy* (Cambridge, Mass.: Abt Associates, 1979).

■ **TABLE 7–4**   Characteristics and Strategy Implications of Products in the Strategy Quadrants

Quadrant	Investment Characteristics	Earning Characteristics	Cash-Flow Characteristics	Strategy Implication
Stars	Continual expenditures for capacity expansion Pipeline filling with cash	Low to high	Negative cash flow (net cash user)	Continue to increase market share, if necessary, at the expense of short-term earnings.
Cash cows	Capacity maintenance expenditures	High	Positive cash flow (net cash contributor)	Maintain share and cost leadership until further investment becomes marginal.
Question marks	Heavy initial capacity expenditures High R&D costs	Negative to low	Negative cash flow (net cash user)	Assess chances of dominating segment; if good, go after share, if bad, redefine business or withdraw.
Dogs	Gradually deplete capacity	High to low	Positive cash flow (net cash contributor)	Plan an orderly withdrawal so as to maximize cash flow.

SOURCE: Reproduced from Subhash C. Jain, *Marketing Planning and Strategy,* 2d ed. (Cincinnati, Ohio: South-Western Publishing, 1985), p. 482. Reprinted with permission of South-Western Publishing Company Copyright © 1985 by South-Western Publishing Company.

The cash generated from cash cows can be used to support those stars which are not self-sustaining. Surplus cash might be used to finance selected question marks toward a dominant market position. Question marks which cannot be funded might be divested. A dog could be restored to a position of viability by shrewdly segmenting the market, that is, by rationalizing and specializing the business into a small niche which the product concerned can dominate. If such is not feasible, the firm will consider harvesting the SBU by cutting off all investment in the business, with consideration given to liquidation of the unit when and if the opportunity develops.

Figure 7–6 shows the consequences of an incorrect strategic move. For example, if a star is not appropriately funded, it could become a question mark, and finally a dog (disaster sequence). On the other hand, if a question mark is given adequate support, it can become a star, and ultimately a cash cow (success sequence).[26]

The product portfolio concept provides the marketer with a useful synthesis of the analysis and judgments necessary as an SBU moves through the product life cycle, and presents the marketer with a provocative source of strategic alternatives. The marketer must remember that strategy is doing the right things—deciding *what* must be done, while tactics are doing things correctly—deciding *how* to do them. Marketing planners must plot the projected positions of each SBU under both present and alternative

---

[26]Jain, *Marketing Planning and Strategy,* p. 482.

■ **FIGURE 7–6**   Product Portfolio Matrix: Strategic Consequences

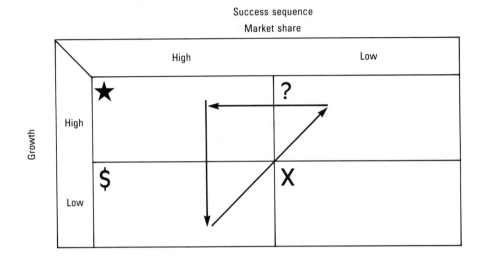

Success sequence

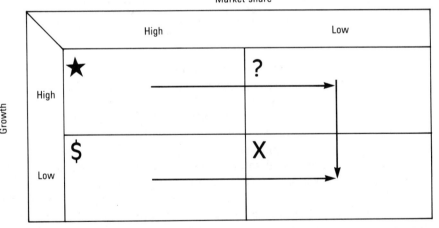

Disaster sequence

strategies, thus enabling them to decide what objectives each SBU should have, the strategies and tactics to use in achieving those objectives, and what resources to assign each strategic business unit.

■ **PRODUCT DELETION STRATEGY**

Any discussion of product development, management, and strategy would not be complete without a brief review of a very difficult marketing decision: when to drop a product, product line, or division. Once product per-

■ **TABLE 7–5**   Statements Explaining the Unsatisfactory Performance of Specific Products Studied

Statement	No. of Companies Citing
Uncompetitive price	7
Production problems (e.g., inferior technology, hard to assemble)	6
Not mass product, uneconomic batches	6
Too costly to produce and market	5
High costs to manufacture	5
Overengineered	4
Competitors dominated the market	4
Customer requirements not as expected	2
Low selling price	2

SOURCE: Reprinted by permission of the publisher from "Revitalizing Weak Industrial Products," by George J. Avionitis, *Industrial Marketing Management* 14 (1985), pp. 93–105. Copyright © 1985 by Elsevier Science Publishing Co., Inc.

formance deviations from established norms are identified and analyzed, management often discovers that weak product performance is seldom the result of one single factor. Rather it generally results from a variety of factors that are frequently interrelated. Table 7–5 shows a range of reasons cited by respondents as the cause of unsatisfactory product performance. Note that a noncompetitive price, production problems (such as inferior technology), and uneconomic batches of the product were the reasons most often cited for unsatisfactory product performance.

The idea that some products entering the decline stage of the product life cycle must be eliminated reflects the strategic thinking that every SBU plays an important part in making the product portfolio viable. When the SBU becomes a drain on financial and managerial resources of an organization, management has three alternatives in product-elimination strategy: harvesting, line simplification, and total-line divestment.[27]

Harvesting

Harvesting strategy is applied to a product or business whose sales volume and/or market share are slowly declining. An effort is made to cut the costs associated with the SBU to help improve the cash flow. Harvesting leads to a slow decline in sales, and when the business ceases to provide positive cash flow, it is divested. The implementation of harvesting strategy would require, where appropriate, reducing maintenance of facilities; cutting advertising and research budgets; curtailing the number and scope of channel intermediaries used; eliminating small-order customers; and reducing service levels in terms of delivery time, sales assistance, etc. DuPont followed the harvesting strategy in the case of its rayon business, and BASF Wyandotte applied harvesting to soda ash.[28]

---

[27]A portion of this discussion is based on Jain, *Marketing Planning and Strategy*, Chap. 13.

[28]K. R. Harrigan and Michael Porter, "End-Game Strategies for Declining Industries," *Harvard Business Review* (July-August 1983), p. 118.

Line Simplification

Line simplification strategy refers to a situation where a product line is trimmed to a manageable size by pruning the number and variety of products and services being offered. It is hoped that the simplification effort will help to restore the health of the line. This endeavor can lead to a variety of benefits, such as potential cost savings from longer production runs; reduced inventories; and a more forceful concentration of marketing, research and development, and other efforts behind a shorter list of products.

The decision to drop an SBU from the product line is difficult to make, but despite the emotional aspects of this decision, the need for objectivity in this matter cannot be overemphasized. According to a classic article dealing with the elimination of weak product items and product lines:

> Putting products to death—or letting them die—is a drab business, and often engenders much of the sadness of a parting with old and tried friends . . . . Too often management thinks of this as something that should be done, but which can be put off until tomorrow . . . . This is why a definite procedure for deletion of products should be set up, and why the authority and responsibility for the various activities involved should be clearly and definitely assigned.[29]

Total Line Divestment

Divestment strategy is a situation of reverse acquisition and is also a key dimension of marketing strategy. Divestment decisions are principally economic or psychological in nature and may allow the firm to restore a balanced product portfolio. If the firm has too many high-growth businesses, its resources may be inadequate to fund such growth. If the firm has too many low-growth businesses, it will frequently generate more cash than is required for investment purposes and will build up redundant equity. For the firm to grow evenly over time, while showing regular earnings increments, a portfolio of both fast- and slow-growing businesses is necessary. Divestment can help achieve this balance.

The use of this strategy is reflected in Allied Signal's selling off of its marine systems defense operation in 1988 because of flat defense spending, tepid earnings, and intensifying competition. Also, the Eaton Corporation has recently put its defense electronics business up for sale.[30]

When the decision is finally made to harvest, simplify, or divest a strategic business unit, a well-planned procedure is essential to the success of such an initiative. This move will likely cause some disruption and create concern among some distributors and customers, in addition to the uncer-

---

[29]Ralph S. Anderson, "The Death and Burial of Sick Products," *Journal of Marketing* 28 (April 1964), pp. 1–7.

[30]"Shakeout Hangs over the Defense Industry as Spending Flattens and Arms Trade Slows," *Investors Daily*, October 21, 1988, pp. 1, 32.

tainy and anxiety experienced by members of the sales force as well as by other employees. Steps should be taken to ensure minimal disruption among both internal and external constituencies.

■ INTERNATIONAL PRODUCT STRATEGY[31]

In breaking into a foreign market, product success calls for a sound framework relating the firm's goals and resources. Because a country in the early stages of industrialization does not necessarily have an adequate pool of trained technicians, a product must be considered in relation to the environment within which it will be used. Equipment that requires a high degree of technical skill to operate, maintain, or repair can be inadequate in a country that lacks a pool of technically skilled labor. An example of this is reflected in a statement reportedly made by a manufacturer of agricultural equipment, commenting on the lack of cooperation of Thailand farmers in combining their plots into larger farms. The U.S. company wants to sell combines for harvesting rice and corn if the farmers can be persuaded to plant similar crops adjacent to each other. However, as the executive commented, "Until the farmers agree to cooperate, there are not going to be opportunities in Thailand to sell the large grain combines that we and other major companies manufacture." As competition increases on the international level, U.S. companies must become more marketing-oriented to survive.

The life cycles of products also tend to vary in different markets. This could produce a longer overall product life cycle as a product in a mature stage of its domestic life cycle may be perceived as new and thus be in the introductory stage of the product life cycle in a foreign market. Yesterday's product in the United States may be today's product in another part of the world. Additionally, used capital equipment or that which new technology makes obsolete might be sold overseas.

Concept Questions

1. How is the diffusion process related to the adoption process?
2. What is the basic value of product-portfolio analysis to the business marketer?
3. What types of activities are involved in implementing a product deletion strategy?

SUMMARY

1. Product development, management, and strategy are important parts of the business to business marketing process, with the major concerns being both to measure and predict success and to execute proper strategy over the life of the product.

---

[31]This section is from Philip R. Cateora, *International Marketing*, 6th ed. (Homewood, Ill.: Richard D. Irwin, 1987), pp. 387–402.

2. Marketers are now beginning to replace engineers as having the most important role in the development of many new product ideas. Technology push and market pull are the two major approaches to new product development. Technology push results when the driving force of a new product's development is the perceived potential of the technology itself, and market pull is primarily the result of marketing research methodologies of interviewing prospective users about their needs and then developing solutions to those perceived market needs. The new product development process includes seven stages: new product strategy development, idea and concept generation, screening and evaluation, business analysis, product development, product testing, and product commercialization and introduction.

3. New product development, evaluation, and management must follow good management practice if effectiveness, efficiency, and a reasonable likelihood of success are to be achieved. The major options available to the business marketer in organizing the new product development process include a product manager system, a new product committee, a new product department, and a new product venture team.

4. The information derived from product life-cycle analysis is generally used to suggest appropriate marketing strategies over a particular product's life span. Experience and learning curves can be used in conjunction with product life-cycle analysis to determine more specifically what is happening to a product as it moves from one stage in its life cycle to the next. Stages in the product life cycle include product introduction, market growth, market maturity, and sales decline.

5. Technology, competition, changes in the level of business activity, and the utilization of plant capacity can have a marked impact on a firm's decision to expand, contract, or maintain the current product mix. The effective marketer must understand each of these market forces in order to make appropriate decisions with regard to possible product mix changes.

6. Marketers have the responsibility of deciding how quickly prospects will adopt a new product, and to what extent they will replace the old one. To perform such a task, marketers frequently study both the adoption process and the diffusion process. The adoption process is the decision-making activity of the buying firm through which the new product or innovation is accepted; it includes the stages of awareness, interest, evaluation, trial, and adoption or rejection of the product. The diffusion process shows how a product is accepted by an industry over time.

7. The business to business firm should regularly review its product portfolio, developing strategic alternatives for each of the company's current products, businesses, and new business possibilities. The Boston Consulting Group categorizes each product or business division in a company according to four types of strategic business units (SBUs),

including stars, cash cows, question marks, and dogs. Strategies have been formulated for use with each of these four categories.

8. When to drop a product, product line, or company division is a very difficult task for the marketer. Common product-elimination options include harvesting, line simplification, and total line divestment.

9. In breaking into a foreign market, product success calls for a sound framework relating the firm's goals and resources. The life cycles of products tend to vary in different markets. This could produce a longer domestic life cycle, as a product in the maturity stage of the domestic life cycle may be perceived as new, and thus be in the introductory stage of the product life cycle in a foreign market.

KEY TERMS

adoption process	new product committee approach
diffusion process	new product department approach
divestment strategy	new product venture team
experience curve	approach
harvesting strategy	product management approach
learning curve analysis	strategic business unit
line simplification strategy	technology push
market pull	

REVIEW QUESTIONS

1. Why are effective product management and strategy so important today? What are the major concerns of product management and strategy?

2. Why was there a reluctance in the past to give marketing personnel a major role in the design and development of new products? Discuss three major styles in organizing the new product development process. Identify two approaches to new product development. Describe each of the seven stages in the new product development process.

3. Identify and discuss four major options which marketers have in organizing the new product development process. Which option is most commonly utilized?

4. What is the fundamental value of product life-cycle analysis? How are learning curve analysis and experience curves used in product life-cycle analysis? Identify and describe each of the four stages involved in the product life cycle.

5. How do terminology, competition, changes in the level of business activity, and the utilization of plant capacity impact upon possible changes in a firm's product mix?

6. What is meant by the adoption process and the diffusion process? How can they be utilized together? Identify and describe the stages in the adoption process. What factors influence the rate of adoption—diffusion?

7. Define product portfolio analysis. According to the Boston Consulting Group approach to product management, what is a strategic business unit? Identify four categories into which each strategic business unit within a firm can be placed and indicate appropriate strategies for use with each of the four categories.

8. What are some common reasons for product failure? Indicate and explain three strategic approaches for the elimination of weak products.

9. What is necessary to product success when breaking into a foreign market? How can the life cycles of products vary between domestic and international markets?

CHAPTER CASES

Case 7–1 Chemicals, Inc.*

On July 11, 1988 the board of directors at Chemicals, Inc., of St. Louis, Missouri, met to decide what action should be taken to improve the characteristics of one of its products—Plantlife, a powdered plant food for flowers.

The board consisted of the president, sales manager, production manager, and two outside men who were successful in other lines of business activity. The president, a young forceful man in his early thirties, was of the firm conviction that his board of directors should make all important decisions of this nature.

Plantlife had been introduced to the market, consisting of growers and florists, during the summer of 1985 through 500 wholesalers. While sales were relatively small during the first year, a few jobbers, particularly in the South, complained that the powder, normally of a white powder, was progressively turning brown. Furthermore, they said that when the brown powder was put into the proper solution for application, it killed the plant. The firm replaced all the brown merchandise it could locate, but continued with the same formula for the winter months because it had no immediate substitute.

The research department discovered that a sulfate compound in the powder was turning to sulfuric acid under conditions of high heat and humidity when stored for any length of time. The acid would then proceed to burn the remainder of the powder and, in turn, burn the plant upon which a solution was poured. Unfortunately, the sulfate compound was an essential ingredient in the powder; without it the solution would not be suffi-

---

*Richard H. Buskirk, *Cases and Readings in Marketing*, 2nd ed., 1970, Holt, Rinehart, and Winston.

ciently acidic to perform its job properly. The problem was to find a sulfate compound that would not be affected by humidity but would grow into proper solution when needed. For technical reasons the solution had to have a pH of about six. The research department developed a substitute which filled the bill; however, there were two objections to it. First, the resulting mixture was identical in results to those of the major competitor. Second, the new mixture left a gummy residue in the bottom of the mixing container. The company had been using the fact that its product was cleaner to use than those of its competitors in its sales promotional campaign. The present Plantlife formula was demonstrably superior to all competitive products on the market in several ways. It had been tested by a number of universities and found to be superior. It was being recommended by many leaders in the floral industry.

The sales manager was strongly in favor of ceasing production of the present product immediately and going to the substitute proposed by the research department. He claimed that it was only a matter of time before every jobber would have a sour experience with Plantlife and would go back to using a competitor's product. He said that once that happened, no amount of personal selling would ever lure them back into the fold. Sales had been increasing steadily, and he wanted to do nothing to jeopardize long-run success.

The production manager, who was in charge of research, claimed that he was presently pursuing another line of attack using a nonsulfuric compound. However, he had only begun tests on several mixtures containing it. Normally, before any product change was authorized, extensive testing was completed using the formula on all types of plants under all types of conditions, and with all types of water. The production manager was highly hopeful that the new acid would prove to be what the firm was seeking—a superior, nonbrowning product. However, he voted for the promotion of the substitute until the tests could prove the worth of the new acid.

The two outside members were strongly against changing the formula until a better, proven product was available. They saw no reason to change to a formula that had no advantage over the competition and was so obviously a change; the gumming precipitate could not be hidden.

With the board deadlocked on what course of action to take, the president had to cast the deciding vote. He asked how long it would be until the first tests on the new acid would be completed, and he was told that it would be one week before any data would be available. Because the big selling season was to start in August, a decision had to be made quickly so that promotional plans could be altered.

The firm had been anticipating this problem and carrying a minimum inventory. Many chemicals to be eliminated from the formula could be returned for credit on the new ones. The costs of production would be about the same for the new formula as for the old one.

Questions

1. Analyze the advantages and disadvantages of each proposal.
2. What actions should the president take?

Case 7–2   Mathewson Machine Works, Inc.*

Mr. R. F. Rowell, sales manager of the Mathewson Machine Works, was considering the advisability of dropping the Hewson Clinitron blood sugar determination machine from the company's product line. The sales of this new product have been below expectations, and Mr. Rowell seriously questioned whether any additional sales effort would be profitable.

The product in question, the Hewson Clinitron, was an automatic machine for making blood sugar screening tests for the detection of diabetes. To perform a test for the detection of diabetes, the physician or technician merely collected 0.1 cc of capillary blood from the fingertip or earlobe, delivered the blood to a test tube containing five cc of water, and placed the test tube in the machine for automatic clinical processing. If after processing the blood specimen contained more than a minimum threshold amount of sugar, the Clinitron registered a positive reaction and thus detected the possibility of diabetes in the patient. The Hewson Clinitron automatically processed such screening tests at the rate of 120 per hour, when used at full capacity.

The speed of accuracy of the Clinitron mass screening tests led to the development of a simple technique which made possible quantitative determinations of the blood sugar content, within diagnostic limits, for the diagnosis of diabetes. Whereas the screening tests diagnosed the possibility of diabetes as revealed by a positive reaction indicating an undetermined amount of sugar in the blood, these quantitative determinations of the blood sugar level by the Clinitron made possible a more definitive diagnosis of diabetes. The machine performed these quantitative determinations in five minutes, as contrasted with the manual laboratory method of several hours.

The Mathewson Company bought the design and patent rights from the private inventors who developed it. During the following year the company invested considerable capital in improving its design and developing the commercial model.

The company undertook the production of the machine from a manufacturing rather than a sales point of view. It had the required production facilities and technical know-how, but was not well equipped to handle the sales function. The company estimated the manufacturing cost of the product at $850 and set the sales price at $1,175, to allow for a commission to sales agents. The Clinitron would be most useful and logical to big medical laboratories and hospitals needing to make a large volume of blood sugar screening tests and quantitative blood sugar determinations. Under these circumstances Clinitron might reduce the staff by one laboratory technician, thus effecting an actual cost saving.

The Mathewson Company exhibited Clinitron at the Southwestern States Medical Exposition in Dallas, Texas, during the first year, and the machine was the subject of lengthy newspaper articles in both the Dallas and Oklahoma City papers. The company conducted several mass screening tests with the Clinitron, and in one such survey the machine was in operation approximately 40 hours, performing screening tests of 4,300 blood specimens. This test was performed with one attendant running the machine, and the doctors considered the results very satisfactory.

The company established a laboratory equipment division to handle the manufacturing and sales operation of the new product. At this time the company, in cooperation with its advertising agency, compiled a hospital mailing list and had 7,000 announcements printed for distribution. The announcement described the Clinitron, stated that the Mathewson Company would manufacture it, and that it would be available in the near future. Although the mailing list comprised 2,923 hospitals, the company sent out 6,133 announcements, since several staff members of each hospital received an announcement.

A short time after mailing the first announcement, the company sent a personalized follow-up to the same mailing list. This letter included a business reply card, which the company requested the recipient to sign and return, if he or she was interested in the Clinitron. Mr. Rowell considered the returns on this follow-up letter very encouraging, since the company received many inquiries, and the medical profession evidenced considerable interest in the Clinitron.

Mr. E. J. Richards, an able and experienced salesperson, who had been with the Mathewson Company for three years, handled the selling of the Clinitron. He spent almost a year traveling about the United States following up the inquiries received concerning the Clinitron. He spent a month in Chicago, and reported that his experience in that city was typical of all his efforts; he was enthusiastically received by prospective buyers and much interest was shown in the product, but sales were few and difficult to achieve. The hospital managers, who exhibited great interest in the Clinitron, felt that the price of $1,175 was too high. They pointed out that in most instances the installation of the Clinitron would not effect economies through reduction in laboratory personnel.

In an effort to increase sales, the Mathewson Company appointed several large and well-known distributors who supplied the medical field to handle the product. The use of these distributors did little to increase the sales of Clinitron. The only advertising of the product was one insertion in *Industrial Medicine and Surgery,* a medical trade journal. The company sent additional mailings to federal, state, and municipal public health agencies, other potential government customers, and to colleges and universities.

Mr. Richards demonstrated the Clinitron before several local and regional medical association meetings and at a meeting of the Association of Industrial Physicians and Surgeons. He also arranged to demonstrate the product before a national meeting of the American Medical Association, although he encountered considerable difficulty in arranging this demonstration, since the association did not ordinarily permit the showing of commercial products at its meetings. It was only due to the interest and importance of the Clinitron to the medical profession that such a demonstration was possible.

The Mathewson Company sold 23 Clinitron machines during the 28 months following the product's introduction. Of these machines, 10 were sold to the U.S. government. The medical profession continued to be interested in the machine and placed occasional orders with the company, but sales were still far below expectations. The Mathewson executives and Mr. Rowell, who were considering whether the company should continue to sell the product, believed that they could not reduce the manufacturing and selling costs of the machine, at least until the sales increased considerably.

Questions

1. Should the Mathewson Company continue to make and sell the Clinitron?

2. Could it have avoided the experience described?

---

*Ralph S. Alexander, James S. Cross, and Ross M. Cunningham, *Industrial Marketing*, 2nd ed., © 1961, R. D. Irwin. Used by permission.

SUGGESTED READINGS

Burt, David N., and William R. Soukup. "Purchasing's Role in New Product Development." *Harvard Business Review* 63 (September/October 1985), pp. 90–97. Discussion of purchasing's role in new product development, including suggested methods of integration.

Cardozo, Richard N., and Jerry Wind. "Risk Return Approach to Product Portfolio Strategy." *Long Range Planning* (UK) 18 (April 1985), pp. 77–85. Managerial model and suggested guidelines for product-line decisions.

Child, Robert W. "New Products—Making a Good Thing Better." *Canadian Business Review* (Canada) 12 (Summer 1985), pp. 31–34. Case study of various types of new product strategies used by Dow Chemical of Canada.

Choffray, Jean Marie, and Gary L. Lilien. "A Decision-Support System for Evaluating Sales Prospects and Launch Strategies for New Products." *Industrial Marketing Management* 15 (February 1986), pp. 75–85. French case study of business to business product development and diffusion.

Cooper, Robert G. "Industrial Firm's New Product Strategies." *Journal of Business Research* 13 (April 1985), pp. 107–21. Empirical study of the dimensions of new product strategy in 122 Canadian firms.

———. "Overall Corporate Strategies for New Product Programs." *Industrial Marketing Management* 14 (August 1985), pp. 179–93. Empirical study of five types of innovation strategy in business to business product development.

Cooper, Robert G., and Elko J. Kleinschmidt. "An Investigation Into the New Product Process." *Journal of Product Innovation Management* 3 (June 1986), pp. 71–85. Study of 13 tasks involved with 252 new product case histories at 123 business to business product manufacturers.

de Brentani, Ulrike. "Do Firms Need a Custom-Designed New-Product Screening Model?" *Journal of Product Innovation Management* 3 (June 1986), pp. 108–19. Comparison of four major product evaluation models, noting that similarities far outweigh the differences among them.

Drozdenko, Ronald, and Sidney Weinstein. "From Experience: The Role of Objective In Vivo Testing in the Product Development Process." *Journal of Product Innovation Management* 3 (June 1986), pp. 120–26. Three case studies involving the quantifying of product testing and potential product advantages.

Englewood, Christopher. "New Product Development for Service Companies." *Journal of Product Innovation Management* 3 (December 1986), pp. 264–75. Survey and applications of product introduction techniques.

Espey, James. "A Multinational Approach to New Product Development." *European Journal of Marketing* (UK) 19 (no. 3, 1985), pp. 5–18. Case study of a new product development team in the liquor industry.

Friedman, Hershey H., and Joshua Krauz. "A Portfolio Theory Approach to Solve the Product-Elimination Problem." *Mid-Atlantic Journal of Business* 24 (Summer 1986), pp. 43–48. Discussion of financial factors related to weak products, and guidelines for candidates for product deletion.

Gagliano, Caren Calish. "How to Mine and Refine New Product Ideas." *Business Marketing* 70 (November 1985), pp. 102–12. Case study of an approach to new product planned growth in the Netherlands.

Gupta, Ashok K.; S. P. Raj; and David Wilemon. "A Model for Studying R&D-Marketing Interface in the Product Innovation Process." *Journal of Marketing* 50 (April 1986), pp. 7–17. Discussion of a conceptual model of organizational structure and climate.

Kleizen, Hendrikus G.; George Beaton; and Russell Abratt. "Pharmaceutical Product Management in 1990: Will There Be Any Changes?" *European Journal of Marketing* (UK) 19 (no. 7, 1985), pp. 5–10. Forecasting the future of product management in the South African pharmaceutical market.

Mercer, J. A. T. "Product Life Cycles of the Windsurfer Market." *European Journal of Marketing* (UK) 19 (no. 4, 1985), pp. 13–22. Case study of a successful test of the PLC concept in the United Kingdom.

Moore, William L. "New Product Development Practices of Industrial Marketers." *Journal of Product Innovation Management* 4 (March 1987), pp. 6–20. A survey of the processes, problems, and strategic planning processes of business to business marketers engaged in new product development.

More, Roger A. "Developer/Adopter Relationships in New Industrial Product Situations." *Journal of Business Research* 14 (December 1986), pp. 501–17. Examples, problems, interorganizational framework, and implications for management regarding developer/adopter relationships arising from new business to business product situations.

Paul, Ronald N. "Improving the New Product Development Process—Making New Technology Push Work." *Journal of Business Marketing* 2 (Fall 1987), pp. 59–62. Discussion of the legitimacy of technology push in developing new products.

Polhill, Frederick. "New Product Development: Is the 3M Approach Inimitable?" *Industrial Marketing Digest* (UK) 10 (Fourth Quarter 1985), pp. 13–24. Case study of product teams and entrepreneurship.

Ronkainen, Ilkka. "Using Decision-Systems Analysis to Formalize Product Development Processes." *Journal of Business Research* 13 (February 1985), pp. 97–106. Guidelines for minimizing risk in evaluating new product ideas.

Sykes, Hollister B. "Lessons from a New Venture Program." *Harvard Business Review* 64 (May/June 1986), pp. 69–74. Case study of internal ventures, looking at determinants of success with a single product focus in an entrepreneurial environment.

Yoon, Eunsang, and Gary L. Lilien. "New Industrial Product Performance: The Effects of Market Characteristics and Strategy." *Journal of Product Innovation Management* 2 (September 1985), pp. 134–44. Presentation of a conceptual model for original and reformulated new products, with guidelines for new product managers.

Chapter **8**

Business to Business Price Planning and Strategy

LEARNING OBJECTIVES

After reading this chapter, you should be able to:

- Explain the pricing methods and strategies most commonly utilized by price setters.
- Discuss the concept of price elasticity and the role of cost-benefit analysis in demand determination.
- Relate the changes which take place in the pricing element of the marketing mix throughout the various phases of the product life cycle.
- Describe conditions under which a price-leadership strategy would be used.
- Comprehend the importance and operation of competitive bidding in setting prices in appropriate markets.
- Communicate the value of leasing as an alternative to purchasing.
- Distinguish among the various types of price adjustments commonly given in purchasing transactions.
- Appreciate the nature of the pricing function in international markets.

CHAPTER OUTLINE

Business to Business Pricing: An Overview
Major Factors Influencing Price Strategy
  Competition
  Cost
  Demand
  Pricing Objectives
  Impact on Other Products
  Legal Considerations
Pricing Methods and Strategies
  Marginal Pricing
  Economic Value to the Customer (EVC)
  Break-Even Analysis
  Target Return-on-Investment Pricing
Demand Assessment and Strategy
  Price Elasticity of Demand
  Cost-Benefit Analysis
Pricing across the Product Life Cycle (Life-Cycle Costing)
  Introduction Phase: New Product Pricing Strategies
  Growth Phase
  Maturity Phase
  Decline Phase

Price Leadership Strategy
Competitive Bidding in the Business to Business Market
  Closed versus Open Bidding
  A Probabilistic Bidding Model
Leasing in the Business to Business Market
  Advantages of Leasing for the Buyer
  Advantages of Leasing for the Seller
  Types of Lease Arrangements
  Types of Leases
Pricing Policies in Business to Business Pricing Strategy
  Trade Discounts
  Quantity Discounts
  Cash Discounts
  Geographical Price Adjustments
International Marketing Pricing Strategy

■ BUSINESS TO BUSINESS PRICING: AN OVERVIEW

Price planning is not a precise science and, despite the importance attached to the task, is not an easy job. Because there are so many variables to consider whose precise influence cannot be anticipated, pricing decisions are often made by guesswork, intuition, or reliance on such methods as traditional markup percentages. However, even under the most favorable conditions, we need to study systematically a large number of both internal and external variables if effective price strategy is to take place. Like other components of marketing strategy, price planning and strategy involves intelligent input concerning environmental as well as operational conditions.

■ MAJOR FACTORS INFLUENCING PRICE STRATEGY

As shown in Figure 8–1, important factors influencing price strategy include competition, cost, demand, the impact of price on other products, and legal considerations. Each of these is discussed below.

Competition

There are two kinds of competitive factors that influence price. One factor is the competitive effect on demand for the marketer's product. This includes competition from directly comparable products—Apple Computer against IBM, Moore Business Forms against Uarco Inc., and UPS against Federal Express. There is competition from substitute products—plastic against steel, and synthetic against natural substances (synthetic versus crude rubber, for example). The other competitive factor is the reaction of competitors to any price move the marketer might make. If the marketer raises the price, will the competition hold its price level and hope to pick up customers? If the price is lowered, will the competition ignore the change, or move in aggressively and possibly retaliate with a lower price?

Cost

Fixed and variable costs are of major concern to the marketer charged with establishing price levels. If a manufacturer is a low-cost producer relative to the competition, the firm will earn additional profits by maintaining prices at competitive levels. The additional dollars generated can be used to promote the product aggressively, hoping to increase the overall visibility of the business. On the other hand, if the costs are high in relation to competition, the manufacturer may be in no position to reduce prices, since such action can lead to a price war which it will probably lose. Various elements of cost must be differently related in setting prices, with the analysis demonstrating how computations of full cost, incremental cost, and conversion can vary. The analysis will show how these costs affect product-line prices.

■ **FIGURE 8–1**   Major Factors Influencing Price Strategy

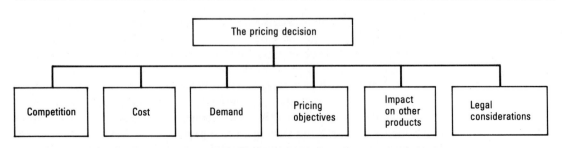

Demand

Demand is based on a variety of considerations, of which price is just one. Some of these considerations are as follows:

1. Ability of customers to pay.
2. Willingness of customers to pay.
3. Benefits that the product provides the customers.
4. Prices of substitute products.
5. Potential market for the product.
6. Nature of nonprice competition.
7. Segments in the market.[1]

All of these factors are interdependent, and it is not easy to estimate their relationship to each other precisely. However, they do point out that contemporary business buyers are highly sophisticated, and that they consider a wide variety of factors in deciding exactly what products to buy.

Pricing Objectives

An important step in pricing strategy is to determine goals and objectives prior to setting price points or levels. The principal pricing objectives of most firms are the following:

General Profit.   Profit is probably the most often stated company objective. A profit-maximization goal is likely to be far more beneficial to the firm if practiced over the long run. If short-run profit is the goal, there is a tendency to cut cost, sometimes to the detriment of quality and customer service. A firm entering a new geographic market or introducing a new product or product line may be well advised to set low prices initially, so as to build a large customer base. In this case the goal would be to optimize profits over the long run, focusing attention on the demand curve.

Achieve Return on Investment.   Products may be priced to achieve a certain percentage return on investment. This criterion is typically selected as a goal by firms which are leaders in their industry—firms such as General Motors and Alcoa. With this approach an organization prices its products to achieve a specific rate of return on investment. Alcoa, DuPont, General Electric, General Motors, Johns-Manville, and U.S. Steel all price many products to yield a target return. This objective makes it simpler to measure and control the performance of separate divisions, departments, and products. The trend of using a target return as a pricing objective has brought the following results:

---

[1]Subhash C. Jain, *Marketing Planning and Strategy,* 2d ed. (Cincinnati, Ohio: South-Western Publishing, 1985, p. 716.

- Increased awareness and concern for the relationships among investments, capital, and profits in planning and budgeting.
- The use of simple, explicit standards in measuring the returns of divisions, departments, and product groups.
- The use of cost-plus pricing to ensure that target returns will be achieved.[2]

It must be noted, however, that this approach is not appropriate for all firms.

Maintain or Increase Market Share.   Maintenance of, or changes in, market share is a popular objective because market share is measurable and may be a better indicator of general financial corporate health than return on investment, especially when the total market is growing. Intermediaries prefer to handle rapidly moving products and tend to drop those falling behind. Gaining market share because of a good reputation for quality and customer service generally will affect long-run profits favorably.

These objectives are not necessarily mutually exclusive, nor is this list by any means complete. Other objectives, such as overhead absorption, demand regulation, the establishment of market leadership, image projection, line-extension differentiation, and cash generation, may work toward achievement of the firm's overall marketing objectives. If maintaining or increasing market share is a strong objective, then pricing action will reflect this orientation.

Impact on Other Products

Often the purchase of one product increases the likelihood of the purchase by the same customer of another product or product line. One product may enhance the value or the effective use of the other product, in addition to the possibility that some buyers might encounter savings in time and effort by purchasing two or more products from the same source. If, for example, the buyer is buying a particular grade of tool steel from a local distributor to do a particular job, that buyer would be inclined to buy other grades of tool steel from the same supplier as the need arose. There is a strong likelihood that the buyer would also buy needed cutting tools and lubricants from that supplier. These complementary products would in all likelihood be price-inelastic, as the supplier inventory and delivery capabilities would more than offset a possible price advantage gained by the buyer by shopping around. This scenario may not hold true if the purchase involved a major new-buy situation or when the quantity to be bought is large enough to make the price element a major buying determinant.

[2]William Lazer and James D. Culley, *Marketing Management* (Boston: Houghton Mifflin, 1983), p. 552.

■ **EXHIBIT 8–1**   Robinson-Patman Act (1936)

SECTION 2(a)   Makes it illegal to discriminate in price among different buyers of commodities of like grade and quality when the effects result in a reduction in competition at the sellers' level, at the buyers' level, or at the buyers' customers' level. Different prices can be charged if they do not exceed differences in the costs of serving different customers. The power to establish maximum limits on quantity discounts granted to any customer or class of customers—regardless of differences in the costs of serving—is given to the FTC.

Section 2(b)   Continues the Clayton Act's provision of "meeting competition in good faith."

Section 2(c)   The granting of "dummy" brokerage allowances—given by a seller to a buyer or a brokerage firm owned by the buyer—is illegal.

Section 2(d) and (e)   Supplementary services or allowances such as advertising allowances must be made to all purchasers on a proportionately equal basis.

Section 2(f)   It is illegal for buyers knowingly to induce discriminatory prices from sellers.

SOURCE: William Lazer and James D. Culley, *Marketing Management: Foundations and Practices.* Copyright © 1983 by Houghton Mifflin Company. Used with permission.

Legal Considerations

Business marketers should be prepared to justify price levels, along with quantity and trade discounts. As shown in Exhibit 8–1, under the **Robinson-Patman Act** quantity discounts are legal if the resulting price differentials do not exceed the cost differentials in manufacturing, selling, and delivering the product to buyers who are in competition with each other. Furthermore, although the act does not discuss trade discounts specifically, several court cases seem to uphold the legality of offering separate discounts to separate classes of buyers, as long as the discounts are offered in return for services rendered (i.e., marketing functions performed). Marketers should be aware of possible legal problems that might arise in using certain types of discounts and allowances. Care is needed to avoid engaging in illegal price discrimination, along with such practices as price fixing, the exchange of price information among competitors, and predatory pricing.

Price Fixing.   Price fixing is illegal per se. Collusion, or the practice of several competitors setting a price, is a direct violation of the Sherman Antitrust Act. Such price fixing is illegal even if the fixed prices are fair. Price fixing is more likely to happen when the number of firms in a particular industry is small, and the product is relatively homogeneous (as in the case of oligopolies). When there are many firms, or when heterogeneous products are involved, competitors find it difficult to agree on what the fixed price will be.

Exchanging Price Information.   This is related to price fixing and occurs when competitors exchange information regarding prices, inventory levels, and the like. It becomes illegal when it leads to price agreements, however, as this is tantamount to price fixing.

Predatory Pricing.   This practice involves the cutting of prices (usually by a larger producer) to a point which is at or below cost for the purpose of eliminating competition. It is an attempt to monopolize the market; in most cases it is considered illegal.

■ PRICING METHODS AND STRATEGIES

Once a complete study has been made of all the variables that can have a major impact on pricing in business markets, marketing managers can turn their attention to the development of specific pricing methods and strategies which are likely to appeal to these markets. In business to business pricing neither cost nor demand approaches can succeed without regard for each other. Generating enough revenue to cover costs is a function of having a competitive cost structure as well as sufficient demand. In the long run all costs must be covered; yet unless there is sufficient demand for the goods, there will not be revenues to cover the costs. We will examine several pricing methods and strategies.

Marginal Pricing

A firm often has an opportunity to gain additional business on a price basis. **Marginal pricing,** also known as **contribution pricing,** is a basic conceptual approach to setting prices, with the aim being to maximize profits by producing the number of units at which marginal cost is just less than or equal to marginal revenue. The product is sold at that price. If the amount of additional revenue the firm receives from selling one additional unit is more than the marginal cost of producing that unit, then a profit is made. If the marginal revenue attained by producing an additional unit is less than the marginal cost of producing it, the firm will lose money on that additional unit, and it should not be produced. Consider the case of Chainco, an original equipment manufacturer (OEM) of tread chain for crawler tractor vehicles.

Chainco's regular business is the manufacture of tread chain for OEMs that produce crawler tractors for construction, agricultural, and military markets. Chainco employs a full-absorption cost system, which means that sales volume, revenue, and costs of manufacture are preplanned, and that variable and fixed costs are allocated over a program period, usually one year. This accounting method allows Chainco to calculate standard costs and levels of profitability of all their products for the program period. This approach is typical of many companies and is characterized by an annual forecasting and budgeting ritual, with updating of standard costs.

Chainco limits its planned government business to 10 percent of total forecast. Government items are distinguished as such and have standard costs, including allocation of appropriate program and standby fixed costs. At midyear, Chainco received a bid invitation from the Department of the Interior for a considerable amount of crawler chain of a type similar to that manufactured for OEM customers. This was a one-time sale opportunity that would not require selling expense or the normal allocation of administrative expense and fixed costs. They decided to use a marginal-pricing approach and bid the proposal on the basis of out-of-pocket variable and fixed costs, plus profit.

■ **FIGURE 8–2**   Marginal Pricing

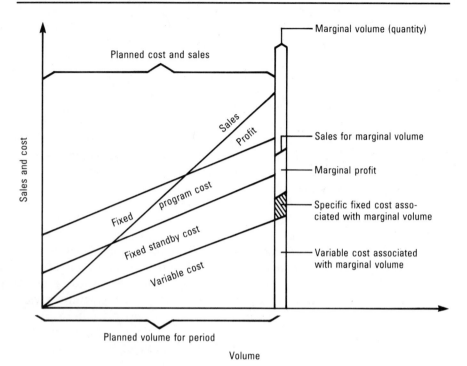

Pricing objective: Recover variable cost for marginal volume with add-on
for profit and/or to recover from negative variance.

Pricing strategy: Depending on demand and capacity situation, price to
gain volume to reduce idle capacity with profit add-on depending on
specific situation.

Legend: Sales: Gross revenue from sale of profit
         Profit: Gross profit above designated cost
         Variable cost: Material, labor, variable overhead, and variable
         selling expense
         Fixed standby cost: Planned operating cost under zero-volume
         condition
         Fixed program cost: Planned cost for R&D, marketing, advertising
         and improvement programs

Using this approach, Chainco was awarded the contract. The bid price
was less than standard cost for the items.[3]

Was this transaction a sound business deal? The answer is yes. Marginal
pricing is often used by contract bidders to gain unplanned business or to
utilize idle capacity. Figure 8–2 illustrates the factors involved in this approach. The overall objective of marginal pricing is to recover variable cost
for marginal volume with add-on for profit and/or to recover from negative

---

[3]Subhash C. Jain, *Marketing Planning and Strategy,* p. 716.

variance. The graph shows the difference between regular business—planned volume for a period—and marginal business. In marginal pricing adjusted fixed costs and marginal profit are substituted for conventional amounts.

Economic Value to the Customer (EVC)

Many customers buy on price, which is visible and measurable. Some suppliers compete on the same basis for the same reasons. However, a strategic advantage based on the total value delivered to the customer is far less easily duplicated by competitors. As companies like 3M and Hewlett-Packard have shown, a value-based strategy can be a uniquely effective way over time to gain a commanding lead over the competition. Recognizing this fact, some firms use a relatively new method of analyzing their products' economic value to the customer (EVC).

This economic value is illustrated in Figure 8–3 when two products, X and Y, are compared. Because of favorable start-up costs and postpurchase costs, as well as an additional incremental value of $100 for product X, the buyer (customer) should be willing to pay twice as much for product X ($600) than for product Y. From the manufacturer's viewpoint it costs $300 to produce product X. Therefore, any price in excess of $300 constitutes a profit. Since any price under $600 gives the buyer a better deal than what will be realized from buying product Y, the supplier of product X has a

■ **FIGURE 8–3** The Economic Value (EVC) to the Customer Concept

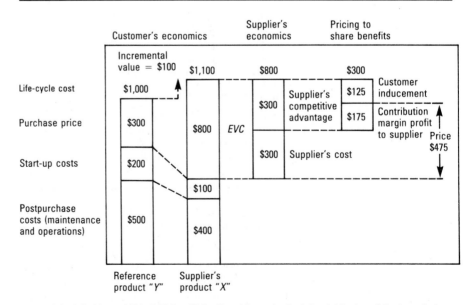

SOURCE: John L. Forbins and Nitin T. Mehta, "Value-Based Strategies for Industrial Products," *Business Horizons* 24 (May-June 1981), p. 33.

$300 competitive advantage. In addition, Supplier X could price the product to the customer at $475, which would result in $175 in profit, and a $125 advantage over product Y for the customer.[4]

Adding value in this way can also mean making the product easier to use, making it more profitable, or giving it some other value advantage. Most buyers will pay a higher price if they perceive a greater significant value or benefit to them than what they would receive from buying a competitive product.

Break-Even Analysis

Break-even analysis ascertains the point (break-even point) at which a firm's revenue will equal its total fixed and variable costs at a given price. Using various prices, a buyer can utilize the following formula to calculate the number of units that would have to be sold at each price to break even:

$$\text{Break-even point (BEP)} = \frac{\text{Fixed cost}}{\text{Unit price} - \text{Unit variable cost}}$$

Calculating a Break-Even Point.   Consider, for example, a company that manufactures a water sealer used to stop leaks in cement retainer walls. In 1990 the company sold 1,600,000 gallons of the sealer at a price of $3.00 per gallon with a variable production cost per gallon of $1.50. The fixed manufacturing costs were $1,550,000.

In 1991 more automated equipment will be used in production. This will increase the fixed manufacturing costs for the year to $1,785,000. The variable production cost per gallon has been estimated at $1.30 per gallon, and sales volume has a forecasted increase of 12.5 percent.

In 1990 the break-even point was 1,033,333 units, calculated as follows:

$$\frac{\$1,550,000}{\$1.50} = 1,033,333 \text{ units}$$

In 1991 the break-even point will be 1,050,000 units, calculated as follows:

$$\frac{\$1,785,000}{\$1.70} = 1,050,000 \text{ units}$$

Break-even analysis is a tool used by the marketer to determine the level of sales required to cover all relevant fixed and variable costs. This analysis indicates the impact different pricing strategies will have on profit margins, and also identifies the minimum price below which losses will occur. Price should not be set without first determining what will happen to profits at various price levels.

---

[4]John L. Forbes and Nitin T. Mehta, "Value-Based Strategies for Industrial Products," *Business Horizons* 24 (May–June 1981), pp. 32–42.

Target Return-on-Investment Pricing

Some firms set annual return-on-investment (ROI) targets such as an ROI of 20 percent. **Target return-on-investment pricing** is a method of setting prices to achieve such an investment goal, and is one of the most widely used methods of establishing price strategy. Price is determined by adding a desired rate of return on investment total costs. A break-even analysis is performed for expected production and sales levels, and a rate of return is added on.

Assume that a small business owner sets a target ROI of 10 percent, double that achieved the previous year. The owner considers raising the average price of an industrial widget to $54 or $58—up from last year's average of $50. To do such a thing, the owner can improve product quality, which will increase cost but will probably also affect the decreased revenue from the lower number of units which can be sold next year.

To handle this wide variety of assumptions, the use of computerized spreadsheets to project operating statements based on various assumptions is clearly in order. Table 8–1 shows a computerized spreadsheet which results from software programs such as VisiCalc and Lotus 1–2–3. The assumptions are shown at the top, and the projected results at the bottom. A prior year's operating-statement results are shown in the column headed "Last Year," and the assumptions and spreadsheet results for four different sets of assumptions are shown in columns A, B, C, and D.

■ **TABLE 8–1**   Results of a Computer Spread-Sheet Simulation to Select Price to Achieve a Target Return on Investment

Assumptions or Results	Financial Element	Last Year	Simulation A	B	C	D
Assumptions	Price per unit (P)	$50	$54	$54	$58	$58
	Units sold (Q)	1,000	1,200	1,100	1,100	1,000
	Change in unit variable cost (UVC)	0%	+10%	+10%	+20%	+20%
	Unit variable cost	$22.00	$24.20	$24.20	$26.40	$26.40
	Total expenses	$ 8,000	Same	Same	Same	Same
	Owner's salary	$18,000	Same	Same	Same	Same
	Investment	$20,000	Same	Same	Same	Same
	State and federal taxes	50%	Same	Same	Same	Same
Spread sheet simulation results	Net sales (P × Q)	$50,000	$64,800	$59,400	$63,800	$58,000
	Less: COGS (Q × UVC)	22,000	29,040	26,620	29,040	26,400
	Gross margin	$28,000	$35,760	$32,780	$34,760	$31,600
	Less: total expenses	8,000	8,000	8,000	8,000	8,000
	Less: owner's salary	18,000	18,000	18,000	18,000	18,000
	Net profit before taxes	$ 2,000	$ 9,760	$ 6,780	$ 8,760	$ 5,600
	Less: taxes	1,000	4,880	3,390	4,380	2,800
	Net profit after taxes	$ 1,000	$ 4,880	$ 3,390	$ 4,380	$ 2,800
	Investment	$20,000	$20,000	$20,000	$20,000	$20,000
	Return on investment	5.0%	24.4%	17.0%	21.9%	14.0%

In choosing a price or another action using spreadsheet results, the owner must: (1) study the results of the computer simulation projections; and (2) assess the realism of the assumptions underlying each set of projections. For example, the owner sees from the bottom row of Table 8–1 that all four spreadsheet simulations achieve the aftertax target ROI of 10 percent. Yet after more thought the owner judges that it would be more realistic to set an average price of $58 per unit, allow the unit variable cost to increase by 20 percent to account for increased quality, and settle for the same unit sales as the 1,000 units sold last year. In this computerized spreadsheet approach to target ROI pricing, the owner selects simulation D, and has a goal of 14 percent after-tax ROI.

■ DEMAND ASSESSMENT AND STRATEGY

Before deciding just what type of pricing method or strategy to utilize in a particular market, the marketer must have a clear understanding of the nature of the demand in that market. Demand refers to the amount of a good or service which a buyer or buyers are willing and able to purchase at a particular moment at each possible price. Demand is more than a desire to purchase; it is the ability to purchase as well.

Price Elasticity of Demand

At lower prices we may assume that more is bought. But how much more? Similarly, at higher prices, less is bought. Yet how much less is actually bought—much less or only a little less? To answer a question such as this one, a marketer should make use of the **price elasticity of demand** concept, which states simply (but broadly) that demand is elastic if quantity is highly responsive to price, but inelastic if not. In other words, elasticity is the relative change in the dependent variable divided by the relative change in the independent variable. The dependent variable is quantity demanded; the independent variable is price.

Price elasticity of demand (E) is expressed as follows:

$$E = \frac{\text{(Initial quantity demanded} - \text{New quantity demanded)}/\text{Initial quantity demanded}}{\text{(Initial price} - \text{New price)}/\text{initial price}}$$

Price elasticity of demand assumes three forms: elastic demand, inelastic demand, and unitary demand. **Elastic demand** exists when a small percentage decrease in price produces a larger percentage increase in quantity demanded. Price elasticity is greater than 1 with elastic demand. **Inelastic demand** exists when a small percentage decrease in price produces a smaller percentage increase in quantity demanded. With inelastic demand, price elasticity is less than 1. **Unitary demand elasticity** exists when the percentage change in price is identical to the percentage change in quantity demanded. In this instance price elasticity is equal to 1.

Price elasticity of demand is determined by a number of factors. First, the more substitutes a product or service has, the more likely that product will be price-elastic. Plastic or steel may be a substitute for each other in particular situations, so one or the other can be said to be price-elastic. Second, products and services considered to be necessities are generally price-inelastic. For example, office supplies, in general, are price-inelastic, whereas new office furniture is price elastic. For the product category of office supplies, although price-inelastic, the demand for a specific brand, such as BIC pens, may be highly elastic. Thus product categories and individual brands within the category may have totally different elasticities of demand. Price elasticity is important to the marketing manager because of its relationship to total revenue and price setting strategies. For instance, with elastic demand, total revenue increases when price decreases, but decreases when price increases. With inelastic demand, total revenue increases when price increases, and decreases when price decreases. Finally, with unitary demand, total revenue is unaffected by a slight price change.[5]

Cost-Benefit Analysis

Cost-benefit analysis (not to be confused with value analysis) is the technique of assigning a dollar value to the costs and benefits of a product or service, along with the customer's usage of the product or service. When used in determining demand, cost-benefit analysis is an analysis of benefits received and costs incurred by the customer in buying and using an industrial product or service. The comparison of costs and benefits can be used to gain the customer's perspective of the product or service, thereby allowing the individual marketer the opportunity to set prices more realistically. Some firms see the buyer's perception of value, not the seller's cost, as the key to pricing. They use the nonprice variables in the marketing mix to build up perceived value in the buyer's mind. Price is set to capture the perceived value. (See Exhibit 3–2 for an example of perceived-value pricing.)

If the marketer charges more than the buyers' perceived benefits of what the product or service is worth, company sales will suffer. Other firms may underprice the marketer's product or service. In such a situation the product or service will sell well, but less revenue is generated than would be the case if price were raised to the perceived-value level.

Concept Questions
1. What is the basic purpose of the Robinson-Patman Act?
2. Why is marginal pricing used by contract bidders?
3. What is the meaning of cost-benefit analysis in demand determination?

---

[5]Ibid., pp. 32–42.

■ PRICING ACROSS THE PRODUCT LIFE CYCLE (LIFE-CYCLE COSTING)

In addition to controllable internal factors, we need to consider external factors in developing prices for new products, along with changes in both environments which may require a review of the prices of products already on the market. If a large, dominant firm in the industry raises or lowers prices, other firms in the industry will be forced to examine their prices, as the product or product line moves through the stages of the product life cycle. The nature of the demand for the product or service in question is one of the most important considerations in the pricing decision, and the price maker must determine the precise relationship between changes in price and demand. In order to make the best decisions concerning price policy and specific pricing problems, the marketer should endeavor to learn as much as possible about the character of demand, and how demand might be affected by adjustments in price in both the short and the long run, as the product moves through the product life cycle.

Introduction Phase: New Product Pricing Strategies

A new product usually enjoys its greatest degree of differentiation during the introductory stage of the product life cycle (PLC), with demand being more inelastic at this stage than at any other stage of the PLC. However, the substantial investment which the firm must recover forces the price setter to decide just how fast it will be necessary to recover that investment. Whether an investment will be recovered quickly or over the product life span depends on such factors as the nature of the product, the projected product life, the nature of potential competition, and the financial strength of the firm. Two opposite pricing strategies for introducing a new product are: (1) **market skimming**—setting a relatively high price which will encourage competitive entry, and (2) **market penetration**—setting a price at or near the point it will eventually reach after competition develops. With market penetration, the firm attempts to gain a large volume of initial sales even though profit per unit may be low.

Price Skimming.   With price skimming, the introductory price is set relatively high, thereby attracting buyers at the top of the product's demand curve. This permits the recovery of research and development costs more quickly as the firm attempts to skim the market. DuPont is an often cited, prime user of a price skimming practice. On a new discovery such as cellophane and nylon, the firm determined the highest price it could charge, given the benefits of the new product over other products customers might buy. DuPont set prices that made it just worthwhile enough for some segments of the market to adopt the new material. After the initial sales slacked off, the firm lowered the price to draw in the next, price-sensitive layer of customers. In this way DuPont skimmed a maximum amount of revenue from the various segments of the market. As demonstrated in Fig-

■ **FIGURE 8–4**   Price Skimming

If the original skimming price is within the expected price range 1, the marketer will peel off customers along the A portion of the demand curve. If the price is lowered within expected price range 2, the marketer will peel off the second layer of customers along the B portion of the demand curve.

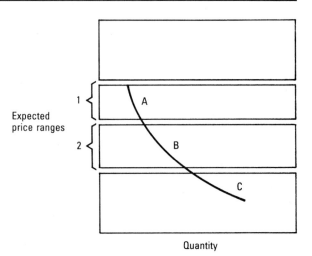

If the original skimming price is within expected price range 1, the marketer will peel off customers along the A portion of the demand curve. If the price is lowered within expected price range 2, the marketer will peel off the second layer of customers along the B portion of the demand curve.

ure 8–4, a skimming strategy assumes that layers of customers can be peeled off the demand curve.

A price skimming maneuver is not without potential problems, however. The high initial price tends to attract competition, as other firms see that the product is selling well at a relatively high price. Consequently, competitors tend to introduce rival versions. By the time the marketer is ready to peel off the next layer of customers, rival offerings may well be on the market. Therefore, a skimming strategy will be more effective when the product has a strong patent position or when there are other barriers to market entry, such as an extremely complex technology or very high capital requirements.

Market Penetration Pricing.   Despite the many advantages, a skimming price policy is not appropriate for all new product introductions. High prices may maximize profits during the early part of the introductory phase of the PLC, but may prevent sales to many of the buyers upon whom the firm relies. The penetration pricing strategy uses a low price as an entering wedge. Such an approach is likely to be desirable under any of the following conditions: (1) when sales volume of the product is very sensitive to price, even in the early stages of introduction; (2) when it is possible to achieve substantial economies in unit cost of manufacturing and distributing the product by operating at a large volume; (3) when a product faces threats of strong potential competition very soon after its introduction; and (4) when there is no elite market—that is, no class of buyers willing to pay a higher price to obtain the newest and the best.[6]

---

[6]Joel Dean, "Techniques for Pricing New Products and Services," in *Marketing Management Readings,* vol. 3, ed. Benson P. Shapiro, Robert J. Dolan, and John A. Quelch (Homewood, Ill.: Richard D. Irwin, 1985), pp. 160–73.

While a penetration pricing policy can be adopted at any stage in the product life cycle, this strategy should at least be examined before a new product is marketed at all. Texas Instruments is a prime user of market penetration pricing. This firm historically has set a price as low as possible, wins a large share of the market, experiences falling costs through experience related to the learning curve concept, and cuts its price further as costs fall. According to this theory, as the cumulative production volume of a product increases, the per unit cost of producing that product will decline at a predictable rate because of the accumulated experience in producing the product. Costs will drop, workers will become more productive, and operations in general will become more efficient.

In contrast to DuPont's skimming strategy, Dow Chemical has used penetration pricing for some products. Dow prices low; builds a dominant market share; stresses low-margin, commodity products; and focuses on the long term.[7]

Growth Phase

A product in the growth phase of the PLC is generally faced with severe competitive pressures as buyers look at price as being more important in the buying decision. The benefits of economies of scale and the effects of the experience curve referred to earlier might allow the firm to lower price as a competitive strategy. Competition is aggressive as this is a period of rapid market acceptance and increasing profits. Profits tend to peak toward the end of the market-growth phase, and the producer faces a trade-off between high market share and high current profit.

Maturity Phase

To price appropriately in this phase, the marketer needs to know when the product is approaching maturity. The marketer may find it desirable to reduce prices as soon as symptoms of deterioration appear. Some of these symptoms are as follows:[8]

1. Weakening in brand preference. This may be evidenced by a higher cross-elasticity of demand among leading products; the leading brand is able to continue demanding as much price premium as it initially did without losing any position.

2. Narrowing physical variation among products as the best designs are developed and standardized.

3. Market saturation; the ratio of replacement sales to new-equipment sales serves as an indicator of the competitive degeneration of products.

4. The stabilization of production methods, indicated by the slow rate of technological advance and high average age of equipment.

---

[7]William Lazer and James D. Culley, *Marketing Management* (Boston: Houghton Mifflin), p. 556.

[8]Dean, "Techniques for Pricing New Products and Services," p. 170.

Decline Phase

This phase of the PLC presents the price setter with a number of opportunities. Cost control becomes increasingly important as demand drops, possibly allowing the marketer to leave the price alone, while maintaining short-term profit objectives as the product dies a natural death. In the absence of tight cost control, the strategy may be to raise price, taking advantage of the segments with inelastic demand. A final pricing strategy could be to use the product as a loss leader. Pricing the product at cost or even under cost, much as is done in consumer retail pricing strategy, might well help sell complementary products in the line.

■ PRICE LEADERSHIP STRATEGY

In pricing a firm's products over their respective life cycles, marketing managers must decide whether to pursue their task as a market leader. **Price-leadership strategy** prevails in oligopolistic situations and is the practice by which one or a very few firms initiate price changes, with most or all of the other firms in the industry following suit. When price leadership prevails in an industry, price competition does not exist. The burden of making critical pricing decisions is placed on the leading firm; others simply follow the leader.

Price leadership is found most often in industries whose products are similar, even standardized and, therefore, considered by customers to be good substitutes for each other. In such industries a firm would lose market share if it charged a higher price than its competitors. Price leadership is a way of coordinating prices without colluding. This practice is at once a sign of so much competition in an industry that all firms involved have to sell at exactly the same price in order to stay in business or of so little competition that firms are able to coordinate their prices as they would under a collusive agreement. Usually the leader is the firm with the largest market share, such as U.S. Steel Corporation or IBM, or the firm that makes the first upward move. Implicit in the very fact of leadership is a willingness to live and let live. Price wars are rare, as price deviation is quickly disciplined.

Successful price leaders are characterized by the following description:[9]

1. A large share of the industry's production capacity.
2. A large market share.
3. Commitment to a particular product class or grade.
4. New, cost-efficient plants.
5. A strong distribution system, perhaps including captive wholesale outlets.

---

[9]Stuart U. Rich, "Price Leaders: Large, Strong, but Cautious about Conspiracy," *Marketing News,* June 25, 1982, p. 11.

6. Good customer relations, such as technical assistance for buyers, programs directed at end users, and special attention to important customers during shortage periods.

7. An effective market information system which provides analysis of the realities of supply and demand.

8. Sensitivity to the price and profit needs of the rest of the industry.

9. A sense of timing to know when price changes should be made.

10. Sound management organization for pricing.

11. Effective product-line financial controls, which are needed to make sound price leadership decisions.

12. Attention to legal issues.

Price leadership requires certain things of leaders. The presence of a specific and consistent pricing strategy, the use of controlled power, and the recognition of the rights of followers to their respective market positions will sustain a leadership position. The threat of independent pricing action is always there, ready to break out if the leader fails to make the right decisions. The leader must be aware that if the wrong decisions are made, followers will, in all likelihood, destroy that position of leadership.

■ COMPETITIVE BIDDING IN THE BUSINESS TO BUSINESS MARKET

Business buyers often engage in competitive bidding. **Competitive bidding** is a process whereby a buyer will request price bids from interested suppliers on a proposed purchase or contract. This is an invitation to negotiate for the best combination of quality, service, and price. This process is used not only for custom-engineered products but also for standard manufactured products, components, and services. The buyer sends inquiries or requests for quotes (RFQ) to firms able to produce in conformity with requested requirements. The marketer must make the decision on whether or not to bid on a specific supply requirement or job as the bidding process requires that quotes be received in final form by a certain deadline. Competitive bids from several firms for basically identical items will vary, even when internal cost structures might be essentially the same for all competitors. The market price level is, therefore, not a specific value for a given item, but rather a wide display of prices with fairly well-defined empirical limits for each industry. Also important in deciding whether or not to bid is excess capacity and alternative opportunities to utilize this capacity. Related to this is the extent to which competitive bidders have excess capacity and, therefore, would be expected to bid low. For the marketer, this could mean substantial opportunity along with substantial potential pitfalls. As explained in the "Business to Business Marketing in Action" box, conjoint analysis is an analytical tool which enables marketers to understand the bidding process better, particularly the reasons why some bids are rejected.

BUSINESS TO BUSINESS MARKETING IN ACTION

Conjoint Analysis Can Explain Why Some Bids Are Rejected

Conjoint analysis can help business marketers understand the criteria prospective clients use when choosing suppliers. Selection criteria can be an especially perplexing issue when requests for proposals are solicited. After the winning bid is selected, the other bidders may find it difficult to understand why their bids were rejected.

The best way to gain that knowledge is through conjoint analysis. It yields answers superior to those developed through structured and unstructured postbidding interviews with clients, in which attempts to rationalize selecting the winning bid may cloud the postbid analysis conducted by marketing researchers.

By contrast, conjoint analysis is largely nonverbal. Respondents choose from packages of attributes and features, so it best replicates the bidding process.

Complex trade-offs are the meat of conjoint analysis. Any conjoint procedure has respondents evaluate various packages or sets of attributes. Once these attributes are combined, the number of possible variations can be in the hundreds. Therefore, a computer program is used before data gathering begins to reduce the packages systematically, so there is a need to present all possible alternatives. Based on its use to reduce the number of combinations, each respondent will typically evaluate 16 to 36 combinations.

After ranking the choices, the buyer's judgments are "decomposed" into separate utility charts which graphically depict the results.

In any business bidding case, options are built from as few as five to as many as 20 factors involved in bidding. Each factor will then have two to four (sometimes more) levels or choices.

An orthogonal array creates the packages to be ranked. The array allows the number of packages shown to be minimized. After all the respondents make their choices, the data are then analyzed through a second computer program. If desired, the results can be organized for specific clusters—by price-sensitive compared to service-sensitive segments, for example. Conjoint analysis techniques can be applied in just about any industry.

SOURCE: Gabriel M. Gelb, "Conjoint Analysis Helps Explain the Bid Process," *Marketing News* 22 (March 14, 1988), pp. 1, 31. Used with permission.

Closed versus Open Bidding

Government units (federal and local) and most public institutions are required to buy product and services on the competitive bidding system. In such a situation the contemplated purchase is advertised in advance, giving the potential supplier the opportunity to consider submitting a bid. Many of these bids are made public; thus price competition is stressed. A price setter often is required to submit a performance bond along with the bid to assure that quality and service will not suffer because of the emphasis on price. Such a requirement may discourage some marketers from competing in this arena.

Competitive bidding can take the form of closed bidding, which is a series of sealed bids, all of which are opened, reviewed, and evaluated at the same time. Again price is stressed, with the lowest bid usually winning the contract. Although the lowest bidder is not guaranteed the contract, this bidder will normally win the business if the bid is for standard products or services or if the product is to be made to exact buyer specifications. Competitive bidding can also take the form of open bidding, which is more informal, allows for negotiation, and is often used when there is much flexibility with regard to buyer specifications. Complex technical requirements utilize an open bidding process, as does the purchase of products where specific requirements are hard to define precisely.

Whether or not to bid, as mentioned earlier, can present the marketer with a dilemma. A number of criteria in determining whether or not to bid on a job should include the following:

1. Is the dollar value of the job large enough to warrant the expense involved in making the bid?
2. Are the product or service specifications ("specs") precise enough so that the cost of production can be accurately estimated?
3. Will the acceptance of the bid adversely affect production and the ability to serve other customers?
4. How much time is available to prepare a bid?
5. What is the likelihood of winning the bid, considering the presence and strength of other bidders?[10]

A Probabilistic Bidding Model

Once the marketing manager has determined that a potentially profitable bidding opportunity is present, a bidding strategy must be developed. A **probabilistic bidding model** is a mathematical technique used to determine prices in a bidding situation; it assumes that competitors will behave in the future as they have in the past. This bidding model provides an objective procedure for evaluating potential profits of different pricing alternatives by drawing on past data and by making assumptions as to how competitors will behave in a bidding situation.

---

[10]Adapted from Donald W. Dobler, W. L. Lee, and D. N. Burt, *Purchasing and Materials Management,* 4th ed. (New York: McGraw-Hill, 1984).

All probabilistic bidding models focus on three criteria: (1) the size of the bid; (2) the profit expected if the bid wins; and (3) the probability that the submitted bid will win. The optimum bid is the one that will return the highest profit to the firm and can be expressed with the following formula:

$$E(x) = P(x)Z(x)$$

where x = Dollar amount of the bid
  $Z(x)$ = Profit if the bid is expected
  $P(x)$ = Probability of the bid being accepted at this price
  $E(x)$ = Expected profit at this price[11]

The most difficult part of using this formula is estimating the probability of a given bid being the lowest one submitted. This factor is $P(x)$, shown above, and success will determine to a large degree on the marketer's ability and experience in competitive bidding. A relatively high bid price, with the resulting large expected profit, will have a low probability of being accepted in a competitive situation. A low bid would probably show the opposite—a high probability of being accepted, but projecting little or no profit. The purpose of a probabilistic bidding model is to find the bid with the optimum combination of profit and probability of acceptance.

In the equation noted earlier, the expected profit equals the probability of winning with a bid of x, multiplied by the profit associated with that bid. To demonstrate the basic model, we use two hypothetical competitors. The Anderson Company is considering bidding on a project against one known competitor, the Zephyr Company. Because the contract will be awarded to the lowest bidder, Anderson wishes to determine the probability that its bid will be lower than Zephyr's bid. The first step is to obtain information on previous relationships between Anderson's estimated direct costs and Zephyr's bids on similar projects. These data are shown in Table 8–2. The second step is to analyze the data in Table 8–2 to determine the probability that Zephyr will submit a bid higher than any given percent of Anderson's estimated direct cost. The result of this analysis is presented in Table 8–3 and Figure 8–5.

If Anderson submits a bid of 140 percent of estimated direct costs, as Table 8–3 and Figure 8–5 indicate, there is a 55 percent probability that such a bid will be lower than Zephyr's bid. If Anderson submits a bid of 110 percent of estimated direct costs, its bid will probably be lower than Zephyr's. Because the probabilistic bidding model considers only direct costs, the expected contribution margin of a bid must be determined. This computation is done by multiplying the difference between the bid price and the estimated direct costs by the probability that the bid will be accepted. To determine the optimum bid, the contribution margin or contribution margin percent on each bid under consideration must be multiplied by the probability that the bid will be lower than that of a competitor.[12] A

[11]The following discussion is based on W. J. Morse, "Probabilistic Bidding Models: A Synthesis," *Business Horizons* 18 (April 1975), pp. 67–74.
[12]Ibid., p. 69.

■ **TABLE 8–2**   Relationship of Zephyr's Bids to Anderson's Estimated Direct Cost

Project	Zephyr's Bid	Anderson's Estimated Direct Cost	Percent
1	19,800	15,000	132
2	88,400	65,000	136
3	62,800	40,000	157
4	33,750	25,000	133
5	72,500	50,000	145
6	11,100	10,000	111
7	64,860	47,000	138
8	12,080	8,000	151
9	53,760	32,000	168
10	99,400	70,000	142
11	29,700	22,000	135
12	60,900	42,000	145
13	39,900	30,000	133
14	29,800	20,000	149
15	23,250	15,000	155
16	34,440	21,000	164
17	47,520	36,000	132
18	43,200	30,000	144
19	41,160	28,000	147
20	73,750	59,000	125

SOURCE: W. J. Morse, "Probabilistic Bidding Models: A Synthesis," *Business Horizons,* April 1975, Table 1, p. 68. Used with permission.

bidder usually has several known or unknown competitors, and the model can be extended for these situations.

Models such as the one presented above are only one tool available to the business marketer; like other quantitative techniques, they usually cannot replace the professional judgment of the price setter. Other factors, some quantifiable and others nonquantifiable, must also be taken into consideration.

Concept Questions

1. What is a price leadership strategy?
2. How is price leadership sustained?
3. What is the purpose of a probabilistic bidding model?

■ LEASING IN THE BUSINESS TO BUSINESS MARKET

In addition to the choice of whether or not to engage in competitive bidding, buyers must also decide in appropriate situations whether to buy or to lease an asset. In such situations, many customers choose to lease rather than to purchase. For the astute marketer, leasing can provide a very viable alternative to selling capital equipment. In FASB Statement No. 13, as

Bid as a Percent of Estimated Direct Cost	Number of Higher Bids	Percent Higher (Probability of Underbidding)
110	20	100
115	19	95
120	19	95
125	19	95
130	18	90
135	15	75
140	11	55
145	9	45
150	6	30
155	4	20
160	2	10
165	1	5
170	0	0

SOURCE: W. J. Morse, "Probabilistic Bidding Models: A Synthesis," *Business Horizons,* April 1975, Table 2, p. 69. Used with permission.

■ **FIGURE 8–5**   Probability of Underbidding One Known Competitor

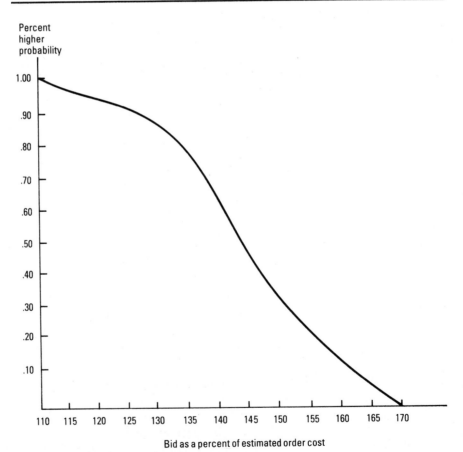

SOURCE: W. J. Morse, "Probabilistic Bidding Models: A Synthesis," *Business Horizons,* April 1975, Figure 1, p. 70. Used with permission.

amended and interpreted through May 1980 (latest change), a lease is defined "as an agreement conveying the right to use property, plant, or equipment, usually for a stated period of time."[13] A lease involves a lessee and a lessor, with the lessee being the party who acquires the right to use the property, plant, or equipment; and the lessor being the party relinquishing the right in return for some form of consideration.

In the business to business market, leasing strategy is employed by most capital goods and equipment manufacturers, including those which market production machinery, postage meters, packaging equipment, textile equipment, copiers, etc. As an example, Farmland Industries in its 1988 financial statements reported leased assets including "railroad cars, automobiles . . . three fertilizer manufacturing facilities, electronic data processing equipment, and other manufacturing facilities." Indeed, almost any asset that can be acquired through purchase can be obtained through leasing. Of the 600 companies recently surveyed, 542 companies or approximately 90 percent reported some form of lease arrangement.[14]

Advantages of Leasing for the Buyer

From both the buyer's and seller's point of view, there are several advantages of leasing over purchasing. The following advantages pertain to the buyer.

No Down Payment.   Lease agreements are frequently structured so that 100 percent of the value of the equipment is financed through the lease, making this an attractive alternative to a company which does not have sufficient cash for a down payment or which wishes to use available capital for other operating or investing purposes. Because cash flow is critical to the survival and growth of a business, its management is very important.

Avoids Risk of Ownership.   There are many risks of ownership, including casualty loss, obsolescence, changing economic conditions, and physical deterioration. The lessee may terminate the lease (usually with a predetermined penalty), and thus avoid assuming the risk of these events. This flexibility is especially important to the buyer in a business where innovation and technological change makes the future usefulness of a piece of equipment or facility highly uncertain. A good example of this condition in recent years has been the electronics industry with its rapid change in areas such as computer technology, robotics, and telecommunications.

Tax Benefits.   Many tax provisions grant benefits to owners of property. For example, prior to the 1986 Tax Reform Act, tax laws provided for investment tax credits which allowed owners of equipment a direct credit

---

[13]"Accounting for Leases," FASB statement, no. 13, as amended and interpreted through May 1980 (Stamford, Conn.: FASB, 1980), par. 1.

[14]Certified Public Accountants, *Accounting Trends and Techniques* (New York: American Institute of Certified Public Accountants, 1988), p. 188.

against income taxes payable, either in the current period or in future periods through carryover provisions. If a lessor sells the asset, the benefits go with the property, but lease agreements can specify who gets the benefits. This flexibility makes it possible for the tax credits to be a significant element in lease negotiations. Further, by deducting lease payments, the lessee can write off the full cost of the asset. The tax deduction can be accelerated, since this is often spread over the period of the lease rather than the actual economic life of the equipment.

Advantages of Leasing for the Seller

Increased Sales. By offering potential customers the option of leasing products, the marketer can significantly increase sales volume. Leasing can be a vehicle to attract customers that otherwise might find a product unaffordable. Market growth can be boosted since many more customers can afford to lease products than can afford to buy them.

Ongoing Business Relationship with the Lessee. In leasing situations the lessor and lessee maintain contact over a period of time, and long-term business relationships may be promoted through leasing.

Residual Value Retained. In many lease arrangements title to the asset does not pass to the lessee. The lessor benefits from economic conditions that can result in a significant residual value at the end of the lease term. The lessor may lease the asset to another lessee or sell the property and realize an immediate gain. A lessor may also realize a profit from unexpected increases in residual values.

Types of Lease Arrangements

There are three basic ways of leasing equipment. First, the firm can lease directly to the customer, financing the lease arrangements itself. In essence, the seller acts as a financial institution would, operating on the basis of monthly or quarterly payments—much like repaying a debt to a financial institution. Second, several large firms have established leasing subsidiaries to provide this service to the customer (John Deere and General Electric, for example). Third, lease transactions are arranged for customers through a lending institution which is involved in leasing to the business market. Examples of companies using such a practice include General Finance Corporation, U.S. Leasing, and C.I.T. Financial. This is called a *direct financing lease* and involves a lessor who is primarily engaged in financial activities, such as a bank or finance company.

Types of Leases

The two types of leases from the lessor's standpoint are operating leases and direct financing leases.

Operating Lease.   An **operating lease** is usually short term and cancellable. The lessor gives up the physical possession of the asset, but the transfer is considered temporary in nature. As such, the lessor continues to carry the leased asset as an owned asset on the balance sheet, and the revenue from the lease is reported as it is earned. Depreciation of the leased asset is matched against the revenue. Generally, the lessor provides maintenance and service, and the lease does not contain a purchase option. Under an operating lease the lessor retains substantially all the risks and benefits of ownership.

Direct Financing Lease.   A **direct financing lease** is noncancellable, usually long term, and fully amortized over the period of the contract. The sum of the lease payments exceeds the price paid for the asset by the lessor. The lessee is responsible for operating expenses and is usually given the option of purchasing the asset; often a portion of the lease payments is applied toward the purchase of the asset.

■ PRICING POLICIES IN BUSINESS TO BUSINESS PRICING STRATEGY

Another important decision faced by firms is the marketing manager's choice of what pricing policies to follow. The prices charged by the marketer are influenced by the different types of customers, the characteristics of the channel system, and the different geographic regions served. Initially, the price setter must be concerned with net price, which is the list price minus allowances for trade-ins and other cost-significant concessions made by the buyer, such as volume purchases and order pick-up versus delivery. The establishment of a list price provides the base from which discounts can be subtracted. Discounts come in many forms, with trade, quantity, and cash discounts being the most prevalent. In theory, discounts are simply cost savings realized by the manufacturer and passed on to intermediaries.

Trade Discounts

A **trade discount** is a deduction from the list price offered to an intermediary in return for services performed. Generally speaking, the more services performed by the intermediary, the higher is the trade discount. These services include inventory holding, the providing of customer credit, technical support for the manufacturer, and missionary sales work. A note of caution, however, is in order here. As price setters contemplate trade discount strategy, they should give considerable thought to the Robinson-Patman Act. As pointed out in Exhibit 8–1, this piece of legislation takes a dim view of price discrimination practices, such as giving a different discount schedule to basically the same types of customers. Discounts must be nondiscriminatory, and while the Robinson-Patman Act is difficult to police and enforce, the price setter should at least be aware of possible ramifications if charged with a violation of this act.

Quantity Discounts

A **quantity discount** is a deduction in the list price which a manufacturer gives either to channel intermediaries or to OEM users for buying in large amounts. Cost savings can be found in inventory storage, transportation cost per unit, sales calls, follow-up service, and order processing. The two primary types of quantity discounts available are *noncumulative discounts,* which are discounts taken on each and every order made, and *cumulative discounts,* which are given on a series of orders over a particular period of time. Quantity discounts are considered to be legal as long as sellers can demonstrate that their costs are reduced by selling in large volume. In the case of cumulative quantity discounts, savings are harder to prove in that the granting of such discounts does not necessarily result in reduced storage or order-processing costs. Manufacturers, with judicial support, may claim that they legally provide cumulative quantity discounts to meet similar competitive offerings.

Cash Discounts

A **cash discount** is a price reduction strategy to encourage buyers to pay their bills promptly, with a discount of 2/10, net 30 being common. (Payment is due within 30 days, but the buyer can deduct 2 percent from the total invoice amount for payment within 10 days). This strategy typically improves the seller's liquidity and reduces credit collection costs and bad debts. Again, as listed in Exhibit 8–1, the seller must be aware of the provisions of the Robinson-Patman Act, which stipulate that the same terms must be offered to all buyers, large and small alike.

Geographical Price Adjustments

Shipping costs heavily impact the ultimate cost of products to the buyer, with prices being adjusted upward or downward, depending on who pays the transportation bill (the buyer or the seller). Transportation fees are an especially important factor when pricing large bulky products, such as machinery and equipment which must travel a long distance. This part of the ultimate cost of the product is usually settled through a negotiated agreement between the buyer and the seller. Several alternative price strategies are available to sellers, as the rate structure of transportation in the United States is highly complex because of class and commodity rates, local and joint rates, contract and transit rates, etc. There are separate rate tariffs (or price lists) for various geographic regions; and shipments are classified into a number of groupings called *classes* for rate quotation purposes. Given the complexity of the rate structure, the determination of the applicable (or lowest) rate for a shipment between two points is sometimes difficult and has become an important function of traffic management. Traffic management personnel must have knowledge of transportation tariffs, classifications, and rate structures.

■ INTERNATIONAL MARKETING PRICING POLICY

Business to business price setters are becoming just as concerned about pricing in world markets as they have been in domestic markets. World trade is becoming increasingly important to the health of our economy and to the growth of U.S. companies. Every billion dollars in U.S. exports generates about 25,000 jobs. Further, small firms represent the largest pool of potential exporters. A recent study shows that of 32,000 companies that export, 52 percent are small businesses with fewer than 100 employees.[15] Selling abroad requires time, personnel, planning, market research, attention to detail, hard work, and a focused attention on the role of pricing as a competitive tool. Differing tariffs, costs, attitudes, and methods of price quotation can often confuse the marketing executive. Pricing activity varies by company, by product, and by competitive conditions, among other things. Becoming a successful exporter depends upon the determination and commitment the entire company is willing to give to the endeavor.

Several additional factors impact international pricing policy. Pricing products in the international environment must be done with full attention to cost considerations. The price of raw materials can fluctuate rapidly, and widely fluctuating exchange rates are an especially important consideration. Taxes and tariffs must be considered by the international trader, as these serve to discriminate against the importing of all foreign goods. Inflation must be considered, especially in countries experiencing rapid inflation or exchange variation. To effectively work this into a final price is no easy task indeed. Channel length and infrastructures must also be considered, as channels are both longer and underdeveloped in many parts of the world. Long distribution channels (and transportation costs) add an additional burden to the job of effective, competitive price setting in international markets.

As a major part of the economic adjustment mechanism in the U.S. economy during the decade of the 1990s, firms must discover new markets, create new products, find new markets for old products, and find profitable new markets for new products. The same qualities that cause firms to succeed in domestic markets can be brought to bear on their ability to export profitability. However, to make this happen, marketers must realize that pricing is one of the most complicated decision areas encountered by international marketers. Pricing in this market will require detailed knowledge of costs and regulations (both present and anticipated), a keen sense of market strategy, and knowledge of exchange rate fluctuations on a day-to-day basis.

Concept Questions

1. What is a lease?
2. What are the major influences on the business price setter?

---

[15] "Focus on the Facts: Opportunities in Exporting," U.S. Small Business Administration in Cooperation with AT&T., no. 7, 1988.

SUMMARY

1. Because there are so many variables to consider whose precise influence cannot be anticipated, pricing decisions are often made by guesswork, intuition, or reliance on such methods as traditional markup percentages. The major factors upon which the success of pricing strategy is based include competition, cost, demand, pricing objectives, impact on other products, and legal considerations. An important step in pricing strategy is to determine goals and objectives prior to setting price points or levels. The principal pricing objectives of most firms include profit generation, a satisfactory return on investment, and the maintenance or increase of market share. Often the purchase of one product increases the likelihood of the purchase of another product or product line by the same customer. Marketers should be prepared to justify price levels, along with quantity and trade discounts.

2. Among the pricing methods and strategies commonly used by price setters are marginal pricing, break-even analysis, and target return-on-investment pricing. Contract bidders often use marginal pricing to gain unplanned business or to utilize idle capacity. A value-based strategy, such as the relatively new method of analyzing a product's economic value to a customer, can be a uniquely effective way to gain a commanding lead over the competition. Break-even analysis is undertaken to determine the point at which a firm's revenue will equal its total fixed and variable costs at a given price. Target return-on-investment pricing is a method of setting prices to achieve a particular percentage return on capital invested in the product in question.

3. Demand refers to the amount of a good or service that a buyer or buyers are willing and able to purchase at a particular moment at each possible price. Demand is elastic if quantity is highly responsive to price, and inelastic if it is not. Unitary demand elasticity exists when the percentage change in price is identical to the percentage change in quantity demanded. When attempting to determine demand, cost-benefit analysis is an analysis of benefits received and costs incurred by the customer in buying and using the product or service.

4. A new product generally enjoys its greatest degree of differentiation during the introductory stage of the product life cycle. Pricing decisions at this stage of the product's life center either on price skimming or market penetration pricing, depending on the nature of the market and the type of customer involved. There are specific price considerations which the marketer must ponder during each phase of the product life cycle with respect to profit, demand, and marketing strategy.

5. The price-leadership strategy prevails in oligopolistic situations, and is the practice by which one or a very few firms initiate price changes, with one or more of the other firms in the industry following suit. Price leadership is found most often in industries where products are

similar and even standardized; therefore, they are usually considered by customers to be good substitutes for each other.

6. Competitive bidding is a process whereby a business buyer will request price bids from interested suppliers on a proposed purchase or contract. Government agencies and most public institutions are usually required to use the competitive bidding system in buying products and services. Competitive bidding can take the form of either closed (sealed bid) bidding or open bidding. A probabilistic bidding model is a mathematical technique used to determine prices in a bidding structure; it assumes that competition will behave in the future as it has in the past.

7. Many customers choose to lease an asset rather than purchase it; and for the business marketer, leasing can provide a very viable alternative to selling capital equipment. In the business to business market, leasing is employed by most capital goods and equipment manufacturers. There are several advantages of leasing over purchasing from both the buyer's and seller's points of view. Two primary forms of business leases are the operating lease and the direct financing lease.

8. The business marketer must be concerned with net price, which is the list price minus allowances for trade-ins and other cost-significant concessions. The establishment of a list price provides the base from which discounts can be subtracted. Discounts come in many forms, with trade, quantity, and cash discounts being the most prevalent. Geographical price adjustments are also frequently made to the list price.

9. World trade is growing increasingly important to the health of our economy and to the growth of U.S. companies. Pricing products in the international environment must be done with full consideration of applicable costs, inflationary pressures, and channel length and infrastructure in each world market.

KEY TERMS

break-even analysis	operating lease
cash discount	price elasticity of demand
competitive bidding	price leadership strategy
cost-benefit analysis	probabilistic bidding model
direct financing lease	quantity discount
elastic demand	Robinson-Patman Act
inelastic demand	target return-on-investment
marginal (contribution) pricing	pricing
market penetration	trade discount
market skimming	unitary demand elasticity

REVIEW QUESTIONS

1. Why is price planning not a precise science? Identify and describe the six major factors influencing pricing strategy. Discuss three common pricing objectives. What is meant by a complementary relationship?

2. Explain the pricing methods of (1) marginal pricing, (2) EVC, (3) break-even analysis, and (4) target return-on-investment pricing. What is the fundamental reason for using each of these methods?

3. What is price elasticity of demand? Distinguish among elastic, inelastic, and unitary demand. How can cost benefit analysis be utilized in determining demand for products?

4. Differentiate between price skimming and market penetration pricing. Under what circumstances would you use each one? What are the primary price considerations in each phase of the product life cycle?

5. What is a price leadership strategy? In what kinds of industries is such a pricing strategy commonly found? How does a company maintain its price leadership position?

6. What is the competitive bidding process, and what types of organizations typically use such a process? Identify five criteria which should be used by a firm considering whether or not to bid on a particular piece of business. What is the fundamental difference between an open bid and a closed bid?

7. What is a probabilistic bidding model? What kind of assumption does such a model make? On what three criteria do all probabilistic bidding models focus?

8. What is involved in a leasing agreement? What type of organization uses leasing transactions most frequently? Identify three advantages of leasing from a buyer's perspective, and three from a seller's perspective. Distinguish between an operating lease and a direct financing lease.

9. How is net price determined? Identify and discuss the three most prevalent types of price discounts. When are transportation fees an important pricing consideration?

10. Why is world trade becoming increasingly important to the health of our economy and to the growth of U.S. businesses? What are some important factors which business to business marketers should consider in setting prices for international markets?

CHAPTER CASES

Case 8–1 The Loctite Corporation*

Loctite is a highly profitable and rapidly growing manufacturer and marketer of adhesives, sealants, and related specialty chemicals, with annual sales of almost $200 million. The company's growth has been in the won-

---

*Philip Kotler/Gary Armstrong, *Principles of Marketing*, 4e, © 1989. Reprinted by permission of Prentice Hall, Inc., Englewood Cliffs, N.J.

der glues, specifically the anaerobic type, which cures quickly in the absence of air, and the crazy glues (cyanoacrylates), which cure instantly upon exposure to moisture present in trace amounts on surfaces to be bonded. In the business market this product sells for over $60 per pound. A pound contains roughly 30,000 drops and is generally applied a few drops at a time. Consumer packages are much smaller, containing about $\frac{1}{10}$ of an ounce and selling for up to $2 per tube, or about $20 or more per ounce.

The company's phenomenal success has attracted competitors, including some large and aggressive ones, such as Esmark and the 3M Company. Competitive anaerobic and cyanoacrylate products are marketed in most countries where the company conducts business. The company has patent protection on its anaerobics in the United States and to a lesser extent in a number of foreign countries. Nearly all competitive anaerobic sealants and adhesives are sold at prices lower than Loctite's. Although the company has selectively reduced prices to meet competition from time to time, it believes that attention to technical sales and customer needs has generally enabled it to maintain its market position without significant price reductions.

The company plans to intensify its application engineering approach, which helped it to overtake Eastman Kodak in the more competitive crazy glue, or cyanoacrylates, market. This approach casts well-trained, technical service personnel as customer problem solvers using Loctite's products, often especially formulated for the customer's application. The company has three principal user markets for its products: the business to business market, the consumer market, and the automotive aftermarket. In the Industrial Products Group, approximately 60 percent of sales are made through independent distributors, some of which sell adhesives and sealants made by others. The remainder of the sales are made directly to end users. The company maintains close and continued contact with its distributors and major end users to provide technical assistance and support for its products. In the United States and Canada sales are made through approximately 120 technically trained district managers and sales engineers and through approximately 2,800 independent distributors.

The Industrial Products Division faces the problems of pricing three new products. The details are as follows:

Bond-a-matic.   This is an instant glue applicator for assembly lines and is targeted at small and medium-sized manufacturers that put a lot of parts together. The product avoids adhesive clog, a common and costly problem. The company is so confident of the product's performance that it will mail a demonstration kit for a 30-day free trial. It should be priced low enough so that it can be bought by the production managers without approval for a capital expenditure.

Quick Repair Kit.   This includes an assortment of materials to make quick minor repairs requiring fast-curing adhesive and/or sealants to keep equipment running and minimize waste of materials in small shops and factories. The kit includes a pair of Vice-Grip pliers as a premium.

Quick Metal.   This is a puttylike adhesive for temporary repair of worn metal bearings and other machine parts. Equipment is ready to run in 1 hour compared with 12 hours for metalizers, the most commonly used alternative method. Loctite claims that the product can save the user $4,000 in time and labor. It is packaged in 50 cc tubes.

All these products are to be sold through the Industrial Product Division's distributors. In determining the suggested price to be charged by the distributors for each product, assume the following hypothetical data:

	Bond-a-matic	Quick Repair Kit	Quick-Metal
Cost to make	$27.00	$6.25	$1.50
All other costs	23.00	5.75	3.50
Total cost per unit	$50.00	$12.00	$5.00

Distributor

Usual gross margin on this type of product, 33⅓ percent of selling price.

Questions

1. What factors should be considered in determining the price Loctite should suggest its distributors charge their customers?
2. What price would you recommend Loctite suggest its distributors charge?

Case 8–2   The Gallison Company*

The Gallison Company makes and markets materials used by a variety of firms. Total sales are about $80 million annually. While not a business giant, the Gallison Company is in tip-top financial condition by any of the ratio tests ordinarily used to measure financial strength. It enjoys excellent management that is aggressive and forward-looking without sacrifice of the hardheaded conservatism that lends soundness to judgment. For many years the company has been a leader in research in its industry and enjoys an enviable record in the development of new products and new processes.

The Gallison Company has avoided making and marketing the heavy tonnage materials produced by its industry, most of which carry narrow margins of gross profit, require no special skills in production, and demand little or no technical service in marketing. It has concentrated on the specialty part of the business, consisting of highly complex items with wide gross profit margins that require unusual research skills to develop, special know-how to produce, and excellent technical service to market. At all times a large percentage of the firm's sales are in products developed within the past 5 to 10 years.

In marketing many of its new products, the Gallison Company follows a policy common in the trade to which it belongs. This is to charge a very

*Ralph S. Alexander, James S. Cross, and Ross M. Cunningham, *Industrial Marketing*, 2nd ed., © 1961, pp. 379–82. Used by permission.

high price in relation to cost during the early stages of market development, and to reduce prices as the cost advantages of volume production economies accrue or when competition begins to develop. This policy has the advantage of enabling the company to write off speedily the capital expenditures in research, equipment, and market-development work.

About two years ago the Gallison Company put on the market a material which greatly reduced the cost of the end products of the customer industry and vastly increased their flexibility and efficiency in use. The company sold this material in pieces that the buying firms mechanically processed into smaller units, which then were incorporated into their end products.

Three other companies had been researching this material. One of them was the giant of the industry. The other two were "captive" firms, subsidiaries of concerns in the using industry. The research efforts of all four bore fruit at about the same time. There was a pronounced difference in the production processes, however, which created a significant difference in the flexibility of their marketing operations.

The production processes of all four companies started with a raw material heavily impregnated with impurities. The Gallison Company developed a method, on which it obtained a valid patent, whereby in one process it removed all impurities and got practically pure material. The competing companies used a series of processes, each of which removed a part of the impurity content. At the end of each of the last five of these, a usable grade of the material was obtained; the last process yielded a grade roughly comparable to the material Gallison got by its single process.

This situation gave Gallison a considerable cost advantage in making the purer grades of the material. In order to obtain the less pure grades, however, Gallison had to put impurities back into the product by a process known in the trade as *slagging*, which dissipated some, but not all, of its cost advantage. Since Gallison's lower grades were tailor-made, however, it could control more precisely the exact characteristics of its material.

Four other smaller noncaptive companies have since come into the business, but none of them has become a significant factor. Gallison and its giant competitor together have about 90 percent of the noncaptive business.

The using industry includes about 50 firms, of which 5 control the bulk of the demand. One of the captive producers is owned by a large user, the other by a medium-sized firm in the customer industry. Neither of the captive producers sells on the open market, although either may do so.

The material is bought both on individual order and on annual contracts covering all or a designated part of the requirements of the buying firm. Because of the newness of the business, buying habits have not yet settled into a dependable pattern. The annual contracts usually contain some sort of a clause allowing the buyer protection against price changes in the supplying industry.

During the past week to 10 days, rumors have been circulating to the effect that the industry giant's prices, which have been the same as Gallison's, would be reduced. No definite information was available until yesterday when a Gallison salesperson telephoned, reporting that a customer had shown a new price list and allowed the salesperson to copy the prices from it. The salesperson reported the giant's new prices, which are shown in the following table; the table also shows Gallison's price list. Several of these prices match those which other Gallison salespeople had reported hearing about yesterday.

Grade	Gallison Price (per pound)	Giant's New Price (per pound)
1	$1,398	$1,400
2–A	858	850
2–B	858	850
2–C	858	850
3	635	595
4	499	467
5	330	270

Gallison had only one Grade 2. The giant's split of Grade 2 into three subgrades represents a departure from the accepted grading system. Gallison can make these subgrades to somewhat more exacting standards and at a somewhat lower cost than other producers, according to the best information available to the company's executives. The marketing executives estimate that this greater exactitude of quality is worth about 5 percent of the quoted price to the average customer.

The marketing executives have also compiled the following estimates of the present market situation, and the direction and extent of the industry's probable development.

Grade	Industry Poundage	Gallison's Share	Probable Growth
1	500	500	Little
2–A	800	4,800	Very great
2–B	3,200	4,800	Great
2–C	4,000	4,800	Moderate
3	5,000	4,250	Not much
4	2,000	1,000	Not much
5	30,000	3,000	Little, if any

In the absence of dramatically revolutionary developments in the using industry, of which there is no present hint, the evidence seems irrefutable that during the next five years there will be a tremendous increase in demand. As the table indicates, most of this may be expected in Grade 2. All the new prices quoted by the giant are still far enough above Gallison's cost to allow a highly satisfactory margin of gross and net profit.

The Gallison executives wonder what to do about the situation. The company has a written statement of pricing policy that contains the following pertinent clauses: "We will remain competitive in our prices for material similar to our own when offered by major competitors. Generally, we will follow list price declines rather than lead them. We will meet published list price declines within a few days after publication."

The officials of the company are aware that since the Gallison executives made these policies, they can violate them or unmake them, if occasion warrants.

Question

1. What should the officials of the Gallison Company do about the company's current pricing policies?

SUGGESTED READINGS

Abratt, Russell, and Leyland F. Pitt. "Pricing Practices in Two Industries." *Industrial Marketing Management* 14 (November 1985), pp. 301–6. Survey of pricing models in the chemical and construction industries of South Africa.

Dhebar, Anirudh, and Shmuel S. Dren. "Dynamic Nonlinear Pricing in Networks with Interdependent Demand." *Operations Research* 34 (May/June 1986), pp. 384–94. Mathematical models for optimizing pricing decisions for a new product.

Goetz, Joe F., Jr. "The Pricing Decision: A Service Industry's Experience." *Journal of Small Business Management* 23 (April 1985), pp. 61–67. Survey of pricing strategy, pricing objectives, competitive pricing, and cost-based prices in a service industry.

Graham, Gord. "Push-Button Price Lists." *Canadian Business* (Canada) 59 (March 1986), pp. 91–93. Case study of cost and price computer applications in the Canadian appliance industry.

Greenley, Gordon E. "The Contribution Method of Price Determination." *Quarterly Review of Marketing* (UK) 12 (Autumn 1986), pp. 1–6. A discussion of the contribution method of price determination, including an application of this pricing method.

Krupp, James A. G. "ROI Analysis for Price Breaks." *Journal of Purchasing and Materials Management* 21 (Spring 1985), pp. 23–25. Discussion of trade-offs, quantity discounts, and industry carrying costs.

Lee, Hau L., and Meir J. Rosenblatt. "A Generalized Quantity Discount Pricing Model to Increase Suppliers' Profits." *Management Science* 32 (September 1986), pp. 1177–85. Mathematical model dealing with the joint problem of ordering and offering price discounts.

Meyerowitz, Steven A. "Tightening the Reins on Distributors' Prices." *Business Marketing* 71 (May 1986), pp. 94–100. Discussion of resale price maintenance, nonprice vertical restraints, and antitrust laws.

Polastri, Riccardo P. "Estimating the Effects of Inflation on Prices: A Practical Approach." *Journal of Purchasing and Materials Management* 21 (Spring 1985), pp. 9–16. Example of forecasting techniques, historical pricing, and use of the correlation approach and a producer price index.

Rao, Ram C., and Frank M. Bass. "Competition, Strategy, and Price Dynamics: A Theoretical and Empirical Investigation." *Journal of Marketing Research* 22 (August 1985), pp. 283–96. Price and market share dynamics of new products, and an empirical analysis of the price paths of eight semiconductor parts.

Shipley, David D. "Dimensions of Flexible Price Management." *Quarterly Review of Marketing* (UK) 11 (Spring 1986), pp. 1–7. Large survey dealing with the pricing policies and turbulent environment of manufacturing firms in the United Kingdom.

Washburn, Stewart A. "Understanding Competitive Price Changes." *Business Marketing* 70 (December 1985), pp. 92–97. Guidelines for price increases and price slashing.

———. "Establishing Strategy and Determining Costs in the Pricing Decision." *Business Marketing* 70 (July 1985), pp. 64–78. Guidelines for, and analysis of, strategy selection and cost determination in the pricing decision.

Wilcox, James B.; Roy D. Howell; Paul Kuzdrall; and Robert Britney. "Price Quantity Discounts: Some Implications for Buyers and Sellers." *Journal of Marketing* 51 (July 1987), pp. 60–70. A taxonomy of price quantity discounts and implications of price quantity discounts for the ordering behavior of buyers and the formation of alternative channels of distribution.

Chapter 9

Business to Business Marketing Channel Participants

LEARNING OBJECTIVES

After reading this chapter, you should be able to:

- Recognize the functions of marketing channel members.
- Understand the nature of channel decisions.
- Appreciate the role and importance of direct channels.
- Comprehend the role and importance of various types of indirect channels.
- Discuss the nature of, and contributing factors to, channel cooperation.
- Relate the reasons for channel conflict and the available remedies.
- Explain the nature of channel activities in international markets.

CHAPTER OUTLINE

Functions of the Channel
Intermediary
    Buying
    Selling
    Storage
    Transportation
    Sorting
    Financing
    Risk Taking
    Market Information
The Nature of Channel Decisions
Direct Channels
    Sufficiency of the Sales-Volume
     Base
Indirect Channels
    The Business to Business
    Distributor
    The Manufacturers' Representative
    (Agent)
    Sales Agents and Brokers
    Facilitating Agencies

Both Direct and Indirect Channels
Channel Cooperation
    Methods of Channel Cooperation
Channel Conflict
    Nature of Channel Conflict
    Conflict Management and
     Resolution
    A Legal Perspective of Channel
     Conflict
    Typical Problem Areas in the
     Manufacturer-Intermediary
     Relationship
International Channel Decisions
    Types of Indirect Channel
    Intermediaries

■ FUNCTIONS OF THE CHANNEL INTERMEDIARY

Business to Business channel strategy must be an integral part of the firm's total operating system, meshing with production, finance, research, purchasing, and other functions of the business so as to make the maximum contribution to company objectives. Marketing managers are learning that channels can create differential advantages, especially in instances in which competitors' products, prices, and promotional efforts are almost homogeneous.[1] The types of outlets available and the functions these outlets perform represent the structural elements of channel strategy.

The current body of marketing literature recognizes the fundamental importance of distribution channel management and policies to manufacturers and distributors. From the earliest times to the contemporary fast-paced and dynamic marketplace of today, geographically separated buyers and sellers have required the capability to move or to transfer goods and

---

[1]Philip Maker, "Distribution: Key to Strategy," *Industrial Distribution* 71 (December 1981), p. 29.

commodities physically. For the great majority of products and services, a number of channel functions must be performed. Therefore, as shown in Figure 9–1, the marketing functions of buying, selling, storage, transportation, sorting, financing, risk taking, and market information feedback must be carried out within the channel system. The types of organizations that perform these functions and tasks are an important channel management consideration. A brief explanation of these functions will create a framework from which we can study the various channel alternatives available to the business to business marketer.

Buying

Some channel members buy products for resale to other intermediaries, to a final user, or for their own use. Most act as purchasing managers or buyers, trying to determine how much of a particular product their customers will need over the next week, month, quarter, or other time period for which they must plan and buy. Buying in advance is most often a risky undertaking, as they are betting that their customers will indeed buy the material or parts on hand.

Selling

Intermediaries must be innovative in their use of the interpersonal skills of persuasion and problem solving as they close sales and develop strong business relationships. In most cases the channel intermediary is picked because of the experience, knowledge, and expertise of the company in this area.

■ **FIGURE 9–1**   Basic Channel Functions

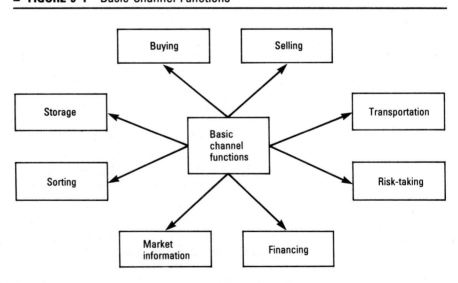

Storage

Effective inventory management requires a proper balance among buying, selling, and production. An inventory commitment is composed of stock to satisfy average or typical customer purchase requirements and to provide for a safety buffer to cover unexpected demand variations and other types of customer buying emergencies. Stock must be in convenient locations to ensure timely delivery and must also be protected to prevent deterioration and loss.

Transportation

The business marketing manager is broadly concerned with managing the physical flow of the product through the intermediary and into the hands of the user. (When title passes, the marketing manager is no longer responsible for transport to the user; this function is assumed by the channel intermediary.) A vast array of transportation alternatives are available for intermediaries to use within their physical distribution systems; the most common modes are rail, motor carrier, water, pipeline, and air. Each of these modes will be examined in detail in Chapter 10.

Sorting

Most intermediaries buy in large quantities, and then break these large shipments into smaller lots for resale to users. The term **breaking of bulk** is commonly used to describe this function performed by intermediaries who take physical possession of the goods. This procedure allows the intermediaries to buy large quantities at reduced prices and to resell the goods at a price which will allow them to make a profit.

Financing

If the intermediary invests in inventory, sells and delivers the merchandise to the user, and provides acceptable credit terms, then he or she is financing the exchange process. Most intermediaries who take title to, and then resell merchandise, allow the user quite liberal terms in paying for the purchase. Thirty days is standard, with 60, 90, and even 120 days not uncommon. Most of these intermediaries operate small businesses and know their customers well. They offer extended terms quite often and tend to be lenient with credit. They are, in a sense, financing the purchase for their customers, much like a local department store or specialty shop finances a final consumer's purchase of a new suit, with payment due (or at least partial payment due) in 30 days.

Risk Taking

Because of obsolescence and deterioration, risk is inherent in the ownership of inventory, with this phenomenon being especially true today because of such rapid advances in technology and the so-called knowledge explosion. Those intermediaries who buy in bulk and take title are betting that the merchandise will not become obsolete and will not deteriorate prior to its resale to the user. The intermediaries in this situation must buy in large enough quantities to make the resale at a profit, while at the same time being careful not to buy in such large quantities that either obsolescence or deterioration could occur before resale to the customer. The amount of risk involved generally depends upon the type of products handled.

Market Information

Communication is a two-way function in the distribution channel, with messages relaying the need for exchange action, and also serving to report progress toward desired end results. Channel communication is necessary and should be continuous as products are transferred and stored in anticipation of future transaction requirements. Information on assortment, quantity, location, and time become important, and must be communicated between channel members if market opportunity is not to be lost. The accuracy of information concerning availability of merchandise, pricing conditions, product quality, and competitive conditions is so important that it might determine what type of channel intermediary the business marketer will use. The number of channel members who perform each of the identified marketing functions will influence the total operating expenses incurred not only by the manufacturer but also by a particular channel member. Each of the eight functions discussed earlier must be performed at least once in every channel, and some may be performed by several channel members.

Channel management and physical distribution management, as shown in Figure 9–2, fit under the distribution strategy variable of the marketing mix. The two components together comprise the distribution element of the marketing mix. Although channel management and distribution management are closely related, they are actually quite different, and frequently there is considerable confusion in regard to the distinction between them. (Distribution management will be discussed in detail in Chapter 10.) **Channel management** is a much broader and more basic component of the distribution strategy variable of the marketing mix than is physical distribution management. Channel management is concerned with the entire process of setting up and operating the organization responsible for meeting the firm's distribution objectives. **Physical distribution management,** on the other hand, is more narrowly focused on providing product availability at the appropriate times and places in the marketing channel. Quite often

■ **FIGURE 9–2**   Marketing Mix Strategic Variables with the Distribution Variable
Divided into Channel and Physical Distribution Components

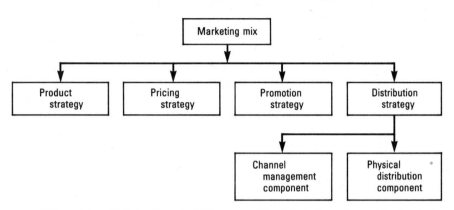

SOURCE: Table, p. 9, from *Marketing Channels: A Management View,* 2nd ed., Copyright © 1983 by The Dryden Press, a Division of Holt, Rinehart & Winston, Inc. Reprinted by permission of the publisher.

channel management must be well under way before physical distribution strategy can even be considered.

■ THE NATURE OF CHANNEL DECISIONS

The business to business marketing manager must regularly perform a critical reappraisal of the channels of distribution in use, with a careful eye on how well each channel member is carrying out assigned functions. If the marketing manager changes the channel structure, a whole complex of marketing decisions is affected. Channel decisions are, by necessity, long-term arrangements. Channel management involves a semipermanent working relationship with either another function within the firm or the same relationship with an outside firm. To change or disrupt a long-term working relationship, while perhaps necessary, can become somewhat difficult and expensive.

Such amending should be done only for sound and serious reasons in that a bad decision may cause market share to suffer. The exercise of choice in channel selection should be done with utmost care. However, if change is later required, the marketing manager must be in a position to execute that change, causing the firm as little disruption as possible. The marketing manager must have some alternative channels of distribution available. Thus a discussion of both direct and indirect channels follows.

Concept Questions

1. What is the basic difference in nature between channel management and distribution management?
2. What kind of time commitment is involved in channel contracts?

■ DIRECT CHANNELS

One alternative channel decision which the marketing manager can make is the selection of a direct channel of distribution. **Direct channels** involve direct selling (i.e., no external intermediary involved) to the user, with or without the use of sales branches. A direct sale would include both generalists and specialists.[2] (Generalists sell the entire product line to all customers, whereas specialists concentrate on particular products, customers, or industries.) A **sales branch** is broadly defined as an off-site manufacturer's sales office, operating within a major market area, staffed with some technical personnel, and having the ability to ship most orders immediately from stock.

■ SUFFICIENCY OF THE SALES-VOLUME BASE

Whether the sales-volume base is sufficient to support a direct-selling program is a matter of judgment. The variables that affect this judgment are absolute sales volume, the breadth and depth of the product line, the relative concentration or dispersion of potential customers, the size of the customers, and the amount of business that can be expected from each of them. If, at one extreme, the line of products that the manufacturer sells to any one market segment is narrow, and if potential customers are small and geographically dispersed, it is likely to be uneconomical to sell directly. At the other extreme, if the manufacturer's product line is broad, if customers are geographically concentrated, and if many buyers have the potential for purchasing in large quantities, it would be difficult to make a case for selling through independent distributors.

Usually, selling direct can be justified if any two of these three conditions are satisfied. Under such circumstances, the marketer generally finds it less expensive to employ direct sales representatives than to give a margin or a commission to an independent.

In sharp contrast to consumer goods, most manufactured business to business goods (as much as 60 to 70 percent) are sold directly to users. This trend will continue and become self-evident as marketing observers analyze the reasons for direct sale. Rockwell International's Municipal and Utility (M&U) Division markets water, gas, and parking meters to local municipalities and gas utilities through a direct sales organization. The direct sales approach is viable because the customers are large and well defined; the customers often insist upon direct sales; sales involve extensive negotiations with high-level utility management; and control of the selling job is necessary to ensure proper implementation of the total product package and to guarantee a quick response to market conditions. In fact, using a direct sales force allowed the company to change its price schedule five times in six months, and to negotiate all the important contracts required by those price changes.

---

[2]Howard Sutton, "Rethinking the Company's Selling and Distribution Channels," The Conference Board, Report no. 885, 1986, p. 1.

■ **FIGURE 9–3**   Alternative Choices of Indirect Channels

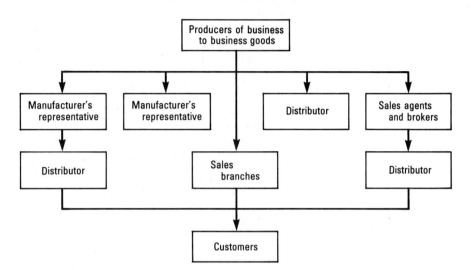

■ INDIRECT CHANNELS

A second alternative channel decision which a marketing manager can make would be the use of **indirect channels.** Indirect channels are warranted when the market is widely scattered, when many firms must be contacted, when small orders are common, and when goods are made for inventory rather than to fill specific orders. Once the manufacturer has determined that indirect channels are appropriate, the paramount question becomes, "which type of indirect channel should be chosen?" As can be noted in Figure 9–3, distributors, manufacturers' representatives (agents), and **sales agents** and **brokers** are possible choices, depending upon the nature of the industry involved and the distribution structure required.

The Business To Business Distributor

Business to business distributors are intermediaries who buy and take title to products, who usually keep inventories of their products, and who sell and service these products. They are the most important single force in distribution channels, numbering approximately 12,000 and accounting for approximately $50 billion in sales volume.[3] One study found that only 24 percent of all business to business marketing firms sell their products directly to end users exclusively; the remaining 76 percent use some type of intermediary, of which distributors are the most prominent.[4] (See Table 9–1 for a more comprehensive profile of the business to business distributor.)

---

[3]"Profits Up despite Lagging Sales," *Industrial Distribution* 77 (July 1987), p. 33.
[4]"Industry Markets Goods through Dual Channels," *Industrial Distribution* 75 (April 1985), p. 15.

■ TABLE 9–1   Profile of the Business to Business Distributor

Characteristics	General Line	Specialist
Median sales	$2,430,000	$2,239,750
Sales from stock	65.5%	60.0%
Number of invoices per year	13,000	7,500
Average invoice	$187	$299
Collections—median number of days outstanding	42	45
Year-end receivables value	$239,600	$268,000
Average monthly inventory values	$397,000	$309,000
Median inventory turnover on stock sales	3.5	4.0
Total number of employees	18.0	15.5
Number of outside salespersons	4	4
Number of inside salespersons	3	2
Square feet of warehouse space	15,000	10,000
Percent with 1 stocking location—no branches	67%	63%
Percent with 2 stocking locations—1 branch	13%	16%
Percent with 3 stocking locations—2 branches	8%	9%
Percent with 4 to 6 stocking locations—3 to 5 branches	8%	10%
Percent with 7 or more stocking locations—6 or more branches	4%	2%
Computerized operations	59.2%	55.1%
Percent of computerized users with own equipment	39%	93%
Percent of computerized users using outside services	11%	7%
Computer applications		
Accounts receivables	92.4%	90.1%
Sales analysis	89.4%	87.6%
Billing	88.6%	84.5%
Accounts payables	85.6%	73.9%
Customer analysis	73.8%	75.8%
Inventory records	78.8%	78.9%
Unit sales pricing	68.9%	57.8%
Purchasing	67.4%	54.7%
Sales order processing	65.2%	60.2%
Payroll	54.5%	45.3%
All others	61.4%	60.2%

SOURCE: Reprinted from *Industrial Distribution*, July 1984, Copyright © (1984) by Cahners Publishing Company, pp. 43–51.

Distributors receive compensation for their services through a margin in the form of the difference between what they pay to the manufacturer and what they charge their customer. This is called a *trade discount*. In addition to the traditional channel functions previously identified and explained, many distributors offer an interesting additional portfolio of services. The most frequently offered of these services are stockless purchasing, literature updating, systems engineering, and guidance on such issues as pollution control.

The distributor is, first of all, a merchant intermediary, taking title to the goods for the purpose of resale. Operating generally as full-service wholesalers, distributors perform the same tasks that a manufacturer would have to provide in selling directly to the user and very often at a lower final cost to customers. The distributor would undertake the performance of buying, selling, storage, transporting, sorting, financing, risk taking, and market information, with this full-service channel member becoming an expert in the provision of the above-mentioned functions. In many ways distributors are similar to wholesalers in consumer channels. Ingersoll-Rand, for example, uses distributors to sell its line of pneumatic tools.

Frequently, the use of distributors lowers the final cost to customers. Because the distributor breaks bulk, provides inventory and delivery services, as well as appropriate personnel, the use of a distributor is often less expensive than using branch houses and company salespeople. In turn, the distributor's lower costs often are passed on to customers in terms of lower prices.

There are two major types of business distributors: **general-line distributors,** who handle a wide variety of supplies and minor equipment, and sell to a broad spectrum of customers; and **limited-line distributors,** who handle fewer, high-volume items such as steel, paper, or chemicals.[5] Such limited-line distributors are often called **jobbers.** Although they take title, they do not necessarily carry the goods in inventory. In this situation jobbers have the manufacturers drop ship the goods directly to the jobbers' customers. Limited-line distributors also include specialists who carry a line of particular goods, such as electrical wiring supplies or who serve a particular industry, such as shoe manufacturers.

Limitations to Using Distributors   After reading and thinking about the previous section, we might get the idea that signing on a distributor is a relatively easy task, and that once such a distributor has been obtained, the marketer has no additional distribution problems. Unfortunately, such is not the case, because for many manufacturers, the use of a distributor might not make sense at all. Exhibit 9–1 examines a number of problems involved in the use of distributors, ranging from overlapping territories to distributors' lack of appreciation for manufacturers' operational policies, procedures, and problems. Distributors are typically very difficult to control. They are generally independent business people; they do not particularly like to, and sometimes will not, take directions from others; and they usually carry or handle competing products. On many occasions they will not emphasize the marketing manager's products in particular. Additionally, the average distributor often does not possess the technical or service know-how to handle high-tech products. The "Business to Business Marketing in Action" box describes how Japan's Epson Corporation, a leading manufacturer of computer printers, replaced all its distributors with other distributors they felt would do a more effective job of selling their new computer product line to retail outlets.

Distributors also seek products that will ensure high inventory turnover and profit margins. Naturally, they tend to stress lines that meet these criteria in their sales efforts.

[5]Victor P. Buell, *Handbook of Modern Marketing,* 2d ed. (New York: McGraw-Hill, 1986), pp. 4–8.

■ **EXHIBIT 9–1**   Problems with the Use of Business to Business Distributors

1. While the manufacturer might desire to retain larger customers as house accounts, the distributor wants access to these accounts.
2. The sophistication and managerial practices of many smaller distributors operating mom-and-pop type businesses are often questioned.
3. Manufacturers desire to keep somewhat high industry levels in distributors' warehouses, whereas distributors wish to minimize such levels.
4. Distributors like to carry second lines in an effort to provide greater selection among competitive offerings for their customers, while manufacturers want distributors to feature their products, and not those of their competitors.
5. Distributors' networks often contain overlapping territories.
6. Distributors frequently demand many small and/or rush orders.
7. Distributors often do not seem sensitive to the operational policies, procedures, and problems of manufacturers.
8. Many distributors do not see manufacturers' promotional advice as relevant and ignore manufacturers' sales representatives.

SOURCE: Reprinted from *Industrial Distribution,* June 9, 1984, Copyright © (1984) by Cahners Publishing Company, p. 30.

Trends for Distributors   In talking with a number of distributors, we learn that the following major changes are taking place: (1) more heavy (capital) equipment, such as large machinery, is being marketed through distributors; (2) manufacturers are increasing their support of distributors, including sales aids, sales training, and other field-support services; (3) distributors are becoming more sophisticated as more and more college graduates and many quality engineers join their ranks. Available computer software has also contributed to the growing sophistication of distributors; (4) a trend toward specialization among distributors is now more evident. As distributors sell increasingly larger amounts of a particular product line, they tend to gain a great deal of expertise in that specific field. This phenomenon tends to feed on itself, as they expand that particular expertise to meet the additional demand created. This development of expertise seems to be a natural tendency as the distributor spends more and more time, money, and effort selling and promoting a certain line or type of product; and (5) manufacturers using distributors are tending to depend more on them for a wide variety of marketing activities, including research, new product development, and additional market coverage. Table 9–2 discusses new directions in distributor operations. Among the more important new directions are the emergence of larger, more sophisticated distributors; the rising popularity of distributor outlet chains; and the growing concentration of efforts in restricted product lines.

Despite the limitations mentioned earlier, the distributor's status as a full-service institution has brought this marketing intermediary recognition as an expert in the performance of many vital marketing functions. Generally speaking, distributors compare favorably with manufacturer's sales branches as far as costs of distribution are concerned. At the same time they offer a more complete product line, provide possibly better market coverage, and aid in the development of small accounts. Table 9–3 summa-

BUSINESS TO BUSINESS MARKETING IN ACTION

Creating a Team of Distributors for Epson Products

Epson Corporation of Japan, a major manufacturer of computer print-ers, wanted to expand its product line by adding computers. Epson was not pleased with its existing distributors. Jack Whalen, general manager at Epson, secretly recruited a pool of new distributors to replace the current ones. He employed a recruiting company, Hergen-rather and Company, and advised its leader as follows:

- Search for applicants who have had two-step distribution expe-rience (factory to distributor to dealer) in either brown goods (televisions, etc.) or white goods (refrigerators, etc.).
- The applicants should be CEO types who are willing and able to set up their own distributorships.
- They would be offered an $80,000 yearly salary plus bonus, and $375,000 to help them set up in business. Each would add $25,000 of his or her own money, and each would get equity in the business.
- They would handle only Epson products, but might stock the software of other companies. Each distributor would have a training manager and a fully equipped service center.

Hergenrather and Company found it difficult to locate motivated qualified prospects. An advertisement placed in *The Wall Street Jour-nal* that did not reveal the company name yielded close to 1,700 re-sponses, mostly from unqualified job seekers. The Yellow Pages were then utilized to secure names of current distributors. Hergenrather thereupon telephoned managers who were second in command. Inter-views were arranged, from which a list of qualified prospects was identified. Whalen interviewed each of these prospects and chose those he considered to be the best twelve. Hergenrather and Com-pany was paid $250,000 for its efforts.

Terminating Epson's current distributors was the concluding stage in the process. This would be perhaps the most difficult step, at least from a tactical point of view, since the existing distributors had no knowledge of Hergenrather's activities. All current distributors were given a 90-day notice of their replacement, regardless of the length of time they had been in Epson's employ. Although most were shocked, they also had no contract in force. Whalen knew these existing dis-tributors could not successfully handle Epson's extended product line and saw no other action as feasible in this situation.

SOURCE: Arthur Bragg, "Undercover Recruiting: Epson America's Sly Distributor Switch," *Sales and Marketing Management*, March 11, 1985, pp. 45–49. Used with permission.

■ **TABLE 9–2**   New Directions in Distributor Operations

Changes in Distributor Operations	Impacts on the Manufacturer
Larger size	Larger, more sophisticated distributors are emerging.* A small number of well-managed distributors can reduce a manufacturer's logistical costs and yield greater effectiveness of dollars spent on training and support. However, there will be fewer uncommitted distributors.
Distributor "supermarkets"	The distributor chain operation is an emerging force in American industry. This is a chain of regional or national outlets owned and/or managed by one corporation.† Chains may carry multiple brands rather than one exclusive name; can offer private labels in a number of brand categories; can use price discounting; and can offer wide and deep territories. A shift of power to the chain is a likely result.
Specialization	Concentrating efforts in restricted product lines is a growing trend. Specialist distributors present buyers with efficient service, expert knowledge, and a multitude of brands in a narrow product line. These factors more closely tie end-user customers to the distributor from a manufacturer's point of view. A shift on control or market power to the specialist is again likely to occur. The business to business marketer might find the need to grant price concessions, heavy advertising, or direct sales controls to the end user so that the manufacturer's brand might be only one of many which the specialist handles.

SOURCE: *Ronald H. Michman, "Trends Affecting Industrial Distributors," *Industrial Marketing Management* 9 (July 1980), p. 214; and †J. Main, "The Chain Reaction That's Rocking Industrial Distribution." *Sales and Marketing Management* 114 (February 23, 1976), pp. 41–45. Used with permission.

rizes the activities of some of the major firms distributing business to business goods. Extensive market coverage, with the ability to sell in great volume, is evident.

The Manufacturers' Representative (Agent)

A **manufacturers' representative,** often called a *manufacturers' agent,* is a firm selling part of the output of one or more manufacturers whose products are related, but noncompetitive. (See Exhibit 9–2 for a brief profile of a manufacturers' representative.) Such representatives enter into a formal written agreement with each manufacturer covering price policy, territories, order-handling procedures, delivery service, warranties, and commission rates. They know each manufacturer's product line and use their wide contacts to sell the manufacturer's products.[6] Representatives comprise sales organizations which work independently and generally represent several different smaller companies within a particular industry or geographic area. Fred Holloway, manager of Yarway Corporation's Metering Pump Division of Blue Bell, Pennsylvania, values the 20 manufacturers' representatives who represent him for a simple marketing reason. Says Hollo-

---

[6]Philip Kotler, *Principles of Marketing,* 3d ed. (Englewood Cliffs, N.J.: Prentice-Hall, 1986), p. 473.

■ **TABLE 9-3** Activities of Major Business to Business Distributors

Company	1974 Net Sales in Distribution	Estimated Number of Outlets	Area Served	Major Products
Associated Spring Corporation Bristol, Conn. *Distribution Group*	$73.7 million *36% of total company sales*	14 warehouses	United States and Canada	Automotive aftermarket, welding supplies, industrial maintenance supplies, industrial aerosols, special purpose hardware and fasteners
Bearings, Inc. Cleveland, Ohio *Bearings, Inc. Dixie Bearings, Bruening Bearings, Inc.*	$156.2 million	131 distribution centers	Essentially national; 25 states excluding California	Bearings, industrial power transmission components, specialized seals, lubricants, bearing retaining devices, and tools
Curtis Knoll Corp. Cleveland, Ohio	$104.3 million *91% of total company sales*	15 warehouses plus *auto jobber outlets*	United States and *foreign markets*	Automotive aftermarket products, and industrial maintenance products such as alloy plate and bar stock, tools, chemicals, cleaning insecticides, and paper
Ducommun, Inc. Los Angeles, Calif.	$210.3 million *97.2% of total company sales*	12 processing centers	United States for electronic; western and southwestern states for metal	Metals, tools and industrial supplies; and electronic parts and components to industrial users
W. W. Grainger, Inc. Chicago, Illinois	$283.9 million *90% of total company sales*	134 branches	United States	Electric motors and accessories, fans, blowers, pumps, air compressors, hand and bench tools, arc welders, material handling and storage equipment
Kaman Corp. Bloomfield, Conn. *Reliable Bearings & Supply; Western Bearings, Inc., BIT Co.*	$45.5 million *30.1% of total company sales*	51 outlets	11 western states, Hawaii, and British Columbia	Bearings, seals, hydraulic components, lubricants, rubber products, power transmission, and material handling equipment.

■ TABLE 9–3 Activities of Major Business to Business Distributors *(concluded)*

Company	1974 Net Sales in Distribution	Estimated Number of Outlets	Area Served	Major Products
Lamson Products, Inc. Niles, Illinois	$33.4 million	5 distribution centers	United States	Expendable maintenance, repair, and replacement fasteners parts, chemicals, electrical supplies, and shop supplies
Motion Industries, Inc. Birmingham, Ala.	$71.9 million	50 sales & warehouse facilities	9 states in south and southwest	Bearings, mechanical and fluid power transmission equipment, including hydraulic pneumatic products, material handling components, and related parts and supplies
Noland Company Newport News, Va.	$226.3 million	52 outlets	11 southeastern states	Plumbing and heating, electrical, industrial, and refrigeration supplies
H. K. Porter Company, Inc. Pittsburgh, Pa. *Banks-Miller Supply Co. Tidewater Supply Co.*	$54.0 million *16% of total company sales*	17 warehouses	Southern region	35,000 items of industrial equipment and supplies
Premier Industrial Corporation Cleveland, Ohio *Newark Electronics Cadillac Electric Supply*	$137.1 million *90.7% of total company sales*	10 distribution centers	United States	Industrial maintenance products such as fasteners, welding supplies, industrial cleaning supplies, specialty oils and greases; electronic and electrical parts, components, and equipment
Union Camp Corporation New York, N.Y. *Moore Handley Corp.*	$123.0 million *13.5% of total company sales*	48 home improvement and building supply centers	Southeastern states	Retail distributor of building materials, appliances, and accessories for the home; wholesale distributor of hardware; direct supplier of industrial and electrical supplies and machine tools

SOURCE: "The Chain of Events in Industrial Distribution," *Marketing News*, Chicago: American Marketing Association, January 20, 1976, p. 7. Used with permission.

■ **EXHIBIT 9–2**   A Brief Profile of a Manufacturer's Representative

Company	Central Southwest Bottling Company
Location	Claremore, Oklahoma
End-user market	Bottling industry
Estimated average commission	8 to 12 percent
Geographic market coverage	Oklahoma, Texas, Arkansas, Kansas, Louisiana, New Mexico, Colorado
Products handled	Plastic cases, decappers, empty bottle inspectors, bottle filler replacement parts, conveyors, and case packers
Companies represented	Medium-sized and small bottle and bottling parts' manufacturers throughout the eight-state service area

way, "Manufacturers' reps tend to be more knowledgeable about markets. They have a closer relationship with the key buying influences in the markets we want to penetrate. Sales costs are not the prime factors for us." Holloway admits that if he had a direct sales force, he would probably have stricter control over field selling; he also wishes that he did not have to compete for selling time with the other manufacturers whose products his reps also carry. "But our reps give us the market coverage we believe we could not win otherwise," he says.[7]

However, not all firms using manufacturers' representatives are small. Manufacturers like National Semiconductor, ITT, Corning, Monsanto, Teledyne, and Mobil Oil are also included. National Semiconductor began using manufacturers' representatives in the early 1960s when the firm's sales were less than $50 million, and the company continues this practice as they enter the 1990s, even though it has become a billion dollar manufacturer. Manufacturers' representatives generally do not take title to the goods they handle, nor do they provide an inventory function. They operate strictly on a commission basis and usually limit their sales efforts to a defined geographic area. Advantages of a firm's using a manufacturers' representative include predictable selling expense; incurrence of little or no cost until sales are forthcoming; cost savings from manufacturers not having to utilize their own sales forces; and a greater intensity of territorial coverage in that the representative is able to make a profit in a smaller territory because of the multiple lines represented.

Limitations to Using Manufacturers' Representatives

Again, one might think that it is an easy task for a manufacturer to acquire a representative and thus entirely eliminate distribution problems. Fortunately, marketing managers realize that such is not the case because, for many manufacturers, the use of manufacturers' representatives or agents is not appropriate.

Representatives or agents often are difficult for the manufacturer to control. If the manufacturer's product line requires special care, representa-

---

[7]Thomas C. Reinhart and Donald R. Coleman, "Heyday for the Independent Rep," *Sales & Marketing Management*, November 1978, pp. 51–54. Reprinted with permission from *Sales & Marketing Management* magazine, copyright 1978.

tives often are unwilling to provide such treatment. Additionally, only partial representation is secured because the representative carries other manufacturers' lines. There is also the possibility of the representative severing the relationship, leaving the manufacturer with no distributive contact in the territory. Costs, too, could be greater than just the commission charged, since extra services demanded, such as the carrying of inventory, require additional compensation. Also, the representative generally prefers to concentrate on large customers and large orders. As a result, if the manufacturer has several small customers in an area, these accounts can easily be slighted by very infrequent sales visits. Lack of available inventory also often creates a problem, as this type of intermediary is of little use when service or parts are needed quickly.

Trends for Manufacturers' Representatives   Many manufacturers' representatives entering the field today have an engineering background and are experts in technical sales skills. They are selling mostly technical goods or services; they are representing fewer manufacturers; and they have expanded authority, making some of the marketing decisions usually made by the manufacturer. Typically, the representative has not stocked the goods they sell except for quickly needed replacement parts. However, there is a tendency toward "stocking reps" who provide at least a limited warehouse service. This practice will tend to increase costs, moving this type of institution a step closer to becoming a distributor. The majority of representatives are males, but more females are now beginning to enter the field. Commission rates are rising, and the current rate is about 10 percent.

Manufacturers' representatives can, in many cases, provide inexpensive coverage to more remote areas and to areas where demand cannot sustain a full-time company salesperson. Furthermore, this type of organization can serve to expand territories by introducing the respective manufacturers' product lines in their preliminary developmental stage. This activity might permit expansion and growth almost on a pay-as-you-go basis, via a commission on sales made.

Sales Agents and Brokers

Sales agents and brokers, like manufacturers' representatives, provide a sales effort; they seldom carry inventory (unless on consignment), generally do not take title, and operate on a commission basis. The major difference between manufacturers' representatives and sales agents and brokers would be that sales agents and brokers may assume responsibility for more marketing functions, including promotional and pricing responsibilities. Additionally, sales agents and brokers tend to handle the entire output of several directly competitive manufacturers. Sales agents and brokers generally have no geographic restrictions on their territories and will provide market data and product-development guidance.

Sales agents and brokers may take over the entire selling function of the manufacturer. For example, Stake Fastener Company, a California-based producer of industrial fasteners, has an agent call on users rather than employing its own sales force. Such a situation is especially appropriate where seasonal representation is desired; where marketing and sales skills are needed recurrently; where the major interests and skills of the manufacturer are in production; where a limited product line is offered; and where the market is widespread.

Brokers are most prevalent in the food industry. Their operation is typified by a seafood broker handling the pack from a salmon cannery. The cannery is in operation for possibly three months of the year. The canner employs a broker each year (the same one if relationships are mutually satisfactory) to find buyers for the salmon pack. The broker provides information concerning market prices and conditions, and the canner then informs the broker of the desired price. The broker seeks potential buyers among chain stores, wholesalers, and others. When the entire pack has been sold, the agent-principal relationship is discontinued, possibly until the following year.[8]

Facilitating Agencies

Facilitating agencies facilitate the flow of goods from the manufacturer to either the channel intermediary or the final user. Facilitators include advertising agencies; public relations firms; transportation and warehouse facilities; banks; and others that, although not actually in the channel, help the flow between buyers and sellers. Advertising agencies and public relations firms provide the necessary marketing communications, including catalogs and product literature, advertising, direct mail, trade shows, publicity, and public relations. Transportation and warehouse facilities, when viewed as part of the logistics function, should maximize customer service and minimize distribution cost. Banks and other financial institutions serve as facilitating agencies when they provide the capital to purchase or lease products. Some firms, such as General Motors, General Electric, and Westinghouse directly provide the financing function themselves.

Facilitating functions assist the marketer in supporting organizational operations and in performing the exchange function. Potential customers must be made aware of new product offerings and must receive the product in the right quantity, at the right time, and in undamaged condition. Many of these same potential customers require financing such as unique leasing arrangements. The role of facilitating agencies should be clear.

■ BOTH DIRECT AND INDIRECT CHANNELS

At this point in the discussion of distribution strategy, we need to raise again the question of whether or not the business to business marketing manager should use direct channels, indirect channels, or a combination of

---

[8]William J. Stanton and Charles Futrell, *Fundamentals of Marketing,* 8th ed. (New York: McGraw-Hill, 1987), p. 357.

the two. If indirect channels are selected, should the manufacturers' representative or agent be used, or should sales agents and brokers be employed? These, of course, are not easy questions for the marketing manager to answer. A wrong decision can easily impair market penetration and lead to serious erosion in market share.

Planning and managing a mixed distribution system require business to business marketers to give special attention to the following four questions:

1. What specific functions must the distribution system perform?
2. Where in the system might these functions be carried out most economically?
3. How do different customers buy, and which elements in the system can be most effective in meeting their needs?
4. What legal constraints must be observed in relationships with independent resellers?

Direct selling to user-customers is preferred in more concentrated market areas having the sales potential to support fixed selling expenses. Independent distributors carrying multiple lines might then be the choice in thinner market areas where their broader product lines provide the base for operating profitably.

When a company's independent distributors and its own sales force operate in the same geographic area, the roles of each can differ in several ways. Each seeks to serve somewhat different kinds of customers. The company sales representatives target accounts which want or need significant technical assistance and a direct relation with its factory source, while distributors serve the customers for whom local sources of supply, credit, and highly personalized attention are important.

The roles of the direct sales force and independent distributors are complementary in other ways as well. The direct sales force often is utilized to perform "missionary selling" in an area and to develop sales volume that will ultimately go through distributors. Further, the company might assume certain distribution functions it can perform more economically than individual distributors. For example, many companies maintain field stocks on which distributors may draw, thereby reducing the inventory levels distributors must keep in their warehouses. Some manufacturers, such as Ford, General Motors, and International Harvester keep computerized records of dealer inventories to enable dealers to draw on each other's stock to meet customers' orders quickly.

Concept Questions
1. Under what circumstances should direct channels be used?
2. What is the primary role of facilitating agencies?
3. How can the roles of the direct sales force and independent distributors be complementary?

■ CHANNEL COOPERATION

Whether direct, indirect, or both direct and indirect channels are used, how can business marketing managers design and operate the firm's distribution channels in order to foster enthusiastic **channel cooperation**? The essence of the marketing concept is customer orientation at all levels of distribution, with a particular emphasis on the idea of partnership to foster that orientation. The characteristics of the highly competitive markets of the 1990s will put a premium on the operation of harmonious manufacturer-dealer relationships.

The channel member's role must be thoroughly defined in the firm's marketing strategy. By putting the principles of the marketing concept to work for them, the firm attempts to inspire a feeling of mutual interest and trust with channel members that helps convince them that they are essential members of the marketing team. In view of this mutuality of interest, firms have to base their distribution programs not only on what they would like from channel members but also on what channel members would like from them. To get maximum exposure for their lines from channel members, the firms need to put in place policies that serve their channel members' best interests and, therefore, their own.

Methods of Channel Cooperation

How do suppliers project their organizations into their respective distribution channels? How do suppliers make organization and channel into one? One means of achieving such a goal is, again, for the supplier to foster a sense of partnership with its distributors. Armstrong World Industries of Lancaster, Pennsylvania, is a good example of a manufacturer that stresses the partnership concept in building a highly motivated team of channel members. In the firm's floor covering division, for instance, all products are sold through independent wholesale distributors whom Armstrong views as partners in a quest to maintain a strong leadership position in the many types of floor coverings sold. Suppliers can also accomplish this difficult task by doing many things for their resellers which they typically do for their own organizations. Suppliers sell, advertise, plan, train, and promote for these firms. A brief elaboration of these methods follows.

Use of Missionary Salespeople   **Missionary salespersons** aid the sales of channel members as well as bolster the whole system's level of activity and selling effort. Training of resellers' salespeople and executives is an effective weapon of cooperation. The channels operate more efficiently when all are educated in the promotional techniques and uses of the products involved.

Involvement in the Planning Function of Channel Members   Such involvement is another powerful weapon of the supplier. Helping resellers set quotas, studying the market potential for them, forecasting a member's sales volume, inventory planning and protection, etc. are all aspects of planning assistance. For instance, American Hospital Supply helps its customers (hospitals) manage inventory and streamline order processing for hundreds of medical supplies.

Promotional Aid   Aid in promotion through the provision of advertising materials, such as mats, displays, commercials, literature, direct-mail pieces, ideas, funds (cooperative advertising), sales contests, store layout, push money (PMs or spiffs), is another form of cooperation.

Acting as a Management Consultant   The large supplier can serve as a management consultant to channel members, dispensing advice in all areas of business, including accounting, personnel, planning, control, finance, buying, paper systems or office procedures, and site selection. Aid in financing would include extended credit terms, consignment selling, and loans.

By no means do these methods of coordination take a one-way route. All members of the channel, including supplier and reseller, see their own organizations meshing with the others, and so provide coordinating weapons in accordance with their ability. Therefore, the manufacturer would undertake a marketing research project for the channel member, and also expect the resellers to keep records and vital information for the manufacturer's use. A supplier would also expect the channel members to service the product after the sale.

■ CHANNEL CONFLICT

When the firm is not able to achieve cooperation among its various channel members, channel conflict arises. **Channel conflict** can be described as a situation in which one channel member perceives another channel member to be engaged in behavior preventing or impeding the other from achieving a set goal. It is, in essence, a state of frustration brought about by a restriction of role performance. The degree to which the behavior of one channel member could potentially destroy, thwart, or hinder the goal attainment of another is a function of a goal incompatibility, domain dissension, and differences in perceptions of reality between them, as well as the extent of their interdependence. Most marketing managers agree on the importance of channel control. In both business to business and consumer goods markets, manufacturers want control of distribution channels for better execution of their marketing strategies. Intermediaries have been assumed also to want control of the channel to avoid being bound by manufacturer-determined strategies.[9] The stage is set for conflict!

With respect to conflict versus cooperation in marketing channels, Gattorna has identified some critical factors underlying possible conflicts between channel members as follows:

---

[9]Gul Butaney and Lawrence H. Wortzel, "Distributor Power versus Manufacturer Power: The Customer Roles," *Journal of Marketing* 52 (January 1988), pp. 52–63.

1. Communications, structures, and decision-making processes.
2. Manipulation of channel members by other members of the same channel.
3. Introduction of new innovations (including new technology) that are resisted by barriers to change.
4. Denial of legitimate claims for reallocation of power and functions.
5. Differences between channel members in primary business philosophy.
6. The exchange act itself, specifically in terms of reaching agreement on terms of trade.[10]

These factors carry the seeds for conflict. Each channel member has a set of objectives and goals which are very often incompatible with those of other channel members. For example, large manufacturers tend to be growth-oriented, whereas small or medium-sized distributors are more interested in maintaining the status quo. The likelihood of conflict is high in such situations because, in their pursuit of policies congruent with dynamic goals (e.g., increased market share and higher investment returns), the larger manufacturers may well adopt innovative programs that contradict the more static orientation of the smaller or medium-sized manufacturers.

Ideally, the cooperation necessary to reduce conflict within a channel system should be present in whatever ways are needed to assist in doing the overall job better. Examples of typical channel-conflict problems are detailed in Exhibit 9–3. The cooperation necessary to reduce such conflicts might be in the form of the simplification of ordering procedures, pricing, billing, or in a more involved area, such as securing promotional materials from the manufacturer's advertising program. Other areas of cooperation to reduce channel conflicts might appear in such diverse activities as market research, sales analysis, assistance in customer identification and determination of potential, product education, technical assistance, training programs, and delivery. Whatever type of cooperation is needed should be known, and should be provided to the fullest extent possible. Again, when and if conflict exceeds a certain level, one of the parties will choose to pull out of the network.

Nature of Channel Conflict

Channel conflict most frequently takes the form of tension and disagreements between channel members. For example, from a wholesaler's perspective, manufacturers do not understand that the primary obligation of wholesalers is to serve their customers, and that serving the manufacturer is secondary. Manufacturers, on the other hand, feel that wholesalers too often pay them only lip service and often openly compete with them for business.

---

[10]J. Gattorna, "Channels of Distribution Conceptualizations: A State of the Art Review," *European Journal of Marketing* 7 (1978), pp. 470–512.

■ **EXHIBIT 9–3**   Issues Embodied in Conflict Incidents Occurring in the Manufacturer-Distributor Dyad

Manufacturer Complaints
1. Lack of service by distributor's personnel
2. Ineffective communication
3. Warranty administration
4. Distributor cash flow tightness
5. Documenting rebates and payments
6. Loss and damages in delivery
7. Documenting advertising expenditures
8. Weak market penetration by distributor
9. Violation of sales policy
10. Gaps in product line

Distributor Complaints
1. Product unavailability
2. Lag time in new product development
3. Ineffective communication for problem solving
4. Product quality and defects
5. Faulty sales forecasting
6. Damages due to packing
7. Off-season financing burden

Conflict management is not only essential but it will also result in better performance of the channel system. A major source of conflict might be in the transactional process since it is natural for the seller to desire a higher price than the buyer wants to pay, or for the buyer to want a lower price than the seller is willing to accept. The conflict in regard to price can be resolved when one party influences the other party's position, or when both parties compromise on a price somewhere between the two extremes. Changes in other factors, such as the amount of service to be provided by the seller, may be necessary before the transaction can be completed. When conflicts are viewed in a rational perspective, firms will discover many more reasons for cooperation, rather than resorting to acts that contribute to conflict in the channel structure. The underlying reason for conflict is that two independent companies are involved, each of which has its own mission, objectives, and perspectives on how its business should be run. Compromise should not heighten conflict; it should reduce it. Negotiated solutions should be mutually satisfying to both parties or the conflict has not been properly resolved.

Conflict Management and Resolution

For the business to business marketer, the problem of how to manage conflict must be resolved. The firm faced with a conflict situation with another channel member has several strategies available to manage the conflict.

Some of these strategies include waiting to see if the conflict issue and cause subside. This offers the firm the opportunity to monitor the conflict situation and to use the time to develop a well thought-out plan of action to resolve the conflict. The use of various bargaining techniques that require compromise to solve the conflict often is useful. Organizational changes often are necessary not only to reduce conflict but also to serve as a warning system to identify stress in an early stage before it becomes a conflict. Possible organizational changes may include the appointment of a distributor ombudsman, the appointment of an advisory board, and/or the short-term exchange of people between firms to develop more empathy in channel relationships. A reorganization of the entire channel system is also often considered. This strategy would include the deletion and the addition of specific members of a channel system, such as distributors or manufacturers' representatives (agents). As mentioned earlier in the chapter, this action can have serious ramifications, resulting in loss of market share. Such action should be studied and carefully evaluated prior to its implementation.

The shortening of product life cycles, especially in areas such as telecommunications, information processing, and other high-tech products puts pressure on manufacturers for rapid market penetration. This causes conflict. Turbulent channel conflict must be managed and resolved by employing strategies that are collaborative rather than combative.[11]

A Legal Perspective of Channel Conflict

The very existence of different kinds of marketing institutions depends not only on their relative effectiveness in performing particular marketing functions but also on the methods and terms upon which they can buy and sell. Legislation which influences either the effectiveness with which marketing institutions compete or the methods and terms employed by sellers can be expected to have repercussions on the use of particular channels of distribution. With regard to most of the legal limitations referred to in this section of the chapter, we should note that the antitrust-enforcement agencies have been highly successful in terms of the number of court cases they have won when they have brought suit against alleged offenders. Furthermore, for a firm to defend itself adequately once charged with a violation, it generally must spend a large sum of money in preparing its case, given the complexity of the defenses available. The costs involved might, in fact, exceed the benefits of the company's winning the case. Business to business marketing managers might spare themselves considerable difficulties by devoting some of their energies toward the avoidance of being in conflict with antitrust laws or with the edicts of the antitrust-enforcement agencies.

Major issues with potential legal ramifications would include exclusive dealing contracts, exclusive territorial arrangements, refusals to deal, and the like. The opportunities for channel conflict are limitless.

---

[11]Allan J. Magrath and Kernneth G. Hardy, "Avoiding the Pitfalls in Managing Distribution Channels," *Business Horizons* 30 (September-October 1987), pp. 29–33.

Typical Problem Areas in the Manufacturer-Intermediary Relationship

To avoid conflict while promoting effective channel strategy is difficult and sometimes seems impossible. A number of basic policy rules must be made, and their enforcement must be carried out by the marketing manager. These rules involve such potential problem areas as service and technical assistance, house accounts, inventory levels, provision of marketing information, training and support services, and second product lines carried. A brief review of each of these potential problem areas follows.

Service and Technical Assistance   Service and technical assistance are big factors in the business market and, out of necessity, must extend into the channel of distribution. As an example, the marketing manager can be forced to use a direct channel strategy because he or she cannot find intermediaries who want to provide service and technical assistance, or because of difficulty in finding an intermediary capable of providing such service. In other cases the marketing manager might choose a particular intermediary, especially a distributor, on the basis of proven service facilities or personnel. In a similar vein the marketing manager might be prohibited from using a manufacturers' representative because of the reluctance of many of these intermediaries to provide such service and technical assistance. If the product line requires significant service and/or technical assistance, the marketing manager must be sure that the desired service is available, and that it is equal to, or better than, the service offered by other manufacturers and intermediaries competing for the same market.

House Accounts   A **house account** can be loosely defined as "a customer with whom the manufacturer would rather deal directly (usually because of volume and/or service requirements), while turning the balance of the territory over to an intermediary." House accounts can be a touchy area, especially if the account is a very large or profitable one which the intermediary would desire to have as a customer. Here, in essence, the manufacturer tells the intermediary that all present and potential accounts within a defined geographical territory belong to the intermediary except . . . . One would not have to stretch his or her imagination too far to realize that a loose, inconsistent policy regarding house accounts, in all likelihood, presents a potential legal problem area in the manufacturer-intermediary relationship.

Inventory Levels   What should the policy be regarding how much inventory a stocking distributor will carry? Too little might result in lost sales due to stockouts, while too much might well jeopardize an intermediary's cash flow. Should the marketing manager allow an intermediary to return obsolete or excess inventory? If such returns are allowed, should there be a restocking charge? The basic objective of the inventory function is to have products available to end users when they need them. Thus the crucial problem is to determine the level of customer service desired or needed, and then to determine the balance between service and inventory availability and the costs associated with carrying the inventory. The higher the field inventory level, the higher the cost of invested dollars, potential obsolescence, and storage costs. This area is a ripe one for spawning manufacturer-intermediary conflict.

Marketing Information and Feedback   The marketing manager must consider the information flow available between and among firms in the physical product-flow network. Will the marketing manager expect market feedback to assess trends in distribution patterns, to discern customer needs, to assess the effect of promotional campaigns, to obtain feedback as to company image, and to gauge competitive pressures? Some marketing managers expect market feedback from their channels of distribution and make this expectation a very specific channel objective. This operating procedure could well lead to channel members being selected on the basis of their willingness to provide such feedback. We might view such a managerial approach toward the collection of feedback as rather unrealistic in expecting a nonstocking intermediary, such as a manufacturers' representative, sales agent, or broker working strictly on a commission basis to take time from the selling effort to search out market information, trends, and the competitive posture in a particular territory, region, or industry. However, can the marketing manager expect or even demand this service from the inventory-stocking distributor? If a certain level of service is not forthcoming, might there be channel conflict brewing? This potential problem area must be discussed, settled, and agreed upon prior to the execution of basic channel decisions.

Training and Support Services   Most intermediaries expect, even frequently demand, merchandising assistance from the manufacturer. Marketing managers who want to stimulate and to hold intermediary interest must consider developing advertising and sales promotion programs. Also, effective sales meetings and training programs must be considered as incentives for both sales and technical training. Factory training of intermediary sales personnel is indispensable. A substantial amount of knowledge can be acquired through programmed learning techniques at relatively low cost. Programmed learning exercises, combined with commercially available sales training packages, will enable most intermediary personnel to become thoroughly familiar with a supplier's product line. This kind of training is important because the sales personnel working for an intermediary tend to favor the manufacturers' product lines about which they are most knowledgeable and with which they are most comfortable.

What training and support services' policies should the business to business marketing manager adopt? What is affordable? Should the policies call for joint training programs with both the manufacturer and the intermediary sharing the cost? Will cooperative advertising be utilized, and will missionary sales work be required? Each of these areas can and often will lead to channel conflict if they are not effectively addressed early in the channel selection process. Reasonable and well thought-out answers to the above questions should enable the marketing manager to develop inventory policies attractive to intermediaries.

Second Lines Carried　The stocking of competing lines of merchandise can also constitute a problem area in the manufacturer-intermediary relationship. Manufacturers tend to favor intermediaries who can afford them some measure of protection from competition, and one way in which to gain this fragile security is to pick intermediaries who will limit the number of competing lines they carry. The marketing manager is confronted with the task of persuading the channel member to do a job comparable with the manager's own direct sales force, if such a force exists. To obtain this degree of control, the marketing manager generally has to provide such services and incentives so that the intermediary will not want to, or have to, pick up competing lines.

Business to business marketing managers whose marketing and sales programs increase channel member profits, who treat distributors as customers when negotiating transactions, and who treat distributors as partners when in pursuit of specific customers will usually find that such intermediaries accept direction willingly.[12] Some firms recognize the partnership concept between manufacturers and intermediaries by preparing formal contracts to be signed by both parties. Columbus-McKinnon Corporation, a large industrial firm, makes the following agreement with its distributors:

> The distributor will maintain an inventory that gives four turns based on last year's sales; will purchase at least $15,000 a year from the supplier; and will actively promote the sale of the supplier's products. The supplier [Columbus-McKinnon], in turn, extends the latest discount service and freight; contributes a specific amount to joint advertising; works a specified length of time with each distributor salesperson; and helps develop annual sales targets.[13]

■ INTERNATIONAL CHANNEL DECISIONS

World trade is increasingly important to the health of our economy and to the growth of U.S. companies. Every one billion dollars in U.S. exports generates about 25,000 jobs.[14] Exporting not only creates jobs but also provides firms with new growth, new markets, and additional profits. Manufacturers introducing a product to a foreign market face that same difficult decision—should the product be marketed directly through a company sales force or company distribution division, indirectly through independent intermediaries, or through a combination of the two. To an economist this is a question of vertical integration in which the choice is between

---

[12]For a related discussion of manufacturers treating their intermediaries as partners, see Philip Kotler, *Principles of Marketing*, 3d ed., 1986, pp. 429–30.

[13]Duffy Marks, "Post Carborundum: Distributors Evaluate Their Vendor Relations," *Industrial Distribution* 7 (June 1983), p. 35.

[14]"Focus on the Facts: Opportunities in Exporting," U.S. Small Business Administration in Cooperation with AT&T, No. 7 of a series.

primarily captive agents (direct) or primarily independent intermediaries (indirect).[15] As with domestic distribution, the former option generally affords the firm more control than the latter.

When transcending national borders, marketers face a host of constraints. People speak different languages; rules and regulations differ; and economic conditions and political stability can cause problems. However, for the first time in many years, U.S. companies are strategically positioned to profit from exporting their products and services to many nations. The U.S. and Foreign Commercial Service (US & FCS) is the U.S. government's only international trade agency with a worldwide delivery system, which will analyze a foreign market, conduct customized in-country studies of a firm's competition, and help marketers choose the best channel of distribution overseas. (International trade specialists are based in 66 major U.S. cities and 126 locations abroad).[16] Trade specialists overseas do on-the-spot market research, including customized individual studies for qualified agents and/or distributors. They speak the host-country language; understand local customs, traditions, and trade regulations; and can be a particularly valuable resource when establishing overseas distribution outlets. The personalized search for qualified foreign representatives will identify up to six prospects who have examined product literature and have expressed interest in representing the firm.

Types of Indirect Channel Intermediaries[17]

With an indirect channel, the marketer deals with one or more domestic intermediaries, who in turn move and/or sell the product to foreign intermediaries or final users. These domestic intermediaries are grouped under two broad categories: (1) **domestic agents** (who do not take title) and; (2) **domestic merchants** (who take title but not necessarily possession). An agent represents the manufacturer, whereas a merchant (e.g., a distributor) represents the manufacturers' product. The merchant has no power to contract on behalf of the manufacturer, but the agent can bind the manufacturer in authorized matters to contracts made on the manufacturer's behalf.

Agents can be further classified, with some representing the buyer and others representing the manufacturer. Those who work for the manufacturer include export brokers, manufacturer's export agents or sales representatives, export management companies, and cooperative exporters.

---

[15]Erin Anderson and Anne T. Coughlan, "International Market Entry and Expansion via Independent on Integrated Channel of Distribution," *Journal of Marketing* 51 (January 1987), pp. 71–82.

[16]For more information, see "It Makes Good Business Sense," U.S. Department of Commerce, International Trade Administration, U.S. and Foreign Commercial Service, Washington, D.C. 20230.

[17]This section is largely from Sak Onkvisit and John J. Shaw, *International Marketing: Analysis and Strategy* (Columbus, Ohio: Charles E. Merrill Publishing, 1989), pp. 506–9.

Agents who look after the buyer's interests include purchasing (buying) agents/offices and country controlled buying agents.

Finally, legal regulations, image, product characteristics, intermediaries' loyalty and conflict, and local customs are additional factors that affect channel decisions. Business to business marketers must keep in mind that no matter how desirable the product might be to the foreign market, it must be made accessible to buyers. Much must be taken into account in designing and developing an international channel of distribution.

Concept Questions

1. How does the marketing concept relate to channel cooperation?
2. What form does channel conflict normally take?
3. What does the practice of exporting goods and services provide for the U.S. economy?

SUMMARY

1. From earliest times geographically separated buyers and sellers have required a capability to move or to transfer goods and commodities physically. The marketing functions of buying, selling, storage, transportation, sorting, financing, risk taking, and market information feedback must be carried on within the channel system. Each channel function must be performed at least once in every channel, and some might be performed by several channel members.

2. Business marketers must decide whether to use direct or indirect channels. Channel decisions, by their very nature, are long term, so a careful consideration of channel needs and requirements is essential for the marketing manager.

3. Direct channels involve direct selling to the business user, with or without the use of sales branches. In sharp contrast to consumer goods, most manufactured business to business goods are sold directly to users.

4. The use of indirect channels is warranted when the market is widely scattered, when many firms must be contacted, when small orders are common, and when goods are made for inventory rather than to fill specific orders. If the marketer decides to use an indirect channel, he or she has a variety of options, including distributors; manufacturers' representatives (agents); sales agents or brokers; and facilitating agencies. There are, of course, both advantages and limitations to each of these options, and the marketing manager must carefully weigh his or her requirements in light of what each of these intermediaries can offer.

5. Whether to use direct or indirect channels continues to be a question of utmost importance to the business marketer. Direct selling to user-customers might be preferred in more concentrated market areas, whereas independent distributors carrying multiple lines might then be the choice in thinner market areas.

6. Channel cooperation, in essence, is the application of the marketing concept to the channel area in marketing. Business marketers must be aware of methods by which channel cooperation can be achieved.

7. The business to business marketing manager must constantly be vigilant in looking for evidence of present and potential conflicting situations within the channel, and be alert to ways in which such conflict can be reduced and/or avoided through greater efforts toward channel cooperation. In attempting to reduce channel conflict, the marketer must be ever mindful of the legal issues involved in catering to the needs and desires of channel members.

8. World trade is increasingly important to the health of our economy and to the growth of U.S. companies. Every one billion dollars in U.S. exports generates about 25,000 jobs. Exporting not only creates jobs, but it also provides firms with new growth, new markets, and new profits. In transcending national borders, marketers face a host of constraints, including different languages, rules, regulations, and economic and political environments. Often indirect channel intermediaries are utilized in international business marketing.

KEY TERMS

breaking of bulk	indirect channels
broker	jobber
business to business distributor	limited-line distributor
channel conflict	manufacturers' representative
channel cooperation	missionary salesperson
channel management	physical distribution management
direct channels	sales agent
domestic agent	sales branch
domestic merchant	
general-line distributor	
house account	

REVIEW QUESTIONS

1. Identify and briefly discuss each of the eight functions of distribution channels.

2. What is a direct channel? Under what general conditions would direct channels be utilized?

3. What is an indirect channel? Under what general conditions would indirect channels be utilized?

4. Define industrial distributor. What are the major limitations on the use of distributors? What major trends are currently associated with distributors?

5. Identify manufacturers' representatives (agents). What are the major limitations on the use of manufacturers' representatives? Discuss the major trends currently related to the work of manufacturers' representative?

6. How are sales agents and brokers used as intermediaries in indirect channels of distribution? What is the role of facilitating agencies in business to business marketing channels? What are some examples of facilitating agencies?

7. How can industrial firms apply the marketing concept to their channel activities? What are some possible reasons for channel conflict? What are four common methods for securing cooperation in a marketing channel? When can channel conflict benefit overall channel performance? Discuss several methods for reducing channel conflict and promoting greater channel cooperation.

8. Discuss six typical problem areas in the manufacturer-intermediary relationship.

9. What purposes does the exporting of business goods and services serve? What constraints are faced by marketers as they cross national boundaries? Distinguish between two types of indirect channel intermediaries used in international marketing.

CHAPTER CASES

Case 9-1 Xerox: A Distribution Strategy Fails*

For many decades Xerox has been the leading manufacturer of photocopiers. Over the years it has expanded the company's product mix to include word processors, electronic typewriters, computers, and other information-oriented items. In the face of intensive competition, especially from Japanese firms, Xerox still accounted for 45 percent of all copier sales during 1983. However, competitors have forced prices down and made significant inroads in the small copier market.

Until 1980 Xerox employed only a direct channel of distribution. A company sales force visited large and medium-sized business accounts. Xerox had no store outlets and did not market through independent channel members. The small-business and home-office markets were virtually ignored. Then Xerox determined that a dual channel of distribution would enable it to increase the market for the firm's products. The Xerox sales force would continue to visit larger customers, and company-owned stores would attract small-business customers.

The first Xerox store was opened in a Dallas shopping center in 1980, with Xerox announcing plans to add 50 new stores each year. The stores would carry the company's full product mix: copiers, word-processing

*Reprinted with permission of Macmillan Publishing Company from *Marketing,* 2d ed. by Joel R. Evans and Barry Berman. Copyright © 1982, 1985 by Macmillan Publishing Company.

equipment, printers, small computers, electronic typewriters, and telephone-answering machines. The target market was defined as doctors, lawyers, accountants, and other small businesses, including people with home offices.

In mid-1983 Xerox reached agreement with Businessland, Inc. (an independent chain of business centers) to distribute its copiers and typewriters in 13 stores in California, Arizona, and Texas. This was Xerox's first move toward establishing a nationwide network of independent distributors. At the same time Xerox began marketing a portable computer to bank customers by inserting ads with their monthly bank statements.

At the end of October 1983, Xerox decided to sell off its retail stores and concentrate on direct distribution and independent channel members. Xerox was unsuccessful with its stores for a number of reasons: only 54 outlets had been opened (compared with 3,000 independent business centers); operating costs were higher than anticipated; competitors offered a better variety of products and brands; and its computer line was weak. As one expert noted, "A manufacturer can't do everything. He needs to get distribution, the quickest and widest possible."

Questions

1. Evaluate Xerox's decision to become involved with dual distribution.
2. What are the pros and cons of company-owned versus independent channels of distribution?
3. Tandy (Radio Shack) operates a company-owned distribution channel. It owns manufacturing, wholesaling, and retailing facilities. Why has Tandy succeeded, where Xerox has failed?
4. What criteria should Xerox consider when examining potential channel members (independent business centers)?

Case 9–2   The Childers Machine Company*

The Childers Machine Company, which is located in New England, manufactured a line of high-quality, precision industrial grinders priced from $25,000 to $200,000, through machine-tool manufacturers' agents. The company had always sold through these channels; and although executives had considered selling direct to industrial users through their own sales force at various times, they had always decided against it. In the fall of 1987, the Buffalo agent, whose territory comprised western New York state, decided to retire and liquidate his distributorship. This brought about the necessity of securing new distribution channels for the area.

The company produced precision-maintained parts capable of grinding to extremely close tolerances and held a position of prestige among the ranking manufacturers in the machine-tool industry. Although many product improvements had been made since the company was founded in 1900, the basic line remained unchanged.

*Ralph S. Alexander, James S. Cross, and Ross M. Cunningham, *Industrial Marketing,* 2d ed., © 1961, R. D. Irwin. Used by permission.

The Childers Company maintained its own design, engineering, and cost departments, where it designed its standard model grinders and made all subsequent improvements. These departments were also responsible for the product and development engineering work involved in the special-purpose or custom-made machines which the firm manufactured for its customers. These special-purpose machines were produced in lots of two or more. The sale of such machines required agents with not only technical selling ability but managerial ability and adequate financing as well.

In selling these special-purpose grinders, the agent determined the general type of machine which should be used and then submitted data to the Childers Company engineers on the amount of grinding required, the number of surfaces to be ground, their planal relationships, and the desired production in pieces per hour. With this and other pertinent technical data, the engineering and cost-estimating departments prepared bids in advance, which the company submitted to customers for their approval.

Fifteen agents carried the Childers line, each handling from 15 to 18 lines of noncompeting machine tools. These firms covered the entire United States, each with a definitely assigned sales territory, and together employed 250 salespeople. They neither stocked the machines of the manufacturing firms they represented, nor did they retain replacement parts for these machines. Eric Gordon, sales manager of the Childers Company, believed that his agents were the finest in the trade, and a bond of friendship and close cooperation existed between the Childers Company and its various agents and salespersons.

Mr. Gordon stated that the agents selling the Childers line neither handled used machinery nor offered trade-in allowances on old machines. The better manufacturers of machine tools demanded such a policy from their representatives because (1) they did not wish to be identified with outlets handling used machine tools, and (2) they desired such a policy as an assurance that the agents would not push second-hand machines instead of new equipment.

The technical training of the agents' sales force varied greatly, as some were graduate engineers and others had not finished college. However, Mr. Gordon stressed the selling rather than the technical ability of his agents' salespeople, and pointed out that many of the salespersons with less formal education were currently earning tens of thousands of dollars per year in commissions.

The Childers Company maintained a staff of four demonstrators, whom Mr. Gordon assigned to specific job installations on which they supervised the installation and adjustment of machines and demonstrated their operation. These employees had no formal engineering training, but rather were skilled mechanics with a thorough knowledge of the Childers line.

Mr. Gordon visited his agents on regularly scheduled trips, attended sales meetings, talked with the individual salespersons, and generally kept them up to date on matters pertaining to the Childers line. One major purpose of these trips was to assure that his products received at least their proportionate share of the salesperson's selling time and attention. Mr. Gordon accomplished this by determining the number of calls per day which the salesperson made, and by accompanying them on some of these calls. He observed and corrected their sales techniques and introduced new selling points for Childers's equipment.

The Childers Company budgeted 2 percent of their sales for trade-paper advertising, reprints, and promotional literature. In addition, agents spent approximately 1 percent of sales for direct-mail advertising, including the expense incurred in sending the circulars and reprints supplied by the company. Mr. Gordon believed that these figures were representative of the industry.

He further pointed out that, as should be expected, an agent's major cost resulted from selling expenses and salespersons' salaries. A good machine-tool salesperson earned from $25,000 to $75,000 per year. According to Mr. Gordon, the average salesperson's commission was from 11 to 12 percent of the selling price to the customer, and the average net profit on sales after taxes was approximately 2 percent.

Salespersons handling the Childers line had to be well versed in metallurgy, and thoroughly familiar with the various types of metals and alloys and their respective cutting characteristics. In addition, they had to know the cutting speeds, rates of production, and other technical aspects of their own as well as their competitors' machines. A machine-tool salesperson was expected to give unbiased technical advice regarding the machine best suited to meet the customer's requirement, even though the agent for whom he or she worked did not handle that particular machine.

It was customary in the machine tool trade for an agent to remit payment to the manufacturer within 30 days after shipment of the machine, although the agent often extended 90-day credit to the buyer. Sometimes the agent financed the purchase by accepting a percentage downpayment (often 25 percent) and receiving the balance in installments spread over perhaps one or two years. During the payment periods the agent retained clear title to the machine and charged an interest rate that covered the cost of obtaining capital.

Mr. Gordon estimated that his agents financed approximately 10 percent of their sales, although the percentage varied in different territories. He also stated that an agent needed sufficient liquid capital to carry approximately 30 days' sales. Since an agent often had annual sales of $100 million or more, the size of the capital or line of credit needed may be realized. The agents often assigned their accounts receivable to commercial banks as security for loans.

Such financing required strong agents who were able to maintain large lines of credit. Thus manufacturers selling through these channels were primarily concerned with securing and maintaining a few important outlets who were financially strong and solvent and able to maintain themselves during recessions. Other important considerations were the agents' prestige and recognition in the industry and the quality of their sales efforts.

In 1983 the president of the large agent firm covering New York state, New England, and northern New Jersey decided late in life to liquidate his business and retire. This agency employed 20 salespeople, and the capital stock was held largely by the president, who had made no provision for the continuation of the firm.

When the president decided to retire, the executives in this agency included a treasurer, sales manager, and secretary, none of who had the ability to assume the presidency. The machine-tool manufacturers whose product lines this firm handled all sent representatives to a joint meeting where the problem was discussed. As a result of this meeting, it was decided to bring a person in from the outside, who had the prerequisite financial backing and managerial ability, to undertake the presidency of a new organization.

In the meantime the managers of the Buffalo and Syracuse territories expressed a desire to buy out their respective branches and set up independent agencies which would handle all of New York state with the exception of metropolitan New York City. These offers were accepted, and subsequently a suitable individual was found who, with the executives of a former agency, formed the managerial nucleus of a new one, comprising the territory of New York City, New England, and northern New Jersey.

The above situation proved satisfactory until the fall of 1987, when the president of the Buffalo agency decided to retire. Neither of the two salespeople in this firm had the necessary financial backing or executive ability to manage a selling organization. This situation focused attention not only on the Buffalo territory but also on the Syracuse outlet, which was likewise a one-person firm employing two salespeople. Mr. Gordon feared a repetition of the Buffalo situation in the Syracuse territory some five years hence when the president of the latter agency would reach retirement age.

Not only was the Childers Machine Company without coverage in the Buffalo area but this was also true of each of the 17 other manufacturers whose product lines this firm handled. Mr. Gordon stated that there were no other desirable agents in the Buffalo area to take over these lines.

Regarding Syracuse, Mr. Gordon stated that he knew of one outlet in the area which would be glad to take on the Childers line. However, he was reluctant to use this firm, since it handled used machine tools to a large extent. He further pointed out that any immediate plans concerning distribution in Syracuse should provide for and incorporate the existing Syracuse agent. Thus, while he wished to insure against a repetition of the retirement of the Buffalo agent, with resulting lack of distribution in that area, Mr. Gordon did not wish to abandon this Syracuse agent with whom the Childers Company had maintained friendly relations for many years.

Questions

1. What should Mr. Gordon and the other machine tool manufacturers do to secure distribution in the Buffalo territory?
2. What action, if any, should be taken in the Syracuse territory?

SUGGESTED READINGS

Bialaszewski, Dennis, and Michael Gialiourakis. "Perceived Communication Skills and Resultant Trust Perceptions within the Channel of Distribution." *Journal of the Academy of Marketing Science* 13 (Winter/Spring 1985), pp. 206–17. Survey of distributors under the supervision of a single channel manager with implications for the trust relationship within a marketing channel.

Butaney, Gul, and Lawrence H. Wortzell. "Distributor Power versus Manufacturer Power: The Customer Role." *Journal of Marketing* 52 (January 1988), pp. 52–63. Empirical study of how both customer market power and manufacturer market power have a role in determining distributor power.

Carter, Joseph R. "Communicate with Your Vendors." *Journal of Purchasing and Materials Management* 22 (Winter 1986), pp. 16–22. Focus on exchange of information with an example of a systematically designed communication system.

Constantin, James A., and Robert F. Lusch. "Discover the Resources in Your Marketing Channel." *Business* 36 (July, August, September 1986), pp. 19–26. Discussion of channel management, marketing support systems, and interorganizational marketing relationships.

Coughlan, Anne T. "Competition and Cooperation in Marketing Channel Choice: Theory and Application." *Marketing Science* 4 (Spring 1985), pp. 110–29. Empirical study of vertical marketing channels in the product-differentiated, duopolistic international semiconductor industry.

Fine, Seymour H. "The Industrial Distributor Is Also Human." *Journal of Business and Industrial Marketing* 2 (Spring 1987), pp. 55–60. Study finding that producers of business to business goods are increasingly experiencing the need to develop stronger personal relationships with their distributors.

Gaski, John F., and John R. Nevin. "The Differential Effects of Exercised and Unexercised Power Sources in a Marketing Channel." *Journal of Marketing Research* 22 (May 1985), pp. 130–42. Empirical study of the use of power and the presence of satisfaction and conflict within a marketing channel.

Hague, Paul. "Sharpening the Distributor Network." *Industrial Marketing Digest* (UK) 11 (Fourth Quarter 1986), pp. 145–50. Evaluation of distribution networks with suggestions for improvement.

Howell, Roy D.; Robert R. Britney; Paul J. Kuzdrall; and James B. Wilcox. "Unauthorized Channels of Distribution: Gray Markets." *Industrial Marketing Management* 15 (November 1986), pp. 257–63. Theoretical discussion of alternative channels of distribution, including a price-quality discounts, problems, and corrective strategies.

Lele, Milind. "Matching Your Channels to Your Product's Life Cycle." *Business Marketing* 71 (December 1986), pp. 60–69. Discussion of the value added by the channel versus the low cost of the channel.

Lucas, George H., Jr., and Larry G. Gresham. "Power, Conflict, Control, and the Application of Contingency Theory in Marketing Channels." *Journal of the Academy of Marketing Science* 13 (Summer 1985), pp. 25–38. Theoretical discussion of the behavioral dimensions of interorganizational channel relationships.

Lusch, Robert F., and Robert H. Ross. "The Nature of Power in a Marketing Channel." *Journal of the Academy of Marketing Science* 13 (Summer 1985), pp. 39–56. Survey of the relationship between food brokers and food wholesalers.

Michie, Donald A., and Stanley D. Sibley. "Channel Member Satisfaction: Controversy Resolved." *Journal of the Academy of Marketing Science* 13 (Winter/Spring 1985), pp. 188–205. Study of channel conflict and resolution in the business to business marketing channel.

Miler, Richard Lee; William F. Lewis; and J. Paul Merenski. *Journal of the Academy of Marketing Science* 13 (Fall 1985), pp.1–17. Theoretical discussion and model development of channel relations.

Ransan, V. Kasturi; Andris A. Zoltners; and Robert J. Becker. "The Channel Intermediary Selection Decision: A Model and Application." *Management Science* 32 (September 1986), pp. 1114–22. Decision framework and normative model of an intermediary network, including a business to business marketing application.

Reddy, N. Mohan, and Michael P. Marvin. "Developing a Manufacturer-Distributor Information Partnership." *Industrial Marketing Management* 15 (May 1986), pp. 157–63. Case study of support services and the sharing of information in the machinery industry.

Shugan, Steven M. "Implicit Understandings in Channels of Distribution." *Management Science* 31 (April 1985), pp. 435–60. Model of learning, influence attempts, retail prices, and channel member profits in a channel of distribution.

Skinner, Steven J., and Joseph P. Guiltinan. *Journal of Retailing* 61 (Winter 1985), pp. 66–88. Survey of manufacturers of farm supplies who are contractually affiliated with dealers.

Sutton, Howard. "Marketing: Changing Channels." *Across the Board* 23 (January 1986), pp. 12–13. Trends in independent distribution, warehousing distribution, and telemarketing.

Walker, Bruce J.; Janet E. Keith; and Donald W. Jackson, Jr. "The Channels Manager: Now, Soon, or Never?" *Journal of the Academy of Marketing Science* 13 (Summer 1985), pp. 82–96. A job description and impediments to the implementation of the channels manager concept.

Chapter **10**

Business to Business Physical Distribution Management and Strategy

LEARNING OBJECTIVES

After reading this chapter, you should be able to:

- Discuss the importance of physical distribution (logistical) management.
- Comprehend the significance of deregulation policies.
- Appreciate the strategic role and importance of customer service.
- Differentiate between public and private warehouses.
- Understand the significance of inventory control in the distribution function.
- Explain what is involved in an order-processing cycle.
- Determine when to use intensive, selective, and exclusive distribution policies.

CHAPTER OUTLINE

Physical Distribution in the
Business to Business Market
    The Nature of Physical Distribution
Traffic Management: An Overview
Functions of Traffic Management
    Mode and Carrier Selection
    Routing
    Claims Processing
    Operation of Private Transportation
Deregulation
Customer Service
    Customer Service Standards
    Examination of Cost Trade-Offs
    The Impact of Logistical Service on
      Channel Members
Warehousing
    Private or Public Warehouses?

Inventory Control
    The EOQ Model
    Just-in-Time Concept
Order Processing
    The Order-Processing Cycle
    Shortening the Order-Processing
      Cycle
    Vendor Stocking
Intensive, Selective, and Exclusive
Distribution
    Intensive Distribution
    Selective Distribution
    Exclusive Distribution
International Distribution
Conclusion

■ PHYSICAL DISTRIBUTION IN THE BUSINESS TO BUSINESS MARKET

Regardless of which channel the marketing manager picks, if the right product is not delivered to the right place, in the right quantity, by the right transportation mode, at the right price, and under the proper conditions, the buyer will be unhappy. Eventually, unhappy buyers lead to reduced market share, and reduced market share leads to a change in marketing management. To avoid this potential problem area, the marketing manager should do the following: (1) understand the importance of physical distribution in overall marketing strategy; (2) understand the role of logistics in physical distribution strategy; and (3) understand the importance of maintaining specific customer service levels, while still maintaining desired profit levels.

The Nature of Physical Distribution

Physical distribution has been defined as "adding value through the management of materials, inventory, warehousing, transportation, and customer service."[1] Physical distribution has the potential to enhance the

---

[1]Victor P. Buell, *Handbook of Modern Marketing,* 2d ed. (New York: McGraw-Hill, 1986), pp. 4–8.

production, marketing, and profit performance of any company which produces a tangible product. The major roadblock to realizing this potential lies in the outdated perception that physical distribution is nothing more than a semantic upgrading of the traffic function. As a result, physical distribution too often has been viewed in its narrow, historical context as the cost function which moves raw materials and finished goods to meet manufacturing schedules. Although services can provide benefits which are partially intangible, they still must have supplies, raw materials, and inventory control systems. For example, the primary mission of a health care institution is to provide quality patient care. In order to provide the proper level of care, management must develop a good physical distribution system. The "Business to Business Marketing in Action" box describes how physical distribution is a critical component in the major success of Rhode Island Hospital.

BUSINESS TO BUSINESS MARKETING IN ACTION

Physical Distribution as the Artery of Hospital Service

The Rhode Island Hospital is a large New England hospital with 719 beds, a budget of over $168 million, and a staff of 5,000 persons. It provides the typical medical and surgical services of a hospital plus medical research projects and medical education programs. To support this level of activity, the hospital has an investment in inventories of over two million dollars and purchases over twenty-four million dollars' worth of materials per year (about 14 percent of total operating costs) with 25,000 to 30,000 purchase orders.

The physical distribution organization consists of six departments: Purchasing, General Stores and Inventory, Central Services, Laundry, Dietary, and Print Shop. They are integrated into the Materials Management Department, whose mission is to balance and coordinate the independent materials functions into a single work force in order to achieve high-quality service at the lowest cost. The focus of the department is on transportation and processing efficiency through the integration of functions and on the awareness of the total cost of supplying items to patients, including purchase, receiving, storage, and final disposal.

Purchasing is a key physical distribution activity in the hospital because purchasing expenditures account for roughly one eighth of operating costs. Purchases are made directly from suppliers, but this hospital and others are able to secure better prices on some items by collectively buying in volume through cooperatives such as the Hos-

continued

pital Association of Rhode Island. Advance buying is a common hospital purchasing practice. Although inventory storage costs increase, the benefits of buying before price increases can more than offset these added inventory costs. With the large number of purchase orders that are processed annually, the hospital computer controls its inventory levels system and types purchase orders automatically from the machine.

The General Stores and Inventory group is responsible for the receiving and storekeeping activities as well as delivery of the material to nursing stations. This group, under the Director of the Materials Management Department, is responsible for over 70 percent of the total inventory investments. Unique to the hospital setting is that departments outside the control of materials management maintain their own inventories. In this case, the Dietary Food and Pharmacy Departments carry and keep close control over stocks for their own purposes. Inventory levels are controlled by scientific procedures and computerized record keeping.

Central Services is a function that is unique to hospital physical distribution. In effect, it is the management of sterile goods inventories. Inventories in a hospital are of two types: sterile and nonsterile. The nonsterile stocks are managed by the General Stores and Inventory groups in much the same way as they are in a business firm. However, sterile goods must be handled more carefully to prevent contamination. The Central Services group, in addition to stock keeping, prepares "kits" of dressing and sterile materials for burn patients, operating rooms, nursing units, and other special purposes.

SOURCE: Ronald H. Ballon, *Basic Business Logistics* (Englewood Cliffs, N.J.: Prentice-Hall, 1987), p. 51. Reprinted with permission.

Physical distribution management is often referred to as *logistical management*. Originating in the military, the word *logistics* refers to the design and management of all activities (basically transportation, inventory, and warehousing) necessary to make materials available for manufacturing, and to make finished products available to customers as they are needed, and in the condition required. Logistics thus embodies two primary product flows: (1) physical supply, or those flows which provide raw materials, components, and supplies to the production process; and (2) physical distribution management, or those flows which deliver the completed product to customers and channel intermediaries.[2]

---

[2]For a comprehensive discussion of business logistics, see Ronald H. Ballou, *Business Logistics Management,* 2d ed. (Englewood Cliffs, N.J.: Prentice-Hall, 1985); Douglas M. Lambert and James R. Stock, *Strategic Physical Distribution Management* (Homewood, Ill.: Richard D. Irwin, 1982); and Roy D. Shapiro and James L. Heskett, *Logistics Strategy* (St. Paul, Minn.: West Publishing, 1985).

One of the earliest attempts to define physical distribution was made in 1962 by Peter Drucker:

> Physical distribution is simply another way of saying the whole process of business. You can look at a business—particularly a manufacturing business—as a physical flow of materials. This flow is interrupted when we take the stuff and cut it or shape it, handle it, store it. These are turbulences which interrupt the flow . . . and materials may flow from the iron ore to the galvanized garbage can. But the flow runs through all functions and all stages, and this is the fundamental reason why it isn't being managed. It does not fit into the traditional structure of a functional organization.[3]

Although Peter Drucker's definition is dated, it is still valid today. Additionally, the following definition has been developed by the Council of Logistics Management:

> Physical distribution is the term employed in manufacturing and commerce to describe the broad range of activities concerned with the efficient movement of finished products from the end of the production line to the consumer, and, in some cases, includes the movement of raw materials from the source of supply to the beginning of the production line. These activities include freight transportation, warehousing, materials handling, protective packaging, inventory control, plant and warehouse site selection, order processing, market forecasting, and customer service.[4]

Not all marketing managers would agree with either of these definitions. However, all would agree to the far-reaching effects of their respective physical distribution systems. Many may not even agree on what their physical distribution system should do, or how it should perform. All would most likely admit that their company might present a unique marketing situation which could probably benefit from a creative application of physical distribution knowledge and experience.

■ TRAFFIC MANAGEMENT: AN OVERVIEW

Transportation is such a pervasive force that it is often taken for granted. Transportation costs have been a concern of marketers for many years, but there has been more talk and theory development than action. However, the increased sophistication of computers, marketing information systems, and integrated channel networks has led to a greater appreciation of the potential profit contribution of the traffic or physical distribution manager. This person is responsible for coordinating and integrating all movement of materials, including transportation, internal movement (materials handling) and warehousing, and seeing to it that the process of implementing a total systems approach is being carried out. Transportation management,

---

[3]Peter F. Drucker, "The Economy's Dark Continent," *Fortune,* April 1962, p. 103.

[4]The National Council of Physical Distribution Management, Oak Brook, Ill., 1985.

traffic management, or physical distribution management (whichever title fits a particular situation), is not only a dominant aspect of the economy but is also an outstanding career choice area.

■ FUNCTIONS OF TRAFFIC MANAGEMENT

The functions of traffic management are broad and vary in intensity with the type of industry, the type of product shipped, and the size and number of shipments transported. A brief discussion of mode selection, routing, claims processing, and the operation of private transportation follows.

Mode and Carrier Selection[5]

The five basic transportation modes are road, rail, water, pipeline, and air. Each plays an important role in the movement of freight; each specializes in certain commodities or geographical freight movement; and each competes for a segment of the freight transportation industry. Table 10–1 shows that each mode also has some major advantages related to such criteria as cost, speed, flexibility, distance traveled, and dependability. A brief profile of each of the major transportation modes available to manufacturers follows.

Motor Carriers   The **motor carrier (truck transport)** is the primary mover of shipments up to about 30 tons. There are approximately 35,000 regulated carriers in the United States in addition to independent trucking and private carriage operations owned by firms that transport their own products in company-owned vehicles. Truckers handle everything from heavy machinery to liquid petroleum, refrigerated products, agricultural commodities, motor vehicles, and building materials.

The strategic advantage of motor carriage is the complete door-to-door service provided. Trucks carry only about one quarter of all ton-mile traffic, but about three quarters of the total dollar value of merchandise transported. Trucks are faster than rail, but are more expensive to use. The greatest disadvantage of motor carrier use is the carrier susceptibility to interruptions by bad weather.

Rail Transport   **Rail transport** competes for large shipment sizes, particularly bulk commodities, as distances increase over 500 miles. A financially healthy rail system is essential to some agricultural and industrial producers if they are to remain competitive in markets across the country. Railroads dominate the other modes of transportation in terms of ton-miles carried, but have lost higher-valued traffic to other modes and now account for only about 12 percent of freight dollars. Among the advantages to rail shippers are more flexible rates and improved service through the use of more sophisticated equipment than was the case a decade ago.

---

[5]This section is largely from Eric N. Berkowitz, Roger A. Kerin, and William Rudelius, *Marketing,* 2d ed. (Homewood, Ill.: Richard D. Irwin, 1989), Chap. 14.

■ **TABLE 10–1**   Major Advantage by Transportation Mode

Mode	Major Advantages
Motor	Speed of delivery
	Diversity of equipment
	Great flexibility
	Frequency of movement
	Transfer of goods to other carriers
	Convenient both to shipper and receiver
Rail	Mass movement of goods
	Low unit-cost of movement
	Dependability
	Long-haul moving
	Wide coverage to major markets and suppliers
	Many auxiliary services, such as switching and in-transit privileges
	Transfer of goods to other carriers
	Specialized equipment
Water	Very low unit-cost of movement
	Movement of low unit-value commodities
	Long-haul moving
	Mass movement of bulk commodities
Pipeline	Lowest unit-cost of movement
	Mass movement of liquid or gas products
	Long-haul moving
	Large capacity
	Most dependable mode
Air	Frequent service to major markets
	Large capability (40,000 to 200,000 pounds in one aircraft)
	Overnight service within continental United States
	Most rapid speed of any carrier
Intermodal	Combines major advantages of two or more modes
	Cost savings
	Lower loss and damage claims due to containerization
	Extends service to more shippers and receivers
	Reduced handling and storage costs

SOURCE: Warren Rose, *Logistics Management* (Dubuque, Iowa: Wm. C. Brown, 1979), p. 71. Used with permission.

Water Transport   Although somewhat slower than other modes, **water transport** competes with rail transport for bulk-freight movement across the Great Lakes, along the St. Lawrence Seaway, and along coastal areas. The percentage of freight handled by water has remained fairly stable over the years (approximately 15 percent), and water transport is indispensable for overseas freight movement of all shipment sizes. Rates are low, but so is transit speed. Water transportation is available only to firms shipping certain commodities that have access to the river systems, the Great Lakes, or ocean ports.

Pipeline Transport   **Pipeline transport** provides low-cost transportation and is utilized primarily for oil-related and chemical-related liquids such as natural gas. However, a variety of products, from liquids to solids, such as coal (in the form of slurry, which is ground-up coal mixed with water to form sludge), can be transported via this mode. Probably the greatest advantage of pipelines, other than cost savings, is dependability. Routes are fixed, tend to be concentrated regionally, and are seldom affected by weather conditions. Speed is slow, but pipelines are second only to railroads in ton-miles carried domestically.

Air Transport **Air transport** offers rapid freight movement, with the airfreight buzzword being *time-sensitive*. Although air freight is costly, its speed may create savings in lower inventory levels to offset the increased cost. Items that can be carried are limited by space constraints and have to be delivered and picked up at the destination. A wide variety of products are shipped through this mode, such as electronic parts, small but specialized machinery, and replacement parts.

Intermodal Transport **Intermodal transport** uses two or more transportation modes to move a product. A shipment of subassemblies destined for Japan might move through a combination of air, rail, water, and truck, before reaching its final destination. *Birdybacking* (air and truck), *piggybacking* (rail and truck), and *fishybacking* (water and truck) are popular and economical intermodal forms of transport.

Routing

If the traffic manager has title to the goods (either inbound or outbound), then decisions concerning specific routes over which shipments are to move become the responsibility of that individual. A practice related to specifying routing instructions is the use of FOB (Free on board) terms, which specify which party, the shipper or the receiver, controls carrier selection and routing of a given shipment. The term *FOB origin* specifies that the receiver is responsible for all transportation charges, and *FOB destination* indicates that the shipper is liable. Under FOB origin, the freight receiver selects carriers and specifies routing. If management considers traffic control important, it will negotiate FOB origin terms for inbound traffic, and FOB destination terms for outbound traffic.[6]

Claims Processing

Freight claims are made against carriers for loss or damage to freight in transit, for unreasonable delay in the movement of freight, and for freight charges which have been improperly assessed.[7] The physical distribution function within the firm must present loss or damage claims to carriers as soon as possible after receipt of a shipment, as there is a time limit for filing a claim, in addition to the very real possibility of cases of divided responsibility for damage or shortage between the shipper and the carrier. The procedure of carriers in regard to over, short, and damaged freight

---

[6]Wayne Kenneth Talley, *Introduction to Transportation* (Cincinnati: South-Western Publishing, 1983), p. 93.

[7]Because of the complexity of rate structures, many companies hire outside freight auditors to examine their freight bills at a commission rate of 50 percent of the amount of claims recovered.

vary to such an extent that the most logical practice for a traffic manager to follow seems to be one based upon past experience with the individual carrier.

Operation of Private Transportation

Many firms have instituted private carriage operations rather than using for-hire transportation. **Private transportation** (i.e., the user and the carrier are one in the same) frequently offers potential savings in transportation costs, possibly better service because of the flexibility of routes and schedules, greater speed along with a reduction of loss and damages, and accessibility to transportation equipment when needed. Inadequate transportation service and uncertain delivery times may force the firm to use its own trucks. This investment may be significant (although leasing is common), but may be necessary for service improvement.

Concept Questions
1. What is physical distribution?
2. What is meant by logistical management?
3. What is intermodal transport?

■ DEREGULATION

Because of the movement toward deregulation that began in the late 1960s, transportation carriers no longer could rely on federal agencies to set prices. This, in turn, has stimulated price competition and has made it difficult for inefficient firms to survive. Deregulation of the transportation industry has brought about a tremendous change in the competitive environment of that industry and has forced carriers to become more customer-oriented. Before deregulation of trucking, rail, and air freight services, carriers were not permitted to compete on price, to guarantee delivery time, to vary routing, or to grant long-term, confidential-rate contracts. Without delivery-date guarantees, inventory management techniques such as JIT were impossible.

Benefits from deregulation have been widespread. Real bottom-line opportunities stemming from deregulation of the transportation industry have also become widespread.[8] Costs have fallen for all modes, with air freight costs down by 50 percent since 1980, and with business savings of $63 billion per year in reduced trucking costs and $5 billion in reduced rail costs. Robert Delaney, former vice president at Leaseway and now a consultant at the megathink tank, Arthur D. Little, Inc., in Cambridge, Massachusetts, has spent the past couple of years working up ways to quantify the savings from deregulation. Some of his findings are as follows:

- Before deregulation, 40 percent of a safety stock was required to offset transit time variance.

---

[8]Peter J. Walters, "The Purchasing Interface with Transportation," *Journal of Purchasing and Materials Management*, Winter 1988, pp. 21–25.

- Deregulation of transportation services has created a direct savings of $90 billion in logistics costs to U.S. businesses. This estimate is based on annual surveys of 300 manufacturers which indicate that the ratio of transportation expenditures to sales revenues has dropped by 21 percent since 1981.
- A reduction has occurred in manufacturing cycle time, something the Japanese have been working on for years.
- Deregulation has spurred a great deal of efficiency. The frequent delivery of parts and components, direct to work stations in small lot sizes (which is routine today), requires the support of reliable transportation systems not available for most of the 1980s.
- Freight has become just like any other buy: a transportation procurement strategy must be developed that supports all other procurement strategies within the firm.[9]

Regulatory reform has spawned innovations that are being used to save time and money, and to improve service, as has been previously noted. One such cooperative effort between purchasing and transportation that could not have been accomplished before deregulation has yielded excellent results for a glass products manufacturer, Ball Corporation in Muncie, Indiana. The transportation of soda ash from the mine to the company's manufacturing destinations cost several thousand dollars per rail car prior to deregulation. The single railroad serving the mines would not negotiate its rates because regulation effectively removed the threat of competition in this market. However, since deregulation, Ball's purchasing and transportation people have worked together with the supplier and a second railroad to produce more competition and lower costs. With the eased entry requirements resulting from the Motor Carrier Act, a trucking company began operations and agreed to carry the soda ash from the mine to a newly renovated transfer station 200 miles away on the other railroad's line. From there, the railroad delivers the product to Ball's plants. This saves the firm $7 per ton, an annual saving of $126,000 at one site alone.[10] A closer correspondence between traditional purchasing concerns and traditional transportation or traffic management concerns has evolved. Many firms now view transportation as a commodity to be purchased in the market from alternative suppliers, much like any other commodity.[11]

As the pace of deregulation intensified in the 1980s, attempts were made to slow down or even reverse the process (reregulation). In many cases it has been firms within deregulated industries that have wanted to slow the process. However, deregulation will prosper and expand as other industries, including banks, other financial service institutions, and telecommunications have been deregulated recently. More are sure to follow.

---

[9]Peter Bradley, "Deregulation's Future: All Roads Lead to Lower Costs," *Purchasing,* 105, no. 1 (July 28, 1988), pp. 54–81.

[10]Peter J. Walters, "The Transportation-Purchasing Interface," *Distribution* 87 (January 1988), pp. 56, 60.

[11]Edward A. Morash, "Using Transportation Intermediaries for Industrial Purchasing Decisions," *Journal of Business and Industrial Marketing,* Fall 1987, pp. 15–27.

■ CUSTOMER SERVICE

Customer service as it relates to the physical distribution function consists of providing products at the time and location corresponding to the customer's needs. The customer service levels which might be provided range from very good to very poor. A 100 percent level of satisfaction would indicate that all customers are completely satisfied with product availability.

The ideal solution to the problem of physical distribution system design is to develop minimum cost systems for a range of acceptable levels of customer service, and then to select the service level that makes the greatest contribution of sales less physical distribution costs. Customers would be 100 percent satisfied if a wide range of products were available at the right time and place in sufficient quantities to meet the needs and wants of all who are willing and able to buy. Of course, this condition rarely occurs since the costs would be prohibitive. Yet it is possible to achieve high levels of customer satisfaction with properly designed distribution systems.

Customer Service Standards

Firms operating effective logistics systems should develop a set of written customer service standards. These serve as objectives, and provide a benchmark against which results can be measured for control purposes. In developing these standards, the place to start is with the customers. What are their service needs? What do competitors offer them? Are the customers willing to pay a bit more for better service? After these questions are answered, realistic standards can be set, and an ongoing measurement program established to monitor results. Typical standards relate to time, reliability, and loss or damage. They must be quantifiable and measurable because during the control process, deviations from standards must be noted and investigated.

Company efforts to improve customer service cover a broad range of matters, some of which are far more dramatic in their impact than others.[12] One effective means of service improvement is to identify the causes of customer service complaints, and then to institute changes to eliminate or minimize the customer service breakdowns. Exhibit 10–1 offers major categories, such as sales, traffic, warehousing, packaging, and inventory control, into which primary service complaints can be placed.

As part of business to business marketing strategy, the establishment of a customer service policy is extremely important because so many facets of customer service interface with other functions of the firm. A broad range of topics which affect customer service, such as credit rules, complaint procedures, minimum orders, order cycles, inventory returns, stock-

---

[12]Charles A. Taff, *Management of Physical Distribution and Transportation* 7th ed., (Homewood, Ill.: Richard D. Irwin, 1984), p. 251.

■ **EXHIBIT 10–1**   Typical Customer Service Complaints

Traffic and Transportation
Damaged merchandise
Carrier does not meet standard transit time
Merchandise delivered prior to date promised
Carrier fails to follow customer routing
Carrier does not comply with specific instructions
Carrier neglects notification of bad order car
Errors present on the bill of lading
Condition or type of rolling equipment not satisfactory

Inventory Control
Stockouts
Contaminated products received
Product identification errors
Poor merchandise shipped

Warehousing and Packaging
Merchandise delivered late
Problem with containers in packaging plants
Special promotion merchandise not specified in delivery
Warehouse release form errors
Shipping incorrect types and quantities of merchandise
Papers not mailed promptly to headquarters
Field warehouse deliveries of damaged merchandise

Sales Order Service
Delayed shipments
Invoice errors
Sales coding errors
Brokerage errors
Special instructions ignored
No notification of late shipments
Name and address errors

SOURCE: Charles A. Taft, *Management of Physical Distribution and Transportation*, 7th ed., (Homewood, Ill.: Richard D. Irwin, 1984) p. 252. Used with permission.

outs, and proposed deliveries, must be carefully examined. A helpful checklist as an evaluation tool in establishing customer service policy is shown in Exhibit 10–2.

Examination of Cost Trade-Offs

Trade-off analysis can be defined as "the examination of the costs associated with each component of the physical distribution system for the purpose of ascertaining that combination of components which will yield the lowest possible cost for a particular level of customer service." The cost trade-offs in product physical distribution must be examined to determine how and to what extent each component will be utilized in the physical

■ EXHIBIT 10–2   Customer Service Policy Checklist

Note: This checklist is intended only as a general guide to the formulation of customer service policy and makes no attempt to separate elements of external policy from those of internal policy. It also recognizes the overlap between terms of sale and customer service policy. Some elements of customer service policy may be influenced by legal requirements and/or trade customs, and, in that regard, should be interpreted by individual firms in the light of their own situation.

Credit Rules Affecting Customer Service
____ Must credit be established prior to acceptance of orders?
____ If open-account orders are acceptable, are there limits?
____ Are there credit limits for established accounts?
____ When will orders not be filled for credit reasons?
____ Is a responsible credit person readily accessible to customers?

Conditions Governing Acceptance of Orders
____ Are there any restrictions on method of receiving orders? (These might include requirements for placing orders through salespeople, brokers, etc., or a prohibition of telephone orders.)
____ Will the customer be required to order from a specific order-receiving location?
____ What information is required on the order?
____ What authority is required? (Formal purchase order, or restrictions on telephone or verbal orders.)
____ Are COD orders accepted?
____ Are there legal limitations? (This would include restrictions applicable to controlled substances, export-import, licensing, or other credentials required by the purchaser.)
____ What is the policy when purchase orders conflict with terms of sale?

Materials in Short Supply
____ Is there a suitable allocation policy?
____ Is it legal?
____ Is there a single person in charge who is accessible to customers, customer service personnel, and salespeople at all times?

Materials in Short Supply
____ Has the mission of the customer service organization been fully defined?
____ Do the managers have the tools necessary to accomplish their tasks, including personnel, information systems, communications, etc.?
____ Do they have sufficient authority?
____ Are there formal selection and training policies for personnel?
____ Are customer service representatives to be assigned by account, or by product line?
____ Is there a policy whereby customer service managers spend a certain amount of time in the field contacting customers on location?

SOURCE: Warren Blanding, *Customer Service Newsletter* (Washington, D.C.: Marketing Publications); also found in Charles A. Taff, *Management of Physical Distribution and Transportation,* 7th ed. (Homewood, Ill.: Richard D. Irwin, 1984), p. 253. Used with permission.

distribution system. The interrelationships of various logistical system components are illustrated in Figure 10–1. The arrows indicate the trade-offs between activities that must be evaluated in (1) estimating customer-service levels; (2) developing purchasing policies; (3) selecting transporta-

■ FIGURE 10–1   Cost Trade-Offs Required in Marketing and Logistics

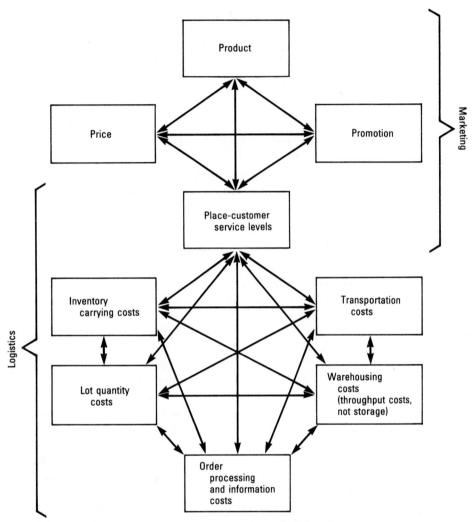

Marketing objective: Allocate resources to the marketing mix in such a manner as to maximize the long-run profitability of the firm.

Logistics objective: Minimize total costs given the customer service objective.

Where total costs equal: transportation costs + warehousing costs + order processing and information costs + lot quantity costs + inventory carrying costs.

SOURCE: As shown in James R. Stock and Douglas M. Lambert, *Strategic Logistics Management,* 2d ed. (Homewood, Ill.: Richard D. Irwin, 1987), p. 42. Used with permission.

tion policies; (4) making warehousing decisions; and (5) setting inventory levels.[13]

---

[13]Douglas M. Lambert and Howard M. Arbitage, "Managing Distribution Costs for Better Profit Performance," *Business,* September-October 1980, p. 46.

Analyzing the costs of alternative combinations of physical distribution system components is essential to guiding the design of the system:

> Storing all finished goods inventory in a small number of distribution centers helps minimize warehousing costs, but leads to an increase in freight expense. Similarly, savings resulting from large-order purchases may be entirely offset by greater inventory carrying costs. In a nutshell, reductions in one set of costs invariably increase the costs of other logistical components. Effective management and real cost savings can be accomplished only by viewing distribution as an integrated system and minimizing its total cost.[14]

Because some components of the physical distribution function are more important than others in a given firm, trade-off analysis must be directed to those components which make up the major portion of distribution costs.

The Impact of Logistical Service on Channel Members

Many firms have not yet achieved an effective customer service strategy. Failure to support markets in terms of service offered can be a costly practice, with some firms hesitant to offer different levels of service, or hesitant out of fear of violating provisions of the Robinson-Patman Act. This fear seems to stem from the fact that it is necessary for a firm to cost-justify its customer-service policies, and most of these companies do not have the needed cost information.[15] Demand is often thought of in terms of sales; yet advertising, product, price, and customer service can also have a significant impact on demand. Customer service is often the physical distribution component which determines whether or not present customers remain customers. Both order getting and order filling (physical distribution) are required for the long-range financial success of the firm.

Logistical service levels affect the relationship between the manufacturer and customer as well as the operations of channel members. Inefficient service to intermediaries either increases their costs, by forcing them to carry higher inventory levels, or results in stockouts, leading to a loss of business. Poor logistical support in the channel negates the marketing effort of the firm by constricting potential sales and antagonizing intermediaries. Both the length and consistency of the order-cycle period (time from the placement of orders to the receipt of products) affect the level of distributor inventories, which generally represent their highest asset investment. As shown in Figure 10–2, this is one of the largest distribution expenses. Distributors rarely remain loyal if poor logistical service is harm-

---

[14]Ibid., p. 47.

[15]See Douglas M. Lambert, *The Distribution Channels Decision* (New York: National Association of Accountants and Hamilton, Ont.: Society of Management Accountants of Canada, 1978); Douglas M. Lambert and John T. Mentzer, "Is Integrated Physical Distribution Management a Reality?" *Journal of Business Logistics* 2 (no. 1, 1980), pp. 18–27; and Douglas M. Lambert and Howard M. Armitage, "Distribution Costs: The Challenge," *Management Accounting*, May 1979, pp. 33–37 and 45.

■ **FIGURE 10–2**   Breakdown of Logistical Cost for Business to Business Products

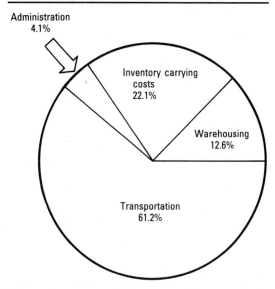

Transportation costs, warehousing costs, and inventory carrying costs account for the bulk of all physical distribution costs for a combination of consumer and business to business products. In the past decade, the share going to transportation costs has grown. (From the Council of Logistics Management, October 1986). Used with permission.

ful to end users. Inventory control systems should be linked to manufacturers' information systems, and if intermediaries are to receive a sufficient level of logistical service, information systems must provide accurate sales forecasts. Alert marketing managers must learn and be ever vigilant for the telltale symptoms of a poor physical distribution system. Table 10–2 indicates that inventory and customer service represent the most common areas of weakness in business to business physical distribution systems.

■ **WAREHOUSING**

Decisions regarding the location of warehouse facilities offer tremendous opportunities for acquiring increased market share, while at the same time generating cost savings. Decisions on warehouse location affect delivery time to customers and the ability to meet customer-service expectations. Marketing decisions on the number and location of warehouses, as part of distribution strategy, are important in improving customer service and in supporting the inventory decisions of the firm. Warehousing is an important facilitating activity; a good warehouse location eliminates (or reduces) the need for costly air freight by keeping products readily available in local markets.

The following example demonstrates the role of warehousing in physical distribution. W. W. Grainger manufactures and distributes its own motors,

■ **TABLE 10–2**   Symptoms of a Poor Physical Distribution System

Symptom	Explanation
1. Slow-turning inventories	Inventory turnover should be comparable to that of similar firms.
2. Inefficient customer service	Costs are high compared with the value of shipments; warehouses are poorly situated; inventory levels are not tied to customer demand.
3. A large number of interwarehouse shipments	Merchandise transfers increase physical distribution costs because they must be handled (packed, unpacked, stored, and verified) at each warehouse.
4. Frequent use of emergency shipments	Extra charges add significantly to physical distribution costs.
5. Erratic customer service	Large variations in the order cycle exist; customers cannot depend on the supplier for consistent delivery times.
6. Too-high inventory levels	Too much capital is tied up in inventory. The firm must bear high insurance costs, interest expense, and high risks of pilferage and product obsolescence. Merchandise may not be fresh.
7. No backhaul opportunities	The firm uses its own trucking facilities; however, trucks are only full one way.
8. Peripheral hauls	The firm uses its own trucking facility; however, many hauls are peripheral or too spread out.
9. Large group of small orders	Small orders are often unprofitable. Many distribution costs are fixed.

SOURCE: Joel R. Evans and Barry Berman, *Marketing*, 2d ed. (New York: Macmillan, 1985), p. 359. Used with permission.

fans, blowers, and other products and parts as well as those of other producers. Sales in 1983 were over $860 million, an increase of nearly three times over sales of a decade earlier. One of Grainger's major strategic advantages is its distribution system—"having the right thing in the right place at the right time."[16] Grainger has 9,800 products and 2,400 parts that could present a distribution nightmare unless properly managed. Grainger's distribution is described as follows:

> All merchandise is gathered through 1.6 million square feet of warehouses near its Skokie, Illinois, headquarters. (This hub was duplicated with a 1.4-million-square-foot building which opened in Kansas City in 1983). There it is arranged into assortments shipped at least weekly, in full truckloads, to the stores. With less volume, Grainger would have to settle for half-filled trucks or less-frequent deliveries. The weekly deliveries, in turn, enable branches to satisfy buyers without holding huge inventories on their own.[17]

Private or Public Warehouses?

When space is owned or leased, such space is classified as a **private warehouse.** Private warehouses are primarily used when an organization's sales volume is relatively stable so that investment in a fixed facility is justified.

---

[16]William Baldwin, "Dollars from Doodads," *Forbes*, October 11, 1982, p. 56.

[17]Ibid., p. 56.

Private warehouses might offer property appreciation or tax advantages through depreciation of the facility, in addition to giving the marketing manager total control over the warehouse operation as opposed to a public warehouse operation.

The alternative to owning or leasing storage space is the use of a **public warehouse.** These firms are operated by professional managers who provide warehouse services on a fee basis. Manufacturers offering a narrow product line to many market areas often find it economical to ship products to public warehouses instead of maintaining privately owned or leased warehouse facilities near production facilities. The use of a public warehouse is often the most economical way to serve marginal markets, or markets the firm is beginning to develop but that do not yet justify an investment in a private facility. Exhibit 10–3 identifies a number of important factors influencing the choice of a public warehouse. Additionally, many public warehouses have begun to offer a variety of logistical services to their clients beyond the physical handling and storage of materials and merchandise. For example, Distribution Centers, Inc. (DCI), which operates out of Columbus, Ohio, maintains warehouse facilities in a number of major markets. DCI will repackage products to meet end-users' orders, label the orders, and arrange local delivery for them. DCI can also link its

■ **EXHIBIT 10–3** Factors Influencing the Choice of a Public Warehouse

The Warehousing Education and Research Council has published a paper by William R. Folz, senior vice president of Tri-Valley Growers, which offers some advice on finding the right warehouse facility. The recommendations below are from his paper:

1. First, review the reasons for your requirement. Examine why you want to use a public facility.
2. Develop a list of warehouses you want to contact.
3. Contact each warehouse by telephone and set up a personal visit.

   a. *Housekeeping.* Develop a perception of what the facility looks like every day. Is there an ongoing plan for good sanitation?
   b. *Equipment.* Review equipment age, maintenance, number of makes, and equipment selection. A high percentage of old equipment may mean increased downtime and maintenance costs. A good maintenance program is a must. Keep in mind that the existence of a high number of makes may indicate a lack of purchasing strategy. Also, note whether the kind of equipment you require is readily available.
   c. *Operations control.* Study the procedures that the warehouse uses to control costs and improve efficiency.
   d. *The facility.* The building should be well maintained and meet your needs in terms of sprinklers, rail siding, dock doors, etc.
   e. *Management clerical procedures.* Review administrative and clerical controls and procedures for inventory management, customer service, claims, shipment logs, etc.
   f. *Insurance.* Know your insurance needs and inquire about the operator's coverage.
   g. *Proximity to rail yard/major highways.* Study the facility's transportation access.

4. Obtain outside references. Talk to other users of a facility to ask their opinion of the services provided.
5. Ask about the warehouse's financial condition. If you are potentially a large customer, you can demand financial information, and the operator will probably provide it.

SOURCE: "How to Choose a Public Warehouse," *Distribution,* September 1984. Used with permission.

computer with that of the manufacturer to facilitate order processing and inventory updating.[18] More than 15,000 public warehouses operate in the United States today.[19]

Concept Questions

1. What changes has deregulation brought about in the transportation industry?
2. Why is the establishment of a customer-service policy so important?
3. What effect do decisions on warehouse location have on customer service?

■ INVENTORY CONTROL

Business firms recognize that too high an inventory level causes high carrying costs and potential obsolescence. (Carrying costs arise when stocks of goods for sale are held; they consist of the opportunity cost of the investment tied up in inventory, and the costs associated with storage, such as space rental and insurance.) For example, in the early 1980s in the earth-moving and farm equipment industries, John Deere Company had an average of 59 days' inventory, Caterpillar Tractor had 88 days', and Massey-Ferguson an amazing 110 days' inventory.[20] Conversely, too low an inventory can result in high restocking and production costs as well as the risk of lost sales and customer goodwill. The level of inventories is related to such factors as the movement and storage of materials. The amount of inventory in storage, transit, and processing can be substantially altered through coordinated management of the production, physical distribution, and sales functions. Capital costs in inventory, transportation and storage, and costs of inventory obsolescence are traded off in order to control total costs and maintain minimal inventory levels consistent with production needs.[21] It does not seem reasonable to expect a firm to be able to fill and ship every order from inventory.

Because of this inventory cost trade-off, most marketing managers seem to accept the **80/20 axiom:** 80 percent of the sales are generated by 20 percent of the product line. The major implication of the 80/20 axiom is that business to business marketers must manage their inventory selectively, treating fast- and slow-moving items differently. If a company has half its inventory committed to products which provide only 20 percent of the unit-sales volume, significant gains can be made by reducing invento-

---

[18]Michael D. Hutt and Thomas W. Speh, "Realigning Industrial Marketing Channels," *Industrial Marketing Management* 12 (July 1983), pp. 171–77.

[19]J. W. Farrell, "Computers Cut Distribution Network Down to Size," Traffic Management, February 1986, pp. 64–67.

[20]Graham Sharman, "The Rediscovery of Logistics," *Harvard Business Review,* September-October 1984, pp. 71–79. See also Roy Shapiro, "Get Leverage from Logistics," *Harvard Business Review,* May-June 1984, pp. 119–26.

[21]Charles A. Taff, *Management of Physical Distribution and Transportation,"* p. 18.

ries of the slow sellers to the point where their turnover rate approximates that of the fast sellers.[22] Inventory represents a sizeable investment for most companies, so the goal of inventory management is to minimize both the investment and the fluctuation in inventories, while at the same time filling customers' orders promptly and accurately.

The EOQ Model

Inventory control analysts have developed a number of techniques to help the physical distribution manager effectively control inventory. The most basic of these techniques is the **economic order quantity model** (the EOQ model). This particular technique emphasizes a cost trade-off between two costs involved with inventory: inventory handling costs, which increase with the addition of more inventory, and order costs, which decrease as the quantity ordered increases. As Figure 10–3 indicates, these two cost items are traded off to determine the optimal order quantity of each product. The EOQ point in Figure 10–3 is the point at which total cost is minimized. By placing an order for this amount as needed, firms can minimize

■ **FIGURE 10–3**   Balancing Order Costs and Holding Costs for Inventory

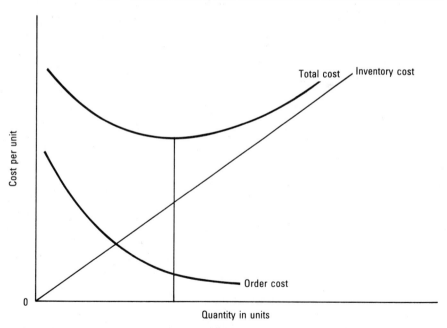

SOURCE: "Balancing Order Costs and Holding Costs for Inventory," from *Marketing*, 3d ed., by David L. Hurt and Louis E. Boone, Copyright © 1987 by The Dryden Press, a Division of Holt, Rinehart & Winston, Inc. Reprinted by permission of the publisher.

[22]James L. Heskett, "Logistics—Essential to Strategy," *Harvard Business Review* 56 (November-December 1977), p. 89.

their inventory costs.[23] The EOQ model has received widespread attention in the past two decades and is widely used in industry today.

   Calculating the EOQ.   The following formula is utilized to determine the EOQ:

$$EOQ = \sqrt{\frac{2RS}{IC}}$$

where

    EOQ = The economic order quantity (in units)
       R = The annual rate of usage
       S = The cost of placing an order
       I = The annual inventory-carrying costs, expressed as a percentage
      C = The cost per unit of the item. The unit might consist of a single item or a prepackaged box, containing a dozen items, a gross, or even more.

In the formula, R is an estimate based upon the demand forecast for the item. S is calculated from the firm's cost records. I is also an estimate based upon the costs of such items as handling, insurance, interest, storage, depreciation, and taxes. Since the cost of the item may vary over time, C is also likely to be an estimate. By inserting specific data into the formula, the EOQ can be determined. Consider, for example, the following data:

$$R = 5,500 \text{ units}$$
$$S = 7.50$$
$$I = 10 \text{ percent}$$
$$C = \$12.90$$

$$EOQ = \sqrt{\frac{(2)(5,500)(7.50)}{(12.90)(.10)}}$$

$$= 252.9 \text{ units}$$

Since the EOQ model involves a mathematical formula, the calculation often results in a fractional answer that must be rounded to the next whole number to determine the economic order quantity. Thus, the EOQ in the above example would be rounded to 253 units.

Just-in-Time Concept

The **Just-in-Time (JIT) approach** introduced in Chapter 2 is a fairly new concept affecting inventory control, purchasing, and production scheduling. This concept is a system practiced by Japanese organizations, and only recently has attracted the attention of top management in many U.S. com-

---

[23]This section of the chapter is based on David L. Kurtz and Louis E. Boone, *Marketing* (New York: Dryden Press, 1987), pp. 576–78.

panies, in which the buying firm reduces the amount of inventory it keeps on hand by ordering more frequently and in smaller amounts. The basic idea of JIT is that carrying any inventory is "evil" because it uses up capital, and covers up many problems, such as poor quality, erratic delivery, poor communications, etc. JIT inventory management makes sure that each person involved in the manufacturing process gets what is needed just in time.[24] For instance, a Bendix plant recently adopted a JIT system and was able to convert 10,000 square feet of floor space from storage to manufacturing usage.[25] Black & Decker, IBM, Firestone, General Motors, Harley-Davidson, and many smaller firms are experiencing decreasing costs and higher quality with the system. General Motors claims to have saved $2 billion in one year with its use of the JIT system.[26]

To be effective in the firm's inventory control function, just-in-time purchasing and production scheduling require very careful managerial monitoring. A high level of cooperation and coordination is called for between suppliers and producers, and then between production and marketing people in the manufacturing firm.[27] To implement the JIT concept in the United States, suppliers often have to maintain warehouses nearer to their customers (although the use of warehouses is generally inconsistent with the JIT concept). Public warehouses could be used to advantage here because of their flexibility and their proximity to many industrial parks. Because production schedules require timely supplies, shipments must arrive on time, or plants may have to be shut down. Different transportation modes have different degrees of reliability, so the choice of mode is very important. Exhibit 10–4 describes how General Motors uses both railroads and trucks in its JIT systems.[28]

■ ORDER PROCESSING

The establishment of an effective order-processing system is of major importance to the logistics efforts of firms. Accurate and efficient processing of orders is one important measure of customer satisfaction, and quick order turnaround time is increasingly becoming a competitive service offering for most firms. Shipping wrong orders, less than full orders, or dam-

---

[24]Craig Waters, "Why Everybody's Talking about Just-in-Time," *Inc.*, March 1984, pp. 77–90. See also Doug Harper, "Zero Inventory Poses Questions for Distributors," *Industrial Distributor,* January 1985, p. 49; and Summer Aggarwal, "MRP, JIT, OPT, FMS?," *Harvard Business Review,* September-October 1985, pp. 8–16.

[25]G. H. Manoochehri, "Improving Productivity with the Just-in-Time System," *Journal of Systems Management,* January 1985, pp. 23–26.

[26]Lewis Schneider, "New Era in Transportation Strategy," *Harvard Business Review,* March-April 1985, p. 124.

[27]For a more detailed discussion of the JIT concept, see Chan K. Hahn, Peter A. Pinto, and Daniel J. Bragg, "Just-in-Time Production and Purchasing," *Journal of Purchasing and Materials Management,* Fall 1983, pp. 2–10; and Richard J. Schonberger, and Abdolhossein Ansari, "Just-in-Time Purchasing Can Improve Quality," *Journal of Purchasing and Materials Management,* Spring 1984, pp. 2–7.

[28]Berkowitz, Kerin, and Rudelius, *Marketing,* p. 395.

■ **EXHIBIT 10–4**   Planning Rail and Truck Service for Just-in-Time Systems

Dependable restocking of supplies is a requisite in just-in-time (JIT) inventory systems to avoid production shutdowns, because these systems typically operate with minimal inventories of raw materials and parts. For a JIT system to be most effective, suppliers must be located close to the production plant. Then the dependability of delivery will be improved.

General Motors (GM) felt that overnight delivery to its Lansing, Michigan, Oldsmobile assembly plant was essential to implement its JIT system. GM combines various parts in a shipment coming from Kalamazoo, Michigan, 118 miles from its Lansing plant. These parts are shipped and delivered the evening prior to the next day's production, allowing Oldsmobile producers to function with only a single day's inventory of such parts. GM needs, then, dependable overnight delivery of these items at low costs. GM's answer was in Conrail's Mini-Train, a small train making no stops between Kalamazoo and Lansing. The train left Kalamazoo at 6 P.M. and had the parts available for use in Lansing by the next morning.

Problems with labor relations or bad weather can create real problems in meeting the tight delivery schedules necessary for a JIT system. For example, GM produces the Pontiac Fiero in Pontiac, Michigan, but buys plastic body panels for the Fiero from the Budd Company in Ohio, a distance of 131 miles. These panels are truck-delivered to Pontiac five times each day. When a February snowstorm covered Michigan, the panel deliveries were held up, slowing the Fiero assembly plant from its typical 20-hour day to an 8-hour day.

Savings from the use of JIT systems can be major. GM estimates that it saved $1 billion in a two-year period by decreasing its average inventory by $30 billion.

SOURCE: "Freight Transportation: A Revitalized Industry Emerges," *Forbes*, August 1, 1983, pp. Ad 1–12; Jeremy Main, "The Trouble with Managing Japanese Style," *Fortune*, April 2, 1984, pp. 50–56; Mike Meyers, "Low Inventory Manufacturing Arrives Just-in-Time," *Minneapolis Star and Tribune*, March 11, 1984, p. 10. Used with permission.

aged merchandise, as well as slowness and delays in processing orders, can result in a loss of considerable customer goodwill for organizations engaged in business to business marketing.

The Order-Processing Cycle

A customer's order is the starting point for any order-processing system. A company salesperson generally transmits the customer's order (via a computerized system) to the firm. As the order enters the system, physical distribution managers must carefully watch both the flow of goods and the flow of information. The warehouse manager must then be notified to check inventory and assemble the order. In some cases, where current inventory is not sufficient to fill an order, back ordering must be done. While an order is being assembled, a variety of paperwork must be completed, such as a bill of lading, an invoice, notification to the customer that the order is being processed, and an indication of when the customer can expect receipt of the order. If the customer does not place regular orders, credit checking will also be required. A computerized order-processing system is all but mandatory today for most distribution systems. Figure 10–4 provides a configuration of such an order-processing system. This type of information system provides very useful information to management in terms of customer analysis, product planning, and market behavior.

■ **FIGURE 10–4**   Computer-Based Order-Processing System

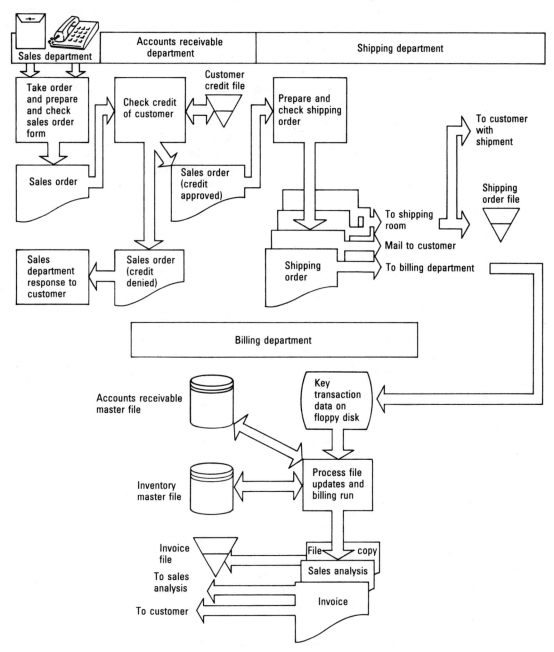

In addition to the physical movement of finished product to customers, information flow and accounting transactions must be managed: orders flow into sales and credit is checked; after approval, shipping orders instruct the warehouse to ship to the customer; finally, the billing department issues invoices for payment. (From Donald H. Sanders, *Computers Today,* New York: McGraw-Hill, 1983, p. 77.)

Shortening the Order-Processing Cycle

Industrial engineering studies of how sales orders are processed can serve to shorten the order-processing cycle. The following key questions should be raised in this connection: (1) What happens after receiving a customer's purchase order? (2) How long does it take to check a customer's credit worthiness? (3) What are the procedures for inventory checking, and how much time is involved? (4) How quickly do production personnel learn of new stock requirements? (5) Do sales managers have an accurate picture of current sales? General Electric operates a computer-oriented system which, upon the receipt of a customer's order, checks the customer's credit standing, and whether or where the items are in stock. The computer issues an order to ship, bills the customer, updates the inventory records, sends a production order for new stock, and relays the message back to the sales representative that the customer's order is on its way— all in less than 15 seconds.[29]

Vendor Stocking

Vendor stocking is a practice in which the supplier maintains an inventory of frequently requested materials for customers, thereby reducing their inventory carrying costs. This service provides major benefits both to suppliers and their customers. The Vallen Corporation, a distributor of industrial safety and health products, carries enough inventory on 250 items for Dow Chemical's Freeport, Texas, operation to satisfy 95 percent of Dow's requisitions immediately, with deliveries every two hours. If Dow needs a certain type of plastic container, the materials manager transmits the order to Vallen's nearest branch office through the use of computer terminals. Such a capability removes Dow's need to shop by telephone, place rush orders, and maintain a stockroom.[30]

■ INTENSIVE, SELECTIVE, AND EXCLUSIVE DISTRIBUTION

A business to business marketing manager can choose from one of three possible distribution alternatives in regard to the degree of market exposure a product item or a product line is to receive. Intensive, selective, or exclusive distribution can be used to reach the desired number of channel members within a specified geographic region. Table 10–3 shows the characteristics of each of these degrees of distribution. A marketer's decision in regard to the number of distributors to use is primarily based on the size of a market and the market share held by channel members. A brief examination of intensive, selective, and exclusive distribution follows.

---

[29]Philip Kotler, *Principles of Marketing*, 3d ed. (Englewood Cliffs, N.J.: Prentice-Hall, 1986), p. 434.

[30]William Baldwin, "Dollars from Doodads," *Forbes,* October 11, 1982, p. 56.

■ **TABLE 10–3**   Intensity of Channel Coverage

Characteristics	Exclusive Distribution	Selective Distribution	Intensive Distribution
Objectives	Strong image, channel control and loyalty, price stability	Moderate market coverage, solid image, some channel control and loyalty	Widespread market coverage, channel acceptance, volume sales
Channel members	Few in number, well-established, reputable distributors	Moderate in number, well-established, better distributors	Many in number, types of distributors
Customers	Few in number, brand-loyal	Moderate in number, brand-conscious	Many in number, convenience-oriented
Marketing emphasis	Personal selling, good service	Promotional mix, good service	Advertising, nearby location, items in stock

SOURCE: Joel R. Evans and Barry Berman, *Marketing,* 2d ed. (New York: Macmillan, 1985), p. 352. Used with permission.

Intensive Distribution

With **intensive distribution** the marketing manager attempts to gain access to as many resellers as possible, or to establish as many of the company's own reselling units as possible within a particular geographic area. There are many cases where the expertise of the intermediary does not matter, but where maximum exposure does. For example, the Building Service and Cleaning Products Division of the 3M Corporation intensively distributes its Scotch-Brite surface conditioning products through distributors throughout the United States and Canada. This product line (abrasives) is used by a multitude of firms in several different industries, and various grades and sizes must be available for use on very short notice. If the user cannot purchase that product immediately from a nearby source, a substitute will be used. On a standardized type of product with low unit cost, little sales effort might be required. Ready availability and immediate delivery become important. For instance, a manufacturer of nuts and bolts would desire widespread distribution of the product since the buying habits of the user will be predicated on convenience of purchase. In this situation the dominant factor is place utility, since brand insistence would typically be relatively weak. Generally, distribution saturation is attempted if the product price is relatively low, and if buyers frequently purchase the product, but are willing to accept a substitute product. The marketing manager, in this event, will often use multiple channels to saturate the market with the product. The channel policy of intensive distribution might cause the firm to use less than optimum channels from a single channel profitability criterion, but intensive distribution can increase the firm's total profitability based on all its channels in the market area.[31]

Selective Distribution

With **selective distribution,** the marketing manager distributes the product to a limited number of resellers in a particular geographic region. The marketer is attempting to select only the better intermediaries in utilizing a selective distribution policy. He or she tries to preserve the company image, while obtaining quality of representation, service, and adequate volume. Several screening criteria are utilized to locate the correct dealers. An accessory-equipment manufacturer looks for firms that are able to service its product properly. An electronics manufacturer looks for service ability and a quality dealer image. On the negative side, poor credit risks and chronic complainers are quickly removed from consideration.[32]

The goodwill of the intermediary is important as well as the competency of the intermediary's sales force and the composition of the area as to potential customers. With this type of arrangement, a better than average selling effort is expected, and adequate market coverage may be realized with more control and reduced costs than is the case with intensive distribution. Materials-handling equipment, electric motors, power transmission equipment, and tools fall into the category of straight or modified rebuy situations. The time spent in evaluating sources for these products is not great, yet the purchase is not always simple and repetitive. The buyer needs advice about applications, maintenance, and repair, and the buyer usually demands rapid product delivery, repair, and service. The manufacturer wants to be represented by a distributor who can satisfy these customer requirements.

While various reasons exist for choosing the selective method of distribution, primary reasons are as follows:

1. Distributors generally give preferential treatment to the brand because of relatively limited competition.
2. The intermediary, from a status standpoint, finds it advantageous to distribute the product in the local business community.
3. The intermediary may well join in cooperative advertising campaigns, thus reducing costs to the manufacturer and at the same time enlarging the promotional effort.

As noted above, the more selective the distribution pattern, the greater is the expected selling effort by the intermediary. Conversely, the more intensive the distribution pattern, the less is the selling effort expected on the part of one reseller. A good rule of thumb seems to be that the more expensive the product, the lower is the stockturn; or the more important

---

[31]Ronald D. Michman and Stanley D. Sibley, *Marketing Channels and Strategies* (Columbus, Ohio: Grid Publishing, 1980), p. 320.

[32]Carl McDaniel, Jr. and William Darden, *Marketing* (Boston: Allyn & Bacon, 1987), p. 413.

the repair service is, the greater should be the tendency for the business to business marketer to choose a highly selective distribution pattern.

Exclusive Distribution

When an **exclusive distribution** policy is used, the marketing manager can exercise more control over pricing, promotion, credit, and other marketing functions by limiting the number of intermediaries handling his or her products in a particular geographic area. Where a strong selling effort is required, where service is a major factor, where full inventory stocks are needed, where the capital investment is large, and where intermediary protection is important, an exclusive arrangement might be feasible. In these situations the manufacturer will assure the intermediary that no sales will be made in a particular territory except through that specific intermediary. The manufacturer agrees to permit the intermediary to be his or her exclusive representative in a certain territory; in return, the intermediary agrees to sell the manufacturer's products aggressively. Pettibone tower cranes and Skytrak extendable boom forklifts are examples of business products sold by exclusive distribution.

The basic reasons for manufacturers' granting exclusive distribution agreements to intermediaries are as follows:

1. To obtain market access if intermediaries believe that protection against intrabrand competition is needed, and if they would decline to handle the product without such a stipulation.

2. As a motivational means to increase the distributor's sales efforts.

3. To control the character and uniformity of resellers' operations.[33]

■ INTERNATIONAL DISTRIBUTION

International distribution costs can account for 25 to 35 percent of the sales volume of a product, a significant difference from the 8 to 10 percent for domestic shipments.[34] Furthermore, U.S. firms can become easily frustrated by the physical distribution problems overseas, including but not limited to, the enormous amount of paperwork involved. Delays, port congestion, inefficient materials-handling equipment, and poor road and rail networks also contribute to this frustration.

To move a product between countries and within a country, there are three fundamental modes of transportation: air, water (ocean and inland) and land (rail and truck). To move goods between continents, ocean or air transportation is needed. When countries are connected by land (e.g., the countries of North America), it is possible to use rail and highway to move merchandise from location to location, such as from the United States to Canada. In Europe, rail (train) is an important mode because of the con-

[33]Michman and Sibley, *Marketing Channels and Strategies,* p. 320.

[34]John F. Magee, William C. Copacino, and Donald B. Rosenfield, *Modern Logistics Management* (New York: John Wiley & Sons, 1985), p. 193.

tiguity of land areas and the availability of a modern and efficient train system.[35] The marketer must understand that there is no one ideal transportation mode. Each mode has its own special kinds of hazards.[36] Of course, moving merchandise across the ocean is a much more complex task than moving merchandise across the United States.

Concept Questions

1. What does the EOQ model of inventory control emphasize?
2. Why is the establishment of an effective order-processing system so important to the physical distribution function?
3. What market factors determine a business to business marketer's decision in regard to the number of distributors used?

■ CONCLUSION

Physical distribution costs account for a substantial portion of the firm's marketing expense. An ideal physical distribution system minimizes total costs, while simultaneously providing timely traffic management, appropriate customer service levels, convenient warehousing, carefully controlled inventory, efficient order processing, and effective channel design. A well-designed and well-operated physical distribution system can aid the firm both in capturing and maintaining a sizeable market share and in developing strong customer goodwill.

SUMMARY

1. Physical distribution has the potential to enhance the production, marketing, and profit performance of any company which produces a tangible product. Logistics, another term for physical distribution, embodies two primary product flows: physical supply and physical distribution management.

2. The functions of traffic management are broad and vary in intensity with the type of industry, the type of product shipped, and the size and number of shipments transported. Primary functions of traffic management include mode selection, routing, claims processing, and the operation of private transportation.

3. Deregulation of the transportation industry has brought about a tremendous change in the competitive environment of that industry and has forced carriers to become more customer-oriented. Benefits from deregulation include reduced logistics costs, greater efficiency, and reduction in manufacturing cycle time.

4. Customer service standards serve as objectives and provide a benchmark against which results can be measured for control purposes. The establishment of a customer service policy is extremely important be-

---

[35] Sak Onkvisit and John J. Shaw, *International Marketing Analysis and Strategy* (Columbus, Ohio: Merrill Publishing, 1989), p. 547.

[36] *Ports of the World: A Guide to Cargo Loss Control*, 13th ed., pp. 46–47.

cause so many facets of customer service interface with other functions of the firm, such as credit rules, complaint procedures, minimum orders, order cycles, inventory returns, stockouts, and proposed deliveries.

5. Decisions regarding the location of warehouse facilities offer tremendous opportunities for acquiring increased market share and generating cost savings. Either private warehouses or public warehouses are used, depending upon the objectives of the firm.

6. Business firms realize that too high an inventory level causes high carrying costs and potential obsolescence, and that too low a level can result in high restocking and production costs, as well as in the loss of both sales and customer goodwill. The economic order quantity model and just-in-time inventory control model are commonly used today to maintain efficient inventory levels throughout the fiscal year.

7. Accurate and efficient processing of orders is an important measure of customer satisfaction, and quick turnaround time in processing orders is becoming a competitive service offering for many firms. Physical distribution managers are continually looking for ways to reduce the time involved in the order-processing cycle so as to reduce costs and to promote greater customer goodwill.

8. Marketers must decide the degree of market exposure they desire their products or product lines to have. The three primary choices include intensive, selective, and exclusive distribution, and the marketing manager must decide exactly which type of exposure offers the most appropriate benefits.

9. International distribution costs can account for 25 to 35 percent of the sales volume of a product. Furthermore, U.S. firms can become easily frustrated by the physical distribution problem overseas, including but not limited to, the enormous amount of paperwork involved. Air, water, and land are the three fundamental transportation modes in international markets, and the business to business international marketer must understand that there is no one ideal transportation mode.

KEY TERMS

air transport	pipeline transport
customer service	private transportation
economic order quantity model	private warehouse
80/20 axiom	public warehouse
exclusive distribution	rail transport
intensive distribution	selective distribution
intermodal transport	trade-off analysis
just-in-time (JIT) approach	vendor stocking
motor carrier (truck transport)	water transport
physical distribution	

REVIEW QUESTIONS

1. Discuss three different definitions of physical distribution.
2. Identify five functions of traffic management. Briefly discuss six methods of transportation available to business to business marketers. What are the basic advantages of using private transportation?
3. What are some of the changes which the deregulation of the transportation industry has brought about? What happened as a result of the intensified deregulation of American industry during the 1980s?
4. Explain what is meant by customer service in physical distribution management. How does a firm decide what level of customer service it should provide for its customers? Why is a company's establishment of a customer service policy so important? How does cost trade-off analysis help to provide a minimum-cost physical distribution system?
5. What is the difference between a private and a public warehouse? How does the marketing manager decide whether to use a private or public warehouse?
6. How is the 80/20 axiom related to inventory management? Describe how the EOQ model and the just-in-time concept of inventory management operate in business to business marketing.
7. What is involved in the order-processing cycle? What are the basic questions a physical distribution manager should ask in attempting to shorten the order-processing cycle? How does vendor stocking serve to reduce the time necessary to process an order?
8. Identify three levels of market exposure commonly used in distribution. When would a physical distribution manager use each one?
9. What are some of the ways in which a firm can become frustrated with physical distribution problems in overseas markets? What are the three forms of transportation commonly utilized in international business to business marketing?

CHAPTER CASES

Case 10–1   Gorman Products, Inc.*

The Gorman Products company was created by the merger of Gorman Cookware, a small midwestern manufacturer of kitchen utensils, and the Electronics Products Company of Houston, Texas. The latter had annual sales of approximately $40 million, most of which consisted of subcontracts of missile components for the company, which held the prime contract from the Defense Department. Gorman cookware sales were $20 million.

By direction of the executive board of the merged company, unified corporate policies and procedures were to be established to the maximum extent possible. Mr. Ritchey, corporate purchasing manager, was uncertain

*Gary J. Zenz, *Purchasing and Management of Materials*, 5th ed., 1981, John Wiley and Sons, pp. 485–86.

how to proceed in establishing policies dealing with controlling the quantity of purchased materials and supplies. To illustrate his problem a major purchase from each of the two original companies will be described.

One of Gorman's principal purchases is the chemical Teflon, which is used in coating its pots and pans. Fluctuations in Teflon usage had been as high as 70 percent from one period to the next, and future usage was predicted to increase greatly, thus accentuating the problem of purchasing the correct quantity. A further problem was presented by the fluctuating price of Teflon. In the past, Gorman had followed a policy of holding a 90-day supply of such items as a hedge against large price fluctuations. The generally accepted reordering period for all inputs was set at two weeks.

The purchasing department was in charge of inventory control. Storage space was a problem, and even though no critical shortages had resulted in the past, any sudden changes in the production rate could lead to such a problem. No physical inventory was taken, but the purchasing department felt that this was unnecessary so long as accurate records were kept.

Two of the most important purchases of Electronic Products were printed circuits, costing approximately 2 cents each, and transistors, some of which cost as much as $500 each. Approximately 80 transistors were needed monthly, and printed circuits were used at the rate of 600 per month. Management policy had been to reorder these items every two months. The delivery cycle on both items had ranged from two to five weeks over the past four years. Quantities of printed circuits and transistors ordered were based on carrying one week's supply as a safety factor.

The corporate controller informed Mr. Ritchey that an inventory carrying charge of 24 percent was being assessed by management, and that the average ordering cost was $6.

Questions

1. Should there be uniform policies on purchasing quantities?
2. What should be done about the difference in reordering periods between two weeks and two months?
3. Should EOQ formulas be applied to printed circuits and transistor purchases?

Case 10–2 *Shapely Sack Company, Inc.**

The Shapely Sack Company produced a large variety of paper sacks that were sold throughout southern Michigan and northern Ohio and Indiana. Shapely had been formed in 1947 in response to the demand for non-hygroscopic paper sacks by the then burgeoning midwestern concrete industry. Although cement sacks were still the main source of revenue (65 percent of gross sales), Shapely had recently diversified its production. The company currently obtained 30 percent of its revenue from the sales of complete lines of paper sacks to many independent grocery retailers and discount stores in south central Michigan. Shapely recognized its depend-

---

*William J. Stanton and Charles Futrell, *Fundamentals of Marketing,* 8th ed., McGraw-Hill, 1987, pp. 412–14.

ence on the production and sale of cement sacks. However, fluctuations in the construction industry prompted Shapely to consider future expansion into relatively more stable industries.

The sales manager for Shapely had been in contact with representatives of Big Drum Foods, Inc. This was one of the largest and fastest-growing midwestern supermarket chains, with outlets in Wisconsin, Illinois, and Michigan. Big Drum officials indicated their dissatisfaction with the quality of their present paper goods, and expressed a desire for an offer from Shapely for all or part of their paper sack requirements. These requirements were equivalent to 75 percent of Shapely's present production.

Shapely's president, Jerry Dominic, was very much interested in a contract with Big Drum. Shapely was in an excellent financial position to undertake a large expansion in production capacity. Before making any arrangements with Big Drum, however, Mr. Dominic wanted to be certain that Shapely would be able to meet or exceed Big Drum's requirements while maintaining its high standards of service to present customers.

Mr. Dominic organized a committee whose task was to provide recommendations on the advisability of taking all, or only selected parts, of Big Drum's business. The committee consisted of a representative from each of the company's functional areas: production, traffic, finance, and sales. Recognizing that the work of the committee would be analytical in nature, Mr. Dominic appointed to the committees recent college graduates who would be most proficient with the latest quantitative techniques. The sales manager, because of his established rapport with key executives in Big Drum, was to act as the committee chairman.

As background information to aid the committee in its deliberations, Mr. Dominic provided the following descriptive summary of Shapely's current operations:

1. *Production facilities.*   Recently moved into a new plant in Kalamazoo, Michigan; present production—550,000 pounds of paper sacks per week. Plant capacity—693,000 pounds per week. Plant capacity expandable by 20 percent with moderate investment in new paper-pressing and chemical-treatment equipment.

2. *Warehouse facilities.*   Warehouse locations centered in areas of high cement production: Flint, Michigan; Mansfield, Ohio; and Fort Wayne, Indiana. Inventories in warehouses based on a four-week supply; Flint warehouse handles half of plant production. The other warehouses handle one-quarter each. Shipment from plant to warehouses is by company-owned truck, scheduled and supervised by the traffic department. Distribution from the warehouse to the customers is made by public carrier (truck), under the control of the warehouse supervisors.

3. *Supplies.*   All raw materials used in the production of paper sacks are received by rail from sources in the upper peninsula of Michigan and from Canada. No difficulty is anticipated in the immediate future in securing whatever quantities of raw materials may be required.

4. *Customer service requirements.*   Shapely's reputation is founded upon producing a very high quality product and upon the self-imposed requirement that 100 percent of all orders be filled within three days. Within this requirement, Shapely's emphasis is upon the cement aspect of demand, and deliveries to cement firms are made as soon as possible after the receipt of the order. Shapely is in the process of enlarging its private fleet of trucks to be able to ensure future performance according to these standards. At present, the number of customers served by the warehouses are as follows:

Flint:	270 cement plants, 412 supermarkets, 115 discount stores. All Michigan customers are served from the Flint warehouse.
Mansfield:	204 cement plants. All Ohio customers are served from the Mansfield warehouse.
Fort Wayne:	197 cement plants. All Indiana customers are served from the Fort Wayne warehouse.

5. *Control.*   Reports are made daily by the warehouse superintendents to the company headquarters on the number and sizes of orders received on the previous day. In addition to this telephonic report, which is made to the finance department, the superintendents forward weekly activity reports and customer service complaints to the sales department. The sales department then coordinates with the production and traffic departments to ensure that warehouse resupply is adequate.

Prior to the first committee meeting, the sales manager distributed a memorandum. It described the sales and service requirements that Big Drum Foods, Inc., had indicated would form a prior condition to its contracting with Shapely. The following is a description of the geographical characteristics of Big Drum's retail system, and a summary of the conditions mentioned in the memorandum.

Big Drum's outlet system consists of 1,040 supermarkets uniformly dispersed throughout Wisconsin, Illinois, Indiana, and Michigan. Owing in part to Big Drum's double-bagging policy, paper sack requirements vary from 350,000 to 430,000 pounds per week, with an average requirement of about 416,000 pounds per week. It is expected that efforts to expand within this region will, in a few years, result in approximately 1,500 outlets, with an anticipated paper sack requirement of about 675,000 pounds per week. According to Big Drum's present inventory policies, the stores should not fall below a two-day supply. Unless an individual store is forced to resort to this safety stock prior to its usual delivery date, deliveries are made on a once-a-week basis.

Distribution to the stores can be made directly by the supplier, or through the 21 Big Drum distribution centers. If distribution is to be made directly to the stores, the price at which Shapely is currently selling to grocery outlets would be acceptable. If distribution is to be made through the distribution centers, a substantial price discount would be required.

As the recent college graduate appointed to represent the traffic department, J. R. Kowalski was wondering how he should prepare himself for the committee meeting. More specifically, he wondered: (a) What factors the committee should consider? (b) What additional information would be required? (c) What problems might he encounter within the committee? and (d) In what ways might the committee's recommendations differ from those of an outside consultant in physical distribution?

Question

1. What specific suggestions would you make to Mr. Kowalski in response to each of the four points that concern him?

SUGGESTED READINGS

"Automated Warehousing—Option for the Evolutionary Approach." *Retail and Distribution Management* (UK) 14 (July/August 1986), pp. 49–53. Trends in new technologies and automated storage retrieval systems in the United Kingdom.

Bertrand, Kate. "The Just-in-Time Mandate." *Business Marketing* 71 (November 1986), pp. 44–55. Trends and guidelines for sharing proprietary information, and a discussion of partnerships between vendors and customers and foreign competition.

Buffa, Frank P. "Restocking Inventory in Groups: A Transport Inventory Case." *International Journal of Physical Distribution and Materials Management* (UK) 16 (no. 3, 1986), pp. 29–44. Model comparison and test of an inventory theoretic cost model; four grouping methods are considered.

———. "Inbound Logistics: Analyzing Inbound Consolidation Opportunities." *International Journal of Physical Distribution and Materials Management* (UK) 16 (no. 4, 1986), pp. 3–32. Discussion of, and guidelines for, materials handling and cost reduction.

Calantone, Roger J., and Michael H. Morris. "The Utilisation of Computer-Based Decision-Support Systems in Transportation." *International Journal of Physical Distribution and Materials Management* (UK) 15 (no. 5, 1985), pp. 5–18. Survey of marketing and sales managers as to the use of computer-assisted decision making in the use of transportation.

Christopher, Martin. "Implementing Logistics Strategy." *International Journal of Physical Distribution and Materials Management* (UK) 14 (no. 1, 1986), pp. 52–62. Discussion of the total systems concept of physical distribution and customer service.

Frazier, Robert M. "Quick-Response Inventory Replenishment." *Retail Control* 54 (August 1986), pp. 19–29. Discussion of inventory management, problems, lead times, shorter buying cycles, and vendor relationships.

Gattorna, John, and Abby Day. "Strategic Issues in Logistics." *International Journal of Physical Distribution and Materials Management* (UK) pp. 3–42. Discussion of trends and issue management in logistics planning.

Haley, George T., and R. Kirshnan. "It's Time for CALM: Computer-Aided Logistics Management." *International Journal of Physical Distribution and Materials Management* (UK) 15 (no. 7, 1985), pp. 19–32. Discussion of trends in computer-based modeling in logistics management.

Hinds, Ed. "Linking Strategic Elements: Marketing and Distribution." *American Salesman* 31 (December 1986), pp. 24–30. Case study of just-in-time inventory control and quality control.

Jones, Thomas C., and Daniel W. Riley. "Using Inventory for Competitive Advantage through Supply Chain Management. *International Journal of Physical Distribution and Materials Management* (UK) 15 (no. 5, 1985), pp. 16–26. Discussion and case studies of inventory management and the planning and control of an entire supply chain.

LaLonde, Bernard J., and Raymond E. Mason. "Some Thoughts on Logistics Policy and Strategies: Management Challenges for the 1980s. *International Journal of Physical Distribution and Materials Management* (UK) 15 (no. 5, 1985), pp. 5–15. Discussion of current trends in strategic logistics management, to include cost reduction, information systems, problem solving, and some new principles.

Langley, C. John, Jr. "Information-Based Decision-Making in Logistics Management." *International Journal of Physical Distribution and Materials Management* (UK) 15 (no. 7, 1985), pp. 41–55. Discussion involving information systems, quality control, resource planning, and the use of microcomputers in logistics management.

Lele, Milind M. "Inventory Management: How to Control Your Critical Marketing Backfield." *Business Marketing* 71 (May 1986), pp. 40–51. Discussion of service-inventory cost trade-offs, using a simulation approach with a computer-based model.

"Material Handling: A Big Life Ahead." *Purchasing World* 30 (September 1986), pp. 67/M1–70/M4. Trends in inventory control and production planning, in regard to automated storage retrieval systems and robots.

Mentzer, John T. "Determining Motor Carrier Backhaul Markets." *Industrial Marketing Management* 15 (August 1986), pp. 237–43. Discussions and examples of, and guidelines for, information systems for determining motor carrier backhaul markets.

Peters, Melvyn. "Information Technology in Delivery Control." *International Journal of Physical Distribution and Materials Management* (UK) 16 (no. 3, 1986), pp. 45–56. In-depth interviews with distribution managers in 30 United Kingdom companies, involving current usage of information technology in distribution firms.

Sandler, Lester, and Thomas Tanel. "Toward Selective Inventory Control." *Purchasing World* 30 (April 1986), pp. 52PW15–52PW21. Discussion of stockouts, the Pareto Principle, demand categories, and strategic planning.

Schary, Philip B. "A Strategic Problem in Logistics Control." *International Journal of Physical Distribution and Materials Management* (UK) 15 (no. 5, 1985), pp. 36–50. Discussion of logistics control systems, involving the limitations of conventional cost accounting, and the use of management information systems and data traces.

Stenger, Alan J. "Just-in-Time: Make Sure You Know What You're Getting Into," *Purchasing World* 30 (March 1986), pp. 64–67. Discussion of the advantages, disadvantages, and inflexibility of just-in-time inventory control.

Sterling, Jay U., and Douglas M. Lambert. "A Methodology for Assessing Logistics Operating Systems." *International Journal of Physical Distribution and Materials Management* (UK) 15 (no. 16, 1985), pp. 3–44. Case study of a non-computer-based assessment system with implications for the provision of more effective and efficient customer services.

Tersine, Richard J.; Marsha H. Nelson; and Susan J. Willer. "Enhancing Productivity with Automated Storage and Retrieval Systems." *Journal of Purchasing and Materials Management* 21 (Fall 1985), pp. 19–24. Discussion of increased productivity and efficiency in warehousing and materials management.

Todd, Arthur W. "Buying Inbound Transportation: Part II." *Purchasing World* 30 (October 1986), pp. 60–64. Discussion of liability and accounting issues.

"Ton-Miles to Go before Any Real Hikes." *Purchasing World* 30 (April 1986), pp. 39–40. Survey results of a study of demand trends in the transportation industry, including rates and transportation modes.

van Amstel, M. J. Ploos. "Physical Distribution and Product Characteristics." *International Journal of Physical Distribution and Materials Management* (UK) 16 (no. 1, 1986), pp. 5–13. Investigation of linkages between physical distribution and product characteristics.

Voorhees, Roy Dale, and John I. Coppett. "Marketing Logistics: Opportunities for the 1990s." *Journal of Business Strategy* 7 (Fall 1986), pp. 33–38. Discussion and trends in negotiated logistical services.

Cases for Part Four

CASE 1: S.C. Johnson and Son, Limited (R)

Four months ago, in November, George Styan had been appointed division manager of Innochem, at S.C. Johnson and Son, Limited[1] (SCJ), a Canadian subsidiary of S.C. Johnson & Son, Inc. Innochem's sole product line consisted of industrial cleaning chemicals for use by business, institutions, and government. George was concerned by the division's poor market share, particularly in Montreal and Toronto. Together, these two cities represented approximately 35 percent of Canadian demand for industrial cleaning chemicals, but less than 10 percent of Innochem sales. It appeared that SCJ distributors could not match the aggressive discounting practiced by direct-selling manufacturers in metropolitan markets.

Recently, George had received a rebate proposal from his staff designed to increase the distributor's ability to cut end user prices by "sharing" part of the total margin with SCJ when competitive conditions demanded discounts of 30 percent or more off the list price to end users. George had to decide if the rebate plan was the best way to penetrate price-sensitive markets. Moreover, he wondered about the plan's ultimate impact on divisional profit performance. George either had to develop an implementation plan for the rebate plan or draft an alternative proposal to unveil at the Distributors' Annual Spring Convention, three weeks away.

■ THE CANADIAN MARKET FOR INDUSTRIAL CLEANING CHEMICALS

Last year, the Canadian market for industrial cleaning chemicals was approximately $100 million at end user prices. Growth was stable at an overall rate of approximately 3 percent per year.

"Industrial cleaning chemicals" included all chemical products designed to clean, disinfect, sanitize, or protect indus-

[1]Popularly known as Canadian Johnson Wax.

trial, commercial, and institutional buildings and equipment. The label was broadly applied to general purpose cleaners, floor maintenance products (strippers, sealers, finishes, and detergents), carpet cleaners and deodorizers, disinfectants, air fresheners, and a host of specialty chemicals such as insecticides, pesticides, drain cleaners, oven cleansers, and sweeping compounds.

Industrial cleaning chemicals were distinct from equivalent consumer products typically sold through grocery stores. Heavy-duty products were packaged in larger containers and bulk and marketed directly by the cleaning chemical manufacturers or sold through distributors to a variety of end users. Exhibit 1 includes market segmentation by primary end user categories, including janitorial service contractors and the in-house maintenance departments of government, institutions, and companies.

■ BUILDING MAINTENANCE CONTRACTORS

In Canada, maintenance contractors purchased 17 percent of the industrial cleaning chemicals sold during 1980 (end user price). The segment was

■ **EXHIBIT 1**   Segmentation of the Canadian Market for Industrial Cleaning Chemicals

By End User Category

End User Category	Percent Total Canadian Market for Industrial Cleaning Chemicals (end user value)
Retail outlets	25%
Contractors	17
Hospitals	15
Industrial and office	13
Schools, colleges	8
Hotels, motels	6
Nursing homes	5
Recreation	3
Government	3
Fast food	2
Full-service restaurants	2
All others	1
Total	100% = $95 million

By Product Category

Product Category	Percent Total Canadian Market for Industrial Cleaning Chemicals
Floor care products	40%
General purpose cleaners	16
Disinfectants	12
Carpet care products	8
Odor control products	5
Glass cleaners	4
All others	15
Total	100% = $95 million

growing at approximately 10–15 percent a year, chiefly at the expense of other end user categories. *Canadian Business* reported, "Contract cleaners have made sweeping inroads into the traditional preserve of in-house janitorial staffs, selling them on the strength of cost efficiency."[2] Maintenance contract billings reached an estimated $1 billion last year.

Frequently, demand for building maintenance services was highly price sensitive, and since barriers to entry were low (small capitalization, simple technology), competition squeezed contractor gross margins below 6 percent (before tax). Variable cost control was a matter of survival, and only products bringing compensatory labor savings could command a premium price in this segment of the cleaning chemical market.

A handful of contract cleaners did specialize in higher margin services to prestige office complexes, luxury apartments, art museums, and other "quality-conscious" customers. However, even contractors serving this select clientele did not necessarily buy premium cleaning supplies.

■ IN-HOUSE MAINTENANCE DEPARTMENTS

Government

Last year, cleaning chemical sales to various government offices (federal, provincial, and local) approached $2 million. Typically, a government body solicited bids from appropriate sources by formally advertising for quotations for given quantities of particular cleaning chemicals. Although bid requests often named specific brands, suppliers were permitted to offer "equivalent substitutes." Separate competitions were held for each item and normally covered 12 months' supply with provision for delivery "as required." Contracts were frequently awarded solely on the basis of price.

Institutions

Like government bodies, most institutions were price sensitive owing to restrictive budgets and limited ability to "pass on" expenses to users. Educational institutions and hospitals were the largest consumers of cleaning chemicals in this segment. School boards used an open-bid system patterned on the government model. Heavy sales time requirements and demands for frequent delivery of small shipments to as many as 100 locations were characteristic.

Colleges and universities tended to be operated somewhat differently. Dan Stalport, one of the purchasing agents responsible for maintenance supplies at the University of Western Ontario, offered the following comments:

> Sales reps come to UWO year 'round. If one of us (in the buying group) talks to a salesman who seems to have something—say, a labor-saving feature—we get a sample and test it. Testing can take up to a year. Floor

[2]"Contract Cleaners Want to Whisk Away Ring-Around-the-Office," *Canadian Business*, 1981, p. 22.

covering, for example, has to be exposed to seasonal changes in weather and traffic.

If we're having problems with a particular item, we'll compare the performance and price of three or four competitors. There are usually plenty of products that do the job. Basically, we want value—acceptable performance at the lowest available price.

Hospitals accounted for 15 percent of cleaning chemical sales. Procurement policies at University Hospital (UH), a medium-sized (450-bed) facility in London, Ontario, were typical. UH distinguished between "critical" and "noncritical" products. Critical cleaning chemicals (i.e., those significantly affecting patient health, such as phenolic germicide) could be bought only on approval of the staff microbiologist, who tested the "kill factor." This measure of effectiveness was regularly retested, and any downgrading of product performance could void a supplier's contract. In contrast, noncritical supplies, such as general purpose cleaners, floor finishes, and the like, were the exclusive province of Bob Chandler, purchasing agent attached to the Housekeeping Department. Bob explained that performance of noncritical cleaning chemicals was informally judged and monitored by the housekeeping staff:

> Just last year, for example, the cleaners found the floor polish was streaking badly. We (the Housekeeping Department) tested and compared five or six brands—all in the ballpark price-wise—and chose the best.

Business

The corporate segment was highly diverse, embracing both service and manufacturing industries. Large volume users tended to be price sensitive—particularly when profits were low. Often, however, cleaning products represented such a small percentage of the total operating budget that the cost of searching for the lowest cost supplier would be expected to exceed any realizable saving. Under such conditions, the typical business customer sought efficiencies in the purchasing process itself, for example, by dealing with the supplier offering the broadest mix of janitorial products (chemicals, paper supplies, equipment, etc.). Guy Breton, purchasing agent for Securitech, a Montreal-based security systems manufacturer, commented on the time economies of "one-stop shopping":

> With cleaning chemicals, it simply isn't worth the trouble to shop around and stage elaborate product performance tests. I buy all our chemicals, brushes, dusters, toweling—the works—from one or two suppliers . . . buying reputable brands from familiar suppliers saves hassles—back orders are rare, and Maintenance seldom complains.

■ DISTRIBUTION CHANNELS FOR INDUSTRIAL CLEANING CHEMICALS

The Canadian market for industrial cleaning chemicals was supplied through three main channels, each characterized by a distinctive set of strengths and weaknesses:

a. Distributor sales of national brands.

b. Distributor sales of private label products.

c. Direct sale by manufacturers.

Direct sellers held a 61 percent share of the Canadian market for industrial cleaning chemicals, while the distributors of national brands and private label products held shares of 25 percent and 14 percent, respectively. Relative market shares varied geographically, however. In Montreal and Toronto, for example, the direct marketers' share rose to 70 percent and private labelers' to 18 percent, reducing the national brand share to 12 percent. The pattern, shown in Exhibit 2, reflected an interplay of two areas of channel differentiation, namely, discount capability at the end user level and the cost of serving distant, geographically dispersed customers.

Distributor Sales of National Brand Cleaning Chemicals

National brand manufacturers, such as S.C. Johnson and Son, Airkem, and National Labs, produced a relatively limited range of "high-quality" janitorial products, including many special purpose formulations of narrow market interest. Incomplete product range, combined with shortage of manpower and limited warehousing, made direct distribution unfeasible in most cases. Normally, a national brand company would negotiate with middlemen who handled a broad array of complementary products (equipment, tools, and supplies) by different manufacturers. "Bundling" of goods brought the distributors cost efficiencies in selling, warehousing, and delivery by spreading fixed costs over a large sales volume. Distributors were, therefore, better able to absorb the costs of after-hour emergency service, frequent routine sales and service calls to many potential buyers, and shipments of small quantities of cleaning chemicals to multiple destinations. As a rule, the greater the geographic dispersion of customers, and the smaller the average order, the greater the relative economies of distributor marketing.

Comparatively high gross margins (approximately 50 percent of wholesale price) enabled national brand manufacturers to offer distributors strong marketing support and sales training along with liberal terms of payment and freight plus low minimum order requirements. Distribut-

■ **EXHIBIT 2** Effect of Geography on Market Share of Different Distribution Channels

Supplier Type	Share Nationwide	Share in Montreal and Toronto
Direct marketers	61%*	70%
Private label distributors	14	18
National brands distributors	25†	12

*Dustbane	17%	†SCJ	8%
G.H. Wood	13	N/L	4
All others	13	Airkem	3
Total	61%	All others	10
		Total	25%

ors readily agreed to handle national brand chemicals, and in metropolitan markets, each brand was sold through several distributors. By the same token, most distributors carried several directly competitive product lines. George suspected that some distributor salespeople only used national brands to "lead" with and tended to offer private label whenever a customer proved price sensitive, or a competitor handled the same national brand(s). Using an industry rule of thumb, George estimated that most distributors needed at least 20 percent gross margin on retail sales to cover sales commission of 10 percent, plus delivery and inventory expenses.

Distributor Sales of Private Label Cleaning Chemicals

Direct-selling manufacturers were dominating urban markets by aggressively discounting end user prices—sometimes below the wholesale price national brand manufacturers charged their distributors. To compete against the direct seller, increasing numbers of distributors were adding low-cost private label cleaning chemicals to their product lines. Private labeling also helped differentiate a particular distributor from others carrying the same national brand(s).

Sizable minimum order requirements restricted the private label strategy to only the largest distributors. Private label manufacturers produced to order, formulating to meet low prices specified by distributors. The relatively narrow margins (30–35 percent wholesale price) associated with private label manufacture precluded the extensive marketing and sales support national brand manufacturers characteristically provided to distributors. Private label producers pared their expenses further still by requiring distributors to bear the cost of inventory and accept rigid terms of payment as well as delivery (net 30 days, FOB plant).

In addition to absorbing these selling expenses normally assumed by the manufacturer, distributors paid salespeople higher commission on private label sales (15 percent of resale) than on national brands (10 percent of resale). However, the incremental administration and selling expenses associated with private label business were more than offset by the differential savings on private label wholesale goods. By pricing private label chemicals at competitive parity with national brands, the distributor could enjoy approximately a 50 percent gross margin at resale list, while preserving considerable resale discount capability.

Private label products were seldom sold outside the metropolitan areas where most were manufactured. First, the high costs of moving bulky, low-value freight diminished the relative cost advantage of private label chemicals. Second, generally speaking, it was only in metro areas where distributors dealt in volumes great enough to satisfy the private labeler's minimum order requirement. Finally, outside the city, distributors were less likely to be in direct local competition with others handling the same national brand, reducing value of the private label as a source of supplier differentiation.

For some very large distributors, backward integration into chemical production was a logical extension of the private labeling strategy. Recently, several distributors had become direct marketers through acquisition of captive manufacturers.

Direct Sale by Manufacturers of Industrial Cleaning Chemicals

Manufacturers dealing directly with the end user increased their gross margins to 60–70 percent of retail list price. Greater margins increased their ability to discount end user price—a distinct advantage in the price competitive urban marketplace. Overall, direct marketers averaged a gross margin of 50 percent.

Many manufacturers of industrial cleaning chemicals attempted some direct selling, but relatively few relied on this channel exclusively. Satisfactory adoption of a full-time direct-selling strategy required the manufacturer to match distributor's sales and delivery capabilities without sacrificing overall profitability. These conflicting demands had been resolved successfully by two types of company: large-scale powder chemical manufacturers and full-line janitorial products manufacturers.

Large-Scale Powder Chemical Manufacturers. Economies of large-scale production plus experience in the capital-intensive manufacture of powder chemicals enabled a few established firms, such as Diversey-Wyandotte, to dominate the market for powder warewash and vehicle cleansers. Selling through distributors offered these producers few advantages. Direct-selling expense was almost entirely commission (i.e., variable). Moreover, powder concentrates were characterized by comparatively high value-to-bulk ratios, and so could absorb delivery costs even where demand was geographically dispersed. Thus, any marginal benefits from using middlemen were more than offset by the higher margins (and associated discount capability) possible through direct distribution. Among these chemical firms, competition was not limited to price. The provision of dispensing and metering equipment was important, as was 24-hour servicing.

Full-Line Janitorial Products Manufacturers. These manufacturers offered a complete range of maintenance products, including paper supplies, janitorial chemicals, tools, and mechanical equipment. Although high margins greatly enhanced retail price flexibility, overall profitability depended on securing a balance of high- and low-margin business, as well as controlling selling and distribution expenses. This was accomplished in several ways, including:

> *Centering* on market areas of concentrated demand to minimize costs of warehousing, sales travel, and the like.
>
> *Increasing* average order size, either by adding product lines which could be sold to existing customers, or by seeking new large-volume customers.
>
> *Tying* sales commission to profitability to motivate sales personnel to sell volume, without unnecessary discounting of end user price.

Direct marketers of maintenance products varied in scale from established nationwide companies to hundreds of regional operators. The two largest direct marketers, G.H. Wood and Dustbane, together supplied almost a third of Canadian demand for industrial cleaning chemicals.

■ S.C. JOHNSON AND SON, LIMITED

S.C. Johnson and Son, Limited (SCJ), was one of 42 foreign subsidiaries owned by the U.S.-based multinational, S.C. Johnson & Son, Inc. It was ranked globally as one of the largest privately held companies. SCJ contributed substantially to worldwide sales and profits and was based in Brantford, Ontario, close to the Canadian urban markets of Hamilton, Kitchener, Toronto, London, and Niagara Falls. About 300 people worked at the head office and plant, while another 100 were employed in field sales.

Innochem Division

Innochem (Innovative Chemicals for Professional Use) was a special division established to serve corporate, institutional, and government customers of SCJ. The division manufactured an extensive line of industrial cleaning chemicals, including general purpose cleansers, waxes, polishes, and disinfectants, plus a number of specialty products of limited application, as shown in Exhibit 3. Last year, Innochem sold $4.5 million of industrial cleaning chemicals through distributors and $0.2 million direct to end users. Financial statements for Innochem are shown in Exhibit 4.

■ INNOCHEM MARKETING STRATEGY

Divisional strategy hinged on reliable product performance, product innovation, active promotion, and mixed channel distribution. Steve Remen, market development manager, maintained that "Customers know our products are of excellent quality. They know that the products will always perform as expected."

At SCJ, performance requirements were detailed and tolerances precisely defined. The Department of Quality Control routinely inspected and tested raw materials, work in process, packaging, and finished goods. At any phase during the manufacturing cycle, Quality Control was empowered to halt the process and quarantine suspect product or materials. SCJ maintained that nothing left the plant "without approval from Quality Control."

"Keeping the new product shelf well stocked" was central to divisional strategy, as the name Innochem implies. Products launched over the past three years, represented 33 percent of divisional gross sales, 40 percent of gross profits, and 100 percent of growth.

■ EXHIBIT 3   Innochem Product Line

Johnson Wax is a systems innovator. Frequently, a new product leads to a whole new system of doing things—a Johnson system of "matched" products formulated to work together. This makes the most of your time, your effort, and your expense. Call today and see how these Johnson systems can give you maximum results at a minimum cost.

For all floors except unsealed wood and unsealed cork

Stripper:	**Step-Off**—powerful, fast action
Finish:	**Pronto**—fast-drying, good gloss, minimum maintenance
Spray-buff solution:	**The Shiner Liquid Spray Cleaner or The Shiner Aerosol Spray Finish**
Maintainer:	**Forward**—Cleans, disinfects, deodorizes, sanitizes

For all floors except unsealed wood and unsealed cork

Stripper:	**Step-Off**—Powerful, fast stripper
Finish:	**Carefree**—Tough, beauty, durable, minimum maintenance
Maintainer:	**Forward**—Cleans, disinfects, deodorizes, sanitizes

For all floors except unsealed wood and unsealed cork

Stripper:	**Step-Off**—for selective stripping
Sealer:	**Over & Under-Plus**—undercoater-sealer
Finish:	**Scrubbable Step-Ahead**—brilliant, scrubbable
Maintainer:	**Forward**—cleans, disinfects, sanitizes, deodorizes

For all floors except unsealed wood and cork

Stripper:	**Step-Off**—powerful, fast stripper
Finish:	**Easy Street**—high solids, high gloss, spray buffs to a "wet look" appearance
Maintainer:	**Forward**—cleans, disinfects, deodorizes
	Expose—phenolic cleaner disinfectant

For all floors except unsealed wood and unsealed cork

Stripper:	**Step-Off**—for selective stripping
Sealer:	**Over & Under-Plus**—undercoater-sealer
Finishes:	**Traffic Grade**—heavy-duty floor wax
	Waxtral—extra tough, high solids
Maintainer:	**Forward**—cleans, disinfects, sanitizes, deodorizes

General cleaning:
Break-Up—cleans soap and body scum fast
Forward—cleans, disinfects, sanitizes, deodorizes
Bon Ami—instant cleaner, pressurized or pump, disinfects

Toilet-urinals:
Go-Getter—"Working Foam" cleaner

Glass
Bon Ami—spray-on foam or liquid cleaner

Disinfectant spray:
End-Bac II—controls bacteria, odors

Air freshener:
Glade—dewy-fresh fragrances

Spot cleaning:
Johnson's Pledge—cleans, waxes, polishes
Johnson's Lemon Pledge—refreshing scent
Bon Ami Stainless Steel Cleaner—cleans, polishes, protects

All-purpose cleaners:
Forward—cleans, disinfects, sanitizes, deodorizes
Break-Up—degreaser for animal and vegetable fats
Big Bare—heavy-duty industrial cleaner

continued

■ EXHIBIT 3 *(concluded)*

Carpets:
- **Rugbee Powder & Liquid Extraction Cleaner**
- **Rugbee Soil Release Concentrate**—for prespraying and bonnet buffing
- **Rugbee Shampoo**—for power shampoo machines
- **Rugbee Spotter**—spot remover

Furniture:
- **Johnson's Pledge**—cleans, waxes, polishes
- **Johnson's Lemon Pledge**—refreshing scent
- **Shine-Up Liquid**—general purpose cleaning

Disinfectant spray air freshener:
- **End-Bac II**—controls bacteria, odors
- **Glade**—dewy-fresh fragrances

Glass:
- **Bon Ami**—spray-on foam or liquid cleaner

Cleaning:
- **Break-Up**—special degreaser designed to remove animal and vegetable fats

Equipment:
- **Break-Up Foamer**—special generator designed to dispense Break-Up cleaner

General cleaning:
- **Forward**—fast-working germicidal cleaner for floors, walls, all washable surfaces
- **Expose**—phenolic disinfectant cleaner

Sanitizing:
- **J80 Sanitizer**—liquid for total environmental control of bacteria; no rinse necessary if used as directed

For all floors except asphalt, mastic and rubber tile. Use sealer and wax finishes on wood, cork, and cured concrete; sealer-finish on terrazzo, marble, clay, and ceramic tile; wax finish only on vinyl, linoleum, and magnesite.

Sealer:	**Johnson Gym Finish**—sealer and top-coater, cleans as it waxes.
Wax finishes:	**Traffic Wax Paste**—heavy-duty buffing wax
	Beautiflor Traffic Wax—liquid buffing wax
Maintainers:	**Forward**—cleans, disinfects, sanitizes, deodorizes
	Conq-r Dust—mop treatment
Stripper	**Step-Off**—stripper for sealer and finish
Sealer:	**Secure**—fast-bonding, smooth, long-lasting
Finish:	**Traffic Grade**—heavy-duty floor wax
Maintainer:	**Forward or Big Bare**
Sealer-finish:	**Johnson Gym Finish**—seal and top-coater
Maintainer:	**Conq-r-Dust**—mop treatment

Disinfectant spray:
- **End-Bac II Spray**—controls bacteria, odors

Flying insects:
- **Bolt Liquid Airborne** or **Pressurized Airborne,** P3610 through E10 dispenser

Crawling insects:
- **Bolt Liquid Residual** or **Pressurized Residual,** P3610 through E10 dispenser

Rodents:
- **Bolt Rodenticide**—for effective control of rats and mice, use with Bolt Bait Box

■ **EXHIBIT 4**

S.C. JOHNSON AND SON, LIMITED
Profit Statement of the Division
(In thousands)

Gross sales:	$4,682
Returns	46
Allowances	1
Cash discounts	18
Net sales	4,617
Cost of sales	2,314
Gross profit:	$2,303
Advertising	75
Promotions	144
Deals	—
External marketing services	2
Sales freight	292
Other distribution expenses	176
Service fees	184
Total direct expenses	873
Sales force	592
Marketing administration	147
Provision for bad debts	—
Research and development	30
Financial	68
Information resource management	47
Administration management	56
Total functional expenses	940
Total operating expenses	$1,813
Operating profit	$ 490

Mixed Distribution Strategy

Innochem used a mixed distribution system in an attempt to broaden market coverage. Eighty-seven percent of divisional sales were handled by a force of 200 distributor salespeople and were serviced from 50 distributor warehouses representing 35 distributors. The indirect channel was particularly effective outside Ontario and Quebec. In part, the tendency for SCJ market penetration to increase with distances from Montreal and Toronto reflected Canadian demographics and the general economics of distribution. Outside the two production centers, demand was dispersed and delivery distances long.

Distributor salespeople were virtually all paid a straight commission on sales, and were responsible for selling a wide variety of products in addition to S.C. Johnson's. Several of the distributors had sales levels much higher than Innochem.

For Innochem, the impact of geography was compounded by a significant freight cost advantage: piggybacking industrial cleaning chemicals with SCJ consumer goods. In Ontario, for example, the cost of SCJ to a distributor was 30 percent above private label, while the differential in British

Columbia was only 8 percent. On lower value products, the "freight effect" was even more pronounced.

SCJ had neither the salespeople nor the delivery capabilities to reach large-volume end users who demanded heavy selling effort or frequent shipments of small quantities. Furthermore, it was unlikely that SCJ could develop the necessary selling distribution strength economically, given the narrowness of the division's range of janitorial products (i.e., industrial cleaning chemicals only).

■ THE REBATE PLAN

The key strategic problem facing Innochem was how best to challenge the direct marketer (and private label distributor) for large-volume, price-sensitive customers with heavy service requirements, particularly in markets where SCJ had no freight advantage. In this connection George had observed:

> Our gravest weakness is our inability to manage the total margin between the manufactured cost and consumer price in a way that is equitable and sufficiently profitable to support the investment and expenses of both the distributors and ourselves.
>
> Our prime competition across Canada is from direct-selling national and regional manufacturers. These companies control both the manufacturing and distribution gross margins. Under our pricing system, the distributor's margin at end user list on sales is 43 percent. Our margin (the manufacturing margin) is 50 percent on sales. When these margins are combined, as in the case of direct-selling manufacturers, the margin becomes 70 percent at list. This long margin provides significant price flexibility in a price-competitive marketplace. We must find a way to profitably attack the direct marketer's 61 percent market share.

The rebate plan George was now evaluating had been devised to meet the competition head-on. "Profitable partnership" between Innochem and the distributors was the underlying philosophy of the plan. Rebates offered a means to "share fairly the margins available between factory cost and consumer price." Whenever competitive conditions required a distributor to discount the resale list price by 30 percent or more, SCJ would give a certain percentage of the wholesale price back to the distributor. In other words, SCJ would sacrifice part of its margin to help offset a heavy end user discount. Rebate percentages would vary with the rate of discount, following a set schedule. Different schedules were to be established for each product type and size.

The rebate plan was designed to be applicable to new, "incremental" business only, not to existing accounts of the distributor. Distributors would be required to seek SCJ approval for end user discounts of over 30 percent or more of resale list. The maximum allowable end user discount would rarely exceed 50 percent. To request rebate payments, distributors would send SCJ a copy of the resale invoice along with a written claim.

The rebate would then be paid within 60 days. Currently, Innochem sales were sold by distributors at an average discount of 10 percent off list.

Proponents of the plan maintained that the resulting resale price flexibility would not only enhance Innochem competitiveness among end users but would also diminish distributor attraction to private label.

As he studied the plan, George questioned whether all the implications were fully understood and wondered what other strategies, if any, might increase urban market penetration. Any plan he devised would have to be sold to distributors as well as to corporate management. George had only three weeks to develop an appropriate action plan.

CASE 2:　Rosemount, Inc.: Industrial Products Division

In January 1975, John Williamson, vice president of marketing at Rosemount, Inc., listens intently as marketing department personnel identify opportunities that might fit into the long-range strategy for the company's Industrial Products Division. The meeting is a significant one for Rosemount as it must lead to a final version of a comprehensive marketing plan for 1975 that can shift attention from one product line (the Model 1151 series), which had provided dramatic growth for the company during the past five years, to new products and markets. The Model 1151 product line consists of expensive, high-precision electronic pressure transmitters.

Potential new products include (1) an original equipment manufacturer (OEM) offering of the Model 1151, (2) an inexpensive electronic gage pressure transmitter—the Model 1144, and (3) an electronic pressure transmitter designed for nuclear applications—the Model 1153. These products are all in late stages of development. A variety of new markets for current and new products are also under consideration. Rosemount has limited resources available to allocate to further research and development and to marketing efforts; therefore, an assessment of the products and markets with greatest potential is vital to the company.

■ THE COMPANY

Rosemount, Inc., was a spinoff of the University of Minnesota. During the Korean War, the university's Aeronautical Engineering Department operated the Rosemount Aeronautical Research Laboratories at Rosemount, Minnesota. In these labs students and engineers from the University of Minnesota worked on projects for the rapidly growing aerospace industry.

This case was made possible through the cooperation of Rosemount, Inc. The case was prepared by William Rudelius, University of Minnesota, and Steven Hartley, University of Denver, as a basis for class discussion rather than for illustration of the appropriate or inappropriate handling of administrative situations. Copyright © 1982 by the Case Development Center, School of Management, University of Minnesota.

One Rosemount project, sponsored by the U.S. Air Force, developed a temperature sensor for military aircraft. Unable to find a manufacturer for the new design, the Air Force offered the original project members a contract to produce the sensor they had designed. Shortly thereafter, in early 1956, Rosemount, Inc., was formed—with one product and one customer.

Early Years.   That first contract provided the means for Rosemount to gain expertise in manufacturing sensors for precise temperature measurement. This, in turn, enabled Rosemount's participation in the U.S. space program starting in the late 1950s. As the space program grew, the need for advanced space technology provided the opportunity for Rosemount to gain research, development, and manufacturing expertise in sensing devices. Engineering excellence became the basis for success and provided the foundation for growth. In 1960 pressure-measurement technology developed by Rosemount allowed the company to introduce high-quality pressure sensors. Again, primary applications were in the space and aircraft markets.

By 1966 Rosemount's annual sales had reached $8.5 million. However, a severe problem was the overwhelming dependence on the U.S. space and defense programs. So in the late 1960s Rosemount tried to apply its unique temperature- and pressure-measurement technology to industrial markets. Several of these markets were growing and needed expensive, high-accuracy instruments.

Present Situation.   Currently, Rosemount provides its products to four primary markets—commercial aviation, defense-and-space, energy, and process-and-manufacturing. Sales during fiscal year 1974 were well distributed among the four markets, exceeding a total of $32 million (see Exhibit 1). Rosemount considers this recent diversification into four markets to be a key strength for the company.

■ PRODUCT LINES

John Williamson feels that now is the time for Rosemount to assess opportunities for its present and prospective product lines. He leans forward in his chair as George Mills, head of the Product Planning Group, and technical executives summarize opportunities for four key product lines.

Model 1151 Series.   As with temperature-related products, Rosemount elected to concentrate on high-quality technology when developing the pressure-related products. Using electrical capacitance to measure changes in pressure, the Rosemount Model 1151 series of pressure sensors established new standards of accuracy and reliability in a wide variety of applications. Very simply, the basic function of the Model 1151 is to monitor pressure, convert the pressure to an electrical signal, and transmit the signal to a control or monitoring station. The primary component of any pressure-measurement device, the sensor, is responsible for the first steps. Because a change in pressure is proportional to such properties as temperature, velocity, weight, force, and strain, many types of sensors are avail-

■ **EXHIBIT 1** Rosemount Financial Data *(in thousands)*

Summary of Earnings	1970	1971	1972	1973	1974
Net sales	$13,388	$15,324	$19,012	$23,977	$32,875
Cost of sales	7,628	8,382	10,278	13,296	18,315
Research and development costs	4,137	942	847	780	1,125
Selling, general, and administrative expenses*	3,744	4,450	5,526	7,051	9,135
Interest expense	151	134	133	237	623
Net income before taxes	849	1,576	2,268	2,792	3,462
Income taxes	393	757	1,194	1,393	1,895
Net income after taxes	456	819	1,074	1,399	1,567
Instrument sales by market:					
Commercial aviation	1,540	2,309	2,671	3,128	3,616
Defense and space	6,100	6,615	8,011	8,180	8,876
Energy	1,330	1,815	3,218	5,114	5,851
Process and manufacturing	3,880	3,880	3,648	4,990	10,916
Total instrument sales	12,850	14,619	17,548	21,412	29,259†
Pressure transmitter sales	100	600	1,350	3,740	8,533†

*Marketing and sales personnel = 10 percent, advertising = 3 percent of selling, general and administrative expenses.

†Figures include noninstrument sales, and instrument sales include nonpressure transmitter sales.

SOURCE: Company financial statements

able. The Rosemount product uses a unique technique in which the capacitance, varying directly with pressure, is converted to an electrical signal.

Rosemount manufactures an entire series of Model 1151 transmitters that are used to measure different types of pressure. They include: differential pressure (differences in pressures at two different points in a pipe or system), gage pressure (pressure in excess of atmospheric pressure), and absolute pressure (pressure above zero pounds per square inch). Of the many models, the differential pressure type accounts for more than 80 percent of Rosemount pressure transmitter sales.

Now in 1975 the Model 1151 has become the standard product offering for Rosemount and also a standard of the pressure-transmitter industry. In his presentation George Mills attributes the wide acceptance of the product and rapid growth in its sales to four key benefits: (1) high-quality performance, (2) ruggedness of design, (3) economical purchase and installation, and (4) reduced maintenance cost. Other benefits, such as specifications, materials of construction, and available options, also give the Model 1151 series a competitive advantage.

Model 1153 Series. In 1971 Rosemount initiated a program to develop a pressure transmitter qualified for nuclear applications—the Model 1153 series. One reason for this decision was the increased acceptance of the Model 1151 in the power-generating industry. Thus, extending the product line to include nuclear applications in the power-generating industry appeared to be an obvious move.

The design and manufacture of the sensor component of the Model 1151 and of the Model 1153 were very similar. But the transmitter component for the Model 1153 required major changes from the Model 1151 design. These transmitter changes were needed to enable the product to meet specifications established by the government for all instrumentation utilized in nuclear power facilities. Specifically, the standards require rigorous aging, radiation, and seismic tests. During the past three years a large portion of Rosemount's research and development (R&D) resources have been allocated to this effort. Although some success has been achieved, additional work is required to "qualify" the product fully for nuclear applications. The estimated unit variable cost for the Model 1153 was $560. Rosemount hoped to achieve a 14 percent pretax return on sales goal with this product.

Model 1144 Series.   The proposed Model 1144 pressure transmitter represents an inexpensive version of the more reliable Model 1151 gage pressure transmitter. The Model 1144 would not have differential pressure-measurement capability. Preliminary design efforts indicated that the Model 1144, which would utilize pressure technology developed for the Model 1151, would meet most performance specifications of competitive products. The new design, which requires an additional $150,000 in research and development to reach the production stage, could also be priced below most other gage pressure transmitters. However, because the Model 1144 would be similar in function to the Model 1151—an extremely successful product to date—several managers have expressed concern about further development of the inexpensive model. The primary concern was the possibility that Model 1144 sales would reduce those of the Model 1151—that is, the products would compete with, rather than complement, each other. The estimated unit variable cost for the Model 1144 was $280. An 8 percent pretax return on sales objective was set for this product.

OEM Model 1151 Series.   The OEM Model 1151 series pressure transmitter would simply be a Rosemount Model 1151 pressure transmitter with a different color paint. These transmitters would then be resold by another firm for use with its own products. Such an arrangement would (1) allow Rosemount to estimate production needs (through OEM production contracts) and (2) gain sales in new markets. A disadvantage, again, would be the possibility that the OEM products would compete directly with regular Rosemount products. The estimated unit variable cost for the OEM Model 1151 was $345. An 18 percent pretax return on sales objective was set for this product.

Support Costs

Each of the product line alternatives would require different levels of marketing, manufacturing, and R&D support. Mr. Mills had solicited rough estimates of these costs from various R&D, manufacturing, and marketing personnel and now presented them to John Williamson and the others in a summary table (see Exhibit 2). Although the information represented subjective judgments, George felt that it was important to get a "feel" for the costs involved. In addition, he noted that Rosemount achieved a 41 percent

■ **EXHIBIT 2**   Estimated Financial Data on The Alternative New Products

Product	R&D	Manufacturing	Incremental Fixed Costs ($)		Miscellaneous Marketing Support
			Personal Selling	Advertising	
OEM					
1151	0	$ 10,000	0	0	$40,000
1144	$150,000	$ 50,000	$ 50,000	$60,000	$40,000
1153	$250,000	$100,000	$200,000	$40,000	$40,000

SOURCE: Estimates made by casewriters.

contribution margin and a 10.5 percent pretax return on sales in 1974 (see Exhibit 1).

■ COMPETITION

Number of Competitors

The number of competitors listed under the SIC heading of 3,823 "Industrial Instruments for Measurement, Display and Control of Process Variables and Related Products" was 119 in 1974. These companies manufacture a large number of products, including sensors, actuators, indicators, recorders, controllers, and transmitters.

Exhibit 3 depicts Rosemount's major competitors in the pressure-transmitter market. Foxboro, the largest competitor, offers a range of products from individual instruments to integrated process management and control systems. Foxboro also offers customized control panels and a host of customer support services, including repair, maintenance, and training programs. Despite the dominance of Foxboro in the pressure-transmitter market, Rosemount had been able to gain considerable market share over the past four years.

■ **EXHIBIT 3**   Pressure Transmitter Market *(percent share of North American sales)*

	1970	1971	1972	1973	1974
Fischer and Porter	10%	10%	10%	9%	8%
Foxboro	50	48	44	38	32
Statham	0	0	3	4	5
Honeywell	5	5	7	9	10
Leeds and Northrup	3	5	5	5	5
Rosemount	<1	3	6	12	20
Taylor	15	15	13	11	9
Other*	16	14	12	12	11
Total	100%	100%	100%	100%	100%
Market size (in millions)	$15	$18	$20	$26	$32

*Includes Bourns, Barton, Bell and Howell, Westinghouse, Bailey, Robertshaw, and Teledyne-Tavis.

SOURCE: Estimates made by casewriters from company records.

Competitive Products

Exhibit 4 provides information about competitive product offerings. For example, only Statham, Bourns, Bell and Howell, and Teledyne-Tavis offer a gage pressure transmitter similar in price and performance to the Model 1144. All other competitors offer products that compete directly with the Model 1151. None of the companies currently offer both products. Information regarding competitors' developmental efforts is difficult to obtain; however, two important points have been raised by Rosemount personnel. First, with the exception of the nuclear-qualified transmitter, the new products being considered by Rosemount could easily be added by competitors. Second, several competitors are probably spending research and development resources on the development of a new "generation" of pressure-measurement technology that, if successful, could greatly reduce the position of the Model 1151 series in the marketplace.

Annual Sales of Pressure Transmitters

Sales in the control instrument industry have been increasing at an annual rate of approximately 20 percent—reaching $1.5 billion in 1973. Instruments account for 60 percent of the industry sales, while 8 percent of the instrument sales are from electronic pressure transmitters. Currently, the North American market (United States and Canada) represents 38 percent of all pressure-transmitter sales. Pressure-transmitter sales in the United States and Canada grew at a rate of approximately 20 percent during the past four years. Market forecasts indicate that sales will continue to increase at a rate of at least 20 percent through 1980. Overseas markets are also expected to grow, although foreign manufacturers are challenging the

■ **EXHIBIT 4**   Competitive Product Information and Prices

| Manufacturer | Type of Pressure Transmitter | | | |
	High Priced	OEM	Low Priced	Nuclear Qualified
Bailey	yes	no	no	no
Barton	yes	no	no	no
Bell and Howell	no	no	yes($435)	no
Bourns	no	no	yes($450)	no
Fischer and Porter	yes($585)	no	no	no
Foxboro	yes($560)	no	no	yes
Honeywell	yes($565)	no	no	no
Leeds and Northrup	yes	no	no	no
Robertshaw Controls	yes	no	no	no
Rosemount	yes($555)	?($465)	?($430)	?($900)
	Model 1151	OEM 1151	Model 1144	Model 1153
Statham	no	no	yes($485)	no
Taylor	yes($600)	no	no	no
Teledyne-Tavis	no	no	yes($440)	no
Westinghouse	yes	no	no	no

Estimates made by casewriters from company records and competitors' sales literature.

once-dominant U.S. firms. In fact, non-U.S. firms are even expanding in the U.S. market. These changes have been attributed to growth of the world market and increased technological and business skills in Western Europe and the Far East.

■ MARKETS

Although Rosemount has diversified into four major instrument markets, the majority of Rosemount and industry electronic pressure-transmitter sales are to the energy and process-and-manufacturing markets (see Exhibit 5).

Energy

Rosemount shipments to the energy market rose 63 percent in 1973 over 1972. Because of significant long-term growth potential, development efforts directed at the energy market have been encouraged. The market consists of three submarkets—electrical power generation, oil and gas production and distribution, and oil and gas refining—that have varied sales records.

Electrical Power Generation. The electrical power generation submarket consists of government- and investor-owned utilities. Rosemount's Model 1151 competes primarily with Foxboro, Leeds and Northrup, Bailey, and

■ **EXHIBIT 5** Pressure Transmitter Sales in North America by Market *(in thousands)*

Industry	1970	1971	1972	1973	1974
Process-and-manufacturing	6,200	7,900	8,200	12,900	6,500
Pulp-and-paper	3,000	3,700	4,400	5,200	6,200
Chemical	3,200	4,200	3,800	7,700	10,300
Energy	8,600	9,900	11,300	12,900	15,000
Oil and gas production and distribution	5,300	6,100	6,700	7,700	9,000
Oil and gas refining	1,600	2,000	2,500	3,000	3,600
Electric utilities: fossil	1,600	1,700	1,900	2,000	2,100
Electric utilities: nuclear	100	100	200	200	300
Other	300	500	400	600	600
Total	15,100	18,300	19,900	26,400	32,100
Rosemount					
Process-and-manufacturing	100	500	580	1,550	4,140
Pulp-and-paper	0	200	260	620	1,240
Chemical	100	300	320	930	2,900
Energy	0	40	600	1,532	2,200
Oil and gas production and distribution	0	0	235	955	1,615
Oil and gas refining	0	0	65	162	195
Electric utilities: fossil	0	40	300	415	390
Electrical utilities: nuclear	0	0	0	0	0
Other	0	0	20	38	60
Total	100	540	1,200	3,120	6,400

■ **EXHIBIT 6**   Projected Growth of Electrical Power Generating Capacity *(domestic and foreign)*

	1975	1976	1977	1978	1979	1980	1981	1982	1983	1984	1985
Total electric generating capacity											
at peak (millions of kilowatts)	476	502	528	555	584	613	641	675	707	745	773
Annual growth (%)	6.0	5.5	5.0	5.1	5.2	5.0	4.6	5.3	4.7	5.4	3.8
Plant construction:											
Fossil fuel											
Number	37	39	39	38	35	31	29	27	26	21	26
Size (megawatts × 1,000)	15.0	16.0	16.1	15.3	15.6	15.7	12.7	14.6	12.8	11.6	14.8
Nuclear											
Number	5	7	8	6	11	11	12	15	16	20	12
Size (megawatts × 1,000)	5.0	6.5	7.7	5.9	11.0	12.3	13.4	15.8	18.3	23.6	14.1

SOURCE: Company estimates.

Westinghouse products for the fossil-fueled utilities, while only Foxboro offers a competitive product for the nuclear power utilities. Leeds and Northrup and Bailey currently dominate the fossil-fueled segment of the market, but marketing managers feel that the lower-priced Model 1144 would be very attractive to these customers.

Although electric utilities will continue to account for a major portion of the U.S. market for electronic transmitters, they will represent a steadily declining share as market growth decreases (see Exhibit 6). This growth pattern reflects a fundamental change in the demand for electric power in the United States; historically, demand grew at an annual rate of 7 percent. Moreover, now in 1975 the United States is just coming out of the 1973–1974 international oil embargo, and energy experts expect a shift from fossil-fueled power generation to nuclear power generation. Each type of power plant requires approximately $150,000 worth of electronic pressure transmitters. Twenty percent of Rosemount's sales to the energy market are to electric utilities.

Oil and Gas Production and Distribution (Pipeline).   The market for instrumentation utilized in the production and pipeline distribution of oil and gas is projected to have a favorable growth pattern of 15 percent annually through 1985. Underlying this growth pattern is an increasing level of capital expenditures to increase the production of oil and gas in the United States to make U.S. citizens less dependent on foreign oil. Although few new production fields are anticipated during the forecast period, modernization and upgrading projects for existing facilities as well as some replacement projects will continue to be a substantial factor in future market growth. Similarly, the number of new oil and gas pipeline installations will be limited. Pipeline expenditures will consist of small-scale projects directed at expansion, modernization, upgrading, and replacement.

Despite increased capital expenditures, Rosemount has not been extremely competitive in oil and gas production and distribution. Currently, none of the pressure-transmitter manufacturers dominate the submarket. However, because a production field can require up to 600 transmitters for use on injection and recovery wells, low-priced transmitters such as those

■ **EXHIBIT 7** Projected Sales of Pressure Transmitters to Oil and Gas Markets *(domestic and foreign, in millions)*

	1975	1976	1977	1978	1979	1980	1981	1982	1983	1984	1985
Oil and gas production and distribution	40.8	47.3	54.2	62.0	71.9	85.1	97.7	112.0	129.4	148.8	170.7
Oil and gas refining	16.5	17.6	18.5	19.5	20.7	21.8	23.1	24.8	26.1	27.8	29.4

SOURCE: Company estimates.

offered by Bourns, Statham, and Bell and Howell have a slight competitive advantage. Exhibit 7 provides electronic pressure-transmitter sales projections through 1985.

Oil and Gas Refining. The least successful submarket for Rosemount has been oil and gas refining. What was previously believed to be a shortage of refining capacity has actually become an excess. Uncertainties of supply, existence of government regulation, and reduced demand for gasoline all were contributing factors. This situation became apparent only recently as refineries trimmed, postponed, or cancelled their expansion plans. Foxboro and Honeywell have become the major suppliers of pressure transmitters to this submarket by also selling supervisory control computers. Rosemount is not yet able to supply a control system and therefore cannot assume responsibility for an entire refinery. Taylor and Fischer and Porter also serve as secondary suppliers to the oil and gas refining market. The Fischer and Porter company has expressed interest in purchasing Rosemount transmitters as an OEM product. Several Rosemount market managers feel that this may be the best alternative for gaining access to orders requiring complete systems.

Process-and-Manufacturing

The combined market for measurement and control instrumentation in the process-and-manufacturing industry now exceeds $250 million in the United States alone. Although most sales are made to the chemical and pulp-and-paper industries, the market includes other industries such as mineral processing and food-and-beverage. The products manufactured by these industries have little in common, but their requirements for control systems and instruments are quite similar. Because accuracy and stability are of great importance in process-and-manufacturing plants, buyers look for very high performance specifications.

Rosemount is not yet a dominant supplier in this market. In fact, only recently has any progress been made against Taylor, Fischer and Porter, and Foxboro—the established competitors in the market. To encourage acceptance, Rosemount has adopted a "concentration" strategy that directs most marketing efforts at major, multinational companies (e.g., International Paper, Boise Cascade, DuPont, Union Carbide). Small firms are contacted through system suppliers and original equipment manufacturers.

Rosemount's annual sales to the process-and-manufacturing market increased over 110 percent from 1973 to 1974. Marketing managers feel that the market has additional growth potential for Rosemount as long as capital expenditures are at a high level. Both the paper and chemical industries have focused on pollution abatement in recent years, absorbing many of the capital equipment resources. Thus, growth potential for the next two or three years appears favorable.

Pulp-and-Paper Manufacturers. U.S. pulp and paper consumption has grown at a rate of about 4.5 percent over the past several years. Industry experts now believe that the pulp-and-paper industry is approaching 95 percent of capacity utilization. Significant increases in capital spending also indicate that plans for expansions and new plants are in progress. Although recent increases in consumption have brought the industry to record production levels, the rate of increase is declining. Growth rates are likely to continue to decline because domestic per-capita consumption is already quite high, many markets appear to be saturated, and the population is increasing at a slower rate. Future growth will come from foreign markets where per-capita consumption is still low.

Chemical. Although capital expenditures in process-and-manufacturing have fallen somewhat below expectations, oil companies seem to be diverting funds from refining to petrochemical production. Several factors may account for this shift in spending. First, refining capacity is adequate. Second, worldwide shortages of petrochemicals (particularly feedstocks and fertilizers) were caused by the 1973 Arab oil embargo. Capital spending for 1975 is expected to rise to 15.3 percent of sales, or about $4.3 million.

■ CURRENT MARKETING STRATEGY

Despite Rosemount's recent growth and the apparent success of the Model 1151 series, Mr. Williamson feels that a marketing plan is essential for future growth. Historically, the company has used over 50 percent of its research and development budget to develop new applications for current products, to test competitive products, and to investigate potential technical improvements in current temperature- and pressure-measurement technology. New product efforts typically receive "project" status to be reviewed on an annual basis. Marketing resources are allocated to areas of potential growth. As the number of new product and market alternatives increases, the need for an explicit allocation procedure increases. Focused marketing and research and development efforts seem increasingly important.

Appeals and Product Features Stressed

Company salespeople identify several factors that are critical in competing with other instrument manufacturers:

1. *Reputation*. Reputation is considered the strongest competitive factor. Users looked for reliable and fast service.
2. *Knowledge*. Thorough knowledge of the user's industry is considered critical. Users expect suppliers to know where instruments are required to maintain production efficiency or product quality and where instruments are unnecessary, thus reducing costs.
3. *Technology*. Product reliability and quality are extremely important to users, particularly in applications where product failure would shut down the factory or system or where production quality would be greatly reduced.
4. *Price*. Competitive bidding always plays a role in contract negotiations but is less important than other factors. In fact, many users do not even consider bids from unestablished suppliers.

Sales Efforts

Sales of new products or to new users are very difficult. Users of pressure transmitters are extremely loyal. If the equipment they have been using is reliable and functional, they are reluctant to change suppliers. Users are loyal because they feel the suppliers know their processes and needs. Reeducating a new supplier is too costly in terms of time and does not insure that the new supplier will be reliable. Even a reputation for high-quality performance in one industry is rarely enough to make a sale to a user in another industry.

Because users expect salespeople to be knowledgeable about Rosemount products, competitive products, and industry applications, significant sales training is required. The marketing department (1) provides regular product-line education sessions for new salespeople and (2) distributes evaluations of competitive products whenever possible. Salespeople often develop expertise in particular industries or applications. Introducing new products or markets has significant implications in terms of marketing costs as new technical information will be required or new customers will have to be called on.

■ PLANNING MEETING

A corporate planning meeting is scheduled for the last week of January, and Mr. Williamson must recommend and support specific resource allocations. First, he must set goals for Rosemount's industrial products and markets for 1975. Second, he must identify the market segments on which marketing effort must be focused and the product lines to which R&D effort will be allocated.

Questions

1. What product-line alternatives are available to Williamson?
2. What are the favorable and unfavorable effects of adding each of the new products to Rosemount's product line?
3. How can Rosemount segment the market for its line of pressure transmitters?
4. How can Rosemount use a product-market matrix to aid in the assessment of "where it is now," "where it wants to go with its new product," and "how it will get there"?

PART FIVE

Promoting and Selling the Goods

Chapter 11 · The Personal Selling Function in
Business Marketing Strategy

Chapter 12 · Business to Business Sales
Management

Chapter 13 · Advertising and Sales Promotion
Strategy in Business Markets

Chapter 11

The Personal Selling Function in Business Marketing Strategy

LEARNING OBJECTIVES

After reading this chapter, you should be able to:

- Appreciate the scope and nature of the salesperson's daily activities.
- Understand the nature of the cost of a business to business sale.
- Uncover a sales prospect's important buying needs.
- Identify different sales approaches for reaching the buyer.
- Discuss important current trends in business to business personal selling.
- Describe the selling process and its associated activities.
- Comprehend how to sell effectively in international markets.

CHAPTER OUTLINE

Learning Objectives
How Personal Selling Differs
between Consumer and Business
Goods' Markets
A Profile of Personal Selling
  Selling
  Cooperative Relationships with
    Channel Members
  Planning
  Decision Making
  The Management of Communication
The Cost of Personal Selling
  The Cost to Close a Business to
    Business Sale
Understanding Buyer Behavior
  Understanding Buyer Needs
  Methods to Uncover Important
    Needs of Buying Center Members
The Selling Spectrum
  Different Approaches to the Sales
    Presentation

Types of Sales Positions and Selling
  Styles in the Business Market
Some Contemporary Trends in
Business Selling
  The Importance of Systems Selling
  The Importance of Telemarketing
  The Emergence of Saleswomen
  The Usage of Terminals and Laptop
    Computers
  The Rapid Growth of Audio-Visual
    Aids
The Personal Selling Process:
A Business Salesperson's
Perspective
  Preliminary Activities
  Face-to-Face Activities
  Follow-Up Activities
International Business to Business
Selling

■ HOW PERSONAL SELLING DIFFERS BETWEEN CONSUMER AND BUSINESS GOODS' MARKETS

Personal selling involves persuasive and deliberate contact between a buyer and a seller for the specific purpose of creating an exchange between them. Personal selling is widely utilized in the sales of both consumer and business goods. In the case of most consumer goods, such as shampoo, clothing, and automobiles, personal selling is used as a complement to other elements in the promotional mix that also includes advertising, publicity, public relations, and sales promotion. On the other hand, personal selling is generally the primary or most fundamental means of selling business goods, such as photocopiers, computer systems, and machine parts. The other elements of the promotional mix are frequently employed to support or to augment the persuasiveness of the personal selling function.

So that we might understand why personal selling typically plays a more important role in selling to business buyers than to final consumers, Table 11–1 examines some important differences in the nature of the marketing

■ **TABLE 11–1**   Differences between Business and Consumer Goods' Marketing

Factors	Business-to-Business Customers	Final Consumers
Customer size	Relatively few customers	Many consumers
Products	Technical and sophisticated, requiring explanation through personal contact	Less sophisticated, relying on mass media for explanation
Purchase size	Large volume	Small volume
Price	Negotiated pricing	One-price policy
Distribution channels	Shorter, more direct	Longer, less direct
Promotion	Personal selling is emphasized with support from business mass promotion	Advertising is emphasized with support from personal selling
Relationships	Formation of both personal and professional relationships	Less personal and enduring relationships

mix elements between final consumers and business buyers. First, there are far greater numbers of final consumers than there are business buyers, and indirect methods of creating a sale are more frequently successful when greater numbers of buyers are available. Second, business buyers most often buy more technical and more sophisticated products and services than do final consumers, who require more explanation and personal demonstration. Third, final consumers generally make smaller-volume purchases than do business buyers, who often have special product or service design needs, and who like to negotiate price rather than adhering to the typical, one-price policy so common in final consumer purchasing. Fourth, final consumers are normally reached through longer, less direct distribution channels, whereas business buyers seem to be more effectively approached through shorter, more direct distribution channels, involving more frequent contact with salespeople. Fifth and lastly, final consumers tend to develop less personal and enduring relationships with the majority of salespeople with whom they come into contact, as opposed to business buyers, who frequently form both a professional and personal relationship with the salespeople from whom they buy repeatedly over a period of years.

In short, final consumers often see salespeople merely as convenient sources of supply of particular and usually ordinary products and services. On the other hand, organizational buyers more typically view business salespeople not only as product and service experts from whom they can seek purchasing and inventory advice but also as good friends and the critical link between the manufacturer and themselves.

■ A PROFILE OF PERSONAL SELLING

How exactly do salespeople spend their time during the course of a work-day? The salesperson's day is quite long, averaging over nine and one half hours. In time spent on the job, less than 40 percent is taken up by actual face-to-face selling, while approximately one third is used in traveling and waiting for interviews. These statistics, when combined with the approximate $250 cost per industrial sales call, paint a picture of a busy executive who must make every minute count when in a face-to-face selling situation with a buyer.[1]

To gain a real understanding of the role of a business to business salesperson, we must understand both the scope and the nature of their daily activities. The contemporary salesperson faces more intense competition and a more well-informed and sophisticated prospect than ever before. This individual performs many types of activities, including selling, maintenance of distributor relationships, planning, decision making, and managing communications. Several of these activities will be examined briefly.

Selling

Selling includes both servicing established accounts and prospecting for new accounts. The salesperson describes the product, and offers the reasons why it should be bought. Additionally, the salesperson is frequently called upon to provide consulting services. For example, salespeople are often asked to demonstrate how their products mesh with the product design and operational aspects of the customer's firm, since the products being sold will either become part of the customer's products or be used in producing them.

Cooperative Relationships with Channel Members

Salespeople must also maintain cooperative relationships among various members of the distribution channels with whom they are involved, or face the consequences of channel conflict which will often lead to problems involving delivery service, damaged or deteriorating goods, and misunderstandings about the specific role of each of the channel members. Salespeople sometimes find themselves helping customers, who have become personal friends over several years of professional association, with various managerial problems, ranging from inventory control to the recruitment, motivation, and retention of sales personnel. More so than ever before, a salesperson who basically calls on wholesalers is asked to assist customers in their selection of appropriate resellers.

Planning

In light of the intense competition involved in most types of business selling, salespeople are now spending a major portion of their time planning activities. Effective planning on the part of salespeople involves scheduling and routing sales calls, determining the frequency of contact with established accounts, and assigning the proper amount of time to spend in prospecting for new accounts. Also included are the evaluation of tapped and

---

[1]*The Wall Street Journal,* January 6, 1988, p. 1.

untapped sales potential within the total sales territory, providing assistance to the sales manager in budgeting and in sales forecasting for a particular sales territory over a specific period of time, and taking on the role of master strategist in the decision-making process of establishing goals, objectives, strategies, and techniques by which a certain territory can be fully and profitably reached.

Decision Making

Highly relevant to each of the sales activities discussed above is a fourth one, *decision making*. Salespeople must choose how to allocate their time in the most productive and efficient manner. Choices must be made in light of various constraints and opportunities, and frequently the more structured decisions are aided through formal rules or models. For example, a company does not enjoy the same rate of net profit on every sale. In most firms a large proportion of the orders, customers, territories, or products account for only a small share of the profit. This relationship between selling units and profits has been referred to as the *80–20 principle,* in that 80 percent of a firm's profits are accounted for by 20 percent of their selling units. When this axiom is applicable, salespeople will tend to devote the lion's share of their time to that most profitable 20 percent of the selling units.

A final aspect of decision making concerns the unstructured or unexpected demands placed upon salespeople. Problems in production or shipping, changing customer needs, competitive movements, labor disputes, conflicting demands from multiple customers, and a whole host of other economic, political, or climatic factors, require that the salesperson be able to make quick decisions with information which is both limited and imperfect.

The Management of Communication

Another type of activity performed by salespeople is the *management of communication.* The salesperson plays an important communication role in the link between the customer and the manufacturer or distributor. A typical salesperson generally has contact with the entire buying center in the customer's organization. As is shown in Exhibit 11–1, this buying center is comprised of purchasing agents, materials managers, or groups of customers responsible for company purchases. To reach many of these decision makers, the salesperson must successfully penetrate the walls erected by the various company gatekeepers, such as receptionists, secretaries, telephone operators, and even the higher layers of the buying center that include the deciders and influencers. During both presale and postsale activities the salesperson must frequently deal with accountants, clerks, distribution personnel, and production managers. Within their own respective organizations, salespeople must deal with their immediate supervisor, advertising staff, accountants, marketing researchers, shippers, and a variety

■ **EXHIBIT 11–1**   Who Participates in the Business-to-Business Buying Process?

Users.   Users are the members of the organization who will use the product or service. In many cases, the users initiate the buying proposal and help define the product specifications.

Influencers.   Influencers are persons who affect the buying decision. They often help define specifications and also provide information for evaluating alternatives. Technical personnel are particularly important as influencers.

Buyers.   Buyers are persons with formal authority for selecting the supplier and arranging the terms of purchase. Buyers may help shape product specifications, but they play their major role in selecting vendors and negotiating. In more complex purchases, the buyers might include high-level officers participating in the negotiations.

Deciders.   Deciders are persons who have formal or informal power to approve or select the final suppliers. In routine buying the buyers are often the deciders, or at least the approvers.

Gatekeepers.   Gatekeepers are persons who control the flow of information to others. For example, purchasing agents often have authority to prevent salespersons from seeing users or deciders. Other gatekeepers include technical personnel and even personal secretaries.

SOURCE: Philip Kotler, *Principles of Marketing*, 3d ed. (Englewood Cliffs, N.J.: Prentice-Hall, 1986), pp. 218, 380, 383. Reprinted with permission.

of other support personnel. Most salespeople are also expected to be expert communicators in recruiting and training new salespeople; in responding to constant requests for information from new, established, and potential customers; and in efficiently generating the required paperwork necessary to process orders, to document expense reports, to file progress reports, and to keep customers informed of new and innovative products and trends within their company and industry.

The salesperson, in summary, is required to impart a positive image of the company and its products, and to convince others in an assertive manner to buy from the company. The typical salesperson, then, must be highly skilled in interpersonal communication.

The Cost of Personal Selling

The average cost of business to business sales calls rose by 9.5 percent between 1985 and 1987, from $229.70 to $251.63, according to the Laboratory of Advertising Performance (LAP), a division of McGraw-Hill Research. Additionally, the cost of personal selling has risen 160 percent over the past decade. Note that this is a conservative estimate because it does not include costs such as sales training and the hidden paycheck (e.g., insurance and retirement benefits). Respondents in this LAP study included 836 vice presidents of sales and sales managers of business to business companies.[2]

Another useful way to comprehend the enormous cost of the personal selling function is to consider that it takes at least $20,000 to train a sales-

---

[2]"Average Business-to-Business Sales Call Increases by 9.5%," *Marketing News*, September 12, 1988, p. 5.

person effectively, and that there is an average annual turnover of 300,000 salespersons. A simple calculation will show that this training and subsequent loss of salespeople cost approximately $6 billion per year.[3]

The Cost to Close a Business-to-Business Sale

Another approach we might take in looking at sales costs is to examine the cost to close a sale. The 1987 statistic of $251.63 was estimated without consideration as to whether a sale was made or not. Since only about 6 percent of sales are made via one sales call, 9 percent by two calls, and 33.5 percent by three calls, the cost to close a sale is significantly higher than the $251.63 figure quoted above. The McGraw-Hill Research Department researched 787 business to business marketing companies and ascertained that an average of 4.3 calls are needed to close a sale, for a total cost of $883.22. The cost to close a sale has recently been found to be as much as $2,000 in some cases.[4] This study also found that total costs to close a sale varied by industry. For example, an average of 3.8 calls were necessary to close a sale in the lumber industry, and an average of 5.6 calls were typical in business services.[5] Because the cost of personal selling can vary so significantly, depending on such factors as the type of product and industry, the size of the firm, and the degree of personal contact with prospects necessary to close a sale, companies must constantly monitor and assess the best methods by which to distribute and sell their products and services.

Concept Questions

1. How do organizational buyers typically view business salespeople?
2. How does one gain a real understanding of the role of a salesperson?
3. Why is the cost to close a sale higher than the average cost of a sales call?

■ UNDERSTANDING BUYER BEHAVIOR

Buyers use a decision-making process very similar to that used by final consumers. Both are interested in products and services that provide the type of benefits for which the buyer is searching. Any buyer is interested in what the product will do for them. **Benefit selling** appeals to the customer's personal motives by answering the question, what's in it for me? Benefit selling is facilitated by the use of **benefit segmentation,** which is

---

[3]Statistics provided courtesy of Professor George W. Wynn, School of Business, James Madison University, Harrisonburg, Virginia.

[4]"Sales Tactics Take on a New Look as Corporations Rethink Strategy," *The Wall Street Journal,* April 28, 1988, p. 1.

[5]Henry Bernstein, "How to Recruit Good Salesmen," *Industrial Marketing* 50 (October 1965), p. 70. Also see John A. Byrne, "Motivating Willy Loman," *Forbes,* January 30, 1984, p. 91.

dividing the total target market into individual groups according to the particular utilities or benefits expected from a specific product or service. For example, in the case of an industrial janitorial service, one group of companies may be looking for dependability and reliability, while another may be looking for the use of specific cleaning procedures. The marketer who is able to use benefit selling to reach prospective customers is demonstrating a willingness to understand and meet the buying needs and objectives of those prospects.

Understanding Buyer Needs

Buying center members seek to buy for many reasons. Some of the more common reasons usually evolve from some aspect of the cost and quality of the product. Specific primary buying needs and motives include increasing profits, increasing sales, producing a quality product, improving the operation's efficiency to create cost reductions, helpfulness of the salesperson's service, payment, trade-in allowances, delivery, and buying a product at the lowest price. Salespeople must determine each prospect's important buying needs, if they hope to be successful. They can then develop a sales presentation which emphasizes their respective product's features, advantages, and benefits, and which explains how their product can fulfill those needs.

A salesperson's initial task when first meeting the prospect is to differentiate between important buying needs and those of lesser or no importance. Figure 11–1 illustrates the concept that buyers have both important needs and other types of needs that are not primary reasons for buying a product. A salesperson must determine the prospects' important needs and concentrate on emphasizing product benefits that will satisfy these needs. Benefits that would satisfy a prospect's unimportant needs should be deemphasized in the sales presentation. If, for example, buying center members say that price is important, but a salesperson determines that

■ **FIGURE 11–1**   Seller Matches Buyers' Important Needs to Products' Benefits and Emphasizes These Needs in Sales Presentation

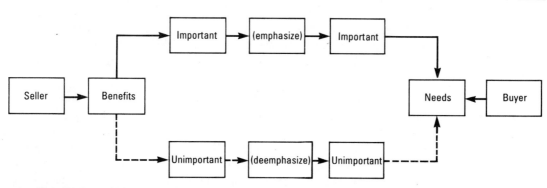

SOURCE: Charles M. Futrell, *ABC's of Selling* (Homewood, Ill.: Richard D. Irwin, 1988), p. 78. Used with permission.

they can afford the product and are also interested in quality, then the salesperson must emphasize the quality of the product being sold.

People buy for reasons other than what the product will actually do, or because of its price. Although customers usually buy the product to solve a rational need that the salesperson perceives to be important, they may also buy to satisfy an emotional need, which is not so easily recognized. It is important to understand this sales concept and to learn to determine the prospect's important buying needs. Some of the most common psychological buying needs include fear, risk proneness or risk aversion, security, curiosity, a desire to succeed, and self-preservation.

Methods to Uncover Important Needs of Buying Center Members

A salesperson must determine which buying needs are most important to the customer. How can this be done? Several methods are frequently utilized to uncover important needs:

- *Ask Questions.* Questions can often bring out needs that the prospect would not reveal or does not know exist. The salesperson asks, "Is a faster, more feature-oriented copier important to you?" "Yes, it is," says the buyer. "If I could give you the quickest, most multi-featured copier currently on the market, would you be interested?" However, care must be exercised as salespeople cannot play 20 Questions with the prospect. There are only so many questions which can be asked before the prospect will begin to show signs of irritability.

- *Observe.* Look at the prospects and study their surroundings. Experienced salespeople can determine a great deal about people by observing such things as the way they dress, or where they live or work.

- *Listen.* Prospects may drop leading remarks like, "I would really like to have a more efficient payroll system than the one I am now using."

- *Talk to Others.* Ask others about a prospect's needs. For example, ask an office manager's secretary about the manager's level of satisfaction with a personal computer.

- *Combination.* A skillful salesperson may talk to others, listen to a prospect, probe with questions, and make careful observations—all in an effort to uncover the prospect's needs.

Once a salesperson has ascertained a prospect's major buying need, he or she is ready to relate the customer's needs to his or her product's benefits. Salespeople can effectively sell to buyers only after they have determined the buyers' needs and motivations, and have identified the problems they are attempting to solve in purchasing a particular product or service. Basically, this is what selling is all about.

It is usually not an easy task for salespeople to learn the customer's needs and to demonstrate how their respective product or service benefits

---

■ **EXHIBIT 11–2**   Uncovering the Behavioral Styles of Buyers

---

What behavioral styles do buyers exhibit when interacting with salespeople? Buyers can be classified into the following categories:

- The *hard bargainer* obtains several price quotations or uses several sources of supply for the same item; salespeople may find it difficult to make a sale.
- The *sales job facilitator* is amenable to a salesperson's solicitations and even attempts to make the transaction go smoother.
- The *straight shooter* behaves with integrity and propriety; these buyers rarely use their buying power to obtain concessions.
- The *socializer* enjoys the personal interaction of the buyer-seller relationship.
- The *persuader* will attempt to market his or her own company to salespersons to stimulate a favorable impression of the buying firm.
- The *considerate buyer* displays compassion and concern for the salesperson; these buyers may be willing to accept substitute products.

A mutually beneficial exchange relationship results when the salesperson tailors selling strategy to a buyer's behavioral style.

SOURCE: Alan J. Dubinsky and Thomas N. Ingram, "A Classification of Industrial Buyers: Implications for Sales Training," *Journal of Personal Selling and Sales Management* 1 (Fall-Winter 1981–82), pp. 46–51. Used with permission.

---

directly and fully speak to such needs. Buyers and other members of the buying center typically have a multitude of different needs, and may not clearly understand or see their unconscious needs or problems. The salesperson's challenge is to understand the behavioral style of each prospective buyer and to convert the customers' apparently unconscious needs into recognized and understood needs. Exhibit 11–2 offers several behavioral styles which prospective buyers typically exhibit when interacting with salespeople.

Buyers and sellers are engaged in a special and unique relationship. As the salesperson attempts to understand and to meet a prospect's needs, that same prospect is evaluating the particular supplier's capability and rating the salesperson according to the buyer's likes and dislikes. Exhibit 11–3 identifies the characteristics of both outstanding and least desirable salespersons, according to a select group of purchasing managers. Outstanding salespeople were thought to have such qualities as thoroughness and good follow-through, and the least desirable salespeople often used high-pressure selling tactics and talked too long about irrelevant matters. Only an understanding of the dynamic nature and interdependency of this buyer-seller relationship will enable the salesperson to have a true understanding of buyer behavior.

■ THE SELLING SPECTRUM

Different Approaches to the Sales Presentation

After the earlier steps in the sales process of prospecting and qualifying have been completed, several general approaches to the sales presentation must be considered. Three major approaches to the sales presentation are

■ **EXHIBIT 11–3** Buyers Rate Salespersons: Likes and Dislikes

A sample of 300 purchasing managers was asked to identify the characteristics of both outstanding and least desirable salespersons:

The characteristics attributed to the outstanding salesperson were as follows:

- Thoroughness and follow-through
- Complete product knowledge
- Willingness to pursue the best interests of the buyer within the supplier firm
- Sound marketing knowledge and willingness to keep the buyer informed

Among the characteristics that can alienate buyers are as follows:

- Hard-selling, high-pressure tactics
- Talking too long about unrelated matters
- Exhibiting little interest in meeting the buyer's real needs

SOURCE: Larry Giunipero and Gary Zenz, "Impact of Purchasing Trends on Industrial Marketers," *Industrial Marketing Management* 11 (February 1982), pp. 17–23. Used with permission.

■ **TABLE 11–2** The Buying/Selling Process

Problem-Solving Model	Formularized Model (AIDA)	Buying-Decisions Model
Sell the interview	Attention	Decides to pay attention
Establish a need or problem	Interest	Decides there is a need
Solve the problem	Desire	Decides product or service will solve need
		Decides the company is acceptable
		Decides the salesperson is acceptable
Close	Action	Decides to buy

SOURCE: James R. Young and Robert W. Mondy, *Personal Selling: Function, Theory, and Practice* (Hinsdale, Ill.: Dryden Press, 1978), p. 158. Used with permission.

found in the (1) formularized model (AIDA), (2) buying-decisions model, and (3) problem-solving model. Table 11–2 reveals the process used in the three models. Each furnishes an insight into the buying/selling process, but from a different point of view.[6]

The Formularized (AIDA) Model. (AIDA is an acronym for Attention, Interest, Desire, and Action.) In the **formularized (AIDA) model** the salesperson takes the prospect through the first three stages in order to evoke action (purchase) from the consumer. An inherent danger in this type of sales presentation is that the mental states of the salesperson and the prospect may not be tuned in to the same stage of the selling formula. For example, the salesperson might assume that the prospect is at the interest stage, when, in fact, the prospect may already be at the desire stage. In this type of situation, the salesperson may well lose the sale because of

---

[6]James R. Young and Robert W. Mondy, *Personal Selling: Function, Theory, and Practice* (Hinsdale, Ill.: Dryden Press, 1978), pp. 156–60.

the prospect's impatience or inability to engage in spontaneous purchase action. However, the formularized model seems to be well suited for use by a relatively new salesperson who is too inexperienced to recognize the buying motives of individual prospects.

The Buying-Decisions Model.   The **buying-decisions model** assumes that the prospect will make a series of smaller, individual decisions before making the final decision either to accept or to reject the product. Therefore, the salesperson will tailor the presentation to achieve a number of decisions aimed at an ultimate decision to purchase the product or service in question. For instance, a photocopier salesperson would lead an office manager toward the final decision of investing in a new copying machine by having him or her decide such issues as how large a copier is needed, what features are necessary for the copier to have, how much usage is the copier likely to receive, how clear must the reproductions be, and how much is the office manager prepared or willing to spend on a photocopier. Once the prospect has made these decisions, it is much easier for the salesperson to promote the features and benefits of the product in such a way that will lead the potential buyer to a positive purchasing decision. Once again, a possible weakness in this model is that the salesperson and the prospect may be at different stages of decision making at any given time. The salesperson must carefully lead the prospect through each of the prepurchase decision stages in order to keep the model going in a positive direction. Only the successful closing of the sale can prevent the prospect from regressing to an earlier prepurchase decision stage.

The Problem-Solving Model.   The **problem-solving model** centers on the specific needs, motives, and objectives of the prospect. There must be an air of mutual trust and respect between the salesperson and the prospective customer. As such, the problem-solving model is quite similar to the need-satisfaction theory of personal selling. The salesperson must skillfully integrate product knowledge into the solution of the problem so as to exert **expert power** (the degree of perceived knowledge, information, and skill possessed by the power holder) over the prospect. Expert power of the salesperson has been found to be a stronger determinant of perceived trust by the customer than has **referent power** (the degree of perceived attraction between the salesperson and the customer).[7] A prospect who can accord a salesperson expert power is much more likely to allow the closing of a sale because he or she generally feels more comfortable in accepting the judgment of the salesperson that his or her product or service will solve the prospect's purchasing need or problem. In this case, "what you know" seems to be, for once, more important than "who you know." The problem-solving model seems to be a particularly useful sales model when *creative selling* (helping the customer buy) is needed.

---

[7] P. Busch and D. T. Wilson, "An Experimental Analysis of a Salesman's Expert and Referent Bases of Social Power in the Buyer-Seller Dyad," *Journal of Marketing Research* 13 (February 1976), pp. 3–11.

Types of Sales Positions and Selling Styles in the Business Market

Reaching business markets effectively requires a great variety of salespeople and selling styles. The following represent the major types of salespeople employed to serve this market; account representatives, detail salespeople, sales engineers, nontechnical products sales representatives, service salespeople, and agent salespeople. (Table 11–3 offers a brief description of the activities of each of these salespeople.) Another way to look at the business selling function is to classify salespeople by the tasks they perform. Sales tasks are activities carried out by salespeople and can be classified into two broad categories: creative selling and service selling. **Creative selling** deals with arousing demand and influencing patronage, and **service selling** assists the customer in bringing the sale to completion.[8]

A useful classification proposed in the classic article by H. Robert Dodge might include four types of sales tasks: development, missionary, maintenance, and support.[9] Figure 11–2 arranges these tasks in a continuum, with examples of each type of sales task. **Sales development** refers to the creation of customers through methods such as motivating a customer to change suppliers, whereas **missionary sales** provides necessary personal

■ **TABLE 11–3**   Classification of Business-to-Business Sales Personnel

Account representatives	Salespeople who call on customers who are already established.
Detail salespeople	Salespeople who provide details relative to promotional activities. Such a salesperson might visit the offices of medical doctors and attempt to inform them of the specific possibilities of a new drug. These salespeople seldom get credit for a sale; instead, the credit usually goes to an intermediary.
Sales engineers	A title originally bestowed to increase esteem of those who held it is that of *sales engineer.* This title has come to signify that the salesperson has technical know-how relative to the construction and/or application of the product. Salespeople in such areas as heavy machinery, electronic parts and equipment, and raw materials often bear this title.
Nontechnical business products sales representatives	Individuals who sell nonsell, nontechnical, tangible products, such as floor wax.
Service salespeople	Service salespeople are in the business of selling services, that is, intangibles. They may sell such things as management consulting and advertising. There is also the *missionary salesperson* classification, which is defined in this text.

SOURCE: Arthur Meridan, "Optimizing the Number of Industrial Salespersons," *Industrial Marketing Management* 11 (1982), pp. 63–74. Used with permission.

[8]Eugene M. Johnson, David L. Kurtz, and Eberhard Scheuing, *Sales Management: Concepts, Practices, and Cases* (New York: McGraw-Hill, 1986), p. 55.

[9]H. Robert Dodge, "The Role of the Industrial Salesman," *Mid-South Quarterly Review,* January 1972, pp. 11–15.

■ **FIGURE 11–2**   Continuum of Business-to-Business Sales Tasks

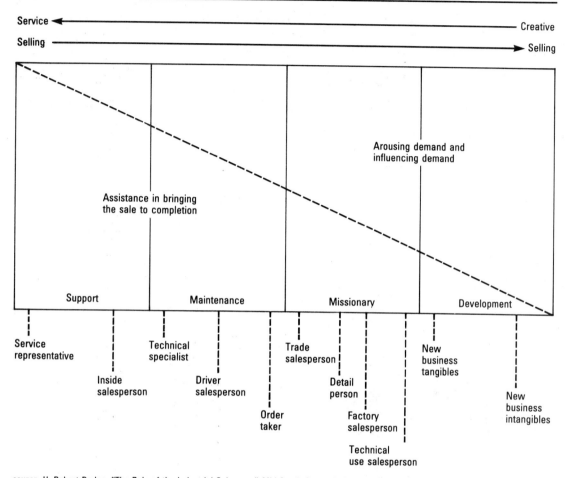

SOURCE: H. Robert Dodge, "The Role of the Industrial Salesman," *Mid-South Quarterly Review,* January 1972, p. 13. Used with permission.

selling assistance. **Maintenance selling** involves the continuation of present sales volume from existing customers, and **support sales** provides continuing service to the buyer and occasionally involves selling directly to the buyer by suggesting a replacement item rather than the repair of an older product. All these tasks are important, and each makes a significant contribution to the total marketing effort.[10]

Figure 11–3 provides a model of career paths in business to business selling, and Exhibit 11–4 briefly describes the activities of various levels of business sales job titles. The two career paths shown in Figure 11–3 seem quite similar, but in reality are quite different. The sales career path leads to a position which may or may not involve aspects of the sales manager's job, such as the planning, direction, organization, and control over the activities of others. This is an important distinction, as the best sales-

---
[10]Ibid., p. 13.

■ FIGURE 11–3   Career Paths in Business-to-Business Selling

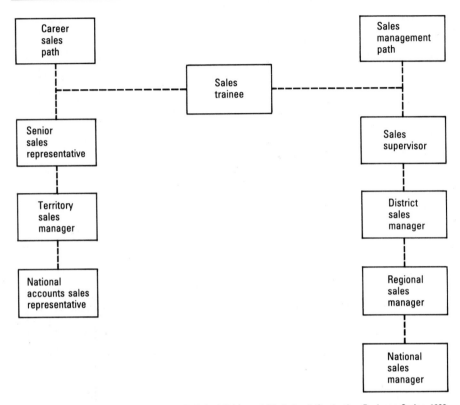

SOURCE: Vincent L. Pesce, Jr., "Careers in Technical Sales and Marketing," *Graduating Engineer,* Spring 1980, p. 105. Used with permission.

person does not always make the best sales manager. Different skills must be acquired before successful salespeople can make the necessary adjustments to being successful sales managers. We will explore this topic in detail in Chapter 12.

Among the major selling styles utilized in reaching markets are consultative selling, negotiation, systems selling, telemarketing, and team selling. (See Exhibit 11–5 for a brief definition of each of these styles of selling.) Because of their increasing popularity and usage by marketers, more complete discussions of *systems selling* and *telemarketing* follow.

■ SOME CONTEMPORARY TRENDS IN BUSINESS SELLING

The Importance of Systems Selling

Salespeople have increasingly recognized that buyers prefer to buy a whole solution to their purchasing problem and not make all the separate deci-

■ EXHIBIT 11–4   Typical Business-to-Business Sales Titles

Top-Level Marketing Management

Marketing vice president.   Typically, the top marketing executive in the company or division.

Sales vice president.   Sometimes another title for marketing vice president, but sometimes the top sales executive who will report to either the president or the marketing vice president.

Top-Level Line Sales Management

National sales manager.   The top sales executive responsible for all sales-force related activities.

General sales manager.   Another title for national sales manager.

Middle-Level Line Sales Management

National account sales manager.   Usually responsible for a separate, high-quality sales force which calls on national accounts. Often the only person in the national account sales force and responsible for actual selling; but the accounts are so large that the position needs a relatively high-level manager.

Regional, divisional, or zone sales manager.   These are titles for high-level field sales managers to whom other field sales managers report. Occasionally, the titles are used for first-level sales management jobs in which salespeople are managed.

Market sales manager.   A sales manager responsible for salespeople calling on a specific group of accounts. Often this position has marketing responsibility in addition to sales management and perhaps sales responsibility. A company which specializes its sales force by market will have one market sales manager to head each separate sales force.

Product sales manager.   The same as market sales manager except that the job is organized around a product line instead of a customer category. The product sales managers are usually more involved with product-oriented decisions than are market managers.

Lower-Level Line Sales Management

District or field sales manager.   The first-line sales manager to whom the salespeople report.

Upper-Level Sales Positions

Account executive, key account salesperson, national account salesperson, and *major account salesperson.*   These people are responsible for selling to major accounts.

Typical Sales Positions

Salesperson, field salesperson, territory manager, account representative, and *sales representative.*   All are typical titles for the salesperson responsible for selling and servicing a variety of accounts.

Staff Sales Management

These positions are usually functionally oriented and include titles, such as *manager of sales training, sales analyst,* etc. The typical staff responsibilities include training, recruiting, and sales analysis. More general staff positions include the title, *assistant to the national sales manager.* Assistant national sales managers may be either line or staff managers. Staff positions may occur at any level in the organization. Some companies with divisional sales forces, for example, have a job of *corporate vice president of sales* who has no line sales management responsibility. Other companies have *regional* or *area sales vice presidents* responsible for aiding salespeople from various divisions with major account sales. This is found, for example, in some weapons marketers where various product-oriented divisions call upon the same buying organization.

SOURCE: Benson P. Shapiro, *Sales Program Management: Formulation and Implementation* (New York: McGraw-Hill, 1977), p. 7. Used with permission.

■ **EXHIBIT 11–5** Common Business-to-Business Selling Styles

- *Consultative selling* occurs when the salesperson assumes the role of a consultant, helping to improve the profitability of the client. The consultative salesperson, by becoming an expert on the client's business operations, providing analytical expertise, and solving problems, attempts to offer a level of value beyond competitors.
- *Negotiation* describes a selling style designed to maximize the benefits of a transaction for both buyer and seller. The goal is to form a salesperson-customer partnership with common objectives, mutually beneficial strategies, and a common defense against others outside the partnership.
- *Systems selling* has evolved to meet the rising sophistication and increased materials management concerns of organizational buyers. The salesperson for a business forms' supplier might begin by defining a prospect's record and information needs, then prescribe a package of machines and forms, offer a recommended layout of facilities, establish a training program for employees, and design operating procedures and maintenance arrangements.
- *Team selling* occurs when the business to business seller assembles a team of personnel with functional expertise that matches the specialized knowledge of key buying influences within the customer firm. The mode of operation adopted by the selling team varies by selling situation. Occasionally, the entire sales team will take part in the presentation to the buying center, while in other cases, they are contacted at various points in the selling process when the salesperson requires technical expertise.

SOURCES: Thomas R. Wotruba, "The Changing Character of Industrial Selling," *European Journal of Marketing* 14 (1980), pp. 293–302; W. J. Hannaford, "Systems Selling: Problems and Benefits for Buyers and Sellers," *Industrial Marketing Management* 5 (1976), pp. 139–45; Lee Adler, "Salesmen Must Be Consultants, Too," *Industry Week,* March 18, 1974, pp. 40–43; and Lee Adler, "Systems Approach to Marketing," *Harvard Business Review* 45 (May-June 1967), pp. 105–118. Used with permission.

sions involved. Consequently, many firms have adopted the practice of **systems selling** as a marketing tool. Systems selling has two components. First, the supplier sells a group of *interlocking products*. For example, the supplier sells not only glue, but applicators and dryers as well. Second, the supplier sells a system of production, inventory control, distribution, and other services to meet the buyer's need for a smooth-running operation. Systems selling is a key marketing strategy for winning and holding accounts.[11]

Systems selling is a key marketing strategy in bidding to build large-scale projects, such as dams, steel factories, irrigation systems, sanitation systems, pipelines, utilities, and even new towns. Companies such as Bechtel, Fluor, and other project engineering firms must compete on price, quality, reliability, and other attributes to win awards. The award often goes to the firm which best meets the customer's real needs. Consider the following:

> The Indonesian government requested bids to build a cement factory near Jakarta. An American firm made a proposal which included choosing the site, designing the cement factory, hiring the construction crews, assembling the materials and equipment, and turning over the finished factory to the Indonesian government. A Japanese firm, in outlining its proposal, included all of these services plus hiring and training the workers to run the

[11]Philip Kotler, *Marketing Management: Analysis, Planning, Implementation, and Control,* 6th ed. (Englewood Cliffs, N.J.: Prentice-Hall, 1988), p. 212. Also see Albert L. Page and Michael Siempliski, "Product Systems Marketing," *Industrial Marketing Management* 12 (1983), pp. 89–99.

factory, exporting the cement through their trading companies, and using the cement to build some new office buildings in Jakarta. Although the Japanese proposal involved more money, its appeal was greater, and they won the contract. Clearly, the Japanese viewed the problem not as one of just building the cement factory (the narrow view of systems selling), but of running it in a way which would contribute to the country's economy. They saw themselves not as an engineering project firm, but as an economic development agency. They took the broadest view of the customer's needs. This is true systems selling.[12]

It is likely that systems selling will continue to be popular in business to business markets as buyers increasingly appreciate the opportunity to find quick, convenient, and total solutions to their buying problems.

The Importance of Telemarketing

Telephone sales, or **telemarketing,** now plays integral cost-cutting and revenue-generating roles in many corporations. By the late 1990s it will be a widely used tool by most organizations in virtually every industry. Telemarketing's major impact today is in business to business applications, not only in soliciting and retaining business customers but also in managing and servicing accounts, taking orders, and conducting surveys among other marketing functions. Companies using the technique include IBM, Merrill Lynch, General Electric, and Allstate. (See Exhibit 11–6 for more descrip-

■ **EXHIBIT 11–6**   Telemarketing—The Wave of the Future in Outside Selling?

The job of outside selling—the kind where the salesperson goes to the customer, in contrast to inside (or across the counter) selling—is changing dramatically these days. Instead of the traditional in-person sales call, a growing number of sales representatives are using the telephone and/or the computer to talk with customers. In effect, outside selling—especially outside business selling—is going electronic.

The prime factor accounting for this change is the dramatic increase in the cost of keeping salespeople on the road. Some companies estimate that their travel expenses—transportation, hotel, and meals—are higher than their sales representative's compensation (salary, commission, and bonus).

Telephone selling, of course, has been used by many companies for decades. What is new today, however, is the innovative use of communication systems involving the telephone, television, and sometimes the computer, to aid a company's selling effort and other marketing activities. The term *telemarketing* has been coined to describe these marketing communication systems.

Raleigh Bicycles used telemarketing to reduce the amount of personal selling needed for contacting its dealers. In the first year, sales force travel costs were reduced by 50 percent, and sales in a single quarter were up by 34 percent. Avis uses computer-assisted telemarketing programs in its fleet-leasing operations to locate and qualify prospects, and to generate good leads for its salespeople. The program cuts sales force costs, substantially improves the sales force's available selling time, and reduces the time required to close a sale by one month. The B. F. Goodrich Chemical Group provides yet another example of the use of telemarketing to support field sales. Goodrich uses a "telemarketing center" for order-taking, customer service, and information dissemination purposes. When customers contact the company, a center

continued

---

[12]Ibid., p. 212.

■ **EXHIBIT 11-6** *(concluded)*

specialist calls up the customer's account file on a computer screen, records the order, checks the inventory supply, and talks with production and shipping to schedule shipment when necessary. Field sales personnel are then provided current inventory data and estimated arrival times of customer orders. Field sales representatives can then schedule follow-up visits to high-volume order accounts, thus increasing both the number and the quality of personal and professional contacts between B. F. Goodrich and its best customers.

Some companies—Louisiana Oil and Tire Company, for example—have increased sales and reduced costs by taking their field salespeople away from their traveling jobs and bringing them into the office. Industrial Fabricators of Jackson, Tennessee, has done the same. This company replaced its field sales force of 39 individuals with an in-house telemarketing department of 14 persons. With this change, sales of industrial-strength wiping cloths went up 25 percent, while selling costs decreased by 30 percent. In the office these representatives have been trained to sell by telephone. In effect, personal selling and order taking are being moved from the field to a well-trained inside sales force. The field selling in these firms is shifting to sales promotion work, such as instructing customers or providing technical advice and service.

In some companies, telemarketing is making the order-taking sales representative virtually obsolete. For instance, American Hospital Supply and some of its customers have a sophisticated mainframe computer capacity so that the buyer's computer can talk to American Hospital's computer. The buyer's computer can determine product availability and shipping dates; and, finally, can even place an order. No salespeople are involved, and there is a lot less paperwork. Ford, Chrysler, General Motors, and American Motors are jointly developing a system whereby a manufacturer and its large suppliers will communicate electronically. This system will eliminate many personal sales calls and a mountain of paperwork.

In Europe, firms in the automobile, chemical, steel, and shipbuilding industries are developing electronic communication systems involving manufacturers, suppliers, and even customs agents and shipping agents.

The examples cited above will save millions, and perhaps even billions, of dollars of personal selling expenses, and other communications expenses. Furthermore, these telemarketing processes are expected to increase the operating efficiency and time responsiveness of the participating industries.

SOURCES: "Rebirth of a Salesman: Willy Loman Goes Electronic," *Business Week*, February 27, 1984, pp. 103–104; "Detroit Tries to Level a Mountain of Paperwork," *Business Week*, August 26, 1985, p. 94; John I. Coppett, and Roy Dale Vorhees, "Telemarketing: Supplement to Field Sales," *Industrial Marketing Management*, August 1985, pp. 213–16; Roy Vorhees and John Coppett, "Telemarketing in Distribution Channels," *Industrial Marketing Management* 12 (1983), p. 106; "Industrial Newsletter," *Sales & Marketing Management* 131 (November 14, 1983), p. 32; Ed Zotti, "There's Madness in Their Methods," *Advertising Age*, November 28, 1983, pp. M54–M57, and Lawrence Strauss, *Electronic Marketing* (White Plains, N.Y.: Knowledge Industry Publications, 1983). Used with permission.

tive examples of firms currently using telemarketing as part of their promotional mix). The rapid expansion of telemarketing is most attributable to the ever increasing cost of making a sales call in person. Additionally, the typical sales representative makes an average of four to five sales calls per day, while a telecommunicator makes an average 10 to 15 phone contacts in one hour. Although the final sale will not always be closed on the telephone, telemarketing will screen prospects on whom the company can focus its sales and marketing efforts.

At Fairfield, Connecticut-based General Electric Company, telemarketing permeates so many business operations that "determining senior management's role in setting telemarketing strategy is a question we are dealing with right now," according to Richard J. Huether, GE's manager of telemarketing development.[13] At GE, telemarketing is teamed up with direct mail, fliers, and other promotional approaches. Says Huether, "I hesitate to say that what we are doing is replacing salespeople. We, instead, are better utilizing the strengths of our sales organization. Many of our people are engineers, and taking orders isn't the best use of their time."[14] Business to business firms spent $28 billion on telemarketing in 1986, so telemarketing will likely continue to be a big sales' buzzword throughout the 1990s.[15]

The Emergence of Saleswomen

Business to business sales was once considered to be exclusively a man's world. Many of the reasons why women were excluded from business selling for so many years were based on sexual stereotypes which included "tradition," women's "inability" to travel and to be away from home overnight, their presumed lack of technical knowledge, sexual exploitation, the priorities of marriage (either getting or staying married), and children. These last two factors were presumed to cause excessive absenteeism and turnover. Yet during the last decade, selling seems to have finally tapped this vital source of new sales power—women. Although much of the initial pressure to hire women for sales positions came from the Equal Employment Opportunity Act and affirmative action guidelines, the success of women in these positions has induced many companies to employ increasing numbers of saleswomen. The Bureau of Labor Statistics reports that there has been a dramatic increase in the number of females selling commodities other than retail products. Brown and Bigelow, a manufacturer of advertising specialty items, had no saleswomen until the mid-1980s. Today, 25 percent of its salespeople are women.

More and more women are moving into sales, assuming positions that were formerly strictly the domain of males. Contemporary saleswomen are selling everything from high-tech computer systems and aluminum siding to steel, lumber, and machine parts. Diane Reader, a senior sales representative with Ricoh copiers, recently sold 184 percent of her quota, placing her among the top five salespeople in the company, and earning her a trip to Japan, the company headquarters.[16]

A 1978 study compared the responses of 169 salesmen and 20 saleswomen in similar jobs in regard to job satisfaction, job-related self-confidence, perceptions of the management control system, and career goals.[17] The findings in this study clearly revealed that saleswomen do differ from

---

[13]Rick Burnham, "Telemarketing's Role Grows in Corporations," *Investor's Daily,* October 13, 1988, pp. 1, 34.

[14]Ibid., pp. 1, 34.

[15]B. Donath, "The $100-Billion Marketing Mix," *Business Marketing* 71 (June 1986), p. 4.

[16]Rayne Skolnik, "A Woman's Place Is on the Sales Force," *Sales and Marketing Management,* April 1985, p. 34.

their male counterparts in how they view their jobs. In contrast to the males in the study sample, the women expressed greater importance for independence in their work and for meeting different people; relatively low satisfaction in the areas of co-workers and supervision; lower self-confidence on many of the job-related measures used in the study, such as promotion possibilities and looking forward to a secure future; and a less favorable view of their firm's management control system. The findings of this study suggested that saleswomen are different from their male counterparts in similar jobs, and that sales managers should take those differences into consideration in their leadership style, management control systems, and training programs.

A 1984 study examined how purchasing managers rated salesmen and saleswomen in a variety of job-related criteria.[18] Responses from the study sample indicated that men were rated higher on (1) knowledge of the companies being sold to, (2) product knowledge, (3) understanding of the buyer's problems, (4) provision of technical assistance, and (5) presentation of new ideas to buyers. Comparatively, women were rated higher on (1) being vigorous and having a lot of drive, (2) knowing how to listen, (3) preparing for sales presentations, (4) following through on deliveries, (5) personalizing the sales presentation, (6) willingness to expedite rush orders, and (7) not bypassing the purchasing people. A careful analysis of this study seems to indicate that saleswomen are rated somewhat higher than their male counterparts in providing postsale services, attentiveness to detail, enthusiasm for their jobs, and a socially comfortable selling environment. It also indicated that women are competent and effective in field selling, and that many purchasing professionals do not harbor negative feelings in regard to their employment.

The Usage of Terminals and Laptop Computers

Portable computer terminals, which include a keyboard, a flat display screen, a hard-copy printer, and an acoustical coupler, can be fitted into a regular-sized brief case. These terminals are now widely utilized in selling because they enable sales representatives to solve customer problems during the sales presentation; to communicate with their home or branch offices; to process invoices; and to check on delivery times, past sales records, current prices, and call schedules.[19]

The use of portable computers to solve customer problems is demonstrated in the following example. Valmont Industries, a manufacturer of

---

[17]John E. Swan, Charles M. Futrell, and John T. Todd, "Same Job—Different Views: Women and Men in Industrial Sales," *Journal of Marketing* 42 (January 1978), pp. 92–98; See also Paul Busch and Ronald Bush, "Women Contrasted to Men in the Industrial Salesforce: Job Satisfaction, Values, Role Clarity, Performance and Propensity to Leave," *Journal of Marketing Research* 15 (August 1978), pp. 438–48.

[18]John E. Swan, David R. Rink, G. E. Kiser, and Warren G. Martin, "Industrial Buyer Image of the Saleswoman," *Journal of Marketing* 48 (Winter 1984), p. 114; See also "Women Often Better Reps, Miller Reports," *Industrial Marketing*, June 1977, p. 1.

[19]Douglas J. Dalrymple, *Sales Management: Concepts and Cases*, 2d ed. (New York: John Wiley & Sons, 1985), p. 107.

irrigation systems, equips its dealer salespeople with portable computers for use when they call on farmers. Before the terminals were used, salespeople spent four or five hours with a hand calculator and a long formula to get a solution to the customer's irrigation problems. Now the salesperson plugs the portable computer into a wall socket in the farmer's home, attaches a telephone to the terminal's acoustical coupler, and telephones Valmont's home office. The salesperson types in the information on the farmer's problem, and in about 10 minutes, the central computer sends back a printed analysis of what equipment is needed and how much it will cost the farmer. Valmont's district offices can also be contacted in this same manner. Salespeople can also use the portable terminals to check their electronic mailboxes on a daily basis. Valmont leases the terminals on a monthly basis, and realizes a savings of time rather than of money.[20]

Permanent terminals are also widely used in selling. These terminals are hard-wired to central computers, usually at the home or district office. Salespeople can use them at various sales offices to plan sequences of sales calls, and to identify customer needs and wants. The most highly desirable usage of permanent terminals would be for customers to install their own on-site terminals and connect them to the salesperson's mainframe computer system. In this way, the customer could order directly, and much paperwork and time would be saved for both buyer and seller.[21]

General Electric's Sentry System has been designed to sell electrical supplies and equipment to industrial contractors and to commercial accounts. Using this system, General Electric agrees to stock specific items at prenegotiated prices. If customers wish to place an order, they first log in on a terminal. The computer then asks a series of questions, and the buyer itemizes the order. Next, the computer informs the buyer of the total value of the order and processes it for delivery on the next working day. The Sentry System has been designed for large-order and/or frequent-order customers. Customers must rent the terminals; consequently, the system is not very feasible for small accounts. When General Electric's salespeople call on Sentry System accounts, they are able to spend their time introducing new products and solving customers' problems rather than writing up orders.[22]

Laptop computers generally weigh between 6 and 18 pounds; because they are now as fully functional as desktop machines and offer portability, they appear to be taking market share away from desktop computers. Zenith Data Systems Z-183 combines a hard-disk drive with long battery life and a readable screen, while Grid's Gridlite Model 1032 uses a high-impact plastic case, weighs only nine pounds, and uses a simple 720K floppy-disk drive. In Canada, Bernie E. Beleskey has rigged his own office

[20]*Sales & Marketing Management,* March 14, 1983, pp. 22–24.

[21]Douglas J. Dalrymple, *Sales Management: Concepts and Cases,* 2d ed. (New York: John Wiley & Sons, 1985), p. 108.

[22]Thayer C. Taylor, "GE Posts a Sentry to Give Customers Better Service," *Sales & Marketing Management,* December 6, 1982, pp. 46–48.

on wheels in a 1984 GMC van, complete with telephone, fax, and laptop computer. He racks up 3,700 miles per month as marketing director for Investment Center Financial Corporation, a seller of financial services. Beleskey likes his setup so much that he hopes to sell the same package to some of the 180 agents he supervises.[23] As we move through the 1990s, additional major advances in technology can be expected.

The Rapid Growth of Audio-Visual Aids

Over the last 15 years one of the fastest growing trends has been the stepped-up use of such audio-visual aids as filmstrips, movies, and videotape cassettes. Since people receive over 80 percent of their knowledge from their sense of sight, salespeople who use visual reinforcement as they talk are in a better position to communicate product benefits to prospects.[24] These devices have also assisted the salesperson in making more selling points in less time. While filmstrips and movies have been long utilized in sales training programs, many more companies are now sending them to the field with the salesperson. Used primarily in the past for heavy equipment selling, audio-visuals have gained considerable appeal during the last few years because of their increased portability and simple design.

Concept Questions

1. How can business to business salespeople uncover buyers' most important needs?
2. What is meant by systems selling?

■ THE PERSONAL SELLING PROCESS: A BUSINESS SALESPERSON'S PERSPECTIVE

In order to get a real sense of the personal selling process in business markets, we must simplify the description and focus on the important elements. From the perspective of the salesperson, a sequence listing of the most fundamental steps in personal selling can be generated. Of course, each firm in each different selling situation would have its own set of unique steps. For instance, a Xerox photocopier salesperson roughly follows five steps: approach, survey, demonstration, proposal, and close.[25]

Exhibit 11–7 offers one way in which the personal selling process can be envisioned from the point of view of the salesperson. For ease of explanation, this process has been divided into the three broad activities of *preliminary activities, face-to-face selling activities,* and *follow-up activities.*[26]

---

[23]*Business Week*, October 10, 1988, p. 104.

[24]*Exchange*, no. 17 (Stamford, Conn.: Xerox Learning Systems), p. 3.

[25]G. David Hughes and Charles H. Singler, *Strategic Sales Management* (Reading, Mass.: Addison-Wesley Publishing, 1983), p. 82.

[26]Richard P. Bagozzi, *Principles of Marketing Management* (Chicago: Science Research Associates, 1986), pp. 434–37.

Preliminary Activities

Review current accounts.
   Estimate potential for new purchases.
   Decide on who needs to be visited.
Identify new prospects in one's territory.
Assess customer needs, resources, possible points of resistance, etc.
Plan selling activities.
   What to say, how to say it, order of presentation, how to handle objections, etc.
Make call schedule.
Make appointments.
Perform needed research.
Evaluate one's own and competitors' products (e.g., attributes, price).
Assess home firm's ability to adapt product, meet delivery schedules, etc.

Face-to-Face Activities

Introduction
   Gain attention and build awareness of one's offering in customer.
   Create rapport and positive atmosphere.
   Obtain knowledge of customer needs, etc., and confirm or disconfirm hypotheses formed in
      preliminary activities.
   Convey information to customer.
   Build interest and create desire on part of customer to learn more.
   Tune in to nonverbal and symbolic communication as well as to the literal and the functional.
   Answer questions.
   Provide transition to next step.
Presentation
   Describe or demonstrate product or service.
   Specify attributes and benefits.
   Point out advantages vis-à-vis competition.
   Monitor overt and nonverbal evaluative responses of customer.
   Answer objections and adjust offer, if possible.
   Involve prospect in process actively (e.g., ask questions, encourage response, probe for likes
      and dislikes).
   Provide transition to next step.
Close
   Ask for commitment.
   Answer objections.
   Make offers and counteroffers.
   Reiterate benefits and promises.
   End on a positive note.

Follow-Up Activities

Complete and fill orders.
Ensure that all support arrangements are made.
Evaluate individual successes and failures to identify reasons behind each one.
Take measures to correct weaknesses.
Measure customer satisfaction with delivery, product performance, service, etc.
Take measures to reduce dissatisfaction (e.g., handle complaints).
Evaluate overall aggregate performance with respect to personal and firm goals.
Relate this to individual actions and the interpersonal process, make corrections in overall style,
   planning, presentation, etc.
Maintain relations with customers, supervisors, support people, etc.
Do research and continually renew one's knowledge and skills.

SOURCE: Richard P. Bagozzi, *Principles of Marketing Management* (Chicago: Science Research Associates, 1986),
p. 435. Used with permission.

Preliminary Activities

The **preliminary activities** arm the salesperson with the tools necessary to close a sale effectively as well as the ability to create the type of sales situation most favorable to meeting actual customer needs and wants. The first task is to review customer accounts to ascertain what customer needs to be serviced next, and to screen out current customers who could be placing larger orders of the same merchandise, or procuring new or established other product items and product lines which the seller has to offer. Salespeople can also simultaneously identify new prospects as they carefully scan their respective sales territories. During these preliminary activities, salespersons must also allocate sufficient time to the formal assessment of customer needs, resources, limitations, and likely objections to sales points. In other words salespeople are attempting to monitor and to update their profile of each account on an individualized basis.[27] This type of activity also enables salespeople to tailor their sales presentations to meet the needs and wants of the prospect by turning each product feature into a critical customer benefit. Salespersons should then make sure that they are thoroughly familiar with their own respective product mixes as well as with the respective product offerings of competitors. After satisfying these preliminary sales activities, sellers are then ready to generate a call schedule, make appointments, and design the form and content of the face-to-face activities involved in the selling process.

Face-to-Face Activities

Observe in Exhibit 11–7 that **face-to-face selling activities** are presented as a sequence of three primary steps: *introduction, presentation,* and *close.* In the introduction stage the salesperson attempts to capture the attention of his or her prospect; to create a positive selling atmosphere; and to build a comfortable professional, and perhaps personal, rapport with the prospect. (See the "Business to Business Marketing in Action" box for a discussion of the use of humor in setting the mood for a sales presentation.) Additionally, the salesperson must glean information about the customer's specific needs and wants in order to set the stage for the upcoming sales presentation.

The presentation stage focuses on actually getting down to business. The salesperson tries to present his or her product or service in the most favorable light to individual members of the buying center, and each product feature is associated with a customer benefit that will hopefully be of some importance to the prospect. Alert salespeople will constantly study their prospects, looking for both verbal and nonverbal cues as to how the presentation is progressing, and as to how the prospects are receiving the information the salespersons are disseminating. Certain cues from prospects, such as yawns, frequent checking of their watches, frowns, wrinkled foreheads, or raised eyebrows, should never go unnoticed or ignored by

---

[27]"The New Supersalesman: Wired for Success," *Business Week,* January 6, 1973, pp. 45–49.

BUSINESS TO BUSINESS MARKETING IN ACTION

Humor Can Be Your Best Sales Tool: Salespeople Say the Key Is Knowing Your Customers

For Rich Little, it's impersonations. For Mark Russell, satire. And for Robin Williams, insanity.

All of these entertainers have one thing in common. They know how to make people laugh. As a salesperson, you're never going to be expected to bring the house down on opening night. But you are expected to maintain relations with customers.

In their book, *The Magic of Thinking Big in Selling* John Doherty and Robert G. Hoehn say there's nothing like a well-placed joke to put you and your prospect at ease. The authors maintain that when you recognize a humorous situation and respond to it with a smile or a casual comment, prospects tend to relax and pay more attention to your sales presentation.

One of the real benefits of using humor, say the authors, is that it gives you total control of the selling situation. A lighthearted approach invites your customers to loosen up, listen, and ask questions. It creates a positive frame of mind that will ultimately put you in a better position to close sales.

Ed Weiss, a salesperson with Raritan Supply Company of Edison, New Jersey, agrees with the authors, saying that during his 35 years in sales, humor has been his most effective tool. "I'm not afraid to tell a joke, even when I first meet somebody," says Weiss. "It's not effective for me to go into a situation and pound on business. As far as I'm concerned, the guy who won't laugh at a joke has a problem— a problem that I'm not in a position to fix."

Tom Bullock, a sales manager at the Kaner Company in Los Angeles, maintains that any business day is a good time for a joke. "This is a tough business with people screaming about delivery schedules and under a lot of strain to get production moving. One of the best ways to reduce the tension is to use humor."

The key to using humor in business, says Roger Thibault of Valcourt Industrial Supply Company, Fall River, Massachusetts, is to know whom you're talking to. Says Thibault, "Be real careful when you use ethnic humor. If somebody is serious and doesn't have time for your antics, know when to back off."

However, Mario Mendoza, a salesperson at the Kalamazoo, Michigan, branch of GRS Industrial Supply Company, may have said it the best. "Nobody is going to buy a $100,000 machine if they don't feel comfortable with the person they are buying from. Humor is an extension of your personality, and that, in the end, is what we all sell."

SOURCE: Steven Zurier, "Strictly for Salesmen," *Industrial Distribution* 77 (February 1988), p. 51. Used with permission.

salespersons. Such feedback generally serves as rather definitive evidence as to the ineffectiveness of the sales presentation from the prospect's point of view.

Almost inevitably, the prospect will raise one or more objections to various selling points made by the salesperson. Frequently, these objections can be turned into actual reasons for buying the product or service.[28] But they can at times also mean that the product or service features and benefits outlined by the salesperson might be unclear to, or even disbelieved by, the prospect. In these latter cases, the salesperson may succeed or fail in closing the sale based on how well he or she has formerly thought out and practiced possible responses. Exhibit 11–8 outlines a four-step method

---

■ **EXHIBIT 11–8**   The Four-Step Method of Handling Sales Resistance

Step 1—Establishing Readiness

Prospect
   That price is far too high.
Salesperson
   Everything seems to cost more today, doesn't it?
Prospect
   You're sure right about that.
Salesperson
   Your firm expects you to make profitable purchases?
Prospect
   Yes, I do my best.
Salesperson
   This means you have to analyze carefully the full value in any proposition, doesn't it?
Prospect
   Yes, but I still say that your price is out of line.

Step 2—Clarifying the Objection

Salesperson
   Might I ask what you consider a fair price based on your value analysis?
Prospect
   Well, I don't have exact figures, but I'd say about 30 cents less a unit.
Salesperson
   What unit value would you place on our guarantee of uniform quality from batch to batch?
Prospect
   I don't know, but that doesn't amount to much. We test a sample out of each delivery ourselves.
Salesperson
   That sounds like a good precaution if you are not certain of quality. What does that cost?
Prospect
   I'd say about 5 cents prorated over the normal order.
Salesperson
   From a cost standpoint, what is your optimum order quantity?
Prospect
   About 1,000 units.

---

[28]Daniel K. Weadcock, "Your Troops Can Keep Control and Close the Sale—by Anticipating Objections," *Sales & Marketing Management,* March 17, 1980, p. 104.

■ **EXHIBIT 11-8**   *(concluded)*

Salesperson
   Would it increase your unit cost to order 4,000 at a time?
Prospect
   There would be some more dollars tied up on inventory.

Step 3—Mentally Formulating the Order

Salesperson
   (Our price breaks 30 cents a unit at 4,000 quantity. The buyer's estimate of testing cost is 5 cents. I can meet the price if I can get an order for 4,000 with delivery in modules of 1,000 as needed).

Step 4—Questioning to have the Prospect Answer the Objection

Salesperson
   If you could eliminate testing incoming purchases, it would save you at least 5 cents a unit, wouldn't it?
Prospect
   This is right, but we would need to be certain of quality if we did.
Salesperson
   Would a guarantee covering replacement of goods plus any and all costs or damages through faulty quality be attractive?
Prospect
   Yes.
Salesperson
   Would you place an order if you could save 5 cents under your own unit value estimate?
Prospect
   I sure would.
Salesperson
   By ordering 4,000 units, you gain the advantage of our volume price, which is 30 cents less per unit than when purchases are in smaller quantities. We will guarantee quality as I have outlined above so you can save the 5 cent unit cost of testing.

SOURCE: W. J. E. Crissy, William H. Cunningham, and Isabella C. M. Cunningham, *Selling: The Personal Force in Marketing* (New York: John Wiley & Sons, 1977), pp. 297–98. Used with permission.

by which the salesperson can handle sales resistance. These four steps include establishing readiness, clarifying the objection, mentally formulating the order, and using questioning to have the prospect answer the objection. During the entire sales presentation, and particularly during the time that objections to selling points are being raised, the salesperson must diligently work to get the prospect actively involved in the presentation, and genuinely interested in learning more about the product or service the salesperson is attempting to sell. Some of the methods the salesperson can use to involve and to interest prospects include: (1) stopping the presentation for a moment to inquire whether or not prospects have understood a particular product or service feature and resulting benefit; (2) probing for likes and dislikes and for general customer preferences in regard to the product or service being sold; and (3) giving prospects an opportunity to handle the product, or to explain any questions or problems that they might be having with the selling points offered by the salesperson. Generally speaking, during the presentation stage salespeople strive to convince prospects that it is in their best interests to purchase the particular product or service the salesperson is offering.[29]

The ultimate and most critical step in the face-to-face interaction is the closing. Of course, the purpose of any close is to ask the prospect for a formal commitment to purchase. Any number of closing techniques may be utilized in an effort to finalize the sale, including a restatement of product or service features and benefits, repeating successful responses to prospects' objections, and better arranging the terms of sale to suit the needs and desires of the prospect. Exhibit 11–9 describes some additional closing techniques commonly used in selling. Whether salespeople are successful or not in actually obtaining the close, they should strive to conclude the sales interview on a highly positive note. This type of effort will typically lead to future opportunities for them and their prospects to meet again, and perhaps to reach a sales agreement at that time.

■ **EXHIBIT 11–9** Closing Techniques Used in Business to Business Selling

---

Closing is simply asking for an order. There are many ways to do this. The professional industrial salesperson knows several closing techniques from which to select one that fits the specific prospect and selling situation. Some effective closing techniques are described below.

The *alternate proposal close* offers the prospect a choice between details. "Do you prefer a truck or rail shipment?" "Will the standard drill suit your needs, or would you prefer to go with the superior model that you have been examining?" The philosophy of this close is to ask for a relatively minor decision.

The *assumptive close* assumes that the prospect will make a commitment. After receiving a positive buying signal and verifying this with a trial close, the salesperson proceeds to write up the order or complete a shipping form. Then the prospect is asked to "sign your name here so that I can process the shipment."

The *gift close* provides the prospect with an added inducement for taking immediate action. "If you sign the purchase order today, I'm sure we can have the order delivered to you next week."

The *action close* suggests that the sales representative take an action that will consummate the sale. "Let me arrange an appointment with your attorney to work out the details of the transaction."

The *one-more-yes close* is based on the principle that saying yes can become a habit. The salesperson restates the benefits of the product in a series of questions that will result in positive responses. The final question asks the prospect to complete the sale.

The *balance-sheet close* is an effective technique to use with procrastinators. The salesperson and the prospect list the reasons for acting now on one side, and the reasons for delaying action on the other. If the salesperson has built a persuasive case, the reasons for immediate action will outweigh the reasons for delaying. Then the salesperson can ask for the order.

The *direct close* is clear and simple. The salesperson asks for a decision. Many salespeople feel that this is the best approach, especially if there are strong positive buying signals. Frequently, the salesperson summarizes the major points that were made during the presentation prior to asking for the close.

SOURCE: Eugene M. Johnson, David L. Kurtz, and Eberhard Scheuing, *Sales Management: Concepts, Practices, and Cases* (New York: McGraw-Hill, 1986), p. 80. Used with permission.

---

[29]G. Ray Funkhouser, "A Practical Theory of Persuasion Based on Behavioral Science Approaches," *Journal of Personal Selling and Sales Management*, November 1984, pp. 17–25.

Follow-Up Activities

A most important point to mention at this time is that the selling process does not end with the close. Exhibit 11–7 indicates that salespersons must attend to a wide variety of **follow-up activities** once the sale has been completed. A truly successful sale requires that an order be completed and that all support arrangements (product design, order processing, credit approval, shipping, delivery, etc.) be completed in a timely manner. After the sale, if the selling company is actively following the tenets of the marketing concept, customer satisfaction with both the product or service sold and the entire selling process must be evaluated, with changes made when and where appropriate and necessary. Salespeople should reflect upon the reasons why their sales presentations resulted in an exchange or a failure. If salespersons are unable to close the sale, they should carefully and thoughtfully examine those individual and collective factors that most likely accounted for the no-sale situation. Such reflection revolves around both the situation and the salesperson (self). Exhibit 11–10 details many of the worst mistakes salespeople can make in planning and implementing a sales call. Some, and perhaps many, changes might have to be made in each of the various stages of the selling process. Follow-up activities usually also involve the salesperson's maintaining strong and positive relationships with as many members of the buying center as possible. Again, this type of activity most often results in future opportunities for the salesperson to meet with numerous members of various buying centers, in an effort to consummate previously lost sales. In conclusion, salespeople should constantly be monitoring both their internal and external environments to note changes in competitive activities, governmental regulations, the economic climate, customer preferences, market behavior, etc. They should continually work to sharpen and refine their product knowledge, selling skills, and communications effectiveness.

■ INTERNATIONAL BUSINESS-TO-BUSINESS SELLING

International markets will present both special problems and tremendous opportunities for salespeople as we move through the 1990s. In the United States we carefully study both our customers and the culture to which they belong. Should we do any less for our customers and prospects in international markets? Examples of selling mistakes made by U.S. salespeople abound. Accepting a Japanese executive's business card and casually placing it in a pocket or wallet would be considered rude by that individual. The Japanese believe that the name, written or spoken, is something close to sacred. Similarly, presuming that all French executives sitting in a business meeting speak English, without first asking in French whether they do so, is a tactical blunder because the French are extremely proud of their heritage and their language.[30]

---

[30]"Helpful Hints and Faux Pas in International Sales," *Information World*, September 16, 1985, p. 30.

■ **EXHIBIT 11–10**   The Seven Deadly Sins of Business to Business Selling

When purchasing agents were asked as part of a survey to indicate the types of selling behavior that most typically accounted for lost sales opportunities, they listed the following "deadly sins":

1. *Lack of product knowledge.*   Salespeople must know their own product lines as well as the buyer's, or nothing productive can take place.

2. *Time wasting.*   Unannounced sales visits are a nuisance. When salespeople start droning on about golf or grandchildren, more time is wasted.

3. *Poor planning.*   Even a routine sales call should be preceded by some homework—maybe to see if it's really necessary.

4. *Pushiness.*   This includes prying to find out a competitor's prices, an overwhelming attitude, and "backdoor selling."

5. *Lack of dependability.*   Failure to stand behind the product, to keep communications clear, and to keep promises.

6. *Unladylike or ungentlemanly conduct.*   "Knocking" competitors, "boozing" at a business lunch, sloppy dress, and poor taste are not professional.

7. *Unlimited optimism.*   Honesty is preferred to the hallmark of the "Good News Bearers" who will promise anything to get an order. Never promise more than you can deliver.

A few of the more vigorous comments from purchasing agents who were disenchanted with certain behavioral characteristics of business salespeople:
- "They seem to take it personally if they don't get the business, as though you owe them something for constantly calling on you."
- "I don't like it when they blast through the front door like know-it-alls, and put on an unsolicited dog-and-pony show that will guarantee cost saving out in limbo somewhere."
- "Many salespeople are willing to give you the delivery date you want, book the order, and then let you face the results of their short quote."
- "They try to sell you, rather than the product."
- "After the order is won, the honeymoon is over."
- "Beware of the humble pest who is too nice to insult, won't take a hint, won't listen to blunt advice, and is selling a product you neither use nor want to use; yet, won't go away."

SOURCE: Charles M. Futrell, *ABC's of Selling* (Homewood, Ill.: Richard D. Irwin, 1984), p. 348. Used with permission.

International salespeople must deal with differences in language and currency, political and legal uncertainties, different kinds of buying wants and needs, and dissimilarities in culture and national policies. "Knowing your customer" is just as important abroad as it is at home, whether selling computers in North Africa, equipment and installations in Western Europe, or raw materials in Asia. U.S. salespeople must realize that they are the foreigners in other countries and conduct themselves accordingly. They must recognize, appreciate, and be sensitive to the differences between how business is conducted in the United States, and how it is conducted in each country in which they are working. Increased international selling by U.S. firms will force salespeople to become familiar with foreign languages, cultures, and politics.[31]

---

[31]"Partnership Selling: The Wave of the Future," *Marketing News*, December 19, 1988, p. 17.

Concept Questions

1. What is the ultimate and most critical step in face-to-face sales interaction?
2. What is an example of a mistake which a U.S. business sales-person might make in a foreign market?

SUMMARY

1. Personal selling involves persuasive and deliberate contact between a buyer and a seller for the specific purpose of creating an exchange between them. Personal selling is the primary promotional tool utilized in business to business selling and is generally supported by the other elements such as advertising, publicity, public relations, and sales promotion. In this manner business selling differs greatly from consumer selling, which relies much more heavily on mass selling tools and advertising in particular.

2. Business to business selling can only be truly appreciated when both the scope and nature of salespeople's daily activities are understood. Such activities typically include selling, maintenance of distributor relationships, planning, decision making, and managing communication.

3. The cost of a sales call has been rising rapidly over the last decade as has the cost of personal selling in general. Because the cost of personal selling can vary so significantly, depending on such factors as the type of product and industry, the size of the firm, and the degree of personal contact with prospects necessary to close a sale, companies must constantly monitor and assess the best methods by which to distribute and sell their products and services.

4. Buyers seek to buy for many reasons, which include increasing profits and sales, producing a quality product, helpfulness of the salesperson's service, trade-in allowances, etc. Once the salesperson has identified the prospect's important buying needs, he or she can specifically tailor a sales presentation to that prospect and capitalize on his or her product or service's features, benefits, and advantages that most directly match that prospect's buying needs, wants, and preferences.

5. The salesperson can use different approaches to his or her sales presentation, depending upon the type of customer or the selling situation involved. These approaches include the formularized, buying-decisions, and problem-solving models. Reaching business markets effectively also requires a great variety of salespeople and selling styles. A careful analysis of selling tasks can aid the salesperson in deciding what priorities to place on which selling activities to ensure a more successful sales effort.

6. Personal selling is constantly evolving and growing ever more complex. Among the most important contemporary trends in selling are systems selling, telemarketing, the increasing presence of saleswomen, the sales assistance provided by both portable and permanent computer

terminals, and the rapid growth of audio-visual aids as helpful tools during the sales presentation.

7. The selling process can be examined in a variety of ways, but understanding it from the salesperson's viewpoint seems highly appropriate. The selling process basically involves three main selling activities: preliminary activities, face-to-face activities, and follow-up activities. Each of these involves a multitude of tasks and plays an important role in the effective selling of business products and services. The salesperson should constantly monitor both his or her internal and external environments, looking for important changes in the buyer-seller interactive process, and should continually sharpen and refine his or her product knowledge, selling skills, and communications effectiveness.

8. International markets will present both special challenges and tremendous opportunities for salespeople during the 1990s. International salespeople must learn to deal effectively with international markets in terms of differences in language and currency, political agendas, laws, buying wants and needs, culture, and national policies. U.S. salespeople must know their international customers just as well as they know their domestic clients.

KEY TERMS

benefit segmentation	missionary sales
benefit selling	preliminary activities
buying-decisions model	problem-solving model
creative selling	referent power
expert power	sales development
face-to-face selling activities	service selling
follow-up activities	support sales
formularized (aida) model	systems selling
maintenance selling	telemarketing

REVIEW QUESTIONS

1. How does the use of personal selling differ in consumer goods' markets and business goods' markets? What is the primary promotional element utilized in selling to each of these two markets?

2. Discuss the five primary activities salespeople typically perform on a daily basis. Why is decision making so intertwined with the other four activities?

3. What factors cause the cost of personal selling to vary so significantly?

4. Explain the importance of using benefit selling in reaching buyers effectively. Discuss five methods by which a salesperson can identify the important buying needs of his or her prospects.

5. Describe three major models commonly used in making sales presentations. Under what circumstances would the use of each one seem most appropriate?

6. Identify and define four basic types of sales tasks: development, missionary, maintenance, and support. Discuss four major selling styles used in reaching business markets.

7. Define systems selling and explain its importance in selling. Why has telemarketing become such a major force for penetrating both new and established markets?

8. Why were saleswomen not utilized in business selling for so many years? Why are they increasing in such large numbers today? How are portable and permanent computer terminals currently being employed in sales? What constitutes the ideal customer application of the availability of permanent computer terminals for selling? What is the value of laptop computers?

9. Why have audio-visual aids gained such popularity as tools to use in making sales presentations over the past decade? Which types of visual-aid equipment are used most frequently in business selling?

10. Distinguish among preliminary activities, face-to-face activities, and follow-up activities in the selling process. How do selling tasks differ among the introduction, presentation, and close stages of face-to-face selling activities. Why are follow-up activities an illustration of the use of the marketing concept in selling to buyers?

11. What are the primary differences between conducting business in U.S. markets and transacting business in international markets? Why is it just as important for U.S. salespeople to know their international customers as well as they know their domestic customers?

CHAPTER CASES

Case 11–1   Douglas & Co.*

Bill Edwards smiled to himself—but he was worried. Bill remembered how red Compton's face had gotten when he told the Division Director why he did not want the position as Internal Sales Manager (see Exhibit 1).

A dead-end job; I'd be nothing more than a telephone operator and message center. I prefer to stay in sales; I want to be the Sales Training Manager and eventually the Regional Marketing Manager.

Compton was barely able to contain himself. Compton's reply through clinched teeth—"We'll see about that."

---

*Source: This case was prepared by Professors Lawson E. Barclay and Paul C. Thistlewhaite of Western Illinois University. Copyright © 1977 by Western Illinois University. Used with permission.

■ EXHIBIT 1

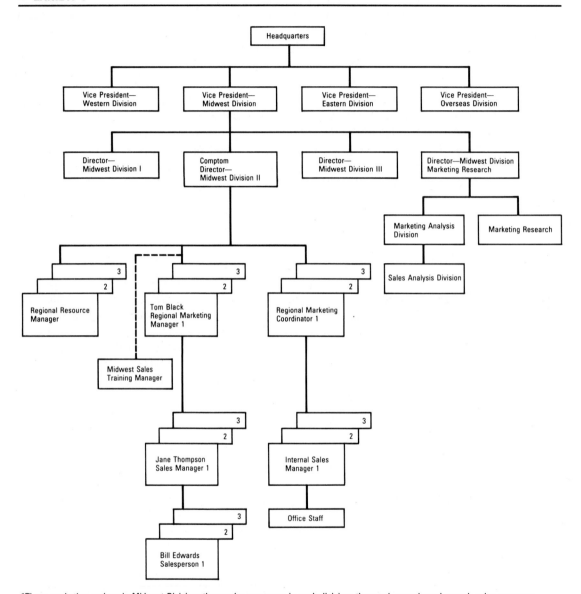

*Three marketing regions in Midwest Division; three sales managers in each division; three salespeople under each sales manager.

Except for the last six months, Bill's career with Douglas & Co. had been on a steady rise. He had been impressed with Douglas & Co. since high school. Douglas & Co. was a worldwide company providing consulting and contract sales/service for government and business projects. For the past 11 years, Bill had been associated with Douglas & Co. First, the Douglas Scholarship & Co-op Program in college; and now, almost six years since he had graduated, as a company employee. What had happened to change a promising future?

With just over two years' experience (one year in the field-training program and over a year on his own in the field) Bill was selected for one of the overseas divisions. After becoming accustomed to the overseas operation, Bill made an outstanding record for himself in the operational sales and service area. He developed new accounts and expanded the service to present accounts—all with increased sales and profits. He was respected and well liked by his contemporaries and superiors alike. In recognition of his work and capability to work with others, Bill was selected to become the Sales Training Manager for his overseas division. Sales Training Managers were usually one of the more successful and older field salespeople. As Sales Training Manager, Bill was recognized for his outstanding contributions to the training and development of the overseas division sales force.

Then, the transfer to the Midwest Division occurred. The transfer was both a step up and a step down. Bill was to become a Field Sales Service Representative again. The Midwest Division was the "darling" of the company and was located at the company headquarters. A transfer to the Midwest Division presented an opportunity to be recognized by the upper echelon of the company. It had been established five years previously and was staffed with experienced and successful personnel. As a member of the Midwest Division, chances and opportunity to be promoted were greatly enhanced. Thus, it was considered a "mark of distinction" to be selected to join the Midwest Division. Bill had mixed emotions about the transfer.

That was almost two years ago. Things had gone from bad to worse. Because the operation and clientele of the Midwest Division were "unique," it had its own special training program. After completing a six-month period of supervised field operations, Bill was allowed to go on his own. As Bill adapted to the Midwest Division operations and gained his independence for his own accounts, things improved.

The Midwest Division had two informal groups within its sales and marketing staff—the "old heads" and the "young turks." The "old heads" were composed of the initial "cadre" who were part of the original Midwest Division staff and the other experienced personnel who had several years of experience in other Douglas divisions/departments and joined the Midwest Division after it was organized. The "young turks" were composed of those field representatives who had demonstrated outstanding ability or promise in the training program or in their short period of field sales/ service experience. The two groups worked and socialized together—but yet—a dividing line existed. Bill fell in with the "young turks."

Bill established a normal routine. His sales and business experience went well. However, there were problems in the organization. The key positions were staffed by the "old heads." The assistant positions were filled by the "young turks." Whenever a key position was vacated, another "experienced" person was put in his or her place. The inexperienced "young turk" remained an assistant. Bill wanted to move up in the organization. He wanted to be recognized for his contributions. Salary was not the problem. Bill knew that he could be more than just a field salesperson—even in the Midwest Division.

The Market Analysis Division had been assigned a special project that required inputs from the field sales force. Bill saw this project as an opportunity to broaden his operational base and to demonstrate his value other than as a field salesperson. The project had been initiated by the Headquarters Division-Market Research, although it was conducted by the Midwest Market Research Division. The project planned to reexamine the regional sales potential, sales territory size, and sales force size for the entire company. Thus, Bill felt that with his experience with one of the Eastern Divisions, the Overseas Division and now the Midwest Division, he could make a valuable contribution to the project. Bill was more than happy to work on this project even though he was expected to maintain normal sales coverage of his accounts.

The Sales Analysis Division Manager requested that Bill work a minimum of two or three days a week on the project. The request was approved by Tom Black, Regional Marketing Manager, with the understanding that Bill was still responsible for his accounts. Bill's initial contributions to the project were of immense value. At first, Bill was able to work on the project two to three days a week, but he had trouble covering his accounts in the remaining time. To accomplish his normal duties and work on the project, Bill began working longer days and weekends. However, as the project continued, Bill contributed and worked on the project when he could. Instead of two or three days a week, Bill was only able to work on the project one day a week—sometimes not even that.

As the project proceeded, Bill spent less and less time with the Sales Analysis Division. After gathering data and input from the field, the project dealt with determinal analysis for company allocation of staff and budgets—an area in which Bill's practical field experience was lightly considered. After three months, the Sales Analysis Division Manager advised Black that, although the project was continuing, Edwards's lack of commitment in time and interest was of little value to the project. They did not want him anymore.

Bill's declining performance on the special project combined with the problems of customer account coverage, and the general lack of enthusiasm had been noticed by Jane Thompson, his Sales Manager. Thompson spoke with Bill concerning the need to remotivate himself and work to the level of his capabilities. Edwards expressed his frustration and his desire to do more than just field sales.

Shortly after Edwards's and Thompson's meeting, the Internal Sales Manager position became vacant by "resignation." The Internal Sales Manager was responsible for coordination of personnel, equipment, and other resources with field sales orders and requirements. The position was supposed to make decisions concerning special commitments, priority of commitments, and allocations of available resources. Thompson spoke with Bill and advised him that he could have the position if he desired.

Edwards:

No way I want that job. I know why that manager left. There was no way to make a decision without checking with the Marketing Coordinator and the Division Director. The one time this was done, both of them jumped in. No way.

Thompson:

But it gives you an opportunity to correct that 'problem' on the special project with the Sales Analysis Division.

Edwards:

What do you mean 'problem'; they did not need me over there. I do not care. I don't want that Internal Sales Manager position.

Thompson:

Maybe you had better think it over—both Black and Compton feel like you ought to give it a try.

Edwards:

No way.

Thompson:

Since Black is not available, you had better talk to Compton. I'll make an appointment for you this Friday.

And now Bill was worried. The meeting with Compton had not gone well at all. Bill still had a sales job at Douglas—but for how long?

The "fast mover" had "spun out."

Questions

1. Who is to blame for the present state of affairs?
2. What should the company do with Bill Edwards?

Case 11–2   Barton Laboratories*

On Wednesday, February 14, Dave Gibson, a senior marketing major, spent a day with Michael Hanson of Barton Laboratories. Mike Hanson is district sales manager of Barton's southern New England territory, which includes Connecticut, Rhode Island, and southeastern Massachusetts. Hanson manages a team of 14 sales representatives, who are responsible for promoting the use of Barton's products to the medical community in their territories. Most of the rep's time is spent calling on physicians, hospitals, and pharmacies.

Barton Laboratories is one of the eight major divisions of its parent company, Barton-Morris, Inc. For over 35 years Barton Labs has been a major marketer of antibiotics. More recently the company has promoted two other areas of new product development—analgesics (pain killers) and anticancer drugs. Domestic and international sales of pharmaceutical and health care products accounted for slightly over half of the parent company's income last year, or roughly $1.2 billion.

---

*Eugene M. Johnson, David L. Kurtz, and Eberhard Scheuring, *Sales Management,* 1986, McGraw Hill, pp. 92–95.

The day began at 8:15 A.M. when Gibson met Hanson and Bill Petrarca at the Ramada Inn in Seekonk, Massachusetts. Petrarca is the territory sales rep for New Bedford, Cape Cod, and the Islands. Hanson began by filling in Gibson on Barton Labs and his responsibilities. He explained that his normal routine is to spend four days each week in the field with reps, and the fifth at home, catching up on paperwork. Hanson was to spend this particular day making several calls with Petrarca.

Hanson explained that one call on the schedule was of special interest to both Bill and him. Middleboro Hospital was in the process of considering a changeover from a competitor's product to a drug produced by Barton for the treatment of a certain class of ailments. This changeover would mean a significant sales boost for Barton at Middleboro Hospital, so significant that Hanson wanted to be there to help conclude the deal as quickly as possible. The next stop was to be another hospital in the area, where they would make several routine calls. Petrarca pointed out that on Wednesdays the main thrust of the day's efforts is to call on hospitals and pharmacies rather than physicians in private practice, who generally take the day off.

Before they left the Ramada Inn, the trio got into a brief discussion of the pharmaceutical industry and what makes selling drugs so different from selling most other products. It became clear to Gibson that pharmaceuticals are highly technical products by nature, and that the technology is constantly changing. Hanson and Petrarca both feel that a major function of the sales rep is to keep physicians informed and current on all product advancements. This function is complicated, however, by the Food and Drug Administration's regulations on just what a sales rep is allowed to say in a presentation.

Further complicating a pharmaceutical sales rep's job is the fact that reps never actually make sales when they visit physicians' offices. Sales success or failure for an individual rep can be determined only by reviewing sales data for the territory. Of course, it is possible to confront a doctor and ask point-blank if the doctor will really use the drug, but, as Petrarca suggested, the answer to such a question is often yes whether or not the doctor truly intends to use the drug.

At 9:30 A.M., the men arrived at Middleboro Hospital. They went to the office of the chief pharmacist, Joe Burkett. The meeting began with an informal discussion of the opportunities in pharmaceutical for a pharmacist. Apparently, Burkett was considering a career change, and Hanson recognized that people like him could be good candidates for positions with Barton Labs in the future. Then Petrarca and Burkett began to discuss the progress that had been made to convince the hospital's medical staff to accept the proposed changeover to the new Barton drug. Burkett was clearly in favor of the new drug because it was of equal quality and less expensive than the competitor's product. Petrarca inquired about each of the six doctors on the new drug committee and how they felt about the change. He made suggestions to Burkett on how he should handle the few remaining holdouts who were reluctant to accept the switch. During the early part of the discussion, Hanson did not say a word, but paid close attention to what was being said. Then, at one point, a question about side effects of the drug came up that Petrarca seemed to stumble over. Hanson jumped in and quoted some recent research findings concerning the side effects of the drug. He concluded his explanation by citing a toll-free telephone number that could be used by anyone on the new drug committee who had doubts about the new drug's side effects. The number was for Barton's research facility in upstate New York. Petrarca and Hanson thanked Burkett for his help and then left.

Outside in the car, Hanson and Petrarca talked about what had just taken place. Hanson encouraged the sales representative to get in touch with each of the physicians on the new drug committee one more time. He wanted to try to clear up the side-effects problem. In general, though, they both felt that the sale would be made.

At 11 A.M., the trio arrived at the next call, Union Hospital. Petrarca explained that this would be a more routine call. The first stop was the hospital pharmacy, where they chatted with the two pharmacists and checked the inventory of Barton products. In a semiserious voice Petrarca scolded them for not pushing a certain drug enough. It was clear that he was probing for a reason for its poor performance in this hospital. By now, Gibson was beginning to realize that Petrarca's 13 years of experience with Barton Labs had made him skillful in obtaining helpful information from sources that did not have to provide it. In fact, he seemed to be part politician and part detective.

From here, the three men went to the operating room, where a doctor they wanted to see was completing an operation. When it became apparent they would have to wait, the trio went into the nurses' lounge where they could relax. Normally, the nurses' lounge would be strictly off limits to all visitors, but Petrarca was on such good terms with everyone that Gibson sensed that no doors in the hospital would be closed to him. The two nurses in the lounge talked freely with Petrarca about exactly which doctors were not using Barton's new analgesic, and why. The salesperson made mental notes of everything. Then the doctor Petrarca was waiting for came out of surgery, and he ran to catch him. The doctor was obviously in a hurry, and Petrarca managed to get in only a few words on the run. The doctor asked him to come back some other time.

From surgery, the men went to talk to Dr. Suryanarayan. Petrarca warned the others that this doctor was a particularly difficult man to talk to because of his poor English, which seemed to become worse whenever salespeople called. The doctor was on his way to lunch, but Petrarca managed to speak to him briefly. Petrarca ran through a quick presentation on one of Barton's new drugs and gave the doctor some literature. The doctor spoke to him, but was very difficult to understand. After a few minutes, Dr. Suryanarayan excused himself and left.

It was almost 1 P.M. when the three men left Union Hospital. Hanson offered to take the other two men to lunch. During lunch, he shared some of his views of file sales management. He told Gibson that the biggest problem that every manager faces is motivation. "The toughest part of a sales rep's job is just getting out of bed in the morning," he said. In addition to this, Hanson believes it is important to manage by support and cooperation rather than by conflict. He does not believe in simply telling his people to meet their quotas—or else. He prefers to work with them on weaknesses, to improve performance and reach common goals. On the subject of high turnover of sales people, Hanson feels that new people are too sensitive and take failures too personally. Such a person simply cannot survive in the long run. In summing up his feelings, Hanson made a comment on the life-style that goes along with a career in selling. He pointed out that although the work is hard and the job is certainly not for everyone, the rewards are great. As he put it, "We work hard to play hard!"

QUESTIONS

1. Review Gibson's day with Hanson and Petrarca. Do you feel that Hanson and Petrarca were effective in their jobs?

2. What is your reaction to Hanson's views of the field sales manager's job? Does it appear that he practices what he preaches?

SUGGESTED READINGS

Dunn, Dan T., Jr., and Claude A. Thomas. "Strategy for Systems Sellers: A Grid Approach." *Journal of Personal Selling and Sales Management* 6 (August 1986), pp. 1–10. Discussion of, and guidelines for, a problem-solution grid related to systems selling.

Hafer, John, and Barbara A. McCuen. "Antecedents of Performance and Satisfaction in a Service Sales Force as Compared to an Industrial Sales Force." *Journal of Personal Selling and Sales Management* 5 (November 1985), pp. 7–17. Discussion of the conflicting results of two studies comparing performance of members of a service sales force and of a business to business sales force.

Hite, Robert E., and Joseph A. Bellizzi. "Differences in the Importance of Selling Techniques Between Consumer and Industrial Salespeople." *Journal of Personal Selling and Sales Management* 5 (November 1985), pp. 19–30. Comparative analysis of differences in the importance of selling techniques between consumer and business to business salespersons.

King, Bob. "Ploys and Counterploys in Sales Negotiation." *Industrial Marketing Digest* (UK) 10 (Third Quarter, 1985), pp. 101–5. Guidelines for negotiation techniques between business to business salespeople and their customers.

Merrett, Bernie. "Industrial Companies Talk to Clients But Seldom Listen." *Sales and Marketing Management in Canada* 26 (December 1985), pp. 19–20. Discussion of market surveys, market research, and problem identification.

Moncrief, William C. "The Key Activities of Industrial Salespeople." *Industrial Marketing Management* 15 (November 1986), pp. 309–17. Survey of shared versus industry specific sales activities.

Mouritzen, Russell H. "Client Involvement through Negotiation: A Key to Success." *American Salesman* 32 (May 1987), pp. 16–18. Guidelines for relationships and negotiation skills in personal selling.

Schurr, Paul H., Louis H. Stone, and Lee Ann Beller. "Effective Selling Approaches to Buyers' Objections." *Industrial Marketing Management* 14 (August

1985), pp. 195–202. Survey of business to business salespeople, price objections, indecision, and techniques for handling resistance.

Shipley, David D., and Julia A. Kiley. "Industrial Salesforce Motivation and Herzberg's Dual factor Theory: A UK Perspective." *Journal of Personal Selling and Sales Management* 6 (May 1986), pp. 9–16. Divergent findings in a survey of 114 business to business salespeople as to job satisfaction and dissatisfaction.

Spekman, Robert E., and Wesley J. Johnston. "Relationship Management: Managing the Selling and Buyer Interface," *Journal of Business Research* 14 (December 1986), pp. 519–31. Discussion of competitive advantage, cross-functional interdependencies, and decision processes.

Swan, John E., and Johanna Jones Nolan. "Gaining Customer Trust: A Conceptual Guide for the Salesperson." *Journal of Personal Selling and Sales Management* 5 (November 1985), pp. 39–48. Discussion of exchange relationships and a model of trust among business to business salespersons and their customers.

Swan, John E., I. Frederick Trawick, and David W. Silva. "How Industrial Salespeople Gain Customer Trust." *Industrial Marketing Management* 14 (August 1985), pp. 203–11. Survey and model development of trust attributes critical salesperson behaviors, and sales techniques.

Taylor, Thayer C. "Laptops and the Sales Force: New Stars in the Sky." *Sales and Marketing Management* 138 (April 1987), pp. 50–55. Sales productivity applications for portable computers.

Wagle, John S. "Using Humor in the Industrial Selling Process." *Industrial Marketing Management* 14 (November 1985), pp. 221–26. Guidelines for the use of humor in business to business sales presentations.

Chapter **12**

Business to Business Sales Management

LEARNING OBJECTIVES

After reading this chapter, you should be able to:

- Identify the changes which take place when a salesperson is promoted to sales manager.
- Explain the common forms of sales force organization.
- Understand the critical role of recruitment, selection, and training of the sales force in sales management.
- Realize the great importance of effective direction and motivation of the sales force.
- Appreciate the role of continuous monitoring and evaluation of sales performance.
- Tell how to build an effective sales force in a foreign country.

CHAPTER OUTLINE

Learning Objectives

Business to Business Sales Management: A Leadership Challenge

Selecting the Sales Manager
  Perspectives
  Goals
  Responsibilities
  Satisfaction
  Job Skill Requirements
  Relationships

Basic Types of Sales Organizations
  The Line Organization
  The Line and Staff Organization
  The Functional Organization
  The Centralized versus Decentralized Organization
  Organizing by Specialization

Staffing the Sales Force
  Determining Sales Force Size
  Recruitment and Selection

Training and Development of the Sales Force
  Purposes of Sales Training

What the Training Program Should Cover

Who Should Do the Training?

Evaluating Sales Training

Directing and Motivating the Sales Force
  Providing Leadership
  Sales Quotas
  Compensation and Motivation

Sales Force Analysis and Evaluation
  Why Analyze and Evaluate Salespeople?
  Who Should Analyze and Evaluate Salespeople?
  When Should It Be Done?

Managing U.S. Salespeople in International Markets
  Selection
  Orientation and Training
  Compensation

■ BUSINESS TO BUSINESS SALES MANAGEMENT: A LEADERSHIP CHALLENGE

Few areas in the business sector are in more need of a more systematic approach to problem solving than the sales management function, as it is still one of the most difficult activities within the firm to manage. The first qualification for a sales manager is leadership; as Figure 12–1 indicates, this individual must not only attempt to allocate financial resources efficiently but must also attempt to allocate, maintain, direct, and control a large group of people who are often rather independent, and who are not in daily contact with management. Effective sales management is critical to the successful allocation of scarce resources in a free, competitive economy. As noted in Chapter 11, personal selling involves persu-

■ **FIGURE 12–1**   The Leadership Functions of Sales Managers

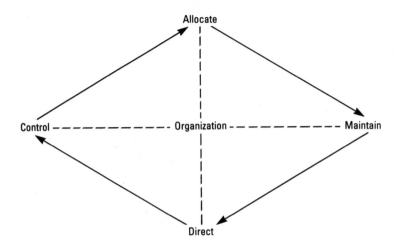

asive and deliberate contact between a buyer and a seller. Sales management, on the other hand, involves a multitude of challenges, as an orientation toward people is the first and foremost concern. Management of the sales function has often been described as both an art and a science, requiring the sales manager to walk a tightrope between subjective creativity and objective detachment.

■ SELECTING THE SALES MANAGER

The primary reason firms face difficulty in selecting a sales manager is that many changes accompany a promotion from subordinate to supervisor. Selling skills and management skills are different, and not all good salespeople make good sales managers. Yet many firms still tend to promote individuals in this way. The qualities that make a good, effective sales manager are often significantly different from those needed by a salesperson.[1] Changes accompany this promotion, some of which are immediate and apparent, while others are less obvious. As a result, it may take a longer time for some people to make the necessary adjustment. The following are some of the major changes which occur when a salesperson is promoted to sales manager.[2]

Perspectives

Selling is doing, traveling, constantly testing your own individual abilities, and being in control of your own destiny. Successful sales managers, how-

---

[1]For another perspective, see Alan M. Schechter, "Thinking, Acting Like a Manager Is a Prime Requisite in Transition," *Marketing News*, September 27, 1985, p. 14.

[2]Adapted from Charles Futrell, *Sales Management*, 2d ed. (New York: Dryden Press, 1988), pp. 10–11.

ever, must delegate, coach, counsel, and keep the big picture in mind. Plans and decisions must be made that consider the impact of those plans and decisions on the goals and well-being of the sales team and the organization as a whole.

Goals

The sales manager must be concerned with the total organization, whereas the salesperson's focus is on meeting personal goals. This is not to imply that the sales manager does not have personal goals, but only to highlight the fact that his or her personal goals must be meshed with the personal goals of the different salespeople in accomplishing overall organizational goals and objectives.

Responsibilities

Progressive firms recognize that the sales management function is related to traditional marketing activities such as pricing, distribution, product development, information collection, and advertising, in addition to other business activities and disciplines. The sales manager recognizes the necessity of making a sale at a profit, in addition to monitoring customer reactions to company products, service, and policies, and the sales methods employed by the individual salespeople.

Satisfaction

The salesperson receives much satisfaction in making the sale after, in many cases, several months of hard work. The sales manager, however, receives satisfaction from seeing people succeed, especially if the sales manager indirectly contributed to that success through guidance, training, and perhaps prodding.

Job Skill Requirements

The sales manager must not only exhibit a superior knowledge of products, policies, and selling techniques but must also become proficient at communicating, delegating, planning, managing time, directing, motivating, and training others—no easy task!

Relationships

New relationships must develop, as the sales manager not only must get things done through the sales force but must also work with and through internal peers, such as the manufacturing manager, purchasing manager, engineering manager, and financial manager, to name just a few. For the sales manager to do an optimal job, top management support is important. Managerial performance criteria, such as profit accountability and decision-oriented reports from top management can help significantly in enabling sales managers to increase the productivity and profitability of the sales force.

■ BASIC TYPES OF SALES ORGANIZATIONS

Just as important as selecting exactly the right type of sales manager is choosing the most appropriate sales organization plan. The sales force can be organized in several ways, with the key to organizational design being consistency and coherence. Developing the structure is not an easy task, and the final decision depends on the needs and objectives of the firm. Although there are many variations, the line organization, the line and staff organization, and the functional organization are the most common and most basic. We will study each of them in turn. Then we will discuss modifications to these basic types of organizational methods based on the need to centralize or decentralize, or to organize by activity, product, customer, geographic territory, or some combination of the above.[3]

The Line Organization

The **line organization** is the simplest design. It is often used by small firms and, as shown in Figure 12–2, has a clear line of authority from the highest level of sales management down to the salesperson. In its simplest form a line organization prescribes that the sales manager should recruit, hire, train, and supervise the salespeople, in addition to designing sales territories, forecasting sales levels, and carrying out other functions or special projects as assigned by top management. When the firm is small, this organizational structure is efficient, effective, and very flexible. However, as the firm grows, and as problems become more complex, the line organization tends to overburden the managers.

■ **FIGURE 12–2**   A Simple Line Organization

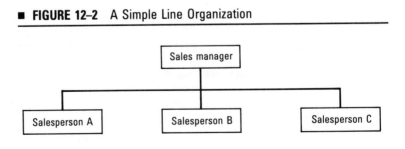

---

[3]Adapted from C. Robert Patty, *Sales Manager's Handbook* (Reston Publishing, 1982), pp. 285–300.

■ **FIGURE 12–3**   A Line and Staff Organization

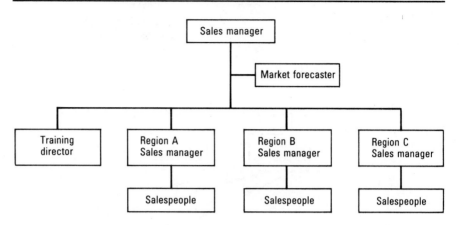

The Line and Staff Organization

When highly specialized skills are needed (advertising, marketing research, etc.), and when the volume of work becomes overwhelming for one
person, **line and staff organization** emerges. The line function is primary,
while the staff function is supportive in nature. Staff people provide the
manager with specialized skills and report to the line position they support. Sales analysts and training directors are directly supportive of field
sales, so these people typically report directly to the general sales manager, as demonstrated in Figure 12–3. A staff specialist can only recommend policy or action.

The Functional Organization

With the **functional organization,** the staff specialist is given line authority
to control a function. As an example, the training specialist would have
authority over the salespeople for all training. Each specialist is, we hope,
highly qualified, so that out of this structure should come improved performance in each functional area. Figure 12–4 offers a diagram of the sales
management activity organized by function.

The Centralized versus Decentralized Organization

The **centralized versus decentralized organization** decision concerns the
organizational location of the responsibility and authority for specific sales
management tasks, such as planning, forecasting, budgeting, and recruiting. For example, RIBCO Industries, an industrial supply firm located in
Providence, Rhode Island, allows the individual, company-owned sales
branches to do most of the planning and recruitment at the local level,
while sales forecasting and financial budgeting are performed at headquar-

■ **FIGURE 12–4**   A Functional Organization

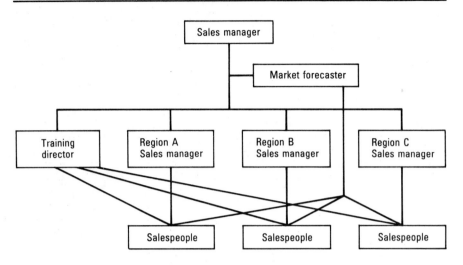

ters. Generally, some functions are centralized at company headquarters, while others are spread among branch or field offices. The following factors might influence this decision: cost, the size of the sales force, geographic size of the market, the role of personal selling in the promotional mix, the need for decentralized inventories, and the need for service.[4]

Organizing By Specialization

In addition to the various types of sales force organizations we have analyzed, some firms find that additional efficiencies and economies may accrue through organization by (1) geographical specialization, (2) sales activities, (3) product specialization, (4) customer specialization, or (5) combination organizations. This form of organization is commonly referred to as **organization by specialization.**

Geographical Specialization.   **Geographic specialization** is the most common way to organize a field sales force, with each territory being treated virtually as a separate company or profit center. Note that three separate and distinct territories (Dallas, Chicago, and Omaha) have been established in the example of geographic organization shown in Figure 12–5. Some firms may have further breakdowns between the general sales manager and the salespeople by having branch, district, or field sales manager units. Advantages of this form of organization include smaller territories whereby salespeople learn more about their customers and their needs; better cultivation of local markets; faster reaction time to external environmental changes; and usually, better service at less expense. Some disadvantages might include lack of a salesperson's knowledge of all products

---

[4]For an interesting discussion of sales force organizational structure, see Ram C. Ras and Ronald E. Turner, "Organization and Effectiveness of the Multiple-Product Sales Force," *Journal of Personal Selling and Sales Management*, May 1984, pp. 24–30.

■ **FIGURE 12–5**   A Sales Force Organized on a Geographic Basis

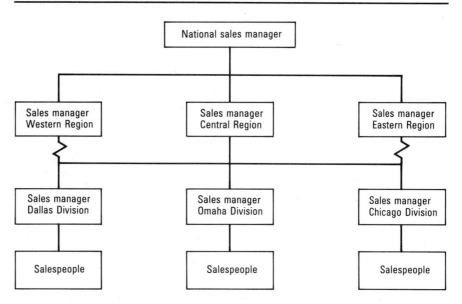

within a line; too much time spent on products and customers that are easier to sell; and the disadvantage arising from the creation of multiple offices, with the resulting duplication of services and administrators.

Sales Activities.   A company can grow by selling additional products to present customers, or by searching for new customers and selling present products to them. Many companies have found it useful to separate these two functions into separate sales groups, thus allowing the firm to place special emphasis on searching out and selling new accounts. The company may choose to divide the group when (1) there is significant difference in the skills needs, or (2) fast growth through acquiring new accounts is considered necessary.

Product Specialization.   Organization by **product (product line) specialization** is often reserved for large and diverse product lines, where technical knowledge is important to maintain efficiency. General Electric and Westinghouse have used this structure effectively, as have IBM and Xerox. A company may have regional, district, and even area managers within each product or product line sales force. A typical sales force organized in this manner appears in Figure 12–6. Notice that there is a product manager and salespeople for both Product A and Product B, but that the advertising department and marketing services department handle appropriate needs for both products. Product specialization allows salespeople and sales managers to concentrate their efforts on particular product lines or individual items. This allows a high degree of specialized attention, which will increase the efficiency of each product or product-line sales force substantially. It also allows for decentralization, whereby decisions can be made by those closest to the problems. On the downside however, two or more

■ **FIGURE 12–6**   A Sales Force Organized on a Product Basis

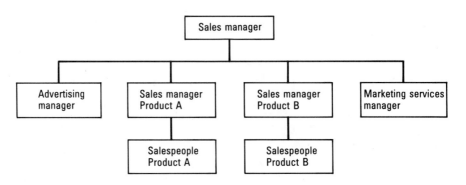

salespeople may be calling on the same customer, which may not only up-set the customer but might also cause an expensive duplication of sales effort resulting from having more than one representative in the same geographic locality.

Customer Specialization.   With **customer specialization,** a salesperson sells an entire product line to selected buyers. This approach is consistent with the marketing concept and with the emphasis on customer satisfaction, as the salesperson is knowledgeable about the unique problems and needs of each group of customers. In addition, special attention is paid to major customers.[5] Greater feedback of new product ideas and new marketing methods may also accrue through the customer-oriented sales force organization. The biggest disadvantage would be the potential for overlapping territories along with a concomitant increase in costs.

Combination Organizations.   Combinations of types of sales organizations allow the company to choose the structure that best serves immediate objectives. Figure 12–7 illustrates a sales force organized by territories, products, and customers. Most firms develop some type of combination organization as they grow in size. General Foods, DuPont, and National Cash Register all use a combination sales organization.

Concept Questions
1. Why are selling skills and management skills different?
2. What are the four basic methods of organizing a sales force?

■ STAFFING THE SALES FORCE

After a company has decided upon the most appropriate way to organize its sales function, it must turn its attention to the recruitment and selection

---

[5]For further discussion, see John Barrett, "Why Major Accounts?" *Industrial Marketing Management* 15 (1986), pp. 63–73. Also see Thayer C. Taylor, "Xerox's Sales Force Arms a New Game," *Sales and Marketing Management,* July 1985, pp. 48–51.

■ **FIGURE 12–7**   Sales Force Organized by Territories, Products, and Customers

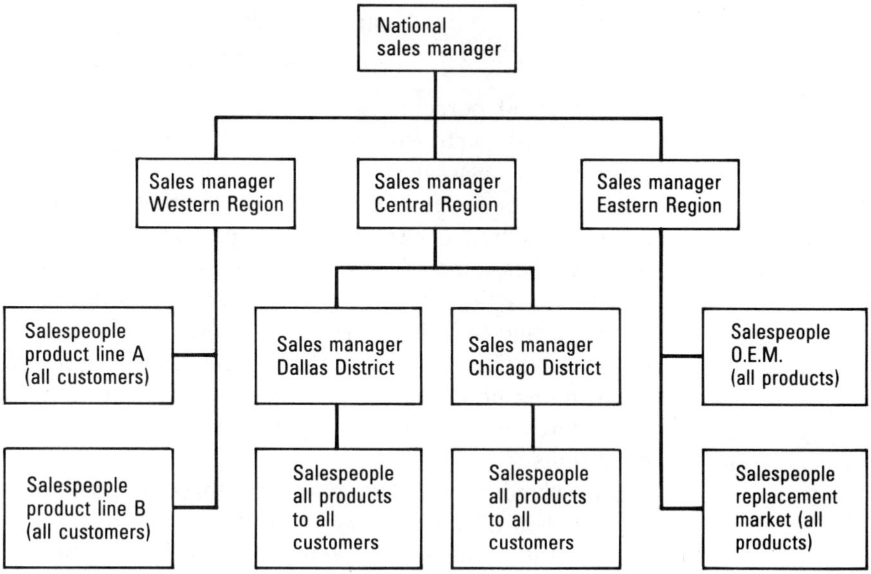

of competent sales representatives. Sales managers may be very competent and refined in other skills, but they will be doomed to failure if they hire poorly qualified salespeople on whom training, compensation, and motivation techniques have a negligible impact. If sales managers were given a choice of skills at which to become proficient, recruitment and selection would certainly have to be among the most popular choices.

Determining Sales Force Size

A firm must be as careful in buying the services of salespeople, as it is in making and buying the products that these people sell. The number of salespeople to hire depends primarily on two things: growth and turnover. Growth dictates the need for additional sales volume, while turnover creates a need for replacements. Turnover rates vary among industries, and range from a low of 5 percent for transportation equipment firms to a high of over 20 percent in business services sales forces.[6] Exceptionally high turnover levels may indicate problem areas with sales management. As noted earlier, management of the sales force is both an art and a science; excessive turnover indicates potential problems in hiring, training, compensating, and motivating the sales force.

---

[6]"Business-to-Business Sales Force Turnover Rate Rises to 9.4%" in *Laboratory of Advertising Performance*, Report #8054.1 (New York: McGraw-Hill, 1986).

Turnover Expected.[7] For many firms, turnover is a persistent problem. The formula for sales force turnover is as follows:

$$\text{Turnover} = \frac{\text{Number of salespeople hired during the period}}{\text{Average size of sales force during the period}}$$

Thus, a 50 percent turnover (which would be totally unacceptable in most sales departments) would result if 100 people were hired in a year, assuming the average size of the sales force was 200. A 50 percent turnover rate does not necessarily mean that half of the sales force was replaced during a particular period of time; perhaps only 50 to 75 positions had to be filled, but some of these had to be replaced twice. Generally speaking, a firm can reduce the turnover rate by upgrading the job, screening more carefully, and tailoring supervision more closely to the requirements of the job. In addition to growth and turnover, other considerations involved in determining how many salespeople to hire are increases or decreases in the incidence of competitive activity, changes in products, and economic conditions.

Still, Cundiff, and Govoni identify three rational methods of approaching the problem of determining the optimal size of the sales force: the workload method, the sales-potential method, and the incremental method.[8] The *workload method,* sometimes called the *buildup method,* categorizes accounts based on their sales and potential importance. The frequency and length of sales calls are determined for each category, with larger accounts (or those with large-volume potential) being called on often (every two weeks or perhaps once per month). Small accounts (or those with low-volume potential) may be called on every three months or longer. This method incorporates several factors in determining the number of sales personnel needed, including:

- Number of accounts in the territory.
- Number of sales to be made.
- Frequency of sales calls on given customers.
- Time intervals between sales calls.
- Travel time around the territory.
- Nonselling time.[9]

The number of accounts multiplied by call frequency equals the total number of sales calls per year that the sales force must make. The necessary interview time is estimated by subtracting time devoted to nonselling activities (such as travel time) from total work time available. The necessary interview time is found by adding together the total time needed for each customer category. In the final step, the yearly interview time available to

---

[7]This discussion of turnover is from Robert F. Hartley, *Sales Management* (Columbus, Ohio: Charles E. Merrill Publishing, 1989), p. 213.

[8]Ronald R. Still, Edward W. Cundiff, and Norman A. P. Govoni, *Sales Management: Decisions, Strategies, and Cases,* 9th ed. (Englewood Cliffs, N.J.: Prentice-Hall, 1981), pp. 63–68. Also see Richard F. Wendel and Walter Garman, *Selling,* 3d ed. (New York: Random House Business Division, 1988), pp. 576–77.

[9]Charles Futrell, *Sales Management,* 2d ed. (New York: Dryden Press, 1988), p. 289.

a sales representative is divided into the total number of hours of customer interview time the firm needs. The result is a fairly accurate estimate of the number of salespeople needed. This method, although simple and easy to use, does not recognize the fact that all customers do not have similar characteristics and requirements.[10]

In the *sales potential method,* the yearly sales volume is divided by the volume each salesperson can be expected to accomplish. The resulting number is adjusted for turnover among sales force personnel and territorial differences in travel time. A major drawback of this method is that sales volume depends on the number of salespeople selling for the firm.[11]

The *incremental method* of determining sales force size is based on the assumption that an additional salesperson may be hired if profit contributions from sales made by that person exceed the costs of hiring him or her. The major element to consider is total incremental or marginal cost relative to the incremental or marginal revenue of the territory. This method is theoretically attractive, but impractical because of the difficulties encountered in estimating marginal sales directly produced by the added salesperson, in addition to the difficulty of estimating marginal costs and costs of production and distribution.[12]

Finally, other factors (including instinct) must also be considered when estimating the number of salespeople needed in the next year or two. Other internal and external conditions, including the level of economic activity and labor relations, may impact the decision heavily.

Recruitment and Selection

Once sales managers have determined the size of the sales force, they must then become concerned with the **recruitment and selection** process. The task of recruiting is to find and attract qualified applicants for sales positions, while selection is a screening or sequential filtering process whereby candidates who do not meet the hiring criteria are not given further consideration in the hiring process.

Recruitment.   The task of finding and attracting qualified applicants for sales positions is a difficult and time-consuming task; improved sales recruiting is a major goal of most sales managers. The cost of inefficient sales recruiting not only will drain company resources but will also cause an inordinate amount of time to be spent in this process. An important first step in the recruitment process is to analyze the job thoroughly and to prepare a list of qualifications needed for successful performance. Such a process tends to ensure that new recruits have a reasonably good chance of being successful in a particular sales situation. Three specific procedures should be followed at this point in the process: (1) conduct a job analysis; (2) prepare a written job description; and (3) develop sales job qualifications for selectees (a **job specification**).

---

[10]Ibid., p. 290.

[11]Wendel and Gorman, p. 576.

[12]Futrell, *Sales Management,* p. 291.

Conduct a Job Analysis. A **job analysis** refers to a careful and objective study and written summary of the selling job in question. It is a definition of roles or activities to be performed, and the determination of the personal qualifications needed for the position. It is commonly used in the preparation of job descriptions, the writing of job specifications, recruitment and selection, performance evaluations, training and development, and compensation.

Prepare a Written Job Description. As noted above, the job analysis is used, among other things, to develop a job description. A **job description** details the components of the sales job and the functions or activities salespeople must perform, such as prospecting, traveling, selling, and providing service assistance. The job description should be committed to paper; should be acceptable to salespeople and management; and should be specific, inclusive, short, quick, and easy to read. In summary, it is a detailed statement of the job in terms of specific functions and activities. It is a profile of the sales job, showing the functions that must be performed, and how much time, effort, and attention should be placed on each function or activity of the job.

Develop Sales Job Qualifications. The duties and responsibilities outlined in the job description should now be put into a set of qualifications that the job seeker should have in order to perform the sales job satisfactorily. The qualifications spell out critical characteristics needed, and would include decisiveness, energy and enthusiasm, maturity, assertiveness, sensitivity, and openness, among others. Some positions would require a high level of enthusiasm, while others might involve little supervision, possibly necessitating the hiring of a mature, experienced person.

Sources of Sales Recruits. Several sources of sales recruits are often used, with referrals coming from both outside the company through friends, customers, and suppliers, as well as from internal sources. The most frequently used sources are (1) company sources, (2) company salespeople, (3) educational institutions, (4) professional associations, (5) suppliers and customers, (6) employment agencies, and (7) advertisements. Each can be compared once enough time has elapsed to determine which method gets the best recruit for the money spent.

Selection. Once the firm has accumulated a pool of candidates, the next step is to select and lure the best salespeople for the job at hand. Figure 12–8 shows how hiring criteria for sales jobs are used to guide the process of selecting salespeople from a pool of available applicants. Too often sales managers think of the managerial function of hiring as a one-way decision, whereas it is really only effective when it involves decision making on the part of the applicant as well as on the part of management. Both parties have a financial stake in making the right decision, as the company will be

■ **FIGURE 12–8**   A Model for Selecting Salespeople

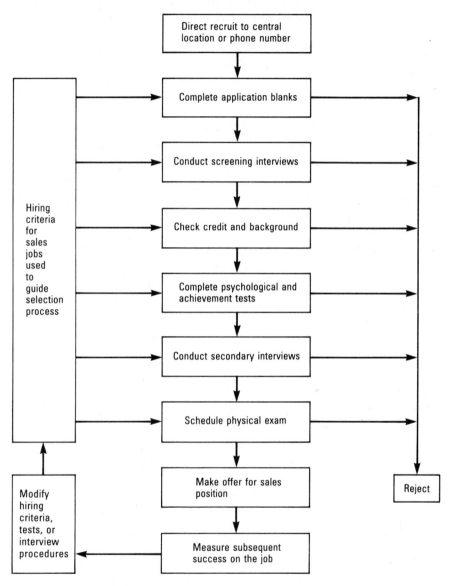

SOURCE: Douglas J. Dalrymple and Leonard J. Parsons, *Marketing Management: Strategy and Cases,* 4th ed. (New York: John Wiley & Sons, 1986), p. 675. Used with permission.

investing in the applicant, and the applicant is gambling a segment of his or her occupational lifetime in the hope of realizing an optimal return. Information retrieved from application forms, interviews, background checks, and tests is compared with a set of hiring criteria. Those best meeting such standards will receive the job offer, while those who do not will be rejected. Usually the process begins with a review of the application forms; it then moves on to interviews and background checks, and concludes with some psychological and achievement tests.

While firms might vary in the time sequence of the steps outlined above, the selection interview inevitably becomes the final step in the employment decision. The sales manager must now resolve moot points, make judgments on the capabilities and overall talents of the candidates, and decide whether or not a candidate will fit as a member of the sales team. At the same time, there are many legal and ethical restrictions on the uses of various traditional selection tools. Also, if applicants are rejected, they should feel that the rejection was in the best interests of both the company and themselves.

■ TRAINING AND DEVELOPMENT OF THE SALES FORCE

Now that sales representatives have been properly recruited and carefully selected, the sales manager (either directly or indirectly) has the responsibility of training and developing the sales force. Willie Loman, the tragic 1940s hero of Arthur Miller's *Death of a Salesman,* worked for a small family-owned business. In preparation for his selling position, he received only a calling card and a sample case; the rest was up to him. Willie represented the end of a somewhat romanticized era for salespeople, as today the salesperson needs more than friends, a good shoe shine, and a pleasant style to obtain orders. **Sales training** is imperative and must be conducted on a continuous basis. Even the best, most experienced salesperson requires training on product knowledge, competition, and new selling techniques, along with a host of other mandatory knowledge and skills development. To be successful, salespeople need training in many different topical areas in addition to product knowledge, policies, and procedures.[13]

Purposes of Sales Training

Companies are primarily interested in training to increase sales, productivity, and profits. H. O. Craffard, president of Plantations Plastics, Riverside, Rhode Island, expressed this interest in the following way:

> I support training, retraining, and other development activities that will achieve results. I am interested in, and will support activities that provide rewards to the employee, higher return to the stockholders, and enable continued growth of the business. In other words, I am interested in that which affects the bottom line. Although training cannot always be evaluated as readily as some other functions, better training is eventually reflected in on-the-job results.[14]

---

[13]"Study Reveals Sales-Training Needs of Business Marketers," *Marketing News,* March 13, 1989, p. 6.

[14]From a personal interview in 1989 with H. O. Craffard of Plantation Plastics, Riverside, Rhode Island.

There are specific purposes of training other than improving general sales volume. These purposes tend to relate to the type of training being offered and include the following:

- To improve morale, thereby reducing absenteeism and turnover.
- To create and foster an information flow from headquarters or the field sales office to the salesperson, and to encourage feedback from the salesperson.
- To improve knowledge in the area of product, competition, customer, time and territory management, and selling techniques.
- To increase sales in a particular product, product line, or customer category.
- To encourage and develop future sales managers.

All training programs should be designed and conducted with specific purposes or goals in mind. In order to provide adequate training for all members of the sales force, a comprehensive program needs to be established that will provide instruction in the skills and information needed by such a sales force. Training and retraining should never be done just to say that one has such a program, as such thinking might well be self-defeating, and the more senior members might reject it. Hire the right salespeople, train them well, retrain them when appropriate—and the sales management task will generally become somewhat easier. The objectives of many training programs reflect new selling strategies. For example, the major goal of DuPont's sales training is "to make would-be representatives aware of the importance of developing customer relationships."[15] DuPont's trainees focus heavily on learning everything possible about their customers' businesses.

What the Training Program Should Cover

The basic principle in sales-training priorities has been to direct the major part of training to those areas deemed necessary for the salesperson to do an adequate selling job. However, as sales organizations become more complex, more computerized, and more international, this role of the sales manager in a training effort is compounded, and new priorities may have to be set. The sales manager must choose and rank priorities in decoding what information to impart, what skills to teach, and when to teach them. Although specific content may vary, an analysis of training needs usually reveals the necessity of training in a combination of the following general areas: (1) company knowledge, (2) product knowledge, (3) selling techniques, (4) customer knowledge, (5) competitive knowledge, and (6) time and territory management.

Company Knowledge.   A sales prospect will want to know if the firm will stand behind its product offerings, so salespeople without basic knowledge of their companies may give the impression of incompetence on the part

---

[15]"DuPont Turns Scientists into Salespeople," *Sales & Marketing Management,* June 1987, p. 57.

of the entire organization. Facts about the firm's history, size, and reputation provide needed assurances, especially to the business customer contemplating the purchase of expensive equipment that will require costly installation and servicing. Also, knowledge of the firm's history and capabilities can increase morale, confidence, and efficiency among the firm's sales representatives. Salespeople need to know and understand the policy on allowable returns, advertising allowances, freight costs, payment terms, cancellation penalties, and minimum orders.

Product Knowledge. Because of the importance of product knowledge in addition to the accelerating nature of technological change, most sales managers provide ongoing or continuous product training to their sales forces. Product information stressed in company training programs tends to highlight special features, end uses, applications, and optional equipment. Also stressed would be advantages compared to competitive offerings. Product features must be turned into customer benefits so the salesperson requires enough product knowledge to feel confident in presenting the goods or services.

Additionally, when a firm changes the organizational structure, changing from a sales organization built around products to a market-oriented organization, additional training for experienced sales representatives may be needed. Xerox Corporation has retrained 4,000 of its sales representatives who sell the firm's entire product line. The firm changed to a market-oriented organizational structure, and to implement this strategy, spent close to $20 million annually on its sales training program.[16]

Selling Techniques. To be successful, selling techniques must be based on how people buy; most sales managers believe that a logical, sequential series of steps exists that, if followed, will convert a prospect into a customer. The *selling process* is an adaptation by a salesperson to the decision process of business buyers; it is a starting point in understanding the use of numerous persuasive communications techniques. Sales managers (or trainers) teach the use and application of several broad selling techniques involving selling benefits, using benefits, being organized, qualifying prospects, obtaining appointments, and employing proper presentation format, among others. Salespeople, both beginners and "old pros" alike, must be reminded that selling is a process, which starts with prospecting, moves forward through several steps to the sale, and ends with follow-up and service.

Customer Knowledge. Sales trainees are taught who the customers are, where they are, and how important they are. Experienced salespeople need additional essential knowledge concerning changes in the segments in which they are selling, and trends and changes that might be noted over time, and which need to be addressed. With both groups, sales by product or product line should be reviewed for each customer or customer class, noting trends that are up or down, and why such is the case. Each major

---

[16]Thayer C. Taylor, "Xerox's Sales Force Learns a New Game," *Sales & Marketing Management,* July 1, 1985, pp. 48–51.

customer or prospect is studied, with discussions centered on members of the buying center, buying policies and procedures, buyer attitudes, and strategies to be employed either to sell the prospect or to expand sales to present customers. Market research findings are shared with salespeople by exploring test market results, product and competitive sales, and buyer behavior findings.

Competitive Knowledge. New sales recruits must be introduced to different types of customers, their needs, their buying motives, and their buying habits. Sales management must provide information on competitors' products, policies, services, competitive advantages and disadvantages, warranties, and credit policies, among other things. "Know thy competition" is wise counsel to both recruits and seasoned sales professionals alike. Does the company's copier cost more than competitors', run faster, last longer? Will your company's automatic packaging machinery, while costing more initially, run longer and with less service or breakdown problems than the competitors' machinery? Does your refuse removal company pick up daily, while the competition picks up once or twice a week? Questions such as these must be answered in any honest appraisal of the competition. Accurate knowledge allows the salesperson to approach prospects with the greatest needs for your product or service. Accurate competitive knowledge allows the business to business salesperson to feel more confident, and to present company features and benefits more forcefully and more effectively. Knowledge increases the probability of success, while ignorance increases the probability of failure.[17]

Time and Territory Management. A **sales territory** represents a group of current and potential customers, and in order to achieve optimum efficiency and effectiveness in servicing accounts within a specific territory, salespeople must plan and control activities carefully. An effective sales manager and/or trainer knows that prime selling time is too precious to waste. The problem of effective time and territory management is particularly important for territorial salespeople, as the cost of a salesperson's time has been increasing steadily and rapidly over the past several years. As noted earlier, it has been estimated that the cost of sales call exceeds $250 today, so selling effectiveness in the light of escalating selling costs has resulted in a focus on time and territory management as a top-priority training endeavor.

Who Should Do the Training?

Sales training programs are normally conducted at a central companywide site by professional trainers, in the field by branch managers and sales personnel, or by private consulting organizations and professional trainers. In general, the training site, relative sophistication of the facilities, and professionalism of the trainers are determined by the particular training

---

[17]Robert J. Calvin, *Profitable Sales Management and Marketing for Growing Businesses* (New York: Van Nostrand Reinhold, 1984), pp. 24–26.

needs involved, and by the size of the firm's sales training budget. One study indicates that about 63 percent of all company sales-training programs are in-house, only about 6 percent are outside only, and the remaining 31 percent involve both in-house and outside personnel.[18] The following sections will cover the three most widely used modes of sales training mentioned above.

Home Office Sales Training.   Many large firms have a **sales training department** which acts as a sort of nerve center for all sales training activities undertaken by the company. Most of these centralized training facilities are designed to supplement the basic sales training done in the field by a field sales manager or branch manager, acting as a liaison between the home office and the field. Training policies and procedures for the entire sales organization emanate from this training unit, with the sales training director usually reporting to either the national sales manager or the vice president of sales. (For example, Uarco, Inc. has its home office training facility located in Barrington, Illinois, and ADP has its facility in Roseland, New Jersey.) These centralized training units concentrate on professionalizing the selling skills of sales representatives who have several months or even many years of experience, in addition to training field sales managers wishing and/or needing to update their training skills. These facilities have classrooms, closed circuit television and videotapes, projection equipment, and nearby facilities for housing trainees during the training period.

Many small companies cannot afford to hire staff trainers. This fact, along with the tendency of staff trainers to schedule far more training than is required, necessitates close supervision of trainees to minimize this potential problem.

Field or Local Sales Training.   **Field or local sales training** exposes the trainee to the real world sales environment, whereby the techniques learned in a formal training session can be tried, with additional necessary training pinpointed and provided as necessary. A note of caution is in order here. Too many companies put new salespeople in out-of-the-way corners of field sales offices, providing little attention, supervision, and training, while expecting sales orientation and training to take place automatically through absorption of the sales-office atmosphere. This mentality and modus operandi should be avoided, as trainees may feel disillusioned, and may question their choice of employment. However, on the plus side of the ledger, field or local sales training moves the learning process closer to the customers. It introduces a measure of realism as the recruits will observe top salespeople selling to customers similar to those the recruits themselves will encounter in their own, yet to be determined, territories.

Private Consulting Organizations and Professional Trainers.   Many **private consulting firms** provide sales training services which are sold to business and industry, and which are conducted by professional trainers, most of whom have extensive experience in the areas they teach. Most private con-

---

[18]Jack Gordon, "Where the Training Goes," *Training*, October 1986, p. 50.

sultants who provide sales training services develop custom-made programs tailored to the client's products, personnel, and sales policies. These programs are given periodically, and the charge to the firm is normally negotiated on a per student basis. Many outside suppliers exist, but perhaps the most popular are Learning International, Wilson Learning Corporation, Forum Company, and Dale Carnegie. Learning International, for example, has worked with 80 percent of the *Fortune* 500 business to business corporations. Dale Carnegie conducts programs that are licensed through franchises. Many companies, such as DuPont, use more than one outside supplier.[19] In addition to consulting organizations, many business schools within institutions of higher learning provide sales training for businesses on a fee basis. Trainers are typically business school faculty members, and the price approximates that charged by private firms. Bryant College in Smithfield, Rhode Island, with its Center for Management Development, along with the Daniel Management Center at the University of South Carolina, The Center for Professional Development at Clemson University, and The Management Development Center at the University of Tulsa, among others, are recognized for their expertise in sales training, along with a host of other disciplines and specialty areas offered. Some institutions of higher learning provide training of this kind not only as a service to the business community but also as a partial answer to financial exigency.

Evaluating Sales Training

The costs of sales training are substantial; the sales training budgets of many large companies involve hundreds of thousands of dollars or more. Whether or not this investment is paying off presents the problem of determining, and, where possible, measuring the contributions made through sales training. A three-step evaluation process is suggested at this point:

1. Set objectives (both overall and specific) for the company sales training program.
2. Determine whether the objectives as set, are being met, or have already been met.
3. Try to measure the effect of training on profitability.

Some objectives cannot be measured, or at the very least, are difficult to measure, while other performance criteria can be measured without much difficulty. Exhibit 12–1 lists some criteria a company might use in order to measure the effectiveness of a sales training program. Although not all of these criteria are used by every company, many are helpful in evaluating the effectiveness of a sales training program.

A training program is designed to take a salesperson from the present level of competence to some desired level of proficiency. If the program is successful, objectives will have been met, and the salesperson will be able

---

[19]Thomas R. Wotruba and Edwin K. Simpson, *Sales Management* (Boston: PWS-Kent Publishing, 1989), p. 356. Also see Jeremy Main, "How to Sell by Listening," *Fortune,* February 4, 1985, pp. 52–54.

■ **EXHIBIT 12–1**   Specific Criteria to Measure When Determining the Effectiveness of Sales Training

Absenteeism	Number of calls
Average commission per sale	Number of lost customers
Average size of the sale	Percentage of objections overcome
Average time to "break-even"	Product mix sold
Bad debt ratio	Qualitative call improvement
Competitive investigations	Ratio of carload sales to total sales
Complaint letters	Referral rate
Compliment letters	Reduced cost of training
Developing new product demand	Reduced training time
Earnings of salespeople	Reduction in legal actions
Implementation of promotional programs	Sales force turnover
Improvement in sales rank position	Sales forecasting accuracy
Improvement of call quality	Sales/phone call ratio
Increased active selling time	Sales/travel ratio
Items per order	Sales volume
New customers per week/month	Volume increase for existing accounts
New/old customer ratio	Volume of returned merchandise

SOURCE: C. Robert Patty, *Sales Manager's Handbook* (Reston Publishing, 1982), pp. 118–20. Used with permission.

to perform some new skills successfully. If performance is not up to expectations, then perhaps parts of the training program should be changed. Both of these scenarios suggest that the business sales executive must constantly review current training programs to see if they are still pertinent, relevant, and practical. If a particular training program has remained exactly the same over a long period of time, it is entirely possible that it no longer satisfies the needs of the marketplace, the company, and the salespeople. Frequent evaluation and reevaluation help to assure that training needs and development programs remain sensitive to the changing internal and external environment.

Learning International suggests measuring the effect of training they provide by using a control group which is not involved in the program and an experimental group which receives the training. The calculation of training benefits is as follows:

$$TE = \frac{CES - CCS}{100 + CCS}$$

where:

TE = Training effect
CES = Change in environmental training group (%)
CCS = Change in control group (%)

For example, the training group in a specialty industrial chemicals firm increased its sales by 13.4 percent, while sales in the control group rose by only 6.4 percent. The training effect was then a 6.5 percent increase, measured as follows:

$$TE = \frac{13.4 - 6.4}{100 + 6.4} = \frac{7.0}{106.4} = 6.5\%$$

If the two groups were well matched at the start of the training experiment, the result can be attributed to the training program. A disadvantage of this method is that it does not demonstrate how long the effects of the training will last.[20]

Concept Questions

1. What is the best-known quantitative method for staffing the sales force?
2. What are some common purposes of sales training?

■ DIRECTING AND MOTIVATING THE SALES FORCE

At this point it is generally assumed that the sales manager has hired capable sales people, has trained them well, has effectively organized the sales force, and has assigned these salespeople to territories that will optimize sales. Now the sales manager must effectively direct and motivate each salesperson to capitalize fully on his or her potential. Is the sales quota system fair? Is the compensation system important? Is it fair? All of these factors and more will play an important part in a sales force's performance; it may sound simple in theory, in reality it is very difficult for sales managers to accomplish. This section of the chapter will attempt to present many of the interrelated factors which influence sales force performance, and will identify what can be done to achieve optimal performance from the members of the sales force.

Providing Leadership

Leadership means getting others to work willingly and enthusiastically to achieve the objectives of the organization. It is not just good management; it is also a matter of establishing values, sharing visions, creating enthusiasm, maintaining focus on a few, clear objectives, and building a sales force that works as a team. The "Business to Business Marketing in Action" box describes how Strong Tool Company of Cleveland, Ohio, has developed both its inside and outside sales staffs into an integrated team. Successful business to business sales managers vary greatly in style, from an autocratic to a laissez-faire type of leadership. Figure 12–9 indicates some of the trade-offs between the use of authority by the sales manager and the amount of freedom allowed the salesperson. Exhibit 12–2 discusses some of the more important characteristics of both strong and weak leadership.

Keep in mind that any sales manager may use a variety of leadership styles, depending on the persons he or she is dealing with. A particular sales manager may be autocratic but friendly with a new sales trainee, democratic with an experienced employee who has many good ideas, and laissez-faire with a trusted, long-term employee. Much research has been conducted in an ongoing effort to find out what makes a person an effective

---

[20]Ibid., pp. 363–64.

BUSINESS TO BUSINESS MARKETING IN ACTION

Building a Sales Staff into a Team

Your outside salespeople boast that they are the ones who bring in the business. On the other hand, the inside salespeople claim that without them, the accounts would never be maintained. Sound familiar?

Bill Gerhauser, operations manager at Strong Tool Company in Cleveland, Ohio, says his company tries to ease the tension between the two sales staffs by having the inside salespeople meet with their assigned outside counterparts at least once every business day.

Says Gerhauser, "Our goal is to open the lines of communication so that each side understands the other's problems. The fact is that it's possible to be an inside salesperson and not understand the big picture. The problem we have is that instead of explaining how our customers operate, the outside salespeople often assume that the inside salespeople already have this knowledge."

To remedy this situation, Gerhauser notes that on a selective basis, Strong Tool's outside salespeople bring inside salespeople along with them on their sales calls. Gerhauser says it's hard to put a dollar value on the success of the program, but maintains that the tactic works, particularly on the more complicated accounts.

"We make it clear to our outside salespeople that taking an inside salesperson along with them on an account is simply one option they can use in putting together a sales program," Gerhauser explains. "But for building rapport with an important customer, you can't beat it."

John Monoky, a sales consultant from Toledo, Ohio, says that while some distributors have opted for a strategy similar to Strong Tool's during the past few years, many still experience poor relations between the two sales departments. He claims that a large portion of this animosity stems from managers who narrowly view the inside sales function.

Notes Monoky, "Distributors ask their inside people to sell, but don't give them any exposure to what they are selling, or provide the necessary sales training. Then they hold up the prize of an outside sales job. Just because someone is an excellent inside salesperson doesn't mean they will succeed out in the field."

Monoky maintains that one way to build a sales staff that works well together is to take a hard look at the types of personalities that succeed in sales positions. For example, Monoky says that the best outside salespeople are good time managers, have excellent verbal skills, and are entrepreneurial in nature.

continued

> "These are the people who work best in an environment which permits a great deal of freedom," Monoky adds, "the kind of individuals who enjoy dealing with people face to face."
>
> Conversely, the profile of an inside salesperson is one who's detail-oriented, works best in a structured environment, enjoys working over the telephone, and is managerial in nature.
>
> "The classic personality for an inside salesperson is the kind of person who would love to spend their day playing with a personal computer," Monoky notes.
>
> SOURCE: Steve Zurier, "Build a Sales Staff That Works as a Team," *Industrial Distribution* 77 (April 1988), p. 67. Used with permission.

leader. There is no such thing as leadership traits that are effective in all situations, nor are there leadership styles that always work best. The style to use at a particular time depends on the sales manager, the salespeople, and both the internal and external macro- and microenvironments confronting the sales manager.

Sales Quotas

A **sales quota** is simply a goal—something set for a particular product line, division, or sales representative. It is a management tool that, if correctly

■ **FIGURE 12–9**   A Continuum of Leadership Styles for Sales Managers

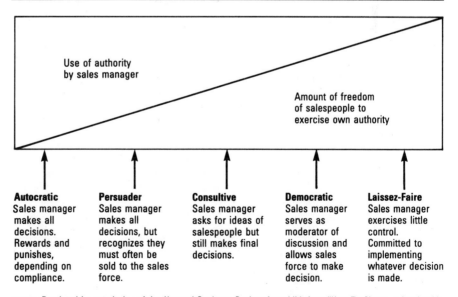

Autocratic	**Persuader**	**Consultive**	**Democratic**	**Laissez-Faire**
Sales manager makes all decisions. Rewards and punishes, depending on compliance.	Sales manager makes all decisions, but recognizes they must often be sold to the sales force.	Sales manager asks for ideas of salespeople but still makes final decisions.	Sales manager serves as moderator of discussion and allows sales force to make decision.	Sales manager exercises little control. Committed to implementing whatever decision is made.

■ **EXHIBIT 12–2**   The Twelve Golden Rules and the Seven Deadly Sins of Leadership

1. *Set a good example.* Your subordinates will take their cue from you. If your work habits are good, theirs are likely to be too.
2. *Give your people a set of objectives and a sense of direction.* Good people seldom like to work aimlessly from day to day. They want to know not only what they're doing but why.
3. *Keep your people informed* of new developments at the company and how they'll affect them. Let people know where they stand with you. Let your close assistants in on your plans at an early stage. Let people know as early as possible of any changes that'll affect them. Let them know of changes that won't affect them but about which they may be worrying.
4. *Ask your people for advice.* Let them know that they have a say in your decisions whenever possible. Make them feel a problem is their problem, too. Encourage individual thinking.
5. *Let your people know that you support them.* There's no greater morale killer than a boss who resents a subordinate's ambition.
6. *Don't give orders.* Suggest, direct, and request.
7. *Emphasize skills, not rules.* Judge results, not methods. Give a person a job to do and let him or her do it. Let an employee improve his or her own job methods.
8. *Give credit where credit is due.* Appreciation for a job well done is the most appreciated of "fringe benefits."
9. *Praise in public.* This is where it'll do the most good.
10. *Criticize in private.*
11. *Criticize constructively.* Concentrate on correction, not blame. Allow a person to retain his or her dignity. Suggest specific steps to prevent recurrence of the mistake. Forgive and encourage desired results.
12. *Make it known that you welcome new ideas.* No idea is too small for a hearing or too wild for consideration. Make it easy for them to communicate their ideas to you. Follow through on their ideas.

THE SEVEN SINS OF LEADERSHIP

On the other hand, these items can cancel any constructive image you might try to establish.

1. *Trying to be liked rather than respected.* Don't accept favors from your subordinates. Don't do special favors trying to be liked. Don't try for popular decisions. Don't be soft about discipline. Have a sense of humor. Don't give up.
2. *Failing to ask subordinates for their advice and help.*
3. *Failing to develop a sense of responsibility in subordinates.* Allow freedom of expression. Give each person a chance to learn his or her superior's job. When you give responsibility, give authority too. Hold subordinates accountable for results.
4. *Emphasizing rules rather than skill.*
5. *Failing to keep criticism constructive.* When something goes wrong, do you tend to assume who's at fault? Do you do your best to get all the facts first? Do you control your temper? Do you praise before you criticize? Do you listen to the other side of the story?
6. *Not paying attention to employee gripes and complaints.* Make it easy for them to come to you. Get rid of red tape. Explain the grievance machinery. Help a person voice his or her complaint. Always grant a hearing. Practice patience. Ask a complainant what he or she wants you to do. Don't render a hasty or biased judgment. Get all the facts. Let the complainant know what your decision is. Double-check your results. Be concerned.
7. *Failing to keep people informed.*

SOURCE: "To Become an Effective Executive, Develop Leadership, and Other Skills," *Marketing News,* April 1984, p. 1. Used with permission.

used, should stimulate the sales effort in terms of physical units, dollars, or both. Quotas can be a powerful means of motivating salespeople if handled correctly. There are several different uses for quotas, including: (1) to provide incentive, (2) to provide a basis for compensation, and (3) to evaluate a salesperson's performance.

Quotas are based on company and sales objectives established during a particular planning process, with quotas being determined for virtually any result and time period relevant to a particular selling job. Quotas can be in the form of sales quotas, expense quotas, profit quotas, or activity quotas. Quotas must be established fairly, be within the reach of salespeople, be easy to understand and control, and be consistent with company revenue goals. Sales quotas are a quantitative tool that must be used to direct, control, motivate, and evaluate sales activities and salespeople. Sales quotas should uncover strengths and weaknesses in the selling structure, improve the compensation plan's effectiveness, control selling expenses, and enhance sales contests. Finally, many sales and marketing managers advocate the joint setting of quotas between sales managers and salespersons. If the salesperson has no part in the establishment of the quota, there is less chance that the quota will be a meaningful motivator, as the salesperson may judge the quota as being too high or too low.

Compensation and Motivation

Employees listen closely when the president of Electro-Scientific Industries Inc. in Portland, Oregon, reports sales and profits; few in the audience fail to grasp the subtleties of pretax and aftertax profits. This degree of awareness is not surprising, as the employees are paid 25 percent of the pretax profits each quarter, with a fourth of that going straight into their pockets, and the rest into retirement or stock ownership accounts. They are not alone. Raychem, Tektronix, Johnson Wax, Lowe's Companies, Hewlett-Packard, Goldman-Sachs, Marion Labs, *Reader's Digest,* and Quad/Graphics, among others, are paying out some portion of pretax profits to all employees, either outright or into trusts.[21]

A sound, solid equitable compensation plan is essential to successful management of the sales force. However, there is some confusion and disagreement about the role of financial incentives as motivators. Some sales managers feel that salespeople are motivated strictly by financial rewards, while others feel that financial compensation is relatively unimportant as a true motivator of behavior. An accurate analysis probably lies somewhere in between these two extremes. In terms of payment plans, the trend seems to be away from straight-salary and straight-commission compensation plans. Today, most company sales compensation plans feature salary plus incentive in the form of a commission or a bonus, as Figure 12–10 indicates.

---

[21]T. C. Hayes, *New York Times,* May 6, 1984, p. F17.

■ FIGURE 12–10   Alternative Sales Compensation and Incentive Plans, 1985
(percent of companies using plans)

Method	All Industries		Consumer Products	Business Products	Other Commercial Industry
	1985	1984	1985	1985	1985
Straight salary	17.4%	17.1%	9.3%	14.1%	30.4%
Draw against commission	6.5	6.8	7.5	6.0	7.0
Salary plus commission	30.7	29.0	22.4	35.8	23.4
Salary plus individual bonus	33.7	33.6	45.8	32.5	29.3
Salary plus group bonus	2.7	2.3	4.7	2.1	2.9
Salary plus commission plus individual or group bonus	9.0	11.2	10.3	9.5	7.0
Total	100.0%	100.0%	100.0%	100.0%	100.0%

Note: Some year-to-year differences reflect changes in the organizations reporting.

SOURCE: "Alternative Sales Compensation and Incentive Plans, 1985," May 6, 1984, by the New York Times Company. Reprinted by permission.

Most discussions with sales executives would reveal a consensus that (1) compensation is the most important element in motivating a sales force; and (2) a properly designed and applied compensation package must be geared to both the needs of the company and the products and services the firm sells, while at the same time allowing the company to attract good salespeople and keep them motivated to produce at increasing rates. Although compensation is clearly fundamental to the motivation of salespeople, the issue is far more complicated than simple payment rewards. The amount of satisfaction and the sense of personal achievement individuals feel from performing tasks are also important for motivation. We suggest that sales team members can be motivated through the following additional factors:

1. Task clarity.
2. Recognition of achievement of short-term objectives with incentive pay (bonuses, stock options, and so on).
3. Recognition of achievement of long-term objectives with status-enhancing rewards (title, promotions, etc.).
4. Job enrichment rewards (trips to professional conferences).[22]

The motivational impact of the factors listed above relates to both monetary incentives and peer and public recognition of achievement. Thus a more broad-based and relevant motivational effect is achieved.

Sales Force Analysis and Evaluation

All firms evaluate their salespeople—whether the firm is large or small; whether it is in consumer, business to business, government, or export

---

[22]Based on Leon Winer, "Motivating Industrial Sales Reps: A Six-Point Plan," *Marketing News,* February 19, 1982, p. 7.

sales; whether it sells goods or services; and whether it employs one or several thousand salespeople. The evaluation may be formal or informal, the form may be simple or complex, and its conclusions based on objective criteria or on executive opinion. Whatever its scope, sales force analysis and evaluation takes place in all companies, because without it the supervision of salespeople is impossible.[23]

Why Analyze and Evaluate Salespeople?

What does a sales manager expect to accomplish through sales force analyses and evaluations? The following list suggests desired outcomes:

1. To determine areas where each salesperson needs improvement.
2. To assess the validity of the standards used.
3. To spot people who are ready for promotion, salary raises, or assignment to new territories and responsibilities.
4. To supply evidence on salespeople who should be disciplined or terminated.
5. To check the effectiveness of the sales compensation plan, training, supervision, recruitment, territory assignments, and operating procedures.[24]

Evaluation plans should be tailored to the specific company for which it is being used. In one company sales calls made per day may be an important criterion of performance, while in another it may be the number of new accounts opened. Regardless of what specific tasks are analyzed and evaluated, the overall evaluation program should be realistic, motivational, participatory, flexible, and specific. It is better to have no formal analysis and evaluation program than to have a poorly designed and administered one.

Who Should Analyze and Evaluate Salespeople?

Most sales managers would agree that the salesperson's immediate superior should be the primary evaluator. Most evaluations would include constructive criterion as supplied by the immediate supervisor, and would also include recommendations for any raises and promotions. Some companies use an entire regional management group and a home office personnel specialist to evaluate salespeople, as shown in Figure 12–11. The specialist would ensure that approved evaluation procedures are followed, and that each person being evaluated is treated fairly.

---

[23]Eugene M. Johnson, David L. Kurtz, and Eberhard Scheuing, *Sales Management* (New York: McGraw-Hill, 1986), pp. 434–35.

[24]Albert H. Dunn and Eugene M. Johnson, *Managing Your Sales Team* (Englewood Cliffs, N.J.: Prentice-Hall, 1980), p. 197.

■ **FIGURE 12–11** Possible Management Input into Salesperson's Performance Evaluation

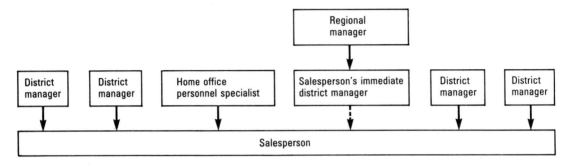

◄---- Direct input performance evaluation.

◄────── Indirect input performance evaluation.

SOURCE: Table, p. 699, from *Sales Management*, 2nd ed., by Charles Futrell, Copyright © 1988 by The Dryden Press, a Division of Holt, Rinehart & Winston, Inc., Reprinted by permission of the publisher.

When Should It Be Done?

Informal evaluation should be almost a daily occurrence, as mistakes should be brought to the salesperson's attention as soon as possible. Other than for routine corrections, a formal evaluation program should be conducted on a regular basis; the time required to evaluate, and the activities involved in the evaluation cycle, will be the primary determinants of formal evaluation frequency. As a general rule, a minimum of one formal evaluation should be completed yearly for each salesperson.

■ MANAGING U.S. SALESPEOPLE IN INTERNATIONAL MARKETS

In order to develop an effective sales organization in another country, the sales manager must appreciate and understand the normal sales manager-salesperson roles, and the expectations of salespeople in that country. Such relationships differ from one country to the next. The U.S. philosophy, which emphasizes individuals' theoretical control over their own destinies, is completely alien to other cultures. U.S. salespeople expect pay based on merit and promotion in accordance with performance compared to other salespeople in the same firm. In other nations, such as Japan, the sales manager-salesperson relationship may be much like a family relationship—the salesperson expects job security, seniority, and reward for loyalty.[25]

After formulating a policy for the management of a sales force in a foreign country, the sales manager must implement this policy through the selection, orientation and training, compensation, and motivation of such salespeople.

---

[25]Edward W. Cundiff and Marye Tharp Hilger, *Marketing in the International Environment* (Englewood Cliffs, N.J.: Prentice-Hall, 1984), pp. 337–38.

Selection

Selection is crucial to the success of an overseas appointment. It is desirable to establish the selection criteria, and to adapt the criteria carefully to ensure that the right person is chosen. Exhibit 12–3 lists considerations

■ **EXHIBIT 12–3**   Interview Criteria for International Candidates

Motivation

- Investigate reasons and degree of interest in wanting to be considered.
- Determine desire to work abroad, verified by previous concerns such as personal travel, language training, reading, and association with foreign employees or students.
- Determine whether the candidate has a realistic understanding of what working and living abroad requires.
- Determine the basic attitudes of the spouse toward an overseas assignment.

Health

- Determine whether any medical problems of the candidate or family might be critical to the success of the assignment.
- Determine whether the candidate is in good physical and mental health, without any foreseeable change.

Language ability

- Determine potential for learning a new language.
- Determine any previous language(s) studied or oral ability (judge against language needed on the overseas assignment).
- Determine the ability of the spouse to meet the language requirements.

Family considerations

- How many moves has the family made in the past between different cities or parts of the United States?
- What problems were encountered?
- How recent was the last move?
- What is the spouse's goal in this move?
- What are the number of children and the ages of each?
- Has divorce or its potential, death of a family member, etc., weakened family solidarity?
- Will all the children move; why, why not?
- What is the location, health, and living arrangements of grandparents, and the number of trips normally made to their home each year?
- Are there any special adjustment problems that you would expect?
- How is each member of the family reacting to this possible move?
- Do special educational problem exist within the family?

Resourcefulness and initiative

- Is the candidate independent; can the candidate make and stand by decisions and judgments?
- Does the candidate have the intellectual capacity to deal with several dimensions simultaneously?
- Is the candidate able to reach objectives and produce results with whatever available personnel and facilities, regardless of the limitations and barriers that might arise?
- Can the candidate operate without a clear definition of responsibility and authority on a foreign assignment?
- Will the candidate be able to explain the aims and company philosophy to the local managers and workers?

continued

■ **EXHIBIT 12–3**   *(concluded)*

- Does the candidate possess sufficient self-reliance, self-discipline, and self-confidence to overcome difficulties or handle complex problems?
- Can the candidate work without supervision?
- Can the candidate operate effectively in a foreign environment without normal communications and supporting services?

Adaptability

- Is the candidate sensitive to others, open to the opinions of others, cooperative, and able to compromise?
- What are the candidate's reactions to new situations, and efforts to understand and appreciate differences?
- Is the candidate culturally sensitive, aware, and able to relate across the culture?
- Does the candidate understand his own culturally derived values?
- How does the candidate react to criticism?
- What is the candidate's understanding of the U.S. government system?
- Will the candidate be able to make and develop contacts with his peers in the foreign country?
- Does the candidate have patience when dealing with problems?
- Is the candidate resilient; can he bounce back after setbacks?

Career planning

- Does the candidate consider the assignment other than a temporary overseas trip?
- Is the move consistent with the candidate's progression and that planned by the company?
- Is the candidate's career planning realistic?
- What is the candidate's basic attitude toward the company?
- Is there any history or indication of personnel problems with this employee?

Financial

- Are there any current financial and/or legal considerations which might affect the assignment, e.g., house purchase, children and college expenses, car purchases?
- Are financial considerations negative factors, i.e., will undue pressures be brought to bear on the employee or family as a result of the assignment?

SOURCE: David M. Noer, *Multinational People Management* (Washington, D.C.: Bureau of National Affairs, 1975), pp. 55–57. Used with permission.

of selection. Potential candidates could be rated as either satisfactory or unsatisfactory according to each of the criteria listed. The salesperson showing the highest satisfactory ratings overall could be the final choice. Additionally, the candidate's spouse should be involved in the selection process right from the beginning. Many failures arise from the spouse's reluctant transfer in the first place and an inability to adapt to the host country's conditions.

Further, before accepting the overseas assignment, candidates and their spouses should be given an opportunity to visit the country in question. Even a trip of a week or so can be helpful to them in arriving at a more comfortable decision.[26]

---

[26]Rosalie L. Tung, "Selection and Training of Personnel for Overseas Assignment," *Columbia World Journal of Business* Spring 1981, pp. 68–78.

Orientation and Training

Sales personnel selected for overseas assignments should be oriented to the new job and provided with appropriate training. Essentially, orientation should cover the terms and conditions of the assignment, language training, and cultural training.[27] The salesperson should be given a clear and concise overview of the company's overseas policies and procedures, compensation program, information on housing, schools, and transportation in the host country, and information on moving arrangements. The salesperson should also receive basic language training since language is the key to a country's culture, and permits understanding of both the fundamental and the subtle differences among the customs and values of various foreign markets. Squibb, IBM, Kodak, and NCR give special attention to the sales training function.

Finally, both academic and interpersonal cultural training should be given. Academic training involves the provision of books, films, slides, maps, and brochures about the country in question; interpersonal training includes making arrangements for the candidate and his or her family to visit the host country, and to meet with those individuals living in the United States who are very familiar with the country of assignment.[28]

Compensation

Salespeople away from their home country cost the firm more because they must be paid additional compensation. This extra compensation covers three factors. First, it is a premium for climatic conditions in the host country, separation from friends and extended family, cultural shock, and subjection to situations of political instability and economic risk in conditions of unstable currencies. Second, it is an allowance for housing, children's schooling, return trips home on a periodic basis, income tax, and overall cost-of-living expenses. Third, there are certain prerequisites common in host countries for particular positions (like car and driver, servants, and club memberships). Here again, NCR and IBM (among others) are pioneers in the motivation and compensation of their overseas sales force.

Considering the expenses involved in transferring non-native salespersons to host countries, the company should make a careful study of the conditions of each country and undertake regular reviews of any changes. The overhead expenses involved in keeping watch on changes in costs, taxation, facilities, and currency values are by no means negligible. Experts in the field are high-priced, and their travel budgets are large. Nevertheless, the cost is a sound investment if, as a result of a reasonable compen-

---

[27]See Burton W. Teague, *Selecting and Orienting Staff for Service Overseas* (New York: Conference Board, n.d.). See also Jefferey L. Blue and Ulric Haynes, Jr., "Preparation for the Overseas Assignment," *Business Horizons,* June 1977, pp. 61–67.

[28]Subhash C. Jain, *International Marketing Management,* 2d ed. (Boston: Kent Publishing, 1987), p. 582.

sation program, the salespeople have confidence in the home office's policy toward them. These necessary prerequisites secure their profitable contribution to the company's performance.[29]

In addition to the criteria listed above for a specific position, the typical candidates for an international sales assignment are married, have two school-aged children, are expected to stay overseas three years, and have the potential for promotion into higher management levels. These characteristics are the basis of most of the difficulties associated with getting the best of the qualified to go overseas, keeping them there, and assimilating them on their return.[30]

Concept Questions

1. What is the value of leadership in sales management?
2. Why should the performance of a sales force be routinely evaluated?
3. What is the difference between U.S. and Japanese salespeople in the way in which they perceive job motivation?

SUMMARY

1. The first qualification for a sales manager is leadership, as this person must attempt to allocate financial resources efficiently. He or she must also attempt to allocate, maintain, direct, and control a large group of people who are both independent and not in daily contact with management.

2. Some of the major changes that occur when a salesperson is promoted to sales manager include changes in perspectives, goals, responsibilities, sources of satisfaction, job skills requirements, and professional relationships.

3. Common forms of organization of the sales force include line organization, line and staff organization, functional organization, centralized versus decentralized organization, and organization by specialization. Organization by specialization can be along the lines of geographic specialization, sales activities, product specialization, customer organization, or some combination of these.

4. One of the most important of all the sales manager's tasks is the recruitment and selection of competent salespeople. The sales manager should first determine the size of the sales force. Then the task of recruitment includes the conducting of a job analysis, the preparation of a written job description, the development of job qualifications, and tapping various internal and external sources of sales recruits. Next,

---

[29]Ibid., pp. 584–85.

[30]Herbert Huffen, "So You Still Want an Overseas Assignment," *Across the Board,* June 1985, p. 64.

the right salespeople must be selected, which involves decision making on the part of the applicant as well as the sales manager.

5. Sales training must be continuous and include instruction in product knowledge, competitive knowledge, new selling techniques, development of sales skills, and knowledge of time and territory management. Companies are interested in providing sales training for a variety of reasons, but primarily to increase sales volume, productivity, and profits. Sales training is generally provided by home office sales trainers, field or local sales trainers, and/or private consulting organizations and professional trainers. Because the costs of sales training are substantial, careful evaluation of the effort should be undertaken on a regular basis.

6. The sales manager must effectively direct and motivate each salesperson to capitalize on his or her potential. Sales managers must provide proper leadership, personal and professional support, and attractive compensation. Appropriate sales quotas should be set for each salesperson as part of an effective overall supervision and motivation function.

7. An evaluation program for the evaluation of salespeople should be tailored to the specific company for which it is being used. The overall evaluation program should be realistic, motivational, participatory, flexible, and specific. Both formal and informal evaluations should be completed on a regular basis.

8. To develop an effective sales organization in a foreign country, the employer must understand the normal sales manager-salesperson roles and the expectations of salespeople in that country. Such relationships vary from country to country. After formulating a policy for the management of a sales force in a foreign country, the sales manager must implement this policy through the selection, orientation and training, and compensation of such salespeople.

KEY TERMS

central versus decentralized organization

customer specialization

field or local sales training

functional organization

geographic specialization

job analysis

job description

job specification

leadership

line organization

line and staff organization

organization by specialization

private consulting firms

product specialization

recruitment and selection process

sales quota

sales territory

sales training

sales training department

REVIEW QUESTIONS

1. Identify and discuss six types of changes that can occur when a salesperson is promoted to sales manager.

2. Differentiate among the five major types of sales force organization. Identify five means by which a sales force can be organized by specialization.

3. Explain how the size of a sales force can be determined by the workload method, the sales potential method, and the incremental method. How is sales force turnover determined?

4. What is the role of a job analysis, a job description, and a job specification in recruiting salespeople? What are some common sources of sales recruits? Explain how the selection process for salespeople is conducted.

5. Identify six fundamental purposes of sales training. Discuss six areas of instruction that should be included in any sales training program.

6. Describe three types of sales training methods. What are the steps involved in the sales training evaluation process? What method for determining the effect of sales force training does Learning International suggest?

7. How does a sales manager utilize leadership skills in directing and motivating the sales force? What are sales quotas, and how do sales managers establish them? How is compensation related to the successful management of the sales force? How often should a sales manager evaluate the sales performance of the individual members of the sales force?

8. How are recruitment and selection of salespeople carried out by U.S. sales managers in international markets? What is involved in orientation and training programs in international markets? How do perceptions of job motivation differ between Japanese and U.S. salespeople?

CHAPTER CASES

Case 12–1   Teletronic Electronics*

Chris White was New Orleans' district sales manager. He was 51 years old and had been with Teletronic Electronics (TE) for 21 years. TE was a distributor of several thousand different types of small electrical parts, such as fuses, batteries, and wiring. In 1977 a company recruiter hired Judy Luby as a salesperson and assigned her to White. This made a total of nine salespeople White was responsible for, with accounts in Louisiana, Arkansas, and Mississippi.

---

*Charles Futrell, *Contemporary Cases in Sales Management,* 1981, The Dryden Press, pp. 225–28.

The First Female Salesperson

Luby graduated from Texas A&M University, majoring in industrial distribution. She was active in campus organizations, while maintaining her 3.86 grade point average. Luby had worked in her father's business, an electronic distributorship like TE, located in Dallas, the last three summers. Luby wanted to be on her own, so she turned down her father's offer of a job after graduation. She was excited about her job and felt that she had a lot to offer. Even though she was the first woman to work for White, and one of only six women employed by TE, Luby felt that she could do the job as well as any man.

Sales Training

Luby attended a three-week training program, learning about products, policies, competition, and selling. Each week trainees were tested. Luby scored top in her class with a 97 percent average. Trainers rated her exceptionally high on her personality, motivation, ability to get along with others, self-discipline, and selling ability. She made several suggestions on sales techniques based on what she had learned while working at her father's business that were eventually used throughout the company.

When White received a summary of Luby's excellent training scores and comments from the trainers, he remembered a young man several years ago who wanted to tell him how to run his sales job. He thought, "Why me? Why do I get stuck with these generous ones who know all? And a female! Why, I'm old enough to be her father!"

White Drops By

Luby was assigned the New Orleans sales territory and rented a very nice apartment. About three months after she began work, White dropped by Luby's apartment to drop off some business forms she had requested. She was going out of town Monday and would not receive them by mail in time. White saw Luby talking to several people by the swimming pool in her building. She seemed very glad to see him. Luby was in her bathing suit, as were two of the four people, two male and two female, she was with, and whom she introduced to White. White discovered they worked for two of their largest customers. Luby asked White whether he would like to go for a swim, but he said "No," left the forms, and went back to his office steaming. The next week a letter went out to all salespeople reminding them to work a full day. That Friday Luby stopped by the office and said she had sold them both a large order. White said it was not professional for a young woman to conduct business in that manner. Luby became so mad she began to cry.

White Won't Pay

Expense vouchers are sent to White for approval. Several small items, not normally approved, had been paid for by Luby herself. For example, she had sent flowers to several buyers who had been in the hospital, and had sent expensive birthday cards to several of her customers. Recently, however, she submitted vouchers for several dinner and entertainment expenses that were not approved. When Luby asked White to pay for two season tickets to the New Orleans Saints' home games, he blew up. Luby explained that she had taken several customers to the games, and felt that it had turned into business entertainment. White said "No" and told her he would pay for standard expenses in the future.

It was not a week later when the wife of a buyer for one of their largest customers called the office requesting Luby's address. White took the call and was glad he did. The woman was upset because Luby had taken her husband to a football game and he had come home late that night quite intoxicated. The buyer told his wife he had been out with a salesman from TE. His wife found out it was a saleswoman and she was furious. White called Luby that night and explained the situation. She apologized and said it would not happen again.

At that time Luby asked White whether the company would pay for her to take courses at a local university. White said "No" and told her he was not in favor of that because it would take away from her job. After all, he didn't even have a college degree and had been successful. Luby said she had already enrolled in an evening graduate level sales management course that would count toward an MBA. For her class project she had collected sales data from the other salespeople in the district and developed a plan to geographically restructure sales territories and their accounts. Luby said the professor would have it graded in three weeks, and she would like to take his comments and present the final plan to White. "However," Luby said, "we'll have to meet at the university one morning because I have the data on their computer. There are some things I'd like to show you." White said he was not interested, and told her she needed his approval to collect such information. He suggested she reconsider taking evening courses.

Job Performance

At the end of her first year on the job, Luby was number 4 out of 295 salespeople in terms of percentage of sales increase. Corporate management wanted to move women into management, and asked White whether Luby would be a good candidate. He said it was too soon to know, and also commented that he personally had doubts that she could fit in and work as part of a team. White said that she likes to do things on her own and that he didn't think she could hold up under pressure.

Luby's Suggestion Goes to the Home Office

Two weeks later White received a telephone call from the national sales manager, Sam Moore. Moore said he had received Luby's report on realigning sales territories and felt it was excellent. In fact, he wanted to fly down next month and talk with White and Luby about realigning sales territories for the entire sales force using Luby's suggestions. Moore asked White whether he had read the report. White said "No, because Luby has only been with us one year and I don't feel she has the background to make such a suggestion."

After White hung up the telephone he went into a rage. "That, that know-it-all has gone too far. She has by-passed me and made me look bad. I have put up with all of this I can stand. I am the boss and I don't care what Moore says, she and I are going to have it out." White told his secretary to call Luby and have her at the office at 9:00 the next morning.

Questions

1. Why is White behaving this way?
2. Why is Luby behaving this way?
3. What will White do at the meeting? Is it the right thing to do?
4. Ideally, what should White do?

Case 12–2   Duncan Business Machines*

Duncan Business Machines is a small company in an industry full of giants. The home office is in San Jose, California. The company sells and installs plain-paper copiers. Minuite Company is the sole manufacturer of the machines under Duncan's patents.

Breaking with powdered-toner technique that Xerox set as a standard, Duncan and its partners—after five years and $13 million of research and development—in October 1987 brought to market an innovative machine using a liquid-toner transfer method that hitherto had been shunned because of uneven copy qualities. This patented liquid-toner technique gave Duncan several pluses that it converted into marketing advantages. For example, manufacturing costs are low, enabling the first model, the Duncan 140, to sell for less than $5,000, or 50 percent under the price of the Xerox 3100, against which the Duncan 140 was positioned. Not only was the Duncan copier cheaper to make, but the liquid-toner technique was also more durable, adding to the life of the machine and lowering the maintenance cost.

The timing of this new copier was significant because of a dramatic shift in use among copy-machine customers. Decentralized copying became popular as users almost overnight chose to purchase relatively inexpensive and slow convenience machines to decentralize copying operations. To avoid waiting at a central machine, they decided to put smaller units on different floors for quicker access.

In addition to the copier, most customers decided on buying the Duncan service package. This service was an added expense of $400 for their first model, the 140. Here they had another price advantage over the competition. Xerox, the giant of the industry, had a service package price of $1,000 for its comparable model; this sum was added onto their already twice as expensive copier.

---

*C. Robert Patty and Robert Hite, *Managing Salespeople,* 3rd ed., 1988, pp. 64–65. Reprinted by permission of Prentice-Hall, Inc., Englewood Cliffs, New Jersey.

All of this paid off nicely for Duncan. In 1987, prior to introducing the revolutionary Duncan 140, the company had operating revenues of $64 million and suffered a pretax loss of $4 million. In 1988 the company had operating revenues of $81 million and a pretax profit of $8 million. Things were on the up and up for Duncan.

With this kind of results in one year, and with new prototypes in the planning stage, Duncan seems to be in an unbelievable position. The two key people responsible for this kind of profitability were Mary S. Smatter, sales manager, and Jack Cardoza, vice president of marketing. They have just received a detailed report on projected growth for the next two years and seemed to be troubled. Why were they troubled? What could be the problem? Operating revenues are expected to climb to $160 million and pretax income to $30 million by 1990. With this kind of growth many problems can arise. What kind of service force and sales force will be needed to handle this magnitude of increase in demand? Mrs. Smatter and Mr. Cardoza regard this as a very important question, one that will receive preferential treatment in the days ahead.

Duncan has been using a direct-sales strategy. Each of the 40 branches has a sales manager who reports directly to one of six regional managers. The six regional managers, in turn, report directly to Mrs. Smatter, the general sales manager.

Mr. Cardoza, vice president of marketing, is the coordinator of the service centers needed to repair, deliver, and service the copying machines.

With this feeling of trouble ahead, both Mr. Cardoza and Mrs. Smatter called all six regional sales managers to a major conference. They asked the regional managers to make a study of their branch sales managers and service centers. Out of this meeting top management hoped to gain some understanding of future problems, and of what corrective action might be taken.

It soon became obvious that there was little coordination between the salespeople and the service centers. Because of this, many problems were arising. Repair schedules were rarely met. Many times salespeople promised the customers delivery on a certain date without knowing that there were no copiers in inventory at the service center. There was a general bad feeling and lack of trust between the sales force and service people. Some of the service people were joining the forces of the competition. The general team effort among all employees, both sales and service, was slowly deteriorating. Sales were starting to skid, and customers were expressing dissatisfaction with both the service and the unkept delivery promises. There was a need for action. The selling and service areas of the company needed a definite restructuring. Lack of motivation and decreasing dealer loyalty were problems that needed answers and solutions, if Duncan were to continue growing.

The day after Smatter and Cardoza held their conference, Mr. Kline, Duncan's president, called the two in for a report and recommendations.

Questions

1. What do you see as the problem?

2. What alternatives do Smatter and Cardoza have?

3. What alternative would you choose? Explain your assumptions and defend your choice.

SUGGESTED READINGS

Apasu, Yao. "The Importance of Value Structures in the Perception of Rewards by Industrial Salespersons." *Journal of the Academy of Marketing Science* 15 (Spring 1987), pp. 1–10. This study uses value structures to explain industrial salespersons' perception of rewards. Recruitment and selection of salespeople may also be based partly on values.

Berry, Dick. "A Method To Portray and Analyze Sales Performance." *Industrial Marketing Management* 16 (May 1987), pp. 131–44. A study of ratio analysis, market changes, data series, and plot sequencing.

Blumel, Robert T. "Pull Your Pay Stub and See How You're Faring." *Purchasing World* 30 (December 1986), pp. 33–39. Salary survey including statistical data, trends, and compensation criteria.

Castleberry, Stephen B., and John F. Tanner, Jr. "The Manager-Salesperson Relationship: An Exploratory Examination of the Vertical-Dyad Linkage Model." *Journal of Personal Selling and Sales Management* 6 (November 1986), pp. 29–37. Implications for organizational behavior, management style, and leadership are offered.

Chonko, Lawrence B. "Organizational Commitment in the Sales Force." *Journal of Personal Selling and Sales Management* 6 (November 1986), pp. 19–27. An examination of expectancy theory, motivation, and measurement of sales force performance.

Cron, William L., Alan J. Dubinsky, and Ronald E. Michaels. "The Influence of Career Stages on Components of Salesperson Motivation." *Journal of Marketing* 52 (January 1988), pp. 78–92. Researchers have found that career stage is related to salespeople's attitudes, work perceptions, and performance. This study addresses this area and provides implications for sales management practice and research.

Dubinsky, Alan J., and Thomas N. Ingram. "From Selling to Sales Management: A Developmental Model." *Journal of Business and Industrial Marketing* 2 (Spring 1987), pp. 27–36. Presentation of a model that sales executives can use in developing potential sales managers. Valuable sales management skills are identified, and methods for providing skill development are offered.

Jenkins, Steven. "Key Account vs. Field Sales: Resolving the Conflict." *Industrial Marketing Digest* (UK) 11 (Fourth Quarter 1986), pp. 105–10. Guidelines, standards, approaches, and techniques for account development.

———. "Sales Management: How to Land a Key Account." *Industrial Marketing Digest* (UK) 12 (First Quarter, 1987), pp. 137–42. The use of negotiations and sales techniques in planning, organizing, and implementing business to business sales.

Kelley, Bill. "Keeping Salespeople on the Road." *Sales and Marketing Management* 138 (April 1987), pp. 56–61. Survey of operating and maintenance costs of automobile fleets in many companies.

Sales and Marketing Management 138 (June 1987), pp. 41–68. Fourteen articles on America's best sales forces. Case studies of many companies in many industries.

Smith, Daniel C., and John E. Prescott. "Couple Competitive Analysis to Sales Force Decisions," *Industrial Marketing Management,* 16 (February 1987), pp.

55–61. Case study and discussion of performance measures based on predetermined criteria.

Taylor, Thayer C. "Hewlett-Packard Gives Sales Reps a Competitive Edge." *Sales and Marketing Management* 138 (February 1987), pp. 36–41. A company analysis of automation, use of portable computers in business to business sales, and sales force productivity.

Templeton, Jane. "Peer Prestige Puts Pow in Salespower." *Sales and Marketing Management* 138 (June 1987), pp. 76–78. Analysis of the use of employee rewards in motivating salespeople.

Waldrop, Heidi. "The Rewards of Noncash Incentives." *Sales and Marketing Management* 138 (April 1987), pp. 110–12. Survey of executives as to the effectiveness of using noncash incentives to motivate the sales force and to stimulate increased productivity.

Chapter **13**

Advertising and Sales Promotion Strategy in Business Markets

LEARNING OBJECTIVES

After reading this chapter, you should be able to:

- Appreciate the role of promotion in business marketing, and how it differs from the role of consumer promotion.
- Identify the steps involved in creating a promotion plan.
- Explain how objectives are set for a promotion campaign.
- Differentiate among the various promotion tools available to the promotion campaign manager.
- Recall two primary methods of measuring the effectiveness of promotion campaigns.
- Relate the role of advertising, publicity, and sales promotion in the development of international business to business promotion campaigns.

CHAPTER OUTLINE

Learning Objectives
An Overview of Business to
Business Promotion
Creating a Promotion Plan
Setting Objectives for a
Promotional Plan
Developing the Promotion Budget
 Prioritizing the Promotion
 Expenditure
Determining and Implementing
the Promotion Mix
 Advertising
 Publicity
 Sales Promotion

Measuring the Effectiveness of the
Promotion Campaign
 Pretesting and Posttesting
 Responses to Advertisements
Following Up and Modifying the
Promotion Campaign, If Necessary
Promotion Strategy for International
Markets
 International Business to Business
 Advertising
 International Publicity and Sales
 Promotions

■ AN OVERVIEW OF BUSINESS TO BUSINESS PROMOTION

Advertising, publicity, and sales promotion are communication methods used by marketers to remind or persuade existing and potential customers that the product or service exists, as opposed to personal selling, which is verbal communication with a prospective customer. In the business market, advertising, publicity, and sales promotion pave the way for the sales call. In this chapter, and as shown in Figure 13–1, **business to business**

■ **FIGURE 13–1** Business to Business Promotion and the Flows of Information and Persuasion

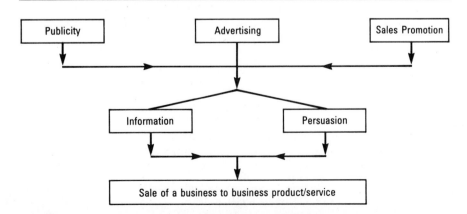

promotion refers to the use of the promotional tools of advertising, publicity, and sales promotion as seller-generated efforts to gain information, while delivering marketing messages to markets. Such promotional methods cost per thousand (CPM) is relatively inexpensive when compared to the cost of personal selling. Additionally, these methods reach many customers quickly and make widespread distribution possible.

Business markets tend to be geographically concentrated with relatively few companies purchasing large amounts. Although only 10 percent of U.S. manufacturing firms employ more than 100 workers, they supply approximately 80 percent of the value added by U.S. manufacturing. These relatively few large buyers represent a potentially lucrative market for marketers. Because of the geographic concentration of these markets and the substantial purchasing volume of most firms, personal selling dominates the promotion mix. Consequently, the role of promotion traditionally has been to support the personal selling function. Business to business promotion can and should aid sales representatives in introducing new products, product lines, and services to either established or potential customers.

Organizational buyers, who tend to be part of a much larger buying center or decision-making unit, purchase in large quantities and base their purchases on relatively exact specifications. Therefore, purchasing managers are considered by some to be less susceptible to promotional appeals that stress brand names. Professional buyers are nonetheless human, and are often subject to the same appeals found effective in consumer advertising. However, not all business markets are concentrated, nor do all firms purchase in large volume. The cost of sending salespeople to many scattered business accounts can be prohibitive. Promotion must assume the selling function for small orders or low-margin products. Carle Instruments is one company that has experienced success using promotional techniques to sell business goods.

Carle Instruments markets products designed for business use and university research. Customers do not buy in large volume; consequently, sales efforts must be spread over many buyers. Because Carle found both its sales force and industrial distributors to be ineffective, it turned to print media and publicity. Using an advertising agency to create high-quality, integrated promotional pieces, Carle answers inquiries promptly and courteously by telephone or personal letter. As the only sales tool employed, promotion must both create a company image and tout the benefits of Carle's products.

Carle is but one company of many which have found that good products and services can be effectively marketed without a sales force. Business buyers have responded favorably to direct mail inquiries—a development that keeps sales costs to a minimum. Many firms are shifting more of their personal selling budget to direct techniques to minimize selling costs, while making personal selling more effective.[1]

---

[1]William G. Nickels, *Marketing Communication and Promotion*, 3d ed. (Columbus, Ohio: Grid Publishing, 1984), p. 145.

■ **FIGURE 13–2**   Steps in a Business to Business Promotion Campaign

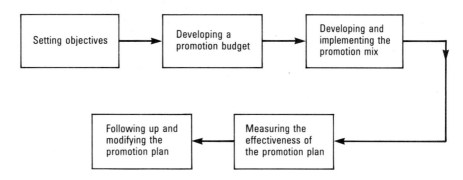

■ CREATING A PROMOTION PLAN

Effective promotion often helps sales, while ineffective promotion can waste millions of dollars and even seriously damage the company image. Figure 13–2 demonstrates that creating a promotion plan involves the following five steps: (1) setting objectives, (2) developing a promotion budget, (3) determining and implementing the promotion mix, (4) measuring the effectiveness of the promotion program, and (5) following up and modifying the promotion campaign, if necessary. This process results in a promotion campaign, which is a carefully planned sequence of promotions centered around a common theme and geared to specific objectives.

■ SETTING OBJECTIVES FOR A PROMOTIONAL PLAN

Promotional campaigns need specific, realistic objectives. The establishment of appropriate objectives should be the starting point for every such campaign. It is difficult, and probably imprudent, to plan a promotional program unless marketers first establish the objectives they are trying to attain. These promotion objectives tend to vary greatly. While it is difficult to quantify such objectives as "friendly image," baseline marketing research can provide initial measures to gauge almost any campaign. Whenever possible, it is preferable to express objectives in dollar amounts. (Objectives need to be "bottom line" in nature.) An objective to generate a certain number of sales leads often results in leads that do not produce sales or profits. For instance, the marketing objective of a promotional campaign may be to generate $3.5 million in sales with a 15 percent ROI (return on investment). Total sales volume and market share are widely utilized sales indices offered by firms such as A. C. Nielsen, Market Research Corporation of America, and Audits and Surveys, Inc. Market-share and sales-volume data assist a marketing manager in determining whether or not a firm's objectives are being met.[2]

---

[2]Carl McDaniel, Jr., and Wiliam R. Darden, *Marketing* (Boston: Allyn & Bacon, 1987), p. 568.

■ DEVELOPING THE PROMOTION BUDGET

After the marketing manager has established promotion goals and has identified appropriate market segments, a solid, cost-effective promotion budget must be developed. This is not a simple or an enviable task, as there are no concrete guidelines or guaranteed techniques to ensure maximum success.

Ideally, the budget needs to be set at a point where the last dollar spent on promotion equals profits from the sales produced by that dollar (i.e., marginal utility). However, in reality, because of the enormity of associated problems, this marginal concept is all but impossible to apply.[3] Com-

■ FIGURE 13–3   Common Techniques for Setting the Business to Business Promotion Budget

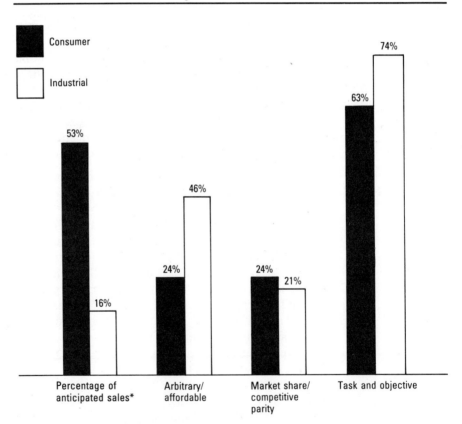

Percents add to more than 100 because of multiple responses.

*Also, 20 percent of the consumer goods firms and 23 percent of the industrial goods organizations use current or past years' sales.

SOURCE: Vincent Blasko and Charles Patti, "The Advertising Budget Practices of Industrial Marketers," *Journal of Marketing*, Fall 1984, pp. 104–10. Used with permission.

---

[3]Ibid., p. 569.

mon techniques for setting budgets include affordable, competitive parity, percentage of sales, and objective and task.[4] As can be seen in Figure 13–3, many firms employ more than one method, although business organizations most commonly use the objective-and-task and affordable methods.

Prioritizing the Promotion Expenditure

Promotion budgets have traditionally been spartan for reasons too numerous, diverse, and illogical to warrant further discussion. It is the marketer's job, however, to set the budget and to insure the most return for every dollar spent. Economists tell us that the first dollar spent on promotion yields the greatest return, with a diminishing rate of return from additional expenditures. However, this is only the case if the money is spent in optimal fashion. Operationally, this requires a prioritization of all promotional efforts in terms of their potential contribution to the firm. How to spend the promotional budget is a tougher and more crucial question than how much to spend. Examine the curve in Figure 13–4 and notice the flatness at the top of the curve. The greatest contribution to the firm is made with the initial dollars spent. A larger budget will often contribute little to profit.

The first step in setting priorities with regard to the promotional dollar is to prioritize the target audience. Figure 13–5 identifies and ranks target audiences, linking the most effective means for reaching each audience.

■ **FIGURE 13–4**   The Contribution of Advertising Expenditures to Profit

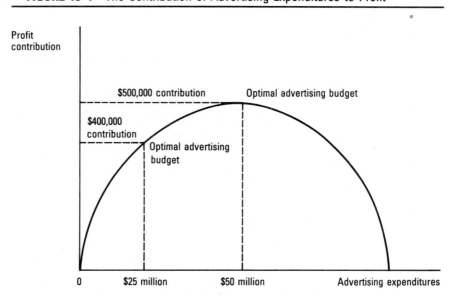

[4]Philip Kotler, *Principles of Marketing,* 3d ed. (Englewood Cliffs, N.J.: Prentice-Hall, 1986), pp. 495–98.

■ **FIGURE 13–5** Identifying Target Audiences and the Most Effective Ways to Reach Them

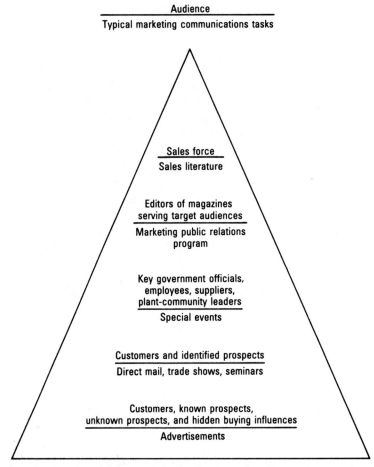

Audience
Typical marketing communications tasks

Sales force
Sales literature

Editors of magazines
serving target audiences
Marketing public relations
program

Key government officials,
employees, suppliers,
plant-community leaders
Special events

Customers and identified prospects
Direct mail, trade shows, seminars

Customers, known prospects,
unknown prospects, and hidden buying influences
Advertisements

Note: How to read: moving downward, size of audience increases. The cost of communicating is more expensive, and ability to isolate influentials is more difficult.
SOURCE: Robert F. Roth, *International Marketing Communication* (Lincolnwood, Ill.: Crain Books, 1982), p. 41. Used with permission.

The astute marketing manager spends budgeted dollars, starting at the top of the pyramid and working down. Advertising, contrary to popular belief, is a low priority item in the business to business promotional budget.

Concept Questions

1. What are the three basic promotion methods used?
2. Why should appropriate objectives be the starting point for any promotion campaign?
3. What is the ideal point at which to set the business promotion campaign?

■ DETERMINING AND IMPLEMENTING THE PROMOTION MIX

Advertising

Nature of Business Advertising.   As pointed out in Table 13–1, **business to business advertising** is considerably different from consumer advertising. Advertising features product-oriented appeals and views the profit motive as a primary purchasing criterion. It assumes a relatively smaller part of the entire selling function than does personal selling and utilizes a smaller percentage of the sales dollar. It also addresses a somewhat limited market, and places greater emphasis on direct mail. Conversely, consumer advertising emphasizes people-oriented appeals, recognizes personal gratification as a primary buying motive, shoulders a greater burden in the total selling effort, spends a larger share of the sales dollar, speaks to a very large and diverse market, and places less emphasis on direct mail.

Goals of Business Advertising.   Advertising generally has one or more of four specific goals:

1.   It is generally designed to make the advertiser favorably known to its current and potential customers.
2.   It often attempts to convey specific and technical information about the characteristics of a particular product or products manufactured by the advertiser.
3.   Either or both of these effects, when achieved, tend to ease the salesperson's job. The company the salesperson represents becomes better known, and the products the salesperson handles become more familiar to potential purchasers as a result of the advertising.
4.   Finally, because of improved sales performance as a result of

■ **TABLE 13–1**   Differences between Business to Business and Consumer Advertising

Business to Business Advertising	Consumer Advertising
Uses rational appeals.	Uses emotional appeals.
Views profit motive as a primary purchasing criterion.	Recognizes personal gratification as a primary buying motive.
Is a smaller part of the entire selling function.	Is a larger part of the entire selling function.
Utilizes a smaller percentage of the sales dollar.	Utilizes larger percentage of the sales dollar.
Addresses a somewhat limited market.	Speaks to a very large and diverse market.
Places greater emphasis on direct mail.	Places less emphasis on direct mail.

advertising, it is usually assumed (or at least hoped) that advertising will help reduce overall selling costs.[5]

We will now discuss in detail each of these objectives.[6]

Advertising should increase customer or potential customer awareness and improve the advertiser's image in their minds. Unlike most consumer advertising situations, business advertising prices are often negotiated. There might be considerable comparative shopping, which may result in competitive bidding. Structural and performance standards may be specified. Often several different specifications from different departments or divisions with differing needs must somehow be fulfilled. Finally, the personality and skill of sharply competitive salespeople often come into play.

What possible effect can advertising have on this process of rationalizing objective and subjective purchasing standards and influences? Advertising can have a significant beneficial effect just in making potential customers aware of potential suppliers, and it can reinforce satisfaction among existing customers. Theodore Levitt makes the following point:

> A company's reputation improves the chances of getting a favorable first hearing and an early adoption of the product. Therefore, corporate advertising that can build upon the company's reputation (other factors also shape its reputation) will help the company's sales representatives.[7]

Advertising should supply information about specific products and services which are of interest to customers. In addition to increasing an advertiser's visibility to potential customers, advertising should provide specific information about the products and/or services of the advertiser that purchasing managers need to know to appraise that advertiser's offerings properly. Two important assumptions are made here. The first is that buyers are looking for detailed information about the products and/or services they buy, and the second is that advertisers know what information is relevant to their customers. As such, it is interesting to discover evidence that advertisers in four product categories studied by Gordon McAleer do not understand the considerations that influence prospective purchasers in their product categories. McAleer studied the buying motivations of four kinds of purchasers: consulting engineers, electrical contractors, architects, and nonresidential building contractors. He then studied the purchasing motives imputed by advertisers to these groups. "The results were disconcerting," McAleer reported, "since the advertising managers did not seem to understand the major considerations which influence the purchase

[5]This section is from William M. Weilbacher, *Advertising* (New York: Macmillan, 1979), pp. 445–46.

[6]Ibid., pp. 446–48.

[7]Theodore Levitt, *Industrial Purchasing Behavior: A Study in Communication Effects,* (Boston: Division of Research, Harvard Graduate School of Business, 1965).

of their products. The finding would indicate that advertising managers are performing their tasks less effectively than they should."[8]

Although the results of McAleer's study cannot be generalized to all areas of business advertising, the evidence indicates that knowledge of buying motives is no less important among business purchasers than among the consuming public. If business advertisers do not know what is going on in the minds of their customers, they would be well advised to find out, so as to keep their advertising messages from being irrelevant and possibly ignored.

Advertising should make the salesperson more productive. One of the fundamental justifications for advertising over the years has been the belief that it smooths the salesperson's entry into both established and prospective customers' firms. According to a recent study by the Advertising Research Foundation and the Association of Business Publishers, increased advertising leads to greater sales and profits.[9] Although it might be difficult to prove in specific situations, there is growing support that the positive interaction between advertising and sales efforts is real and substantial, and is a major reason for investing in advertising. Exhibit 13–1 reflects the advertising on the personal selling effort at IBM.

If advertising improves sales performance, it must reduce selling costs. It is one thing to come to the general conclusion that advertising helps a salesperson's performance, and yet another to quantify just how much savings are generated by such a relationship. No one seems to know just how the advertising-salesperson relationship operates or what the exact economics of the relationship are. However, the subject is important because it means that advertisers must figure out for themselves the proper budget levels for their advertising and personal selling programs. Lilien, Silk, Choffray, and Rao make this point in the following statement:

■ **EXHIBIT 13–1**   The Effects of Advertising on the
                               Personal Selling Effort at IBM

Sales Productivity Study

Advertising/Mail Generated Leads 1981

Average hours to close the order:
Electronic typewriters: without lead 4.4—with lead 1.2
Displaywriter: without lead 19.7—with lead 3.2
Series III: without lead 23.8—with lead 3.4
51XX: without lead 12.8*—with lead 9.5
S/34: without lead 37.5*—with lead 17.5

*Not including prospecting time
SOURCE: Presentation handout by Robert H. Hutchings, manager of advertising and promotion, IBM.

---

[8]Gordon McAleer, "Do Industrial Advertisers Understand What Influences Their Market?" *Journal of Marketing* 38 (January 1974), p. 15.

[9]"Study: Increase Business Ads to Increase Sales," *Marketing News* 22 (March 14, 1988), p. 13.

There is no indication about what the overall budget should be, or about what split between advertising and personal selling expenditures would be most efficient.[10]

Media Selection.   When advertising is used, management must select the **media mix.** The media mix is some combination of the following types of advertising media: print media, broadcast media, and direct marketing.

Print media.   Print media includes business publications, professional publications, trade directories, and general consumer publications, such as *Time, Newsweek, Scientific American,* and *Golf Digest.* Business publications are of two basic types: horizontal and vertical. **Horizontal publications** are intended for buyers who have similar functions in their companies, regardless of their specific industry, such as *Industrial Maintenance and Plant Operation,* which is published for those maintaining and operating industrial plants with more than 50 employees, and *Purchasing,* which is a news magazine for purchasing executives. **Vertical publications** are those discussing current issues and problems of a single industry, such as *Frozen Food Field,* which is edited for management personnel in the frozen food industry, and *Mechanical Contractor,* which is designed to meet the needs of the large heating, plumbing, piping, and air-conditioning contractor.

Professional publications include journals, such as *Architectural Digest,* which is edited for such professionals as physicians, surgeons, dentists, architects, and others. Their editorial range varies from reporting new technical developments to discussing how to run offices more efficiently and profitably. Much advertising is directed to professionals, since they are an important influence in recommending or specifying the products their patients or clients will need.

Industrial trade directories have long been used as an important promotion medium in business advertising. Most industries have their own directory and buyer's guide, with descriptions of products and product lines, and lists of the various firms marketing and selling its product lines. Trade directories are a highly effective way to get particular advertisers' names before their target audiences. Although there are numerous statewide and private trade directories, the best known and most popular is the *Thomas Register of American Manufacturers,* which is comprised of 19 volumes and contains over 60,000 pages with 50,000 product headings and listings from 123,000 business to business companies. One of Thomas's largest customers is General Electric, which buys over 300 sets per year for both its domestic and international concerns.[11] The greatest advantages of industrial trade directories are their selectivity in reporting on individual companies and product titles, and their high credibility and acceptance rate with both large and small advertisers and buyers.

---

[10]Gary L. Lilien, Alvin J. Silk, Jean-Marie Choffray, and Murfidhar Rao, "Industrial Advertising Effects and Budgeting Practices," *Journal of Marketing* 40 (January 1976), p. 24.

[11]"Thomas Register Ranks As King of Catalogs," *Advertising Age,* March 7, 1985, p. 54.

General business publications, such as *Fortune, Business Week,* and *The Wall Street Journal,* cut across a wide variety of industries, and with their business and editorial content address a broad range of issues and concerns of interest to executives in all aspects of business and industry. About 60 percent of the space in general business publications is used for business to business advertising.

Broadcast media. **Broadcast media,** generally thought to be only for consumer goods' advertising, are receiving increasing attention from business advertisers who serve highly geographically concentrated markets, and who want to get around the intense advertising competition in older, more traditional, and well-established business media. Both large and small firms have used radio advertising through the years. Standard Oil of New Jersey attempts to speak to a select audience of managerial decision makers, financial executives, and government officials through appropriate radio stations and time periods. Another veteran radio user is Timken Roller Bearing Company of Canton, Ohio, which runs 15 radio spots a week during morning and evening drive times in the upper Midwest to reach select audiences in cities where there is a great involvement with the automobile and the automotive industry.[12] However, this medium is not appropriate for all business marketers, since costs cannot be justified unless the product has multiple uses across many industries.

Television advertising by business firms has more recently become increasingly popular and more highly visible through the efforts of such industrial giants as IBM, Hewlett-Packard, Xerox, and Federal Express. As the average sales call exceeded $200, one supplier of food equipment began to advertise heavily on television, with classified advertisements in local newspapers; a 24-hour, toll-free answering service; and direct mail as support media.[13] With the sales call now over $250, this type of practice will increase.

Direct marketing.[14] Along with print and broadcast media, business marketers have turned to direct marketing techniques for cost-effective lead generation to facilitate the sale of their products and services. **Direct marketing** includes direct mail, data sheets, catalogs, and telemarketing.

Historically, over 80 percent of the manufacturers of business goods have used direct mail as part of their promotion effort. **Direct mail** is especially important where the market for a product or service is concentrated, because direct mail pieces can be specifically targeted to key individuals and can focus on the key buying motives of that individual. In cases where there is a limited number of potential customers, direct mail offers a relatively less expensive medium in which to maintain contact with them than

---

[12]Kleppner, p. 674.

[13]Joseph Bohn, "Food Equipment Maker Tries Local Television," *Business Marketing,* April 1985, pp. 106–12.

[14]This section is based on Frederick A. Russell, Frank H. Beach, and Richard H. Buskirk. *Selling: Principles and Practices* (New York: McGraw-Hill, 1988). Contribution and further analysis by Bruce Buskirk.

does advertising in business or professional publications. Direct mail is direct marketing only when it elicits a response from the target audience. Otherwise, it is just another advertising medium among magazines, television, and radio. Responses can be either business reply mail or via telephone.

Some of the more common uses of direct mail include rapid distribution for a new product, paving the way for a salesperson's call, an aid to convince distributors to handle a particular product, a means to build strong company image, testing the acceptance of new products, and following up a salesperson's call to emphasize selling points made during the oral presentation. Business services are also frequently promoted through the use of direct mail. Peat-Marwick, a Big 8 accounting firm, with revenues in excess of $3 billion, uses direct mail in selling its services to the financial community. Their direct mail campaigns are not offer-driven, but are instead intended to create awareness and to convey an interest in providing up-to-date tax, auditing, and management services. According to Adrian Dessi, director of marketing services, "We know who we are. Consequently, our direct mail letters are 'chocked-full' of valuable information that directly impacts the business of our clients and prospects."[15]

Direct mail is also a helpful promotional tool for the marketer because it is not very difficult to compile lists of prospects from responses to trade and professional advertisements, and from intracompany telemarketing operations. Mailing lists can also be acquired through industrial directories and mailing list houses, such as Dun & Bradstreet's Marketing Services Division and National Business Lists. Direct mail can also be disadvantageous if appropriate prospects are not clearly targeted and identified, or if direct mail pieces are considered as junk mail and are discarded.

Data sheets are useful because sales representatives often have the answers to many of the highly sophisticated questions posed by technical buyers. Data sheets can be left with appropriate buyers who might make the purchasing decision when the sales representative is not present. Exhibit 13–2 offers some guidelines for advertisers in creating data sheets that sell.

Business catalogs are another segment of direct marketing. Annual growth rates of 20 to 40 percent are not uncommon.[16] Catalogs are created and designed for highly segmented buyers for comparison shopping, for acquiring information on new products or new product applications, and for determining current prices for particular items of interest. Catalogs make the distributor's job a bit easier because it would be difficult for distributors to stock a manufacturer's complete product mix. Historically, buyers have rarely used only a catalog in deciding to make a purchase. However, the increasing ability to communicate economically over long

---

[15]Adrian F. Dessi, "Big-Business-to-Big-Business Direct Mail," *Direct Marketing,* April 1988, pp. 58–60.

[16]J. Schmidt, "Starting Up a Business Catalog," *Direct Marketing* 50 (July 1987), pp. 74–75. See also Cyndee Miller, "Coming Decade Seen As Golden Era for Business-to-Business Mail Order," *Marketing News* 22 (March 14, 1988), pp. 1–2.

■ **EXHIBIT 13–2**   Creating Data Sheets That Sell

1. Include as much technical information as possible. Data sheets should answer all the customer's questions. When the information isn't there, the data sheet is worthless.

2. Good product data sheets explain and highlight technical features to show the customer what benefits he or she will receive when he buys the product.

3. Use photographs. Nothing beats photographs for establishing what something looks like and how it works.

4. Use competitive data sheets to help customers make the comparisons between products.

5. Use 8½″ × 11″ pages so the data sheet doesn't get lost at the bottom of the file folder.

6. Know your reader. Make the content and technical depth of your data sheet compatible with the background and buying interests of your readers.

7. Know where in the buying process the data sheet fits in. Know the environment in which it will be used. Will there be advertising support, public relations, distributors, sales people, catalogs, brochures, direct mail, and word of mouth?

8. Ask for customers' help in preparing the data sheet.

9. Use one writer for the entire project: the ads, the public relations, and the highly technical sheets.

10. Figure out how many people you would like to have read the data sheet, and multiply the number by four to arrive at the number of sheets needed.

SOURCE: See "Data Sheets That Sell," *Sales and Marketing Management,* May 14, 1984, pp. 45–48.

distances, the growing concern over rising inventory costs, and the greater need today for marketers to serve many smaller and geographically diffuse customers are all good reasons why buying through catalogs is becoming more attractive and cost-effective.

A recent survey conducted by the Quick Corporation showed a marketing view of the business mail order industry. Among the findings of the study were the following: (1) business catalogues have increased 20 to 50 percent in recent years; (2) competition is getting fierce, and margins are becoming slim; (3) there is an ever growing number of targeted mailings; (4) databases and compiled lists are being utilized more; and (5) businesses are becoming more comfortable with purchasing through the mail.[17]

Telemarketing as a promotional tool (and form of selling as discussed in Chapter 11) greatly aids the business advertiser in making follow-up calls to check the receipt and effectiveness of various forms of printed and broadcast media, direct mail, data sheets, and catalogs. Coordination between the telemarketing effort and other promotion tools is both important and necessary. Some marketers may not admit it, but they are using telemarketing. "Many companies think telemarketing is a dirty word," says Sandra Pernick, president of Direct Response Corporation, Des Plaines, Illinois, "but all businesses use some form of telemarketing whether they want to call it that or not." The number of structured telemarketing programs has increased dramatically among business marketers to the point that they have become almost routine. "No company should go without

---

[17]J. Miller, "The Shape of Business Cataloging," *Direct Marketing* 50 (August 1987), pp. 100–104.

telemarketing, even if it's as simple as a customer service line," says Pernick.[18] Telemarketers often service telephone hotlines that enable customers to phone in for specific products, services, and price information. According to Joseph Misiura, president of Chicago's SMS Supply Company, "If you don't create an awareness of how effective a selling tool the telephone can be, you'll never improve. We just came to the realization that 90 percent of our communications are over the telephone, and that our inside sales department could be doing a better job of selling."[19]

Telemarketing revenues multiplied 16 times in the last decade and now account for 46 percent of all direct marketing sales.[20] Companies are using telephone systems for promotion, order processing, sales support, and customer service. Telemarketing's potential would seem to be limited only by the imaginations of its users. Telemarketing is not a substitute or replacement for a regular sales force. It should complement and supplement other elements of the promotional mix so that overall promotional efficiency can be improved. Telemarketing as a promotional tool will continue to expand, as we have seen and discussed in Chapter 11.

Advertising Content.   The effective business product or service advertisement contains several elements. First, a short headline presents an interesting or intriguing idea which has enough significance to readers to whom it is addressed that they will wish to pursue the idea further. An explanation or amplification of the headline then develops a limited number of specific appeals that are carefully designed to show potential users that the product or service will be useful to them, and will fill a need or want. The copy then describes the distinctive features of the product or service, offering evidence of the desirability and proof of claims made for it. Finally, the reader is urged to take some action; where feasible, specific courses of action are suggested.[21] Note that the headline, subheadline, and copy of the advertisement shown in Exhibit 13-3 illustrate these concepts.

Excellent photography and clear illustrations increase readership, while strengthening headlines or elaborating on them. Art, however, should not be used for its own sake. Generic images do not convey messages. It is better to use testimonials, case histories, and other copy-heavy advertisements than to be burdened with weak pictures.[22] A recent study by Lebhar-Friedman Research and Information Services of New York City of 481 corporate decision makers found that frequently run colorful advertisements, such as the one shown in Exhibit 13–3, are the best for business

---

[18]Sandra Pernick, "Business Marketers Shouldn't Be Ashamed of Telemarketing," *Marketing News,* March 13, 1989, p. 16.

[19]Steve Zurier, "Strictly for Sales," *Industrial Distribution,* September 1988, p. 65.

[20]Ernan Roman, "The Newest Member of the Media Mix," *Marketing Communications,* June 1987, pp. 72–74, and "Telemarketing," *Marketing Communications,* June 1987, p. 75. See also Louis Weisberg, "Telemarketing: A Growing Art Form," *Advertising Age,* June 27, 1987, pp. S9–S10.

[21]Ralph S. Alexander, James S. Cross, and Ross M. Cunningham, *Industrial Marketing,* 2d ed. (Homewood, Ill.: Richard D. Irwin, 1961), p. 445.

[22]Tenney, p. 12.

■ **EXHIBIT 13–3**   A Well-Created Business to Business Advertisement

advertising. Eight out of 10 respondents said they are more favorably impressed and influenced by four-color than by black-and-white advertisements.[23]

[23]"Study Shows That Frequent Four-Color Ads Attract More Attention in Trade Press," *Marketing News* 22 (March 14, 1988), p. 13.

Use of advertising agencies. **Advertising agencies** are specialist-organizations equipped to provide a range of advertising services to their clients. They work on advertising strategy and campaigns, prepare copy and layouts, study markets, select media, and carry out the physical production of the advertisement, including its placement in selected media.

Most media have historically allowed agencies 15 percent on the cost of the space or time purchased. In the marketing of consumer goods, this commission, plus markups on purchased services, usually represents the total income of the agency available to cover costs of operation and leave a profit. For many marketers of business goods, this method of payment does not result in an amount large enough to cover agency costs, and the contract with the agency includes an additional lump-sum payment proportionate to the services contemplated.

The advertising agency brings the client a wide breadth and depth of experience in business marketing that can seldom be duplicated by the experience of a single company. The agency must also be able to provide the qualities of imagination and innovation in an unusual degree. In Cleveland-based Media II's study of 100 companies in northeastern Ohio, with annual net sales of between $8 million and $100 million, creative marketing services, such as copywriting, art, and logotype creation, were found to be the most important factor in selecting an advertising agency. Creative services outweighed marketing services in importance by 2 to 1.[24]

Contrary to these advantages, advertising agencies are not as universally used by business concerns as they are by consumer goods' firms. Some firms believe that they can save money by avoiding an agency, and also feel that they can probably do a better job themselves because of their greater understanding of their own business and customer base. Advertising agencies, on the other hand, believe that such companies do not know what they are talking about, save less money than they think, and sacrifice creative independence. A fuller discussion of this controversial topic is provided in the "Business to Business Marketing in Action" box. There is little question that the advertising agency has an important place in the marketing of business products. There are some types of activities it cannot perform as well as in-house departments, while there are others it can do better or more economically. If an advertising agency is used, the challenge for marketers is to achieve an effective partnership between the company and the agency. Exhibit 13–4 discusses DuPont's partnership with six advertising agencies.

Publicity

Publicity is defined as "stimulation of demand for a business product or service by planting commercially significant news about it in a print or broadcast medium without payment by the sponsor."[25] Publicity can be a

---
[24]B. Kelley, "Surprising Times in Ohio," *Sales and Marketing Management* 138 (June 1987) p. 109.

[25]Report of the Definitions Committee, Chicago, American Marketing Association, 1960.

BUSINESS TO BUSINESS MARKETING IN ACTION

In-House Advertising Is Causing Agency Concern

Rhode Island–based machine tool builder Brown & Sharpe's gradual weaning away from advertising agencies over the years—culminating recently with longtime agency Marquis/Bennett's decision to resign the account—may represent a trend.

Industrial companies think they can save money—and perhaps do the job better—on their own.

Agencies, on the other hand, assert that such companies don't know what they're talking about, that the companies don't save as much money as they think, and that the companies sacrifice creative independence.

"We've seen a bit of that happening lately, companies going in-house with their advertising," said Stauch-Vetromile principal Fred Stauch, who doesn't like what he sees.

Stauch had no problem reeling off a list of companies, besides Brown & Sharpe, that shun an "agency of record" in favor of doing their own advertising or farming it out piecemeal:

L. G. Balfour Co., the Attleboro, Mass., jewelry manufacturer; Avanti Communications Corp., the Newport maker of high-speed digital communications equipment; Data Translation of Marlboro, Mass.; Augat's Alco Switch Division; Ispe of Mansfield, Mass.; and others.

The lure for Balfour is a "substantial cost reduction," said Jim Lutz, vice president of market development. "It's always tough to compare year to year, but I'd say we have 25 to 40 percent savings" over hiring an agency, he said.

Balfour spends more than $1 million a year on promotional activities—everything from overhead and salaries for its 15 advertising-related employees (managers, artists, photographers, and support staff), to the creation of collateral materials and the placement of print advertising.

Lutz said about 95 percent of Balfour's promotional work is done in-house. He said agencies frequently make informal pitches for some of the company's work, "but we do relatively little media advertising, which in turn makes us less attractive to agencies."

Brown & Sharpe historically has had three advertising agencies—one each for its three divisions.

"It was hard to get any consistency," said Mark De Cellibus, director of corporate communications. "We needed to get some control over the situation. The net result is that we've been able to pull together something I'm proud of, and I think the ad managers (of the three divisions) are too."

continued

The company spends about $1.2 million a year on advertising—again, that's everything from overhead to trade shows.

Bob Bennett, president of Marquis/Bennett, isn't so sure Brown & Sharpe is on the right track.

The company is using "an awful lot of freelancers," he said, so "they don't have a cohesive approach on a corporate level. Lots of people get a piece of Brown & Sharpe, and in my opinion that's not the way to do it."

Bennett said that in 1981 Brown & Sharpe made up 95 percent of his agency's business. He said the account billed between $500,000 and $1 million a year.

By early this year, when Marquis/Bennett decided to resign, the account billed about $290,000, and made up only 10 percent of the agency's business, he said. The agency claims billings of $4.1 million for last year, and projects $5.1 million this year.

Spencer Bennett Nowak has seen a similar erosion of business from one of its biggest clients—East Greenwich R.I.–based Gulton Industries, a maker of thermal printers.

"When we first went to work with them 10 years ago we did almost everything," said agency president Ed Nowak. "Today we just do media and ad creation." He said the account bills less than half the $500,000 a year it once did.

Stauch said he is convinced that such companies are making a mistake.

He said the biggest lure for the companies is reduced costs, "but I don't think anybody has really taken the time to do a cost analysis." Companies not only have to pay salaries and benefits, he said, but they have to buy equipment—desktop publishing systems, for example. "They're just not set up for it."

Stauch also said that the creative product "suffers tremendously" and "doesn't have the pizzazz of work done outside."

He said companies lose their creative objectivity because employees won't stand up to their boss.

"I know it because I've seen it," said Stauch, who has worked with John Hancock in Boston and Procter & Gamble.

De Collibus' response is the recent National Machine Tool Builders Association awards show. "We just found out we won 12 awards there," he said. "It's a unique show in that the work is judged by the end user. I'd say going in-house has lent us good results."

SOURCE Jeffrey L. Hiday, "In-House Advertising Agency Causing Concern," *Providence Sunday Journal*, June 5, 1988, p. F-6. Used with permission.

■ **EXHIBIT 13–4** Du Pont's Partnership with Six Advertising Agencies

With over 600 products, Du Pont is the eighth largest industrial advertiser in the United States and works closely with six advertising agencies: BBDO, Rumrill-Hoyt, Sudler & Hennessey, Barnum Communications, Kelly Advertising, and N. W. Ayer, Inc. Harry E. Davis of Du Pont has said, "I hate to sound trite and talk about the old 'partnership' bit, but because of the way we do it, we and our agencies are really pulling the oars together."

Du Pont does not abide by the standard 15 percent commission structure for advertising agencies. Rather, it has a time-based fee compensation program that it negotiates annually with each agency. The compensation is determined by time rates and direct personnel costs, indirect agency cost allocations, profit margins, and an inflation adjustment. Other expenses such as production are billed at net cost.

Du Pont's cooperative attitude toward its agencies is also facilitated by a two-way performance auditing program. Du Pont annually rates each agency account group on a scale of 1 to 5 according to:

- Background knowledge of markets and products
- Administration of account
- Initiative in developing facts and ideas
- Responsiveness
- Cost consciousness
- Evaluation and recommendation of media
- Quality of art
- Understanding advertising fundamentals
- Quality of copy
- Quality and efficiency of production

- Budget control
- Maintenance of schedules and paperwork
- Attention to detail
- Maintenance of contact
- Use of ad research

To get the other side of the equation, agency people rate Du Pont's performance on:

- Background knowledge of markets and products
- Annual budget preparation
- Determination of marketing and advertising objectives
- Development of facts and ideas
- Stimulation and encouragement of agency personnel
- Constructiveness of criticism
- Scheduling of assignments
- Validity of media requests
- Responsiveness of requests
- Overall administration of work load
- Cost consciousness
- Budget control
- Clarity and completeness of instructions
- Attention to detail
- Maintenance of schedules and paperwork
- Use of ad research
- Maintenance of contact

The responses to both of these questionnaires are studied by senior management at the agencies and in Du Pont's marketing communications department. These senior managers then meet to determine which procedural changes need to be made or which personnel may need new assignments.

SOURCE: Based on Bob Donath, "Managing the Partnership: How Du Pont Works with its Six Advertising Agencies," *Business Marketing*, September 1983, pp. 70, 72, 74, 76. Used by permission.

powerful mass promotion tool for the advertiser. Publicity can serve to help build or add to a firm's prestige; to introduce a new product or service, product or service improvement, or product or service application; to provide the salesperson with easier entry into the offices of current and prospective customers; and to increase the company's visibility and the desirability of its product mix.

Techniques to Secure Publicity. The public relations or advertising department is usually charged with the responsibility for developing favorable publicity that comes to the attention not only of users but also of the com-

■ **EXHIBIT 13–5**   Four Techniques for Getting in the News

Press Release.   An annoucement to the news media of significant changes in a firm or product or to introduce a new product. It is the most popular technique for obtaining publicity.

Exclusive Feature.   An in-depth article or broadcast message about something of interest to a particular public. An exclusive feature could focus on a new concept, an industry trend, a special new technique, and so on. The feature usually does not focus solely on a company's products but will use them as examples to illustrate certain points. An exclusive feature usually requires extensive coordination between public relations personnel and editors or broadcast managers.

Press Conference.   A meeting for the media sponsored by the firm. Press conferences can be overdone and used too often. They should be used to announce major news items such as a new product introduction or the appointment of a new president.

Press Kits.   Sometimes used in connection with a press conference and may include press releases, pictures, tapes and films, product samples, and complimentary passes.

SOURCE: Based on Michael Ray, *Advertising and Communication Management* (Englewood Cliffs, N.J.: Prentice-Hall, 1982), pp. 347–48; David P. McClure, "Publicity Should Be Integrated in Marketing Plan," *Marketing News,* December 10, 1982, p. 6. Used with permission.

pany's suppliers, distributors, employees, creditors, stockholders and investors, and the general public. As shown in Exhibit 13–5, four techniques for getting in the news are the press release, the exclusive feature, the press conference, and press kits. Additionally, publicity can be generated from five major areas: management activities, product promotions, sales activities, manufacturing and engineering, and personnel activities.[26] Management activities which are good sources for publicity include personnel changes and promotions; speeches and special appearances at banquets, graduations, and professional meetings; and stories about the company's history and future. The private lives and interesting activities of managerial personnel, including their hobbies and charitable and volunteer activities, show a different side than the frequently perceived "insensitive corporate giant."

Product promotions provide numerous sources of publicity. New product announcements are perhaps the most common source. For instance, a new product could have three or four uses, each with its own story; or the product may have a unique design or feature which warrants a special story. Sales activities are somewhat harder to publicize, but not altogether impossible. Sources for publicity here include national and regional sales conferences and trade shows, sales training programs, and recognition of key sales personnel. In this area publicity can also be used as a means to raise and maintain the morale of the company's sales force.

Publicity about manufacturing and engineering aspects of the product or company can serve to build confidence in the minds of customers. For instance, a better or unusual method of manufacturing or storing a product; technical employees recognized for their skills; and a flawless safety record—all are useful and effective sources of publicity. Personnel activities with possibilities for publicity include winners of safety, waste reduc-

---

[26]This section is from Robert F. and Virginia N. Lusch, *Principles of Marketing,* (Boston: Kent Publishing, 1987), pp. 446–47.

tion, environmental, and cost-cutting awards as well as employees' community involvement and leisure-time activities.

One of the real advantages of publicity is that the media time or space used is free of charge for the company, but it must be remembered that publicity can be negative, too. For example, McDonnell Douglas Corporation experienced very negative publicity when its DC-10 aircraft resulted in air crashes and the loss of human life, as did Union Carbide with its chemical leak in Bhopal, India. Although publicity can work against a firm at a given time, its effects are usually short term, and through time and positive promotional efforts any damage can generally be reversed.

Sales Promotion

Sales promotion was formerly considered by business marketers as only a set of short-term inducements to create interest among salespeople, intermediaries, and customers. In many firms today, sales promotion ventures well beyond creating short-term value for various prospects. It has become the driving force that links personal selling, advertising, and publicity into a meaningful, integrated promotional program. Although there are many forms of sales promotion, business marketers commonly use trade shows and exhibits; contests, sweepstakes, and games; and advertising specialties.

Trade Shows and Exhibits. In an increasingly competitive world, sales and marketing executives are required to define markets more closely, develop new tactics, strategize more comprehensively, and target selling more selectively. **Trade shows** are a medium to this end. Trade shows produce quantifiable sales results if they are adequately researched and strategically organized for (1) the special dynamics of the trade show environment, and (2) the special dynamics of interaction between exhibitor staff and prospective buyers. Firms selling to a particular industry display and demonstrate their products for the purpose of promoting and selling these products. Other firms (suppliers), such as Kitzing Exhibits Marketing Service, evaluate the sales-producing potential of the firm's promotion resources with a trade show marketing agency. A well-done trade show exhibit can provide access to key decision makers, contact with prospects, and an opportunity to further serve present customers. It also offers an opportunity to publicize a significant contribution to technology or to demonstrate both new and old products. According to Thomas V. Bonoma, executives can gain more from trade shows by understanding the benefits offered and picking the events accordingly. Also, for many firms, trade show expenditures are the major (or only) form of organized marketing communication activity other than efforts by the firm's sales force and/or distributors.[27]

---

[27]Thomas V. Bonoma, "Get More out of Your Trade Shows," *Harvard Business Review* 61 (January-February 1983), p. 75. See also Roger A. Kerin and William L. Cron, "Assessing Trade Show Functions and Performance: An Exploratory Study," *Journal of Marketing* 51 (July 1987), pp. 87–94.

The most recently published figures reveal that more than 35 million people attend over 900 trade shows every year.[28] Furthermore, over 91,000 firms displayed their merchandise and spent in excess of $7 billion for exhibits. The cost per potential customer is about half that of a personal sales call.[29] The participating vendors expect several benefits, including generating new sales leads, maintaining customer contacts and goodwill, introducing new products, meeting new customers, and selling more to present customers. Benefits derived can be broadly grouped into selling and nonselling categories, with selling categories offering access to key decision makers and an expanded opportunity to serve present customers. Nonselling aspects include the availability of intelligence about competitors, and the chance to test new products.[30]

The days of all fun and little work at trade shows seem to have disappeared. Today, marketing-driven corporations are holding exhibit staffs and programs accountable for quotas, goals, and objectives. For example, more money is going into preshow preparation. A case in point was Ex-Cell-O Corporation's gearing up for the International Machine Tool Show. Before the show the company launched an all-out campaign to get 300 VIPs to visit its exhibit and attend a special hospitality event on a cruise ship. Efforts included direct mail, tie-ins with trade advertisements and press events, and a one-on-one sales push in the field. The effort was considered a success when 275 VIPs attended Ex-Cell-O's live production demonstration and cruise.[31] Getting more bang for the trade show dollar is what it's all about. Tools used in the months before a trade show directly affect exposition success or failure. Preshow preparation includes exhibit booth setup; electrical, plumbing, and communications services; audiovisual equipment; and booth decorations and furniture. The exhibiting firm may also want to have a hospitality suite in the headquarters hotel to entertain valued customers, a preregistration procedure for potential and existing customers, and a postshow list of attendees.[32]

Deciding whether to participate. Trade Show Bureau data indicate that, on average, 47 percent of a typical trade show audience plays a role in the decision to buy from at least one major product category at the event, and 18 percent make the final decision. Further, 64 percent of all visitors travel more than 200 miles to attend a trade show, with 29 percent of attendees being owners, partners, presidents, vice presidents, and general managers.[33] Although trade shows are costly, the question a company must answer in considering trade show participation is whether such an en-

[28]John Dickinson and A. J. Faris, "Firms with Large Market Shares and Product Lines Rate Shows Highly," *Marketing News,* May 10, 1985, p. 13.

[29]"How To Win at The Show," *Sales and Marketing Management,* February 4, 1985, pp. 48–50.

[30]Bonoma, "Get More Out of Your Trade Shows."

[31]McDaniel and Darden, *Marketing,* pp. 557–58.

[32]David E. Tester, "Tools of the Trade Don't Belong in the Circular File," *Marketing News,* March 13, 1989, p. 21.

[33]"Trade Shows: A Major Sales and Marketing Tool," *Small Business Report,* June 1988, pp. 34–39; published by Business Research and Communication, Monterey, Calif.

■ **FIGURE 13–6**   Cost per Contact: Sales Call versus Trade Show

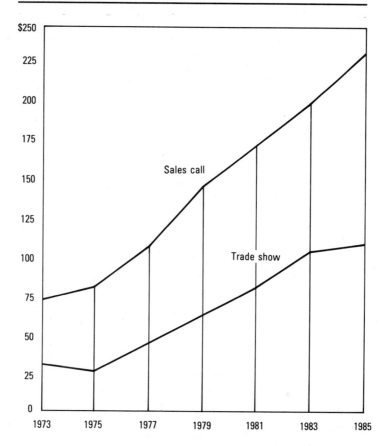

deavor will be profitable. According to the most recent Trade Show Bureau figures (as shown in Figure 13–6), the average cost of a contact with a qualified trade show prospect is approximately $100. This compares with more than $250 reported for a typical face-to-face business sales contact.[34] Further, research indicates that an average three to four calls are required to close a sale in the field. Trade show sales are often completed on the show floor or in a single follow-up call. (A study by Exhibit Surveys found that 78 percent of the attendees at the National Computer Conference had purchased a product within a year after the 1984 exhibition.)[35] Clearly, trade shows can help a firm establish accounts, develop awareness of its products or services, and increase market penetration.

Selecting the show.[36]   There are more than 8,000 trade shows in the United States each year, and entering all of them would be wasteful and

---

[34]Ibid., p. 35.

[35]"The Power of the Trade Show," *Business Marketing* 71 (May 1986), p. 37.

[36]This section is based largely on "Trade Shows: A Major Sales and Marketing Tool," *Small Business Report*, June 1988; published by Business Research and Communications, Monterey, Calif.

quite expensive. The challenge is to select and enter those shows that will help achieve the company's short-term and long-term strategic goals. Show sponsors can provide the expected registered attendance along with a profile of each potential registrant, and his or her business job title and job responsibility. Some additional criteria to consider when determining whether or not to participate include:

Location—The majority of trade show visitors live within 500 miles of the host city. Therefore, evaluate the location to determine who is likely to attend.

Facilities/services available—Telephones and other needed communication equipment, adequate floor space, and electrical and water outlets must be available.

Restrictions—Does the show prohibit certain types of products or display signs, or limit the number of booth personnel that can be used?

Past success—Does the particular trade show have a successful history?

Dates/scheduling—Do the show's dates conflict with other industry events?

Trade show objectives.   The setting of specific trade show objectives is important when making decisions as to what shows to participate in, whom to send, and how much to budget for the effort. Overall objectives might include introducing a new product, increasing market share, and building the firm's image. Once we decide on the objectives, then we need to determine and define specific goals for accomplishing each objective. Specific goals may be to boost sales for a declining product or product line, to identify potential customers, to attract new channel intermediaries, to conduct competitive intelligence, or to conduct research regarding a potential technological innovation.

Trade show budget.   Excluding booth personnel, the average cost to participate in a trade show in 1988 was over $35,000. The cost of an exhibit depends on furnishings required, services required, and hardware needed. A modest exhibit in a single booth space will cost at least $2,500–$5,000, with a multispace exhibit costing $100,000 or more. How much to budget for this effort is a difficult decision to make. Payback is difficult to measure, and tangible results may not be known for months or even years. Gary Lilien's ADVISOR studies provide the practitioner with some help in the difficult job of trade-show budgeting. The level of spending on trade shows is likely to be higher if the product or product line is in the early stages of the product life cycle, if it is experiencing high sales volume, if the firm employs a strongly aggressive marketing plan, and if the product or product line has low customer concentration.[37] The marketing manager must weigh the total cost and time commitment against expected sales and image impact.

Contests, sweepstakes, and games.   **Contests, sweepstakes, and games** are also used by many marketers. These tools provide business customers with a chance to win something—such as cash, trips, or goods—as a result

---

[37]Gary L. Lilien, "A Descriptive Model of the Trade-Show Budgeting Decision Process," *Industrial Marketing Management*, February 12, 1983, p. 29.

of either luck or extra effort. A contest calls for customers to submit an entry—a jingle, an estimate, or a suggestion—to be examined by a panel of judges who will select the best entries. A sweepstakes calls for customers to submit their names in a drawing. A game presents customers with something every time they buy, which may or may not help them win a prize. A sales contest is a contest involving dealers or distributors in order to induce them to redouble their sales efforts over a specific time period, with prizes going to the top performers.[38]

Advertising specialties.   **An advertising specialty** can be defined as *a useful item with a message on it,* such as a pen, a calendar, or the ever-popular back scratcher. From an intensive study of the specialty advertising industry, sampling specialty distributors, suppliers, and users as well as media representatives, advertising agency personnel, and advertising educators, the researchers reached a number of conclusions:

1. Too many advertisements running too close together in business media are creating an ever-increasing opportunity for advertising-specialty programs to replace media advertising. Advertising-specialty products offer a strong alternative to an already overcrowded media situation.

2. Businesses have increasingly realized that in mature markets, especially service businesses, relationships with clients must be established and maintained. Advertising specialties are well suited for both of these promotional objectives.

3. Suppliers have, in recent years, offered the industry a supply of products that are technically superior and can be applied to advertising-specialty programs as promotional vehicles.

4. Users and other relevant publics are gaining a better behavioral understanding of the specialty advertising process. The learning reinforcement-based effects are the source of the most successful advertising-specialty programs.

5. Marketers are only beginning to learn how to design more comprehensive marketing strategies which include advertising-specialty items along with media and public relations efforts.[39]

Historically, advertising specialties have been regarded as mere gimmickry and have not been taken very seriously as an effective sales promotional vehicle. However, this negative image is beginning to change, and the use of advertising specialties appears to be on the rise.

Advertising specialties offer great versatility when used in a planned campaign. Trade show exhibitors can specifically target their audience with an item they will remember. For example, Harris Calorific, a valve manufacturer, had an objective of generating traffic to its exhibit from a select group of 240 dealers attending the American Welding Society's Trade

---

[38]Philip Kotler, *Marketing Management: Analysis, Planning, Implementation, and Control,* 6th ed. (Englewood Cliffs, N.J.: Prentice-Hall, 1988), p. 652.

[39]Charles S. Madden and Marjorie J. Caballero, "Perceptions of the Specialty Advertising Industry: Implications for Business Marketers," *Journal of Business Industrial Marketing* 2 (Fall 1987), p. 42.

Show. Harris was convinced that if its salespeople could spend just a few minutes with each dealer, its dealer network could be greatly increased.

> Prior to the trade show, Harris Calorific mailed a vinyl executive desk folder to selected dealers. Each folder included an invitation for the dealers to stop at the Harris booth. However, the front of the folder was intentionally hot stamped with gold to indicate the place for a personalized nameplate that could be picked up at the booth. This was a tactic instrumental in ensuring exhibit traffic because recipients wanted to pick up their personalized nameplates which could be affixed to enhance the appearance of the folder. As a result, 63 percent of the targeted dealers visited the booth to pick up their nameplates, and Harris quadrupled the number of leads normally generated at the show. The 37 percent who didn't show up were later contacted by Harris representatives. Harris signed up 25 distributors.[40]

The use of prizes, coupled with specialty advertising items, can also be effective. The United States Surgical Corporation (USSC) increased its turnout 36 percent in one year by offering nurses a chance to win a fur coat. A customized folder was mailed to 7,000 members of the Association of Operating Room Nurses. Over 3,000 of these prospects registered for the trade show, with 2,200 visiting the USSC booth. The inside cover of the folder contained a scratch-off circle. Nurses had to remove the circle at the booth to be eligible for 10 different prizes, including a color television set and a fur coat. Everyone who visited the display received a coffee mug imprinted with the company's logo.[41]

As these examples show, it is possible to gain an advantage over the competition with the creative use of specialty advertising.

Concept Questions

1. What is the role of the advertising agency?
2. Why is sales promotion no longer considered to be only of short-term value to the marketer?
3. What is the primary benefit of contests, sweepstakes, and games to the customer?

■ MEASURING THE EFFECTIVENESS OF THE PROMOTION CAMPAIGN

Two of the most commonly used methods of measuring the effectiveness of a promotion campaign are both pretesting and posttesting, and responses to advertisements.

Pretesting and Posttesting

Pretesting of promotional pieces measures, among other things, the subjects' awareness of the product or service at issue through a series of questions about it, or a number of situations to which respondents react,

---

[40]H. Ted Olson, "Trade Show Techniques," *Direct Marketing,* March 1989, pp. 82–86.
[41]Ibid., p. 82.

thereby indicating their current knowledge about the product or service. In posttesting, those who have been exposed to advertisements, publicity pieces, or sales promotion devices are questioned as to their aided recall, unaided recall, recognition, comprehension, believability, and brand awareness (where applicable) in regard to the promotion. If respondents have purchased a product or service as a result of the promotional piece or activity being studied, they will usually be asked to indicate satisfaction with, and frequency of usage of, the product or service.

Responses to Advertisements

Traditionally, one of the most popular methods of measuring the effectiveness of advertising has been through the response the company receives to print and broadcast advertisements, and to direct marketing efforts. For print media, usually coupons or tear-away sheets are put on advertisements placed in various forms of business publications and direct marketing pieces. Advertisers generally assume that if a particular advertisement or direct marketing effort receives a large mail-in or phone-in response, it is an effective promotional piece. Likewise, if an advertisement using a broadcast medium receives a considerable number of inquiries, it is also felt to be successful.

Business marketers, often puzzled by the value of advertising, can now find answers to some long-asked questions. By fielding scaled-down versions of the pioneer controlled ad weight study developed by the Advertising Research Foundation (ARF), marketers can learn:

- Whether they should advertise in the first place.
- If they do advertise, how much is profitable.
- Whether advertising cuts will hurt or help profit.[42]

The $390,000 research project developed by the ARF and its research project partner, the Association of Business Publishers, offers a practical model for testing print advertising. The ARF/ABP weight test measures how different amounts of advertising affect sales for several products. By carefully segmenting markets, matching different levels of media coverage to each segment, and accurately tracking sales, researchers can devise a marginal cost model for their advertising. They can estimate how much profit an additional dollar of advertising will generate. The overall goal of this activity is to know when advertising levels reach the point of maximum profit.[43]

■ FOLLOWING UP AND MODIFYING THE PROMOTIONAL CAMPAIGN, IF NECESSARY

Basic management theory suggests that any process currently being used in business should be periodically reviewed and modified, if necessary.

---

[42]Bob Donath, "How Should You Advertise?" *Business Marketing,* April 1988, pp. 78, 82–86.
[43]Ibid.

Certainly, such is the case with promotion. In order for marketing managers to evaluate the promotional campaign properly, they must return to the objectives which were initially established for the campaign. Were the objectives met? Were they exceeded? Did the campaign fall short of the objectives? If so, by how much?

If the campaign has not met the intended objectives, then each specific segment must be analyzed to determine which stage or stages require further analysis and modification. If the campaign has met or exceeded the stated objectives, it is generally helpful to identify that stage, or stages, in the campaign which were most or least successful in that regard. Even in a successful promotion campaign, some parts of the system might need rethinking and perhaps some modification.

■ PROMOTIONAL STRATEGY FOR INTERNATIONAL MARKETS

International Business to Business Advertising[44]

The promotion of goods and services is also an important part of the marketing mix for international markets. As with domestic markets, the purposes of international promotion are to inform, persuade, and remind customers in overseas markets of the availability of certain business goods and services. The three primary components of international promotion are also advertising, publicity, and sales promotion.

The problems of business and consumer goods marketers are often quite different, as has been pointed out several times in this text. This is especially true in regard to international advertising. Many international advertisers find that only a large agency with offices or affiliates in many markets can do the job adequately. (Table 13–2 lists the 10 largest American agencies in terms of worldwide billings.) Firms planning large campaigns must often deal with a large international agency. Overseas offices are usually staffed with multilingual, multinational personnel, allowing each country to be treated as a distinct market. Agency selection is a time-consuming and laborious job, but it is a critical step for the international advertiser and must be done thoroughly and professionally.

Guidelines to use in developing an international promotional program include the definition of advertising goals; preparation of a campaign plan; review and approval of the plan; copy development and testing; media planning; budget approval; campaign implementation; and measurement of advertising effectiveness. Not an easy job indeed! Many countries have more than one official language (Canada and Norway have two; Belgium, three; and Switzerland, four); people's attitudes and the way they think may be different; and the social, economic, technological, and political environment may be quite different from the one the domestic marketing manager is used to.

---

[44]This section is largely from Courtland L. Bovee and William F. Arens, *Contemporary Advertising,* 3d ed. (Homewood, Ill.: Richard D. Irwin, 1989).

■ **TABLE 13–2**   Top Ten Advertising Agencies by Worldwide Billing

Rank	Agency	Worldwide Billings 1987*
1	Young & Rubicam	4,905.71
2	Saatchi & Saatchi Advertising	4,609.44
3	Backer Spielvogel Bates	4,068.70
4	BBDO Worldwide	3,664.50
5	Ogilvy & Mather Worldwide	3,663.80
6	McCann-Erickson Worldwide	3,418.50
7	J. Walter Thompson Co.	3,221.80
8	Lintas: Worldwide	2,787.20
9	DDB Needham Worldwide	2,581.55
10	D'Arcy Masius Benton & Bowles	2,494.28

*In millions of dollars.

An important decision for international advertisers to make is whether the advertising campaign should be standardized worldwide or localized. Standard advertising has advantages in that a successful campaign in one country is likely to be effective in another as well. Also, standardized advertising is cost-efficient. On the other hand, localized advertising recognizes cultural differences among nations. In the final analysis, the choice between standard and local advertising should be based on such considerations as levels of education, experience and competence of personnel in either the foreign advertising agency or the affiliate of a domestic agency, degree of nationalism and rate of economic growth in the targeted country, customers of the country, attitudes toward authority, and independence of media from governmental control.

International Publicity and Sales Promotion

Publicity programs that give the firm and its products broad exposure to customers and prospects as well as third-party endorsement by the media provide a cost-effective use of a limited promotion budget. Good publicity and good public relations mean adapting to the publics of individual countries. Although positive publicity and effective public relations will minimize a firm's problems in foreign markets, some problems will persist in spite of the best corporate diplomacy and media cooperation and support.

Sales promotion tools tend to stimulate new attitudes toward the promoted product, as few can resist the lure of getting something for nothing. Just the feeling that something can be had for free creates a strong desire for the product among buyers, no matter what country or region they live in. The role of sales promotion in other countries does not vary from what it is in the United States. Yet an appropriate sales promotion program for an overseas market should be geared to the local environment. Historically, sales promotion has been an American phenomenon. However, sales promotion tools are increasingly used today to supplement advertising and personal selling throughout the free world.[45]

Concept Questions

1. How do international advertisers determine whether an advertising campaign should be standardized worldwide or should be localized?
2. What is necessary to have good international publicity and public relations?

SUMMARY

1. Promotion refers to the use of the promotional tools of advertising, publicity, and sales promotion. Promotional tools generally serve to strengthen the personal selling effort and can be very effective in paving the way for sales representatives, in introducing new products and product lines to both established and prospective customers, and in creating goodwill between the selling and purchasing firms.

2. Creating a promotion campaign involves the following five steps: setting objectives, developing the promotion budget, determining the promotion mix, measuring the effectiveness of the promotion plan, and making any necessary changes in the campaign.

3. There is a great need for specific, realistic objectives for any promotion campaign. The establishment of appropriate objectives should be the starting point for every promotion campaign. Whenever possible, it is preferable to state objectives in quantitative terms so that they can be more easily measured.

4. Ideally, the promotion budget should be set at a point where the last dollar spent on promotion equals profits from the sales produced by that dollar. This is only possible, however, if the money is spent in an optimal fashion. Therefore, there must be a prioritization of all promotional efforts in terms of their potential contribution to the firm.

5. A business to business firm can use advertising, publicity, and sales promotion in its promotion mix. Advertising has very specific goals and generally employs printed media, broadcast media, and direct marketing to deliver its message to selected target markets. The advertising agency provides the client with a wide breadth and depth of experience in business marketing, which can seldom be duplicated by a single firm. Yet a number of firms prefer to use their own in-house advertising departments. Publicity can be generated from the five major areas of management activities: product promotions, sales activities, manufacturing and engineering, and personnel activities. Sales promotion has become the driving force which links personal selling,

---

[45]This section is taken from Subhash C. Jain, *International Marketing Management,* 2d ed. (Boston: Kent Publishing, 1987), pp. 564–65, 593; and Vern Terpstra, *International Marketing,* 4th ed. (New York: Dryden Press, 1987), Chapter 12.

advertising, and publicity into a meaningful, integrated promotional program. It includes trade shows and exhibits; contests, sweepstakes, and games; and advertising specialties.

6. Two of the most commonly used methods of measuring the effectiveness of promotion campaigns are pretesting and posttesting, and determining responses to print media advertisements. Pretesting and posttesting methods determine how much respondents knew about the product or service before the advertisement, and how much they learned about it from the advertisement. If an advertisement is successful, usually there will be strong mail or telephone response to the advertisement.

7. In order for marketing managers to determine the degree of success of promotion campaigns, they must first determine if the campaign met its initial objectives. If the objectives were not met, each stage of the campaign should be analyzed to see where the problems are. These parts of the campaign will generally need rethinking and probably some modification.

8. International business promotion also involves advertising, publicity, and sales promotion. International advertisers must determine whether or not to standardize their advertising campaigns worldwide or to localize according to local or nationalistic lines. International publicity must be carefully adapted to local publics, as should international sales promotion. Once considered only an American phenomenon, sales promotion is increasingly used throughout the free world as a supplement to personal selling and advertising.

KEY TERMS

advertising agencies
advertising specialty
broadcast media
business to business advertising
business to business catalogs
business to business promotion
business to business publicity
business to business sales
  promotion
contests, sweepstakes, and games
data sheets

direct mail
direct marketing
general business publications
horizontal publications
industrial trade directories
media mix
professional publications
telemarketing
trade shows
vertical publications

REVIEW QUESTIONS

1. What three promotional tools are commonly utilized in business promotion campaigns? When does promotion play a primary role in sell-

ing business products and services? Why is promotion usually only a support promotional effort for personal selling activities?

2. What are five stages in the development of a promotion plan? What is a promotion campaign?

3. Why is it preferable to express the objectives of promotion in dollar amounts? How are market-share and sales-volume data useful to the marketer?

4. Ideally, at what point should the promotion budget be set? Identify and describe four major methods by which promotion budgets are determined.

5. Discuss four major goals of advertising. How is business advertising different from consumer advertising?

6. Identify three primary media mix elements in business advertising. Discuss four types of print media, two types of broadcast media, and four types of direct marketing efforts.

7. What should an effective advertisement contain? How can advertising agencies be of great value to the firm? Why are many firms reluctant to use advertising agencies? How do advertising agencies counter this reluctance?

8. What purpose does publicity have in the business firm? From what five major areas does a business to business firm generally derive its publicity? How can publicity be negative? Provide a recent example of this phenomenon.

9. How has the perception of sales promotion changed for the business firm from a decade ago to the present? Discuss three types of sales promotion tools used.

10. Discuss two of the most commonly used methods to evaluate the effectiveness of a promotion campaign. What is involved in following up and modifying (when necessary) a promotion campaign? What advertising research questions does the ARF/ABP weight study model answer for the marketer?

11. How does a firm engaged in international operations decide whether or not to standardize a promotion campaign worldwide or to localize it according to national or regional norms of particular markets? What is necessary to have good publicity and public relations in international markets? Why do you think the use of international sales promotion has been increasing at such a rapid rate throughout the free world?

CHAPTER CASES

Case 13–1   *How Diminishing Returns Affect Selection of Media**

Pindar Company is a leading manufacturer of sleeve-type bearings and bushings for use principally in the automotive industry. Its products also

**Charles J. Dirksen, Arthur Kroeger, and Francesco M. Nicosia, *Advertising Principles, Problems, and Cases,* 5th ed., 1977, R. D. Irwin, pp. 360–63.*

are used extensively in the aircraft, farm equipment, diesel engine, and locomotive industries.

The principal products of the company are:

1. *Bearings, bushings, and related products.*   Lined bearings and lined, plain, and graphited bronze bushings are manufactured in a wide variety of types and sizes for use as original equipment and for replacement purposes in internal combustion engines and in many other applications. Rubber-and-metal bearings are manufactured for use primarily in automotive chassis applications.

2. *Electronic components and devices.*   Artificially grown piezoelectric crystals are produced and sold for use in phonograph pickups, microphones, headphones, hearing aids, sonal and underwater listening devices, and other acoustical products. Analyzing and recording instruments, including direct-writing, oscillographs, amplifiers and strain, surface and general purpose analyzers, are manufactured for industrial and research use.

The customers of the company include manufacturers of automotive original equipment, aircraft engines and equipment, railroad locomotives, engines and engine parts, agricultural machinery and equipment, and electrical machinery and equipment. The company sells directly to manufacturers, as well as through distributors, wholesalers, and jobbers of automotive parts and electrical products.

The following tabulation gives the percentage of total sales represented by sales to the principal classes of customers:

Manufacturers of:	Percent of total sales
Automotive original equipment	31
Aircraft engines and equipment	15
Railroad locomotives	5
Other engines and engine parts	11
Agricultural machinery and equipment . . .	10
Electrical machinery and equipment	9
Distributors, wholesalers, and jobbers . . .	19
Total	100

A major portion of the total sales of Pindar has been made to a relatively small number of customers. In the past year, sales to the three largest customers (manufacturers of automotive vehicles) accounted for 25 percent of total sales, while sales to the 10 largest customers accounted for 46 percent of the volume. Sales outside of the United States amounted to 3 percent of total sales.

The bearing and bushing business is highly competitive. Pindar's competitors include not only other independent manufacturers of bearings and bushings but also certain manufacturers of equipment using such items who produce substantial portions of their bearing and bushing requirements. Automotive manufacturers will also sell bearings and bushings for replacement through their own outlets.

As a result, because of the intense competition, the advertising manager of Pindar had followed the policy of dividing his advertising budget so that the leading industrial magazines would be included for each of the major customer classifications. For every classification, he used three or more magazines.

It was his opinion that while such a policy resulted in some duplication of the reading audience, nevertheless Pindar was able to make a greater impact on its potential customers by advertising in the most important specialized magazines for the various groups. In the selection of the magazines for the automotive classification, as an example, he divided his budget in automotive trade publications as follows:

Publication	Percent of advertising budget
A	40
B	30
C	15
D	15

The representative of *Publication A* was dissatisfied with this division because his magazine was recognized as the leading publication in the industry. To show the Pindar advertising manager how he might be able to make his advertising dollar more effective, he prepared a chart (Exhibit 13–1C) on "How the law of diminishing returns affects advertising media." He pointed out that it is uneconomical, under average conditions, to select more than one or two publications to cover the important potential buyers, because, as was indicated in the chart, the number of additional readers becomes smaller as each successive publication is added, and the cost of reaching these extra readers becomes proportionately higher.

He believed that with a limited budget, to divide an advertising schedule between the number one and two magazines in any industrial field resulted in too thin a coverage to obtain good returns from either publication. It would only be when two trade magazines had practically equal circulation, market coverage, editorial acceptance, and space cost that a split schedule on an alternate-month basis would deliver as much, or more, effectiveness than a full schedule in one magazine. It would have to be a very exceptional situation, in his opinion, that would justify a policy whereby a company would advertise in more than the two leading publications.

Pindar had followed for the last 10 years a policy of using the same copy for each of its principal product categories in the industrial magazines which were used for that specific line.

As an example, in the media selected for the automotive classification the advertisements featured an illustration of an engineer looking through a microscope examining a bearing with a headline, "A Pindar Engineer Is Your Best Friend." The copy then stated that no other sector of the industry rendered equal service and know-how.

During the past year the advertising manager had received some negative feedback from a number of purchasing executives who said that it was an-

■ **EXHIBIT 13–1C**   How the Law of Diminishing Returns Affects Advertising
Media Cost for Each Additional Publication

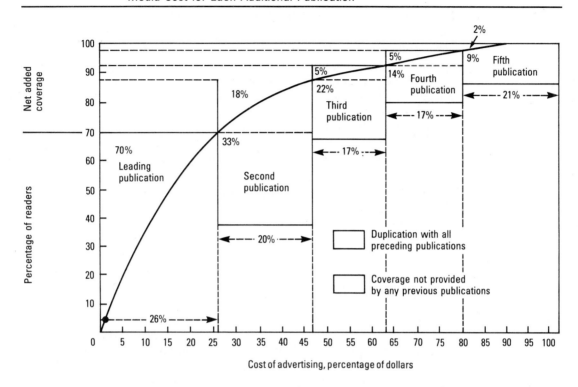

noying to them to see the same advertisement time and time again in several different industrial magazines. It was their contention that repetition turned them off and that no industrial ads were so brilliant and intellectually acceptable that they justified this excessive repetition. It was also their opinion that this practice of repetition resulted in significant diminishing returns because it discouraged them from reading any of Pindar's advertising.

Case Questions

1. Evaluate the advertising policy which the advertising manager of Pindar has been using.

2. On what hypotheses do you believe that the representative of *Publication A* developed the chart for the "law of diminishing returns"?

3. What policy should Pindar follow in deciding on the number of trade magazines to use?

4. What should be the policy of Pindar in repeating the same advertisements in several different industrial magazines?

5. Would this law of diminishing returns operate the same way for TV, radio, and outdoor billboards if similar studies were made for those media?

*Case 13–2 Eagle Steel Supply Company**

Everett Allen, president of the Eagle Steel Supply Company, realized that the market for his company's products and services was showing signs of expansion. Consequently, he was wondering what kind of a promotional program his firm should develop: (1) to take advantage of the growing market opportunities, and (2) to minimize the effects of competition, which was sure to intensify. Located in Detroit, Michigan, the Eagle Company provided Detroit-area industries with customer-made steel products capable of withstanding excessively heavy use in specialized situations.

Basically, Eagle was a service organization. The company did not produce any of the products it sold. Instead, it acted as a liaison between steel users and steel producers in the following manner. During a regular call on a steel user, an Eagle sales person would seek to identify a problem situation that called for a specialty steel product. Or the user company itself—after identifying its need for a high-strength alloyed steel product—might initiate the contact with a specialty steel supplier such as Eagle. The Eagle sales rep would analyze the problem and recommend a particular type of steel.

Eagle then placed an order for this product with a steel manufacturer. There the mill's metallurgists formulated the processes and components which would yield the desired products. Typically, some material (tungsten, manganese, nickel) was mixed with the molten steel to form an alloy that gave the desired flexibility, hardness, or ability to withstand temperature extremes.

Specialty steel products are used in a wide variety of industrial situations involving heavy blows or stresses over long periods of time. For example, alloyed high-strength steel is commonly used in conveyor systems, blast furnaces, and machine parts (gears, bearings, connecting rods, cutting units, etc.). Over the years there has been an increasing demand for these specialized steel products.

In view of this increasing demand, some people wondered why the major users did not deal directly with the large steel producers, thus bypassing such suppliers as Eagle. Mr. Allen gave two reasons why the specialty steel suppliers had developed and continued to thrive. First, the major users found that they did not buy this type of product often enough to have a separate procurement facility. However, when the users did need a specialty product, the tasks of determining specifications and procuring the product were complex. Second, the greatly expanded list of steel alloys available meant that considerable expertise was needed to ensure correct product choice.

The Eagle Company's primary market was the heavily industrialized area within a 60-mile radius of Detroit. However, Mr. Allen considered that Eagle's total market extended out 100 miles from Detroit. Within that 100-mile radius, Eagle had a 22 percent market share, according to Mr. Allen.

---

*William J. Stanton and Charles Futrell, *Fundamentals of Marketing,* 8th ed., 1987, McGraw Hill, pp. 412–14.

Three other specialty steel suppliers competed with Eagle in this market. Allen estimated that their respective market shares were 30 percent, 28 percent, and 20 percent.

Competition in the specialty steel industry typically was on a nonprice basis, because all steel producers generally maintained comparable prices. Companies competed on their ability to analyze a user's problem and then recommend a steel alloy that would solve the problem at a reasonable cost. Personal relationships which sales people built with their customers also were important.

The Eagle Company had experienced significant ups and downs in its sales history. However, since Everett Allen took over six years ago, sales had increased annually to the present level of $2.5 million a year. Net operating profit had increased to 7 percent of sales. Mr. Allen credited much of the sales success to his methods of working with the steel producers. In contrast to previous buying practices, Allen selected only one mill supplier—United States Steel Company. He then maintained intensive written and personal contact with that manufacturer. The net result was that U.S. Steel filled Eagle's orders promptly—sometimes even ahead of orders from other specialty steel firms.

Mr. Allen estimated that the four specialty steel companies could handle only 80 percent of the potential business in the Detroit area and, furthermore, that the market was expanding rapidly. Eagle had built a clientele of steady customers in the automotive, cement, and gravel industries. In addition, new users and new uses of specialty steel offered opportunities for market expansion. Local chemical companies and machine parts makers, for instance, were potential customers.

Up to the present, Eagle's promotional program had consisted primarily of the personal selling efforts of the company's eight sales representatives. No advertising was done at all. In fact, only one of Eagle's three competitors used any advertising, and then only in a very small amount.

With demand outrunning supply in the specialty steel market, Eagle's market prospects looked good. Mr. Allen was smart enough to realize, however, that the current market situation could very well be a short-run phenomenon. Such a market was bound to attract additional competitors and to draw more aggressive, better-trained selling efforts from existing firms. Consequently, he was wondering how he might improve Eagle's promotional efforts in order to capture a satisfactory share of the expanding market.

As one alternative, Mr. Allen considered budgeting $100,000 for an advertising program during the coming year. He consulted a Detroit advertising agency that suggested a program of direct-mail advertising plus placing advertisements in selected trade journals and Detroit newspapers. According to that agency, the proposed advertising program would have several advantages, some of which were:

1. It would make the sales reps' efforts more efficient by using advertising to make the initial customer contact.

2. It would establish company identity and image.

3. It would reach customer personnel now inaccessible to the sales force.

Another alternative was to use the same amount of money to hire, train, and compensate three additional sales people. The total cost per person would be about $40,000, depending on the amount of training the reps needed. If experienced sales reps were hired, then the training costs presumably would be reduced. In that case, any unallocated promotional funds could be used: (1) to further train the present sales people, and (2) to equip the sales force with better sales tools (catalogs, samples, etc.).

An informal market investigation conducted by Mr. Allen revealed the following interesting facts about the purchase decision for specialty steel products:

1. The initial purchase idea comes from the first level of management—a supervisor or general supervisor—which is in closest contact with a company's problems.

2. Buying decisions for specialty steels are made quickly when a need arises. Then the buyer seeks the assistance of a specialty steel company. The purchase is not a long-range, planned affair.

Question

What promotional program should the Eagle Company use to profitably expand its sales volume?

SUGGESTED READINGS

Bly, Robert W. "The 12 Most Common Direct Mail Mistakes . . . and How to Avoid Them." *Business Marketing* 72, June 1987, pp. 122–28. Problems and guidelines in writing direct mail pieces.

Davids, Meryl. "How to Plan and Place Corporate Advertising in Print Media." *Public Relations Journal* 42 (December 1986), pp. 29–30, 33. Guidelines for media purchases and criteria for media selection.

Gordon, Howard L. "Advertising that Really Grabs Buyers." *Business Marketing* 72 (July 1987), pp. 78–89. Copy, emotions, and graphic arts in business advertising.

Li, Richard P. "The Hunt for Direct Marketing Success." *Direct Marketing* 49 (March 1987), pp. 38–42. A study of direct mail campaigns, market segmentation, database management, and statistical modeling.

Nadal, Miles S. "Sales Promotion Gives You the Competitive Edge." *Sales and Marketing Management in Canada* (Canada) 27 (October 1986), pp. 33–34. Advantages, trends, and expenditures in the use of sales promotion for a competitive edge.

O'Keefe, Philip. "Get Discovered with Directories." *Business Marketing* 72 (June 1987), pp. 130–37. Discussion of the value of industrial promotion through trade publications, trade directories, and reference services.

Pfaff, Fred. "How Business Talks to Business: Like It Is." *Marketing and Media Decisions* 22 (May 1987), pp. 83–97. Study of expenditures and innovations in industrial advertising campaigns, and a discussion of trade publications.

Piercy, Nigel. "The Politics of Setting an Advertising Budget." *International Journal of Advertising* (UK) 5 (no. 4, 1986), pp. 281–305. Exploratory study of organizational structure and the power of the marketing department in setting the advertising budget.

Schaefer, Wolfgang. "Readers per Copy of Trade Publications." *European Research* (Netherlands) 14 (1986), pp. 198–201. Discussion of magazine penetration measurements in the Federal Republic of Germany, including a new measurement model.

Seelig, Pat. "Advertising Specialties." *Incentive Marketing* 161 (May 1987), pp. 104–8. Study of many companies using giveaway items imprinted with the company name and coupled thematically with a mass media advertising campaign.

Stoeger, Keith A. "Three, Two, One, Contact!" *Direct Marketing* 50 (June 1987), pp. 114–15. Study and discussion of industrial advertising, and telephone selling, customer relations, and customer services in industrial markets.

Summerfield, Cy. "Business Press Advertising Can Reduce Sales Costs." *Sales and Marketing Management in Canada* (Canada) 27 (September 1986), pp. 33–34. Survey of 461 Canadian advertising executives about the effectiveness of business press advertising in reducing industrial sales' costs.

Swayne, Linda E., and Thomas H. Stevenson. "Comparative Advertising in Horizontal Business Publications." *Industrial Marketing Management* 16 (February 1987), pp. 71–76. Study of the trends in three leading U.S. industries.

West, Reg. "Sales Promotion: Cutting Risks." *Marketing* (UK) 29 (June 11, 1987), pp. 39, 41. Study of new technologies, projective techniques, promotional maps, and quantitative measurement in sales promotion.

Williams, Terry Considine. "I Saw It on Radio—Will Direct Response Radio Return to the Golden Ad Days?" *Direct Marketing* 49 (October 1986), pp. 50–56, 82. Trends in, and advantages of, radio advertising, including per inquiry marketing.

Young, Gary G. "Trade Show Practices: Time for Evaluation." In *Marketing in a Dynamic Environment,* ed. Michael H. Morris and Eugene E. Teeple. (Atlantic Marketing Association, 1986), pp. 1–11. Nationwide survey of trade show practices involving the setting of objectives, show selection criteria, and performance of trade show effort.

Zibrun, S. Michael. "Business-to-Business: A Value-Added Service to Build Opportunity." *Journal of Business & Industrial Marketing* 2 (Winter 1987), pp. 67–76. Overview of telemarketing to add incremental business—its roots, structure, pitfalls, and potential.

Cases for Part Five

CASE 1: Henderson Service Center

Tom Henderson, president of Henderson Steel Service Center, felt it necessary to review his company's marketing and sales strategies. Early in 1979, it was apparent that old assumptions and approaches had to be carefully examined and updated due to a number of ongoing changes in the environment. To be specific:

1. Specialist service centers were becoming more important and assuming major positions in such lines as tubing, spring steel, aluminum, and tool steel—products characterized as being of relatively high technical content, difficult to comprehend technically, consisting of many small volume grades, with considerable risk of obsolescence, and often with limited sources of supply—but, nonetheless, profitable due to their unique characteristics.

2. A decided upsurge in requests for bids, in which major buyers asked for quotes on a six-month supply contract; contracts which unfortunately might not be honored fully and where shipments might not always be in the specified truckload quantities (in short, a price squeeze).

3. The proliferation of brokers and secondary-line houses, who emphasized distress prices, raised havoc with traditional margins, and were in and out of the markets.

4. An ominous industry drift toward commodity selling, in which old trade names (Shelby Tubing, Jalloy) were being superseded by ASTM numbers, with the resulting willingness of customers to accept "or equivalent" products.

5. The merging of small centers into larger, multilocation houses.

6. The accelerated trend toward sophisticated management, particularly in regard to asset management in general and inventories in particular.

Henderson was a medium-sized general line steel center in California whose growth made it increasingly difficult for management to stay on top of the details and to maintain its earlier entrepreneurial touch. As Tom Henderson said, "This is a business of inches—of exact control and doing the little things right—where success is closely tied to service and employee attitudes. How do I keep a balanced effort among the salespeople when growth results in a one-inch catalog; specialists eat away at our specialty markets; and the individual salespeople tend to gravitate toward their favorite products?"

Thus, it was timely that he review the company's sales and marketing strategies. Did his sales programs enhance the all-important company-customer relationships? Tom wanted to be sure that there weren't new approaches that warranted implementation. Indeed, he had a number of specific concerns about his sales strategies.

■ THE STEEL SERVICE CENTER INDUSTRY

As of 1975, there were estimated to be 1,500 steel service centers (SSC) operated by 700 companies and accounting for 20 percent of the country's steel tonnage. The median firm had annual sales of $3 million. The modern steel service center was a vital link in the chain from basic steel producer (the mill) to user. An SSC was both distributor and processor, who not only handled a great range of mill products, but added considerable value to standard mill output. Steel service center processing included, but was not limited to, cutting, sawing, trimming, slitting, blanking, burning, roll forming, and light fabrication.[1] The mills were only too pleased to see most of this small order, specialty business handled by the centers.

Products handled included pipe, spring steel, sheet, tool steel, bar tubing, and structurals, primarily in steel (or aluminum) and involving a great complexity of specifications and basic processing variations—such as cold rolled carbon. Sales were made by the centers to a wide array of primarily industrial customers, including agriculture and commercial establishments. Needless to say, there were many products that were wholesaled primarily (i.e., no processing) by the steel service centers. And as will be shown, there was a wide difference between different types of centers. Separate from the steel service centers were hundreds of brokers—small independents who bought and sold as the opportunity arose, rarely handled the product, and substituted price for service.

A 1974 study by Republic Steel contained some interesting speculations about the future:[2]

Summary

The service center market will be the largest market for steel by 1980, with shipment of 24.8 million tons in a peak year. This will represent a 25 percent increase over 1974's shipments of 19.9 million tons. Shipments of

---

[1]Cutting, sawing, and trimming involved reducing mill dimensions to customer requirements. Slitting was represented by the reduction of a wide roll to a narrow one. Blanking was the process of stamping out custom shapes. Burning would involve the "burning out" of a gear design, as an example, from heavy plate. Roll forming would be typified by forming a gutter or down spout. Light fabrication included such activities as punching predetermined holes in structural beams or bending material to a particular shape.

[2]"Steel Service Centers in 1980," Republic Steel, pp. 2, 3.

flat rolled products will increase by 29 percent, and shipments of hot rolled bar products will show a gain of 28 percent. Both tubing and cold finished bar shipments will increase by 22 percent, while the volume of stainless and pipe through service centers should register gains of 16 percent and 15 percent, respectively.

Seven products accounted for almost 75 percent of total service center tonnage in 1974. These products included the following: C HR Sheets, C CR Sheets, C Plates, C Structurals, C Standard Pipe, C HD Galvanized, and C HR Bars.[3] The largest single item was C HR Sheets, accounting for 18.6 percent of total service center tonnage.

Service centers will continue to increase their share of total steel shipments. Although they dropped sharply in 1975, we believe they will recover and take 20 percent in a peak year by 1980.

Our survey revealed four distinct types of service centers: super processor's large general line centers, small general line centers, and specialty houses. We forecast the biggest growth to take place among the large general line centers between 1974 and 1980 because trends to larger minimum order quantities by the mills and the continuation of absorption and consolidation of smaller centers will combine to promote strength in this market segment. The super processor, although showing good growth, will be hampered somewhat by its dependence on the automotive market. The specialty houses will just about hold their own in the marketplace. The small general line center will remain a significant part of the market, although many may be absorbed by large general line centers.

The survey findings indicate that two major changes are likely to take place in the service center market by 1980. If the mills increase and maintain higher minimum quantity extras as our survey indicates, there will probably be fewer service center companies but more locations, as some small centers are likely to be absorbed by larger centers. Those small centers remaining in the business will probably turn to larger centers as a source of supply, creating a two-tier service center market. The average service center of 1980 will be larger than the one of 1975 and will be more professionally managed.

Service centers will not be involved in any different types of processing in 1980 than they are in now but will experience growth in virtually everything they are doing currently. Slitting and cut-to-length will continue to be bread-and-butter items, but plate burning, blanking, and roll forming should all show good growth. Pickling and tube manufacturing could show limited growth at the service center level.

We forecast good growth in hot rolled bar products, particularly carbon hot rolled bars, through service centers based largely on the fact that the forecasted level of shipments through the rest of this decade will encourage volume rollings by the mills. Such levels of operations encourage increased minimum order quantity extras at the mill level. This activity in turn would cause the small purchaser to use service centers as a source of

---

[3] C HR Sheets = carbon hot rolled sheets
C CR Sheets = carbon cold rolled sheets
C Plates = carbon plates
C Structurals = carbon structurals (beams, columns, joists)
C Standard Pipe = carbon standard pipe
C HD Galvanized = carbon hand dipped galvanized
C HR Bars = carbon hot rolled bars

supply. Good growth in cold finished bars could result from the same type of circumstances.

Cold finished bars should continue their excellent growth through service centers, as will tubing products. Stainless and pipe products will not experience the rapid growth of other products, but will still register impressive gains.

We estimate that the four major captive service centers handled approximately 20 percent of all steel shipped through service centers in 1974. Captives should grow faster than the average for all service centers because they fall into the fastest growing category, the large general line center. However, we do not believe their growth will surpass that of the independent large general line centers.

Foreign-owned companies have been increasing their holdings in the domestic service center market. We estimate that 13 percent to 15 percent of the total tonnage handled by domestic service centers goes through foreign-owned outlets.

In addition to these trends, Mr. Henderson foresaw: (1) continued emphasis upon sophisticated computer systems to control operations; (2) increased equipment improvements and costs of investments; (3) the need to ensure solid supplier relationships, due to limited investment funds for capacity increases among U.S. steel companies; and (4) continued downward pressures on price unless growing commodity selling attitudes could be curbed.

■ THE COMPANY

The Henderson company was headquartered in the San Fernando Valley, north of downtown Los Angeles, having been started by Tom Henderson in 1958 after his discharge from the army. Over the years, Tom had developed the company by internal growth and the acquisition of four smaller firms in San Diego, Bakersfield, Modesto, and San Jose (all in California). Bank financing had been used recently, but in his earlier days, Tom relied for financing upon internal funds and the public sale of 60 percent of the ownership.

It is revealing to see how the firm grew with the acquisitions program (see Exhibit 1).

It is reasonably clear that market share was gained fairly early in each market and then maintained or slowly increased over time. Overall growth was primarily a function of acquisition.

As with all steel service centers, profits were sensitive to volume and mix, with different locations having different experiences. Variable costs exceeded 80 percent, which meant that funds available for overhead and profits were narrowly bounded by margins and direct costs. Peak sales for Henderson occurred in 1974, when total volume reached $29 million; 1976 was a poor year for the company and the industry, and by 1978, volume was still below 1974 but recovering.

Tom Henderson was a strong believer in the fact that true profitability was a function of asset turnover and leverage ratio (i.e., relative amount of

■ **EXHIBIT 1**

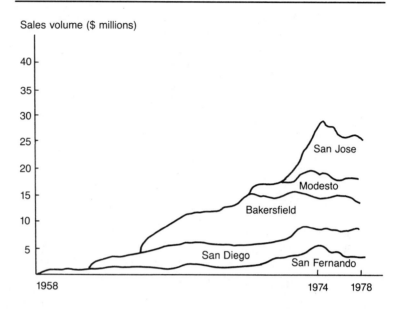

Sales volume ($ millions)

debt) as opposed to solely conventional profit expressions. To be specific, he had drawn up a simple "strategic profit model" which he also used to compare his results to competition (Exhibit 2).

For 1978, to illustrate the model, Tom had drawn the comparisons between his firm and two competitors shown in Exhibit 3.

It was Tom's conviction that strategy should be stated specifically in terms of the model, such as:

Asset Management

Improve asset turnovers to 2.5:

1. Improve inventory turnover to minimum of three times.
2. Eliminate delete when out of items.
3. Maximum use of mother warehouse concept.
4. Maintain accounts receivables at 41 days.
5. Review all fixed assets and remove all nonproductive assets.
6. Study balance of fixed assets to improve their earning power.

Profit Management

1. Tight cost control.
2. Improve plant operating procedure to reduce cost.
3. Better systems to cut out unnecessary work.
4. Improve pricing where possible.
5. Study product lines to emphasize profit opportunities.

■ **EXHIBIT 2**   The Strategic Profit Model*

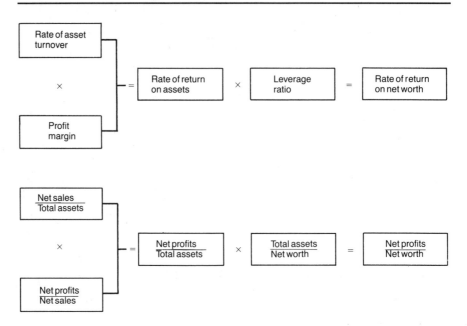

*The strategic profit model excludes leased equipment, fixtures, and facilities. The model also excludes the capital structure of nonconsolidated subsidiaries.

■ **EXHIBIT 3**

Competitor	Asset turnover	×	Percent profit margin	=	Percent return on assets	×	Tax return rate	=	Net return on assets	×	Financial LVRG	=	Net return on equity	×	Earn return rate	=	Reinvest rate	Working capital percent sales
No. 1	2.7		1.7		4.4		53.2		2.4		2.2		5.2		32.6		1.7	17.0
No. 2	2.7		4.7		12.6		54.8		6.9		1.7		12.0		76.5		9.2	13.1
Henderson	1.6		4.1		6.6		53.9		3.6		1.7		6.1		100.0		6.1	22.1

Financial Management

1. Find expansion opportunities that meet or equal our asset and profit objectives.
2. Expand debt to 38 percent of total assets.

■ COMPETITION AND MARKETS

Competition for Henderson was strong—from five majors and 20 times that number of specialists and brokers. It was Henderson's experience that the large, full line houses were strong but reasonable competitors. Market disruption and cost cutting came from the brokers and a fringe handful of smaller firms whose approach to selling centered around "a good deal."

Such tactics were particularly effective with those buyers, who seemed to be increasing in numbers, who preferred to shop around for the lowest offer and who thought that loyalty was for boy scouts.

Henderson's marketing/sales strategy was straightforward. The policy was to carry a good inventory of prime (as opposed to secondary) merchandise, to offer fast response time, and to concentrate on stock parts and cutting at the expense (relatively) of first-stage processing, though 20 percent of sales did come from processing. Whenever the company had to buy out, it examined carefully whether demand for that item would warrant future stocking.

Henderson's markets were diverse, reflecting basic differences among the California territories; 90 percent of the sales, to be specific, were into the farming and farm equipment, railroad, mechanical contractors, industrial equipment, mining, appliance, and furniture segments. Although there were several automobile assembly plants in the state, Henderson had chosen to not go after that very specialized and competitive business. Each market segment represented, obviously, a unique selling problem.

Farm equipment producers in the Henderson territories were six short line firms which manufactured and sold for their own account or acted as suppliers to full line houses (such as Deere). By and large, these manufacturers wanted reliability, on-time service, and product quality, as opposed to minimum cost. The service center salesperson was a critical variable in the selling process, though much of his influence was due to the entertainment between supplier and buyer that was common practice. Apparently, the buyers preferred to purchase "from a friend," all other things being equal, and equated supplier reliability with the salesperson's interpersonal skills. This was not meant to imply that product knowledge and service were unimportant; it was rather that the essential catalyst was the salesperson's personal input. Multiple sourcing and bidding, nonetheless, were common, although trusted salespeople typically got "the last look." Buying decisions were made by the purchasing vice president or his buyer (if the firm were big enough).

Railroads were a good market on the West Coast, but in these firms it was difficult to find who buys. The successful salesperson did lots of legwork in engineering, purchasing, and even top management in order to get drawings. As in the case of the farm equipment segment, the role of the salesperson was critical. Cronyism was common, and most sales relationships had been established slowly over the years.

In the case of both segments, Henderson tried to sell the idea of "cost of position," that is, why invest as a buyer in expensive processing equipment when you can share the capital costs with the buyers by dealing with a service center?

Mechanical contractors (plumbing and heating, sheet and metal working), on the other hand, were easy to sell in that they bought "off the shelf," but they were price buyers of mixed credit reliability who shopped around. The nature of contractors' businesses caused them to be single job oriented. The salesperson's role was minimal in these instances, and entertainment was of little importance.

Appliance manufacturers (mostly in Los Angeles) were somewhat the same. They were tough buyers who appeared to have little loyalty. They were auction oriented and usually purchased flat rolled products with few components. Salespeople were significant only in respect to maintenance and repair.

Furniture accounts had little need for maintenance and repair. Price, not selling, was the name of the game. Theirs also was a fragmented industry of small, unstable producers.

The **industrial equipment** and **mining** segments were more solid and resembled the farm equipment market—sophisticated, insistent upon reliability and service, and sympathetic to constructive salesperson relationships.

■ PRICING, ADVERTISING, AND DISTRIBUTION

Henderson was not a price house, although its prices were competitive. In periods of short supply, in fact, the firm had deliberately refrained from gouging its accounts in the hopes that the ensuing goodwill would carry over into buyer markets. Whether this policy was paying off was not at all clear: in 1977 and 1978, there had been a tendency for Henderson margins to slip and for the field salespeople to sacrifice service for discounted prices. Price pressures were growing. In fact, Tom Henderson figured that one of his most pressing needs was to give his salespeople more backbone to withstand such pressures and to sell service instead.

Advertising was a small but useful adjunct to the firm's strategy. Because there were no obvious regional media that matched Henderson's customer base, emphasis was put upon a modest direct mail campaign (which stressed the service dedication of the company, i.e., "Henderson Means Service"), a biannual house publication which went to employees and customers alike, appearance at all relevant conventions, some public relations, and hopefully, positive word of mouth.

The distribution strategy was simple. There were five warehouses in five cities, each stocked to its own market needs. Particular items could be shipped from branch to branch in a matter of hours and were in order to meet special requests. Buyouts were made whenever necessary.

■ ORGANIZATION

Henderson's organization was probably representative of the industry (see Exhibit 4).

Even though the local plant managers reported to the district managers (for daily administration), they had a dotted-line relationship to the vice president of operations for functional matters. The reporting duality seemed to work.

The sales and service end of the business, because it was of particular concern to Mr. Henderson, deserves more elaboration. Including the San

■ EXHIBIT 4

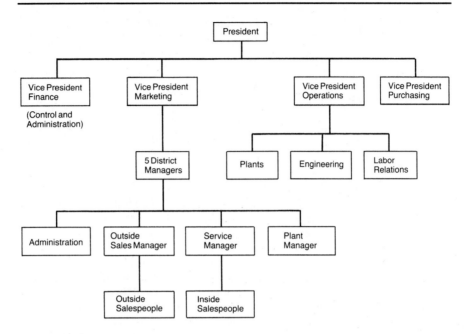

Fernando headquarters, there were five district managers who reported to a marketing vice president. Each manager operated out of a plant and supervised the sales manager, the plant manager, an inside service (sales) manager, and an administrative staff.

Reporting to the outside sales managers were 16 salespeople, for each of whom (with a few exceptions) there was a corresponding inside person. The two worked as a team, although they reported to separate bosses. The team idea was important because most ongoing sales were placed by customers calling in. The role of the outside salespeople was, therefore, to prospect for new accounts, to build established accounts, and to ensure post-purchase service. The inside person's responsibility was to maintain the business.

The district manager was the local authority. He had considerable decision-making leeway, although credit, purchasing, inventory policy, compensation, finance, and labor relations were controlled out of headquarters. The district manager could fire or add to the sales forces (with the concurrence of the marketing vice president), deploy his labor force as he saw fit, and train, supervise, and generally decide sales strategy. He was further responsible for making sure that the plant could meet customer requirements on time.

In a real sense, the district manager was "the leader" and was expected to know intimately the needs of the market. Suffice it to say he reinforced his own observations with data from the field concerning quantity changes, customer new product plans, customer switches in mill purchases, self-fabrication plans, and competitive activity.

The typical district manager earned between $30,000 to $35,000, including a maximum 20 percent of salary bonus based on district profitability. He received a percentage of the profit beyond the plan up to 20 percent of his base pay. Profit was calculated before headquarter's allocations for overhead and support.

■ THE PEOPLE

The five district managers came from different backgrounds. To single out three as representative:

> **San Fernando.** Started in accounting and then to inside selling. After two years, became an outside salesman and after three years, fabrication manager. Next, sales manager in a district and finally, at age 40, to district manager. One year of college but . . . "a very strong manager. Pushes hard, sets high standards, lets everyone know where they stand, good on strategy and market penetration."
>
> **San Jose.** College graduate, age 45, formerly manager of an advertising agency. Joined Henderson at 34 as outside salesman, then sales manager, manager of corporate development (a staff assignment reporting to the president), and finally district manager. "Sales oriented, well liked, polished, comfortable anywhere, runs tight team, well informed."
>
> **Bakersfield.** "Too long in his market. 37 years in the industry, close to retirement, resistant to new techniques but thoroughly conversant with his territory and key accounts. The customers love him, but he is a poor trainer."

The local sales managers had three responsibilities: to supervise and train their salespeople; to handle the key accounts directly; and to establish "executive level" contacts at all accounts. This was a heavy work load, needless to say, and different managers excelled in one or two of the three areas depending upon their strengths and territorial idiosyncrasies.

One of them, for example, said that he saw his major job as exciting the salespeople because "attitude is everything in this business." Another felt that sorting out his 900 accounts was a crucial responsibility because "without organization you can't make any territorial headway." A third defined his role as "keeping the men on plan because it's too easy to deviate and do things your own way."

The salespeople were, of course, the prime contact between account and company. They were scheduled to average eight calls each day and to cover their accounts in a three- to four-week cycle. They determined their own callback patterns and varied them by account. Although it is unfair to single out one, the remarks of Harold Murphy (Modesto) are interesting:

> I used to sell insurance. Didn't do well in that environment. All they cared about was the one-time sale. They weren't concerned with building a lasting sales relationship.
>
> I like to think I'm a personal friend of my customers. The two most important things as a salesman are *credibility* and *sincerity*. Customers have got to believe me, or I'm wasting my time. I try to get my inside

person out to the customers as much as possible too, so she is more than just a voice on the phone. If they're going to call in an order, then they're more likely to call someone pleasant whom they know.

I've got to have good office support. My job is to introduce customers to Henderson Steel. Then after that, I have to depend on shipping, on production, and especially on my inside person. They make me look good. The first order from a potential new customer is often a token for having visited him three or four times, to "see how the salesman will do." Then I have got to have good support to impress him with my service.

The importance of the inside salespeople isn't recognized adequately at Henderson. Bad inside people slow down a salesman, waste his time and effort doing their jobs for them. The customer may not see any difference and sales may not fall, but the salesman has to cover for his inside person. Inside people were strictly a training grounds for outside salesmen in the past. Now people are beginning to see that some people are best suited there. Some want to stay in the inside.

We're number one in Modesto (the inside person and me), and half the credit goes to her. The inside person doesn't get an incentive bonus, though they should, since they really generate sales. I'm going to share part of my bonus with my inside person. She deserves it.

I run my territory on the basis of customer demand. I go where I can do the most good, be most influential, not based on the size of the account or a certain call frequency. I go to customers with a reason in mind, for a specific purpose. Some of my best customers told me when I first visited them three years ago, "Look, we've been buying from Henderson for years. You can't tell us anything new about Henderson and its service. Don't keep just coming around. We'll call you when we need you!" So I visit them maybe once a month and let my inside person deal with them. If they have a problem, then I am right there. They know whatever the problem is, I take care of it.

At one of my most sophisticated accounts, one of my competitors insists on going out every Tuesday morning to their plant. I don't think it's ever influenced a purchase decision. They joked about his coming every Tuesday.

Henderson Steel gives its sales force too much leeway on how to sell, especially the young ones. But I like it loose. I call my manager daily, and I feel good about calling him in to help if needed.

A rundown of the five districts indicated the situation at the start of 1979 as shown in Exhibit 5.

The salespeople specifics are depicted in Exhibit 6.

Tom Henderson provided a thumbnail sketch on each of the individual salesmen and sales managers:

San Fernando

Smith. An old pro; knows the territory; needs incentives to get full attention; overlooks possibilities in established accounts; about 46 years old; has a "good way" about him; the sales manager, but spends most of his time in his territory; has team which needs little supervision.

Smiley. With us three years; young, comer, eager, wants to advance; liked by customers; only 28; tends to high spot the accounts; somewhat weak on product knowledge; sells service aggressively.

EXHIBIT 5

District and Plant	1978 Sales ($000)	1978 Quota	Number of Salespeople (including management)	Sales per Salesperson ($000)	Gross Margin ($000)	Average Gross Margin per Salesperson	Approximate Number of Accounts	Estimated Share of Market
San Fernando	$ 7,188	$ 7,000	3	$2,396	$1,798	599	2,500	12 %
San Diego	3,456	3,850	3	1,155	917	306	2,500	7.5
Bakersfield	4,727	4,650	2 + district manager/ sales manager combined	1,576	1,128	376	1,100	11
Modesto	2,423	2,600	2 + district manager/ sales manager combined	808	591	197	1,500	10
San Jose/Salinas	5,531	5,100	5	1,106	1,330	265	2,400	8
Total	$23,325*	$23,200						

*In addition there were home office house accounts of $2,550,000 handled by the senior management (but serviced locally).

■ EXHIBIT 6

District and Territory	Salesperson	1978 Percent of Quota	1978 Gross Margin	Compensation	As Percent of Gross Margin
San Fernando					
No. 1	Smith	87%	$552,630	$21,166	3.8%
No. 2	Smiley	104	470,912	14,811	3.1
No. 3	South	112	763,215	21,608	2.8
No. 4	Open	—	—	—	—
San Diego					
No. 11	Drudge	61	187,184	—	—
No. 12	Dodge	82	380,747	17,268	4.5
No. 13	Davis	118	320,098	17,963	5.6
Bakersfield					
No. 21	Brown	92	162,165	19,667	12.1
No. 22	Benton	137	468,371	24,055	5.1
No. 23	Bowles*	93	494,120	18,600	—
San Jose					
No. 41	Johnson	86	254,819	22,733	8.9
No. 42	Judas*	65	196,014	16,768	8.6
No. 44	Judd	98	316,592	19,816	6.3
No. 45	James	118	418,211	21,185	5.1
No. 46	Jaedeke	115	143,640	—	—
No. 48	Open	—	—	—	—
Modesto					
No. 51	Murphy	102	301,951	18,355	6.1
No. 52	Minnow*	65	57,853	16,500	28.0
No. 53	Morris*	80	243,582	15,410	6.3

*In territory less than full year. Compensation annualized for comparison.

South. Formerly plant superintendent; has done exceptionally well; best suited to country area and will probably have to be transferred; likes farm and mining contracts; thorough but unimaginative; has several key accounts who think the world of him.

San Diego

Drudge. The sales manager; well trained but emotional; orthodox in his approach; tends to concentrate on his favorite accounts; 38 years old; has potential; has trouble organizing but does reasonably well as SM.

Dodge. A problem—seems to be drinking too much; recently went through a nasty divorce; was once our best man, now I'm not so sure.

Davis. Shop background; formerly inside salesman; 15 years on the job; seems to be getting bored; OK if closely supervised; no apparent potential; has some well-established accounts which he's comfortable with.

Bakersfield

Brown. Combination DM and SM; knows everyone in town; sells entirely on basis of friendship; not running too hard; needs lots of management time; in a tough market; inflexible; close to retirement; good with the petroleum accounts.

Benton. The old pro; a jewel; can always get business; positive; not good on systems or administration; knows markets and products; doesn't want a promotion.

Bowles. Very new in the territory (six months); comes from a competitor where he left under some kind of a cloud; I'm still not comfortable with him—seems slippery, not quite open and honest—though these may be unfair generalizations; I let my DM hire him against my better judgment; has some of our most loyal accounts; shows signs of selling on price.

San Jose

Johnson. Lots of experience; was a sales manager but demoted because he couldn't motivate others; needs supervision; knows his product but is easily discouraged; great at knowing the people; spends lots of time on his real estate investments where he has done well; is well-off financially.

Judas. Came from another company where was a purchasing agent; inside selling for us and has been outside for less than one year; highly religious individual, who occasionally offends others by his inflexible beliefs; not at ease in his territory but seems to be catching on; still a question mark; not fully able to sell on basis of service.

Judd. With us 1½ years from an outside company; good product knowledge but in a tough market; inclined to sell on price; not a strong competitor—wants everyone to like him.

James. An old pro; age 49; lots of experience but needs occasional pumping up; not promotable; the mayor of his town; likes new products and new accounts.

Jaedeke. Recently made SM; too new to judge; has an MBA, which he earned at night; very control oriented; sees the need to concentrate on key accounts and senior managers; well balanced; says he wants to get into marketing management soon; very sharp; should go a long way if handled well.

Modesto

Murphy. 24 years in the industry after a short career in insurance; once a DM but had a nervous breakdown; excellent salesman but very excitable; sees himself as a lady's man; separated from his wife; not fully reliable—some indication that he is slacking off.

Minnow. A new DM; doubles as SM; only three months on the job; has a strong sales background and leads by doing; seems to be a good planner; thorough; tends to be impatient if things don't go his way.

Morris. A new man; just finished his training; college degree; age 24; his father owned and operated a small center but sold out five years ago; seems to be floundering.

■ SALES MANAGEMENT

The Henderson company's hiring procedures were somewhat a function of local management. Although headquarters set some broad parameters, the district managers were pretty much left to their own. Consider, for example, the remarks of one district manager:

> We hire salespeople primarily through employment agencies. They often have no prior steel experience, though some do. Few even have sales ex-

perience; usually they know nothing about sales. We don't require a college degree or screen them with a sales test. What we look for is ambition and good recommendations. Do they want to succeed? The outside salesperson alone is responsible for the territory. Most sales managers, on the other hand, have been with the company many years, since we promote from within.

The training of a new salesperson was supposed to consist of six weeks in the shop learning terminology and the production processes used at Henderson. The content and duration of training varied greatly with the individual managers. Some managers gave trainees two weeks in the plant, some outside selling time, and then four weeks again in the plant. Other managers used six weeks in the plant. One salesman reported that he spent 12 weeks training in the plant, followed by one week each in the credit, billing, and inventory departments. Upon completing the training, the new salesman moved into inside sales. It was not unusual for competition to hire the new employee after his training was completed—at least this was an ongoing threat because a good labor force was at a premium in the industry.

Territorial assignments were largely a function of local needs. A new person might move into an unexpected assignment because of some sudden emergency (i.e., salesperson turnover was 25 percent a year), or territory boundaries might be changed to accommodate a new multilocation account. By and large, however, a salesperson was assigned to a geographic area containing between 500 and 2,500 potential customers and with an industry mix that reflected the local economy.

Sales quotas were established early and were arrived at by adding 10 percent to the person's last year's sales. The marketing vice president recognized that this was a simplistic approach (in fact, the 10 percent figure was only an average; the vice president would vary it by territory depending upon local requirements), but he took comfort in the fact that the resulting target closely reflected what the organization *could* do. Actual results over the years had been remarkably close to the 10 percent average increase, and the firm seemed to be gaining market share (though there were no real data to measure this relative gain).

Sales compensation was tied to the quota. Each person received a salary and a quarterly commission based upon quota. Between 80 and 90 percent of quota, the commission was $10 times the percentage over 80 percent but under 90 percent; $30 between 90 and 100 percent; $35 between 100 percent and 120 percent, and $10 over 120 percent. If a person hit 129 percent of quota during a three-month period, therefore he would receive:

$$\begin{array}{rcl} \$10 \times 10 & = & \$ \ 100 \\ \$30 \times 10 & = & 300 \\ \$35 \times 20 & = & 700 \\ \$10 \times \ 9 & = & \underline{90} \\ \text{Total} & = & \$1{,}190 \end{array}$$

At 98 percent of quota his commission was:

$$\$10 \times 10 = \$100$$
$$\$30 \times 8 = \underline{\ \ 240}$$

$$\text{Total} \quad = \$340$$

One hundred percent of quota was the expected sales target and represented the "10 percent average over last year" previously described. It was hoped that the typical salesperson would earn about 10 percent of salary in bonus.

Sales supervision, as explained, was centered in the local sales manager, who was both salesperson and supervisor. Normally, however, the sales manager carried a lighter customer load than the full-time salespeople. One manager had this to say about his position:

> I don't think a sales manager can also be his own salesman. Our outside salespeople deserve more attention than I can give them. For example, I don't get out often enough to see other customers. I want to travel more with the sales force, and I plan to. I try to have fewer short sessions with them in favor of longer talks.
>
> Now, Tom Henderson thinks the sales manager can also act as salesman. I'm one reason he thinks so. Sales here have gone up since I took over as sales manager. But I'm the only one who knows I am not doing justice to either job. Our sales are good, but they could be even better. Somewhere between supervising three and seven salespeople, a sales manager becomes necessary. I work hard to do both jobs.

■ SOME ALTERNATIVES

As he reviewed his sales strategy, Mr. Henderson singled out a number of issues.

1.   Deployment. Was the company's policy of assigning salespeople contiguous geographic areas the best one? After all, the buying habits of the various segments were different, and some salespeople seemed better equipped to sell to sophisticated buyers, while others were at home with more mundane accounts, such as contractors or farmers. Some people were more comfortable in small-town, small-company environments, while others thrived on the big, complex situations. Finally, it was apparent that different salespeople preferred different tasks. For some, prospecting was the challenge. For others, it was developing more business from existing accounts. A few liked to work with development engineers and others with the more commercial side of the customer's operation.

Without even considering the economics of various territory assignment alternatives, Mr. Henderson pondered what were the best overall ways to organize in today's markets? What were the fundamental advantages and disadvantages of each variation?

A part of the development problem was the additional fact that company sales were concentrated. To be exact, volume was distributed as follows:

Percent of Customers	Percent of Sales
Largest 20 percent	78.5%
Next 30 percent	12.5
Remaining 50 percent	9.0

This concentration was typical of all the district offices. In fact, out of ±10,000 customers throughout the company, 250 represented 60 percent of the sales, while the smallest 2,000 averaged only $500 per year. They represented, on the other hand, 18 percent of the calls.

2. Training and Career Development. A 25 percent turnover of salespeople struck Mr. Henderson as excessively high. He could figure the initial costs of hiring and training a new employee at $18,000. Nor did it make sense that his company should invest heavily in the selection and training of a new salesperson only to have competition raid his ranks with alarming degrees of success. Somehow the company had to convince the new hires that a few more dollars from a competitive firm were a poor trade-off for Henderson's generous retirement and benefit plans. Henderson wondered if more detailed individual career development programs would alleviate the problem and whether ongoing training couldn't be more specifically tied into additional job responsibilities and salary increases. In short, how could Mr. Henderson structure the job, compensation, and career development steps in order to attract and hold superior sales candidates?

One of his friends in the industry sent Tom a summary of a personnel development program that he was using. Excerpts are included below, and Tom wondered whether he should adopt a similar program, one which his friend estimated would add 50 percent to the costs of the normal training program:

Personnel Development Program

The objective of this memorandum is to establish a minimum program to be used in developing new salespeople. The requirements should be expanded to meet the needs of the individual district. For example, those districts with light fab, slitting, etc., should include training in those areas.

The requirements shown should be completed within the time frame of the program, and all portions of one step, including the time involved, must be completed before the change in title is certified.

The district manager will be responsible for arranging outside training, which will have to be adapted to what is available in each area.

Special attention should be directed throughout the program to developing selling skills. Reading material pertaining to products and the industry should be available.

A conference with the district manager is required at the completion of each step of the personnel development program.

Sales trainee—I	0 to 4 months
Sales trainee—II	5 to 8 months
Sales trainee—III	9 to 12 months
Salesperson	Completion

The summary went on to detail each step, listing the specific activities, tasks, and assignments required of the trainees before they could be certified for the next step. Salary adjustments were dependent upon the separate steps. To illustrate, the details under "Sales Trainee I" follow:

STEP 1 0 to 4 Months

A. Company Orientation
1. Salary and review date.
2. Insurance programs.
3. Savings plan.
4. Retirement program.
5. Vacations and holidays.
6. Safety program.
7. Personnel development program written test.

The manager of employee relations will furnish a written test concerning these programs. Completion of this phase will be upon recommendation of the department head and certification by the district manager.

B. Plant Experience
1. People identification.
2. Equipment identification.
3. Equipment capacities.
4. Material identification.
5. Receiving systems.
6. Storage systems.
7. Delivery experience.
8. Order paper flow procedures.

Completion of these requirements will be upon recommendation of the plant superintendent and department head. Certification will be required by the district manager.

3. Future Managers. Closely related to the problem of salesperson retention was that of preparing a cadre of managers suited to the environment of the 1980s. It was Tom Henderson's conviction that the manager of tomorrow would have to be a true professional—able to think for herself or himself, to strategize, to work with profit models, to analyze, and to lead a group of better trained subordinates.

Would such requirements permit the traditional policy of promotion from within, or should the company begin to go outside for highly talented individuals? It was possible to spot attractive candidates from outside the industry, but whether the risk of force-feeding them upon the existing culture was worthwhile was unclear. To avoid this risk, why wouldn't it be possible for Tom to retrain current managers to fit the new pattern? Such a move would, of course, require a special training effort—one which would be costly and which might or might not work.

4. Quotas and Compensation. The quota system, as described, concentrated upon experience (10 percent over last year). Why not, wondered Tom, include some measures of potential? After all, the quality of a particular level of performance was a function of both experience *and* potential. It should be possible, he thought, to qualify quotas by such potential measures as industrial activity, level of employment per district, freight car loadings, and changes in employment. If the company were to include such variables, how should they be worked into the present system? How much weight should be placed upon experience? Upon potential?

And even more critical, if there were changes made in the quotas, how should the salespeople be paid? Was straight salary to be preferred, or did there need to be an incentive payment? Similar or different from what now existed?

Another friend of Tom's had suggested a simple diagram for thinking out the problem of compensation (Exhibit 7).

First, you must decide how much the "average salesperson doing an average job" should earn. In this illustration, it was $20,000 as seen at the bottom right. Across the top, the key salesperson jobs and their relative values were listed. Hence, the $20,000 pie was allocated across the tasks. Finally, all of the possible payment techniques were enumerated vertically. The dollars and payment methods were then matched by asking "How do I best pay for this task, and how much?" Obviously a particular task might warrant more than one payment technique.

The resulting matrix would form the base for telescoping the various payment alternatives into a simpler, less complicated compensation plan. But at least the implications of each sales task and the ideal way of paying for it would have been considered.

5. Organization. It was clear, as pointed out earlier, that company growth had come principally from acquisition. Was it possible, considered

■ **EXHIBIT 7**

Payment alternatives	Tasks and relative importance	1 To maintain sales* 40%	2 To open new accounts* 30%	3 To sell full line* 20%	4 To supply intelligence* 10%
Salary		$?		$?	
Commission			$?		
Contests					
Bonus			$?		
Expense Accounts					$?
Profit Share					
Other					
				$?	
Dollars for Each Task		$8,000	$6,000	$4,000	$2,000

Note: Total Expected Pay = $20,000
*Assumed for this example only.

Tom, to reorganize so as to develop more market share in the existing districts?

For example, would it help to have product managers or even key account managers? After all, business was concentrated both in selected products and customers. Wouldn't specialization in one or both of those dimensions result in better account penetration? But if such a move were to be made, Tom was concerned about how such a modification could be built into the existing structure. Moreover, he estimated that the incremental costs of new managers would be about $60,000 each.

From a field management vantage point, there was the ongoing question of whether the sales managers should supervise and sell, or supervise alone. It was easy to say that supervision was the critical function, but the economics of small districts made it tough to support sales managers who only managed. As the senior salespeople in their territories, their customer know-how was so great that Tom hesitated to set it aside. Could a full-time manager, in other words, pay his own way when he had only two or three salespeople to lead? How best could his job be structured?

6. Product Lines. Finally, Tom thought it important to reconsider his product policies. Specialists were growing as were price-oriented brokers and purveyors of secondary lines. Could Henderson hope to survive unless his firm somehow insulated the impact of these competitors from its major markets? Should the company work with one or more of these specialists, become one, or fight them?

Tom knew that he had raised a number of hard questions. It wasn't easy to answer them, but he thought that a good starting point would be to evaluate the effectiveness of his present strategy and to match that strategy against the needs of the marketplace.

CASE 2:   CSX System

Edwin E. Edel, vice president for corporate communications of CSX Corporation, was experienced in "start-ups." He was the first public affairs director for railroads for the Department of Transportation and was involved in the early phases of AMTRAK. He was vice president for corporate communications at Seaboard Coast Line Industries, Inc., before accepting his present position on November 1, 1980. Two months later, Edel reflected upon this experience, as well as the issues and actions of the past few hectic months, and reviewed his newly completed corporate communications strategy for 1981. Was it an appropriate strategy for the complicated entity that was CSX?

This case was prepared by Margo W. Hoopes under the direction of Associate Professor Paul W. Farris, Colgate Darden Graduate School of Business Administration, University of Virginia. Copyright © 1982 by the Sponsors of The Colgate Darden Graduate School of Business Administration, University of Virginia. Used with permission.

■ BACKGROUND

CSX Corporation was created on November 1, 1980, through the merger of Chessie Systems, Inc., and Seaboard Coast Line Industries, Inc. Its major units were two rail systems—Chessie System Railroads and the Family Lines Rail System. These rails formed a north-south transportation system that covered 27,000 miles and 22 states (see Exhibit 1). The two rail systems accounted for approximately 95 percent of revenues and 85 percent of net income for CSX (Exhibit 2).

CSX also had holdings in natural resources, communications, aviation, and hotel services. CSX Minerals, Inc., held the mineral rights to over

■ EXHIBIT 1   CSX Corporation

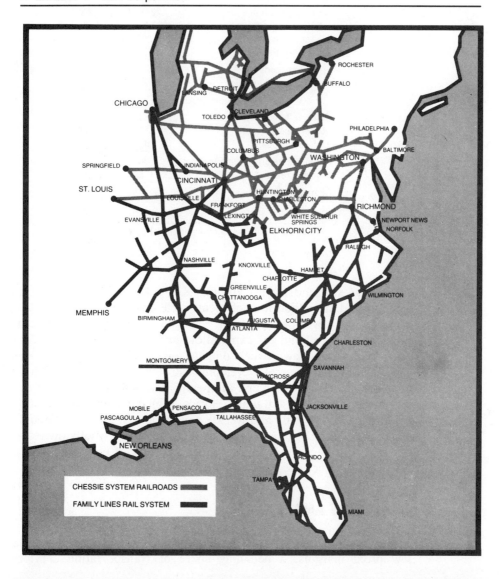

■ **EXHIBIT 2**

Consolidated Statement of Earnings
Year Ended December 31
(millions of dollars except per share amounts)

	1980	1979
Operating revenue:		
Merchandise	$2,948.4	$2.792.4
Coal	1,357.3	1,039.3
Other	191.3	195.3
Transportation	4,497.0	4,027.0
Nontransportation	344.4	326.9
Total operating revenue	4,841.4	4,353.9
Operating expenses:		
Labor and fringe benefits	2,063.1	1,974.7
Materials, supplies, and other	1,395.2	1,202.9
Locomotive fuel	462.2	334.0
Depreciation	158.0	160.7
Transportation	4,078.5	3,672.3
Nontransportation	255.0	253.5
Total operating expenses	4,333.5	3,925.8
Income from operations	507.9	428.1
Other income—net	37.9	46.9
Interest expense	180.7	185.8
Earnings before income taxes	365.1	289.2
Income taxes	83.5	52.1
Earnings for the year	$ 281.6	$ 237.1
Earnings per share	$7.13	$6.12

Primary earnings per share are based on 41,204,845 shares for the year, 1981; 39,498,853 shares for the year, 1980; and 38,742,897 for the year, 1979.

677,000 acres of land in West Virginia, Kentucky, and Maryland, containing an estimated 1.3 billion tons of recoverable coal reserves. CSX Resources managed and developed extensive real estate holdings, directed corporate participation in oil and gas exploration, and managed 350,000 acres of forestry lands. The New River Company operated coal mines in West Virginia, while CSX Mineral Development Company assisted coal companies in acquiring coal reserves and in opening coal mines throughout the territory served by CSX's rail units. Florida Publishing company, another CSX holding, published daily and weekly newspapers in Jacksonville and northern Florida, and the Greenbrier Resort Hotel was a wholly owned subsidiary of CSX. Beckett Aviation managed a fleet of executive aircraft and offered related services in nine major airports.

■ THE RAILROAD INDUSTRY AND CSX

The railroad industry was considered mature at best, characterized by low profit margins, a declining share of transportation services, and labor strife, all of which were brought to public attention with the well-publicized bankruptcy of Penn Central. Ironically, railroading was also perceived as a static, unexciting industry. Industry and management had recently been buoyed by a feeling of optimism, however, due to three factors: deregulation, mergers, and coal. The Harvey O. Staggers Rail Act of 1980 gave railroads the right to change rates within prescribed zones without seeking ICC permission. This right, for which the industry gave up its right to collective rate-making, allowed more aggressive competition in the marketplace.

CSX sold its rail services through a direct sales force that maintained close contact with customers. This sales force was organized into "commodity modules." There was a group of direct salespeople devoted to the paper and lumber industry, another dedicated to "piggyback" services, and still another for the coal industry.

When standard services were required by the customer, the prices were determined by merely referring to the published tariff rates. Other arrangements were quite common, however. For example, contract rates were negotiated for a fixed time and predetermined amount to be shipped, either in trainload or less-than-trainload quantities.

The newly favorable atmosphere for mergers created opportunities for such systems as CSX. The merger made possible more efficient routing of traffic by eliminating high-cost short hauls and frequent switching. Equally important was the creation of a more competitive service and what this meant to marketing and sales.

Due to energy conservation, greater use of gas by utilities, and environmental regulations, there had been little or no growth in coal traffic in recent years. But industry sources predicted that export coal would be a vital source of new business, and European markets promised continuing strong demand for coal. For a major coal hauler, such as CSX, this prediction was particularly significant. Export coal yielded a higher revenue per ton at less expense since it was moved in trainload lots from the mines to port.

The major constraint on greater export coal volume was inadequate port facilities. These delay-causing inadequacies, which might lead European users to look elsewhere for coal, inspired efforts by railroads, mining companies, and the government to increase port facilities. Chessie reopened Pier 15 at Newport News in August 1980, and construction was begun on three new facilities in Baltimore and Newport News. Additionally, four coal companies agreed to build a $60–$100 million coal export facility in Portsmouth, Virginia.

■ THE MERGER

The merger that created CSX placed it in a favorable position in several respects. The 27,000 miles of rail, which connected Michigan with the southern tip of Florida, allowed CSX to offer the better and cheaper service of a single system while enjoying the savings and efficiency obtained from the merger. Management believed this efficiency would lead to improved operating revenues and corporate earnings. CSX was dominant in key natural resources, most significantly as a major carrier and holder of reserves of coal, which promised to become more and more important. In addition to its coal development activities and mineral rights, CSX was the leading carrier of coal in the United States.

The real test of the merger's success would be whether CSX could compete successfully for new traffic. With its 27,000 miles of rail, CSX had the potential to originate and terminate a lot of traffic formerly shared with other lines. A single system reduced or eliminated paperwork, crew changes, locomotive changes, sorting of cars, delays, expense, and sharing of revenue. As a major Seaboard customer said, "The fewer problems that railroads have with the divisions of revenue and the more shipments they can haul on a single-line basis, the better opportunity I have to get improved service and more competitive rates."

CSX expected $70 million in annual operating savings by the third year. Efficient utilization of assets was expected to produce rapid benefits. For example, Louisville & Nashville, a subsidiary line of Seaboard, was frequently short of locomotives and hopper cars. Chessie had a predicted surplus of 30 diesels, which were put at L&N's disposal along with the Chessie-operated hopper car plant in Kentucky.

Southern Railway estimated that it would lose $50 million a year in freight business to CSX because of the merger.[1] In addition, CSX expected the efficiency and resulting lower rates not only to convince shippers to switch business from competitive rail lines but also to capture freight business from truck lines. Growth was anticipated in refrigerated shipments, steel shipments, and grain shipments. Both railroads, however, saw the greatest growth possibility in an operation known as *piggybacking*—hauling of truck trailers and containers on flatcars in high-speed trains over long distances, such as from Jacksonville, Florida, to Philadelphia. As the cost of diesel fuel increased, piggybacking became even more attractive to trucker lines.

The rest of the railroad industry was well aware of the benefits of merger and single-system service. A merger of the Norfolk and Western Railway and the Southern Railway was on the horizon. The merger would probably be approved within the next two years, and CSX would face a direct and possibly stronger competitor in its own regions.

Certain aspects of the merger and the resulting corporation complicated this positive situation, however. Early in the merger discussions it was agreed by Chessie and Seaboard to preserve the identities and general operating independence of each company. The merger was viewed and accepted as a 50/50 partnership. CSX was created by Hays T. Watkins and Prime F. Osborn III, chief executive officers of the two companies, without incurring conversion costs, without affecting the current identities in the marketplace, and with little disruption in day-to-day operations. Even the

---

[1]"CSX: A Gradual Consolidation," *Railway Age,* October 13, 1980.

new name, CSX Corporation, began as a deliberately nondescript, temporary designation. It was adopted because it had been well received prior to and during the ICC merger hearings and because, according to President Hays T. Watkins, "Prime [Prime F. Osborn, chairman of CSX] and I thought it up and like it because it's so anonymous and nondistinctive—the way we want the parent to be in relation to its operating railroads."

The economy and logic of this sort of transition were apparent. There were attendant disadvantages, however, such as the inconsistency of a two-part identity with the image and benefits of the corporate entity; the complications of a multifaceted identity for marketing and communications; the confusion of a two-part identity for customer perceptions; and the added costs of advertising, promotion, and printing.

The seriousness of the identity issue became more obvious when the systems were examined in detail. Both Seaboard and Chessie had evolved over several decades and possessed complex identities composed of their many different elements (see Exhibit 3). For example, the line in Nashville was the L&N Railroad, not CSX or even Family Lines. The Baltimore Railroad was the B&O, not Chessie. The creation of CSX added another layer of complexity to this multifaceted entity. Yet the strength of CSX, its short- and long-term potential for increased growth and profitability, was created by the very fact of its new corporate identity.

■ THE ROLE OF COMMUNICATIONS

Edwin Edel outlined his philosophy of how his function would relate to the communications officers on the company level in an early memo. An initial interim plan covering the period from November 1, 1980, to the end of the fiscal year on December 31, 1980, dealt, of necessity, with start-up issues of a new name, merger details, new headquarters, etc. (see Exhibit 4).

The overall objective of the start-up corporate communications effort was to begin to achieve the recognition, understanding, and support that CSX needed from all of its publics in order to operate successfully as a new business entity. Edel identified several key goals in reaching this objective. They included developing an accurate picture of CSX as the parent company of Chessie and SCL; conveying a reputation for success, good management, even better service, and responsible civic behavior; fostering broad understanding of the benefits of the new corporation and its subsidiaries; and building confidence in both its operations and its people.

Edel's start-up program contained three major elements. First, the new corporate identity required a logo that was a strong and positive symbol communicating the essence of a well-managed company that united two strong and complementary railroads and included a group of diverse non-rail companies. The logo was to reflect unity, strength, innovation, and diversity, and be adaptable to a wide range of uses. It must fit when used in conjunction with subsidiary materials, such as Chessie Railroad advertising.

■ **EXHIBIT 3**   How the CSX Rail System Came Together

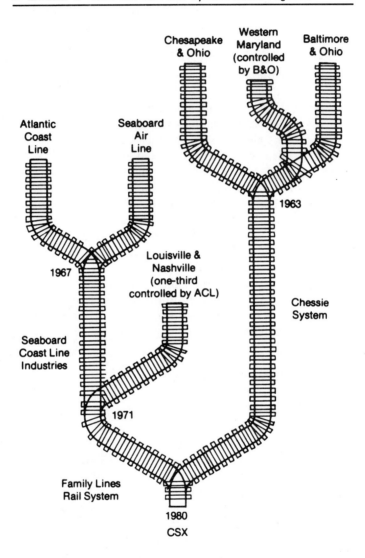

Second, the advertising of the new corporation was to define and explain the corporation to important audiences. The message was to be geared to the business and financial communities, and to emphasize innovation, efficiency, improved operating ratios, and profitability. The advertising was to use both reach and frequency and maintain a continuity in its "look." There was to be an introductory and a sustaining phase.

The third element of Edel's initial plan was a public relations program to disseminate basic information on the new corporation to interested publics. While all required much of the same information, each needed a different treatment as to emphasis and means of presentation. These publics included the following:

■ **EXHIBIT 4**

L&N Merger into CSX to Improve Freight Service

by Ben Eubanks

Louisville and Nashville Railroad's new ability to speed freight to large Northern cities could attract more new industry to Tennessee, L&N officials say.

On Nov. 1, L&N became part of one of the world's largest privately owned railroads, when its parent corporation, Seaboard Coast Line Industries, Inc., and the Chessie System, Inc., merged to form CSX Corp.

CSX will be the nation's No. 1 railroad with assets of more than $7.4 billion and 75,000 employees. It will be No. 2 in track length with 27,000 miles of rail in 22 states stretching between Miami, Fla., and Ontario, Canada.

Direct service will also be available between cities such as Detroit, Chicago, Pittsburgh, St. Louis, Birmingham, and New Orleans. Before the merger, freight traveling from these cities often had to be handled by several different rail services.

Seaboard, concentrated in the Southeast, was comprised of railways such as L&N, Clinchfield, Georgia Railroad called the Family Lines. Chessie's concentration is in the Northeast and has railroads such as the Baltimore and Ohio, Chesapeake and Ohio, and Western Maryland.

Hooper said L&N customers will now get quicker delivery of freight going north since the Cincinnati gateway will be avoided. Before the merger, Seaboard's track ended at Cincinnati and the cars were turned over to other railways.

Hooper said switching through the Cincinnati yard, operated by Con Rail, usually takes two or three days now because of the vast number of railcars passing through the city.

"If we can get through Cincinnati without wasting two days in the gateway we are improving everybody's service," Hooper said.

CSX will be using C&O's (Chessie) Stephens Yard in Cincinnati for its Piggyback Service, which will be expanded with three of the six new routes CSX is planning coming through Nashville. L&N already operates two lines: St. Louis to Atlanta and Chicago to Birmingham.

Hooper said the economics of the CSX line will make it more competitive with trucking lines and may return some business lost several years ago.

"One thing trucks always got us on was quicker delivery and better scheduling," Hooper said. "But these customers will find that with the increasing gasoline and fuel costs and with quicker service time the costs of railroads will become more attractive."

SOURCE: *The Tennessean,* November 16, 1980.

Rail Merger Creates No. 2 Transportation Company in U.S.

By Carole Shifrin
Washington Post Staff Writer

Take the 50 largest transportation companies in the 1980 Fortune Double 500 Directory. Cross off number 11—Seaboard Coast Line Industries—and number 13—Chessie System. Make a new entry: number 2—CSX Corp.—just between Trans World Corp., number 1, and UAL, Inc., old number 2.

The merger of Chessie and Seaboard into CSX was formally consummated this month, less than two years after their joint application to the Interstate Commerce Commission.

Along with the increased competition that is expected to come from rail deregulation legislation, the merger is just one of many developments that is expected to make the rail industry more dynamic that it has been in decades.

SOURCE: *Washington Post.*

Railroad Merger Becomes Final

The merger of Chessie System, Inc., and Seaboard Coast Line Industries, Inc., into CSX Corporation was formally consummated Nov. 1 as members of the new CSX board of directors met for the first time in Richmond, Va.

continued

■ **EXHIBIT 4** *(concluded)*

Prime F. Osborn III, chairman, and Hays T. Watkins, president, termed the meeting "a significant milestone" in the history of the railroad industry. "Our forefathers long dreamed of a strong north-south railroad system that would link the industrial Northeast with the Southeast, tying together these two vital areas of the country. Today that dream is a reality," they said.

SOURCE: *Wilmington Morning Star,* November 9, 1980.

1. Financial and business press.
2. Shareholders.
3. Analysts.
4. Investors.
5. Employees.
6. Trade press.
7. General print media.
8. Electronic media.
9. Legislative and executive branches of federal government.
10. State and local governments in states served.

Next in determining his strategy for 1981, Edel attempted to balance the complicated issues created by the merger with the goals of the new corporation. The role of corporate communications was to create a recognition of CSX as a purposeful, future-directed, and profit-oriented corporation in the business and financial community. The external analyses of CSX available to the financial community predicted growth and increased profitability,[2] and the corporate advertising program was designed to develop a high and positive awareness of CSX. Edel's objective was to enhance CSX's image with both current and potential shippers and the financial community. He had researched the effects of corporate advertising on stock prices, and he believed the research results supported the idea that an advertising campaign could have a measurable impact (see Exhibit 5).

Edwin Edel formulated some specific objectives for corporate advertising in 1981. Taking advantage of the interest inherent in being "new" and the opportunity to take the initiative rather than the defensive, he intended to focus on the following:

Informing individual investors about CSX and its increased importance in the economy.

Establishing increased awareness to facilitate future acquisitions.

---

[2]Examples of such analyses:

"Superior market performance is expected from CSX Corporation as the economy strengthens and the newly formed system attracts greater volume."

"From a valuation standpoint, CSX's P/E ratio of 6.3 for 1980 represents a 36 percent discount to the Standard & Poor's 500. With a favorable outlook for 1981, the stock would appear undervalued at current levels."

"Railroad deregulation, allowing for upward revision of rates and a higher level of coal export loadings, leads to projected increases in 1981 earnings."

"The major port expansions under way both at Chessie and Seaboard indicate that CSX should garner more than its share in the increased coal shipments in future years."

■ **EXHIBIT 5**   Effects of Corporate Advertising

Is Financial/Corporate Advertising Effective?

A survey among professional money managers who are readers of *Barron's* indicated the following:*

1. 81 percent said they take financial/corporate advertising seriously and, as a result, look into a company's investment qualifications.
2. 78 percent said their investigations led them to purchase securities.

Does Corporate Advertising Affect Stock Prices?

A three-year study by E. P. Schonfeld and J. H. Boyd, Jr., professors of advertising and finance, Northwestern University, led to the following conclusions:

1. Corporate advertising has a statistically significant positive effect on stock prices.
2. Based on three years' data, the impact of corporate advertising seems greatest in an up market.
3. Firms that could report *stable* earnings growth had more favorable results from their corporate advertising than those who could not.

A study among some 600 upper echelon executives across the country revealed the following:†

1. *47 percent* of those who had *not* been exposed to a financial corporate campaign had a favorable general impression of the average company.
2. *63 percent,* on the other hand, who had been exposed had a favorable opinion, showing a "lift" factor of 33 percent.

A three-year study, analyzing 460 major U.S. corporations, revealed the following:‡

1. Corporate advertising adds about 4 percent per share to the price of a corporation's stock.
2. About 55 percent of a corporation's stock price is determined by economic performance, such as revenue and earnings growth, dividends, net sales, debt/equity ratio, etc.
3. About 40 percent is due to market influences or company disasters.
4. There is approximately a 30-to-1 return on corporate advertising expenditures.

*SOURCE: Erodos & Morgan, Inc.
†SOURCE: Time, Inc., study.
‡SOURCE: Dr. Jaye S. Niefield, executive vice president, Independent Research.

> *Supporting* the rail and other units of CSX through positive association with the CSX name.
>
> *Creating* awareness and understanding among the "influentials"—that small and exclusive group of security analysts, brokers, investment bankers, and financial writers and editors.

The results of achieving these objectives would be:

> *To establish* CSX as a dominant U.S. corporation, competing successfully with consumer-oriented "nifty-fifty" corporations for investment dollars and management talents.
>
> *To inform* analysts who do not specialize in rails, assist those with less research time and those who do not favor conglomerates while expanding beyond the "railroad holding company" image.
>
> *To support* the selling efforts by creating a recognizable name for prospective rail service customers.
>
> *To anticipate* and preempt the competition. Norfolk/Western and Southern would be a reality in eighteen months at the most, and the lead time would be used to establish CSX's single-system service.

Edwin Edel carefully reviewed the results of an awareness study (Exhibit 6) and telephone interviews (Exhibit 7). He glanced once more through his plan for 1981–82 (see Addendum). Now, as before, the fundamental communications problem centered on the following question: If we must preserve the two railroad identities, how do we "sell" a completely new, complicated corporate identity with clarity and bring simplicity to this maze?

■ **EXHIBIT 6**   Study of *The Wall Street Journal* Subscribers

Method and Sample

One thousand (1,000) survey forms were sent to *W.S.J.* subscribers randomly selected from the newspaper's files. These names were provided on self-adhesive labels and selected by zip code from the top ten (10) major markets. The questionnaire addressed the following areas:
1. Name recognition
2. Areas of business activity

Summary of Findings

Table 1   Corporate Awareness

		Position		
Base: Total Respondents	**Total (269) %**	**CEO (62) %**	**Other Top Management (85) %**	**All Other (104) %**
CSX	18	15	22	19
Esmark	64	58	72	69
TRW	86	92	95	88
PepsiCo	84	79	95	89

Table 2   Corporate Image

	Percentage Who Rate Company as Excellent or Good			
Base: Aware of Company	**CSX (48) %**	**Esmark (171) %**	**TRW (231) %**	**PepsiCo (225) %**
Progressiveness	35	47	68	63
Earnings record	25	23	38	37
Potential investment	29	26	44	40

Table 3   Lack of Familiarity among Respondents Who Claim Awareness of Company

	Base: Aware of Company	Unable to Rate Company %
CSX	(48)	(46)
Esmark	(171)	40
TRW	(231)	26

Table 4 Advertising Awareness among Those Aware of Company

	Base: Aware of Company	Position			
		Total %	CEO %	Other Top Management %	All Other %
CSX	(48)	31	44	26	30
Esmark	(171)	73	68	75	77
TRW	(231)	84	81	86	85
PepsiCo	(225)	79	74	86	74

Table 5 Familiarity with CSX's Business

Base: Aware of CSX	Total (48) %
Railroads	63
Natural resources	35
Coal mining	25
Resorts	23
Publishing	15
Aviation	13
None of the above	15
Don't know	17

■ **EXHIBIT 7** Study of Registered Representatives

The objectives of this study were:

To establish benchmark data on awareness of CSX Corporation among a limited number of registered representatives.

To provide guidelines for developing the design and specifications of further research.

Method/Sample

Data was collected via telephone interviews with 100 registered representatives from East and Midwest United States.

Awareness of CSX

Q#1:   "I'm going to read down a list of companies. As I read each name, please tell me whether or not you are familiar with the company."

Base Total	Familiar with Company Percentage 100
Esmark, Inc.	93
CSX Corporation	44
IC Industries, Inc.	68
NWS Corporation	11
Beckett	24
TRW, Inc.	91
PepsiCo. Inc.	98
Burlington Northern, Inc.	98
None	1

continued

Companies' Progressiveness

Q#2: "I'm going to read down the same list of companies. This time, as I read each name, please tell me how you would rate the company in terms of its progressiveness. Please rate each company either excellent, good, only fair, or poor on progressiveness."

	Base Total	Excellent	Good	Only Fair	Poor	Don't Know No Opinion
Esmark, Inc.	(100)	21	44	14	3	18
CSX Corporation	(100)	4	25	10	—	61
IC Industries, Inc.	(100)	13	28	17	1	41
NWS Corporation	(100)	1	6	6	—	87
Beckett	(100)	3	8	7	—	82
TRW, Inc.	(100)	32	40	10	—	18
PepsiCo, Inc.	(100)	31	35	20	2	12
Burlington Northern, Inc.	(100)	32	41	15	—	12

Earnings Records of Companies

Q#3: "Next, I'd like to ask your opinion of the earnings record of each of these companies. As I read each name, please tell me whether you consider the company's earnings record to be excellent, good, only fair, or poor."

	Base Total	Excellent	Good	Only Fair	Poor	Don't Know No Opinion
Esmark, Inc.	(100)	12	36	17	3	32
CSX Corporation	(100)	4	18	7	1	70
IC Industries, Inc.	(100)	7	31	11	—	51
NWS Corporation	(100)	2	3	4	—	91
Beckett	(100)	1	8	2	2	87
TRW, Inc.	(100)	27	37	5	—	31
PepsiCo, Inc.	(100)	28	28	18	2	24
Burlington Northern, Inc.	(100)	25	34	15	—	26

Companies' Qualities as an Investment

Q#4: "Now, I'd like to ask you to classify the common stock of each company in terms of its quality as an investment. As I read each name, please tell me whether you consider the company's stock suitable for growth-oriented portfolios, suitable for income-oriented portfolios, suitable for speculative portfolios, or not suitable for any portfolio at this time."

	Base Total	Growth Oriented	Income Oriented	Speculative	Not Suitable	Don't Know/ No Opinion
Esmark, Inc.	(100)	58	7	8	5	22
CSX Corporation	(100)	27	9	2	1	61
IC Industries, Inc.	(100)	39	11	8	1	41
NWS Corporation	(100)	5	3	4	1	87
Beckett	(100)	10	2	8	—	80
TRW, Inc.	(100)	70	5	1	1	23
PepsiCo. Inc.	(100)	67	16	5	2	10
Burlington Northern, Inc.	(100)	56	21	5	3	15

Number of Years as a Registered Representative

Q#5: "How long have you been a registered representative?"

Base Total	Percent 100
Less than one year	13
1–5 years	35
6–10 years	16
11–15 years	17
16–20 years	8
21–25 years	6
26+ years	5

Number of Industries Followed

Q#6: "How many industries do you follow regularly as part of your job?"

Base Total	Percent 100
1–5	36
6–10	26
11–15	7
16–20	2
21–25	—
26+	6
No answer	18
None	3
Don't know	2

Number of Companies Followed

Q#7: "In all, about how many companies do you regularly follow as part of your job?"

Base Total	Percent 100
Less than 10	19
11–20	25
21–30	13
31–40	7
41–50	11
51–100	8
101+	7
No answer	7
Don't know	3

ADDENDUM ───────────────────────────────

■ CSX CORPORATION: 1981–1982

Media Objectives

1. Direct advertising to a target audience consisting of (1) the financial community and (2) the broad business community.
2. Provide for both a high impact introductory campaign designed to build awareness quickly and a strong base level continuity campaign designed to sustain awareness levels throughout 1982.

Media Strategy

1. During the Introductory Campaign utilize a combination of financial magazines, business publications, newsweeklies, and selected network television news programs to effectively and efficiently reach large numbers of the target audience.
2. After the introductory awareness effort, utilize a shorter list of publications selected to sustain advertising exposure primarily among the financial community and owners of corporate stock.

CSX Print Media

The following publications are recommended to effectively and efficiently reach CSX target audiences:

Professional Investors	Individual Investors
Barron's	*The Wall Street Journal* (E&MW)
Financial World	*New York Times*
Institutional Investors	*Dun's Review*
Financial Analysts' Journal	*Forbes*
	Fortune
	Business Week
	Money
	Time
	Newsweek
	U.S. News & World Report

These publications will provide a monthly reach of 80 percent of all people who own securities. Frequency of exposure will be 2–3 times per month. Total reach 85 percent: frequency 6–7 times.

Media Budget Summary

	4th Quarter 1981	1982 (12 months)
CSX Corporation:		
Magazines	$1,164,000	$2,868,200
Television	307,000	307,500
	1,471,000	3,175,700
Freight:		
Magazines	118,300	631,200
Industrial:		
Magazines	13,700	195,000
	1,603,000	4,001,900
Production	200,000	300,000
	1,803,000	4,301,900

1981–1982 Corporate Media Plan

I. *Magazines*

A. *Financial Publications*—These magazines are recommended both during the introductory and sustaining campaigns. Each emphasizes the professional investor.

	Circulation	Approximate Unit Cost	1981 Schedule Number of Ads	1981 Schedule Total Cost
Barron's (weekly)	262,000	$ 6,061*	3	$18,182
Financial Analysts' Journal (bimonthly)	19,000	11,236	1	11,236
Financial World (semimonthly)	100,000	11,395	2	22,770
Institutional Investor (monthly)	32,000	15,985	2	31,970
Registered Rep (monthly)	37,000	9,120	1	9,130
				$93,328

*Full-page black and white, all others 4-color spreads.

The above publications, plus three additional magazines, are recommended during 1982 to sustain strong exposure among this primary target.

	Circulation	Approximate Unit Cost	1982 Schedule Number of Ads	1982 Schedule Total Cost
Barron's (weekly)	262,000	$ 6,061	12*	$ 72,732
Financial Analysts' Journal (bimonthly)	19,000	11,236	6	67,416
Financial World (semimonthly)	100,000	11,385	12	136,620
Institutional Investor (monthly)	32,000	19,125	6	114,750

continued

	Circulation	Approximate Unit Cost	1982 Schedule	
			Number of Ads	Total Cost
Registered Rep (monthly)	37,000	9,120	6	54,720
Fortune (financial) (bimonthly)	160,000	23,012	12	276,144
Pensions & Investments (26/year)	32,000	6,411†	6	38,490
Survey of Wall Street Research (bimonthly)	20,500	1,485*	6	8,190
				$769,782

*Full-page black and white.
†Half-page 4-color spread, all others 4-color full-page spreads.

B. *Business Publications*—These magazines are also recommended during both the introductory and sustaining campaigns. Each is a major business publication long established and read by the broad business community.

	Circulation	Approximate Unit Cost	1981 Schedule	
			Number of Ads	Total Cost
The Wall Street Journal	1,325,000	$20,500* 30,625†	2 5	} $163,550
Dun's Business (monthly)	285,000	15,230	2	30,460
Forbes (biweekly)	690,000	43,677	2	87,354
Fortune (26/year)	670,000	52,382	1	52,382
Business Week (weekly)	770,000	53,866	3	161,598
				$495,344

*888-line OpEd.
†Full-page black and white, all others 4-color spreads.

With one exception (*Fortune,* financial, rather than full-run), each of these publications is recommended during 1982 to continue advertising emphasis direct to the corporate business executive and stockholder. In addition, *Harvard Business Review* is recommended as an efficient means of supplementing the 1982 effort.

	Circulation	Approximate Unit Cost	1982 Schedule	
			Number of Ads	Total Cost
The Wall Street Journal	1,325,000	$34,625*	24	$ 834,000
Dun's Business (monthly)	285,000	15,230	6	91,380
Forbes (biweekly)	690,000	46,715	6	280,290
Business Week (weekly)	770,000	57,500	9	517,500
Harvard Business Review (6/year)	225,000	12,190	3	36,570
				$1,759,740

*Full-page black and white, all others 4-color spreads.

C. *Introductory Emphasis Publications*—To build awareness quickly, additional publications are recommended to be discontinued after the first few months of the advertising effort. These publications broaden the campaign's exposure considerably to reach not only the professional investor and the corporate business community but the individual investor as well. These "emphasis" vehicles are judged important to enhance the campaign's overall visibility.

	Circulation	Approximate Unit Cost	1981 Schedule	
			Number of Ads	Total Cost
New York Times (daily)	930,000	$ 18,432*	3	$ 55,296
Money (monthly)	875,000	42,389	1	42,389
Time (top management)	590,000	49,784	1	49,784
Newsweek (weekly)	2,950,000	127,116	2	254,232
U.S. News & World Report (weekly)	2,000,000	86,705	2	173,410
				$575,111

*Full-page black and white, all others 4-color spreads.

During the first quarter of 1982, the upper-management demographic editions of the three newsweeklies are recommended to efficiently extend the high visibility introductory print effort.

	Circulation	Approximate Unit Cost	1982 Schedule	
			Number of Ads	Total Cost
Time (top management)	590,000	$49,784	2	$ 99,568
Newsweek (executive)	575,000	49,467	2	98,934
U.S. News (blue chip)	450,000	37,471	2	74,942
Washington Post (daily)	618,100	9,980*	4	39,920
				$313,364

*Half-page black and white, all others 4-color spreads.

II. *Television*

Like the introductory emphasis publications, television is recommended as a supplementary medium to help build awareness quickly and enhance the visibility of the CSX corporate awareness advertising campaign. The following schedule was placed during 1981:

	Estimated 25-54 Rating	Day	Time	Number of Announce-ments	1981 Total Cost
Network/program:					
ABC/Issues & Answers	2.0	Sun	12 N–12:30 P.M.	2	$20,470
ABC/This Wk w/Brinkley	2.0	Sun	11:30 A.M.–12:30 P.M.	3	30,705

continued

	Estimated 25-54 Rating	Day	Time	Number of Announce-ments	1981 Total Cost
ABC/World News Tonight	7.3	M-F	6:30–7 P.M.	1	40,235
CBS/AM News	1.0	M-F	7:30–9 A.M.	8	46,776
CBS/Dan Rather News	8.1	M-F	6:30–7 P.M.	1	50,406
NBC/Today Show	1.5	M-F	7:30–9 A.M.	6	57,500
NBC/Nightly News	7.3	M-F	6:30–7 P.M.	1	45,400
CNN/Financial News	0.6	T-Th	7–7:30 P.M.	7	10,815
CNN/Inside Business	0.6	Sun	6:30–7 P.M.	7	4,690
				36	$306,997

A similar schedule is recommended in 1982, beginning in mid-January as follows:

	Preliminary Schedule			Number of Announce-ments	1982 Estimated Total Cost
	25-54 Rating	Day	Time		
Network/program:					
ABC/This Wk w/Brinkley	2.8	Sun	11:30 A.M.–12:30 P.M.	6	$ 61,410
ABC/World News Tonight	8.4	M-F	6:30–7 P.M.	1	35,235
ABC/Good AM America	1.8	M-F	7:30–9 A.M.	7	62,662
CBS/Sun Eve. News	6.2	Sun	6:30–7 P.M.	2	44,812
NBC/Today Show	1.5	M-F	7:30–9 A.M.	7	54,180
NBC/Nightly News	7.0	M-F	6:30–7 P.M.	1	31,500
CNN/Financial News	0.6	T-Th	7–7:30 P.M.	8	12,360
CNN/Inside Business	0.6	Sun	6:30–7 P.M.	8	5,360
				40	$307,519

III. *Reach & Frequency Estimates*

	1981		1982		Total	
	(3 months)		(3 months)			
	Reach	Frequency	Reach	Frequency	Reach	Frequency
Introductory Period						
Financial & business publications	50%	1–2×	50%	1–2×	60%	2–3×
Introductory emphasis publications	60%	1–2×	55%	1–2×	65%	2–3×
Total Print	70%	2–3×	70%	2–3×	85%	4–5×
Television News	40%	1–2×	50%	1–2×	60%	2–3×
Sustaining Period			*(average monthly)*			
Financial & business publications	—		30%	1–2×	85%	9–10×

SOURCE: Media Mark Research (MRI) Manager and Administrator; Readership by publication, 25–54; Nielsen Television Ratings, TW & Co. estimates.

CHESSIE/FAMILY LINES (FREIGHT): 1981–1982

Media Objectives

1. Direct advertising to the shipping public and industrial business community (i.e., traffic managers or individuals who make decisions on the shipping of goods in large manufacturing companies).
2. Schedule advertising support on a sustaining basis beginning in the fourth quarter 1981 and throughout 1982.

Media Strategy

Selected business trade publications.

1981–1982 Freight Media Plan:

I. *1981*—The following magazines are recommended:

	Circulation	Approximate Unit Cost	Number of Ads	1981 Schedule Total Cost
Chemical Week	53,000	$10,340	1	$ 10,340
Coal Industry News	10,400	1,245	1*	1,245
Commerce Magazine	N.A.	1,048	1†	1,048
Container News	30,000	4,870	2	9,740
Distribution	61,000	6,480	2	12,960
Handling & Shipping	75,000	6,850	2	13,700
Industry Week	280,000	17,712	2	35,424
Purchasing Magazine	95,200	8,125	1	8,125
Railway Age	22,800	4,745	1	4,745
Traffic Management	70,000	6,250	2	12,500
Traffic World	13,500	4,250	2	8,500
				$118,327

N.A. means not available.
*Jr. Page.
†Full-page black and white, all others 4-color spreads.

II. *1982*—The use of most of the above publications is recommended to continue in 1982. Two publications, *Business Week* (industrial edition) and *Chemical Business*, are also recommended.

	Circulation	Approximate Unit Cost	Number of Ads	1982 Schedule Total Cost
Business Week (industrial)	315,000	$37,200	3	$111,600
Chemical Week	53,000	12,200	3	36,600
Chemical Business	17,350	4,300	3	12,900

continued

	Circulation	Approximate Unit Cost	Number of Ads	1982 Schedule Total Cost
Container News	30,000	4,900	6	29,400
Distribution	61,000	6,500	6	39,000
Handling & Shipping	75,000	6,850	6	41,100
Industry Week	280,000	19,900	8	159,200
Purchasing	95,200	8,125	6	48,750
Traffic Management	70,000	6,250	6	37,500
Traffic World	13,500	4,250	12	51,000
Savannah Port Handbook	N.A.	1,140	1	1,140
Modern Railroad	18,125	5,920	3	17,760
Railway Age	22,800	4,745	3	14,235
				$600,185

III. *Media Cost Summary*

Freight	$118,330	$600,185
Industrial development	13,670*	—
	$132,000	$600,185
Ports campaign reserve		25,000
Rate increase reserve	—	6,000
	$132,000	$631,185

Jacksonville Magazine 11/12 issue @ $989.
Nation's Business Nov. I.D. issue @ $12,673.

■ FAMILY LINES (INDUSTRIAL DEVELOPMENT): 1982

Media Objectives

1. Direct advertising to a broad number of manufacturing companies who may be interested in establishing a manufacturing and/or distributing operation in the 13-state area served by the Family Lines.

2. Utilize vehicles that are likely to generate inquiries regarding Family Lines Industrial Development Services.

Media Strategy

Selected business trade publications.

I. *1982 Industrial Development Media Plan:*
The following publications are recommended:

	Circulation	Unit Cost	Total Number of Ads	1982 Schedule Total Cost
Area Development	32,000	$1,610(5) 1,755(7)	12	$ 20,335
A.I.P.R.	30,600	1,700	10	17,000

continued

	Circulation	Unit Cost	Total Number of Ads	1982 Schedule Total Cost
Chemical Week	53,000	4,025 (2) pg. 1,790 (6) ⅓	8	18,790
Dun's Business Month	285,000	6,525 (2) pg. 2,365 (5) ⅓	8	27,240
Industry Week	280,000	6,961 (2) pg. 2,785 (6) ⅓	8	30,632
Plant Location Annual	42,000	2,650	1	2,650
Site Selection Handbook	28,000	1,865	4	7,460
Plants Sites & Parks	30,900	1,955	6	11,730
The Wall Street Journal (East)	780,000	4,679 (420 li)	3	28.077
		1,560 (140 li)	9	
				$163,914
			Reserve	31,086
				$195,000

■ OTHER CORPORATE COMMUNICATIONS PROGRAMS

Corporate communications programs will be implemented to maintain an easily understood and consistent flow of information on those corporate activities that impact on each public and, thus, move the company toward the aforementioned overall goals. The CSX activities will center on the following:

1. *A broad Financial Relations Program* will improve communications with our stockholders, increase demand for CSX shares, and educate the investment community about our business, our growth opportunities, and the strengths of our management team.
   a. Multicity briefings will be held in January and February with security analysts.
   b. Early-on meetings will be initiated with institutional investors in major on-line and off-line cities.
   c. A corporate profile will be produced for broad distribution.
   d. A new quarterly publication will be initiated and called the *CSX Investor Update*. The publication will be designed to supplement the usual interim reports and to give shareholders, present and future, more timely "product" information in greater depth that can be included in the present interim and annual reports.
   e. A center of information will be installed for analysts and brokers. (An 800 line is recommended in the Finance Department as it opens up communications to brokers, most of whom have to pay for their own phone calls!)
   f. Quarterly and annual results will be disseminated to employees, the trades, and financial and general media.

2. *A Corporate Information Program* will disseminate the news from the top to the various nonfinancial publics.
   a. A new publication, tentatively called *CSX Dialogue,* will be developed to give us a controlled forum on national and other issues that affect the business environment in which we operate. This publication will be directed at not only the investment community but also the political community, transportation professionals, national opinion leaders, and potential shareholders, and can accomplish three things:
      (1) It will provide the opportunity to speak out on any pertinent issue (e.g., energy, worldwide or coal development).
      (2) It will help build long-term credibility.
      (3) It will provide the opportunity for commissioned articles by national authorities to be an important force.
   b. A strong program of public appearances and speeches by top executives will be supported.
   c. A planned flow of information to top-level business writers of all major publications will be initiated and maintained.

3. *A steady flow of news from the two railroad systems* to both external and internal publics will be planned and managed.
   a. Each railroad system now generates news almost every week that is of interest to one or more publics regarding new capital projects, a new traffic record, or a new service, etc. Each railroad group, therefore, will be expected to maintain a steady flow of such stories to be coordinated to obtain the maximum reach without flooding the market.
   b. Each railroad system will maintain its specialized information programs now in place for employees and shippers, for Operation Lifesaver, and regarding safety activities. Again, coordination will be required to obtain the most mileage in reach and budget.
   c. At the same time, a new *CSX Management Digest* will be proposed that will sharpen communications from top management to supervisors and above. As its name implies, this publication will consist of pertinent excerpts and reprints of a whole range of self-help and generally informative items on how to better manage affairs.

Six sample advertisements follow, illustrating the CSX media objectives previously discussed.

PORT AUTHORITY.

Our railroads give shippers throughout the eastern United States direct access to overseas markets with the nation's most extensive rail-port connections—serving 11 throughout the Great Lakes and 26 along the Atlantic and Gulf Coasts. And we have agents in or near each one ready to help you when your ship comes in.

For more information contact John L. Blair, Manager Intermodal Services, The Family Lines Rail System, 500 Water Street, Jacksonville, Florida 32202.

 FAMILY LINES RAIL SYSTEM **CHESSIE SYSTEM RAILROADS**

Family Lines Rail System and Chessie System Railroads are units of CSX Corporation.

CSX CORPORATION

THE LEADER IN COAL.

When it comes to moving America's coal, the CSX railroads are number one. And the outstanding performance turned in last year clearly demonstrates the resourcefulness of our people and the capabilities of our single-system service. Now and in the future.

Our prompt and strong recovery from the 80-day strike in the coal fields enabled us to handle record tonnages. Domestic shipments, driven by the utilities' need to rebuild stockpiles depleted during the strike and hot summer, rose 7 percent to 208.3 million tons. Export shipments continued their phenomenal growth as well, with dumpings of 36.5 million tons for overseas markets.

When it comes to coal, look to the leader. Call the CSX railroads.

For more information, contact Jerry E. Gobrecht, V.P. Coal Traffic, Chessie System Railroads, Terminal Tower, Cleveland, OH 44101. (216/623-2323).

Or John E. Nall, V.P. Coal Traffic, Family Lines Rail System, 500 Water Street, Jacksonville, FL 32202. (904/359-1710). Or call toll free: 800/368-2792.

Get to know us. You'll like the way we do business at CSX.

CSX Corporation

Chessie System Railroads

Family Lines Rail System

Railroads, Natural Resources, Land Development, Aviation Services, Publishing and Resort Properties.
Chessie System Railroads and Family Lines Rail System are units of CSX Corporation.

PART SIX

Trends in Business to Business Marketing

Chapter 14 · Marketing of Business Services

Chapter 15 · Ethical Considerations and Future Trends in Business to Business Marketing

Chapter **14**

Marketing of Business Services

LEARNING OBJECTIVES

After reading this chapter, you should be able to:

- Identify the external environments facing the marketing manager for business services.
- Understand the important characteristics of business services.
- Appreciate the challenges and opportunities found in the marketing of business services.
- Differentiate among various methods by which to classify business services.
- Comprehend the role and importance of international markets for business services.
- Discuss likely future trends in the marketing of business services.

CHAPTER OUTLINE

Learning Objectives
The Marketing of Services: An Overview
The Environments for Business Service Firms
  Economic Environment
  Societal/Cultural Environment
  Competitive Environment
  Technological Environment
  Political/Legal Environment
Important Characteristics of Business Services
  Intangibility
  Perishability and Fluctuating Demand
  Simultaneity
  Heterogeneity
Business Service Marketing— Challenges and Opportunities
  Service Marketing versus Product Marketing

Positioning
Bundling of Services
Service Strategy and the Marketing Mix
New Service Development
Classification of Services
  Seller-Related Bases
  Buyer-Related Bases
  Service-Related Bases
  Classifying Services by Clusters
  People-Based versus Equipment-Based Services
International Marketing of Business Services
  The Risks of International Marketing for Service Organizations
  Problems of Adaption to, and Operation in, Overseas Markets
  Barriers to Trade in Services
The Future of Business to Business Services

■ THE MARKETING OF SERVICES: AN OVERVIEW

Many marketing textbooks devote little, if any, attention to program development for the marketing of business services. For the most part the entire area of business service marketing remains undefined or ill defined. Compared to consumer services research, few published sources exist on the benefits sought and performance of business services.[1] Marketing, however, is slowly coming of age in the service sector, as it becomes obvious that the most basic trend of the last half of the 20th century is the transformation from a product-oriented economy to a service-oriented one. The topical omission from textbooks is usually based on the assumption that the marketing of goods and the marketing of services are the same; as a result, the techniques described for goods must apply to the marketing of

---

[1]Arch G. Woodside, R. Hedley Sanderson, and Roderick J. Brodie, "Testing Acceptance of a New Industrial Service," *Industrial Marketing Management,* February 1988, pp. 65–71.

services as well. In a sense this is true, as the marketer in both cases is concerned with developing a marketing strategy centered around the four controllable decision variables comprising the marketing mix: the product (or service), the price, the distribution system, and the promotional program. Because of the fact that the marketing of services usually requires a different treatment of the marketing mix ingredients, business marketers will be increasingly expected to respond to the unique challenges posed by service marketing. The purpose of this chapter is to acquaint the reader with some of the special problems and opportunities of service marketing. The problems of service firms are so distinct from those of tangible goods firms that a separate chapter is needed to help the reader appreciate both the differences and their effects on business to business marketing strategy.

■ THE ENVIRONMENTS FOR BUSINESS SERVICE FIRMS

The diversity of the environment within which the service marketer must work is reflected in its multiple sectors. There are a number of classification theories, but for our purposes (as shown in Figure 14–1) we will view the environment in five sectors: the economic environment, the societal/cultural environment, the competitive environment, the technological environment, and the political/legal environment.

■ **FIGURE 14–1**   Marketing Environment for Business to Business Service Firms

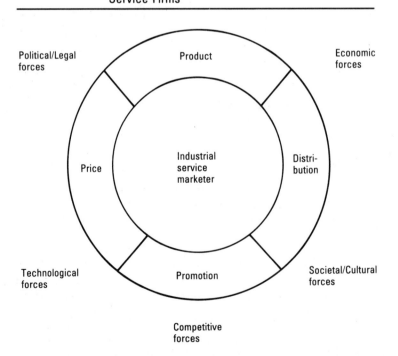

Economic Environment

The **economic environment** includes forces associated with the macro-environment, including such factors as inflation, interest rates, and gross national product (GNP). The sharp increase in spending for business services and the development of service industries have been among the most significant economic trends in the post–World War II economy. Most explanations for this trend have looked at it as the result of a maturing economy, along with the by-products of rapid economic growth. Rapid technological advances, coupled with the knowledge explosion of recent years, have made the servicing of the business sector very profitable, as companies in this field range from suppliers of temporary help to highly specialized management consulting firms. Many times the business service provider can perform a specialized service more efficiently, and at a lower cost than the buying firm can do itself. (See "make or buy" in Chapter 3.)

The growth of business services and the increased spending for business services over the last decade have been spectacular. In recent years business service firms have prospered primarily for two reasons. First, they are frequently able to perform a specialized function more efficiently than would the buying firm itself. Second, many companies are unable to perform certain services for themselves. Marketing research studies, for example, often require the knowledge that outside experts, such as Judson Rees and Associates, Ltd. and Telecommunications Marketing Resource, Ltd., can provide. Temporary employment needs and employment counseling can often be better supplied by service firms such as Accountemps, Kelly Services, and Options, Inc. Technical recruitment can often be more productive by using firms such as Technical Procurement Service Inc., and SAT Recruitment and Placement, Inc. Legal and financial services are well represented, with service firms such as Kennedy Consultants and Schattle Consultants that provide expertise in these areas.

Societal/Cultural Environment

The **societal/cultural environment** contains the forces emanating from society as a whole, and includes both informal forces (the values of society), and more formally organized forces (those growing out of the result of the consumerism movement). The societal/cultural environment has a significant impact on the marketing of business services. A variety of societal/cultural trends are relevant to the increased marketing of business services, such as the growing emphasis on safety and environmental considerations that has widened the market for several business services. The movement toward protecting the physical environment has provided new markets for energy-preserving consultation and products. The demand for on-site monitoring of dust, solvents, metals, asbestos, and noise for both federal and state requirements has increased the demand for testing specialists and consulting firms such as New England Testing Laboratory, Inc., and Enviro Sciences, Inc. Additionally, the need for protection specialists such as

Burns International Security Services and First Security Services Corporation has soared. As mentioned above, most of these firms provide the specialized service more efficiently and at a lower cost than if the buying firm tried to perform these services itself.

Competitive Environment

The **competitive environment** consists of all other service providers who are vying for the patronage of the same customer. A major influence on competitive intensity is the threat of new entrants. If entrance barriers are low, competitors can easily enter the market and intensify competition. Opportunities within the competitive environment include such things as (1) acquiring competing firms; (2) offering demonstrably better value, thus attracting prospective customers away from competitors; and (3) driving competitors out of the industry. The primary constraints in this environment are demand-stimulation activities of competing service providers, and the number of prospects who cannot be lured away from the competition.[2]

Historically, many forms of competition have been almost nonexistent in some service industries:

- Price competition has been severely limited by regulation and trade practices in transportation, telecommunications, and in business, legal, and medical services.
- Many service industries are difficult to enter (health care facilities, educational institutions, etc.).
- A major financial investment may be necessary (utilities).
- Special education or training may be required (professions).
- Government regulations may restrict operations (telecommunications, banking).[3]

The entry of manufacturers into service markets has also increased the intensity of competition for the business service dollar. Some large manufacturers have begun to offer spin-off business services to other organizations—for instance, Dupont, Dow, Alcoa, and other companies noted for their technical expertise, market analytical services and facilities, pollution control systems, and related products or services to other companies. These firms see the special needs of other businesses as an opportunity to profit from their own investments in research and development.[4] The problem of increased competition is the primary impetus for strategy change.

Technological Environment

The vast majority of the economic growth in the United States has resulted from the **technological environment,** through increased productivity

[2]J. Paul Peter and James H. Donnelly, Jr., *A Preface to Marketing Management,* 3d ed. (Plano, Tex.: Business Publications, 1985), p. 20.

[3]Eugene M. Johnson, Eberhard E. Scheuing, and Kathleen A. Gaida, *Profitable Service Marketing* (Homewood, Ill.: Dow-Jones-Irwin, 1986), p. 45.

[4]Ibid., p. 47.

(the output produced by each worker). Technological developments have accounted for tremendous increases in productivity, and this trend should not change in the foreseeable future. How will future increases in productivity be accomplished in a service economy? Theodore Levitt argues that service providers should assume a **manufacturing attitude.** "Instead of looking to service workers to improve results by greater exertion of energy, managers must see what kinds of organizations, incentives, technology, and skills could improve overall productivity."[5] The introduction of wide-bodied jets by some airlines enables them to serve twice as many passengers, while using the same number of pilots and flight engineers. A major challenge to marketers during the 1990s is to implement gains in productivity, while not sacrificing the quality of service. This goal will most likely be realized through improved marketing.[6]

Political/Legal Environment

The **political environment** includes the attitudes and reactions of the general public, business critics, and external organizations such as the Better Business Bureau. The **legal environment** includes local, state, and federal legislation (both real and envisioned), directed at protecting both business competition and the consumer. Political and legal forces are closely interrelated because, as legislation is enacted, legal decisions are interpreted by the courts, and regulatory agencies are created and operated mostly by people who occupy government positions. Business organizations also need to be concerned about making a favorable impression on political officials as political officials may play key roles in securing foreign markets.[7]

■ IMPORTANT CHARACTERISTICS OF BUSINESS SERVICES

There are a number of characteristics which not only distinguish goods and services but also impact business to business marketing program development. Four characteristics are unique to services and influence the way they are marketed: intangibility, perishability and fluctuating demand, simultaneity, and heterogeneity.

Intangibility

Services are intangible, and therefore, abstract. Most business services cannot appeal to the buyer's sense of taste, touch, smell, sight, or hearing

---

[5]Theodore Levitt, "The Industrialization of Service," *Harvard Business Review,* September-October 1976, pp. 63–75.

[6]For an analysis of the industrialization of service via hard, soft, and hybrid technologies, see Theodore Levitt, *The Marketing Imagination,* (Glencoe, IL: The Free Press, 1986), pp. 50–71.

[7]From William M. Pride and O. C. Ferrell, *Marketing: Basic Concepts and Decisions,* 4th ed. (Boston: Houghton Mifflin, 1985), pp. 476–77.

before buying, which places some strain on the seller's marketing organization. Proven strategies of product marketing cannot be applied when the product being marketed cannot be seen, felt, or guaranteed to provide specific and measurable results. Because of the lack of tangibility, business service marketers find it difficult to differentiate their offerings, and as a result, services must be made tangible by visual representation and symbolism. Marketing promotion, through the sales force and the advertising department becomes critical in service marketing since the product itself is incapable of communicating its benefits.[8] Intangible products, such as freight forwarding, consulting, repair, brokerage, or education, can seldom be tried out or tested in advance of purchase. Buyers are forced to view advertising copy, listen to a sales presentation, or consult current users to determine how well a service will perform. Even the most tangible of products cannot be reliably tested prior to purchase. To inspect an automatic order-picking installation in advance, and to have studied, in advance, the vendor's design and quote with other members of the buying center is still not a guarantee of satisfaction in most buying situations. The process of getting precisely what was ordered, having it built, delivered, and installed on time, and then having the installation run smoothly involves more than the tangible product itself. Intangibles can and will make or break the installation's success in most situations. So, it is logical to assume that all products are in some respects intangible. The use of nouns (for example, *hotel* when we mean *lodging rental*) obscures the fundamental nature of services, which are processes, not objects.[9]

Perishability and Fluctuating Demand

Services are perishable: they cannot be stored, and the markets for most business services fluctuate by the day, week, or season. Unused electric power, an empty airplane seat, and an idle machinist in a factory, all represent business that is lost forever. This combination of perishability and fluctuating demand has created some very special problems with regard to strategy implementation for marketers of business services. Key decisions must be made on what maximum capacity level should be available to cope with surges in demand before service levels suffer. Furthermore, decisions must be made in times of low levels of usage on whether spare capacity will be idle, or whether short-term policies (differential pricing, special promotions, etc.) will be adopted to even out fluctuations in demand. Business service marketers thus lose the valuable buffer function of inventory that allows a producer to manufacture for inventory during slow periods and to draw on inventory during periods of peak demand. This unique

---

[8]For suggestions on how to offset the marketing problems created by intangibility in services, see Theodore Levitt, "Marketing Intangible Products and Product Intangibles," *Harvard Business Review,* May/June 1981, pp. 94–102. Also see Betsy D. Gelb, "How Marketers of Intangibles Can Raise the Odds for Consumer Satisfaction," *Journal of Consumer Marketing,* Spring 1985, pp. 55–61.

[9]G. Lynn Shostack, "Service Positioning through Structural Change," *Journal of Marketing* 51 (January 1987), pp. 34–43.

combination of perishability and fluctuating demand offers exciting challenges and opportunities to business service marketers in the areas of product planning, pricing, and promotional strategy. For most service businesses, sales and mass promotional activities must be used extensively to increase sales volume during slack periods, and thereby spread sales out more evenly over time.

Simultaneity

Production and consumption of services are inseparable, with selling coming first, followed by production and consumption simultaneously. Services are used at the same time as they are produced, which typically puts the business marketer of services in very close contact with the customer. As a result of this situation, service customers tend to perceive relatively greater risk when they are shopping for a service. They rely more heavily on the recommendations of others.[10] In the marketing of many business services, a client relationship exists between the buyer and the seller, as opposed to the more typical customer-supplier relationship found in the marketing of tangible products. Physical proximity is essential to the successful delivery of services. An example of this type of relationship would be the business consulting relationship. The buyer considers the suggestions or advice provided by the seller, and the relationship is of an ongoing nature. In addition, since many business service firms are client-serving organizations, the marketing function is very professional as seen in financial, legal, and educational services.

Heterogeneity

It is difficult to standardize services; as a result, output can vary widely in quality. A major problem created by heterogeneity is quality control, whereby the provider of the business service can control the production, but not the quality or the consumption of the service. Service marketers try to control, with some going to great lengths to standardize their services, in addition to investing in high-quality employees. However, even services of the same firm are remarkably dissimilar. Although standardization of some services (for example, insurance, transportation, and utilities) has increased, it is improbable that services will ever become as standardized as most tangible goods in the business to business sector.

In addition to the factors mentioned above, the quality of service performance varies from one business service provider to another. Not all consulting firms, airlines, or insurance companies offer the same level of service. The quality of the service provided will also vary for the same provider from one occasion to another. A group seminar held by a psychological consulting firm such as Nordlie Wilson, Inc. will achieve varying

---

[10]William J. Winston, "Topic: International Marketing—Key to a Successful Professional Service Marketing Program," *Journal of Professional Services Marketing,* Winter 1986, pp. 15–18.

results, depending on client response and cooperation. The variability of business service output makes it difficult for the service firm to establish, maintain, and guarantee quality continuously.

Concept Questions

1. Why is marketing coming of age in the service sector?
2. Why will business to business marketers increasingly be called upon to respond to the unique challenges of service marketing?
3. What does the presence of multiple environments say about the macroenvironment which business service marketers face?

■ BUSINESS SERVICE MARKETING—CHALLENGES AND OPPORTUNITIES

Although marketing functions are basically the same for many services and products, there is a difference in the way business service marketing is organized and implemented in an effort to gain a competitive advantage. American industry is changing. Honeywell Corporation estimates that 30 percent of its revenue comes from services, yet most of us think of the firm as a high-tech manufacturing company. General Telephone and Telegraph has earned over half of its revenue from services since 1974. The growing significance of business service marketing is just starting to be understood. Only in the last few years—thanks to a few scholars and practitioners, along with the American Marketing Association's Services Marketing Division—has the subject been addressed.

Services Marketing versus Product Marketing[11]

As noted earlier, a distinctive feature about business services marketing is that production occurs at the point of sale. This decentralization of service performance puts a different perspective on the role of a centralized-business to business-staff marketing department. A major function of the centralized staff is to get everyone else in the organization to practice marketing. Their role is to facilitate good marketing because with a business service provider, everybody is responsible for the customer.

With a business product, the unit is well defined. This is not so in service marketing. A product can be measured objectively against specifications by checking tolerances and comparing weight, color, shape, and so on. Measuring a service such as an office building cleaning service or a business new-product consulting service, is not so easy. What is clean? What is efficient, feasible, and marketable? In product marketing, once the need is defined, the manufacturing process takes over. With business services marketing, the "product" is not created until the service is performed.

---

[11]The discussion in this section is from Thomas J. Fitzgerald, "Understanding the Differences and Similarities between Services and Products to Exploit Your Competitive Advantage," *Journal of Business and Industrial Marketing* 2, no. 3 (Summer 1987), pp. 29–34.

With an office building cleaning service, delivery occurs when the vendor employees arrive to do the work. Did they do a good job? Is the office clean? Did they arrive on time? With a business product, there is no need for a distribution channel until after a product is manufactured, packaged, priced, and ready to ship. With a business service, the channel of distribution and delivery are one and the same. The employees of the office building cleaning service are at the same time manufacturing and distributing the "product." With a business product, little change can be made without substantial time and money costs in most cases. However, with a service provider, the "product" can be altered quite easily. The office building cleaning service can provide additional services such as window washing and carpet cleaning on very short notice. Finally, in business product development, time is required to develop, test, introduce and provide an inventory buildup. With a business service, the provider distributes the "product," usually within a 24-hour period. Again, the office building cleaning service provides an appropriate example.

Positioning[12]

The image that a business service has in the mind of the user, especially in relation to competitive offerings, follows naturally after identification of the market segment sought. Business firms that have most successfully positioned themselves have answered these questions: To what extent do competitors provide a like service? To what extent are customer expectations met? To what extent does the company, the customer, and the competitor (the Three Cs) relate to one another on dimensions considered important to the customer? When the service provider establishes and maintains a distinctive place for itself and its offerings in the market, it is said to be successfully positioned. In the increasingly competitive service sector, effective positioning is one of marketing's most critical tasks.[13] Effective positioning requires marketing research, something foreign to nearly all but the best-managed business service firms. It is more complicated to research reactions to a service than to a product because potential customers find it harder to put themselves into the role of using a prospective service than that of using a product they can hold and see. One of the regional telephone companies, in preparing for deregulation, learned from its major business users that some firms using phone lines for data-processing purposes were interested in contracts providing 24-hour repair service. Its retail customers, however, which were heavily dependent on phone service only during business hours, wanted a guaranteed minimum response time for service interruptions only during those hours. In the past the company offered a single service contract that treated all business customers alike. Company management concluded that there was a great risk

---

[12]The discussion in this section is from James L. Heskett, *Managing in the Service Economy* (Boston: Harvard Business School Press, 1986), Chapter 2.

[13]G. Lynn Shostack, "Service Positioning through Structural Change," *Journal of Marketing* 51, (January 1987), pp. 34–43.

of losing business to competitors who tailored their telephone service to specific industries' needs. They, in turn, repositioned their service by offering accordingly and by establishing and maintaining a distinctive place for themselves and their offerings in the market. In the increasingly competitive service sector, effective positioning will be one of the business marketer's most critical tasks.

Bundling of Services

Broadly defined, **bundling** is the practice of marketing two or more products and/or services in a single package for a special price.[14] It is most often used by a firm with a broad line of complementary products, and its effectiveness is a function of the degree to which bundling stimulates demand so as to achieve cost economies. Examples of bundling includes the sale of a maintenance contract with computer hardware, with the lease of a truck, or with a piece of machinery. The rationale for bundling is based primarily on the reality that the cost structure of most industrial service businesses is characterized by a high ratio of fixed to variable costs, and by a high degree of cost sharing. (As a result, the same facilities, equipment, and personnel are used to provide multiple services).[15] The objective of bundling is to add value while keeping cost increments small, and thus not to increase price for the added value. Price bundling is a special form of discount pricing where two or more services are combined into a single package and sold at a special price.[16] Bundling as a marketing strategy can impact a business firm's short-term success or failure. We will see an increased use of this marketing tool in the years ahead.

Service Strategy and the Marketing Mix

Since Jerome McCarthy popularized the four Ps in 1964, marketing plans have incorporated these elements as key building blocks for marketing programs.[16] The controllable variables of product, price, place, and promotion have been the key in developing a strategy that involves identifying a target market segment, and then developing a marketing program to deliver that product to members of the segment. All these elements must be combined into a cohesive package by the astute business services marketer.

Product. The development of new services is as important to a business service provider as new products are to a product-marketing firm. Also, the improvement of existing services and the elimination of unprofitable services are key strategies. The development of a product line, which involves the design and introduction of new service offerings, has been cited

---

[14]Joseph P. Guiltinan, "The Price Bundling of Services: A Normative Framework," *Journal of Marketing,* April 1987, p. 74.

[15]John Dearden, "Cost Accounting Comes to Service Industries," *Harvard Business Review* 56 (September-October), pp. 132–40.

[16]E. Jerome McCarthy, *Basic Marketing: A Managerial Approach,* 2d ed. (Homewood, Ill.: Richard D. Irwin, 1964), pp. 38–40.

as one of the more difficult challenges of managers in the service sector.[17] According to those who have provided consulting services both to manufacturing and service firms:

> New product development is inherently more difficult, messier, and less successful in the service sector. In industry, research and development labs can usually come up with new designs that incorporate certain predictable functions and characteristics. On the other hand, when a service firm correctly, if subjectively, perceives a need, it cannot have the same confidence in its ability to deliver all the ingredients that comprise successful new service products. As a result, service organizations are more likely to be conservative about innovations. They focus most of their attention on geographical extensions of their service, or on minor modifications to the primary service package. True inventiveness is rare . . . innovation in the service sector is frequently the result of trial and error . . . original or imitative ideas exist in abundance. Yet, new ideas often ignore the deep and subtle linkages among the variables in the service package. Between imagination and execution lies a dark gulf that has swallowed up many a bright new product.[18]

Despite the difficulties involved, every service industry has companies and managers noted for their ability to foster new product development or the design and implementation of new internal processes. In banking Citicorp is often mentioned, along with Basic One and VISA, as firms providing cash transfer service systems. In financial services Merrill Lynch is often the first to produce new products that are imitated by others, while Dun & Bradstreet relies on new product development for a significant share of its revenue. In communications Dow Jones and Gannett are frequently mentioned; in lodging, the Marriott Corporation.[19]

Some subelements of the controllable-variable product that concern the service firm's management in selecting appropriate strategy development include product-line width-and-depth adjustment, product-line warranties, and product-line naming, logos, and trademarks. Additionally, the strategies for individual product items must be aggregated into marketing plans for individual product lines, product/market domains, and total corporate marketing strategy.[20]

Price.   A second controllable variable of the mix is price, which is important in business service marketing because profitability is more related to the respective net margin of a larger number of services than to total revenues. The price of a service should be related to the achievement of marketing and organizational goals, and should be appropriate for the service firm's overall marketing programs. In setting price objectives for services,

---

[17]James L. Heskett, *Managing in the Service Economy* (Boston: Harvard Business School Press, 1986), p. 84.

[18]"Service Management: The Toughest Game In Town," *Management Practice,* Fall 1984, p. 8.

[19]Heskett, *Managing in the Service Economy,* p. 85.

[20]For a model that management can follow in service (product) development, see G. Lynn Shostack, "Designing Services That Deliver," *Harvard Business Review,* January-February 1984, pp. 133–39.

we must consider a number of factors.[21] The more significant of these are as follows:

1. The planned market position for the service product.
2. The stage of the life cycle of the service product.
3. Elasticity of demand.
4. The competitive situation.
5. The strategic role of price.

The planned market position for the service product. How the service product is "seen" in relation to other like services available will clearly influence price strategy. Price is an important element in the marketing mix and, as noted earlier in the chapter, influences position; services are often "positioned" on the basis of intangible attributes. Price will influence market position.

The stage of the life cycle of the service product. The price of a service will relate to its life cycle, much the same as the price of a tangible product will fluctuate as the product moves through the stages of its life cycle. At introduction, management may opt to use a skimming or a penetration strategy, adjusting prices either upward or downward as competitive pressure dictates. We can anticipate that there will be a need to identify a company's position in the life cycle as well as its major objectives, decisions, problems, and organizational transitions required for the future.

Elasticity of demand. **Elasticity of demand** refers to the responsiveness of demand to changes in price. A business service provider has to understand how elastic or inelastic demand for its services is in response to price changes. If the firm reduces its price and demand is elastic, then the effect would be to reduce margins with no compensating increase in demand. Elasticity will impose limitations on certain price options.

The competitive structure. In situations where there is little differentiation between business service "products," and where competition is intense, price discretion is limited. In other settings tradition and custom may influence the prices charged (e.g., advertising agencies' commission system).

The strategic role of price. Pricing policies have a strategic role aimed at achieving business organizational objectives. Thus the pricing decision on any particular business service should fit in with the firm's strategic objectives. Additionally, any pricing strategy must fit in with the way in which other elements of the marketing mix are manipulated to attain strategic ends.

In the business service sector the marketer must consider the demand for the services; the production, marketing, and administrative costs; and the influence of competition. Price negotiation also forms an important

---

[21]This discussion follows M. G. Christopher, M. M. McDonald, and G. S. C. Wills, *Effective Marketing Management* (Gowers Aldershot, 1980), pp. 108–109; it is adapted from Donald Cowell, *The Marketing of Services* (London: Institute of Marketing and the CAM Foundation), pp. 147–61.

part of many business service transactions, such as financial and legal assistance, equipment rental, insurance, and maintenance and protection services. Variable pricing may also be a viable pricing option.[22] Quantity discounts, payment terms, cash discounts, price bidding, trade discounts, adjustments in price that reflect peak-load pricing (seasonal, yearly, fluctuations in demand and/or supply), and bundling arrangements must also be considered when determining business strategy development with the price element of the marketing mix.

Place.   The function of distribution channels for business services is to make the service available and convenient to the buyer. Because services (unlike tangible goods) cannot be transported, the channel is usually simpler and shorter. An attorney will work directly with a client; insurance will usually be purchased through an agent; and a business loan will be obtained through a bank officer. These are short, direct channels, and are due, in large part, to the intangibility of services, along with the need for continuing personal relationships between providers and users of many services. The objective of channel selection decisions is the same for the marketers of both goods and services—that is, to select channels which will maximize the firm's profit position over the long run.[23] For marketers of business services, this involves providing optimum service and coverage at minimum cost. Business marketers must clearly delineate their markets and understand the buying patterns for their services—when, where, and how the service is purchased, and by whom.

Historically, in business service marketing, little attention has been paid to distribution. However, as competition grows, the value of convenient distribution is recognized. Legal firms, along with accounting firms like Touche-Ross, use multiple locations for the distribution of services. The use of a channel intermediary is another way to broaden distribution. It is now quite common for companies to deposit an employee's paycheck into his or her bank account, thereby becoming an intermediary in distributing a bank's service. We have all seen vending machines at airports whereby insurance firms attempt to expand their distribution network. Travel agents, tourist boards, hotel representatives, and centralized reservation systems are all examples of the use of intermediaries to expand on the place element of the marketing mix.

Promotion.   As noted earlier in the chapter, the fact that many business services cannot appeal to the buyer's sense of touch, taste, smell, sight, or hearing before purchase places a heavy burden on the business marketing organization in general, and on the promotion element of the marketing mix in particular. Since the business to business service firm is selling an idea, not a product, it must tell the buyer what the service will do, since it is often unable to illustrate, demonstrate, or display the service in use. For example, information retailing, as described in the "Business to Business

---

[22]Also see Stephen W. Brown, "New Patterns Are Emerging in Services Marketing Sector," *Marketing News,* June 7, 1985, p. 2.

[23]Victor P., Buell, ed., *Handbook of Modern Marketing,* 2d ed. (New York: McGraw-Hill, 1986), Chap. 24.

Marketing in Action" box, is an underused service with incredible opportunity for growth. MacFarlane and Company, Inc., of Atlanta, and Find S. V. P., Inc., of New York, are two of the better known information retailers. This potential will only be recognized if information retailers can persuade prospective clients that the service provides them with a competitive advantage. Such a situation obviously points out the need for the effective promotion of services.

BUSINESS TO BUSINESS MARKETING IN ACTION

Information Retailers: A Potential Not Yet Realized

Information retailing is an underused service with incredible opportunity for growth. Yet this potential will only be realized if information retailers can persuade prospective clients that the service provides them with a competitive advantage.

Lack of awareness is understandable. Information retailing is fragmented and evolving so rapidly that even a precise definition is hard to develop. An acceptable one appears in "The Information Industry," a report by Paine Webber and the Information Industry Association. The report defines information retailing as the "activities of companies which search computer and manual information sources for their clients, and may provide document fulfillment services as stand-alone profit centers."

Moreover, many businesspeople aren't sure who information retailers are or what they do.

One important and growing segment consists of information brokers. This group searches electronic databases and sometimes augments findings with telephone and/or personal interviews. Firms that provide training, software packages, or help establish an in-house library are included in this group.

Information retailers frequently offer several or all these services, and many do not fit into an identifiable segment. Customers are often able to work with one vendor and select from a menu of services designed to satisfy diverse information needs.

About 28 percent of information users use databases that are business- or economics-oriented, according to the *1985 Survey of On-Line Professionals*. One representative business database, ABI/Inform, is very comprehensive and widely used by business professionals. Anyone with a personal computer, modem, and telephone can access such information, but there are several good reasons to use outside sources. Information vendors can provide needed information

continued

quickly, analyze data rapidly and accurately, and create an interpretative report when required. They can also be objective.

Many businesses already realize these advantages. The proof is in the profits. Dominated by companies with annual sales of less than $1 million, the Paine Webber report estimated total 1987 information retailing revenues at $197 million, with 1990 revenues projected at $230 million, a 21 percent increase.

However, this represents less than 1 percent of the total information industry, which has an estimated worth of $24 billion. With such well-established and easily identified segments as document delivery and computer-based information services accounting for about three-quarters of this market, it's not surprising that the still emerging information retail segment is not clearly focused.

Needless to say, enormous potential exists for information retailers, but there is undoubtedly a need to educate nonusers regarding the benefits of on-line information services.

SOURCE: L. Lyne Smith III, "Information Retailers Must Educate Nonusers about the Service's Value," *Marketing News* 22 (March 14, 1988), p. 10. Used with permission.

Service marketing uses many of the same promotional tools as product marketing. Advertising, personal selling, publicity, and sales promotion are all available for developing an overall promotion plan. The use of publicity and sales promotion corresponds well with strategy implementation in product marketing so that the emphasis must be on the personal selling and advertising elements of the overall promotion mix. The inseparability of production and consumption usually requires face-to-face interaction between the buyer and seller of business services. As one executive puts it, "In a service business, you're dealing with something that is primarily delivered by people-to-people. Your people are as much a part of your product as any other attribute of that service."[24]

The use of advertising by business service providers is not new, as it has been used for years in such fields as transportation and insurance. What is new is its use by firms in the professional services industries, such as attorneys and accountants among others. For years the use of advertising by professional service providers was considered unethical. Such is not the case today. The creative task is to attempt to create and convey a distinct image for the business service provider.

New Service Development

Services comprise all economic activity in which the primary output is neither a product nor a construction. Services substitute directly for man-

---

[24]Gary Knisely, "Comparing Marketing Management in Package Goods and Service Operations," in *Service Marketing,* ed. Christopher H. Lovelock (Englewood Cliffs, N.J.: Prentice-Hall, 1984), p. 21.

ufactured products across a wide spectrum. Few customers care whether a computer accomplishes a function by a hardware circuit or by its software. If anything, they may prefer the software approach, especially when, as with CAD/CAM, it substitutes for production machinery at a fraction of the cost.[25] New services are the lifeblood of any business service organization, with growth requiring a steady flow of new services. If the business service industry is properly nurtured, it will grow and generate much of America's future wealth.

In the past there has been a tendency to develop new business services in a haphazard fashion, reacting to emergency conditions with little thought to long-term growth and true market needs. Strategy options for service businesses, which have been discussed elsewhere in this book, include market segmentation and positioning, among other things. In the context of this chapter, however, it is useful to highlight strategic choices by depicting the alternative directions that business service firms can take in their new service efforts. They can choose to pursue newness either in terms of markets or offerings, or a combination of both. There are accordingly four basic avenues available in this framework:

1. Sell more existing services to current buyers—a share-building strategy (also called market penetration).
2. Sell existing services to market segments not previously served—a market-extension strategy (also called market development).
3. Offer new services to current markets—a line-extension strategy (also called product development).
4. Offer new services to market segments not previously served—a new-business strategy (also called diversification).[26]

Share building.   When this avenue is used, the business to business marketer becomes aggressive, promoting discount pricing or aggressive promotion. There have been accounting wars between the Big Eight public accounting firms; and many professionals, such as business marketing consultants, are aggressively promoting, mostly through direct mail, to attract more clients. This approach is appropriate in growing markets, but expensive; and the effort may be futile in mature markets where market shares have stabilized.

Market extension.   This strategy seeks new groups of buyers with the firm's current business service offering. A firm such as Blue Cross/Blue Shield may go beyond group plans offered through employers to individual coverage sold to self-employed business people. Other firms, such as banking institutions, may decide to take their services abroad.

Line extension.   This strategy is appropriate in mature business service industries where growth is not likely to come from established services.

---

[25]James Brian Quinn and Christopher E. Gagnon, "Will Services Follow Manufacturing into Decline?" *Harvard Business Review,* November/December 1986, pp. 95–103.

[26]Based on Eugene M. Johnson, Eberhard E. Scheuing, and Kathleen A. Gaida, "New Service Development and Management," in *Profitable Service Marketing* (Homewood, Ill.: Dow Jones-Irwin, 1986), pp. 159–82.

An example would be the hospitality industry, where hotels in popular vacation spots develop special packages for business groups during their off-season.

New business. Where a new product department, new product manager, or a business marketing research department has been established, it is within the duties of these units to provide a steady flow of new business service ideas. Although risky, the contemplation of new service offerings allows the business marketer to explore gaps and desires in the marketplace. Competitors are an excellent source of new business service ideas.

Without a steady flow of new service offerings, the business service firm is not likely to survive over the long run. Too many service firms are slow to invest in new market opportunities and research facilities. They have stayed with old concepts and have concentrated on cost cutting rather than providing their customers with services they want and need. Those businesses that are diversifying or segmenting have a strong grasp on how their operations should change over time.

Concept Questions

1. What is a prerequisite to the effective positioning of a business service?
2. What are the two primary objectives in the bundling of business services?

Classification of Services

While there are a variety of models which attempt to classify services, some believe that classifications are not very helpful because they might misdirect marketing thinking and perpetuate a product orientation. Other scholars and practitioners believe that classification is helpful because it serves as a first step in obtaining an understanding of the ways in which markets operate. A classification model should be helpful to many in developing business marketing strategies for services, and for evaluating current strategies and tactics used by business service marketing organizations. Many models for services are derived from those used in the marketing of tangible goods, and some are based on assumptions about what is or is not a service. Figure 14–2 shows three ways of classifying services: seller-related bases, buyer-related bases, and service-related bases.[27]

Seller-Related Bases

Seller-related bases is a common method of classification whereby the marketing organization may be classified according to whether it is private or public, and within each grouping, whether it is profit-motivated or not-for-

---

[27]Donald Cowell, *The Marketing of Services* (London: Institute of Marketing and the CAM Foundation, 1985), pp. 28–30.

■ **FIGURE 14–2**   An Illustration of Some Current Ways of Classifying Services

SELLER-RELATED BASES

Nature of enterprise	Functions performed	Income source
Private, for profit Private, nonprofit Public, for profit Public, nonprofit	Communication Consulting Educational Financial Health Insurance	Derived from market Market plus donations Donations only Taxation

BUYER-RELATED BASES

Market type	Way in which service bought	Motives

Consumer market
Industrial market
Government market
Agricultural market
	Convenience service
	Shopping service
	Specialty service
	Unsought service
		Instrumental—
		    means to an end
		Expressive,—i.e.
		    an end in itself

SERVICE-RELATED BASES

Service form	Human or machine based	High or low contact
Uniform service Custom service	Human centered service Machine centered service	High contact service Low contact service

SOURCE: Donald Dowell, *The Marketing of Services* (London: Institute of Marketing and the CAM Foundation, 1985), pp. 28–30. Used with permission.

profit-motivated. The function performed by the organization may also be used as a basis of classification, as can the income source.

Buyer-Related Bases

Buyer-related bases include the type of market, the way in which the service is bought, and the motives for purchase. The Swan and Pruden model for classifying business services suggests that establishing whether the motives for purchase are instrumental (with the service a means to an end), or expressive (with the service an end in itself), may also provide a useful framework for classifying some services.[28]

---

[28]J. E. Swan and H. O. Pruden, "Marketing Insights from a Classification of Services," *American Journal of Small Business* 2, no. 1 (July 1977).

Service-Related Bases

Service-related bases may be in terms of the form of service, either human-based or equipment-based, or they may involve high or low levels of personal contact.

Apparently there is no one best classification for a particular service, as different people view the same service in different ways at the same time. The bases shown in Figure 14–2 can be further developed to add additional dimensions to those suggested, such as temporal or spatial categories; rational or emotional motives; and high-urgency or low-urgency services. Such additional categories may be determined by judgment or through marketing research.

Classifying Services by Clusters

It has also been argued that development of greater sophistication in business service marketing will be aided if we can find new ways to group services other than by current industry classifications. Christopher H. Lovelock has suggested that a more useful approach would be to segment services into clusters which share certain relevant marketing characteristics—such as the nature of the relationship between the service organization and its customers, or patterns of demand relative to supply—and then to examine the implications for marketing action.[29] His article summarizes several past proposals for classifying services identified in Table 14–1. These proposals represent an attempt to answer one or more of the following questions:

1. What is the nature of the service act?
2. What type of relationship does the business service organization have with its customers?
3. How much room is there for customization and judgment on the part of the business service provider?
4. What is the nature of demand and supply for the service?
5. How is the service delivered?

By addressing each of the five questions posed, marketing managers can obtain a better understanding of their product, of customer relationships, of factors underlying variations in demand, and of the characteristics of their service delivery systems. By recognizing characteristics that their service shares with other service providers, marketing managers will look to new ideas as to how to resolve marketing problems shared in common with firms in other industries.

---

[29]Christopher H. Lovelock, "Classifying Services to Gain Strategic Marketing Insights," *Journal of Marketing* 47 (Summer 1983), pp. 9–20.

■ **TABLE 14–1**   Summary of Models for Classifying Services

Author	Proposed Classification Schemes	Comment
Judd (1964)	1. Rented goods services (right to own and use a good for a defined time period) 2. Owned goods services (custom creation, repair or improvement of goods owned by the customer) 3. Nongoods services (personal experiences or "experiential possession")	First two are fairly specific, but third category is very broad and ignores services such as insurance, banking, legal advice and accounting.
Rathmell (1974)	1. Type of seller 2. Type of buyer 3. Buying motives 4. Buying practice 5. Degree of regulation	No specific application to services—could apply equally well to goods.
Shostack (1977)* Sasser et al.* (1978)	Proportion of physical goods and intangible services contained within each product "package"	Offers opportunities for multiattribute modeling. Emphasizes that there are few pure goods or pure services.
Hill (1977)	1. Services affecting persons vs. those affecting goods 2. Permanent vs. temporary effects of the service 3. Reversibility vs. nonreversibility of these effects 4. Physical effects vs. mental effects 5. Individual vs. collective services	Emphasizes nature of service benefits and (in 5) variations in the service delivery/consumption environment.
Thomas (1978)	1. Primarily equipment-based 　a. Automated (e.g., car wash) 　b. Monitored by unskilled operators (e.g., movie theater) 　c. Operated by skilled personnel (e.g., airline) 2. Primarily people-based 　a. Unskilled labor (e.g., lawn care) 　b. Skilled labor (e.g., repair work) 　c. Professional staff (e.g., lawyers, dentists)	Although operational rather than marketing in orientation, provides a useful way of understanding product attributes.
Chase (1978)	Extent of customer contact required in service delivery 　a. High contact (e.g., health care, hotels, restaurants) 　b. Low contact (e.g., postal service, wholesaling)	Recognizes that product variability is harder to control in high contact services because customers exert more influence on timing of demand and service features, due to their greater involvement in the service process.
Kotler (1980)	1. People-based vs. equipment-based 2. Extent to which client's presence is necessary 3. Meets personal needs vs. business needs 4. Public vs. private, for-profit vs. nonprofit	Synthesizes previous work, recognizes differences in purpose of service organization.
Lovelock (1980)	1. Basic demand characteristics 　—Object served (persons vs. property) 　—Extent of demand/supply imbalances 　—Discrete vs. continuous relationships between customers and providers 2. Service content and benefits 　—Extent of physical goods content 　—Extent of personal service content 　—Single service vs. bundle of services 　—Timing and duration of benefits	Synthesizes previous classifications and adds several new schemes. Proposes several categories within each classification. Concludes that defining object served is most fundamental classification scheme. Suggests that valuable marketing insights would come from combining two or more classification schemes in a matrix.

■ **TABLE 14–1**   *(concluded)*

Author	Proposed Classification Schemes	Comment
	3. Service delivery procedures —Multisite vs. single site delivery —Allocation of capacity (reservations vs. first come, first served) —Independent vs. collective consumption —Time defined vs. task defined transactions —Extent to which customers must be present during service delivery	

*These were two independent studies that drew broadly similar conclusions.

SOURCE: Christopher H. Lovelock, "Classifying Services to Gain Strategic Marketing Insights," *Journal of Marketing* 47 (Summer 1983), pp. 9–20. Used with permission.

People-Based versus Equipment-Based Services

A final classification of services explored in this chapter, as diagrammed in Table 14–2, is based on determining whether the service is people-based or equipment-based.[30] Within **people-based services** we can distinguish between those involving professionals (accountants, consultants, etc.), skilled labor (plumbers, toolmakers), and unskilled labor (janitors). In **equipment-based services** we can distinguish among those involving automated equipment (vending machines, etc.), equipment operated by unskilled labor (taxis, motion picture projectors), and equipment operated by skilled labor (airplanes, computers, etc.).[31] Questions must be asked, such as, "Is the client's presence necessary to the service (industrial psychology versus truck repair)? What about the service provider's motives (profit or not-for-profit) and form (private or public)? These characteristics, when crossed, produce four quite different types of services' organizations.[32]

Regardless of which classification scheme is used, a problem in classifying a business service is the fact that many services are directly tied to a tangible product. An example of this is a consultant's services. This service provider produces a report (a tangible good) as a result of the service provided. The quality of the service is judged both by the actions of the consultant and by the report produced. Other business services are less tied to goods, such as an extermination service, which does not produce a tangible product, and whose quality cannot be judged in the short term. Evaluating business service quality is difficult because of the number of people involved in the evaluation, and because many services have a goods' component.[33]

---

[30]Dan R. E. Thomas, "Strategy Is Different in Service Businesses," *Harvard Business Review,* July-August 1978.

[31]Philip Kotler, *Principles of Marketing,* 3d ed. (Englewood Cliffs, N.J.: Prentice-Hall, 1986), p. 683.

[32]Ibid.

[33]Philip D. Cooper and Ralph W. Jackson, "Applying a Services Marketing Orientation to the Industrial Sector," *Journal of Business and Industrial Marketing,* Summer 1988, pp. 51–54.

■ **TABLE 14–2**   Types of Service Businesses

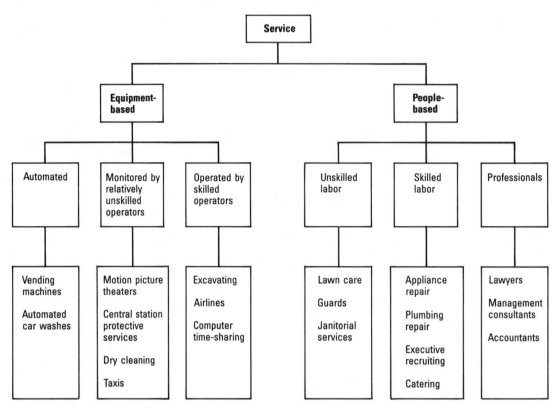

Interest in the study of marketing business services is a relatively recent phenomenon. Marketing expertise in the service sector has significantly lagged behind marketing efforts in the manufacturing sector despite the fact that the service sector is becoming increasingly competitive.[34] This reflects such developments as the partial or complete deregulation of several major service industries in recent years, the removal of professional association restrictions on using marketing techniques (particularly advertising), and the growth of new electronic delivery systems.[35] Because of increased competitive intensity the understanding and use of a strong marketing effort will be essential to survival.

---

[34]Christopher H. Lovelock, "Classifying Services to Gain Strategic Marketing Insights," *Journal of Marketing,* Summer 1983, p. 19.
   [35]Ibid.

■ INTERNATIONAL MARKETING OF BUSINESS SERVICES

Service marketers are battling for foreign as well as domestic markets. Price Waterhouse (accounting), Hertz (car rental), J. Walter Thompson (advertising), Donovan, Newton, and Leisure (legal), and Bechtel (construction engineering) have had a history of aggressively competing for customers in global markets. Other U.S. service firms are expanding their operations. Holiday Inn has negotiated the purchase of 140 sites in Western Europe, where by 1995 it will build hotels, most of which will have 250 to 300 rooms. Ramada Inn and Marriott Hotels plan to add 20 more facilities by the mid-1990s, and Sheraton is attempting to double its holdings to 50 hotels in Europe by the early 1990s.[36] Although the United States is experiencing a large international trade deficit, such published data can be deceptive because the deficit is only reported in merchandise or tangible products. The United States actually exports more services than it imports. Future growth in the business service sector should help offset the large merchandise deficits the United States has experienced.[37] World trade in services is growing rapidly, and in spite of stringent restrictions on some aspects of this trade, its growth has been irrepressible and of strategic importance to many major service firms.

The principles of marketing services internationally are similar to those which would apply to the marketing of services domestically in many respects. The strategies associated with the setting of clear objectives, of defining and selecting target markets, and of developing appropriate and specific marketing strategies and marketing mixes are much the same. What is very different, and what business service providers need to adjust to, are external environmental factors, such as the social, political, economic, legal, and cultural climates. The nature of these environmental forces facing international marketing managers are treated in detail in most international marketing textbooks (albeit in product marketing settings in most cases). Therefore, we will not cover them here. Their absence is in no way a measure of their importance. There are, however, few illustrations of how such influences affect service organizations specifically. Three strands of the available evidence relate to the following: (1) the risks of international marketing for service organizations; (2) problems of adaptation to, and operation in, overseas markets; and (3) barriers to trade in services.[38]

The Risks of International Marketing for Service Organizations

Carman and Langeard have suggested that while internationalization represents a growth strategy for service firms, the following are also true:

---

[36]"U.S. Hotel Chains Are Following the Tourists to Europe," *Business Week,* August 19, 1985, pp. 75–77.

[37]From Robert F. Lusch and Virginia N. Lusch, *Principles of Marketing* (Boston: Kent Publishing, 1987), pp. 591–93.

[38]This section is largely based on Cowell, *Marketing of Services,* pp. 265–75.

1. Out-of-country expansion is a more risky strategy for a service firm than, for example, concentric diversification or new service development in existing markets.

2. Out-of-country expansion is more risky for a service business than it is for a manufacturer of physical items.[39]

They base their argument for the greater risk involved for service-related businesses on the fact that foreign expansion by product manufacturers can be undertaken more gradually, whereas service providers must go to the country, face the customer, and produce the service. The seller must produce on foreign soil and must deal directly with the customer. This situation, in addition to providing on-site quality control, and coping with personnel and know-how difficulties, produce potential problems for service providers that might be minimized for tangible goods producers.

Problems of Adaptation to, and Operation in, Overseas Markets

It has also been suggested that service marketers may have a more difficult time with the host government than product marketers. Service marketers typically provide little capital inflow into the country, little or no technological transfer, and do little to upgrade the training of workers. This is an interesting but perhaps controversial view, and requires more empirical evidence to substantiate such a claim.

Barriers to Trade in Services

The barriers to services marketing that concern us here relate specifically to foreign-produced services and cover discriminatory measures in the fields of banking, insurance, transport, consulting services, and so forth. For example, restrictions on capital movements may deter a service company from setting up a service operation in an overseas country in the first place, just as they may deter a manufacturer from building a factory. In a major study which examined barriers to trade in services and other invisibles, the following general restrictions were identified.[40]

Restrictions on Foreign Competition.   A service organization may be excluded by law, by a restrictive licensing system, by tariffs (i.e., taxes), by takeover, or by nationalization. An example would be the limitation in many countries that reserve internal routes for domestic airlines.

Exchange Control.   Limitations might be exercised over the purchase of foreign exchange for buying foreign-produced services. An example would

---

[39]J. M. Carman and E. Langeard, "Growth Strategies for Service Firms" (Paper presented at the Eighth Annual Meeting of the European Academy for Advanced Research in Marketing, Groningen, The Netherlands, April 1979).

[40]Much of this material is based upon Professor B. Griffith's small but valuable book, *Invisible Barriers to Invisible Trade* (New York: Macmillan, for Trade Policy Research Center, London, 1975).

be restrictions on the amount of foreign currency allowed for overseas travel.

Constraints on Choice of Factor Input Mix.   The amount of capital or local labor that must be employed may be specified. An example would be in the employment of local nationals in a service such as banking.

Governments around the world have played a significant role in restricting the growth of multinational services. Many services have been considered critical to the well-being of a nation's citizens and to its own development, and some governments have seen fit to guarantee the delivery of some quality of service at low prices. National chauvinism, sometimes clothed in such words as *national defense,* has at times been involved.[41] For whatever reasons, a variety of service trade barriers can be found around the world. Additional barriers would be discrimination against shippers wishing to transport foreign cargo, restraints on the international flow of information, the banning of operations by foreign insurance firms, and administrative delays that hinder licensing agreements. Of course, there are many more. Perhaps these potential impediments help explain why services make up so small a share of international trade.

■ THE FUTURE OF BUSINESS TO BUSINESS SERVICES

Today, service industries have assumed the mantle of economic leadership. These industries, which encompass trade, communications, transportation, food and lodging, financial and medical services, education, government, and technical services to industry, account for about 70 percent of the national income, and three-fourths of the nonfarm jobs in the United States. In generating 44 million new jobs in the past 30 years, service industries have absorbed most of the influx of women and minorities into the work force, softened the effects of every post–World War II recession, and fueled every recent economic recovery.[42] This trend will continue because the demand for business services expands as business becomes more complex, and as management further recognizes its need for business-service specialists.

For the next several years the marketing of services will continue to receive attention from practitioners and academics alike, as the forces of deregulation and continued technological change will have a remarkable impact on our economy. Practitioners have learned that many of the ideas and approaches developed for the marketing of tangible goods fit uneasily and uncomfortably into their needs. Academics, seeking new fields in which to develop marketing ideas, will give increased attention to nongoods sectors like nonprofit and service entities. There seems to be common agreement that the broad principles of marketing management are applicable to both of these areas.

---

[41]Heskett, *Managing in the Service Economy,* Chapter 8.

[42]James L. Heskett, "Lessons in the Service Sector," *Harvard Business Review,* March–April 1987.

Finally, the future success and well-being of service marketing organizations will largely be a function of their understanding and reaction to the following propositions:

- There are greater opportunities for future growth and expansion in services than in goods.
- Mass production, industrial design, and systems engineering are being increasingly implemented and adapted to service businesses.
- Use of mass production and systems engineering increases productivity, but leads to increased depersonalization of service marketing.
- The whole range of strategic marketing activities are relevant for service marketing, and their use will tend to satisfy the growing demand for diversity in service-market offerings.[43]

The biggest increases in terms of share of output are likely to be in insurance, banking, finance, and communications. Many factors will influence the continuing development of the service sector in the 1990s, including the attitude of government toward services and technological innovation.

Concept Questions

1. How is classifying services helpful to the business marketer?
2. How is the marketing of services internationally similar to the marketing of services domestically?
3. In what service areas will the greatest increase in share of output occur?

SUMMARY

1. For the most part, the entire area of service marketing remains ill defined. Marketing, however, is slowly coming of age in the service sector, as it becomes obvious that the last half of the 20th century represents the transformation from a product-oriented economy to a service-oriented economy.

2. The major environments for business service firms include the economic, societal/cultural, competitive, technological, and political/legal environments. Each of these environments will impact upon a business service firm's sales and profits, and we need to study carefully the nature, role, and importance of each in developing marketing objectives and accompanying strategies.

3. Four characteristics are unique to services and influence the way they are marketed: intangibility, perishability and fluctuating demand, si-

---

[43]R. Markin, *Marketing: Strategy and Management* (New York: John Wiley & Sons, 1982).

multaneity, and heterogeneity. Services are intangible in that they cannot appeal to the senses. Promotion, through the sales force and advertising department, must communicate the benefits of various business offerings. Services are perishable and cannot be stored. Decisions must be made on what maximum capacity level should be available to cope with surges in demand before service levels suffer. Production and consumption of services are inseparable, with selling coming first, and then production and consumption at the same time. It is difficult to standardize services; as a result, output can vary widely in quality.

4. Although marketing functions are basically the same for many services and products, there is a difference in the way business service marketing is organized and implemented in an effort to gain a competitive advantage. With business services marketing the product is not created until the service is performed. When the service provider establishes and maintains a distinctive place for itself and its offerings in the market, it is said to be successfully positioned. The marketing mix can be applied to business services, just as it can be to business products. The strategies for different services must be incorporated into the entire corporate strategy, and the development of new services is just as important as the development of new products. Business service companies can expand their service offerings through share building, market extension, line extension, and cultivating new business.

5. Classifications of services can be helpful in understanding the ways in which markets operate. They can also be an aid in developing marketing strategies for services, and in evaluating current strategies and tactics used by business service organizations. A number of classifications have been offered, including those which are seller-related, buyer-related, and service-related; classification by clusters, and by people and equipment bases are also possible. There seems to be no one classification for a particular service, with different people viewing the same service in different ways.

6. Service marketers are battling for foreign, as well as domestic, markets. Yet governments around the world have played a significant role in restricting the growth of multinational services. Business service marketers must be alert to new opportunities in international markets, but they must also be aware of the many problems and pitfalls if they are to succeed in such markets.

7. For the next several years the marketing of services will continue to receive great attention from both business practitioners and academicians. The biggest increases in terms of share of output are likely to be in the areas of insurance, banking, finance, and communications. Many factors will influence the continuing development of the service sector in the 1990s, including the attitude of government toward services, and technological innovation.

KEY TERMS

bundling	manufacturing attitude
buyer-related bases	people-based services
competitive environment	political environment
economic environment	seller-related bases
elasticity of demand	service-related bases
equipment-based services	societal/cultural environment
legal environment	technological environment

REVIEW QUESTIONS

1. Identify and discuss the six major environments facing the marketing manager for a business service.

2. Identify and discuss four important characteristics of services. Provide an example of each one.

3. How does business service marketing differ from business product marketing? When is a business service properly positioned? What is meant by the bundling of services?

4. How does each element of the marketing mix contribute to the overall strategy used for a particular business service? Identify and discuss four methods by which a business firm can expand its service offerings.

5. What is the value of classifying services to the business services marketer? Describe three major models of classifying services according to Cowell. Distinguish between people-based and equipment-based services.

6. How are the principles of marketing services internationally similar to those of marketing services domestically? How are they different? Identify the risks and problems associated with the marketing of services abroad.

7. On what four propositions will the future well-being and success of services marketing depend? In what fields will the largest growth of services marketing occur?

CHAPTER CASES

Case 14–1   The U.S. Postal Service*

U.S. postal workers may battle rain, snow, or sleet on any given day, but they aren't very well known for perseverance in making business sales. However, times are changing in government management. The Postal Serv-

---

*Carl McDaniel, Jr., and William R. Darden, *Marketing,* 1987, Allyn and Bacon, Inc., p. 683.

ice now sells two major products to business: overnight mail and the extra-digit zip code called Zip + 4. "With Zip + 4 there is a great deal of interface with business, and we have a cadre of salespeople and customer service representatives to handle the job," says Harold S. Coyne, Jr., general manager of the customer programs division of the central region of the U.S. Postal Service. "We had been doing a lot of [nonmarketing-oriented] in-house training in the past, but we had reached a point where we felt we should look at what we were doing more objectively."

"Putting a new program together was a challenge," says John Steinbrink, senior vice-president of the firm hired for a new training system. "They weren't sure exactly what they wanted, but they realized that they have to act more like a business, and the way to go was to become more marketing and sales oriented. It's been very exciting."

"The Postal Service is asking companies to spend $20,000 or $30,000 in software to be able to use the extra four-digit zip code. So they have to sell people in those companies on the advantages of doing it—such as getting a lower bulk rate," says Hal Fahner, a sales management training consultant. "Selling is a whole new ballgame for the postal employees."

Gene Allen, a supervisor of customer service representatives in Kansas City, says he now has more confidence in conducting his own sales meetings. "Before, my sales meetings were just called sales meetings. Now, they really are more informative about selling techniques," he says. "I do some role playing and use the techniques I learned."

Questions

1. What attitudes on the part of postal employees might need to change in order for them to approach businesspeople in a selling role?
2. In what ways is the situation of the Postal Service sales force different from that of a private, profit-oriented mail-service sales force?

Case 14–2 DataCorp of Virginia, Inc.*

In a meeting with his department managers, the president of DataCorp was wondering what marketing strategies they should adopt in order: (1) to prevent any further loss of customers; and (2) to replace the customers already lost. DataCorp of Virginia, Inc., was an organization that provided computerized banking services for small, independent banks. Founded in 1968 and located in Harrisonburg, Virginia, DataCorp currently served 18 banks in Virginia, West Virginia, and Maryland. Although the company was a subsidiary of the Rockingham National Bank, DataCorp's separate business philosophy was to provide service and flexibility for the independent banker.

DataCorp provided an assortment of computer services related to the following banking activities:

---
*William J. Stanton and Charles Futrell, *Fundamentals of Marketing*, 8th ed., 1987, McGraw Hill, pp. 558–60.

Savings	Deposit system
Installment loans	Payroll
Commercial loans	Amortization schedules
Customer information file	Depreciation schedules
Certificates of deposit	General ledger
Automated clearing house; paperless entry processing	Stockholder accounting

DataCorp currently was preparing to introduce a new service that would enable the company to expand its geographic market by using telephone lines. This new service would enable DataCorp to reach almost anywhere and also to cut the delivery time for reports from hours to minutes.

According to the president, DataCorp was continually striving to improve its computer services, its operational reliability, and its systems flexibility. In order to compete in the field, DataCorp tried to provide the most current and useful data processing aids available. One big advantage for DataCorp, as opposed to in-house systems and competing data-processing companies, was that it used IBM equipment and frequently updated its software systems.

The client relations department, one of nine departments in DataCorp, served as the primary company interface with all client-users (customers). This department was responsible for user training, development of user manuals, and day-to-day problem solving involving users. In addition, this department was responsible for all marketing activities, including marketing research, sales to new clients, and expanding sales to existing clients.

When DataCorp first started out, the managers knew many bankers in Virginia as a result of their association with Rockingham National Bank, the parent company. Prospecting was done by making phone calls to bankers in order to set up appointments with their bank.

In expanding its market area, management currently was using a direct marketing approach. Brochures were sent to banks to familiarize them with the DataCorp name and its data-processing services. The banks were contacted shortly after the brochure was received to set up an appointment. A slide presentation was shown during the meeting to explain the data-processing procedure. Once a bank become a customer of DataCorp, the client relations department took over the account.

The time it actually took to sell the services to a bank ranged from six months to a year. During this period some competitors or technological changes might interfere with the sale. However, the effort and risk were worthwhile, because an established account provided a contribution to gross profit of between $5,000 and $15,000. Once the sale was made, it took a considerable amount of time to adapt the actual work for processing. This also was a problem, because some less sophisticated data-processing alternatives available to the prospective clients required less time to implement.

The president made many of the sales calls involved in obtaining new clients. But he was having a difficult time physically getting to them because they now were spread out over three states—Virginia, Maryland, and West Virginia. He made it a point to meeting personally the bank presidents because he either knew them or had been referred to them by other bank presidents.

Some of DataCorp's customers, mainly small community banks, had merged with other banks or bank-holding companies. A merger typically resulted in a change of data-processing suppliers for some of the participating banks. DataCorp felt the impact of this form of competition more than any other.

Holding companies created a similar problem for DataCorp by purchasing banks and dominating their decisions concerning which data-processing systems and services to use. So far, holding companies had not been a major problem for DataCorp, but they were expected to be an increasing cause of lost sales.

In the changing banking environment the trend was toward bigger, regional-sized banks, which tended to smother the small community banks. The result was a diminishing number of small community banks, which were the major customers for DataCorp.

Another problem was that some banks previously serviced by companies such as DataCorp were going to in-house systems. The reasons for changing to in-house systems were apparently lower costs, easier access, and more convenience. However, banks that had gone to in-house systems were having numerous problems, including a much higher than expected cost of running the equipment and a lack of technically skilled personnel. Some banks that previously had been customers of DataCorp or other services now found themselves in trouble and were turning back to the use of outside services.

Technological changes can have an incredibly fast effect on the marketability of computer services. Consequently, the people of DataCorp were cautious about the future, and sales forecasts were frequently revised. But management was sure that DataCorp could continue to thrive because of the marketing efforts of its staff and their daily contact with clients.

Questions

What changes in marketing strategy should DataCorp adopt in order to:

1. Slow down the loss of customers?
2. Replace lost customers with new accounts?

SUGGESTED READINGS

Adams, Ronald J., and M. Reza Vaghefi. "The Application of Environmental Management Concepts to Hospital Strategic Planning." In *Marketing in a Dynamic Environment,* ed. Michael H. Morris and Eugene E. Teeple. Atlantic Marketing Association, 1986. Current position of hospitals in the United States is described in the context of Porter's model of competitive strategy.

Evans, Kenneth R., and Richard F. Beltramini. "Physician Acquisition of Prescription Drug Information." *Journal of Health Care Marketing* 6 (December 1986), pp. 15–25. Survey of specialists and general practitioners as to their sources of prescription drug information.

Guiltinan, Joseph P. "The Price Bundling of Services: A Normative Framework." *Journal of Marketing* 51 (April 1987), pp. 74–85. Discussion of marketing strategy and complementary relationships in the price bundling of services.

Heskett, James L. "Lessons in the Service Sector." *Harvard Business Review* 65 (March/April 1987), pp. 118–26. Discussion of organizational structure, target markets, quality, and economies of scale in the service sector.

Kastiel, Diane Lynn. "Service and Support: High Tech's New Battleground." *Business Marketing* 72 (June 1987), pp. 54–66. Study of marketing strategy, profitability, and contracts in the computer service industry.

Lynn, Susan A. "Identifying Business Influences for a Professional Service: Implications for Marketing Efforts." *Industrial Marketing Management* 15 (May 1987), pp. 119–30. Survey of CPA firm selection, including marketing strategies used by CPA firms.

McKee, Daryl; P. Rajan Varadarajan; and John Vassar. "The Marketing Planning Orientation of Hospitals: An Empirical Inquiry." *Journal of Health Care Marketing* 6 (December 1986), pp. 50–60. Survey of marketing strategies in hospitals, with a performance measurement using statistical analysis.

Olszewski, Agnes Pauline; Hubert D. Hennessey; Philip Harris Monchar; and Arthur Boudin, "Corporate Culture: A Strategy to Enter Entrenched Markets." *Journal of Business and Industrial Marketing* 2 (Summer 1987), pp. 5–16. Research illustrates a methodology to segment industrial markets on the basis of corporate culture. Application made to the corporate purchase of a financial service.

Raffield, Barney T., III. "Creating Promotional Synergism in the Marketing of Non-Credit, Continuing Education Programs." *Issues in Higher Education* 13 (October 1984), Division of Continuing Education, Kansas State University, Manhattan, Kansas. Discussion of, and guidelines for, promoting continuing education programs to both industrial and consumer markets.

Shostack, G. Lynn. "Service Positioning through Structural Change." *Journal of Marketing* 51 (January 1987), pp. 34–43. Within service systems, structural process design can be used to engineer services on a more scientific, rational basis.

Stern, Aimee. "One-Stop Shopping for Market Services." *Business Month* 129 (March 1987), pp. 60–62. Discussion of consulting, merchandising, and sales promotion services at one location.

Turnbull, Peter W., and Michael L. Gibbs. "Marketing Bank Services to Corporate Customers: The Importance of Relationships." *International Journal of Bank Marketing* (UK) 5 no. 1, 1987, pp. 19–26. Discussion of segmentation and profitability in marketing bank customers to corporate clientele.

Chapter **15**

Ethical Considerations in Business to Business Marketing

LEARNING OBJECTIVES

After reading this chapter, you should be able to:

- Identify the major changes which impact marketing strategy in the future.
- Explain the role of ethics in marketing research.
- Differentiate among various types of ethical issues in business to business pricing.
- Distinguish among ethical issues faced by salespeople in dealing with both their customers and their employers.
- Speak about the ethical problems that can arise in implementing marketing strategy.
- Realize the complexities and ramifications of ethical issues in the international environment.

CHAPTER OUTLINE

Learning Objectives
Marketing Ethics in the Future:
An Overview
    Examples of Corporate Social
    Responsibility
    The Individuality of Ethical
    Standards
Strategy and Tactics in the
Business to Business Marketing
Environment
An Ethical Issue: The
Organizational Buying Function
and Buyer-Seller Relationships
    Ethics Is Not a
    One-Sided Proposition
Ethical Issues in Marketing
Research
    Societal Rights
    Clients' Rights
    Researchers' Rights
Ethics and the Management
of the Pricing Function
    Setting a Price that Meets Company
    Objectives, while Not Taking
    Advantage of the Customer

Altering Product Quality without
    Changing Price
Practicing Price Discrimination with
    Smaller Accounts
Price-Fixing
Obtaining Information on a
    Competitor's Price Quotation in
    Order to Rebid or Requote
Reciprocity
Ethics and the Management of the
Sales Force
    Ethics in Dealing with Customers
    Ethics in Dealing with Employers
Ethics and Advertising Strategy
    Truth in Advertising
    Comparative Advertising
Ethics and International Marketing
    Ethics Differ from Country
    to Country
    The Complexity of International
    Ethical Issues

■ MARKETING ETHICS AND THE FUTURE: AN OVERVIEW

The quantity of discussion on social responsibility and ethics in marketing has increased tremendously in recent years, as marketing is the functional area most closely related to ethical abuse. **Ethics** implies a standard of behavior by which conduct is judged. But standards that may be legal may not always be ethical. Standards or beliefs about what is right and proper often change over time, and this question becomes more important as our economy becomes more competitive and our technology more complex. Furthermore, the factors which affect people's propensity to make ethical or unethical decisions are not fully understood. There is speculation that three general sets of factors influence the ethics of our decisions.[1] First, individual factors such as values, knowledge, attitudes, and intentions are believed to influence our decision. Second, opportunity resulting from the absence of professional codes of ethics, corporate policies regarding ethics, or punishment, may encourage unethical decision making. Third, the values, attitudes, and behavior of significant others, such as peers, supervisors, and top management, affect the ethics of our decisions. Because it is an organized discipline, business ethics provides a solid foundation from which to operate. Even so, the study of ethics is not without problems of interpretation, as major philosophies are sometimes in conflict with one another as to how to resolve a single issue.[2]

What should be the guiding philosophy with regard to ethical considerations as we approach the 21st century? For many years there has been uncertainty within some industries regarding the position that corporate management should take. Three different views of corporate responsibility have been subscribed to:

1. *The invisible hand.*   Under this philosophy, "the true and only social responsibilities of business organizations are to make profits and obey the laws . . . the common good is best served when each of us and our economic institutions pursue not the common good or moral purpose . . . but competitive advantage. Morality, responsibility, and conscience reside in the invisible hand of the free market system, not in the hands of the organizations within the system—much less in the hands of managers within the system."

2. *The hand of government.*   Under this philosophy, "the corporation would have no moral responsibility beyond political and legal obedience . . . corporations are to seek objectives which are rational and purely economic. The regulatory arm of the law and the political process, rather than the invisible hand of the marketplace, turn these objectives to the common good."

3. *The hand of management.*   This philosophy "encourages corporations to exercise independent, noneconomic judgment over matters of morals and ethics which face them in their short- and long-term plans and operations." It seeks "moral reasoning and intent" from the corporation, and for managers to apply . . . individual morality to corporate decisions.[3]

---

[1]O. C. Ferrell and Larry G. Gresham, "A Contingency Framework for Understanding Ethical Decision-Making in Marketing," *Journal of Marketing* 49 (Summer 1985), pp. 87–96.

[2]Donald P. Robin and R. Eric Reidenbach, "Social Responsibility, Ethics, and Marketing Strategy: Closing the Gap between Concept and Application," *Journal of Marketing* 51 (January 1987), pp. 44–58.

[3]Kenneth E. Goodpaster and John B. Matthews, Jr., "Can a Corporation Have a Conscience?" *Harvard Business Review,* January-February 1982, pp. 132–41.

Examples of Corporate Social Responsibility

In companies today examples of all three philosophies can be found. Some firms are totally profit-oriented and leave social results to the marketplace. Others operate within the letter of the law, but provide no moral or ethical leadership. Some managers, however, are going beyond the narrow goals of profit to act as social citizens and ethical leaders, as the trend today is for society to demand moral and ethical leadership from business. As shown in Exhibit 15–1, the American Marketing Association published a Code of Ethics in 1986—an example of many similar codes being proposed by business organizations. Many large corporations such as Caterpillar Tractor, IBM, Johnson Wax, ITT, Security Pacific Corporation, Primerica Corporation, Chemical Banking Corporation, and Champion International Corporation have adopted formal codes of ethics. More are sure to follow.

■ **EXHIBIT 15–1**   The American Marketing Association Code of Ethics

Members of the American Marketing Association (AMA) are committed to ethical professional conduct. They have joined together in subscribing to this Code of Ethics embracing the following topics:

Responsibilities of the marketer

Marketers must accept responsibility for the consequence of their activities and make every effort to ensure that their decisions, recommendations, and actions function to identify, serve, and satisfy all relevant publics: customers, organizations and society.

Marketers' professional conduct must be guided by:
1. The basic rule of professional ethics: not knowingly to do harm.
2. The adherence to all applicable laws and regulations.
3. The accurate representation of their education, training and experience.
4. The active support, practice and promotion of this Code of Ethics.

Honesty and fairness

Marketers shall uphold and advance the integrity, honor, and dignity of the marketing profession by:
1. Being honest in serving consumers, clients, employees, suppliers, distributors and the public.
2. Not knowingly participating in conflict of interest without prior notice to all parties involved.

3. Establishing equitable fee schedules, including the payment or receipt of usual, customary and/or legal compensation for marketing exchanges.

Rights and duties of parties in the marketing exchange process

Participants in the marketing exchange process should be able to expect that:
1. Products and services offered are safe and fit for their intended uses.
2. Communications about offered products and services are not deceptive.
3. All parties intend to discharge their obligations, financial and otherwise, in good faith.
4. Appropriate internal methods exist for equitable adjustment and/or redress of grievances concerning purchases.

It is understood that the above would include, *but is not limited to,* the following responsibilities of the marketer:

In the area of product development and management

■ Disclosure of all substantial risks associated with product or service usage.
■ Identification of any product component substitution that might materially change the product or impact on the buyer's purchase decision.
■ Identification of extra-cost added features.

continued

■ **EXHIBIT 15–1** (concluded)

In the area of promotions:

- Avoidance of false and misleading advertising.
- Rejection of high-pressure manipulations, or misleading sales tactics.
- Avoidance of sales promotions that use deception or manipulation.

In the area of distribution:

- Not manipulating the availability of a product for purpose of exploitation.
- Not using coercion in the marketing channel.
- Not exerting undue influence over the resellers choice to handle a product.

In the area of pricing:

- Not engaging in price fixing.
- Not practicing a predatory pricing.
- Disclosing the full price associated with any purchase.

In the area of marketing research:

- Prohibiting selling or fund raising under the guise of conducting research.
- Maintaining research integrity by avoiding misrepresentation and omission of pertinent research data.
- Treating outside clients and suppliers fairly.

Organizational relationships:

Marketers should be aware of how their behavior may influence or impact on the behavior of others in organizational relationships. They should not demand, encourage or apply coercion to obtain unethical behavior in their relationships with others, such as employees, suppliers or customers.

1. Apply confidentiality and anonymity in professional relationships with regard to privileged information.
2. Meet their obligations and responsibilities in contracts and mutual agreements in a timely manner.
3. Avoid taking the work of others, in whole, or in part, and represent this work as their own or directly benefit from it without compensation or consent of the originator or owner.
4. Avoid manipulation to take advantage of situations to maximize personal welfare in a way that unfairly deprives or damages the organization or others.

Any AMA members found to be in violation of any provision of this Code of Ethics may have his or her Association membership suspended or revoked.

SOURCE: American Marketing Association, Chicago, Ill., 1988. Reprinted with permission.

As we approach the next century, many firms are recognizing that ethical issues and social responsibility find their expression in the daily decisions of marketers, rather than in abstract ideals. Consider the following:

- Arthur Anderson and Company launched a $5 million project to teach ethics to business students. This project "will train college professors to use case studies that emphasize ethics in their courses on management, accounting, economics, finance, and marketing." The project stems from Anderson's desire to instill ethical decision-making standards in its 40,000 U.S. employees, according to Duane Kullberg, managing partner of Chicago-based Anderson.[4]
- DuPont Company, the world's leading producer of "chlorofluorocarbons" (CFCs), has called for a total phaseout of the chemicals to prevent destruction of the earth's protective ozone layer. The company "is convinced that an international treaty calling for 50 percent

---

[4]Lee Berton, "Arthur Anderson Launches Program to Teach Ethics," *The Wall Street Journal,* March 11, 1988, p. 31.

cuts in CFC production over the next decade is not stringent enough to prevent serious damage to the ozone layer." DuPont invented CFCs and sells $600 million worth of them annually, about a fourth of the world's supply.[5]

- Two-thirds of upper-level executives think people are "occasionally" unethical in their business dealings, while another 15 percent believe people are "often" unethical; 16 percent consider people "seldom" without ethics. These are among the findings of a survey of 1,000 corporate executives on ethical behavior commissioned by McFeely-Wacherle Jett, a Chicago-based executive-recruiting firm. Nearly one in four executives believes ethical standards can impede successful careers, while 68 percent agree younger executives are driven to compromise their ethics "by the desire for wealth and material things." Still, 54 percent think that business executives and managers have higher ethical standards and behavior than the general population.[6]

The Individuality of Ethical Standards

Every marketing manager must work out his or her own philosophy of socially responsible and ethical behavior, looking beyond what is legal and allowed, and developing standards based on personal integrity and corporate conscience. Business to business marketing executives of the 1990s will face many challenges, not the least of which will be ethical considerations in their decision-making process. Those marketers that are able to practice socially responsible behavior in carrying out the day-to-day decision-making process, should be in a position to promote legality, fairness, and decency among organizations in the years ahead, as they realize that responsive corporate policy within this area makes good business sense.

■ STRATEGY AND ETHICS IN THE BUSINESS TO BUSINESS MARKETING ENVIRONMENT

In comparing the marketing strategies and tactics of firms today versus 10 or so years ago, the most striking impression is one of general marketing strategy obsolescence. Just a few short years ago computer companies were introducing ever more powerful hardware for more sophisticated uses. Today these same companies emphasize mini- and microcomputers and software; competitors launch new products and customers switch their business; distributors lose their appeal; promotion costs skyrocket; new government regulations are announced, and old ones are being enforced; and consumer groups attack. While all this is going on, and at a time when more than half of the American public believes that the level of business

---

[5]Mary Lu Carnevale, "DuPont Plans to Phase Out CFC Output," *The Wall Street Journal,* March 25, 1988, pp. 2, 11.

[6]Timothy D. Schellhardt, "What Bosses Think about Corporate Ethics," *The Wall Street Journal,* April 6, 1988, p. 27.

ethics has declined significantly in the past decade, it might be the time for both academics and marketers (at least those who have stood idly by) to become involved. While we cannot deemphasize the importance of training, research and development, market development, and other disciplines central to our business system, we must start sensitizing managers to the interface of ethical values and the implementation of business marketing strategy. Such questions as the following should be asked: What laws are being proposed that might affect future marketing strategy? Which government agencies should we be working with in our quest for improved social and ethical behavior? What can the business marketer expect in the areas of pollution control, product safety, advertising, price controls, and other areas relevant to present and future marketing strategy development? What is the attitude of the public toward the firm and the firm's products? In short, what major changes now occurring will impact the implementation of future marketing strategies across several disciplines within the firm in the short, intermediate, and long-term future.

■ AN ETHICAL ISSUE: THE ORGANIZATIONAL BUYING FUNCTION AND BUYER-SELLER RELATIONSHIPS

Organizational buyers and sellers are engaged in activities which come under the continuing scrutiny of superiors, associates, prospective suppliers, the public, and the press. The National Association of Purchasing Management, mindful of the key problems often faced by buying individuals, codified many potential problems into its Code of Ethics. This code is as follows:

1. Interests of the firm are foremost in all dealings. This concept implicitly indicates that personal gain from suppliers in the form of "commissions" (gifts, etc.) clouds the objectivity necessary in making the best decision for the buying firm.

2. Buy without preference or prejudice. This calls for objectivity in vendor selection, and avoiding conflict of interest when the buyer might have a financial interest in one particular vendor.

3. Seek maximum value in purchases. This statement reinforces the objective of receiving the maximum value at the lowest overall price to the buying firm.

4. Maintain a sound policy with regard to gifts. The cost of any gift is a marketing expense to the vendor that must be recaptured through higher prices.

5. Strive for knowledge about materials, processes, and practical methods. This is a reminder that the buyer should not merely process requisitions and purchase orders.

6. Be receptive to competent counsel from colleagues. This is a reminder to be open to new ideas and anything that might improve performance, and to further the goals of the employer.

7. Counsel and assist other buyers. This means seeking improvements, aiding others, etc.

8. Avoid "sharp practice." This includes misrepresentations in order to gain an unfair advantage over a vendor.

9. Subscribe to honesty and truth in dealings. This is similar to the sharp practice point and emphasizes that honesty and truth will benefit the buyer in the future with like action from vendors.

10. Respect obligations. Obligations can range from contractual obligations to verbal understandings.

11. Provide prompt and courteous reception to vendors. A seller's time is as valuable as the buyer's, so a prompt reception of salespeople is encouraged.[7]

Although the typical buying organization has developed the methods of a science, its decisions remain largely a matter of personal judgment. The purchasing manager, through contacts and dealings with salespeople, is the custodian of the firm's reputation for courtesy and fair dealing. The opposite is also true, with the salesperson also being expected to retain his or her firm's reputation for courtesy and fair dealing. A high ethical standard of conduct is essential for both parties. Courtesy and fair dealing beget confidence and cooperation on the part of both buyer and seller. This is something intangible—something that will frequently spell the difference between a merely adequate buying or selling performance: it will also be a major contribution to efficiency and profitability.

Business Ethics Is Not a One-Sided Proposition

Business ethics is certainly not one-sided. Buying personnel are faced from time to time with unethical sales practices—practices that might include: (1) collusive bidding, (2) restrictive conditions in specifications, (3) artificial stimulation of demand, (4) verbal or actual sabotage of competitive products, (5) padding of orders and shipments, (6) the use of highly technical and/or other unfamiliar trade terms and metric measurements, (7) supposedly sample orders which are magnified into excessive quantities, and (8) obscure contract clauses buried in small type.[8] Furthermore, salespeople are not under direct, continuous supervision, but are under constant pressure to produce sales. They are faced with additional temptations offered by the myriad opportunities for unethical behavior invited by their position. Some of the most common areas of misconduct are as follows:

- *Overselling.* Some customers are easily persuaded to buy more or costlier items than they should through the use of sharp practices, as explained in Chapter 4.

---

[7]Adapted from Joseph L. Cavinato, *Purchasing and Materials Management* (St. Paul, Minn.: West Publishing, 1984), pp. 409–11.

[8]Stuart F. Heinritz and Paul V. Farrell, "Ethics of Purchasing," in *Purchasing Management: Selected Readings,* ed. Victor P. Gravereau and Leonard J. Konopa (Columbus, Ohio: Grid, 1973), pp. 223–33.

- *Promising more than can be delivered.* Some salespeople are tempted to promise delivery when such a promise is unrealistic. They hope for the best and give excuses when pressured.
- *Lying.* This may range from exaggerated claims for a product or service to lying about a competitor's situation with regard to delivery, quality, price, etc.
- *Failing to keep confidences.* Some salespeople may reveal information of value to their customer's competitors that should have been kept confidential.
- *Bribes.* Some bribery and the existence of some unscrupulous purchasing people are a fact of life. Bribery, kickbacks, and payoffs are illegal and can get both salespeople and their companies into serious trouble.
- *Gifts.* Many buying firms prohibit employees from accepting any gifts whatsoever. Perhaps more should do the same.
- *Entertainment.* Some entertainment is important and is a necessary part of doing business, as it might serve to strengthen a relationship and build rapport. However, caution is advised.[9]

Bribes, gifts, and the use of entertainment are treated in more detail later in the chapter.

In the buyer-seller relationship the best opportunity to maintain ethical standards is competent buying, supported by training, insistence on purchase contract performance, acceptance testing, and the like. Most sellers respect the buyer who is thorough and honest in the conduct of the buying office or buying center, and they will usually respond in kind.

Concept Questions

1. How can marketing managers become more sensitized to the interface of ethical values and the implementation of marketing strategy?
2. How is the purchasing manager the custodian of his or her firm's reputation for courtesy and fair dealing?
3. What is the best opportunity for maintaining ethical standards in the buyer-seller relationship?

■ ETHICAL ISSUES IN MARKETING RESEARCH

It is important for not only marketing research students but also business practitioners and professors of marketing research to develop an awareness and concern for the ethical issues of the profession. Ethics in this context is concerned with the proper conduct of the marketing research process in business inquiry. As marketing research grows as a form of marketing intelligence, researchers will be forced to examine and scrutinize the ethical

---

[9]Ronald D. Balsley and E. Patricia Birsner, *Selling: Marketing Personified* (New York: Dryden Press, 1987), pp. 421–23.

aspects of their activities. People engaged in marketing research may unknowingly use techniques and practices the general public might consider unethical. Because of this, researchers should examine the profession for activities that may be questionable; that examination should lead to research activities appropriate to the general ethical expectations of society in general. This approach is not only good in an absolute sense, but is also self-serving.[10] Most marketing researchers would prefer to maintain high standards of conduct voluntarily, rather than have standards set and enforced by governmental action.

Societal Rights

Business is a social phenomenon coexisting with many other organizations and entities in society, and as do the others, it has certain responsibilities to this society. These rights include the following: (1) the right to be informed of research results that may impact society as a whole, and (2) the right to expect objective research results. The right to be informed is a very basic right that expresses the fundamental belief that if business and industry discover something, accidentally or otherwise, which may affect the general health and well-being of society in general, then the general public deserves to be informed of this finding. Consider the following:

- DuPont Company has vowed to stop making chlorofluorocarbons by the end of the 1990s. The chemicals, widely used in refrigerants and styrofoam, are suspected of eating away the Earth's protective ozone layer.
- Monsanto Company has promised to reduce all its hazardous air emissions by 90 percent by 1992, though they currently meet federal guidelines.
- Dow Chemical Company and the Sierra Club have endorsed jointly a proposed federal law that would sharply reduce hazardous-waste production. Dow itself has adopted an aggressive waste-reduction program.
- The Chemical-Manufacturers Association has proposed for the first time to set operating and safety standards that its 170 members would have to meet to retain membership.[11]

The right to expect objective research results implies that if research results are made public, then the general public has a right to expect that the research was objective, complete, unbiased, and scientifically sound.

---

[10]Much of the following is drawn from Donald S. Tull and Del I. Hawkins, *Marketing Research: Measurement and Method,* 3d ed. (New York: Macmillan, 1984), Chapter 20; and Duane Davis and Robert M. Cosenga, *Business Research for Decision Making* (Boston: Kent Publishing, 1985), pp. 433–37. These two sources provide excellent treatments of the major ethical issues in the conduct of business research.

[11]Laurie Hays, "Chemical Firms Press Campaign to Dispel Their 'Bad Guy' Image," *The Wall Street Journal,* September 20, 1988, p. 1.

Clients' Rights

For the sake of simplicity, the word *client* will be used to denote either an actual client in the case of a professional research firm, or the researcher's actual employer. Their rights include the following: (1) the right of confidentiality of the working relationship, and (2) the right to expect quality research. The right of confidentiality is basic, as it may benefit competitors if they know that a study is being done. The anonymity of the client must be preserved, whether it is an internal study, or a study commissioned by an outside research firm. The right to expect quality is again a very basic demand, as overly technical jargon, the failure to round numbers properly, unnecessary use of complex analytic procedures, or incomplete reporting, can make good research difficult to understand, and can cloud faulty research. Recently, as reported in *The Wall Street Journal,* two groups of graduate students polled competitors of H. O. Penn Machinery Company in Armonk, N.Y., and Yancy Brothers in Atlanta, both Caterpillar dealers. These dealerships wanted the students to conduct competitive analyses on actual competitors, with the dealers providing the names of the competitors, and even suggesting what questions to ask. The students were able to obtain and analyze information on the competitors' inventory levels, sales volume, advertising expenditures, and even potential new product introductions. The students identified themselves only as university students working on a class project, and when corresponding with the dealers, used university marketing department stationery. Said one of H. O. Penn's competitors: "I wouldn't give out that type of stuff if I knew it were going to someone other than students."[12] Can such practices be eliminated? Probably not. Can they be reduced? We think so.

Several issues can arise in which the researcher, department, or firm needs protection. The right for protection against improper solicitation of proposals could refer to the sharp practices mentioned earlier. Proposals should not be solicited for the specific purpose of driving down prices, nor should a proposal from an outside research firm be given to an in-house research department for implementation. The right to expect accurate presentation of findings again refers to a possible distortion of findings. This not only misleads the client, but is potentially damaging to other involved parties as well. The right to expect confidentiality of proprietary information on techniques is included to help researchers who develop special techniques for dealing with certain types of problems encountered. Examples would be proprietary modeling and simulation techniques.

■ ETHICS AND THE MANAGEMENT OF THE PRICING FUNCTION

Pricing is perhaps the most difficult of all the areas of marketing to examine from an ethical viewpoint because of the complexity of the price vari-

---

[12]Clare Ansberry, "For These M.B.A.s, Class Became Exercise in Corporate Espionage," *The Wall Street Journal,* March 22, 1988, p. 37.

able.[13] There is an expansive realm of ethical issues in pricing; issues may be raised at all levels of the distribution channel, across different market structures and competitive situations, and across industry types. The following is an overview of some of the more important areas of ethical issues in pricing.[14]

Setting a Price That Meets Company Objectives, while Not Taking Advantage of the Customer

Generally speaking, new products should be priced to gain experience and market share, which, if done correctly, should meet stated company objectives in terms of profit and return on investment. As market share increases, lower costs should be the result. If a skimming price strategy is initially used, is the firm under any moral obligation to lower prices without a clear market-oriented reason for doing so (such as competitive entry, competitive price move, etc.)? None of us is in a position to make a judgment on this question, and the question is raised only to point out that if profit goals are overemphasized, line management may perceive that profit should be placed above ethical considerations. We can hope that competitive forces will keep prices and demand for the company products or product lines on an even keel.

Altering Product Quality without Changing Price

As noted in Chapter 3, product quality will usually determine price, as buyers are reluctant to pay for unnecessary product quality. Also, as noted in Chapter 3, an overanxious line manager may be tempted to reduce quality standards as part of a value-analysis effort. Assume that a large equipment manufacturer initiates a major cost reduction effort, substituting plastic for steel in several subassemblies. Though realizing that the life of the equipment may drop slightly, the manufacturer does not point this out to prospective customers, and does not reduce the price of the finished product to reflect the cost savings. (It must also be assumed that price exhibits an inelastic demand curve in this situation.) Is this ethical? Should the possibility of a shortened useful product life be brought to the attention of prospective buyers? Will this decision depend on competitive forces, the stage in the product life cycle, the profitability of the product line, or pressure exerted by top management for increased profitability? We could easily generate glib answers here but in reality it's not easy to produce ready answers to such questions.

---

[13]William J. Kehoe, "Ethics, Price Fixing, and the Management of Price Strategy," in *Marketing Ethics: Guidelines for Managers,* ed. Gene R. Laczniak and Patrick E. Murphy (Lexington, Mass.: Lexington Books, 1985), pp. 71–83.

[14]Adapted from Patrick E. Murphy and Gene R. Laczniak, "Marketing Ethics: A Review with Implications for Managers, Educators and Researchers," in *Review of Marketing,* ed. Ben M. Enis and Kenneth J. Roering (Chicago: American Marketing Association, 1981), pp. 251–66.

Practicing Price Discrimination with Smaller Accounts

Although the **Robinson-Patman Act** makes it unlawful to discriminate in price between commodities of like grade and quality, and prohibits unfair competition (among other things), would someone be naive enough to think that price discrimination against smaller accounts does not happen occasionally with some companies? In an effort to please, or because of a long-standing professional (or even personal) relationship, in addition to both internal and external pressures, the marketer will probably be tempted to treat some customers better than others when price is an issue. Such a marketer, in most cases, would be shocked to learn of a potential violation of the law here, and in all probability, is doing what he or she thinks is best for the company, given the realities of the situation. Although understandable, such an attitude raises serious ethical and legal questions and issues.

Price-Fixing

A way of controlling competition is for a small group of producers to collude for their common good by agreeing on the prices to charge. This practice, known as **price-fixing,** is illegal because it undermines the competitive system to the detriment of the buyer; it is also immoral. If firms join together and use their combined power to fix prices, to drive out competitors, or to earn monopolistic profits at the expense of not only the business buyer but also of the ultimate consumer, the market ceases to be competitive; the result is a decline in, or restriction of, a buyer's freedom to make economic choices. The courts have consistently held that agreements between firms to set prices are **per se violations** of Section 1 of the Sherman Act. This means that there is no defense on economic grounds, and the government only has to prove that there was intent to fix prices to obtain a conviction. Criminal penalties for those convicted of collusive price activity may include a fine, a prison term, or both. Antitrust penalties have become more severe since the enactment of a **federal antitrust statute** that makes it a felony to violate federal antitrust laws. The statute, which took effect on January 1, 1975, increased the maximum penalty that can be imposed against a company from $50,000 to $1 million; it also increased the penalty that can be imposed on an individual defendant from one year in prison and a $50,000 fine to three years in prison and a $100,000 fine.[15] In view of the potential fines, jail terms, legal fees, damages, and loss of goodwill that may result from this practice, there would appear to be no valid justification for a firm to engage in this activity.

---

[15]Douglas J. Dalrymple and Leonard J. Parsons, *Marketing Management: Strategy and Cases,* 4th ed. (New York: John Wiley & Sons, 1986), pp. 484–89.

Obtaining Information on a Competitor's Price Quotation in Order to Requote or Rebid

When competitive bidding is used, requests for bids are usually sent to from three to six potential vendors, depending on the dollar size of the purchase. Bidding is a morally justifiable procedure, providing it is fair. However, keeping it fair is not always an easy task. If the bidding process is top secret, then a violation of secrecy by any of the parties in the process violates the fairness condition of the bidding process. Obviously, the leaking of information to other potential suppliers is unfair, immoral, and unethical, and could be the result of bribery or offers of a cash kickback. Bidding, although used fairly in the vast majority of cases, is open to abuses and must be controlled if it is to be kept fair.

Reciprocity

Many business buyers often select suppliers who also buy from them. An example of **reciprocity** would be a packaging manufacturer who buys needed chemicals from a chemical company that is buying a considerable amount of the packaging firm's product. Reciprocity, by itself, is not illegal. However, the Justice Department and the Federal Trade Commission monitor reciprocity because it may substantially lessen competition. Another example of reciprocity is the way the Canadian government purchased military aircraft from McDonnell Douglas (a U.S. firm). Canada agreed to buy $2.4 billion worth of aircraft, and in return McDonnell Douglas promised to find $2.9 billion of business for Canadian companies.[16] Reciprocity is forbidden if it eliminates competition in an unfair manner. As long as the buyer can show that competitive prices, quality, and service are supplied, then reciprocity probably just makes good business sense. However, if those conditions are not met, then we may have to address the question of ethical standards.

Concept Questions

1. Why should marketing researchers examine their profession for activities that might be questionable?
2. Why is pricing such a difficult area to examine from an ethical viewpoint?

■ ETHICS AND THE MANAGEMENT OF THE SALES FORCE

As key links between their organizations and the buyer, salespeople encounter situations that, on occasion, can lead to unethical conduct. For this discussion we will categorize ethical issues confronting sales person-

---

[16]New Restrictions on World Trade," *Business Week,* July 19, 1982, p. 119.

nel into two broad areas: (1) ethics in dealing with customers, and (2) ethics in dealing with employers.[17] But first, consider the following vignettes:

Scenario 1:   A machinery salesperson faced the following problem. When a newly installed milling machine continued to malfunction, the customer demanded that the piece of equipment be immediately replaced with another new machine. Management within the selling firm decided to replace the machine with a slightly used demo that looked new. The salesperson did not know whether or not to inform the customer of the replacement with the obvious risk of losing the sale, or to defer to management's action, thus not only salvaging the sale, but perhaps even his or her job.

Scenario 2:   A commercial real estate sales person was attempting to sell a building to a client who finally had decided to make an offer on the building. The offer was several thousand dollars below not only the asking price but also the appraised value of the property. Knowing that the seller would decline such an offer, the salesperson considered telling the potential buyer that the seller was considering an offer extended by another potential buyer, even though no such offer existed.

Scenario 3:   A salesperson was attempting to sell cleaning supplies to a large, multiplant manufacturer of widgets. The buyer bluntly told the salesperson that for a private "fee" of $500, the contract could be signed very quickly. The salesperson, being fairly new in the position, told the sales manager what had happened. The sales manager in turn, told the salesperson to do whatever was necessary to get the order, even if that included the payment of a $500 "fee" (bribe!).

These situations are very real for many people in the business to business sales force. Now, as mentioned earlier, we shall return to the two broad areas confronting sales personnel with regard to ethical considerations.

Ethics in Dealing with Customers

Occasionally, salespeople find themselves in the position wherein they are tempted to lower their ethical standards when dealing with some customers; the salespeople may compromise their standards because a customer or competitor is engaged in an unethical strategy. A half-truth or misrepresentation, a subtle demand for a gift or extraordinary entertain-

---

[17]Adapted from Alan J. Dubinsky, "Studying Field Salespeople's Ethical Problems: An Approach for Designing Company Policies," in Laczniak and Murphy, "Marketing Ethics," pp. 41–53.

ment, or some other unethical trick might tempt the salesperson to relax standards, especially when a large order is at stake. The major problem areas involved are bribes, gifts, entertainment, and reciprocity.

Bribes.   The use of bribes, although widespread and considered very acceptable behavior within some cultures, should be refused tactfully, thus allowing salespeople to act in the best interests of their employers, and in fairness to all customers. Bribery not only is unethical, but can also be illegal. A few years ago a large American steel company was fined $325,000 for paying $400,000 in bribes to obtain ship repair business for its domestic shipyards.[18] In addition, it is often difficult to distinguish between a bribe, a gift to show appreciation, and a reasonable commission for services rendered, as bribery today is done in a more sophisticated manner than in the past and is less easy to identify. Bribery as we know it, erupted as an international scandal in the mid- to late 1970s, when there were revelations of payoffs to foreign officials by American companies selling abroad. The resultant political sensitivity in the United States and several foreign countries did much to clean up a bad situation.[19] Bribery distorts the operation of fair bargaining, and salespeople should resist efforts for bribes from the occasional member of the buying center who might want to engage in such activity.

Gifts.   Accepting or giving gifts may or may not be ethical, but the practice of gift giving is under careful scrutiny within many business firms. If the giving of a gift is done as a condition of doing business (subtle or otherwise), then clearly the act is immoral and unethical. Many firms have stopped the practice of giving Christmas gifts to customers, offering instead to contribute to a customer's favorite charity. Some common sense and social intelligence should be good guides in keeping the selling firm within ethical boundaries.

Entertainment.   Although the entertainment of customers and potential customers is quite common and even expected today, it too can pose ethical questions. Is taking a customer to lunch or a ball game fair, reasonable, and expected? If that is deemed to be acceptable, then how about a few days at the company resort or fishing lodge, or a trip to view an equipment installation near Disneyland with the buyer's spouse? Many times members of the buying center resent attempts to influence them unduly and find efforts to obligate them to buy from a particular seller quite offensive. As a general rule, lavish entertainment can become unethical if the attempt is to substitute it for good selling techniques.

Reciprocity.   As explained in Chapter 4, this phenomenon occurs when a buyer gives preference to a supplier who is also a customer; it is usually found in industries in which products are homogeneous and/or there is not a high degree of price sensitivity. The buyer of business goods thus has the

---

[18]*The Wall Street Journal,* July 25, 1980, p. 5.

[19]Thomas Griffith, "Payoff Is Not 'Accepted Practice,' " *Fortune,* August 1976, pp. 122–25.

opportunity to use purchases to generate sales by a threat, overt or implied, or to withdraw patronage unless it is reciprocated. This practice obviously has ethical, and perhaps even legal, implications. Chemical Bank, the New York-based financial institution, with some 270 branches in the United States and 55 offices abroad, has long been noted for its innovative approach both to business ethics and to corporate responsibility. Its purchasing department has procedures to ensure fair and equitable treatment of the bank's suppliers. In order to avoid even the appearance of reciprocity, there is no review to determine which suppliers are Chemical customers before the bank awards contracts. Chemical's own printing subsidiary is expected to compete against other companies for most of the bank's printing orders.[20]

Ethics in Dealing with Employers

In dealing with their own employers, salespeople encounter situations which may lead to unethical conduct. The major problem areas involved are moonlighting, relationships with fellow salespeople, and expense accounts.

Moonlighting.   Salespeople who waste or misuse time (especially those who work on a straight salary compensation plan) are in a sense stealing profits from the employing company. The holding of more than one job, **moonlighting,** may be construed as a misuse of company time, and it therefore raises some potential ethical and moral questions. Employers have a right to expect full-time work from salespeople employed to sell their product, and those that work another job in the evening or have a side business of their own may violate the principal of time accountability. A salesperson who handles another product line (even a noncompetitive product line) is engaged in the unethical practice of **kiting.** The key here is disclosure—that is, informing the employer that extra hours are being spent doing something else. If the employer agrees that the salesperson may engage in other work, or may carry the line of another company, then the salesperson's obligations with regard to ethical behavior have been satisfied. The question of ethics would depend upon the special circumstances surrounding each individual case.

Changing Jobs.   Another area in which salespeople face ethical responsibility is in changing jobs. An active effort by sales managers to "pirate" salespeople away from competitors is likely to be seen as unethical. Companies invest considerable money in training salespeople, in addition to the fact that over a period of time they build up customer knowledge and goodwill of which they may take advantage if they change jobs and accept a position with a competitor. Job switchers have generally had access to confidential information, and perhaps to competitive secrets. If such factors

---

[20]Chemical Bank Programs in Business Ethics and Corporate Responsibility," by the Ethics Resource Center, Inc., in *Corporate Ethics: A Prime Business Asset,* The Business Roundtable, February 1988, pp. 31–40.

are used as a ploy to gain new employment, this practice would be considered unethical of both the prospective employer and the recruiting sales manager.

Expense Accounts. Most companies provide the sales force with sufficient travel and entertainment expense money to cover all justified expenses of doing business, and it is the responsibility of the salespeople and the sales managers to allocate expense dollars effectively. **Expense accounts** present special temptations and are the most frequent area for ethical abuse within a sales organization. The fine line the sales manager must walk with regard to expense account control can be trying. A tight control might cause the salesperson to curtail travel and necessary entertainment to the detriment of the company, while loose control will usually result in selling expense ratios higher than they should be.

Contests. Contests are designed to motivate sales representatives to make more sales of all products, or to make more sales of specific products within a product line. The pressure to win can result in the "stockpiling" of orders until the contest begins, the selling of unneeded product to "friends" for later return for credit, or the overselling of unneeded products to good customers. All these practices are easy to rationalize, and all are unethical.

■ ETHICS AND ADVERTISING STRATEGY

When Winston Churchill took his entrance examination for Sandhurst in 1880, he was given a choice of three essay questions: Riding versus Rowing; Advertisements, Their Use and Abuse; and the American Civil War. (He chose the American Civil War.)[21] That the use and abuse of advertising tools and techniques were up for discussion more than a century ago reveals that today's criticisms of advertising are not new. Indeed, the manager overseeing the firm's promotional strategy has a primary responsibility to create profitable sales for the business unit, along with responsibilities toward the customers themselves. Advertising techniques have often been criticized by those outside the field as a dubious practice involving the use of questionable techniques to accomplish nefarious ends. No business discussion of ethics would be complete without a section of study devoted to ethics and advertising strategy.

Truth in Advertising

Truth in advertising is a complex issue, as most statements supported by a reference to a scientific study would probably be very dull, and may or may not be effective. Advertisements make statements for the purpose of trying to persuade buyers to purchase the product advertised. Persuasion may take place by making statements or by simply creating associations in

---

[21]Randolph S. Churchill, *Winston S. Churchill* (Boston: Houghton Mifflin, 1966), vol. 1, p. 129.

the mind of the buyer. Some business to business advertisements simply show a picture of the product; their aim is that when the buyer sees the name, it will have a positive effect on purchasing. A statement made about a product may be true, may not mislead, and may not deceive. Nevertheless, it may be morally and ethically objectionable. Sometimes what the advertisement does not say is as important as what it does say. It is wrong to advertise and to sell a hazardous product without indicating its dangers.[22] General rules concerning truth in advertising can be summarized in the following way: it is immoral to lie, mislead, and deceive in advertising. It is immoral to fail to indicate dangers that are not normally expected. It is not immoral to use a metaphor or other figure of speech if these will be normally understood as the figurative use of language, nor is it immoral to persuade as well as to inform.[23]

Comparative Advertising

Comparative advertising is an advertisement or sales promotional piece that names the competitors and proceeds to compare one product to another. It can present both potential ethical and legal problems. Because of this, some marketing managers prohibit or at least discourage such practices within their own firms, feeling that such practices serve no real purpose. The customer has to make comparisons in selecting products, and most business copy can provide enough comparative and accurate information to aid that process. If comparisons are made, then clearly the standard should insist on accurate comparisons, as there might be a temptation to imply that a product that is superior to the competition in one characteristic is therefore superior overall. It might be recommended that a more ethical and responsible course of action would be to point out competitive differences, leaving the customer to judge the superiority (or inferiority) of the product offering.

Inherent in the semantics of advertising and promotion in general are the notions of lying, misrepresentation, deception, manipulation, and other questionable practices. Those that are unethical, immoral, or illegal should be labeled as such. Peers or top management influence most ethical decisions related to advertising in particular and promotion in general. Ethical decision making within this area is conceptually complex, and a multiplicity of factors can influence the final outcome. To implement and monitor ethical decision making in advertising in particular and other promotional activities in general, we need to examine all dimensions of ethics, as ethics has both philosophical and organizational dimensions.[24]

---

[22]Richard T. DeGeorge, *Business Ethics,* 2d ed. (New York: Macmillan, 1986), p. 279.
[23]Ibid., p. 280.
[24]Laczniak and Murphy, "Marketing Ethics," pp. 27–39.

■ ETHICS AND INTERNATIONAL MARKETING

In the mid 1970s public shock over disclosures of bribery, kickbacks, and illegal campaign contributions by various corporations led to the development of the **Foreign Corrupt Practices Act** (FCPA), which was signed into law in 1977. This act greatly limits corporate payments of fees to obtain a foreign contract, and a violation of the act is punishable by fines and prison terms. (One of the more notable cases was the Lockheed involvement in payments made to the Japanese in connection with the sale of its L1011 Tri Star and its F-104 Starfighter jets.) Recent past happenings in our global economy are filled with cases wherein large multinational enterprises have used their power in ways which seemed to hurt others. For example, the history of chemicals, metals, and oil contains numerous examples in which a few large firms dominating the market have extracted a heavy rent from their hosts. There have also been cases in which the power of the multinational enterprise has been manifested by its decisions to open or close plants, with powerful effects upon the communities in which such enterprises have operated. Still other cases such as the chemical tragedy in Bhopal, India, have involved the pollution of the environment or the manufacture of harmful products.[25] Some multinationals have also used their power in the political arena, helping to elect candidates and shape legislation. The history of British Steel, Petroleos Mexicanos, Electricité de France, Montedison, and dozens of other large foreign national entities provide ample illustrations of the exercise of power in all of the dimensions that have been mentioned so far.[26] It is perfectly clear that Union Carbide made a serious error of judgment; it is also clear that the Foreign Corrupt Practices Act has attacked, and will continue to attack, a rising tide of extortion and bribery in international business. In addition, our legal standards are not necessarily a reliable guide to overseas conduct.

Ethics Differ from Country to Country

The ethical practices of business tend to vary from country to country. In one study marketers in the United States, Germany, and France were asked to evaluate the ethical standards in marketing of the following countries: the United Kingdom, France, the Federal Republic of Germany, Greece, India, Israel, Italy, Japan, Mexico, and the United States.[27] The results, which are shown in Table 15–1, reveal a significant variation in the

---

[25]Raymond Vernon, "Ethics and the Multinational Enterprise," in *Ethics and The Multinational Enterprise*, ed. W. Michael Hoffman, Ann E. Lange, and David A. Fedo (Proceedings of the Sixth National Conference on Business Ethics, Bentley College, Waltham, Mass.: University Press of America, 1985), pp. 61–69.

[26]Ibid., pp. 61–69.

[27]David J. Fritzsche and Helmut Becker, "Linking Management Behavior to Ethical Philosophy—An Empirical Investigation," *Academy of Management Journal*, March 1984, pp. 166–75, adapted from David J. Fritzsche, "Ethical Issues in Multinational Marketing," in Laczniak and Murphy, "Marketing Ethics," pp. 85–96.

■ **TABLE 15–1** Perceptions of Ethical Standards in Marketing Provided by French, West German, and U.S. Marketers

Country Ranked	Respondents			
	French Median	German Median	U.S. Median	Average Median
United Kingdom	3	3	3	3
France	3	5	5	4[a]
Germany	2	2	2	2
Greece	8	7	7	7[a]
India	8	9	8	8
Israel	6	7	6	6
Italy	7	8	8	8[a]
Japan	5	5	4	5
Mexico	8	9	9	9[a]
United States	3	7	1	4[a]

Note: The data were obtained from respondent's rankings of the countries, with 1 representing the most ethical.
[a]Significance at the .05 level.

perceptions of the various countries. The data shown are the median values of the ranked data from marketers in the three countries. The Federal Republic of Germany is perceived to be the most ethical country by marketers from all three of the countries, followed by the United Kingdom, and then the United States and France. Mexico was ranked lowest, with India and Italy not much higher. While some nationalism is evident, other factors were significant as evidenced by the fact that the French ranked the West Germans as high as the West Germans ranked themselves. If this data is representative of the ethical practices being followed, then it would seem that the level of ethical behavior tends to increase with the level of economic development of the country. Whether this increase is caused by developments in the legal system of the country or by society's expectations and the needs of the participants is unknown. What is clear is that the United States was not ranked as the most ethical or unethical country in the survey. This result could mean different things to different people.

On the international scene, what is legal and what is ethical are not necessarily uniform worldwide. As noted earlier, in several countries the payment of **grease money** to high-level military officials to sell weapons to their government is not illegal, is common practice, and is expected. However, as far as some companies such as Whirlpool are concerned, this practice is both unethical and illegal. As Robert Gunts of Whirlpool Corporation stated in a recent address:

> Whirlpool will forego business opportunities if it takes unethical payments to acquire new business. We make that commitment with eyes wide open, knowing full well that we will lose some business opportunities, particularly when competing against business from nations which do not subscribe to our principles.[28]

---

[28]Robert Gunts, Ethics As a Way of Life," in Hoffman, Lange, and Fedo, pp. 101–6.

It would seem that the types of payoffs mentioned earlier tend to feed on themselves, and there may be no end in sight once the word is out that a company will barter on its principles.

The Complexity of International Ethical Issues

Finally, when we operate in the international environment, ethical issues in business to business marketing become somewhat more complex than when we operate solely within the home country. As described in the "Business to Business Marketing in Action" box, U.S. companies doing business in South Africa are repelled by the common practice of apartheid

---

BUSINESS TO BUSINESS MARKETING IN ACTION

An Ethical Problem in South Africa for U.S. Marketers

The situation in the 1980s that perhaps best illustrated ethical decision making on an international level is that of South Africa. The government of South Africa has long practiced apartheid (separation of the races). The blacks in South Africa protested apartheid throughout the 1980s, and hundreds of people were killed in clashes among blacks who had differences of opinion about the apartheid system and the white ruling government.

Virtually all nations of the world, including the government of South Africa, felt that something had to be done about the system of apartheid. Some small steps were made to change some of the rules, but the changes were few and slow. Protestors in the United States demanded that American organizations, such as universities, stop investing in firms that did business in South Africa. The idea was to pressure the South African government to end apartheid more quickly. The protests grew more insistent when increased violence erupted in South Africa. Soon, protestors called for U.S. firms to pull out of South Africa entirely.

In 1986 an advertisement sponsored by 80 American companies operating in South Africa, including Citibank, IBM, Coca-Cola, and Union Carbide, called for a complete end of all forms of apartheid. One possibility would be for all such U.S. firms to pull their subsidiaries out of South Africa. Many people proposed that very solution. The problem is that U.S. firms employ many black employees and are some of the fairest and most liberal employers in the country. If they were to pull out, it would hurt the economy of South Africa badly. That means both whites and blacks would suffer, and other nations would be less likely to lend money to businesses in the area. The

continued

government might fall, but what would remain would be a country with a weaker business base to build on. This would hurt blacks more than whites in the long run because blacks are in the majority.

American businesses with subsidiaries in South Africa faced a serious ethical problem. Should they stay in South Africa and try to get the government to be more liberal with blacks? They do have a significant influence. Or should they pull out in protest and potentially hasten the end of apartheid, but increase black unemployment and remove a source of pressure on other businesses to be as fair as U.S. businesses are with blacks? American businesses have subsidiaries in many countries with poor race relations or suppressive governments. Should they pull out of all such countries or stay and try to promote change? What is the moral and ethical position for businesses to take relative to other governments? These are the kinds of international ethical questions that will have to be answered in the next decade.

in that country. Many Americans would like all U.S. business activity with South Africa halted until this situation is corrected. However, many black South Africans are dependent upon U.S. business concerns in South Africa for employment. Therefore, a unilateral withdrawal of U.S. companies from South Africa, although honorable in intention, could have a disastrous effect on the very people the action was intended to assist. While the following is not an exhaustive list, some important issues should be addressed when contemplating operations abroad:

Product.   Could the product cause damage to the people or the environment of the host country? What safeguards are in place to ensure that the product will not do this, or will lessen the impact if the unexpected does happen?

Promotion.   Will the promotion be viewed as a bribe or a payoff by the host country?

Distribution.   Is a bribe or payoff required to enter a foreign market; if so, is the company willing to engage in such activity? Will this violate ethical norms as presently set up and in place? Will disclosure impact domestic business?

Price.   Will the price charged in the foreign market be viewed as dumping by the host country? Could the price charged in a foreign market have political, ethical, or moral implications in the domestic market?[29]

---

[29]Adapted from Fritzsche, "Ethical Issues in Multinational Marketing," pp. 85–96.

Concept Questions

1. What is the most ethical way to approach comparative advertising?
2. What led to the development of the Foreign Corrupt Practices Act?
3. What is Whirlpool management's view about making unethical payments to acquire international business?

SUMMARY

1. Ethics means the standard of behavior by which behavior is judged. Standards that may be legal may not be ethical. Standards and beliefs about what is right and proper change over time; this question is becoming more important as our economy becomes more competitive, and our technology more complex.

2. Comparing the marketing strategies and tactics of firms today versus a decade ago, the most striking impression is one of general marketing strategy obsolescence. Marketers must become sensitized to the interface of ethical values and the implementation of marketing strategy. They must learn to recognize the major changes that will impact the implementation of future marketing strategies.

3. The purchasing manager, through contacts and dealings with salespeople, is the custodian of his or her firm's reputation for courtesy and fair dealing. The subject of business ethics equally applies to both buyer and seller. In the buyer-seller relationship the best opportunity for maintaining ethical behavior is competent buying supported by training, insistence on purchase contract performance, and acceptance testing. Most salespeople respect the buyer who is thorough and honest in his or her purchase transactions.

4. People engaged in marketing research may unknowingly use techniques and practices the general public might consider unethical. Because of this, researchers should examine their profession for activities that may be questionable so as to avoid them. Market researchers should be aware of societal rights, clients' rights, and researchers' rights in discharging their professional duties.

5. Pricing is perhaps the most difficult of all the areas of marketing to examine from an ethical perspective because of the complexity of the price variable. Common areas of ethical concern in pricing include: (1) setting a price that meets company objectives while not taking advantage of the customer; (2) altering product quality without changing the price; (3) practicing price discrimination with smaller accounts; (4) price-fixing; (5) obtaining information on a competitive price quotation in order to requote or rebid; and (6) reciprocity.

6. As key links between their organizations and the buyer, salespeople encounter situations that, on occasion, lead to ethical conflict. Salespeople may be tempted to lower their ethical standards in dealing with their customers in such areas as bribes, gifts, entertainment, and reci-

procity. They may be likewise tempted with respect to their employers in such areas as moonlighting, charging accounts, expense accounts, and bribes.

7. A statement made about a product may be true, may not mislead, may not deceive, but may nevertheless be morally and ethically objectionable. What the advertisement does not say may be more important than what it does say. In comparative advertising the marketer should carefully point out differences, leaving the customers to judge the superiority of the product offering.

8. What is considered to be ethical practice can vary from country to country. Ethical issues can become much more complex when we operate in international markets rather than in domestic markets. The international business marketer must adapt each of the elements of the marketing mix to the particular customer and the particular country where the marketing mix is to be used.

KEY TERMS

comparative advertising	moonlighting
ethics	per se violations
expense accounts	price-fixing
federal antitrust statute	reciprocity
Foreign Corrupt Practices Act	Robinson-Patman Act
grease money	truth in advertising
kiting	

REVIEW QUESTIONS

1. What three sets of factors influence the ethics of an individual's decisions? Identify and describe three different views of corporate social responsibility. Provide a business example for each one.

2. What kinds of questions should marketers ask in order to sensitize themselves to the interface of ethical values and the implementation of marketing strategy?

3. How can the purchasing manager be the custodian of his or her firm's reputation for courtesy and fair dealing? What types of unethical sales practices are likely to face buyers from time to time? What types of ethical misconduct are sources of temptation to the salesperson?

4. What three sets of rights should all professional marketing researchers keep in mind as they discharge their activities? How can ethics be applied to the marketing research function?

5. Why is pricing perhaps the most difficult of all the marketing areas to examine from an ethical perspective? Discuss six types of potential unethical conduct in business to business pricing.

6. What are four types of ethical problems salespeople might encounter in dealing with their customers? What are four types of ethical problems they might encounter in dealing with their employers?

7. What are two ways in which "persuasion" may take place in promotion? How can comparative advertising be used in an unethical manner?

8. What led to the establishment of the Foreign Corrupt Practices Act of 1977? What is its primary purpose? What is the Whirlpool Corporation's policy on making unethical payments to acquire new international business?

CHAPTER CASES

CASE 15–1   Manville Corporation*

On August 26, 1982 Manville Corporation, a large construction and forest-products manufacturer, asked for court protection under Chapter 11 of the federal bankruptcy code, despite a net worth of $1.1 billion. Chapter 11 status allows companies to continue their operations and reorganize debt without interference from creditors or other outside parties.

When Manville voluntarily filed for court protection, it was a very profitable firm that had no intention of going out of business or changing the way in which it operated. Rather, Manville sought to halt the lawsuits brought against it by people suffering health problems caused by exposure to asbestos and products made with asbestos that were produced by Manville. By gaining bankruptcy status, all pending lawsuits against the company would be ruled on by a bankruptcy judge rather than by state and federal courts; legal proceedings would be delayed; and new lawsuits could not be brought. Manville planned to remove itself from bankruptcy standing after its legal problems were resolved.

Manville defended its application for Chapter 11 protection in full-page newspaper advertisements appearing on August 27, 1982. Manville offered these reasons for its actions:

- About 16,500 lawsuits were pending, with 500 new lawsuits being filed each month. It was estimated that 32,000 more lawsuits could be brought against the company. The total costs of settling these lawsuits at $40,000 per claim (Manville's average) would amount to more than $2 billion.

- Asbestos-related health problems were not discovered until 1964. Up to then, existing medical knowledge showed that Manville operated properly. The largest group of plaintiffs against the company was shipyard workers using asbestos insulation on ships built or modified during World War II, when asbestos was viewed as safe.

---

*Reprinted with permission of Macmillan Publishing Company from *Marketing,* 2d ed. by Joel R. Evans and Barry Berman. Copyright © 1982, 1985 by Macmillan Publishing Company.

- The U.S. government should be responsible for a compensation program for asbestos-related injuries. Furthermore, it was virtually impossible for the company to defend itself in every state, under different statutes.

Manville's critics believed the firm was not acting in a socially responsible manner and was misusing bankruptcy protection (which was intended for companies with severe financial, not legal, problems). These critics asserted that:

- Manville was trying to force the federal government to develop a bailout plan for the company.
- By cutting off lawsuits, Manville was not allowing plaintiffs to exercise their legal rights.
- Manville "fraudulently concealed" information about asbestos hazards. In 1980 the California Supreme Court ruled that plaintiffs were eligible for punitive damages because of this. These damages could not be covered by insurance, but by Manville itself.

In May 1983 Manville offered a reorganization plan that was not acceptable to its critics. Under this plan Manville asked litigants to negotiate or risk settlements imposed by the bankruptcy court. Although it revised the plan in November 1983, both the original plan and its revision were rejected. By early 1984 Manville was losing the backing of key commercial and trade creditors. Despite all these distractions, Manville reported a $100 million profit for the final quarter of 1983 (while remaining in bankruptcy).

Questions

1. Was Manville justified in applying for court protection? Explain.
2. Should a company be liable for health hazards not discovered until years after a product is introduced? Why or why not?
3. How do you view the large settlements U.S. juries are awarding to plaintiffs in product liability trials? For example, a Texas woman was awarded $2 million by a jury ($1 million in punitive damages) for asbestos-related health problems of her deceased husband.
4. Will Manville's actions have a long-term impact on the company's image? Explain your answer from the perspective of both stockholders and consumers.

Case 15–2   *Cotton Belt Exporting**

While John Welch was growing up in Texas, he was an excellent student. His parents and teachers thought of him as "college capable." In fact, he never seriously considered any option other than college. A reason he chose to major in marketing was because one of his goals was, in his own words, "not to get stuck in Civil Service like my dad did. Private industry is the place for me, where I have more of an opportunity to be promoted

*Douglas J. Dalrymple, *Sales Management*, 3rd ed., 1988, John Wiley and Sons, Inc., pp. 605–7.

on my own merits, and not necessarily on seniority." John entered college and, as usual, did well scholastically.

As college graduation neared, John began to interview with a number of companies. The college placement counselor advised John to make a list of aspects he would find desirable or undesirable in a job. One of the items on his list was that the company and its product or goal had to be socially justifiable. This item had come to mind because many of his classmates were going to work for companies which had engaged in ethically questionable practices. John believed that, in spite of these companies' slightly higher pay scales, he would not want to work for a company that made its money through socially irresponsible means.

Another of the items on his list was that he wanted to travel on the job. His family had traveled in the United States on vacations when he was a child, and he had been to Mexico and Canada; but he wanted to see something of other parts of the world. Although John did not care to live in another country, he did think that a job which took him periodically to other countries for short trips would be desirable.

One day during his senior year, John talked with one of his marketing professors, Dr. Mayfield, about his career goals, and Dr. Mayfield suggested that perhaps John should look into the exporting business. Dr. Mayfield said he had a friend in Memphis who was a vice president in a cotton exporting firm, Cotton Belt Exporting. Things fell into place and John received, and accepted, an offer of a job in the firm.

For the first couple of years, John's responsibilities included traveling throughout the southern United States and California, buying cotton from farmers and gins. But the company promised that once he had proved himself in a couple of positions, he would be promoted into a position where he would be dealing directly with people in foreign countries. After about six years and two positions within the firm, he was promoted to manager of export sales to Japan.

It took John some time to become accustomed to dealing with Japanese businesspeople, but in doing so he became fascinated by the differences in customs. He learned to understand that, just because Mr. Tanaka said yes while John was talking to him, Mr. Tanaka did not mean that he agreed to what was being said—instead, he meant merely that he understood what was being said. Each trip to Japan was a learning experience.

John also became acquainted with the mechanics of selling cotton to Japan. He learned that disagreements between cotton sellers in the United States and cotton buyers in Japan were arbitrated by two associations, one in the United states (the American Cotton Shipping Association) and one in Japan (the Cotton Trade Association). The two associations agreed to many rules for trade but, when their rules conflicted, the cotton contracts themselves specified which rules would apply.

On one trip to Japan, John heard rumors from importers that the Cotton Trade Association was contemplating some rule changes in the near future that could affect his company's ability to trade with Japan. He paid a visit to the association, but his usual contact was on vacation in Hawaii, so he had to see another gentleman, Mr. Kodama. Kodama said that he knew little about the pending changes, but he intimated that, although he was a busy man, for a small fee he could probably find out "many" details. John left the office promising to get back to Kodama.

John considered his options. He decided that, although he had never approved of paying to obtain such information, the urgency of the situation, and the probable need for immediate action dictated that he should make the payment. The next day he returned to Kodama's office with an envelope containing 22,170 yen (equivalent to about $100) which was, from his experience, the going rate for such payments.

Kodama told John that a middle-level government official, Mr. Nakamura, was pressuring the cotton-importing people to diversify their sources of cotton in order to reduce Japan's dependency on any one country. The association reacted by considering rule changes that would encourage leaders to buy from sources other than their largest ones. Since the United States was the largest supplier of cotton to Japan, this action was certain to reduce the total amount of cotton it could sell to Japan.

John checked with his company, and his boss approved John's suggestion that he do some lobbying while he was in Japan. After obtaining the appropriate introductions, John arranged to have lunch with Nakamura. At the restaurant John explained his company's situation, giving Nakamura facts about the promise of larger crops in the United States, reduced prices because of technological advances in production, improved strains of cotton, and so on. After much discussion Nakamura indicated that, having given some thought to the specifics of the problem, he believed he might be able to see John's side of the argument.

Later in the conversation Nakamura began to discuss the increasing cost of living, especially since his son had been admitted to Harvard. He wondered if John's company might see fit to give the boy some type of scholarship—according to the Harvard catalog, his son would need about $20,000 per year to attend school. Nakamura subtly (but unmistakably) intimated that financial aid to his son might help him see the cotton situation more clearly.

John found himself in a dilemma. He had rationalized the payments for information, but somehow this situation seemed different.

Questions

1. In light of John's actions in Japan, what do you think of his attitude toward the companies for whom his friends worked?

2. Was John correct to pay Mr. Kodama for information about pending activities at the Cotton Trade Association? Why or why not?

3. How do you feel about trading college financial aid for Nakamura's son for Nakamura's agreement not to promote changes at the Cotton Trade Association? Why?

SUGGESTED READINGS

Behof, Kathleen. "The Right Way to Snoop on the Competition." *Sales and Marketing Management* 136 (May 1986), pp. 46–48. Guidelines on how to acquire competitive information legally and ethically.

Caywood, Clarke L., and Gene R. Laczniak. "Ethics and Personal Selling: Death of a Salesman as an Ethical Primer." *Journal of Personal Selling and Sales Management,* August 1986, pp. 815–27. Guidelines for, and discussion of, ethical issues and problems in personal selling.

Farmer, Richard N. "Would You Want Your Granddaughter to Marry a Taiwanese Marketing Man?" *Journal of Marketing* 51 (October 1987), pp. 111–16. Reexploration of marketing ethics in contemporary times, with an emphasis on Taiwan as a newly industrialized country.

Felch, Robert I. "Standards of Conduct: The Key to Supplier Relations." *Journal of Purchasing and Materials Management* 21 (Fall 1985), pp. 16–18. Discussion of unethical conduct in negotiations and other purchasing activities.

Halcomb, Ruth. "Incentives and Ethics." *Incentive Marketing* 160 (October 1986), pp. 36–39, 67. Trends in salespeople's abuse of incentives.

Hoffman, Carl C., and Kathleen P. Hoffman. "Does Comparable Worth Obscure the Real Issues?" *Personnel Journal* 66 (January 1987), pp. 83–95. A survey of the perceptions of wage differentials and sex roles among dual career couples.

Kirkpatrick, Jerry. "A Philosophic Defense of Advertising." *Journal of Advertising* 15 (no. 2, 1986), pp. 42–48, 64. A theoretical discussion of social issues and the moral basis of capitalism and egoism.

Lantos, Geoffrey P. "An Ethical Base for Marketing Decision-Making." *Journal of Business and Industrial Marketing* 2 (Spring 1987), pp. 11–16. Discussion of the use of ethics in marketing decision making, with particular emphasis on the roots of ethical philosophies.

Laroche, Michael; K. L. McGown; and Joyce Rainville. "How Ethical are Professional Marketing Researchers?" *Business Forum* 11 (Winter 1986), pp. 21–25. Canadian survey of researchers' attitudes and behavior and of common industry practices.

Murray, Keith B., and John R. Montahari. "Strategic Management of the Socially Responsible Firm: Integrating Management and Marketing Theory." *Academy of Management Review* 11 (October 1986), pp. 815–27. Normative model of corporate social responsibility, and guidelines for moral expectations of target publics.

Painter, Tony. "Sales Promotion: Deciphering the Codes." *Marketing* (UK), 24 (February 13, 1986), pp. 43–45. Self-regulation codes for advertising and sales promotion in the United Kingdom.

Raffield, Barney T., III. "Student Evaluations of the Ethics of Marketing Practices: A Replication with a New Generation and Further Implications for the Role of Marketing Education." In *Marketing in a Dynamic Environment,* ed. Michael H. Morris and Eugene E. Teeple, The Atlantic Marketing Association 2 (October 1986), pp. 290–98. Comparison of 1960s and 1970s students with 1980s students in regard to their perceptions of the ethics of common marketing practices.

Robin, Donald P., and R. Eric Reidenbach. "Social Responsibility, Ethics, and Marketing Strategy: Closing the Gap Between Concept and Application. *Journal of Marketing* 5 (January 1987), pp. 44–58. A study of ethical values and objectives in organizational behavior, corporate culture, and market planning.

Springer, Robert F., and H. E. French, III. "Determining Fraud: The Role of Resale Price Maintenance." *Journal of Business* 59 (July 1986), pp. 443–59. A study of recent antitrust cases, with a discussion of the disadvantages of free pricing and misleading markups.

Trevisan, Richard E. "Developing a Statement of Ethics: A Case Study." *Journal of Purchasing and Materials Management* 22 (Fall 1986), pp. 8–14. A study of ethics in purchasing policies and practices, and in vendor relations.

APPENDIX ———————————————————————————————————

APPENDIX 15A *Future Trends in Business to Business Marketing*

The decade of the 1990s promises to be a significant one for business to business marketers as they try to anticipate trends, deal with technological breakthroughs, and plan long-term strategies. The decade ahead promises continued advances in technological capabilities, expanding worldwide markets, greater deregulation of industry, along with many other challenges and opportunities. The firm which does not anticipate and plan for anticipated change will probably fall into Levitt's marketing myopia trap and lose ground to more astute marketers.[30] According to a 1985 survey of chief executive officers and other top managers, 64 percent believe that marketing is now the most important functional area for their companies.[31] Obviously top management will be looking toward the marketing group for direction as we proceed through this decade.

What will the practice of business to business marketing be like in the mid-1990s? A careful assessment of some of the factors which will affect future marketing performance should be helpful in trying to answer this question, since it is these factors that will, to a large extent at least, influence and guide the firm as it moves through this decade.

Technology

Major changes are occurring in the energy, materials, transportation, information, and genetic (bioengineering) fields. Industries which are not strong on the technology dimension will be particularly vulnerable to competition, both from new industries and from foreign competitors that have made the necessary investment. Most major steel firms still use the blast furnace technology developed in the 1800s. Foreign steel firms and domestic companies that invested in modern manufacturing technology have been highly successful in the past decade.[32] Those which did not invest in such technology will continue to fall behind and become less competitive. A major implication of the so-called **knowledge explosion** will be the introduction of new types of products and services. A majority of American manufacturing facilities will move to significantly greater automation through computerized machine tools, robotic systems, and computer-aided design and manufacturing (CAD/CAM). Because of the anticipated increased use of **CAD/CAM**, manufacturing firms will be able to modify and design products more quickly. Also, because of the growth projected in the

---

[30]Theodore Levitt, "Marketing Myopia," *Harvard Business Review* 53 (September-October 1975), pp. 26–44.

[31]Coopers and Lybrand, "Strategic Marketing Top Priority of Chief Execs," *Marketing News,* January 31, 1986, pp. 1, 17.

[32]Donald R. Lehmann and Russell S. Winer, *Analysis for Marketing Planning* (Plano, Tex.: Business Publications, 1988), p. 50.

area of information and computer-based technology, firms selling computer hardware and software will witness a major growth opportunity. American success in high-tech marketing is too essential to the nation's future to give it the marketing-as-usual treatment. Who marvels now over the automobile or the light bulb? Likewise, future generations will not be impressed with today's technological breakthroughs.

Competition

The last decade has been perhaps the most turbulent period ever faced by marketing managers because of increased foreign competition, dramatic changes in technology, rates of innovation, and large shifts in interest rates and inflation. A by-product of the mounting international competition which American companies will continue to face here and abroad has been, and in all probability will continue to be, the recent trend toward the formation of **research consortia.** Encouraged by relaxed antitrust restrictions and favorable actions by Congress, companies have been banding together to form research and development organizations which, we hope, will speed the development and use of technologies so necessary to making American industry more competitive in the future. An example of one of these research and development consortia is Microelectronics and Computer Technology Corporation, based in Austin, Texas. Since opening in 1983, membership has grown from 12 to 21 firms, including such firms as Honeywell, Control Data, RCA, NCR, Boeing, National Semiconductor, and Eastman Kodak. In 1988 MCC spent $65 million pioneering new technologies in such areas as advanced computer design and semiconductor packaging.[33] The hoped for result of these efforts will be that business firms will better understand their competitors' possible future strategies, thus giving them an advantage over those which tend to be inner-oriented. There seems to be no doubt that marketing executives generally agree that competition, both foreign and domestic, will intensify, and that firms will be spending more of each sales dollar on marketing because of this increased competition.

Finally, there has been a trend toward larger firms, a trend that should continue as we move through the 1990s. By 1995 it is expected that 90 percent of all United States communications facilities will be owned by 15 firms.[34] If small firms are to compete successfully, personal service, better segmentation, and flexibility will, out of necessity, be major differential advantages. Large firms will also continue to diversify since they can develop and apply expensive new technology more easily. Again, smaller firms will be forced to find their niche.

---

[33]"Additional Perspectives: Can Consortia Keep Us Competitive?" An interview with MCC's Bobby Inman, reprinted from *World,* March-April 1986, pp. 40–42, and presented in William L. Shanklin and John K. Ryans, Jr., *Essentials of Marketing High Technology* (Lexington, Mass.: Lexington Books, 1987), pp. 70–74.

[34]"The Revival of Productivity," *Business Week,* February 13, 1984, pp. 92–100.

Government

Domestic political trends foreshadow what the economic environment will be like for business, and also indicate what legal/regulatory approach government will most likely take toward the private sector. One of the most relevant government actions facing marketers in the years ahead is continued deregulation of the marketplace. Banks are almost fully deregulated, and the Federal Communications Commission is deregulating FM radio stations. The success of deregulation could spur the federal government to sell such assets as the Tennessee Valley Authority to private industry. Deregulation might force greater price competition, putting the burden of success or failure on the marketing manager, rather than on government supports and restraints.[35]

Global Events

As the 1990s unfold, business marketers will be exposed to exciting opportunities and risks, as trade barriers fall while worldwide per capita income increases, heightened literacy is experienced, and standardization in measures make overseas investment even more attractive than it is now. Political disruptions, nationalism, improved capabilities of foreign companies, and countries' interest in self-sufficiency, all pose both risk and potential opportunity for firms contemplating entering and/or increasing international involvement.

Telemarketing

The use of telephone selling will continue to expand as marketers continue to discover that it is a productive, yet low-cost method of selling. According to the Direct Marketing Association, more money is spent annually in the United States on telemarketing than on direct mail. In addition to its use as a selling tool, the use of the telephone in marketing will continue to expand by handling reorders, following up of customer orders, and providing customer services. Products which will continue to be important to a telemarketing effort will be standardized, relatively low-priced business products, such as small tools, wire, cable, nuts and bolts, screws, and other basic (MRO) supplies. Telemarketing designed to sell products almost always operates in a straight rebuy situation. This is not likely to change. In some companies telemarketing will make the order-taking sales representative virtually obsolete. For example, American Hospital Supply, through computer usage, can determine product availability, shipping dates, and even place an order. Ford, Chrysler, and GM are jointly developing a system in which a manufacturer and its larger suppliers can communicate electronically, eliminating the personal sales call and reducing paperwork.

---

[35]See Jeanne Saddler, "In Rush to Deregulate, FCC Outpaces Others, Pleases the Industry," *The Wall Street Journal*, December 7, 1983, pp. 1, 21. Also see James Cook, "Profits over Principle," *Forbes*, March 25, 1985, pp. 148–54.

Future telemarketing advances are expected to increase the operating efficiency and time responsiveness of participating industries.

Materials Management

New techniques such as just-in-time inventory (JIT), materials requirements planning (MRP), optimal production technology (OPT), and flexible manufacturing systems (FMS), will greatly impact business strategies as we move through the decade of the 1990s toward the 21st century. Efficiency and competitive advantage will present the marketer with both challenges and opportunities.

Few would doubt that domestic manufacturing processes and materials management techniques have changed dramatically during the 1980s and will continue to do so during the 1990s. Computer technology has enabled manufacturers to operate their production lines and corresponding purchase operations more efficiently and effectively. Marketers may well find that the utilization of such techniques by customer organizations necessitates fundamental changes in the way in which they do business.[36] When marketing to firms using the production operations techniques listed above, the selling firm that is able to guarantee delivery in direct response to production requirements, or who can work with an on-line inventory ordering system, will have a strategic competitive advantage.

Pricing will also be a strategic option of the marketing mix in the struggle for survival as we approach the year 2000. A recent study clearly shows that profitability and maximization of profit have surpassed market share and growth as major pricing objectives and tactics.[37]

Continued Development of the Buyer-Seller Relationship

In the future marketers can look forward to increased sophistication on the part of the buyer and other members of the organizational buying center. Personal relationships have played an important part in business relations in the past, and this trend will continue as the expertise of both buyers and sellers will rise to new levels in the immediate years ahead. More firms will hire engineers for the buying assignment so that they will be able to perform technical buying and analytical work on a comparable plane with the seller. Most of the routine clerical tasks of the past are in management information form, which enables the buyer to devote more time and effort working with the seller on value analysis projects, make-or-buy decisions, and the like. In brief, it is safe to assume that both buyer and seller will find it to their mutual benefit to expand the base upon which their business relationship is built. Formulation of pricing strategies should

---

[36]For an expanded discussion of these potential changes, see Michael H. Morris and Jere L. Dailey, "Implications of Trends in Materials Management for the Industrial Marketer," *AMA Educators Proceedings*, 1986, pp. 212–17.

[37]For an expanded discussion of future strategic pricing activity, see Barbara J. Coe, "Shifts in Industrial Pricing Objectives," *AMA Educators Proceedings*, 1986, pp. 9–12.

be a fundamental goal of business firms looking to increase effectiveness and profitability during the 1990s and beyond.

Promotion, distribution, customer targeting, and segmentation strategy must also be studied as changes in the field are dramatically affecting strategies and operational decisions within these areas. The advent of the computer-integrated database, relationship marketing, the "total quality" philosophy, and electronic data interchange will allow both buyers and sellers to operate more as a team. All of the elements of the marketing mix will be affected.

Cases for Part Six

CASE 1: Rogers, Nagel, Langhart (RNL PC), Architects and Planners

It was August 1984. John B. Rogers, one of the founders and a principal stockholder in RNL, had just completed the University of Colorado's Executive MBA program. Throughout the program John had tried to relate the concepts and principles covered in his courses to the problems of managing a large architectural practice. In particular, he was concerned about the marketing efforts of his firm. As he put it, "Marketing is still a new, and sometimes distasteful, word to most architects. Nevertheless, the firms that survive and prosper in the future are going to be those which learn how to market as effectively as they design. At RNL we are still struggling with what it means to be a marketing organization, but we feel it's a critical question that must be answered if we're going to meet our projections of roughly doubling by 1989, and we're giving it lots of attention."

■ RNL

In 1984, with sales (design fees) of approximately $3,300,000, RNL was one of the largest local architectural firms in Denver and the Rocky Mountain region. The firm evolved from the individual practices of John B. Rogers, Jerome K. Nagel, and Victor D. Langhart. All started their architectural careers in Denver in the 1950s. The partnership of Rogers, Nagel, Langhart was formed from the three individual proprietorships in 1966, and became a professional corporation in 1970.

In 1984 the firm provided professional design services to commercial, corporate, and governmental clients, not only in Denver but throughout Colorado and, increasingly, throughout the western United States. In addition to basic architectural design services, three subsidiaries had recently been formed:

This case was prepared by H. Michael Hayes, Professor of Marketing and Strategic Management, University of Colorado at Denver, as the basis for class discussion rather than to illustrate either effective or ineffective handling of an administrative situation. Copyright © 1985 by H. Michael Hayes.

Interplan, which provides pre-architectural services, programming, planning, budgeting, scheduling, and cost projections, utilized in corporate budgeting and governmental bond issues.

Denver Enterprises, formed to hold equity interests in selected projects designed by RNL and to take risk by furnishing design services early in a project and by participating in the capital requirements of a project.

Space Management Systems, Inc. (SMS), which provides larger corporations with the necessary services (heavily computer system supported) to facilitate control of their facilities with respect to space, furnishings, equipment, and the cost of change.

In 1984, the firm had 72 employees. John Rogers served as chairman, and Vic Langhart served as president. Nagel had retired in 1976. (See Exhibit 1 for an organization chart.) Development of broad-based management had been a priority since 1975. The firm had seven vice presidents. Two of these vice presidents, Phil Goedert and Rich von Luhrte, served on the Board of Directors, together with Rogers and Langhart.

Growth was financed through retained earnings. In addition, a plan to provide for more employee ownership, principally through profit sharing (ESOP in 1984), was initiated in 1973. Rogers and Langhart held 56 percent of RNL stock; a total of 66 percent was held by the four board members. The Colorado National Bank Profit Sharing Trust held 12 percent in its name. The remaining 22 percent was controlled by 23 other employees, either personally or through their individual profit sharing accounts. It was a goal of the firm to eventually vest stock ownership throughout the firm, in the interest of longevity and continuity.

The firm's principal assets were its human resources. Rogers and Langhart, however, had significant ownership in a limited partnership, which owned a 20,000-square-foot building in a prestigious location in downtown Denver. In 1984, RNL occupied 15,000 square feet. Use of the remaining 5,000 square feet could accommodate up to 30 percent growth in personnel. Through utilization of automation and computers, RNL felt it could double its 1984 volume of work without acquiring additional space.

■ ARCHITECTURAL SERVICES

Architecture: the profession of designing buildings, open areas, communities, and other artificial constructions and environments, usually with some regard to aesthetic effect. The professional services of an architect often include design or selection of furnishings and decorations, supervision of construction work, and the examination, restoration, or remodeling of existing buildings.

Random House Dictionary

Demand for architectural services is closely tied to population growth and to the level of construction activity. The population in the Denver metropolitan area grew from 929,000 in 1960 to 1,620,000 in 1980, and it is estimated to grow to 1,958,000 by 1990. Denver's annual population change of 3.4 percent in the decade 1970–80 ranked 10th for major American cities (Dallas and Phoenix ranked 1 and 2). The projected population growth for

■ **EXHIBIT 1**   Corporate Organization

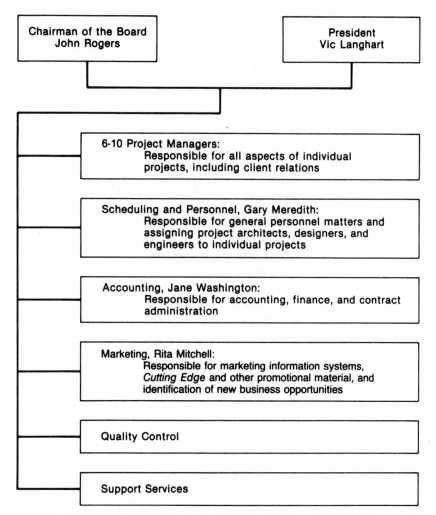

| Chairman of the Board John Rogers | | President Vic Langhart |

6-10 Project Managers:
    Responsible for all aspects of individual projects, including client relations

Scheduling and Personnel, Gary Meredith:
    Responsible for general personnel matters and assigning project architects, designers, and engineers to individual projects

Accounting, Jane Washington:
    Responsible for accounting, finance, and contract administration

Marketing, Rita Mitchell:
    Responsible for marketing information systems, *Cutting Edge* and other promotional material, and identification of new business opportunities

Quality Control

Support Services

Note: RNL does not have a formal organization chart, as such. This exhibit was developed by the case writer to portray the general nature of work assignments and reporting relationships in the firm. As a general rule, project managers report to either John Rogers or Vic Langhart. Most administrative staff functions report to Vic Langhart. At the operational level, Interplan and SMS projects are handled similarly to RNL projects.

the Denver metropolitan area from 1978 to 1983 ranked third in the nation, and Colorado was predicted to be one of the 10 fastest-growing states during the 1980s.

Commercial construction permits grew from 340 in 1970, with an estimated value of $70,818,000, to 1,235 in 1980, with an estimated value of $400,294,000. This growth was not steady, however. Year-to-year changes in dollar value of commercial construction varied from 0.2 percent to 91.6 percent, and the number of permits dropped from a high of 2,245 in 1978 to 1,235 in 1980. Similar patterns of growth and variation characterized industrial construction.

Translating construction growth into estimates of demand for architectural services is difficult. One rule of thumb holds that each additional person added to the population base requires 1,000 square feet of homes, schools, churches, offices, hospitals, manufacturing facilities, retail and shopping facilities, and transportation facilities. In the Denver metro area alone, this could mean 338 million square feet. At $50 average per square foot, total construction expenditure over the decade could reach $16.9 billion, involving as much as $845 million in design fees during the 1980s.

The past and projected growth in demand for architectural services was accompanied by a significant growth in the number of architects in Colorado. From 1979 to 1982, the number of state registrations of individual architects grew from 1,400 to 3,381, an increase of 141.5 percent. Over 100 architectural firms competed actively in the Denver market. (Over 500 architects are listed in the Yellow Pages of the Denver metro area phone directory.) In recent years, a number of national firms (e.g., Skidmore, Owens and Merrill) opened offices in Denver. Other major firms came to Colorado to do one job and then returned to their home offices (e.g., Yamasaki for the Colorado National Bank Office Tower, TAC for Mansville World Headquarters). Of the 26 major firms working on 38 selected jobs in Denver in 1983, 16, or 61.5 percent, were Denver based. Of the other 10, which have headquarters offices elsewhere, all but 2 had offices in Denver.

Major categories of customers for architectural services include:

Industrial.
Commercial.
  Owner.
  Developer.
Government.
  Federal.
  State.
  Municipal.
Residential (note: RNL did not compete in this market).

Within these categories, however, not all architectural work is available to independent firms, and not all architectural work on a project is awarded to one architect. A recent Denver survey, for example, indicated that of 49 commercial jobs under construction with a known architect, 11 were handled by an "inside" architect. Of the remaining 38 jobs, 20 included shell and space design whereas 18 involved space design only. In the 18 space designs, only 50 percent were actually done by architects.

The rapid growth in the construction market in Denver came to an abrupt halt in February 1982. Triggered by the broad realization that the oil boom was over, or had at least slowed significantly, project after project was put on hold. Construction of office space literally came to a halt. Of particular concern to RNL, which had just completed negotiations for a $1 million contract with Exxon, was the Exxon announcement of the closure of its Colorado Oil Shale activities at Parachute, Colorado.

It was against the backdrop of these changes that RNL felt the pressing need to review its marketing activities.

■ MARKETING OF ARCHITECTURAL SERVICES

The basis of competing for architectural work has changed dramatically over the past several decades. As John Rogers recalled:

> At the beginning of my practice in 1956, you could establish an office, put a sign on your door, print calling cards, and have a "news" announcement with your picture in the *Daily Journal* that you had established a new practice of architecture. Beyond that, it was appropriate to suggest to friends and acquaintances that I was in business now and I hoped that they might recommend me to someone they knew. The Code of Ethics of the American Institute of Architects, like many other professions at the time, prohibited any kind of aggressive marketing or sales effort as practiced in recent times.
>
> In fact, after convincing one School Board member (an artist) in Jefferson County that design was important, and then being awarded a commission to design an elementary school, which led to another and another, it was not surprising to read in the *Daily Journal* that the School Board had met the previous evening and had elected me to design a new junior high school, one that I hadn't even known about. I called and said, "Thank you." Marketing expense was zero with the exception of an occasional lunch or courtesy call here and there.
>
> Today, the situation is vastly different. We have to compete for most jobs, against both local firms, and, increasingly, large national firms. Clients are becoming more sophisticated regarding the purchase of architectural services [see Exhibit 2 for a brief description of buyer behavior]. Promotion, of some kind, and concepts such as segmentation have become a way of life.

During the 1960s, development of an architectural practice was a slow process, characterized by heavy reliance on word of mouth regarding professional experience and expertise. Overt communication about an architect's qualifications was limited to brochures. Personal acquaintances played a significant role in the development of new clients. Personal relations between principals and clients were an important part of continuing and new relations. This method of practice development tended to favor local firms, whose reputation could be checked out on a personal basis, and small firms, whose principals could provide personal management and design of client projects.

As Denver grew, the market changed. The advantage of being a successful, local architect and knowing the local business community diminished. Newcomers to Denver tended to rely on relationships with architects in other cities. For local architects there wasn't time to rely on traditional communication networks to establish relationships with these newcomers. The size of projects grew, requiring growth in the size of architectural staffs. Personal attention to every client by principals was no longer possible.

■ **EXHIBIT 2** Buyer Behavior

Purchase of architectural services is both complex and varied. Subject to many qualifications, however, there seems to be a number of steps that most buying situations have in common.

Development of a list of potential architects.

Identification of those architects from whom proposals will be solicited for a specific job (usually called the short list).

Invitations to submit proposals.

Evaluation of proposals and screening of final candidates.

Selection of a finalist, based on proposal evaluation, or invitations to finalists to make oral presentations to an evaluation group.

From a marketing standpoint, the focus of interest is the process of getting on the short list and the process by which the final selection is made.

The Short List

Prospective clients find out about architects in a variety of ways. Those who are frequent users of architectural services will generally keep a file of architects, sometimes classified as to type or practice. Additions to the file can come from mailed brochures, personal calls, advertisements, press releases or, in fact, almost any form of communication. When a specific requirement develops, the file is reviewed for apparent fit. With many variations, a short list is developed and proposals are solicited.

Those who use architects infrequently tend to rely on various business or social networks to develop what is in essence their short list. In either case, a previously used architect is almost always on the short list, provided the past experience was satisfactory.

As the largest single customer for architectural services, agencies of the federal government follow a well-defined series of steps, including advertisement in the *Commerce Business Daily* and mail solicitation of local firms.

The Selection Process

The selection process is significantly influenced by the nature and scope of the work and its importance to the firm. Architect selection on major buildings is usually made at the highest level in the organization: by a principal or the president in a private organization or by various forms of boards in not-for-profit organizations such as churches. In some instances, the principal, president, or board are actively involved in all phases of the process. In others, the management of the process is delegated to others who develop recommendations to the decision makers. On smaller jobs, and those of an ongoing nature (e.g., space management), the decision is usually at lower levels and may involve a plant engineer or facilities manager of some kind.

Regardless of the level at which the selection process is made there seem to be two well-defined patterns to the process. The first, and predominant one, evaluates the firms on the short list, taking into prime consideration nonprice factors such as reputation, performance on previous jobs, and current workload. Based on this evaluation, one firm is selected and a firm agreement is then negotiated as to the scope of the work, the nature of the working relationship, the project team, and specific details as to price. The second, and of limited but growing use, pattern attempts to specify the requirements so completely that a firm price can accompany the proposal. In some instances, the price and the proposal are submitted separately. Evaluation of the proposals includes a dollar differential, and these dollar differentials are applied to the price quotation to determine the low evaluated bidder.

Regardless of the process, there appear to be three main criteria on which firms are evaluated:

■ **EXHIBIT 2** *(concluded)*

1. *The ability of the firm to perform the particular assignment.* For standard work this assessment is relatively easy and relies on the nature of past work, size of the organization, current backlogs, and so forth. For more creative work the assessment becomes more difficult. Much importance is put on past work, but the proposal starts to take on additional importance. Sketches, drawings, and sometimes, extensive models may be requested with the proposal. In some instances, there may actually be a design competition. Much of this evaluation is, perforce, of a subjective nature.

2. *The comfort level with the project team that will be assigned to do the work.* For any but the most standard work there is recognition that there will be constant interaction between representatives of the client's organization and members of the architectural firm. Almost without exception, therefore, some kind of evaluation is made of the project team, or at least its leaders, in terms of the client's comfort level with the personalities involved.

3. *Finally, the matter of cost.* While direct price competition is not a factor in most transactions, the cost of architectural services is always a concern. This has two components. First, there is great concern with the total cost of the project, over which the architect has great control. Second, there is growing concern with the size of the architect's fee, per se.

At least some assessment of the reputation of the architect with respect to controlling project costs is made in determining the short list. Once final selection is made, there is likely to be much discussion and negotiation as to the method of calculating the fee. The traditional method of simply charging a percentage of the construction price seems to be on the wane. Increasingly, clients for architectural services are attempting to establish a fixed fee for a well-defined project. The nature of architectural work, however, is such that changes are a fact of life and that many projects cannot be sufficiently defined in the initial stages to allow precise estimation of the design costs. Some basis for modifying a basic fee must, therefore, be established. Typically this is on some kind of direct cost basis plus an overhead adder. Direct costs for various classes of staff and overhead rates obviously become matters for negotiation. In the case of the federal government, the right is reserved to audit an architect's books to determine the appropriateness of charges for changes.

Concomitantly, there was a growing change in the attitude toward the marketing of professional services. New entrants in the fields of medicine and law, as well as architecture, were becoming impatient with the slowness of traditional methods of practice development. A Supreme Court decision significantly reduced the restrictions that state bar associations could impose on lawyers with respect to their pricing and advertising practices. In a similar vein, the American Institute of Architects signed a consent decree with the Justice Department, which prohibited the organization from publishing fee schedules for architectural services.

Perhaps of most significance for architects, however, was the start of the so-called proposal age. Investigations in Maryland and Kansas, among other states, had revealed improper involvement of architects and engineers with state officials. Financial kickbacks were proven on many state projects. Formal proposals, it was felt, would eliminate or reduce the likelihood of contract awards made on the basis of cronyism or kickbacks. Starting in the government sector, the requirement for proposals spread rapidly to all major clients. In 1984, for example, even a small church could receive as many as 20 detailed proposals on a modestly sized assignment.

■ MARKETING AT RNL

In 1984, RNL was engaged in a number of marketing activities. In addition to proposal preparation, major activities included:

Professional involvement in the business community by principals, which provides contacts with potential clients. This included memberships in a wide variety of organizations such as the Downtown Denver Board, Chamber of Commerce, and Denver Art Museum.

Participation in, and appearances at, conferences, both professional and business oriented.

Daily review of *Commerce Business Daily* (a federal publication of all construction projects) along with other news services that indicate developing projects.

Maintenance of past client contacts. (RNL found this difficult but assigned the activity to its project managers.)

Development of relationships with potential clients, usually by giving a tour through the office plus lunch.

VIP gourmet catered lunches for six invited guests, held once a month in the office. These involved a tour of the office and lively conversation, with some attempt at subsequent follow-up.

Participation in appropriate local, regional, or national exhibits of architectural projects.

Occasional publicity for a project or for a client.

The *Cutting Edge*.[1]

An assortment of brochures and information on finished projects.

Special arrangements with architectural firms in other locations to provide the basis for a variety of desirable joint ventures.

RNL participated in a number of market segments, which it identified as follows, together with its view of the required approach.

Segment	Approach
Government	
City and county governments	Personal selling, political involvement.
School districts	Personal selling (professional educational knowledge required).
State government	Political involvement, written responses to RFPs (requests for proposals, from clients), personal selling.
Federal government	Personal selling, very detailed RFP response, no price competition in the proposal stage.

---

[1] The *Cutting Edge* is an RNL publication designed to inform clients and prospects about new developments in architecture and planning and about significant RNL accomplishments (see Exhibit 3 for an example of an article on a typical issue).

Segment	Approach
Private sector	Personal selling, social acquaintances, referrals, *Cutting Edge*, preliminary studies, price competition.
Semiprivate sector (includes utilities)	Personal selling, *Cutting Edge*, referrals, continuing relationships, some price competition.

■ **EXHIBIT 3**

The Cutting Edge

Planning for Parking

The recent boom in downtown Denver office building has resulted in tremendous increases in population density in Denver's core, bringing corresponding increases in the number of vehicles and their related problems as well.

Auto storage, or parking, is one of the major resulting problems. Most building zoning requires parking sufficient to serve the building's needs. Even building sites not requiring parking are now providing parking space to remain competitive in the marketplace.

RNL's design for this above-grade parking structure at 1700 Grant aided in facilitating lease of the office building.

Parking solutions can range from a simple asphalt lot to a large multi-floor parking structure; the decision is based on many factors including site access, required number of spaces, land costs, budget and user convenience.

For many suburban sites, where land costs are sufficiently low to allow on-grade parking, design entails mainly the problems of circulation and landscaping. Circulation includes issues of easy site access and optimal efficient use of the site. Landscaping, including landforming, can visually screen automobiles and break up ugly seas of asphalt common to poorly designed developments.

At the opposite end of the parking spectrum are downtown sites where high land costs necessitate careful integration of parking into the building concept. This is often accomplished by building parking underground, below the main structure. Parking design, in this case, becomes a problem of integrating the circulation and the structure of the building above. While building underground eliminates the need for

acceptable outer appearance, the costs of excavation, mechanical ventilation, fire sprinklering and waterproofing make this one of the most expensive parking solutions.

Between on-grade parking and the underground structure is the above-grade detached or semi-detached parking structure. This solution is very common in areas of moderate land cost where convenience is the overriding factor.

Site conditions do much to generate the design of an above-grade parking structure, but where possible the following features should ideally be included:

1. Parking is in double loaded corridors, i.e. cars park on both sides of the circulation corridor to provide the most efficient ratio of parking to circulation area;

2. Parking at 90 degrees to circulation corridors rather than at angles, once again the most efficient use of space;

3. Access to different garage levels provided by ramping the parking floors, efficiently combining vertical circulation and parking;

4. A precast prestressed concrete structure (this structure economically provides long spans needed to eliminate columns which would interfere with parking circulation and the fireproof concrete members have a low maintenance surface that can be left exposed).

5. Classification as an "open parking garage" under the building code, meaning that the structure has openings in the walls of the building providing natural ventilation and eliminating the need for expensive mechanical ventilation of exhaust fumes;

6. A building exterior in a precast concrete finish, allowing the designer to combine structure and exterior skin into one low cost element.

RNL recently completed work on the $20,000,000 1700 Grant Office Building for Wickliff & Company. The inclusion of a 415 car parking garage in the 1700 Grant project provided one of the amenities necessary for successful leasing in a very depressed leasing market.

A Publication of RNL/Inception ● by Richard T. Anderson ● Vol. II No. I ● 1576 Sherman Street Denver, Co. 80203 (303) 832-5599

Net fee income and allocation of marketing expenses by major segments is given in the following table. The general feeling at RNL was that there is a lapse of 6 to 18 months between the marketing effort itself and tangible results such as fee income.

	1982		1983		1984 (estimated)		1985 (estimated)	
	Net Fee	Marketing Expense	Net Fee	Marketing Expense	Net Fee	Marketing Expense	Net Fee	Marketing Expense
Government	$ 800	$104	$1,220	$101	$1,012	$150	$1,200	$140
Private	1,376	162	1,261	140	1,200	195	1,616	220
Semiprivate	88	11	118	24	100	25	140	30
Interiors	828	40	670	30	918	100	1,235	110
Urban design	95	20	31	10	170	30	220	40
Total	$3,187	$337	$3,300	$305	$3,400	$500	$4,411	$540

Note: All amounts are in $000s.

Salient aspects of budgeted marketing expense for 1985, by segment, were:

1. *Government.* Heavy emphasis on increased trips to Omaha (a key Corps of Engineers location), Washington, and other out-of-state, as well as in-state, locations plus considerable emphasis on participation in municipal conferences.

2. *Private.* Personal contact at local, state, and regional levels with corporations, banks, developers, and contractors plus local promotion through Chamber of Commerce, clubs, VIP lunches, *Cutting Edge,* promotion materials, and initiation of an advertising and public relations effort.

3. *Semiprivate.* Increased level of personal contact and promotional effort.

4. *Interiors.* Major allocation of salary and expenses of a new full-time marketing person to improve direct sales locally plus other promotional support.

5. *Urban design.* Some early success indicates that land developers and urban renewal authorities are the most likely clients. Planned marketing expense is primarily for personal contact.

Additional marketing efforts being given serious consideration included:

A more structured marketing organization with more specific assignments.

Increased visibility for the firm through general media and trade journals; paid or other (e.g., public relations).

Appearances on special programs and offering special seminars.

Use of more sophisticated selling tools such as video tapes and automated slide presentations.

Increased training in client relations/selling for project managers and other staff.

Hiring a professionally trained marketing manager.

Determining how the national firms market (i.e., copy the competition).

Expansion of debriefing conferences with successful and unsuccessful clients.

Use of a focus group to develop effective sales points for RNL.

Training a marketing MBA in architecture versus training an architect in marketing.

■ RNL CLIENTS

RNL described its clients as:

1. Having a long history of growing expectations with respect to detail, completeness, counseling, and cost control.
2. Mandating the minimization of construction problems, including changes, overruns, and delays.
3. Having an increased concern for peer approval at the completion of a project.
4. Having an increased desire to understand and be a part of the design process.

Extensive interviews of clients by independent market researchers showed very favorable impressions about RNL. Terms used to describe the firm included:

Best and largest architectural service in Denver.

Innovative yet practical.

Designs large projects for "who's who in Denver."

Long-term resident of the business community.

Lots of expertise.

Designs artistic yet functional buildings.

RNL's use of computer-aided design systems was seen as a definite competitive edge. Others mentioned RNL's extra services, such as interior systems, as a plus, although only 35 percent of those interviewed were aware that RNL offered this service. In general, most clients felt that RNL had a competitive edge with regard to timeliness, productivity, and cost consciousness.

Two major ways that new clients heard about RNL were identified. One was the contact RNL made on its own initiative when it heard of a possible project. The other was through personal references. All those interviewed felt advertising played a minor role, and, in fact, several indicated they had questions about an architectural firm that advertises.

Clients who selected RNL identified the following as playing a role in their decision:

Tours of RNL's facilities.

Monthly receipt of *Cutting Edge*.

Low-key selling style.

RNL's ability to focus on their needs.

Thoroughness in researching customer needs and overall proposal preparation and presentation.

RNL's overall reputation in the community.

Belief that RNL would produce good, solid (not flashy) results.

Clients who did not select RNL identified the following reasons for their decision:

RNL had less experience and specialization in their particular industry.

Decided to stay with the architectural firm used previously.

Decided to go with a firm that has more national status.

Other presentations had more "pizzazz."

Overall, clients' perceptions of RNL were very positive. There was less than complete understanding of the scope of RNL services, but its current approach to clients received good marks.

■ MARKETING ISSUES AT RNL: SOME VIEWS OF MIDDLE MANAGEMENT

Richard von Luhrte joined RNL in 1979, following extensive experience with other firms in Chicago and Denver. In 1984, he led the firm's urban design effort on major projects, served as a project manager, and participated actively in marketing. He came to RNL because the firm "fits my image." He preferred larger firms that have extensive and complementary skills. He commented on marketing as follows:

RNL has a lot going for it. We have a higher overhead rate, but with most clients you can sell our competence and turn this into an advantage. I think RNL is perceived as a quality firm, but customers are also concerned that we will gold-plate a job. I'd like to be able to go gold-plate or inexpensive as the circumstances dictate, but it's hard to convince a customer that we can do this.

For many of our clients continuity is important and we need to convey that there will be continuity beyond the founders. RNL has done well as a provider of "all things for all people," and our diversification helps us ride through periods of economic downturn. On the other hand, we lose some jobs because we're not specialized. For instance, we haven't done well in the downtown developer market. We're starting to do more, but if we had targeted the shopping center business we could have had seven or eight jobs by now. One way to operate would be to jump on a trend and ride it until the downturn and then move into something else.

There's always the conflict between specialization and fun. We try to stay diversified, but we ought to be anticipating the next boom. At the same time, there's always the problem of overhead. In this business you can't carry very much, particularly in slow times.

I like the marketing part of the work, but there's a limit on how much of it I can, or should, do. Plus, I think it's important to try to match our people with our clients in terms of age and interests, which means we need to have lots of people involved in the marketing effort.

Oral presentations are an important part of marketing, and we make a lot of them. You have to make them interesting, and there has to be a sense of trying for the "close." On the other hand, I think that the presentation is not what wins the job, although a poor presentation can lose it for you. It's important that the presentation conveys a sense of enthusiasm and that we really want the job.

As comptroller, Jane Washington was involved extensively in the firm's discussions about its marketing efforts. As she described the situation:

There is little question in my mind that the people at the top are committed to developing a marketing orientation at RNL. But our objectives still aren't clear. For instance, we still haven't decided what would be a good mix of architecture, interiors, and planning. Interiors is a stepchild to some. On the other hand, it is a very profitable part of our business. But it's not easy to develop a nice neat set of objectives for a firm like this. Two years ago we had a seminar to develop a mission statement, but we still don't have one. This isn't a criticism. Rather, it's an indication of the difficulty of getting agreement on objectives in a firm of creative professionals.

One problem is that our approach to marketing has been reactive rather than proactive. Our biggest marketing expenditure is proposal preparation, and we have tended to respond to RFPs as they come in, without screening them for fit with targeted segments. From a budget standpoint we have not really allocated marketing dollars to particular people or segments, except in a pro forma kind of way. As a result, no one person is responsible for what is a very large total expenditure.

Another problem is that we don't have precise information about our marketing expenditures or the profitability of individual jobs. It would be impractical to track expenditures on the 500–1,000 proposals we make a year, but we could set up a system that tracks marketing expenditures in, say, 10 segments. This would at least let individuals see what kind of money we're spending for marketing, and where. We also could change from the present system, which basically measures performance in terms of variation from dollar budget, to one that reports on the profitability of individual jobs. I've done some studies on the profitability of our major product lines, but those don't tie to any one individual's performance.

Rita Mitchell, who has an MS in library science and information systems, joined RNL in 1981. Originally her assignment focused on organizing marketing records and various marketing information resources. In her new role as new business development coordinator she had a broader set of responsibilities. According to Rita:

We definitely need some policies about marketing, and these ought to spell out a marketing process. In my present job, I think I can help the board synthesize market information and so help to develop a marketing plan.

I do a lot of market research based on secondary data. For instance, we have access to Dialog and a number of other online databases, using our PC. Based on this research, and our own in-house competence, I think I can do some good market anticipation. The problem is what to do with this kind of information. If we move too fast, based on signals about a new market, there is obviously the risk of being wrong. On the other hand, if we wait until the signals are unmistakably clear, they will be clear to everyone else, and we will lose the opportunity to establish a preeminent position.

With respect to individual RFPs, our decision on which job to quote is still highly subjective. We try to estimate our chances of getting the job, and we talk about its fit with our other work, but we don't have much hard data or policy to guide us. We don't, for instance, have a good sense of other RFPs that are in the pipeline and how the mix of the jobs we're quoting and the resulting work fits with our present work in progress. The Marketing Committee [consisting of John Rogers, Vic Langhart, Phil Goedert, Rich von Luhrte, Dick Shiffer, Rita Mitchell, and, occasionally, Bob Johnson] brings lots of experience and personal knowledge to bear on this, but it's not a precise process.

We have a number of sources of information about new construction projects: the *Commerce Business Daily* [a federal government publication], the *Daily Journal* [which reports on local government construction], the Western Press Clipping Bureau, Colorado trade journals, and so forth. Monitoring these is a major activity, and then we have the problem of deciding which projects fit RNL.

Bob Johnson, a project manager and member of the Marketing Committee, commented:

The way the system works now we have four board members and 12 project managers, most of whom can pursue new business. They bring these opportunities before the Marketing Committee, but it doesn't really have the clout to say no. As a result, people can really go off on their own. I'd like to see the committee flex its muscles a little more on what jobs we go after. But there's a problem with committing to just a few market segments. Right now we're involved in something like 30 segments. If we're wrong on one it's not a big deal. But if we were committed to just a few then a mistake could have really serious consequences.

For many of us, however, the major problem is managing the transfer of ownership and control to a broader set of individuals. Currently the prospective owners don't really have a forum for what they'd like the company to be. My personal preference would be to go after corporate headquarters, high-tech firms, speculative office buildings, and high-quality interiors. But there probably isn't agreement on this.

■ MARKETING ISSUES: THE VIEWS OF THE FOUNDERS

Vic Langhart started his practice of architecture in 1954 and has taught design in the Architecture Department of the University of Colorado. He was instrumental in developing new services at RNL, including Interplan and SMS, Inc., and was heavily involved in training of the next level of management. In 1984, he supervised day-to-day operations and also served as president of Interplan and SMS, Inc. Looking to the future, Vic observed:

Our toughest issue is dealing with the rate of change in the profession today. It's probably fair to say there are too many architects today. But this is a profession of highly idealistic people, many of whom feel their contribution to a better world is more important than dollars of income and so will stay in the field at "starvation wages." We wrestle with the question of "profession or business?" but competition is now a fact of life for us. The oil boom of the 1970s in Denver triggered an inrush of national firms. Many have stayed on, and we now have a situation where one of the largest national firms is competing for a small job in Durango. We're also starting to see more direct price competition. Digital Equipment recently prequalified eight firms, selected five to submit proposals that demonstrated understanding of the assignment, and asked for a separate envelope containing the price.

Our tradition at RNL has been one of quality. I think we're the "Mercedes" of the business, and in the long haul an RNL customer will be better off economically. A lot of things contribute to this—our Interplan concept, for instance—but the key differentiation factor is our on-site-planning approach.

In 1966–68, we were almost 100 percent in education. Then I heard that they were closing some maternity wards, and we decided to diversify. Today we have a good list of products, ranging from commercial buildings to labs and vehicle maintenance facilities. In most areas, the only people who can beat us are the superspecialists, and even then there's a question. Our diversification has kept our minds free to come up with creative approaches. At Beaver Creek, for example, I think we came up with a better approach to condominium design than the specialists. Plus, we can call in special expertise, if it's necessary.

Over the past several years we've had a number of offers to merge into national, or other, firms. We decided, however, to become employee owned. Our basic notion was that RNL should be an organization that provides its employees a long-time career opportunity. This is not easy in an industry that is characterized by high turnover. Less than 10 percent of architectural firms have figured out how to do it. But we're now at 35 percent employee ownership.

I'm personally enthusiastic about Interplan. It has tremendous potential to impact our customers. In Seattle, for instance, a bank came to us for a simple expansion. Our Interplan approach, however, led to a totally different set of concepts.

We've had some discussion about expansion. Colorado Springs is a possibility, for instance. But there would be problems of keeping RNL concepts and our culture. We work hard to develop and disseminate an RNL culture. For example, we have lots of meetings, although John and I sometimes disagree about how much time should be spent in meetings. A third of our business comes from interiors, and there is as much difference between interior designers and architects as there is between architects and mechanical engineers.

In somewhat similar vein, John Rogers commented:

In the 1960s, RNL was primarily in the business of designing schools. We were really experts in that market. But then the boom in school construction came to an end, and we moved into other areas. First into banks and commercial buildings. We got started with Mountain Bell, an important relationship for us that continues today. We did assignments for mining companies and laboratories. In the late 1960s, no one knew how to use computers to manage office space problems, and we moved in that direction, which led to the formation of Interplan. We moved into local and state design work. One of our showcase assignments is the Colorado State Judicial/Heritage Center.

In the 1980s, we started to move into federal and military work, and this now represents a significant portion of our business.

We have done some developer work, but this is a tough market. It has a strong "bottom line orientation," and developers want sharp focus and expertise.

As we grow larger we find it difficult to maintain a close client relationship. The client wants to know who will work on the assignment, but some of our staff members are not good at the people side of the business.

Currently we're still doing lots of "one of a kind" work. Our assignment for the expansion of the *Rocky Mountain News* building, our design of a condominium lodge at Beaver Creek, and our design of a developer building at the Denver Tech Center are all in this category. A common theme, however, is our "on-site" design process. This is a process by which we make sure that the client is involved in the design from the start and that we are really tuned in to his requirements. I see this as one of our real competitive advantages. But I'm still concerned that we may be trying to spread ourselves too thin. Plus, there's no question that there is an increased tendency to specialization: "shopping center architects," for example.

We need to become better marketers, but we have to make sure that we don't lose sight of what has made us the leading architectural firm in Denver: service and client orientation.

PART SEVEN

Comprehensive Cases

Case 1 · Canadair Challenger Jet

Case 2 · The Kingston-Warren Company

Cases for Part Seven

COMPREHENSIVE CASE 1: Canadair Challenger Jet

Mr. James Taylor and Mr. Harry Halton were taking a last-minute look at the marketing strategy developed for Canadair's new Challenger business jet. Mr. Taylor was head of Canadair Inc., the Challenger's marketing arm located in Westport, Connecticut. Mr. Halton, the executive vice president, was the chief engineer, responsible for the design and production of the Challenger at Canadair's Montreal plant. The Challenger was being touted as the world's most advanced business aircraft, incorporating the latest technologies to achieve high speed, longest range, greatest fuel economy, and greatest seating space and comfort. It was early July 1976, and the president of Canadair, Mr. Fred Kearns, wanted senior management's consensus on product design, pricing, advertising, and approach to selling.

The preliminary design of the Challenger was generally complete, but Mr. Halton continued to receive suggestions for additional features from Mr. Taylor and his marketing group, from prospective customers, and from project engineers. Rather than build prototype models by hand, Mr. Halton had decided to begin setting up a full-scale production line. Eventually, three preproduction models of the Challenger would be constructed for testing and demonstration.

Canadair management was considering a number of pricing options. Some executives advocated a very competitive initial price to hasten customer orders, with subsequent price increases. Another group of top executives believed that the Challenger should bear a premium price to reflect its superiority and to recover $140 million in development costs. The advertising agency's proposed copy for the Challenger's print advertisements was feared to be too controversial and the marketing group wondered whether some "softening" of the copy might be advisable. Selling direct to customers, selling direct to customers with a supplementary dealer network, or selling entirely through a dealer network were three possible approaches to sales. Finally, executives recognized that plans

This case was prepared by Mr. Larry Uniac, research assistant, under the direction of Professor Kenneth G. Hardy. Case material of the Western School of Business Administration is prepared as a basis for classroom discussion. Copyright © 1979, The University of Western Ontario.

for service facilities required to maintain the Challenger "in the field," which could mean anywhere in the world, were very sketchy.

Canadair executives wanted 50 orders by September 30, 1976, before committing fully to the Challenger program. However, the major marketing decisions had to be finalized before the sales blitz could begin. If sales by September 30 fell in the range of 30 to 40 units, management might grant an extension on the deadline. However, sales of fewer than 30 units probably would result in scrapping the Challenger program.

■ GENERAL BACKGROUND

Canadair's objective was to sell 410 units, or 40 percent of the market for large business jets over the period from 1978 to 1988. Business jets were changing the way companies conducted business, as executives learned the competitive advantages that a corporate aircraft could provide. What critics had once scorned as a "toy of executive privilege" was increasingly seen as a desirable and advantageous management tool. "Probably more than ever, most businessmen agree with Arco's vice chairman Louis F. Davis, that 'there's nothing like face-to-face communications to keep a business running.' "[1] One observer commented:

> As big as corporate flying has become in recent years, there are strong signs that its role will continue to expand rapidly in years to come. Of the largest 1,000 U.S. companies, only 502 operate their own airplanes versus 416 five years ago. That leaves a sizable virgin market, which sales people from a dozen U.S. and foreign aircraft builders are tripping over each other to develop.[2]

Competitors were skeptical that the Challenger could meet its promised specifications. The unloaded Challenger would weigh only 15,085 pounds compared to 30,719 for the Grumman Gulfstream II (GII), a head-on competitor that was the biggest corporate jet flying, yet still provide a wider cabin. The Challenger would be propelled by less powerful engines than the GII, yet theoretically would fly faster and consume only 50 percent as much fuel. "The Canadians seem to know something the rest of the industry doesn't," commented Ivan E. Speer, group vice president of Aerospace at Garret Corp., the major builder of corporate jet engines.[3] The Challenger was to be powered by Avco-Lycoming engines, a competitor to the Garret Corp.

More simply, it was not known how well the Challenger would fly. Although Canadair had made jets for the military, the company had never built a business jet. Beyond these concerns, production problems could

---

[1]"Corporate Flying: Changing the Way Companies Do Business," *Business Week,* February 6, 1978, p. 64.

[2]Ibid., p. 62

[3]Ibid., p. 64.

arise with a project of this nature and magnitude, but little could be done to anticipate how and when these problems would occur.

■ COMPANY BACKGROUND

Originating as the aircraft division of Canadian Vickers Ltd. in the 1920s, Canadair assumed its own identity in 1944 following a reorganization brought about by the Canadian government. In 1947, Canadair was acquired by Electric Boat Company of Groton, Connecticut, forming the basis for an organization that became General Dynamics Corp. in 1952. Canadair reverted to Canadian government ownership in January 1976 under a government plan for restructuring the Canadian aerospace industry. In 1975, *Interavia* magazine described Canadair as follows: "Once a flourishing company, Canadair is the 'sick man' of the national aerospace industry; employment has steadily dropped since 1970, when 8,400 were on the books, and could fall below 1,000 sometime this year unless new work is found rapidly."[4]

However, uneven employment was characteristic of the entire aircraft industry. In terms of deliveries, quality, innovation, and steady profits, Canadair had an enviable record. Located at Cartierville Airport in St. Laurent, Quebec, approximately 10 miles from the center of Montreal, the plant was one of the largest and most versatile aerospace-manufacturing facilities in Canada. Canadair's activities included the design and development of new aircraft, and contracting for major modifications to existing types of aircraft. Subcontracts for the manufactured component parts and subassemblies for the military and commercial aircraft in production such as the Boeing 747 accounted for a substantial volume of the company's business (Table 1). Exhibit 1 supplies data on earnings for Canadair from 1973 to 1976. Canadair's President reflected on the activities of the company:

> We at Canadair are not really known as a major influence in the international aerospace industry. For various reasons, we have been a major subcontractor or producer of other people's aircraft over a large span of our existence, and our native designs have not been more than a small portion of our overall effort. You may imagine that the elder statesmen of the aerospace industry smiled indulgently when they heard about this radical new aircraft that Canadair was developing.

■ THE CANADIAN AEROSPACE INDUSTRY[5]

The Canadian aerospace-manufacturing industry had specialized capabilities for the design, research and development, production, marketing, and

---

[4] *Interavia,* February 1975, p. 150.

[5] Source: Chairman D. C. Lowe, *A Report by the Sector Task Force on the Canadian Aerospace Industry,* June 30, 1978.

■ TABLE 1 Canadair's Estimated Sales from 1973 through 1976 by Class of Business

	1976		1975		1974		1973	
	Dollars (000)	Per-cent	Dollars (000)	Per-cent	Dollars (000)	Per-cent	Dollars (000)	Per-cent
Aircraft	20,410	46	15,520	42	38,808	68	22,006	63
Component subcontracts	7,783	17	6,716	18	2,945	5	2,967	9
Surveillance systems	9,367	21	6,958	19	9,620	17	8,542	25
Other	7,034	16	7,938	21	5,744	10	1,113	3
Total	44,954	100%	37,132	100%	57,117	100%	34,628	100%

■ EXHIBIT 1

CANADAIR LIMITED AND SUBSIDIARIES
Consolidated Statement of Income
(in thousands)

	Year Ended December 31			
	1976*	1975	1974	1973
Sales	$ 44,594	$ 37,132	$57,117	$34,628
Cost of sales	41,325	42,421	53,264	31,702
Income (loss) from operations	3,269	(5,289)	3,853	2,926
Other income (expense):				
Interest income	240	260	248	356
Miscellaneous income	9	30	61	71
Interest expense	(2,056)	(3,203)	(1,755)	(1,001)
	(1,807)	(2,913)	(1,446)	(574)
Income (loss) from operations before provision for income taxes, loss on discontinued operations of a subsidiary, extraordinary items and share of earnings of Asbestos Corporation Limited	1,462	(8,202)	2,407	2,352
Provisions for federal and provincial income taxes	642	6	1,122	1,056
Income (loss) before loss on discontinued operations of a subsidiary, extraordinary items and share of earnings of Asbestos Corporation Limited	820	(8,208)	1,285	1,296
Loss on discontinued operations of a subsidiary	(385)	(165)	(260)	(280)
Income (loss) before extraordinary items and share of earnings of Asbestos Corporation Limited	435	(8,373)	1,025	1,016
Extraordinary items:				
Income tax reduction	638	—	1,100	1,041
Gain on exchange	—	1,957	—	—
Provision for disposal of a subsidiary company's assets	(988)	—	—	—
Total extraordinary items	(350)	1,957	1,100	1,041
Income (loss) before share of earnings of Asbestos Corporation Limited	85	(6,416)	2,125	2,057
Share of earnings of Asbestos Corporation Limited	—	7,368	6,063	520
Net income	$ 85	$ 952	$ 8,188	$ 2,577

■ **EXHIBIT 1**   (concluded)

Consolidated Statement of Earned Surplus
  (deficit—in thousands)

	Year Ended December 31			
	1976*	1975	1974	1973
Balance at beginning of year	$(14,059)	$ 49,683	$41,495	$38,918
Net income	85	952	8,188	2,577
	(13,974)	50,635	49,683	41,495
Dividend paid	—	25,000	—	—
Unrecovered portion of investment in Asbestos Corporation Limited, representing the excess of carrying value over the amount paid by General Dynamics Corporation	—	39,694	—	—
	—	64,694	—	—
Balance at end of year	$(13,974)	$(14,059)	$49,683	$41,495

* Estimated results for 1976.

in-plant repair and overhaul of aircraft aero-engines, aircraft and engine subsystems and components, space-related equipment and air and ground-based avionic systems and components.

Approximately 100 companies were engaged in significant manufacturing work, but 40 companies accounted for 90 percent of the industry's sales in 1975. Three companies (including Canadair) were fully integrated, having the capability to design, develop, manufacture, and market complete aircraft or aero-engines. With aggregate sales of $785 million in 1976, the Canadian aerospace industry shared fifth place in western world sales with Japan, after the United States, France, the United Kingdom, and the Federal Republic of Germany.

It was economically impractical for Canadian industry to manufacture all the diverse aerospace products demanded on the Canadian market. Through selective specialization, the Canadian industry had developed product lines in areas related to Canadian capabilities and export-market penetration. In 1975, 80 percent of the industry's sales were in export markets, an achievement attained under strong competitive conditions.

The Canadian industry was fully exposed to the competitive forces of the international aerospace market. In some cases, its hourly labour rates were higher than those in the United States. The industry's export-market penetration was vulnerable to the economic forces associated with competitors' industrial-productivity improvements. The industry, like most world aerospace industries, was manufacturing high-cost and high-risk products. There were many hazards: a relatively long-term payback cycle, sporadic government purchasing decisions, tariff and nontariff barriers, monetary inflation, and rapid technological obsolescence.

Aerospace industries throughout the world generally received government support, particularly in the areas of research, development, and equipment modernization. For example, the U.S. aircraft industry benefited from the annual $10 billion Department of Defense budget and the annual $6 billion NASA budget. By contrast, during the nine years ended March 31, 1976, the Government of Canada had provided $349 million to the Canadian aerospace industry through several programs. In short, the Canadian aircraft industry was not subsidized.

There were indications in 1976 that the Canadian aerospace industry was entering a growth cycle. The trend lines of Canadian sales and exports encouraged an optimistic outlook.

■ THE BUSINESS JET INDUSTRY

Continued expansion of business-aircraft activities was expected to continue into the 1980s in what business aviation officials described as the "best growth climate in years."[6] Booming sales of business aircraft in Europe, the Middle East, and Africa were giving rise to a belief that the business aircraft was becoming a true business tool in these regions, much as it had in the United States about a decade earlier.

All forecasts pointed to an enormous upsurge in the sale of business jet aircraft. Exhibit 2 graphs the trends in the U.S. business jet industry from 1956 to an estimate of 1976 and beyond. Exhibit 3 illustrates the trends in

■ **EXHIBIT 2**   Growth Trends in U.S. Business Flying *(semilog paper)*

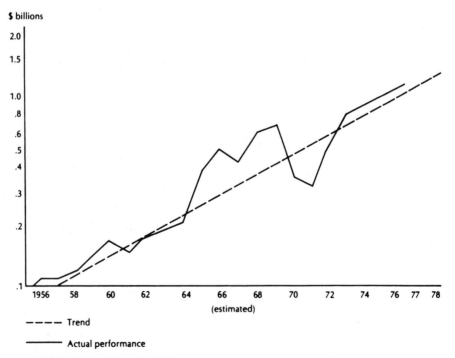

SOURCE: *Aviation Week and Space Technology.*

---

[6] *Aviation Week and Space Technology,* September 11, 1978, pp. 46–56.

■ **EXHIBIT 3** Unit Worldwide Corporate Jet Deliveries *(all models)*

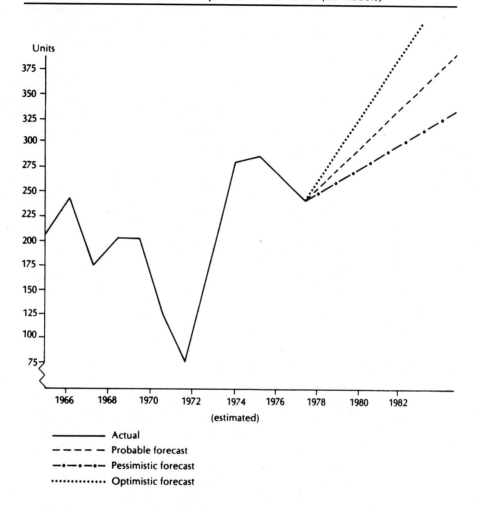

world deliveries of all corporate aircraft from 1965 to 1975, with delivery estimates through 1981. Many factors were contributing to increase the desire for private business aircraft:

Commercial airlines were reducing service drastically as they added the "jumbo" jets. In six years, the number of U.S. cities served by commercial airlines dropped from 525 to 395.

Ninety-seven percent of all scheduled air-carrier passengers in the United States flew out of only 150 airports.

Flights were packed with tourists and other occasional travelers. This made it difficult to obtain reservations and impossible to work en route. The amount of executive time spent traveling was increasing and most of this travel time was being wasted.

Corporate planes provided the management of many companies with new flexibility and shortened reaction time in special situations.

Cost savings could be achieved; for example, Xerox flew 15,000 employees per year on a company-owned shuttle plane between its Stamford headquarters and its Rochester (N.Y.) plant, saving $410,000 annually over commercial air fares.

There was growing concern for the security and protection of top executives from the growing incidence of airplane hijackings.

Finally, many organizations were trading up to newer or larger aircraft to replace outdated, older equipment. Essentially, technology permitted such improvements over the aircraft of 10 years earlier (for example in fuel economy) that the buyers could easily justify the update.

To cash in on the business jet bonanza, several manufacturers were planning to introduce new models. The following business jets would be on the market in some fashion by 1979:

Canadair's Challenger (large category).

Dassault-Breguet Falcon 50 (medium category).

Grumman Gulfstream III (large category).

Rockwell's Sabreliner 80A (medium category).

Cessna's Citation III (medium category).

Gates Learjet's 54/55/56 series (medium category).

■ CORPORATE AIRCRAFT CATEGORIES

More than 100 different aircraft models were offered to the business flyer.[7] Hence the selection of the right aircraft for an individual company was a complex task. John Pope, Secretary of the National Business Aircraft Association, emphasized this advice: "Any aircraft selected involves a compromise, because the worst error you can make is buying more aircraft than you need and underutilizing it."[8] The general categories in order of performance and price were: single-engine piston, multiengine piston, turboprop, turbojet, and turbofan.

> Single-engine piston aircraft, while not usually considered "corporate," did provide starting points for many smaller companies, as well as individuals who combined business and pleasure flying. . . . Multiengine piston aircraft were the next step up, offering the additional security and performance afforded by a second engine. . . . Piston-engine twins were considered excellent entry-level aircraft for smaller corporations, with a relatively high percentage owner-flown. . . . Turboprop aircraft were referred to by some as "turbojets with propellers attached." . . . Turboprops used significantly less fuel than pure jets but could easily cost more than $1 million.[9]

Turbojet and turbofan aircraft flew faster and, for the most part, farther than the other aircraft. A turbojet was not usually a first-time purchase for

---

[7]"Corporate Aviation: The Competitive Edge," *Dun's Review,* January 1979, p. 89.
[8]Ibid.
[9]Ibid.

a smaller company. Prices in this category ranged from $1 million to $7.5 million. The turbofans offered greater low-altitude efficiency than the turbojets. The Challenger, JetStar II, Falcon 50, GII, and GIII were turbofans.

The following rules of thumb were often used to determine the suitability of different planes for different flying needs:

Average Distance per Flight	Appropriate Type of Aircraft for This Distance
150– 200 miles	Single-engine piston
200– 500 miles	Multiengine piston and smaller turboprop
500– 750 miles	Turboprops and small turbojets
750–1,000 miles	Small turbojets
1,000–2,000 miles	Medium-size turbojets
2,000–4,000 miles	Large turbofans and large turbojets

■ CORPORATE JET COMPETITION

The Falcon 50, Gulfstream II and III, and JetStar II seemed to compete directly against the Challenger. Exhibit 4 summarizes sales by segment and

■ EXHIBIT 4   Worldwide Corporate Jet Deliveries *(units)*

Model	1965	1966	1967	1968	1969	1970	1971	1972	1973	1974	1975	1976 Prices (000s)
Small jet market												
Citation 1								52	81	85	69	$ 918
Falcon									1	21	26	1,905
Lear 23	80	18	1									—
Lear 24		24	26	28	33	20	10	16	21	22	18	—
Lear 25				18	25	18	10	23	45	40	14	1,315
Lear 35/36										4	47	1,679
Hansa			3	6	14	4	1	1	5			—
Sabre 40	26	31	5	5	1	6						—
Corvette										6	5	—
Westwind #1151/52/54	30	50	25	10	12	5	4	11	12	12	4	—
Total small jets	136	123	60	67	85	53	29	103	165	190	183	
Medium jet market												
Hawker Siddely 125	43	58	20	32	39	32	18	24	24	25	13	2,075
Sabre 60			11	20	14	6	9	4	4	20	9	2,200
Sabre 75								6	1	10	19	2,406
Falcon 20	14	43	63	38	25	18	7	24	46	17	29	3,005
Total medium jets	87	101	94	90	78	56	34	60	75	72	70	
Large jet market												
JetStar	18	22	18	18	11	2	4	10	6	1	0	5,035
Gulfstream			2	35	36	17	14	14	17	18	20	5,500
Total large jets	18	22	20	53	47	19	18	24	23	19	20	
Grand total	211	246	174	210	210	128	77	194	284	290	273	

model from 1965 to 1975. A schematic layout of each competitive plane is shown in Exhibits 5 and 6. Exhibit 7 compares the salient product differences for the Challenger and its competitors.

The new Dassault-Breguet Falcon 50, with its flight testing scheduled for completion by October 1978 and certification expected in December 1978, was slightly ahead of the Challenger program. The Challenger would probably not be certified until August 1979. Flight tests of the Falcon 50 had shown that its performance figures were better than expected in terms of landing strip required and rate of climb. The Falcon 50 was essentially a modification of the medium-sized Falcon 20, which had been introduced 14 years earlier.

The new Falcon 50 would be available for delivery by March 1979 and its performance in terms of projected operating cost per mile and range

■ **EXHIBIT 5** Cabin Floor Outline

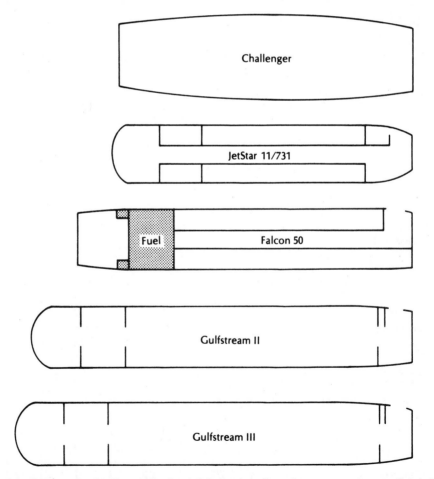

Note: Challenger data based on engineering statistical analysis. For performance guarantees see Technical Specification.

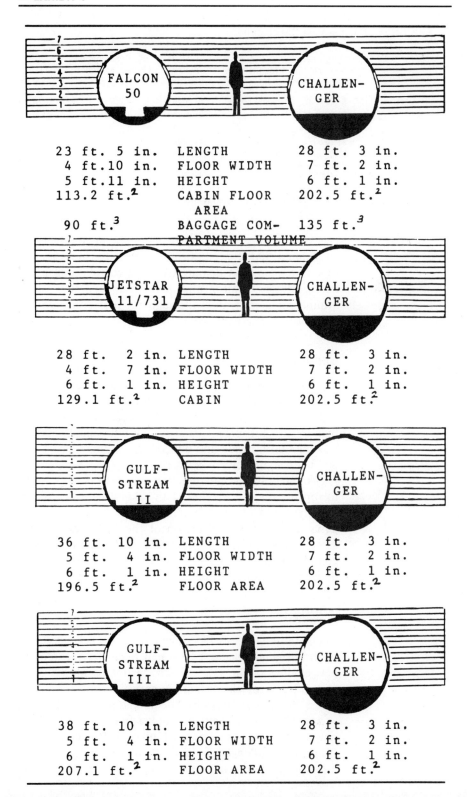

23 ft. 5 in.	LENGTH	28 ft. 3 in.
4 ft.10 in.	FLOOR WIDTH	7 ft. 2 in.
5 ft.11 in.	HEIGHT	6 ft. 1 in.
113.2 ft.^{2}	CABIN FLOOR AREA	202.5 ft.^{2}
90 ft.^{3}	BAGGAGE COMPARTMENT VOLUME	135 ft.^{3}

28 ft. 2 in.	LENGTH	28 ft. 3 in.
4 ft. 7 in.	FLOOR WIDTH	7 ft. 2 in.
6 ft. 1 in.	HEIGHT	6 ft. 1 in.
129.1 ft.^{2}	CABIN	202.5 ft.^{2}

36 ft. 10 in.	LENGTH	28 ft. 3 in.
5 ft. 4 in.	FLOOR WIDTH	7 ft. 2 in.
6 ft. 1 in.	HEIGHT	6 ft. 1 in.
196.5 ft.^{2}	FLOOR AREA	202.5 ft.^{2}

38 ft. 10 in.	LENGTH	28 ft. 3 in.
5 ft. 4 in.	FLOOR WIDTH	7 ft. 2 in.
6 ft. 1 in.	HEIGHT	6 ft. 1 in.
207.1 ft.^{2}	FLOOR AREA	202.5 ft.^{2}

■ **EXHIBIT 7**   Comparative Specifications

	Operating Cost per Nautical Mile	Maximum Range	Cruising Speed	Fuel Consumption 100 NM at Cruise Speed	Noise Decibles*		
					Take-off	Sideline	Approach
Challenger†	$ .93	3,900 nm.	547 mph	4,160 lb.	78	87	90
JetStar II	$1.25	2,800 nm.	538 mph	7,250 lb.	n.a.	n.a.	n.a.
Gulfstream III	$1.16	3,600 nm.	534 mph	6,410 lb.	90	102	98
Gulfstream II	$1.26	3,187 nm.	541 mph	7,723 lb.	90	102	98
Falcon 50	$1.06	3,550 nm.	528 mph	6,200 lb.	87	94	97

*1979 FAA 36 Regulation = Take-off: 89, Sideline: 94, and Approach: 98.
†Initial proposal for first 50 units.
SOURCE: Canadair comparative advertising material (based on statistical analysis).

was second only to the Challenger. The print advertisement for the Falcon 50 claimed that it would be the fastest business jet in the world, although this statement was disputed by the calculations made by Canadair engineers. Messrs. Halton and Taylor believed that the Falcon 50 would be around for some time, although its fuel consumption would be a major competitive disadvantage.

Gulfstream II and III

The Gulfstream II first flew in October 1966 and represented the latest technology at the time of its certification. Its turbojet engines were powerful, but consumed considerably more fuel than used in the more recent high-bypass turbofans used by the Challenger. In addition, engine noise was high both inside and outside the cabin. Since 1966, 173 Gulfstream IIs had been sold around the world.

Grumman had accelerated developmental work on a new Gulfstream III to replace the Gulfstream II in response to new demands on the market and the news of the Challenger. The Gulfstream III would be an aerodynamically modified version of the Gulfstream II, but it would use the same engines. The first prototype of the Gulfstream III was scheduled for completion in August 1979 and the first production unit was scheduled for delivery in March 1980.

JetStar II

The JetStar II, available since January 1976, was a re-engineered version of the original JetStar which had been certificated in 1961. Although the new engines of the JetStar were turbofans, they were medium-bypass fans and not as efficient as high-bypass fans in minimizing fuel consumption. More than 112 JetStars had been sold since 1961.

According to a company spokesman, Lockheed-Georgia anticipated no new changes to its JetStar II in order to meet forthcoming competition from the Challenger, Falcon 50, and Gulfstream III. Lockheed was still attempting to determine its market share in the larger-cabin business fleet,

with the performance and acceptance of the three new aircraft still unknown. JetStar IIs were being built at the rate of one per month and the
earliest promised delivery date was June 1978.[10]

■ THE CHALLENGER PROGRAM

Early in 1976, much of Canadair's subcontract work was nearing completion, and Canadair was not selling enough of its own CL-25 water bombers
to fill the gap. Canadair executives needed an ambitious project if they
were to meet government demands for eventual self-sufficiency. Mr. Halton
commented:

> We knew that we needed to do something in the general-aviation business
> and a market-research study indicated that business aviation would be a
> growth market. In November 1975, Fred Kearns talked with Bill Lear
> about his concept of an advanced business aircraft based on two known
> pieces of technology, the supercritical wing used on military aircraft and
> the high-bypass fanjet engine. In January 1976, I met with Bill Lear and
> by March 1976 we were negotiating options on the Lear design. Jim Taylor
> was hired in April 1976 to head up the marketing for the new aircraft and
> by May he had arranged a selling seminar to which he invited 200 chief
> pilots and senior corporate officers to Canadair's plant to unveil the Chal-
> lenger concept.

Bill Lear, who built the first business jet in 1961, had developed the
original concept of the Challenger around an 88-inch diameter fuselage.
Representatives of the business market for the jet responded to the design
encouragingly. However, Canadair decided to change the rear design drastically for a number of reasons, one of them a fuel-tankage problem. Also,
at the original meeting with 200 chief pilots and executive officers, potential customers expressed demands for roominess. Consequently, Canadair
engineers redesigned the jet with a 106-inch fuselage. As it happened, the
extra width made the plane capable of seating four abreast. Lear disasso-
ciated himself from the Challenger program in response to this change and
dubbed the Canadair design "Fat Albert." Canadair executives recognized
the possibility of creating a "stretch" version of the Challenger that perhaps could carry up to 50 passengers.

It was clear at the beginning of 1976 that in order to finance the project,
at least $70 million would have to be raised in addition to the company's
own $70 million. Projects with this degree of leverage were not uncommon
in the aerospace industry and the Canadian government agreed to *guarantee* a $70-million Eurobond for Canadair. A forecast schedule of invest-
ment outlays is shown in Exhibit 8.

The Challenger's most salient product benefits as conceived by Canadair's marketing and engineering staff were:

---

[10]*Aviation Week and Space Technology,* September 11, 1978.

■ **EXHIBIT 8** CL 600 Challenger Pro Forma* Cash Flow Profile as of June 1976 *(in thousands)*

	Sept. 76–Dec. 79 Not Assignable	Dec. 77–Oct. 80 Lot #1 Aircraft 1–50	Apr. 79–Aug. 81 Lot #2 Aircraft 51–100	Feb. 80–Apr. 82 Lot #3 Aircraft 101–150	Oct. 80–Jan. 83 Lot #4 Aircraft 151–200	Jul. 81–Dec. 83 Lot #5 Aircraft 200–250	Total
Labor, overhead cost	$ 86,400	$ 72,460	$ 28,350	$ 26,350	$ 24,980	$ 25,315	$ 264,855
Material, equipment cost	20,925	81,148	94,970	107,450	113,045	126,100	543,638
Other costs (rentals, service)	21,600	17,550	925	713	760	750	42,298
Program support cost	6,075	18,936	10,440	11,100	12,784	14,475	73,810
Marketing		5,030	2,744	2,938	3,390	3,836	17,938
Finance		31,326	10,700				42,026
Total cost	$135,000	$226,450	$149,129	$148,551	$154,959	$170,476	$ 984,565
Revenue		$205,000	$225,500	$238,500	$253,000	$268,000	$1,190,000
Cumulative	$(135,000)	$(156,450)	$(80,079)	$9,870	$107,911	$205,435	$ 205,435
Date #1 aircraft ordered		Jul. 76					
Anticipated date last aircraft ordered		Nov. 76	Apr. 78	Oct. 79	Apr. 81	Oct. 82	
Delivery date #1 aircraft		Nov. 79					
Anticipated date last aircraft delivered		Sept. 80	Aug. 81	June 82	May 83	Apr. 84	
Assumed average price per aircraft		$4,100	$4,510	$4,770	$5,060	$5,360	$4,750

*This data is presented for case study purposes only and does not purport to represent actual estimating data.

Large wide-body cabin: excellent size for executive, air taxi, third-level
carriers, and cargo.

Fuel economy: lowest operating cost per nautical mile compared with
direct competition.

Long range: long single-stage flight or numerous short-stage flights
without refueling.

Competitive speeds: very competitive, high cruise speed in long-range
configuration.

Low noise levels: most closely meets FAA standards for 1979.

Market Forecast

Canadair was already building a test model for fatigue tests, a test model
for static tests, and three preproduction models for the eventual production
plan which would be as follows:

1979— 6 units
1980—50 units
1981—80 units

The first test unit was expected to fly by April 1978 and the preproduction models were to be available for delivery by the end of 1979. This production plan was adopted in response to an analysis of the market trends
for this category. Table 2 traces the market history of jet sales in the medium and large categories.

The United States was the major market for corporate aircraft. Table 3
summarizes the geographic distribution of corporate-aircraft sales during
1966–1975:

On the basis of this history, Canadair's marketing staff first calculated
pessimistic, probable, and optimistic worldwide sales forecasts for the medium and large jet category from 1978 to 1988, judged to be the Challenger's sales life (Table 4).

Canadair executives then narrowed this down to a forecast for Challenger sales only (Table 5).

The most-probable-sales estimate for this period represented a 40 percent share of the probable world market during 1978–88. In the midterm,

■ **TABLE 2** Market History (units):
             Sales of Medium and
             Large Size Jets
             *(Gulfstream II, JetStar,
             Falcon 20, HS 125)*

1966:	123	1971:	43
1967:	103	1972:	72
1968:	123	1973:	93
1969:	111	1974:	62
1970:	69	1975:	51

10-year total: 850 units

■ **TABLE 3** Distribution of Sales, 1966–
             1975 *(all corporate planes)*

	Units	Percent
North America	565	66.5
Europe	189	22.2
Central and South America	25	2.9
Asia	24	2.8
Africa	37	4.4
Oceania	10	1.2
	850	100.0

■ **TABLE 4**   Worldwide Business-Jet Sales Forecast, 1978–1988 *(Challenger category, executive configuration only)*

	Pessimistic	Probable	Optimistic
North America	600	625	675
Europe	200	225	275
Central and South America	25	40	65
Asia	25	40	65
Africa	50	75	95
Oceania	10	15	20
	910	1,020	1,195

■ **TABLE 5**   Challenger Sales Forecast, 1978–1988 *(executive configuration only)*

	Pessimistic	Probable	Optimistic
North America	150	250	300
Europe	55	80	105
Central and South America	15	20	25
Asia	15	25	35
Africa	20	30	50
Oceania	5	5	10
	260	410	525

Canadair executives could consider a stretched version of the Challenger for the commuter and freight market. Adding this version would raise the probable forecast to 560 units, the pessimistic to 333, and optimistic to 750 units. The average variable cost per unit for the first two hundred units was projected to be $4.1 million per jet but variable costs per unit were expected to show some improvement because of the experience curve effect after the first 200 jets. Exhibit 8 shows a pro forma cash flow for the first 250 Challengers that might be produced. No cost or investment data had been generated on the stretched Challenger model.

Pricing

The marketing staff had prepared several pricing options for the Challenger. It was necessary to finalize pricing for the first 50 orders and work out a *general* pricing plan for the rest of the projected sales. Exhibit 9 contains data on the existing competitive prices and the marketing staff's best estimate of future pricing moves by the competition.

One pricing option for the first 50 orders was to undercut the competition by $1.2 million, setting the price at $4.1 million per Challenger. To some executives, a $1.2 million discount seemed large for such a superior product, even though the Challenger had flown only "on paper." They pointed out that all new aircraft faced this issue of confidence and that most buyers understood the process of designing an all-new aircraft and

■ EXHIBIT 9   Expected Pricing Movement in the Large-Jet Market *(in thousands)*

	1976 Current Price*	Expected BCA Price†							
		1977	1978	1979	1980	1981	1982	1983	1984
Challenger‡	$4,100								
JetStar II	5,345	$5,195	$5,611	$6,057	$6,544	$7,068	$7,633	$8,244	$8,900
Gulfstream III	6,200	?	—	—	—	—	—	—	—
Gulfstream II	5,500	5,900	6,354	6,844	7,371	7,938	8,549	9,208	9,910
Falcon 50	5,750	5,750	5,750	5,750	6,153	6,583	7,044	7,537	8,060

*Average BCA equipped prices.
†Smith and Taylor were less certain of pricing activity after 1980.
‡Initial proposal for first 50 units.
SOURCE: Company records.

the process of gearing up a volume production system. Because the break-even volume under the low-price option was larger than the probable-sales forecast, the price was expected to rise after the first 50 orders.

Alternatively, the Challenger could be priced at parity with the competition. In this case, the price would probably increase in step with inflation and the pricing of competitive products.

Some executives suggested that the Challenger's superior product characteristics required a premium price even in the short run. They believed that the Challenger could maintain a premium over competitive prices in the long run.

The purchase price for each Challenger would include training for captains, maintenance training for mechanics, programmed maintenance assistance from Montreal, and service and support from any of the three planned service facilities. Bill Lear, who had done the initial Challenger design, would receive 5 percent of the *sale* price of the first 50 units sold, 4 percent on the second 50, and 3 percent on all orders beyond the first hundred.

The following terms of purchase were proposed:

1. Each customer would be required to make a 5 percent deposit for each plane ordered. All deposits would be placed in escrow with accrued interest at the Canadian prime rate (10 percent in 1976).
2. One year before delivery, the customer would pay 30 percent of the purchase price.
3. Six months before delivery, the customer would pay 30 percent again.
4. The customer would pay the final 35 percent of the purchase price upon delivery.

Service

After-sale service was an important purchase criterion for the customer. Canadair executives tentatively had decided to build three factory-owned service centres which would service only Challengers. Their cost, $4.5 million each, was included in the planned $140 million investment. One centre would be located in Hartford, Connecticut, where Canadair's U.S. sales office was located, one in the southwestern United States, and one in Europe. The selection of these locations was based on the projection that these areas would provide the majority of Challenger sales. Only technical personnel would operate from these facilities.

The service facilities would have to be completed in time to service the first jets as they were sold at the end of 1979. Canadair would have to service early Challenger buyers very well to enhance its credibility and improve sales prospects. There was some concern at Canadair about whether factory-owned centres were the best way to provide service. Some corporate jet manufacturers such as Gulfstream and Hawker-Siddely utilized service distributors. Hence, the 200 Hawker-Siddely 125s in the United States were serviced by a distributor network of 14 outlets. This method of servicing, if chosen by Canadair, would eliminate the $4.5 million investment in each service facility, but because the Challenger was technically more advanced than its competition, special in-house expertise might offer certain advantages and would not require handing over technical information to distributors who serviced competitive aircraft.

Advertising and Promotion

The advertising and promotion budget for the Challenger program in 1976 was set at about $2.5 million. Because the Challenger was a new and unproven airplane, the marketing staff and its advertising agency had decided to mount a print advertising campaign in the leading technical and business magazines to support the sales force's personal selling activities. Domestic and international advertising campaigns were planned for journals such as *Professional Pilot, Business Week, Business and Commercial Aviation, Interavia,* and *The Wall Street Journal.* All of the Challenger's competitors advertised in these journals, trying to reach the executive in charge of purchasing a business jet and the pilot who would be flying the jet.

To achieve high readability scores for their advertising, Canadair executives were prepared to use a bold, confident, and "challenging" theme. Of the total advertising and promotion budget, $625,000 was to be allocated to print advertising.

To reinforce the print advertising campaign, brochures and other sales literature were printed. An active direct mailing program could be used to solicit inquiries from potential prospects. The Challenger would also be promoted through press releases and press conferences, pilot seminars, photography, and newsletters, so that magazine articles would chronicle the progress of the Challenger engineering and marketing activities.

All competitors generally used this kind of promotion, but with varying degrees of intensity and success. The Falcon 50 marketers had used comparative advertising but had made no mention of the Challenger in their advertising. Canadair executives believed this obvious exclusion was an attempt by the Falcon 50 people to present the Challenger as unworthy of consideration. The JetStar II and Gulfstream II advertising did not use comparative approaches.

Exhibit 10 contains rate and reach data for full-page advertisements (the typical size in the large-jet business) in publications typically used by corporate-airplane advertisers. Media space could be purchased as early as the third week in July.

■ THE SELLING TASK

President Kearns described the selling process this way:

> Each sale *is* different. It isn't like going to the military with a proposal and finding that you have just won a competition and the armed forces are going to buy 225 of your airplanes in the very first contract. It isn't like going to the airlines and selling batches of 10 or a dozen transports at once, all to the same specifications, with the same number of seats and the same colours inside and on the tail! It is, in fact, a matter of doing a complete presentation and proposal for every single prospect you approach. We start out with a prospect list made up of present business-aircraft operators plus other major corporations throughout the world who do not yet operate any aircraft. These organizations often have the need but we in the industry have yet to prove it to them. We gather data on the companies. We get an idea of their current needs by talking to their pilots, or we make some estimates if they have never operated an aircraft.
>
> We study the trips their people make, the points they routinely travel between, the longest and shortest flights, how many go on each trip, etc. Gradually a picture emerges to show us each prospect's specific requirement. And armed with that study, we approach the prospects with our sales proposals.

The first pitch was usually made to a firm's pilot. He generally had only veto power and not purchase power, but his acceptance was crucial. The salesman had to determine how much he would be able to use the pilot to make the sale. Mr. Taylor described three possibilities:

1. The pilot is strongly in your favour. He would act like an in-house salesman for you.
2. The pilot is unsure. The first task is to move him to neutral and then improve his and management's attitudes.
3. The pilot is against the product right off, clearly the least-preferred situation. The first task here is to cool him off and try to get to the chief executive officer and sell him first.

The salesman had to be very perceptive in assessing to what degree the influencers on the selling decision would be involved, and finding out who exactly would make the final decision.

■ **EXHIBIT 10**   Print Advertising Rate Data[1]

Publication	Edition	Circulation (000s)	Distribution	Full Page (1 time)	Half Page	Frequency Discount 7 Times	13 Times
The Wall Street Journal	Eastern	606	Daily	$14,101	$ 7,050		
	Midwest	458		11,366	5,683		
	West	289		7,958	3,534		
	Southwest	168		4,049	2,024		
	North America	1500		36,265	18,132		
Business Week	International	59	Weekly	$ 2,450			
	European	31		1,710			
	Northeast	218		6,180			
	Midwest	182		5,120		10%	5%
	Pacific Coast	131		3,640			
	Southwest	51		1,480			
	Southeast	66		1,900			
	North America	738		9,000			
Fortune	North America	600	Biweekly	$13,710			
	Eastern	201		7,000		8%	4%
	Midwestern	159		5,130			
	Southeastern	60		2,610			
	Southwestern	48		2,210			
	Western	115		3,820			
	International	70		4,020			
	European	46		3,070			
Forbes	North America	665	Monthly	$10,990		7%	4%

Publication	Edition	Circulation (000s)	Distribution	Full Page (1 time)	Frequency Discount 3 Times	5 Times	7 Times	13 Times
Dun's Review	Eastern	90	Monthly	$3,405				
	Central	86		2,665	7%	6%	5%	
	Southern	32		1,515				
	Western	40		1,160				
	All	248		5,405				
Aviation Week and Space Technology	All North America	97	Weekly	$4,343	2.5%	1.8%		4%
Business and Commercial Aviation	All North America	50	Monthly	$2,850		11%		6%
Flight International*	All	47	Weekly	$1,670		6%		6%
Interavia*	All	3	Monthly	$390	14%	22%		

*International circulation.

[1]All rates are for black-and-white ads and are noncontract rates.

SOURCE: Standard Rate and Data Service.

Prospects were identified with the assistance of a *Business and Commercial Aviation*[11] study that measured the impact of company aircraft in the U.S. top 1000 industrials as compiled by *Fortune* magazine.

This summary of the business performance of the *Fortune* 1,000 industrials showed that the aircraft operators, for whatever reason, were more efficient. The 514 aircraft-operating companies controlled 1,778 aircraft in 1975, an increase of 125 over 1974. This study concluded that:

> . . . nearly one half of the nation's biggest corporations are not operators even though their dollar volume of business indicates a cash flow that would support capital equipment such as an aircraft. In some cases, the nature of a firm's activities precludes the need for travel to locations not well served by public transportation; for others, the scheduling flexibility and effective utilization of personnel afforded by business aviation is not a strong incentive in the firm's type of business endeavors. But there are many corporations, we suspect, where the concept of business aircraft still is not appreciated nor fully understood, and it is in this area that a greater knowledge of corporate aviation is needed.[12]

Hence, part of the selling task involved giving a potential customer an education in the advantages of corporate-owned aircraft in general before making a pitch for a particular model.

Another study identified companies owning the most expensive and largest fleets in the United States (Table 6).

■ THE PEOPLE BEHIND THE SELLING TASK

Mr. James Taylor, 55, had been hired by Canadair in April 1976 to market the Challenger concept to the corporate market. Mr. Taylor's fascination with aircraft went back many years. His father had been a test pilot in both World War I and World War II. James Taylor had scored successes for the Cessna Aircraft Corp. and the French-based Dassault-Brequet Aircraft Corp. When Mr. Taylor joined Dassault in 1966, the "Fan Jet Falcon 20" soon became the industry sales leader in terms of both units and dollars. In 1966, Lear had sold 33 jets worldwide through 200 dealers, but in 1967, Mr. Taylor and his four salesmen sold 45 Falcon 20s in North America without the assistance of any dealers. Mr. Taylor believed in direct sales rather than a dealer network because, as he put it: "It is a narrowly defined market. When I sell direct, I have better control over hiring, training, the territory, and the price. I like to bring prospects in for seminars, take a mock-up to key cities, and make extensive use of direct mail."

Joining Cessna in March 1969, he became the architect behind the highly successful "Citation" marketing and product-support programs

---

[11]Arnold Lewis, "Business Aviation and the *Fortune* 1,000," *Business and Commercial Aviation,* December 1978, pp. 1–4.

[12] Ibid.

■ **TABLE 6**   The Most Expensive Corporate Fleets

Company	Number of Airplanes	Fleet Value ($ millions)
Coca-Cola	5	$17.2
3M Co.	7	16.2
Rockwell International	21	15.6
Mobil	28	14.4
IBM	9	13.2
Atlantic Richfield	20	13.0
General Motors	14	12.8
United Technologies	14	12.3
Exxon	16	11.3
Tenneco	26	11.1
ITT	13	10.9
Shell	24	9.7
Diamond Shamrock	3	9.0
Gannett	4	8.9
General Dynamics	5	8.8
U.S. Steel	4	8.8
Conoco	19	8.7
Texaco	8	8.3
Time	9	8.2
Johnson & Johnson	7	8.1
Marathon Oil	14	8.0

SOURCE: Aviation Data Service Inc.

which transformed the aircraft into the world's most successful business jet in its initial four years of production.

Mr. Taylor brought three key people with him to Canadair. Mr. Bill Juvonen had been with Mr. Taylor on three previous marketing programs including the Falcon 20 and the Citation. He became the vice president of sales responsible for Canada and the United States west of the Mississippi. Mr. Dave Hurley had spent five years with Cessna and had worked with Mr. Taylor on two programs. He became the vice president of sales responsible for the eastern half of the United States. Barry Smith had been the director of corporate marketing services for Atlantic Aviation, a company that serviced and distributed such corporate jets as the Gulfstream II, the Hawker-Siddely 125 and the Westwind. He had later worked for James Taylor in the same capacity on the successful Cessna Citation program. Mr. Taylor immediately hired him as vice president, marketing services. Mr. Smith would be responsible for advertising, direct mail, and all the "inside" marketing services. These four men made up the marketing team that would have to sell 50 Challengers before September 30th, 1976.

■ FINAL QUESTION

The Challenger's design was undergoing constant modification. Mr. Taylor described the chief engineer, Mr. Halton, as "the most open-minded engineer I've ever met. For example, one of our customers suggested an APU (auxiliary power unit) system to assure power to the cabin electricals in flight. Harry designed in the APU system. Similarly, traditional aircraft use DC electricals but there are customer advantages in using AC. Harry put in AC. When Harry cannot accommodate one of our design suggestions, he always has good reasons and he takes the time to tell us. Normally, a chief pilot would not want you talking to his boss, but with the Challenger, some pilots not only are talking to their bosses, they are relaying information to us and to them." However, it was time to finalize the design and move ahead on a production system that would produce 80 aircraft per year.

Although Mr. Taylor had been very successful using a direct sales approach, other companies made extensive use of dealer networks, particularly in foreign countries. The "five percenters" (agents) in foreign countries also raised the issue of controlling their selling practices, especially in countries where mordida[13] was almost a standard practice.

The pricing strategy and promotion strategy would have to provide fairly rapid market penetration. Advertising and service expenditures already comprised $16 million of the investment budget; changes in these expenditures would have to promise compensating paybacks. There had to be a high probability that the proposed marketing plan would deliver the sales forecast for the Challenger. Mr. Taylor smiled and commented wryly to his aides: "This is going to have to be the biggest selling job in history. I think we can count on working 6 days a week, 14 hours a day, from now until September 30."

Two manufacturers were rumoured to be looking at the Challenger statistics to see how best to compete with this wide-body turbofan. Messrs. Taylor, Halton, and Kearns sat down on the morning of July 4, 1976, to review the Challenger strategy for the next three months and the longer term.

COMPREHENSIVE CASE 2: The Kingston-Warren Company

In August 1983, John Grant, sales manager for the controls systems group of the Kingston-Warren Company, was reviewing several customer proposals for the CAPS system. CAPS, a computerized order-picking system for warehouses, had been introduced by Kingston-Warren a year ago and had generated significant interest in the order selection trade. The interest had not translated into firm orders, however. John was more than a little puzzled and concerned about the slow flow of actual orders for CAPS. Many proposals had been submitted, often at considerable expense, to prospective customers, and there were still many under active consideration in

---

[13]Mordida represents payments to government officials in return for favors.

This case was written by Kim Borden, Research Assistant, under the direction of Frederick E. Webster, Jr., E. B. Osborn Professor of Marketing, Amos Tuck School of Business Administration, Dartmouth College. Not to be reproduced without permission. Copyright © by Trustees of Dartmouth College.

those customers' organizations. It was proving extremely difficult to actually close the sale. The customer buying process had proven to be very complex and time-consuming. John thought that the level and quality of promotional effort on CAPS had been more than adequate, as had been the level of financial and other forms of support from top management. He was concerned about pricing, the ability of the dealer organization to sell CAPS, and the emergence of several new competitors. Clearly, the economic recession was having an impact on all capital goods markets, but John wasn't sure that an improving economy would help CAPS very much.

The stack of proposals revealed few clues as to why only three systems, out of 25 proposals, had been sold and installed over the past 12 months. As he reviewed the proposals and the sales representatives' correspondence, he felt that each system had been justified economically, solved a customer problem more than adequately, and had been priced competitively. He remembered outlining his strategy to Kingston-Warren's president, Herb Grant, Jr., last year and the initial excitement from the sales representatives.

Herb Grant, Jr., and John Grant had met at the end of June to review the results of the marketing strategy for CAPS over the past year. John and the company's sales representatives had become discouraged after having put so much effort into pushing the CAPS system. John was concerned that the Kingston-Warren dealer network did not have the high-level management contacts in customer companies to effectively sell CAPS, and he was thinking about revising the CAPS dealer policy. In their meeting, the president had also mentioned CAPS pricing. Kingston-Warren had always sold very high-quality materials-handling equipment and had also always commanded the highest price. Herb Grant, Jr., was worried that the recent discounts the control systems group had quoted in order to close a few sales would establish a low price level in the marketplace. He felt Kingston-Warren had put out "confusing" signals in regard to CAPS pricing. During most of the meeting, however, Herb Grant, Jr., had urged John Grant to maintain the current strategy. Despite the sales representatives' frustration and the growing number of competitors, Herb Grant, Jr., honestly believed that the original strategy was sound and well focused.

■ THE COMPANY

The Kingston-Warren Corporation was founded in 1946 to manufacture weatherseals for automobile windows. Located in Newfields, New Hampshire, the company was owned by Herb Grant, and his son, Herb Grant, Jr., managed its day-to-day operations. In 1982, total sales were $40 million, employees numbered 850 people, and the factory and office space occupied a handsome, modern 256,000-square-foot building. Kingston-Warren's proprietary metal roll-forming process, initially developed in 1946, was the basis for many new products developed since that time. The company was organized into three divisions in 1983: automotive, metal products, and materials handling.

The automotive division manufactured rubber and metal/rubber composite channels to weather seal automobile windows. The size of the market for this product was determined by automobile industry sales and usually accounted for about 55 percent of annual company sales. General Motors was the auto division's largest customer, and GM valued Kingston-Warren as a supplier. GM would keep their order quantities constant or increasing at the expense of other weatherseal suppliers during economic downturns. The metal products division produced custom steel components for the television, construction, computer, and electronics industries. The division's customers included IBM, General Electric, RCA, and Armstrong World Industries.

■ THE MATERIALS HANDLING DIVISION

The materials handling division was created 20 years ago when the chairman of Grand Union grocery stores thought it would be a good idea to make an automatic stocking retail shelf. The chairman intended for grocery stores to have inclined shelves so the products would slide to the front of the shelves automatically. In theory, when a customer selected a product, another would slide into place; the goal was to have a store that always looked fully stocked and neat. Kingston-Warren was contracted to manufacture these shelves because of their highly precise roll-forming process. Unfortunately, the application of a gravity-fed shelf did not work well in retail stores. Customers could not replace items they had selected but did not want to buy, and soon the store aisles were littered with grocery items.

Gravity-flow shelving did have another very useful application, however—warehouse order selection systems. Order selection systems involve shelving, a conveyor with totes (bins for collecting items), and a picker. A useful example for explaining order selection systems is a gift item mail-order house. In their catalog, the mail-order house may have 700 different items, each of which is held in inventory at their warehouse. When a customer sends in an order, the order is translated to a "pick list." The pick list will have information about which items are to be picked, the quantity needed for each item, and (usually) information about where the items are located in the warehouse.

The picker will take the pick list and locate the goods on shelves, filling the tote with the necessary items. (See Exhibit 1 for a typical order-picking setup.) Usually, a conveyor runs through the picking aisle, and totes, with the pick list attached, move along a conveyor. A picker will only be responsible for a certain number of items (his or her zone), and several people may be responsible for filling the same order. As items are picked, the corresponding line on the pick list is checked or marked in some way to indicate that item on the order has been filled.

Gravity-flow shelving enhanced this basic system by providing a method to keep inventory (stock) easily available. Each inclined shelf was equipped with roll track, so open cases of goods slid to the front of the shelf. Handling of goods was far more efficient because restocking of gravity-flow

■ **EXHIBIT 1** A Typical Warehouse Order-Picking Situation

GRAVITY FLOW:
Pickers spend 85% of their time doing productive work.

A gravity flow system may cost a little more than conventional shelving, but it dramatically cuts labor costs. How? By decreasing the distance a picker has to walk between the items being picked, and the time spent looking for them (see illustration). Frontage per item is usually reduced to a single case except for a few of the fastest movers.

In a typical gravity flow system, about 85% of the picker's time is spent actively picking and marking order forms—and only 15% walking. Thus, a picker can save as much as three quarters of each hour, often making it possible to eliminate three out of four workers.

Similar savings can be made in restocking goods.

Finally, a gravity flow system makes the most efficient use of floor space. Fewer aisles are required. And 50% or more goods can be stocked in the same area.

----- ORDER PICKER (Shown making ten stops.)
——— RESTOCKER (Shown making six stops.)

GRAVITY FLOW SYSTEM

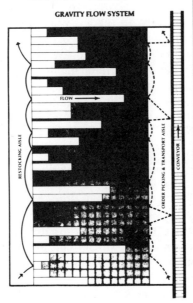

STATIC SHELVING:
Pickers spend 15% of their time doing productive work.

Static shelving systems are relatively inexpensive. The big hidden cost factor is labor—the amount of time and energy spent by people restocking and picking.

In the drawing below, notice how many wasted steps are taken between the items being picked.

In the typical static system, pickers actually waste about 85% of their time walking. That means only about 15% of their time is left for productive work—picking and marking order forms.

Compare the two systems . . .

	GRAVITY FLOW	STATIC SHELVING	GAIN WITH GRAVITY FLOW
Total floor space	equal	equal	none
Items stored (each case, 1 cubic foot)	155	120	29%
Shelves high	5	3	2
Cases per opening	15	12	3
Total cases	2325	1440	61%

STATIC SHELVING SYSTEM

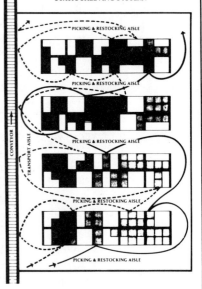

shelves could be handled from the back of the unit, while picking was taking place simultaneously at the front of the shelf. Warehouse space was saved because the available stock was kept in a single row on the shelf, rather than having several cases stacked across the front of the shelf as required in static shelving. As a result of the improved utilization of warehouse space, picker productivity was also greatly increased. Pickers did not have to walk as far, nor did they have to search for products on static shelving. (See Exhibit 2 for typical static and gravity-flow layouts.)

■ **EXHIBIT 2** Gravity-Flow and Static Shelving

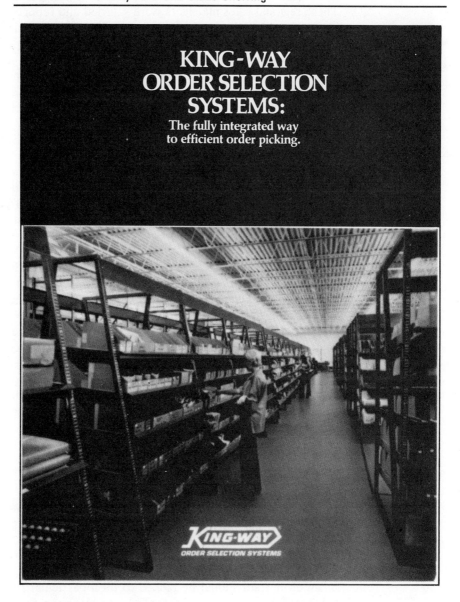

■ KING-WAY SALES AND DISTRIBUTION

Kingston-Warren marketed its gravity-flow shelving and other order selection hardware under the brand name King-Way. The internal sales structure consisted of the president, who supervised the sales activities of all divisions, a vice president of sales for the materials handling division, a sales manager for the control systems group, and four regional sales managers. The regional sales managers were responsible for developing their territories, each of which was roughly one quarter of the United States. These regional sales managers were salaried and reported to the vice president of sales. (See Exhibit 3 for an organization chart for Kingston-Warren.)

Kingston-Warren sold King-Way products through approximately 120 dealers located across the United States. They were independent companies and usually represented a wide range of materials handling equipment and machinery, including fork lifts, dollies, pallets, pallet racks, conveyors, and automated picking systems.

In 1982, sales for King-Way products were $12 million. Customers included firms in a wide variety of industries including health and beauty aids, food and tobacco, hardware, toys, printed matter and stationery, and shoes, for example. Although there was a price list available to dealers for standard King-Way items, approximately 75 percent of the dollar volume of sales was quoted in Newfields by estimators. The quotations were usually part of proposals prepared by the regional sales managers for customer-designed facilities.

Kingston-Warren, considered by many to be the leader in order-picking systems, had installed thousands of systems throughout the world and had an excellent reputation for quality, durability, and functional equipment. Competition had increased over the years, and King-Way, as the highest priced system, had seen some erosion in its share of the market. In recent years, several new manufacturers had entered the market, mostly steel fabricators who sold flow rack and pallet rack at a low price. Kingston-Warren prided itself on selling "total systems" and actively promoted this advantage in its advertising and product focus. Their "Profiling" service was a computer-generated efficient layout for customer order selection systems. (See Exhibit 4.)

■ CAPS: COMPUTER ASSISTED PICKING SYSTEM

In July 1982, Kingston-Warren introduced CAPS, an abbreviation for "computer assisted picking system." CAPS was a microprocessor-based system designed to increase picker productivity and reduce picking errors by doing away with the pick list. Instead of a paper pick list, LED (light emitting diodes) displays on the front of gravity-flow racks indicated how many of an item should be picked to fill a particular order. The complete CAPS system consisted of a control console, zone controllers, bay lamps, and pick modules. (See Exhibit 5.)

The *CAPS Control Console* consisted of a keyboard and CRT screen. Customer order information was passed to this microprocessor from a company's main computer via direct communications line or formatted diskette. The console tracked orders, inventory status, bottlenecks, and backlogs and could be used for entering rush orders, canceling orders, or calling up specific orders. The main function of the controller, however, was to direct the pickers in their activities with LED signals on the face of gravity-flow racks.

■ **EXHIBIT 3**   Organization Chart

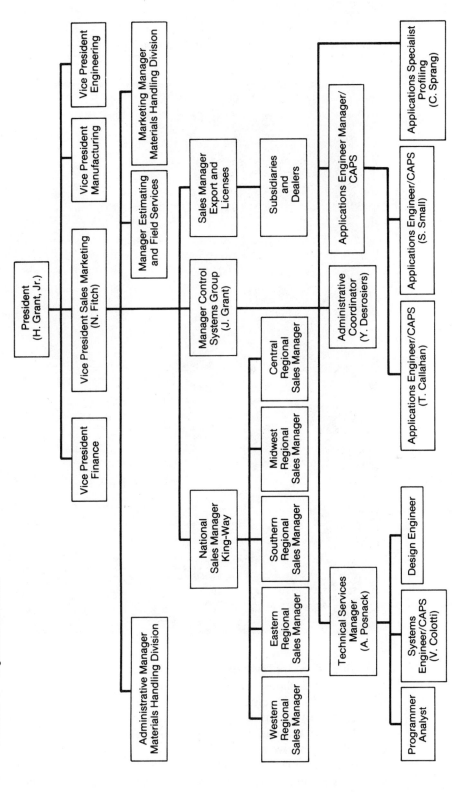

■ **EXHIBIT 4**   An Explanation of the "Profiling" Service

An Exclusive Service

PROFILING is a service which provides the King-Way flow rack user with an essential tool to assist in the planning and installation of King-Way order selection systems. Available only to King-Way users, **PROFILING** can yield significant dollar savings in such areas as floor space, hardware costs, installation labor, stocking and picking.

Using carton data provided by the user, King-Way's computer will "stock" the Flow Rack System—before anyone ever touches a carton! The user can measure the effect of various stocking strategies long before the flow rack is installed, and choose the arrangement that satisfies his requirements best. The finished **PROFILE** tells the installers exactly where to mount each shelf and lane guide; it tells the stockers what cartons to put where; and it provides input to the user's data processing system for recording slot locations.

KING-WAY®
ORDER SELECTION SYSTEMS

A zone is an area where one picker works, and there may be up to 40 zones in a warehouse. The *zone controller* was located in the first bay (shelving unit) of a picking zone and indicated the order number of the order currently being picked in that zone. When the picker had finished with the active order, he or she pushed the "next" button on the zone controller to receive a new order.

The *bay lamp* was located at the top of each bay and, when illuminated, served as a highly visible indicator that there were picks to be made from that bay on the active order. When all the picks had been made in a par-

■ **EXHIBIT 5** The CAPS System

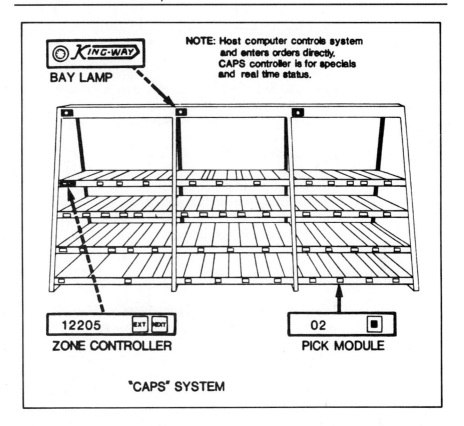

ticular bay, the bay lamp would automatically extinguish. The bay lamps made it easier for pickers to locate bays that had pick activity and ignore those bays without activity.

The *pick module* was positioned at the front of each item in the system— usually a single runway or lane in a gravity-flow shelf. When lit, the pick module indicated to a picker the item to be picked and in what quantity. As the pick was completed, the picker pushed the button on the module to extinguish the quantity number and to signal to the computer that the pick was complete. The pick module could also be used to report shorts and stock-outs.

The advantage of CAPS was that it simplified the picker's job, reducing picking errors and increasing productivity, while also reducing order processing time. CAPS provided a wealth of instantaneous information on inventory and active orders in the order selection system. The system was very flexible and could work in a variety of zone configurations. CAPS easily retrofitted to existing King-Way gravity-flow racks and could be adapted to fit other manufacturers' equipment.

The CAPS system was originally introduced by Dimension, Inc., in 1979. Kingston-Warren was licensed for exclusive worldwide distribution rights (except for Europe other than the United Kingdom and Australia) from

Dimension, Inc., in September 1981. CAPS systems were shipped from the Dimension plant in Reston, Virginia. The first "paperless picking" system had been installed in Rubbermaid's Party Plan warehouse in Chillicothe, Ohio, which supplied products to housewives who acted as dealers by setting up neighborhood parties and taking orders. Several thousand orders were shipped each week, and the average order had 50 items in it. Customer and dealer satisfaction was extremely important in this business, and Rubbermaid had many checking procedures to ensure that orders were shipped correctly. The productivity increases and error reduction results of the Dimension installation were impressive: An initial study showed that picking output rose from 400 items picked per hour to 600 picks per hour, and errors decreased from .5 percent to $\frac{1}{10}$ of 1 percent. These improvements were possible because pickers no longer had to refer to written documents listing the product and quantity ordered. Also, location of items in the warehouse did not need to be memorized. System and installation cost payback was achieved in one year.

■ CAPS MARKETING STRATEGY

John Grant and his colleagues based the preliminary marketing strategy plan for CAPS on a situational analysis covering the company, the supplier, and the external environment. CAPS was to be an integral part of the product line, expanding the King-Way equipment range and furthering the company's goal to continue to be the foremost supplier of order selection systems. Although not a "high-tech" company, Kingston-Warren had the customers and sales network from King-Way to effectively market CAPS. The supplier of CAPS, Dimension, Inc., had already produced and installed computer-aided picking systems, and the technology had been tested and proven. Future research and development expenses would be jointly shared by Dimension and Kingston-Warren, and software improvements that would add different management report options to the basic system were under way.

Materials handling personnel seemed ready for a product that offered greater productivity and less errors but was less costly than fully automated storage and retrieval units. Fully automated order-picking systems had been developed that required no human pickers, but these were prohibitively expensive and prone to breakdowns. A computerized system like CAPS that aided pickers was regarded as an ideal compromise in cost and efficiency. The market for computer-aided picking systems was estimated to reach $23 million by 1988 and to level off after that point. Kingston-Warren, because of their excellent reputation for quality products, expected to achieve a 60 percent market share.

Distribution/Sales Network

Originally, John Grant and his colleagues decided to use the existing sales network of regional sales managers and dealers to sell CAPS. Most of the dealers had been with King-Way for over 10 years and had established relationships with the local companies using order selection systems, their warehouse managers, and often the company engineers who helped design and set up each facility. In addition, Kingston-Warren hired two applications engineers to be specialists in CAPS, to help regional sales managers and dealers lay out system proposals, and to assist in sales calls on request from the dealer and regional sales manager.

Over the past year, it had become obvious that CAPS must be sold to a different organizational level than King-Way products. The investment for a CAPS system was large and usually considered a capital budgeting decision by the customer. The economic return on a CAPS system and approval by the customer's financial officer were at least as important in closing a sale as the recommendation of the warehouse manager. Only 10 or so Kingston-Warren dealers were judged to have well-developed contacts at these levels of customers' organizations. The regional sales managers and applications engineers had had to forcefully step into several situations and do the actual selling of a project. For the dealers, learning about CAPS and assigning or hiring personnel to promote it could be expensive. CAPS was extraordinarily different from most materials handling equipment, and many dealers could not make the transition from a basic industrial product to a high-tech product.

Some dealers had expressed grievances about the commission structure on the CAPS systems. King-Way products were quoted to the dealers at list price minus a standard discount. The dealer's actual commission was determined by the selling price to the customer, which was ultimately determined by the dealer with many transactions below list price. The materials handling equipment market had a "notorious" discount structure, with many commodity items selling at 50 to 60 percent off list. Kingston-Warren offered CAPS to dealers at list minus a discount that was less than half the percentage offered on King-Way but which was consistent with dealer discounts in the computer field. Dealer earnings on a CAPS sale could still be significantly higher than on an average King-Way sale because of the dollar value of the transaction. Dealers reported encountering significant problems with warehouse managers who were expecting a materials handling type discount on the computer-assisted picking system.

The control systems staff was considering setting up a structure involving A and B dealers. A dealers would have to meet several objective requirements before they would be qualified to receive commissions on CAPS sales in their territories. These requirements, yet to be determined, would relate to product training and knowledge, general management and financial capabilities, and size of the dealership. B dealers would receive a finder's fee for sales leads that led to CAPS sales in their territory. These B dealers would not be expected to learn about CAPS, however, nor would they be expected to participate in the sales process after they had passed on the sales lead.

In order to execute the CAPS high-level management sell, Kingston-Warren had put together a senior strike force to help close sales. Depending on the sales situation, the strike force would include the president, the vice president of sales, the vice president of finance, and other senior management officials and technical personnel. In a "textbook" sale, the dealer in the area would make the first contact with the customer, then an applications engineer would arrange a visit to the customer's plant. Proposals and a quotation would be prepared, and then the strike force would be used either during a potential customer's visit to the Kingston-Warren plant or at an on-site call. This approach worked very well because the senior management at Kingston-Warren knew the CAPS product very well and could effectively communicate to the higher management levels in the customer's company.

Pricing

Prices for a CAPS system including hardware, software, spare parts, training, and a one-year warranty were estimated as follows for the purpose of developing a proposal:

SKUs*	List price
500	$185,000
1,000	290,000
2,000	525,000
4,000	975,000

*An SKU is a stock-keeping unit, a single item in inventory. Each item—product, color, size, etc.—would be counted as a separate SKU.

When a customer was quoted a CAPS system, he was supplied an extensive cost justification based on raw data the customer supplied on his order selection system. From Kingston-Warren studies and data from installations, picker productivity improvement and error reduction would be 50 to 100 percent. For analysis, Kingston-Warren used 75 percent productivity improvement and 75 percent error reduction. See Exhibit 6 for an example of a CAPS cost justification.

Most prospective customers for a computer-assisted picking system would solicit bids from several different companies. Few companies had actually awarded purchase orders over the past few years, however, and Kingston-Warren had dropped the price on several bids in the hopes of closing a sale. Competitive companies were also offering low prices, trial periods, extended warranties, and other incentives in the hopes of being able to develop initial "showcase" installations as a way of developing the market. Potential customers seemed hesitant to invest in a computer-aided picking system which they regarded as an unproven technology.

Kingston-Warren initially had planned to follow the high-quality/high-price/market leader strategy on CAPS that had been successful with King-Way. When it became clear that orders were developing much more slowly than expected, Kingston-Warren lowered prices almost to the level of their cost on several proposals, hoping to develop a few "showcase" installations, and to close these orders quickly. Unfortunately, few orders were

■ **EXHIBIT 6** CAPS System Cost Analysis for Wesley Pharmaceuticals, Inc.

	Year 1	Year 2	Year 3	Year 4	Year 5
Pickers	10	10	10	10	10
Average salary	33,680	33,680	33,680	33,680	33,680
Labor costs	336,800	336,800	336,800	336,800	336,800
Productivity increase	.75	.75	.75	.75	.75
Labor savings	144,343	144,343	144,343	144,343	144,343
Picks	1,137,500	1,137,500	1,137,500	1,137,500	1,137,500
Error rate	.0040	.0040	.0040	.0040	.0040
Cost/error	25.00	25.00	25.00	25.00	25.00
Error costs	113,750	113,750	113,750	113,750	113,750
Error reduction	.75	.75	.75	.75	.75
Error savings	85,313	85,313	85,313	85,313	85,313
Maintenance	(5,869)	(7,826)	(7,826)	(7,826)	(7,826)
Total savings	223,786	221,830	221,830	221,830	221,830
Pretax analysis:					
Items	800	0	0	0	0
CAPS investment	(225,000)	0	0	0	0
CAPS savings	223,786	221,830	221,830	221,830	221,830
Cash flow	(1,214)	221,830	221,830	221,830	221,830
Cum cash flow	(1,214)	220,616	442,445	664,275	886,105
ROI	0	0	0	0	0
Aftertax analysis:					
CAPS investment	(225,000)	0	0	0	0
Investment tax credit	22,500	0	0	0	0
Net cost	(202,500)	0	0	0	0
Depreciation	33,750	49,500	47,250	47,250	47,250
CAPS savings	223,786	221,830	221,830	221,830	221,830
Total net savings	126,837	133,630	132,522	132,522	132,522
Net cash flow	(75,663)	133,630	132,522	132,522	132,522
Cum net cash flow	(75,663)	57,966	190,488	323,010	455,532
ROI	0	76.61	147.40	166.84	172.92

actually closed, the bid periods had dragged on, and now Herb Grant, Jr., worried that Kingston-Warren had established a low price precedent in the market. Price competition had increased as the number of competitors had increased over the past year. In one recent bid, one competitor had bid at one half the price of a CAPS system. John Grant wondered how he could compete with this alarming price competition and differentiate CAPS so that it could command a higher price.

Marketing Communications

Advertisements for CAPS had been placed in the major trade journals. During the introductory six months, a full-page, four-color advertisement had been run in each of the two major trade publications. (See Exhibit 7.) After six months, the frequency had been reduced to every other month. The advertising stressed the general concept of computer-assisted picking rather than the CAPS system. Kingston-Warren had received about 100 requests for literature from each ad placed. Two magazine articles, one in

■ **EXHIBIT 7**   An Introductory Advertisement

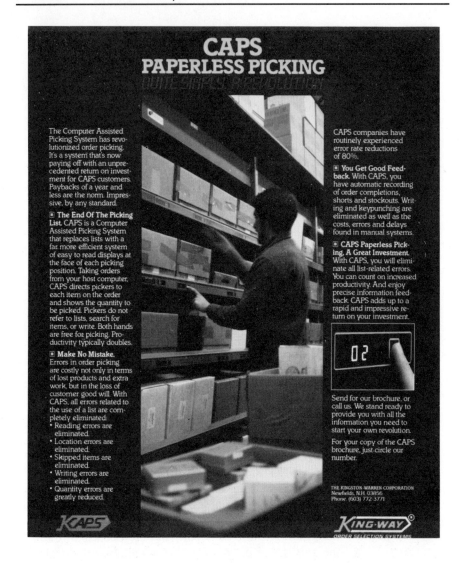

The Howard Way Letter—A Guide for Improving Productivity in Warehousing and Distribution (August 1982) and one in *Modern Materials Handling* (November 5, 1982), gave glowing reports about the CAPS system and features. Glossy brochures were printed and distributed to the dealers, and CAPS was included in general King-Way advertisements and guidebooks.

CAPS had been featured at two materials-handling trade shows, where it was displayed in operation on two King-Way gravity-flow racks. Each trade show had generated 400 to 500 good leads. These people received a follow-up letter giving the name of the local dealer, and the lead was then turned over to the dealer.

Another promotional effort was dealer-sponsored regional sales presentations. Dealers were encouraged to hold one-day miniconferences inviting potential CAPS customers. The regional sales manager, an applications engineer, and several of the corporate officers gave informal talks with visual aids throughout the day. (See Exhibit 8 for daily schedule.) A CAPS system was available for hands-on use and a picking demonstration using the attendees as pickers. These presentations had two objectives—to inform prospective customers of CAPS advantages and to give the dealer a better understanding of the system and its applications. Attendees ranged from vice presidents of distribution to consultants to warehouse managers and foremen, and generally numbered 30 to 50. Six such sessions had been held around the country, and more were planned.

The control systems group and the regional sales managers believed these presentations to be a very effective form of selling. Audience interest and attention had been consistently high, and the prospects were available for an entire day. The cost was not considered expensive at approximately $2,000 per day, split 50–50 with the dealer in the area to give him incentive to bring in good prospective customers and to actively participate in the

■ **EXHIBIT 8**   CAPS Seminar Agenda

FRANK BOUFFORD CO., INC.
MATERIALS HANDLING EQUIPMENT & STORAGE SYSTEMS
HUNTING RIDGE MALL • BEDFORD, NEW YORK 10506 • 914-234-7286 • 914-234-9253

```
FRANK BOUFFORD CO., INC. - "CAPS" SEMINAR AGENDA
        TARRYTOWN HILTON - JUNE 21-24, 1983


     9:00 -  9:15 AM     Welcome & Orientation with KW Tape
     9:15 -  9:45 AM     Kingston-Warren Corporation History
     9:45 - 10:15 AM     CAPS Picking Demo
    10:15 - 10:30 AM     Break
    10:30 - 12:00 Noon   Introduction to CAPS
    12:00 -  1:00 PM     Lunch
     1:00 -  2:30 PM     Introduction to CAPS continued including profiling
     2:30 -  2:45 PM     Break
     2:45 -  3:30 PM     Cost Justification
     3:30 -  4:30 PM     Cocktails with Discussion


                        SPEAKERS
```

	Tuesday	Wednesday	Thursday	Friday
Welcome	Frank Boufford	Frank Boufford	Frank Boufford	Frank Boufford
KW History	Herb Grant, Jr.	Neil Fitch	John Grant	John Grant
Picking Demo	Terry Mackin	Tim Callahan	Terry Mackin	Terry Mackin
Intro to CAPS	Tim Callahan	Al Posnack	Tim Callahan	Tim Callahan
Cost Justification	Al Posnack	Terry Mackin	Terry Mackin	Terry Mackin

seminar. About one month after the seminar, one of the applications engineers would do follow-up calls with the dealer. John Grant felt that it would be possible to hold seminars in New York and Los Angeles three times a year and still not reach every good potential customer in those markets.

Competition

At the time of its introduction, CAPS had only one serious competitor. In August 1983, there were five computer-aided picking systems on the market, and John Grant expected that others would appear over the next year. Many were small companies and had been attracted to the field by the promotion efforts of Kingston-Warren. Acme, the leading manufacturer of warehouse conveyors, was the original competitor and had promoted the picking system that was tied to its own conveyor system. Acme's Pick Pack system was not as flexible as CAPS, but Acme was well respected among materials-handling equipment suppliers. Although Acme had not promoted their product recently, several people at Kingston-Warren thought they were reevaluating the market and would come out soon with a system comparable to CAPS. Others at Kingston-Warren felt that Acme would leave the market and drop the product altogether. This was in part due to the recent takeover of Acme by Consolidated Engineering, Inc., a large, diversified company.

Of the other competitive products, only one, the Bosworth Rackamatic system, had actually been installed. Al Posnack, the technical services manager for control systems, felt that the Rackamatic system was the only system that could rival CAPS for features; he was unsure of its quality, however. Bosworth was a small regional manufacturer of conveyors, flow rack, and other materials-handling equipment, and John Grant believed the Rackamatic might be the product to bring Bosworth up to the level of national supplier. Bosworth had a good understanding of the productivity increases possible with computer-aided picking and was the only manufacturer that could compete with Kingston-Warren in supplying total systems.

The two other competitors, Saturn Automated Industries and Multinational Materials Handlers, were believed to have sold one system, and none of the companies had actually installed a system. Al Posnack believed all of them could deliver a working product, although none could offer the experience that Kingston-Warren had in materials handling. All were small companies buying the equipment and software from outside suppliers.

Difficulties Closing Orders

John Grant pulled five file folders from the stack he was going through. They were in Terry Mackin's territory, and Tim Callahan, one of the CAPS applications engineers, had also worked on these jobs. Both were in the office that day, and John decided to call them in to discuss the five proposals, as well as to discuss his thoughts on the dealers and pricing. Terry had been on the phone all morning, chasing leads and updating the status reports on several jobs. The meeting would have to be brief because several

several more proposals were due out that week and a potential customer was coming in on Friday for a CAPS demonstration. Tim was busy preparing a training session for one of the first CAPS' customers.

That afternoon, John, Terry, and Tim sat down in the conference room over coffee. The first job they looked at was Wesley Pharmaceuticals, Inc. Wesley was a large, international manufacturer of pharmaceuticals, and one of their industrial engineers had first expressed interest in response to a CAPS ad in *Modern Materials Handling*. She had called Kingston-Warren and had been put in touch with Terry, who immediately sent her the CAPS questionnaire. Wesley had numerous picking lines scattered across the United States and Europe and was looking to buy a trial system. Terry started the conversation.

Terry: Good news on this one. It became an order this morning! Not bad for a year's worth of work. Once this one is up and running, I'm sure we'll get other orders from them—both domestically and in Europe. The dealer will be pleased, even though he hasn't done much on this order.

John Grant reviewed the Wesley file that was started a year ago March. All the correspondence was directly from Kingston-Warren to the customer, without so much as a brief note of communication to or from the dealer, which John thought was perhaps for the best, given the dealer in that area. He was fine for flow-rack sales but did not have the contacts in the upper management of his client companies. Terry was obviously annoyed because he had had to do all the work on this order with Tim; but at least it was an order.

John: What do you think of the idea of A and B dealers for CAPS?

Terry: In some ways I'd like to do the whole sell myself—but there are a few excellent dealers. Besides, those who can't sell CAPS do a good job in general with King-Way. We can't afford to lose them—so the finder's fee is a good way of keeping the Bs happy. You asked me earlier about criteria for A dealers. Well, the Pyramid job is a great example. EDS (a King-Way dealer) has got to be one of the classiest outfits in materials handling.

Tim: They've been truly professional with that job. Jay, the dealer's sales representative, is dedicated solely to CAPS and has really taken the time to understand it. He has the features down cold—it has really been a pleasure working with him.

Terry: But we still don't have an order.

John: Have all the right people in every functional area been contacted?

Terry: Yes, and then some. Everybody, from the warehouse foreman on up, is excited, and I'm sure we'll see an order by the fourth quarter. Pyramid is one of the largest home care catalog operations we've looked at. CAPS systems in all their pick lines could save them hundreds of thousands of dollars.

John: But you've been working on this one for more than a year!

Tim: Bad timing again. Once we got all their questions answered—and they had plenty, but none we couldn't solve—the economy turned down.

Terry: Dave, the senior engineer, told me that they had to lay off people for the first time *ever* this summer. The times are just not right to bring in a productivity improvement. They were ready to close in March, after they visited here, but then their market began to decline. But I'm sure we'll see this one yet. EDS is keeping on top of things.

John looked at the Pyramid file that was thick with correspondence from the dealer to Kingston-Warren and from the dealer to the customer. Everything had proceeded smoothly, but still Kingston-Warren would have to wait for the order.

The next job they looked at was Emerson Distributors. Emerson was a distributor of general merchandise and had over 2,000 SKUs in their warehouse. They were updating their static shelving system to flow rack, and the control systems group had put together an add-on CAPS proposal to the King-Way bid. Emerson was building a new warehouse, and the flow-rack order was worth approximately $400,000. Although Kingston-Warren received the flow-rack order, Emerson's president had decided that the company could not justify an additional investment for CAPS at this time. He purchased King-Way, however, with the expressed intention of purchasing CAPS at a later date. The control systems group had used the senior strike force to push this sale, and John Grant felt it had been extremely successful.

Terry next mentioned Manlius Wholesale, a distributor serving a large grocery store chain.

Terry: Pounds, the president, is sold on CAPS, but he must win approval from *his* boss. Manlius is a subsidiary of Eastern Provision, and Pounds perceives CAPS as a radical step for the company—and it *is* very different from their current picking methods. Currently, we're trying to arrange for several people at Eastern Provision to visit our factory, but until we get to this higher level, the job is only barely active. It's strange that Pounds, who does have the authority to commit to this project, is hesitant to do so without corporate approval.

Tim: We even offered him a three-month free trial—and surprisingly he won't take us up on that either.

John: Do you think it will become an order?

Terry: Eventually, but there is still a lot of selling to do. These certainly aren't like King-Way orders where you can usually get a commitment in 100 days.

John: What about Wellington Imports? They sell giftware, don't they?

Terry: Yes, and that job is still pending. The project has been delayed because they've decided to build a warehouse rather than lease one. The prospect still looks good, but it won't be until the first quarter next year that they'll be ready to move on CAPS.

The meeting ended with a discussion of various proposals that were being prepared. Tim and Terry were excited about the upcoming customer demonstration planned for that day. The company that was visiting was a large mail-order house, and the senior management would be attending the presentation. The warehouse manager had become interested in CAPS after attending a trade show where CAPS had been displayed.

John was very concerned about the closure record for CAPS. The Wesley Pharmaceuticals job could be added to the list of sales, but four closed sales in over a year did not seem like a good record. He thought that maybe the lead time for CAPS systems was longer than he had anticipated. There were certainly many good proposals out for CAPS. The A-B dealer system would need approval by the president, and John Grant had to come up with some quantitative criteria for selecting A dealers. Pricing was another issue to be considered. He knew that CAPS would have to be differentiated from its competitors, but had not decided how this should be done. He called Herb Grant, Jr., to arrange a meeting the next day. Although John Grant did not think major changes were needed, he felt he should go over some of the issues with Herb, who had shown signs of also becoming concerned about the lack of firm orders in the face of continuing significant increase in marketing expenses.

Index

A

A. C. Nielsen, 515
ABI/Inform, data base, 616
Abrams, Bill, 231 n
Abratt, Russell, 25, 289, 325
Accountemps, 605
Ace Welding Company, 141
Acme Foods, 19
Adams, Frances, 97
Adams, Ronald J., 633
Adler, L., 170 n
Advertising, 519–26
  agency versus in-house, 528–30
  content, 526–27
  business to business versus
    consumer, 519
  goals of, 519
  media selection, 522–26
Advertising agency, use in
  promotion, 514
Aerojet General, 136
Agarival, Manoj K., 265 n
Airborne Freight Corporation,
  230–31
Airkem, 407
Alcoa, 293, 606
Alexander, Ralph S., 117 n, 526 n
Alijan, George W., 128 n
Allegheny International, 8
Allen, Everett, 548–50
Allen, Gene, 631
Allied Signal, 280
· Allstate, 445
Ally and Gargano, 231
Alwin, Duane F., 192
American Hospital Supply
  Company, 215, 668
American Marketing Association,
  162
  code of ethics, 1986, 639
Ames, B. Charles, 81 n, 235
Amos and Fitch, Inc., 153
Anderson, Erin, 62, 355 n
Anderson, James C., 76 n
Anderson, Ralph S., 280 n
Anderson Company, 310
Ansari, Abdolhossein, 48 n, 387 n
Ansberry, Clare, 646 n
Antitrust laws, 351.
Apasu, Yao, 509
Apodac, Patrice, 256 n
Apple Computer, 12, 45, 232–35,
  269, 292
Arens, William F., 540
Armitage, Howard M., 379 n,
  380 n

Arthur Anderson and Company,
  640
Arthur D. Little, Inc., 374
Atkinson, Bill, 269
Audio visual aids in personal
  selling, 450
Audits and Surveys, Inc., 515

B

Bacon, Kenneth H., 18 n
Bagozzi, Richard P., 450 n
Bailey, Earl L., 162 n
Baldwin, William, 382 n, 390 n
Ball Corporation, 375
Ballon, Ronald H., 369 n
Balsley, Ronald D., 644 n
Banting, Peter M., 113 n
Barclay, Lawson E., 461 n
Barrett, John, 478
Barton Laboratories, 465–68
Bartran, Peter, 192
BASF Wyandotte, 279
Basic One, 613
Bass, Frank M., 326
Bates, Bryan, 143
Bates, Milo, 148–53
Beach, Frank H., 523 n
Beaton, George, 289
Becker, Helmut, 655
Becker, Robert J., 364
Beckett Aviation, 574
Behof, Kathleen, 664
Beleskey, Bernie E., 449
Bell and Howell, 423
Beller, Lee Ann, 468
Bellizzi, Joseph A., 49 n, 468
Beltramini, Richard F., 633
Bendix, 47 n, 387
Bennett, Peter D., 51 n, 53 n
Berg Raingear Company, 97
Berkowitz, Eric N., 33 n, 196 n,
  371 n, 387 n
Berkowitz, Marvin, 25
Bernhardt, Kenneth L., 117 n
Bernstein, Henry, 434 n
Berry, Dick, 271 n, 509
Berton, Lee, 640 n
Bertrand, Kate, 400
Bialaszewski, Dennis, 363
Bidding, competitive
  bidders list, 35, 37
  bids for government
    procurement, 18
  closed versus open, 310

Bidding—Cont.
  conjoint analysis, 308
  criteria for, 310
  probablistic bidding model,
    309–11
  by whom it is used, 307, 309
Bids, soliciting
  quotation request form, 34
  vendor analysis, 35
Big Drum Foods, Inc., 398–400
Birsner, Patricia E., 664 n
Bishop, William S., 13 n
Black, Tom, 464
Black and Decker, 48, 387
Bloomquist, Lars, 147–53
Blue Cross/Blue Shield, 618
Blue, Jeffrey L., 501 n
Blumel, Robert T., 509
Boeing, 667
Bohn, Joseph, 523 n
Boise Cascade, 423
Bonita Baking Company, 187–89
Bonoma, Thomas V., 117 n, 119 n,
  124 n, 196 n, 197 n, 200 n,
  533 n, 534 n
Bonneville, David, 127 n
Boone, Louis E., 6 n, 386 n
Booz, Allen and Hamilton, 262 n
Bordon, Kim, 711–29
Borg Warner, 11
Boston Consulting Group, 275,
  275 n
Bourns, 423
Boyce, Courtland, 540
Bradley, Peter, 375 n
Bragg, Arthur, 339 n
Bragg, Daniel J., 48 n, 387 n
Break-even point, calculating, 299
Breaking of bulk, 331
Breton, Guy, 406
Briety, Edward G., 123 n
Briggs and Stratton Corporation,
  13
Britney, Robert R., 326, 363
Brodie, J., 603
Brookings, California, 147–53
Brown, James R., 7 n
Brown, Stephen W., 615 n
Brown and Bigelow, 447
Buell, Victor P., 337 n, 615 n
Buffa, Frank P., 400
Bullock, Tom, 453
Bundling of products and services,
  612
Burdick, Richard K., 63
Burger, Philip C., 265 n
Burkett, Joe, 466–67

Burnett, Stephen C., 265 n
Burnham, Rick, 447 n
Burns International Security
    Services, 606
Burt, D. N., 288, 309 n
Busch, P., 439 n
Businessland, Inc., 359
Business market versus consumer
    market, 6–12
Buskirk, Bruce, 523 n
Business to business buyers
    changing role of, 113–17
    fewer vendors, 114–15
    long-term contracts, 115
    personality oriented, 14–15
    post-sale support, 15
    rising status of, 115
    single sourcing, 115
    seven rights of, 66–67
Business to business demand
    derived demand, 12
    fluctuating demand, 13
    inelastic demand, 12, 13
    joint demand, 14
Business to business distributors;
    see also Physical
    distribution
    functions of, 335–37
    limitations to use of, 337
    trends for, 338–40
    types of, 337
Business to business goods and
    services
    accessory equipment, 15–16
    business services, 17
    fabricated and component parts,
      16
    maintenance, repair and
      operating supplies (MRO),
      16
    major equipment, 15
    raw materials, 16–17
Business to business marketing
    complexity of, 4–7
    emphasis on personal selling, 9
    foreign competition, 4
    growth of, 4
    impact of technology, 4
    importance of the service sector,
      5
    need for education in, 6
    types of buyers, 4–5
Business to business pricing; *see*
    also Price, strategy factors
    influencing
    variables to be considered, 291

Business to business promotion,
    advertising, publicity, sales
    promotion, 513–14
Business to business services, the
    future of, 607–10, 627–28
Buss, W. C., 121 n
Butaney, Gul, 348 n, 363
Buyer behavior models
    Choffray-Lilien model, 119
    Sheth model, 119
    Webster and Wind model, 117
Buyer needs, 434–37
    important and unimportant,
      435–36
    methods to uncover, 436
    rational versus emotional, 436
Buying center
    decision making unit, 67–68
    importance of information for
      marketers, 68, 70
    members, varied roles of, 67
    new task versus rebuy situation,
      205
Buying process, steps in, 33–37
Buying situations
    modified rebuy, 49, 52–53
    new task buying, 49–52
    straight rebuy, 49, 52–53
Buzzell, Robert D., 214

C

Caballero, Marjorie J., 537 n
CAD/CAM (computer-aided design
    and manufacturing), 666
Calatone, Roger J., 400
Calder, Bobby J., 26
Canadair Challenger jet, 689–711
Canadian Johnson Wax, 403 n
Cardoza, Jack, 508
Cardozo, Richard N., 288
Careers
    in business to business
      marketing, 4–6, 27–28
    in business to business selling,
      440–42
Carle Instruments, 514
Carlson, Neil, 145–47
Carman, J. M., 626 n
Carnevale, Mary Lu, 641 n
Carter, Joseph R., 363
Carusone, Peter S., 143
Casey, M., 132 n
Cateora, Philip R., 281
Caterpillar Tractor, 76–77, 639
Cavinato, Joseph L., 67 n, 84 n,
    91 n, 93 n, 665

Caywood, Clark L., 665
Celley, Albert E., 62
Center for Advanced Purchasing
    Study (CAPS), 114
Central General Hospital, 51–52
Central Maintenance and Welding,
    75
Certified Purchasing Manager; *see*
    CPM
Chainco, 296–97
Chambers, John C., 223 n
Champion International
    Corporation, 639
Chance, David, 114
Chandler, Bob, 406
Channel conflict, 348–54
    conflict management, 350–51
    factors underlying, 348–50
    legal perspective, 351–52
    problems in manufacturer-
      intermediary relationships,
      352–54
Channel cooperation, 347–48
Channel intermediaries
    functions of, 330–31
    risk taking, 332
Channel management, 332–33
Channel strategy, 329
Channels
    direct, 334
    indirect, 335
    international, 354–55
Chemical Banking Corporation,
    639
Chemicals, Inc., 284
Child, Robert W., 288
Childers Machine Company,
    359–62
Choffray, Jean Marie, 121 n, 288,
    522 n
Choffray-Lilien model of buyer
    behavior, 119–22
Chonko, Lawrence B., 509
Christopher, M. G., 614 n
Chrysler, 668
Churchill, Randolph S., 653 n
Citibank, 657
C.I.T. Financial, 314
Citicorp, 613
Clapton, Stephen W., 98
Clearwood Building, Inc., 163
Coaker, James W., 117
Coca Cola, 657
Coe, Barbara J., 669 n
Coleman, Donald R., 343 n
Colgate-Palmolive, 159

Columbus-McKinnon Corporation, 354
Competition, 431
    Japanese strategy, 163
Compton, 461
Computer-aided design and manufacturing; *see* CAD/CAM
Computer spreadsheet for operating statements projection, 300
Computers in personal selling, 4, 48–49
    General Electric's Sentry System, 449
    Valmont Industries, 48–49
Constantin, James A., 363
Consumer markets versus business markets, 3–4, 6–15
Consumer products companies, 3
Contract between buyer and seller, 32
Contribution pricing; *see* Pricing, methods and strategies
Control Data, 667
Cook, James, 668 n
Cooper, Philip D., 623 n
Cooper, Robert G., 288
Coopers and Lybrand, 666 n
Copacino, William C., 393 n
Coppett, John I, 402
Corey, E. Raymond, 117 n
Corning Glass, 133, 343
Cosinga, Robert M., 645 n
Cost benefit analysis, 302
Cost of salespersons versus promotion, 514
Coughlin, Anne T., 355 n, 363
Cowell, Donald, 614 n, 619 n, 625 n
CPM (Certified Purchasing Manager), 10–11
Craffard, H. O., 484 n
Cravens, David W., 124 n, 209 n
Creative selling, 439–40
Crispell, Diane, 192
Cron, William L., 509, 533 n
Cross, James M., 117 n
Cross, James S., 526 n
Crow, Lowell E., 119 n
CSX System Corporation, 572–77, 580–81, 586, 593–94
Culley, James D., 294, 305 n
Cullinane (company), 213
Curry, David J., 214 n
Customers, categories of
    commercial enterprises, 17–18

Customers—*Cont.*
    government organizations, 18–19
    institutions, 19
Cundiff, Edward W., 498 n
Calvin, Robert J., 487 n
Cunningham, Ross M., 526 n

D

Dailey, Jere L., 669 n
Dalrymple, Douglas J., 448 n, 449 n, 648 n
Darden, William, R., 515 n, 534 n
Database sources, 177
DataCorp of Virginia, Inc., 631–33
Davids, Meryl, 550
Davidson, William H., 205 n
Davis, Duane, 645
Day, Abby, 400
Day, George S., 265 n
Day, Ralph L., 25, 98
Dean, Joel, 304 n, 305 n
Dearden, John, 612 n
de Brentani, Ulrike, 288
DEC, 235
Deere and Company, 205–6, 559
De George, Richard T., 654
de Kluyver, Cornelius, 235
Delaney, Robert, 374 n
Delphi method of forecasting, 222–23
Demand assessment, 301
Deregulation, 5
    of transportation industry, 374–75
Dessi, Adrian, 524, 524 n
Dhebar, Anirudh, 325
DHL Corporation, 231
Dickinson, John, 534 n
Diffusion index, 226
Dillon, Thomas F., 98, 144
Dillon, William R., 178
Dion, Paul A., 113 n
Direct customer contact in marketing research, 158–59
Direct financing lease; *see* Leasing versus selling, types of leases
Direct Response Corporation, 525
Discounts, types of, 315–16
Distribution
    international, 393–94
    product positioning by, 215
Distribution alternatives
    exclusive, 393
    intensive, 392–93
    selective, 392–93

Distribution channels in service businesses, 615
Diversey-Wyandotte, 409
Dobler, Donald W., 117 n, 309 n
Dodge, H. Robert, 440, 440 n
Doe, R. Chang, 214 n
Doherty, John, 453
Dolan, Robert J., 272 n, 304 n
Dominic, Jerry, 398
Donath, B., 447 n
Donnelly, James H., Jr., 606 n
Douglas and Company, 461–64
Dow Chemical, 305, 390, 606
Dow Jones, 613
Dowst, Somerby, 115 n
Doyle, Peter, 200 n
Dren, Shmuel S., 325
Drozdenko, Ronald, 288
Drucker, Peter F., 370
DTM Products, 163
Dubinsky, Alan J., 509, 650
Dun and Bradstreet, 524, 613
Duncan, Delbert J., 119 n
Duncan Business Machines, 507–8
Dunn, Albert H., 497 n
Dunn, Dan T., Jr., 468
Du Pont, 3, 206, 279, 293, 303, 423, 485 n, 528, 606, 640, 645
Dwyer, Robert F., 114 n
Dyson, Esther, 269, 270

E

Eagle Steel Supply Company, 548–50
Eastman Kodak, 321, 667
Eaton Corporation, 280
Economic fluctuation, market sensitivity to, 159
Economic order quantity model; *see* EOQ
Edel, Edwin, 572, 577, 580, 582
Edwards, Bill, 461–64
Electronics Products Company, 396–97
Electro-Scientific Industries, 495
Emery Worldwide, 231
England, Wilbur B., 82 n
Englewood, Christopher, 288
Enis, Ben M., 647 n
Enviro Sciences, Inc., 605
Environmental scanner, 132
Environments in business service firms, 605–7

EOQ (economic order quantity model), 385–86
formula for calculating, 386
Eovaldi, Thomas L., 11 n
EPI, Inc., 22
Epson Corporation of Japan, 339
Ericsson, an international firm, 214
Epsev, James, 289
Esmark, 321
Estimate demand; *see* Sales forecasting
Ethical improprieties in purchasing
competitive bidding, 137–38
gifts and kickbacks, 137
presale service and samples, 138
reciprocity, 137
sharp practices, 137
Ethical issues and daily decisions, 640–41
Ethical responsibility, corporate, 638
Ethics
in advertising, 653–54
and international marketing, 655–58
and pricing, 646–49
and sales, 649–53
in marketing research, 644–46
Evans, Kenneth R., 633
Experience curve, 214, 265

F

Faes, W., 25
Facilitating agencies and the flow of goods, 345
Fahner, Hal, 631
Family Lines Rail System, 573
Faris, A. J., 534 n
Faris, Charles W., 49 n, 50 n
Farmer, John Haywood, 144
Farmer, Richard N., 665
Farmland Industries, 313
Farrel, J. W., 384 n
Farrel, Paul V., 32, 37 n, 127 n, 128 n, 643 n
FASB Statement, 313 n
Fearon, Harold E., 82 n, 114 n
Federal Express, 215, 230–31, 233, 292, 523
Fedo, David A., 655 n
Felch, Robert I., 665, 137 n
Femina, Jerry Della, 232
Fenster, Gail, 150–53
Fern, Edward F., 7 n
Ferrell, O. C., 7 n, 607 n, 638 n

Find, S.V.P. Inc., 616
Fine, Seymour H., 363
Finkin, Eugene F., 254 n
Firestone, 48, 389
First Security Services Corporation, 606
Firtle, Neil H., 178
Fitzgerald, Thomas, 610 n
Flax, Steven, 11
Florida Publishing Company, 574
Fluctuating demand, 608–9
FOB
destination, 373
origin, 373
Fodor, George M., 98
Forbes, John L., 299
Ford, John B., IV, 62
Ford Motor Company, 7, 11, 18, 133, 205, 346, 668
Fortunada, Frank, Jr., 187–89
Fortunada, Vito, 187
Franklin, Stan, 60–61
Frazier, Gary L., 44 n
Freborg, Roy, 270
French, H. E., III, 665
French, Warren A., 62
Friedman, Hershey H., 289
Fritzsche, David, 655, 658 n
Fruehauf Trucking Company, 242, 245–46
Funker, G. Roy, 456
Funkhouser, G. Ray, 456 n
Futrell, Charles, 345 n, 448 n, 472 n
Future trends in business to business marketing, 666–70

G

Gagliano, Caren Calish, 289
Gagnon, Christopher E., 618 n
Gaida, Kathleen A., 606 n, 628 n
Gallison Company, 322
Gannet, 613
Garman, Walter, 480 n, 481 n
Gaski, John E., 363
Gattorna, John, 349 n, 400
Gazzara, Ben, 232
Geer Company, 59
Gelb, Betsy D., 608 n
Gelb, Gabriel M., 308 n
General Dynamics, 70, 199
General Electric (GE), 12, 33, 35, 52, 293, 315, 345, 390, 445, 446–47, 522
General Electric's Sentry System, 449

General Finance Corporation, 314
General Foods, 70
General line distributor, 337
General Mills, 3, 4
General Motors (GM), 9–11, 40, 46, 48, 233, 293, 345, 346, 387, 668
General Telephone and Telegraph, 610
General Trailer Company, 241–43
Ghingold, Morry, 62 n
Giallourakis, Michael, 363
Gibbs, Michael L., 634
Gibson, Dave, 465
Giltner, Dave, 145
Gimpert, David E., 19 n
Giunipero, Larry C., 48 n, 49 n
GM; *see* General Motors
GNP, 605
Goetz, Joe F., 325
Goldman Sachs, 495
Goldstein, Frederick A., 192
Goodpaster, Kenneth E., 638 n
Goodwin, George, 269
Gord, Graham, 325
Gordon, Eric, 360–62
Gordon, Howard L., 550
Gordon, Jack, 488 n
Gorman Products, Inc., 396–97
Govoni, Norman A. P., 480 n
Goyder, John, 192
Grabowski, Daniel P., 192
Graham, John L., 13 n, 98
Graham, Sharman, 384 n
Grassell, Milt, 144
Gravereau, Victor P., 643 n
Greenley, Gordon E., 325
Gregory, Robert E., 144
Gresham, Larry G., 363, 638 n
Griffith, B., 626 n
Griffith, Thomas, 651 n
Gross, Irwin, 192
Gross national product; *see* GNP
Grossman, Elliott S., 162 n
GRS Industrial Supply Company, 453
Grubb, John, 163
Grubb, Robert, 163
GTE, 233
Sylvania Division, 133
Guaranteed cost reduction program, 76
Gudebrod Brothers of Philadelphia, 22
Guiltinan, Joseph P., 13 n, 17 n, 19 n, 364, 612 n, 634
Guimaraes, Tor, 193

Gummesson, Evert, 214 n
Gumpert, David E., 19 n
Gunts, Robert, 656 n
Gupta, Ashok K., 289
Government information sources, 171; see also SIC

H

H. O. Penn Machinery Company, 646
H. O. Smith (company), 11
Hafer, John, 468
Hague, Paul, 192, 363
Hahn, Chan K., 48 n, 384 n
Halcomb, Ruth, 665
Haley, George T., 400
Hall, Robert W., 44 n
Hammitt, John, 233
Hanson, Michael, 465–68
Hardy, Kenneth G., 351 n, 689–711
Harley Davidson, 46, 48, 387
Harp, Laurie, 645 n
Harper, Doug, 387 n
Harrigan, K. R., 279 n
Harris, Calorific, 537–38
Harrison, Allen, 95
Hartley, Robert F., 480 n
Hartley, Steven, 415 n
Hashaway, Phil, 78
Howes, John M., 63
Hawkins, Del I., 645 n
Hayes, Michael H., 671–86
Haynes, Ulric, Jr., 501 n
Heinritz, Stuart F., 37 n, 127 n, 643 n
Heinritz, Farrell and Smith, 49 n
Henderson, Bruce, 275, 276 n
Henderson, Tom, 553–54, 556–61
Henderson Steel Service Center, 553–54, 556–61, 566–71
Henkel, Jan W., 62
Hennessey, Hubert D., 634
Hergenrather and Company, 339
Heskett, James L., 369 n, 385 n, 611 n, 613 n, 627 n, 634
Heuther, Richard J., 446
Hewlett Packard, 12, 264, 298, 495, 523
Hiday, Jeffrey L., 530 n
Hilger, Marye Tharp, 498
Hill, Richard M., 117 n
Hills, Gerald E., 124 n
Hindin, Russell, 12 n
Hinds, Ed., 401
Hisrich, Robert, 262 n
Hite, Robert E., 468

Hlavacek, James D., 25, 81 n, 235
Hoehn, Robert G., 453
Hoffman, Carl C., 665
Hoffman, Kathleen P., 665
Holloway, Fred, 340
Holloway Corporation, 43
Honda, 133
Honeywell, 233, 423, 610, 667
Hooper, Margo W., 572
House account, 352
Howard, John A., 119 n
Howell, Roy D., 326, 363
Howell Chuck Company, 140
Huffen, Herbert, 502 n
Hughes, G. David, 450 n
Hunt-Wesson Foods, Inc., 32
Hurwood, David L., 162 n
Hutchinson, Leland, 270
Huthwaite Research Group, 99
Hutt, Michael D., 384 n
Hyatt Legal Services, 615
Hypercard software, 269

I

IBM (International Business Machines), 10, 12, 48, 70, 123, 133, 184, 209, 233, 264, 292, 306, 387, 445, 323, 501, 632, 639, 657
Image, product positioning by, 215
Inelastic demand, 13
Information sources for research, 171–83; see also Hypercard software; Information specialists; and SIC
primary data, 171
secondary data, 171–83
Information specialists, 177
Ingram, Thomas N., 509
Ingrassia, Lawrence, 256 n
Input output analysis, 226
Inspecting goods for quality, 35–36
International Business Machines; see IBM
International business to business selling, 317, 457–58, 625–26
International channels, 354–56
International customers, 19, 22
International distribution, 393–94
International Harvester Company, 205–6
International Paper, 423
International product strategy, 281
International publicity and sales promotion, 541

International segmentation, 205–6
Inventory control, 43, 381–87; see also EOQ, formula for calculating
80/20 axiom, 384
EOQ model, 385–86
JIT, 386–87
manufacturer's information system, 381
warehousing, 381–84
Inventory management
computerized records, 346
inventory level policy, 352
risk taking in, 332
Investment Center Financial Corporation, 450
Investor Update, 593
Ispe, 529
ITT, 343

J

Jackson, Donald W., Jr., 63, 364
Jackson, Ralph W., 144
Jain, Subhash C., 197 n, 277 n, 293 n, 297 n, 501 n, 542 n
James, Barrie G., 214 n
Janson, Robert L., 98
Japan Management Association, 44
Jenkins, Steven, 509
JIT (just in time), 44–49, 386–87
and choice of transportation mode, 387
computerized purchasing, 46
frequent and reliable delivery, 44–45
100% quality, 45
practiced by Japanese organizations, 386
single sourcing, 46
stable production schedules, 46
top management commitment, 48
and use of warehouses, 387
zero inventory, 44
Joachimsthaler, Erecha, 122 n
Jobber, David, 192
Jobbers; see Limited line distributors
Jobs, Steven P., 232–34
John Deere, 314
John Roberts Manufacturing Company, 95
Johns-Manville, 293
Johnson, Eugene M., 440 n, 497 n, 606 n, 618 n
Johnson Wax, 495, 639
Johnston, Wesley J., 119 n, 469

Jones, Michael H., 13 n
Jones, Patricia E., 208 n, 209 n
Jones, Thomas C., 401
Judson Rees and Associates, Ltd.,
    605
Jury of executive opinion, 221
Just in time; *see* JIT

K

Kanban, 48
Kaner Company, 453
Kanet, John S., 62
Kapar, Mitch, 269
Kapp, A., 98
Kasle Steel, 46
Kastiel, Diane Lynn, 634
Kasturi, Ransan V., 364
Kehoe, William J., 647 n
Keith, Janet E., 63, 364
Kelley, Bill, 509, 525 n
Kelley Services, 605
Kelly, I. Patrick, 117 n
Kendall, Donal, 234
Kennedy, Consultants, 605
Kerin, Roger A., 33 n, 196 n,
    371 n, 387 n, 533 n
Kern, Richard, 174
Kiley, Julia A., 469
King, Bob, 468
Kingston-Warren Company, 711–29
Kirkpatrick, Jerry, 665
Kirshnan, R., 400
Kiser, G. E., 448 n
Kleinschmidt, Elko, J., 288
Kleizen, Hendrikus, G., 289
Kleppner, 523 n
Knisely, Gary, 617 n
Knowledge explosion, 135–36, 666
Konapa, Leonard J., 643 n
Kotler, Philip, 4 n, 7 n, 197 n,
    340 n, 354 n, 390 n, 444 n,
    517 n, 537 n, 623 n
Kowalski, J. R., 400
Krapfel, Robert E., 144
Krauz, Joshua, 289
Kriger, Ruth Haas, 63
Krosnick, John A., 192
Krupp, James A. G., 325
Kuehn, A. A., 251
Kullberg, Duane, 640
Kurtz, David L., 6 n, 386 n, 440 n,
    491 n
Kuzdrall, Paul J., 326, 363
Kyj, Larissa S., 98
Kyj, Myroslaw J., 98

L

Laboratory of Advertising
    Performance (LAP), 433
Laczniak, Gene R., 647 n, 665
LaLonde, Bernard J., 401
Lambert, Douglas M., 369 n,
    379 n, 380 n, 401
Lange, Ann E., 655 n
Langeard, E., 626 n
Langley, C. John, Jr., 401
Lantos, Geoffrey P., 665
LaPlace, Peter, 6 n
Laroche, Michael, 665
Lauer, Joachim, 281 n, 235
Layer, William, 264
Lazer, William, 294 n, 305 n
Leading indicators, 225
Learning curve analysis in product
    strategy, 265–68
Leasing, advantages of, 11–12
Leasing versus selling, 311–15
    advantages for buyer and seller,
        313–14
    types of leases, 314–15
    ways to lease equipment, 314
Leavitt, Harold J., 117 n
Leavitt, Theodore, 520, 607, 608 n,
    666 n
Lebhar-Friedman Research and
    Information Services, 526
LeBlanc, Ronald P., 63, 119 n
Lee, Hau L., 325
Lee, Lamar, Jr., 117 n
Lee, W. L., 309 n
Leenders, Michael R., 82 n, 144
Legal considerations in
    purchasing, 55–56
Lehman, Donald R., 666 n
Lele, Milind M., 363, 401
Lewis, William F., 364
Li, Richard P., 550
Lidington, Simon, 192
Life cycle analysis, 227
Lilien, Gary L., 68 n, 121 n, 288,
    289, 522, 536 n
Limited line distributors, 337
Lincoln, Douglas J., 50 n
Lincoln Electric, 76
Little, Rich, 453
Liquid Paper, 6
Loctite, 68 n, 123 n, 320
Logistical management; *see*
    Physical distribution
    management
Logistics; *see* Materials
    management

Loring, James A., 98
Lotus, 270
Lovelock, Christopher, H., 216 n,
    621 n, 621, 624 n
Lowe's Companies, 495
Luby, Judy, 504
Lucas, George H., Jr., 363
Luqmani, Mushtag, 264
Lusch, Robert F., 363, 532 n, 625 n
Lusch, Virginia N., 332, 625 n
Lynn, Susan A., 634

M

MacMillan, Ian C., 208 n
Macro/Micro segmentation,
    199–200
Madden, Charles S., 537 n
Madden, Thomas J., 178
Madison Chemical Corporation, 97
Magee, John F., 393 n
Magrath, Allan J., 351 n
Main, Jeremy, 459 n
Maker, Philip, 329 n
Make-buy analysis
    definition of, 80
    factors in the decision, 80–81
    interdisciplinary committee to
        implement, 82
    reasons to manufacture, 81
    use of vendor expertise in, 81
Management by exception, 33
Management Information of
    Competitor Strategies; *see*
    MICS
Manoochebri, G. H., 48 n, 387 n
Manufacturer-intermediary
    relationship, 352–54
Manufacturer's representative
    limitations to using, 343–34
    operates on commission, 343
    sells manufacturer's products,
        340
    trends for, 344
Manville Corporation, 661–62
Marginal pricing; *see* Pricing,
    methods and strategies
Marion Labs, 495
Market controllable variables, 131
Market demand, definition, 219
Market factor, definition, 218
Market forecast, definition, 219
Market index, definition, 218
Market maturity, signs of, 305
Market potential, definition, 218
Market pull process, 253

Market Research Corporation of America
  source for sales indices, 515
Market selection strategies
  concentrated, 199
  differentiated, 198–99
  undifferentiated, 197–98
Market share, definition
Market skimming versus market penetration, 303–4
Marketing environment
  analysis of uncontrollable variables, 131
  environmental forces and buying decisions, 131–37
  ethical standards, 641–42
  working with government, 642
Marketing ethics, factors influencing, 638
Marketing information system; see MIS
Marketing planning and strategy, 22
Marketing research
  by American Marketing Association, 162
  consumer versus business to business, 157
  international, 184–85
  market characteristics, 161
  market potential, 159
  organization of, 183–84
  research process, 167–70
  sales analysis, 161
Marketing strategy for category of customers, 17–19
Markin, R., 628 n
Marks, Duffy, 354 n
Marriott Corporation, 613
Martin, Christopher, 400
Martin, Warren G., 449 n
Mason, Raymone E., 401
Mason Electronics, 158–50
Massey-Ferguson, 205–6
Mast, Kenneth E., 63
Materials management, 42–49; see also Inventory control and JIT
Mathews, H. L., 123 n
Mathewson Company, 286–88
Matthews, John B., Jr., 638 n
Matthyssens, P., 25
Mayer, C. S., 170 n
Mayfield, Dr., 663
Mayflower Moving and Storage Company, 243–44
Mazda Motor Corporation, 133

McAleer, Gordon, 520–21
McCarthy, E. Jerome, 612
McCuen, Barbara A., 468
McDaniel, Carl, Jr., 392 n, 515 n, 534 n
McDonald, M. M., 614 n
McFeely-Wacherle Jett, 641
McGown, K. L., 665
McKee, Daryl P., 634
McVey, Philip, 49 n
McWilliams, Robert D., 50 n
Mead Corporation, 17
Media II, 528
Mehta, Nitin T., 299 n
Mendoza, Mario, 453
Mentzer, John T., 14, 350 n, 401
Mercer, J. A. T., 289
Meredith, Jack R., 63
Meredith, Lindsay, 144
Merenski, J. Paul, 364
Merrett, Bernie, 468
Merrill Lynch, 445, 613
Meyerowitz, Steven A., 325
Michael, George C., 219
Michaels, Ronald E., 98, 509
Michie, Donald A., 364
Michman, Ronald D., 235, 392 n, 393 n
Microelectronics and Computer Technology Corporation, 667
Micro-Lam, 237–44
MICS (Management Information of Competitor Strategies), 133
Middleboro Hospital, 466–67
Miler, Richard Lee, 364
Miller, J., 525 n
Mills, George, 416–18
MIS (Marketing Information System), 162, 164–67
Missionary salespersons, 347
Mixed distribution systems, 346
Mobil Oil, 343
Modified rebuy, 53–54
Moller, K. E. Kristian, 63
Moncka, Robert M., 125 n
Moncrief, William C., 468
Mondy, Robert W., 438 n
Monsanto, 343, 645
Montahari, John R., 665
Montgomery, David B., 265 n
Moore, Sam, 506
Moore, William L., 289
Moore Business Forms, 292
Morash, Edward A., 375 n
More, Roger A., 289, 403 n
Morgan, James, 77 n
Morita, Akio, 44

Morris, Michael, 400, 669
Morse, W. J., 310 n
Moschitta, John, 231
Motor Carrier Act, 375
Motorola, 73–74, 74 n, 235
Mougel, Mark, 15 n
Mouritzen, Russell H., 468
Muffco, 270
Mullik, Satinder K., 223 n
Multiple sourcing, 123
Murphy, Harold, 562
Murphy, Patrick E., 647 n
Murray, Keith B., 665

N

Nadal, Miles S., 550
Narasimihan, Ram, 63
Narus, James A., 76 n, 193
National Association of Purchasing Management, 114
  Code of Ethics, 642–43
National Cash Register; see NCR
National Labs, 407
National Semiconductor, 343
Naumann, Earl, 50 n
NCR (National Cash Register), 209, 501, 667
Negotiation, 82–88, 99–111
  definition, 82
  maneuvers, strategies and tactics, 85
  objectives of, 84
  preparation for, 88
  qualities necessary for, 82–83
  successful negotiator, summary of behavior, 111
  use of questions, 86–88
Negotiation of specifications, dates, terms and price, 11
Nelson, James E., 171 n
Nelson, Marsha H., 401
Nevin, John R., 363
New England Testing Laboratory, Inc., 605
New product, organization of effort, 260–63
  new product committee, 262
  new product department, 262
  product management concept, 261
  venture team 262–63
New product development
  role of marketing managers, 253
  seven steps in the process of, 254–59

New product development—*Cont.*
technology push or market pull, 253–54
New River Company, 574
New services development, 613, 617–19
New York City, Metropolitan Transportation Authority, 18
Nickels, William G., 514 n
Nissan, 133
Nolan, Johanna Jones, 469
Nordlie Wilson, Inc., 609
Norfolk and Western Railway, 576
Nowak, Ed, 530
Null, Robert O., 263 n

O

O'Brien, Terrance, 235
OEM; *see* Original equipment manufacturers
Office Boss Company, 189–90
O'Keefe, Philip, 550
Olshan, Kenneth, 231
Olshavsky, Richard W., 119 n
Olszewski, Agnes Pauline, 634
O'Neal, Charles, 44 n, 48 n
Onkvisit, Sak, 355 n, 394 n
On-line information systems, 177; *see also* Information sources
list of, 179
Operating cost research, 159
Operating lease; *see also* Leasing versus selling, types of leases
Order-cycle period, 384
Order processing, 387–90
Organization of the textbook, 23
Organizational buyers, 65
Original equipment manufacturers (OEM), 13, 18

P

Pacific Laminated, 242
Page, Albert L., 444 n
Paine Webber, 616, 617
Painter, Tony, 665
Papermate, 6
Parsons, Leonard J., 648 n
Pascarella, Perry, 71 n, 76 n
Paul, Ronald N., 289
Peat Marwick, 524
Peerless Trucking Company, 242, 244–45
Perceived value in pricing, 76

Perdue, Barbara C., 98
Pernick, Sandra, 526 n
Perreault, William D., Jr., 117 n
Persoft, 270
Personal selling
versus advertising, 12
cost of, 433–34
definition, 429
steps in the process, 450–57
Pesch, Michael J., 63
Peter, J. Paul, 606 n
Peters, Melvin, 401
Peters, Tom, 71 n, 76 n
Peterson, Wayne, 245–46
Petrarca, Bill, 466–67
Pfaff, Fred, 550
Phillips, Lynn W., 214 n
Physical distribution
customer service
identifying complaints, 376
trade-off analysis, 377–80
written standards, 376
definition, 367–68, 370
Physical distribution management, 370
as a career choice, 371
Piercy, Nigel, 193, 550
Pindar Company, 544–47
Pinto, Peter A., 48 n, 387 n
Pitt, Leland F., 325
Plank, Richard E., 236
Polastri, Riccardo P., 325
Polhill, Frederick, 289
Pollack, Andrew, 213 n
Pooler, David J., 92 n
Pooler, Victor, H., 92 n
Porter, Michael E., 206, 208 n, 279 n
Positioning in business services, 611
Positioning of products, 209–17
definition, 209
by other factors, 212–17
relative to the competition, 212
Powley, R. H., 62, 143
Precision Cutting Tools, 145–47
Prescott, John E., 509
Price
elastic, 294
elasticity of demand, 301–2
leadership strategy, 306–7
product positioning by, 213–14
skimming, 303–4
strategy, factors influencing, 93, 292–95
versus total cost, 70
Prices for services, 614

Pricing; *see also* experience curve
through life cycle of the product, 303–7
methods and strategies, 296–301
policies, 315
Pride, William M., 7 n, 144, 607 n
Prime, F. Osborne, 576
Primerica Corporation, 639
Proctor and Gamble, 159
Product adoption-diffusion process, 273–75
Product deletion strategy
divestment, 280–81
harvesting, 279
line simplification, 280
Product life-cycle model
technological advances, effect of, 64
sales at different stages, 63
Product management concept, 260–61
Product mix planning
business cycles and seasonal variations, 272
competition, 272
identifying determinants, 268
market factors, 273
operating capacity, 272
technology, 268, 271
Product portfolio
diagnosing, 276
strategic business units of, 275
strategies, 276–78
Product specifications, 33–34
Professional publications
academic, 176
trade, 176
Profit, measures of, 92
Promotion campaign, effectiveness of
modification, if necessary, 540
objectives met or exceeded, 540
pretesting and posttesting, 539
responses to advertisements, 538
Promotional mix in consumer goods selling, 429
Promotional plan, 515–17
Promotional strategy, international, 540
Pruden, H. O., 620 n
Publicity, sources for, 532–33
Purchasing
contract, 35
department policies, 31–33
impact on company profit, 91–93
personnel, motives of, 122–24

Purchasing—*Cont.*
  purchasing organization
    centralized versus
      decentralized, 40
    and size of company, 37–38
  quality acceptance level, 72–74
  records
    access to open orders, 54
    commodity record file, 55
    vendor catalogs and literature,
      54
    vendor experience file, 54
Purolater Courier Corporation,
  231–32

Q

Quad/Graphics, 495
Quality, product positioning by,
  214–15
Quality acceptance level, 70–74
Quality control in services, 609–10
Quelch, John A., 272 n, 304 n
Quick Corporation, 525
Quinn, James Brian, 618
Quraeshi, Zahir, 264

R

Rackham, Neil, 99–100
Raffield, Barney T., III, 634, 665
Rainville, Joyce, 665
Raj, S. P., 289
Ramirez, Anthony, 135 n
Rao, Murfidhar, 522 n
Rao, Ram C., 326
Raritan Supply Company, 453
Ras, Ram C., 476 n
Rathbun, Craig, 98
Raychem, 495
RCA, 667
Reader, Diane, 447
Readers Digest, 495
Reciprocity, legal or illegal, 11, 651
Reddy, N. Mohan, 235, 364
Reeder, Betty H., 123 n
Reeder, Robert R., 123 n
Regulation in business services,
  606–7
Regulatory agencies, 136
Reid, David A., 265 n
Reidenbach, R. Eric, 638 n, 665
Reinhart, Thomas C., 343 n
Reisberg, Jerry, 176
Remen, Steve, 410
Research specialists, internal or
  outside the organization,
  170–71

Rhode Island Hospital, 368–69
Rich, Stuart U., 237, 306 n
Richards, E. J., 287
Ricoh, 447
Ries, Al, 216 n
Riesy, Peter C., 214 n
Riley, Daniel W., 401
Rink, David R., 448 n
Ritchey, Mr., 396–97
Roberts Fibre Company, 142
Robin, Donald P., 638, 665
Robinson, Patrick J., 49 n, 50 n
Robinson-Patman Act, 295, 380,
  648, 665
Robles, Fernando, 236
Rockingham National Bank, 631
Rockwell International (Municipal
  and Utility Division), 334
Roering, Kenneth J., 647 n
Rogers, Mel, 244–45
Rogers, Nagel, Langhart (RNL),
  671–86
Roman, Ernan, 526 n
Ronkainen, Ilkka, 289
Rosemount, Inc., 415–26
Rosenblatt, Meir, J., 325
Rosenfield, Donald B., 393 n
Ross, Robert H., 363
Rothschild, William E., 272 n
Routing; *see* Traffic management
Rowell, R. F., 286–88
Royal Bank of Canada, 269
Rudelius, William, 33 n, 196 n,
  371 n, 395 n, 415 n
Russ, Frederick A., 117 n
Russell, Frederick A., 523 n
Russell, Mark, 453
Ryans, John K., Jr., 136 n, 213 n,
  667 n
Ryder Truck, 159

S

S. C. Johnson and Son, Limited,
  403–15
Saddler, Jeanne, 668 n
Sales agents and brokers, 344–45
  handle entire output of
    manufacturers, 344
  more promotion than
    representatives, 344
  prevalent in food industry
Sales branch, 334
Sales force
  motivating
    compensation plans, 495–96
    evaluation, 496–98

Sales force—*Cont.*
  leadership, 491–93
  sales quotas, 493–95
  recruiting, 481–82
  training
    areas covered, 485–87
    evaluating training, 489–91
    field sales training, 458
    professional trainers, 487, 488,
      489
    purpose of, 484–85
Sales force selection hiring
    criteria, 482
  applications and interviews, 483
  decision by applicant and
    management, 482–83
  psychological tests, 484
Sales force staff, 479–81
Sales forecasting
  basic terminology, 218–19
  decision making, 318
  for each product, 217
  qualitative approaches, 221–23
  quantitative approaches, 223–27
  top-down and bottom-up, 220–21
Sales manager qualifications,
  471–73
Sales organization plans
  centralized versus
    decentralized, 475
  functional, 475
  line and staff, 475
  line organization, 474
  by specialization, 476–78
Sales presentation, major
    approaches to, 438–39
Sales promotion, 533–36
Sales resistance, 455
Salespeople in international
    markets, 498
  extra compensation, 501–2
  language and cultural training,
    501
Salesperson, business to business,
    activities of, 431–33
Saleswomen, 447–48
Sanderson, R. Hedley, 603 n
Sandia National Laboratories, 74,
    74 n, 264
  massively parallel processing,
    computer program, 264–65
Sandler, Lester, 401
Sarathy, Ravi, 236
Saunders, John, 200 n
Schaefer, Wolfgang, 551
Schary, Philip B., 401
Schattle Consultants, 605

Schechter, Alan M., 472 n
Schelhardt, Timothy D., 641 n
Scheuing, Eberhard, 440 n, 497 n,
    606 n, 618 n
Schmidt, J., 524 n
Schmidt, Roland W., 268 n
Schneider, Lewis, 48 n, 387 n
Schoell, William F., 7 n, 10 n,
    13 n, 17 n, 19 n
Schoenberger, Richard J., 47 n,
    48 n, 387 n
Schroeder, Gary D., 63
Schurr, Paul H., 26, 114 n, 468
Schwartz, David J., 14
Scientific Radio Systems, 22
Scudder, Gary D., 63
Sculley, John, 234
Seaboard Coast Line Industries,
    Inc., 572–73
Sears, 10
Securitech, 406
Securities and Exchange
    Commission, 133
Security Pacific Corporation, 639
Seelig, Pat, 551
Segmentation, benefit, 434–35
Segmentation approaches
    macro/micro, 199–200
    nested, 201
Segmentation strategy, 196–97
Segmenting business to business
    markets, 195–209
Selling, personal; see Personal
    selling
Selling an idea versus a product,
    615–17
Selling consumer goods versus
    selling business goods, 430
Selling styles in the business
    market, 440
Sejo, Oh, 114 n
Service
    as an attribute, 74–75
    product positioning by, 215–17
Service marketing mix, the
    controllable variables,
    612–17
Services
    classification of, 619–24
    people based versus equipment
    based, 623–24
Services marketing versus product
    marketing, 610–19
Shanklin, William L., 136 n, 213 n,
    667 n
Shapely Sack Company, Inc.,
    397–400

Shapiro, B. F., 197 n
Shapiro, Benson P., 196 n, 200 n,
    272 n, 304 n
Shapiro, Roy D., 369 n
Shaw, John J., 355 n, 394 n
Shealy, Robert, 144
Sheegan, Steven M., 364
Shelley, Charles J., 236
Shelley, Maynard W., II, 117 n
Sherman Antitrust Act, 295
Sherman Brothers Trucking, 239,
    243–44
Sheth, Jagdish N., 119 n
Sheth model of buyer behavior,
    119
Shingo, Shigeo, 44
Shipley, David D., 326, 469
Shostack, G. Lynn, 608 n, 611 n,
    216 n, 236, 613 n, 634
Shroeder, Gary D., 63
Sibley, Stanley D., 364, 392 n,
    393 n
SIC (Standard Industrial
    Classification), 172–76, 196,
    200, 203
Siempliski, Michael, 444 n
Signode Industries, Inc., 262–63
Silk, Alvin J., 522 n
Silva, David W., 469
Simpson, Edwin K., 489 n
Singler, Charles H., 450 n
Skinner, Steven J., 364
Skolnik, Rayne, 447 n
Slinger, Rodney, 148–50
Small order problem, 88–91
    cost of handling versus cost of
    items sold, 88
    specialty techniques, 89–91
Smatter, Mary S., 508
Smith, Clifton L., 37 n, 127 n
Smith, Daniel C., 509
Smith, David, 63
Smith, Donald D., 223 n
Smith, Lyne, III, 617
Smith, Paul, 236
SMS Supply Company, 526
Social responsibility of managers,
    639
Soukup, William R., 288
Southern Railway, 576
Spin-off services, 606
Speh, Thomas W., 384 n
Spekman, Robert E., 44 n, 200 n,
    468
Springer, Robert F., 665
SPS (statistical process control),
    45

Stake Fastener Company, 344
Stalpart, Dan, 405
Standard Communications
    Equipment, 153
Standard Industrial Classification;
    see SIC
Standard Oil of New Jersey, 523
Stanton, William J., 345 n
Steelcase (company), 215
Steiger Tractor Company, 133
Stenger, Alan J., 401
Sterling, Jay U., 401
Stern, Aimee, 634
Stern, Louis W., 11 n, 215 n
Stevenson, Thomas H., 551
Still, Edward Cundiff, 480 n
Stock, James R., 369
Stoeger, Keith A., 551
Stone, Louis H., 465
Stoynoff, Linda K., 63, 63 n
Straight rebuy, 52
Strategic business unit (SBU),
    275–76
Strategy versus tactics, 277
Stryker, Charles W., 236
Sturdivant, Frederick D., 215 n
Styan, George, 403–15
Summerfield, Cy, 551
Summers, John O., 119 n
Sunbeam, 9
Supplier, as management
    consultant, 348
Supplier-customer relationship,
    9–10
Survey methods, 182–83
Survey of buyer intentions, 222
Surveys in marketing research, 159
Suss, Warren H., 19 n
Sutton, Howard, 334 n, 364
Swan, J. E., 448 n, 469, 620 n
Swayne, Linda E., 551
Sweeney, T. W., 123 n
Sykes, Hollister B., 289
Synergy, definition of, 22
Systems selling, 442, 444–45

                T

Taff, Charles A., 376 n, 384 n
Taiichi, Ohno, 44
Taking title (for purpose of resale),
    336
Talley, Wayne Kenneth, 373 n
Tanel, Thomas, 401
Tandy (Radio Shack), 232, 359
Tanner, John F., Jr., 509

Tatus Farms of Georgia, 22
Taylor (company), 423
Taylor, Rob, 63
Taylor, Thayer C., 449 n, 469, 486 n, 510
Teague, Burton W., 501 n
Technical Procurement Service, Inc., 605
Technology, product positioning by, 212–13
Technology push, 253
Tektronix, 495
Telecommunications Marketing Resource, 605
Teledyne, 343
Telemarketing, 445–47
Templeton, Jane, 510
Templeton Engine Company, 145–47
Terpstra, Vern, 22 n, 542 n
Tester, David E., 534 n
Texas Instruments (TI), 70, 214
Thibault, Roger, 453
Thomas, Claude A., 468
Thomas, Dan R. E., 623 n
Thomas, Harold, 237
Thompson, Jane, 464
Thorelli, Hans B., 265 n
3M Corporation, 298, 321, 391
Timmerman, E., 130 n
Timmins, Jeffrey A., 19 n
Todd, Arthur W., 402
Todd, John T., 448 n
Toro Company, 13
Total cost
  definition, 70
  factors in, 75
Touche-Ross, 615
Toyota, 44, 133
Trade discount, 336
Traffic management
  claims processing, 373–74
  mode and carrier selection, 371, 373–74
  routing, 373
Trailmobile, 242
Transport, intermodal; see Traffic management
Transportation as a commodity, 375
Transportation modes; see Traffic management
Trawick, I. Frederick, 469
Trecha, Steven J., 125 n
Trend fitting, 223
Trevisan, Richard E., 665
Trout, Jack, 216 n

Troutner, Art, 237
Trus Joist Corporation, 237–46
Tull, Donald S., 645 n
Tung, Rosalie L., 500 n
Turnbull, Peter W., 634
Turner, Ronald E., 476 n
Turtletaut, Steven, 147 n

U

Uarco, Inc., 292
Unethical sales practices, 643–44
Uniac, Larry, 689–711
Union Carbide, 423, 657
Union Hospital, 467
Uniroyal, 132
United Airlines, 231
UPS (United Parcel Service), 231, 292
U. S. Leasing, 314
U. S. Government Electric Boat Division, 199
U. S. Postal Service, 630–31
U. S. Steel Corporation, 293, 306
University Hospital, 406

V

Vaghefi, M. Reza, 663
Valcourt Industrial Supply Company, 453
Vallen Corporation, 390
Valmont Industries, 448–49
Value analysis
  improved performance at less cost, 77
  integration of purchasing, production, engineering, 78
  preproduction analysis, 78
  tests involving customers, 78
  use of, 78
Value engineering; see Value analysis
Vamos, Mark, 264 n
van Amstel, J. J. Ploos, 402
Vanderwickee, Peter, 255 n
Varadarajan, P. Rajan, 634
Vassar, John, 634
Vendor rating, 115
  categorical, 128
  cost ratio, 130–31
  weight pointed, 128–29
Vernon, Raymond, 655 n
Visa, 613
Vorhees, Roy Dale, 402
Vose, Carolyn, 403 n

Vyas, Niran, 133 n

W

Wagle, John S., 469
Waldrop, Heidi, 510
Walker, Bruce J., 364
Walline, Jim, 241
Walters, Peter, 374, 375 n
Wang Laboratories, 78
Warehouse facilities
  importance of location, 381–82
  public versus private, 382–84
Washburn, Stewart A., 326
Waters, Craig, 47 n, 387 n
Watkins, Hayes T., 576, 577
Weadcock, Daniel K., 454 n
Webster, Frederick E., Jr., 26, 117 n, 132 n, 711–29
Webster and Wind model of buyer behavior, 117, 119
Weilbacker, William M., 520 n
Wein (company), 97
Weinstein, Sidney, 288
Weisberg, Louis, 526 n
Weiss, Ed, 453
Weitz, Barton, 62
Welch, Joe L., 193
Welch, John, 662–64
Wendel, Richard F., 480 n, 481 n
West, Reg, 551
Westinghouse, 345, 395, 422
Westinghouse International, 185
Whalen, Jack, 339
Wheeler, David R., 236
Whirlpool Corporation, 656
White, Harry R., 223 n
Whitlark, David B., 235
Wilcox, James B., 326, 363
Wilemon, David, 289
Willer, Susan J., 401
Williams, Robin, 453
Williams, Terry Considine, 551
Williamson, John, 415–16, 424–26
Wills, G. S. C., 614 n
Wills, Rich, 231
Wilson, D. T., 123 n, 200 n, 439 n
Wilson, Elizabeth, 200 n
Wind, Jerry, 288
Wind, Yoram, 49 n, 50 n, 117 n
Winer, Leon, 496 n
Winer, Russel S., 666 n
Winston, William J., 609 n
Wong, Anthony, 68 n
Woodruff, Robert B., 124 n
Woodside, Arch G., 133 n, 200 n, 603 n

Wortzell, Lawrence H., 348 n, 363
Wotruba, Thomas R., 489 n
Wright, T. P., 265 n
Wujin, Chu, 62
W. W. Grainger, 381–82
Wynn, George W., 434 n

X–Y

Xerox, 3, 358, 507, 523
Yancy Brothers, 646
Yarway Corporation, 340
Yelle, Louis E., 265 n
Yoon, Eunsang, 289
Young, Gary G., 551
Young, James R., 438 n

Z

Zenith Data Systems, 7, 183, 449
Zephyr Company, 310
Zibron, S. Michael, 551
Zoltners, Andris A., 364
Zurier, Steven, 526 n